Norfolk Record Society
Volume LXXIV for 2010

The Papers of Nathaniel Bacon Of Stiffkey

Volume V
1603–1607

Edited by
Victor Morgan, Elizabeth Rutledge
and Barry Taylor

Norfolk Record Society
Volume LXXIV
2010

First published in 2010
by the Norfolk Record Society

ISBN 978-0-9556357-3-1

Produced by John Saunders Design & Production
Printed in Great Britain by
The MPG Books Group, Bodmin and King's Lynn

To the memory of
JEAN KENNEDY, 1930–2009
City and County Archivist, 1962–1974
Norfolk County Archivist, 1974–1997
Friend and colleague

CONTENTS

MAPS

ACKNOWLEDGEMENTS

Firstly our thanks are due to the British Academy for funding Elizabeth Rutledge in 2006 for a year as a part-time research associate to work on preparation of the volume; to Trinity College, Cambridge, for a generous grant towards publication costs; and to the Norfolk Record Society for continuing to act as the publisher of this series. The School of History at the University of East Anglia has provided the accommodation and office space for the not inconsiderable number of filing cabinets, slip indexes and boxfiles out of which the volumes of this edition are created.

We are grateful to the following persons and institutions for permission to publish manuscripts in their care: the Beinecke Rare Book and Manuscript Library, Yale University; the British Library; the Folger Shakespeare Library, Washington; the Howard Gottlieb Archival Research Center, Boston University; the Norfolk Record Office; the Special Collections Research Center, University of Chicago Library; the Suffolk Record Office (Ipswich and Bury); the late Marquess Townshend of Raynham and the Dowager Marchioness Townshend. We are also grateful to Godfrey Sayers for allowing us to use his redrawing of the map of Blakeney haven and the port of Cley for the dust jacket.

Our thanks are also due to Dr Sheila Adam for generously giving her time and expertise in translating the letter on p.97; to Professor Michael Chisholm for providing background information to the documents concerning proposals for Fenland drainage; to Phillip Judge for drawing the maps; to Scilla Landale for her help in connection with the manuscripts still at Raynham Hall; to Dr Heather Wolfe in connection with manuscripts in the Folger Shakespeare Library. Also to the staff of the Norfolk Record Office for their continued assistance: the current County Archivist, Dr John Alban, not only oversees what probably is the finest provincial record office in England but also, among the multifarious other demands on his institution, continues to facilitate scholarly projects such as this. Similarly, Dr Clive Wilkins-Jones has, as always, been a fount of knowledge about the often unique holdings of the Norfolk Heritage Library, part of the Norfolk County Library Service. We are much indebted to the late Marquess Townshend for his constant appreciation of, and support for, this edition. In the wider academic world Professor Patrick Collinson has provided sage advice and support.

At different times a number of research students have drawn on the resources represented by the Bacon papers and its associated Stiffkey Database. At the same time they have contributed to our understanding of these documents. Mention must be made of Linda Campbell, Jane Key, Alan Metters, Jan Pitman, Peter Smith and Jill Taylor.

As in the case of the previous volumes in this series, the editors mentioned on the title page are only part of the wider team responsible for various stages in the editorial process. We are sorry to have to report the death of one member, Jean

Kennedy, the former Norfolk County Archivist, during the course of the work on this volume. Her particular contribution here was in checking transcriptions, but the project as a whole owes a far wider debt over the years to Jean for her assistance in tracking down Nathaniel Bacon papers and in helping to make them available. Ian Palfrey and Paul Rutledge also checked transcriptions, an essential contribution to any editorial project, and Paul Rutledge is responsible for the index, based in part on the working index initially compiled by Barry Taylor. Emeritus Professor Hassell Smith, with his unrivalled knowledge of the Bacon archive and a lifetime's immersion in the period and in Tudor and early Stuart Norfolk, has, as always, contributed in innumerable ways to the furtherance of the project that he had the vision to initiate.

The General Editors of the edition as a whole, Professor Hassell Smith and Dr Victor Morgan, are much indebted to Mr Barry Taylor and Mrs Elizabeth Rutledge for their work on this volume. As always, Barry has laboured indefatigably in the transcription of documents, in compiling an initial index in order to facilitate on-going editing, and in contributing erudite notes. Elizabeth has been the essential lynchpin of this volume. She has undertaken much of the basic editorial work. In particular she has brought a sharp legally trained eye where often it has been needed. She has also performed the essential function of co-ordinating the editorial process and attempted to keep her fellow editors in order. Anyone who knows us also knows that this last is by no means the least of her achievements. On many days in most weeks, we have eaten together and whatever may have been on the menu, it has almost always been Bacon for lunch, and tea breaks too! Need one add that the conversation was always argumentative and on occasion pugnacious, as it should be.

Victor Morgan

ABBREVIATIONS

NOTE: for the convenience of users the list of abbreviations presented here is cumulative across all the volumes of the edition of the *Bacon Papers* thus far. In some instances manuscripts formerly in private ownership have migrated to public repositories, or changed reference within the same repository. In order to maintain consistency across the edition the old abbreviations have been retained in the list and all such changes cross-referenced under both the old and the new references.

APC – *Acts of the Privy Council of England*, ed. J. R. Dasent (32 vols; London, 1890–1907)

AUL – University of Adelaide, Barr Smith Library, manuscript collection

Bacon Exhibition Catalogue – *The Sources of English Society, the Sir Nicholas Bacon Collection 1250–1700* (catalogue of an exhibition at the Joseph Regenstein Library of the University of Chicago; Chicago, 1972)

Bald, *Donne* – R. C. Bald, *Donne and the Drurys* (Cambridge, 1959)

Barnard – Catalogues of manuscripts offered for sale by P.M. Barnard

Barton, *Anthony Harison* – *The Registrum Vagum of Anthony Harison*, ed. T. F. Barton (NRS, 2 vols, xxxii and xxxiii, 1963 and 1964)

BL Add. – British Library, Department of Manuscripts, Additional Collection

BL Stowe – British Library, Department of Manuscripts, Stowe Collection

Blomefield – Francis Blomefield, *An Essay Towards a Topographical History of the County of Norfolk ...*, ed. Charles Parkin (11 vols, London, 1805–10)

Bodl. – Bodleian Library

Boston (Richards) – Boston University, Mugar Memorial Library, Richards Rare Book and Manuscript Collection

Bowyer, *Parliamentary Diary* – *The Parliamentary Diary of Robert Bowyer, 1606–1607*, ed. D.H.Willson (Minneapolis, 1931)

Boynton, *Militia* – Lindsay Boynton, *The Elizabethan Militia 1558–1638* (London, 1967)

BP, i – *The Papers of Nathaniel Bacon of Stiffkey Volume I: 1556–1577*, ed. A. Hassell Smith, Gillian M. Baker and R. W. Kenny (NRS xlvi for 1978 & 1979; Norwich, 1979)

BP, ii – *The Papers of Nathaniel Bacon of Stiffkey Volume II: 1578–1585*, ed. A. Hassell Smith and Gillian M. Baker (NRS xlix for 1982 and 1983; Norwich, 1983)

BP, iii – *The Papers of Nathaniel Bacon of Stiffkey Volume III: 1586–1595*, ed. A. Hassell Smith and Gillian M. Baker (NRS liii for 1987 and 1988; Norwich, 1990)

BP, iv – *The Papers of Nathaniel Bacon of Stiffkey Volume IV: 1596–1602*, ed. Victor Morgan, Jane Key and Barry Taylor (NRS lxiv, Norwich, 2000)

Brentnall, 'Regional Influences' – David Brentnall, 'Regional Influences in the House of Commons 1604–1610 (University of East Anglia, MPhil thesis, 1978)

Brewer – Manuscripts *penes* R. Brewer, Kenninghall

Cheney & Jones – *A Handbook of Dates for Students of British History*, compiled C.R.Cheney, revised Michael Jones (Royal Historical Society, 2000)

Chicago – University of Chicago Library, Redgrave Collection

CJ – *Journals of the House of Commons*

Clark, *Commonwealth* – *The English Commonwealth 1547–1640. Essays in Politics and Society Presented to Joel Hurstfield*, ed. Peter Clark, Alan G. R. Smith and Nicholas Tyacke (Leicester, 1979)

Clarke and Campling, *Visitation* – *The Visitation of Norfolk anno domini 1664 made by Sir Edward Bysshe, Knt, Clarenceux King of Arms,* ed. A.W. Hughes Clarke and Arthur Campling (NRS, 2 vols, iv and v, 1934)

CMH – *The Cambridge Modern History*, ed. A. W. Ward, G. W. Prothero and S. Leathes (14 vols; Cambridge, 1902–12)

Cockburn, *Assizes* – J. S. Cockburn, *A History of English Assizes 1558–1714* (Cambridge, 1972)

Collinson, *Puritan Movement* – Patrick Collinson, *The Elizabethan Puritan Movement* (London, 1967)

Corder, *Visitation of Suffolk* – *The Visitation of Suffolk, 1561*, ed. J. Corder (2 vols; Harleian Society, new series, ii and iii, 1981, 1984)

Cozens-Hardy, *Mayors* – B. Cozens-Hardy and E. A. Kent, *The Mayors of Norwich 1403 to 1835* (Norwich, 1938)

CPR – *Calendar of Patent Rolls* (London, 1924–1982)

c.s. – *custos sigilli* (Keeper of the Great Seal)

CSPD – *Calendar of State Papers, Domestic*, ed. Robert Lemon and M. A. E. Green (8 vols; London, 1856–72)

CSP Foreign – *Calendar of State Papers, Foreign*, ed. Joseph Stephenson, A. J. Crosby, A. J. Butler, S. C. Lomas, A. B. Hinds and R. B. Wernham (23 vols; London, 1863–1950)

CSP Rome – *State Papers, relating to English Affairs, in the Vatican Archives and Library* ed. J. M. Rigg (2 vols; London. 1916–26)

d. – pence/*denarius* (12*d.* = 1*s.*; 240*d.* = £1)

di. – *dimidius* (a half)

D'Ewes, *Journal* – Simonds D'Ewes, *The Journals of all the Parliaments during the Reign of Queen Elizabeth, both of the House of Lords and the House of Commons*, revised and published by P. Bowes (London, 1682)

DNB – *Dictionary of National Biography*, ed. Leslie Stephen and Sidney Lee (22 vols, London, 1908–9)

Dobell – Catalogues of manuscripts offered for sale by P.J. and A.E. Dobell, Bruton St, London

Eden, *Surveyors* – *Dictionary of Land Surveyors and Local Cartographers of Great Britain and Ireland 1550–1850*, ed. Peter Eden (3 vols, Folkestone, 1975–6)

EH – Manuscripts formerly at Elveden Hall: now in the Suffolk Record Office (Ipswich)

Ellis – Catalogues of manuscripts offered for sale by Ellis, New Bond Street, London

f./ff. – Folio/s

FBL – Francis Bacon Library, formerly at Sutro, now at the Huntington Library, San Marino, California

Felbrigg – R.W. Ketton Cremer, *Felbrigg: the Story of a House* (1962)

Fitzwilliam – Fitzwilliam Museum, Cambridge

Folger – Folger Shakespeare Library, Washington, D.C.

Foster, *Proceedings* – *Proceedings in Parliament 1610*, ed. E.R. Foster (New Haven, 1966)

Fryde *et al.* – *Handbook of British Chronology* (3rd ed.), ed. E.B.Fryde, D.E.Greenway, S.Porter and I.Roy (Royal Historical Society, 1986)

GEC – *The Complete Peerage of England, Scotland, Ireland etc., extant, extinct or dormant*, ed. G.E. Cokayne (revised edition, ed. Vicary Gibbs, 13 vols; London, 1910–49)

GI Admissions – *Register of Admissions to Gray's Inn, 1521–1889*, ed. Joseph Foster (London, 1889)

Halliday – Catalogues of books and manuscripts offered for sale by Bernard Halliday, Leicester

Harvard (Houghton) – Harvard University, the Houghton Library, manuscript collection

Hawes, *City Officers* – *An Index to Norwich City Officers 1453–1835*, compiled Timothy Hawes (NRS, lii, 1986; Norwich, [1989])

HMC – Royal Commission on Historical Manuscripts

HMC Gawdy – HMC 11: Tenth Report, Appendix II, *Gawdy*, 1509–75 (C.4576–iii of 1885)

HMC Salisbury – HMC 9: *Salisbury (Cecil) MSS* at Hatfield, Herts. (24 vols, 1883–1976)

HMC Townshend – HMC 19: Eleventh Report, Appendix IV, *Townshend*, 1499–1791 (C.5060–iii of 1887)

H of C, 1558–1603 – *The History of Parliament: the House of Commons 1558–1603*, ed. P. W. Hasler (3 vols; London, 1981)

Hofmann and Freeman – Catalogues of rare books and manuscripts offered for sale by Hofmann & Freeman Ltd., Sevenoaks, Kent

Hoyle *et al.*, *Heard before the King* – *Heard before the King: Registers of Petitions to James I, 1603–16*, ed. R. W. Hoyle, Danae Tankard and Simon Neal (List and Index Society, Special Series; Kew, 2006)

HRO – Hertfordshire Record Office

HTM – *History Teachers' Miscellany*, ed. H.W. Saunders (7 vols, 1922–9)

Hughes & Larkin, *Tudor Proclamations* – *Tudor Royal Proclamations*, ed. Paul L. Hughes and J.F. Larkin (3 vols; 1964–9)

Huntington – Henry E. Huntington Library, San Marino, California, manuscript collection

Jacob, *Law Dictionary* – G. Jacob, *A New Law-Dictionary* (London, 1762)

Jessopp, *One Generation* – Augustine Jessopp, *One Generation of a Norfolk House* (London, 1913)

J.P. – Justice of the Peace

Judges of England – *The Judges of England 1292–1990*, compiled Sir John Sainty (Selden Society Supplementary Series 10, 1993)

Key, 'Dorothy Bacon' – 'The Letters and Will of Lady Dorothy Bacon, 1597–1629', ed. Jane Key, in *A Miscellany* (NRS lvi for 1991; Norwich, 1993), pp.77–112

£ – pound sterling/*libra* (= 240*d.*, or 20*s.*)

Larkin & Hughes, *Stuart Proclamations* – *Stuart Royal Proclamations, vol.I: Royal Proclamations of King James I, 1603–25*, ed. J.F.Larkin and Paul L Hughes (1973)

Levack, *Civil Lawyers* – Brian P. Levack, *The Civil Lawyers in England 1603–1641: a Political Study* (Oxford, 1973)

l.h.s. – left-hand side

li. – *libra* (a pound, currency or weight)

LJ – *Journals of the House of Lords*

MacCulloch, 'Suffolk' – D. N. J. MacCulloch, 'Power Privilege and the County Community: County Politics in Elizabethan Suffolk' (Cambridge University, PhD thesis, 1977)

MacCulloch, *Suffolk* – Diarmaid MacCulloch, *Suffolk and the Tudors: Politics and Religion in an English County 1500–1600* (Oxford, 1986)

MacCulloch, *Redgrave Hall* – *Letters from Redgrave Hall. The Bacon Family, 1340–1744*, ed. Diarmaid MacCulloch (Suffolk Records Society 50, 2007)

Maggs – Catalogues of manuscripts offered for sale by Maggs Bros

Metcalfe, *Visitations of Suffolk* – *The Visitations of Suffolk made by Hervey, Clarenceux, 1561, Cooke, Clarenceux, 1577, and Raven, Richmond Herald, 1612*, ed. Walter C. Metcalfe (Exeter, 1882)

Metters, 'Rulers and Merchants' – A. Metters, 'The Rulers and Merchants of King's Lynn in the Early Seventeenth Century' (University of East Anglia, PhD thesis, 1982)

Millican, *Freemen* – *The Register of the Freemen of Norwich, 1548–1713*, ed. Percy Millican (Norwich, 1934)

Myers – Catalogues of manuscripts offered for sale by Myers & Co

NA – *Norfolk Archaeology*

Norf. Official Lists – *Norfolk Official Lists, from the Earliest Period to the Present Day*, ed. Hamon Le Strange (Norwich, 1890)

NRO – Norfolk Record Office

NRO Acc Sotheby – Purchase from Sotheby and Co: Acc Sotheby 28/12/1967 and subsequent accessions

NRO AH – Deposit by A. Hamond. Now NRO HMN

NRO AYL – Aylsham Collection

NRO BCH – Deposit by B. Cozens-Hardy

NRO BRA – Deposit by British Records Association

NRO BUL – Bulwer Collection

NRO DS – Duleep Singh papers

NRO E&T – Deposit by Emett & Tacon. Now NRO MC 1868

NRO FX 245 – Photocopies of manuscripts formerly owned by the late P. Millican, formerly NRO PM xerox

NRO GRM – Deposit by G.R. Martyn. Now NRO MC 1872

NRO HBL – Bradfer-Lawrence Collection

NRO HMN – Hamond Collection, formerly NRO AH

NRO MC – Minor Collections
    NRO MC 934 formerly TSB
    NRO MC 1082 formerly Sotheby 11/01/74
    NRO MC 1370 formerly Christie 14/05/82
    NRO MC 1868 formerly E&T
    NRO MC 1872 formerly GRM

NRO MF 4/1 – Microfilm of manuscripts *penes* Mr P.C. Pearson in 1965, formerly NRO PCP

NRO NAS/NNAS – Norfolk and Norwich Archaeological Society Collection. NRO NAS now refers only to the Frere Manuscripts, a part of this collection. The whole is now NNAS

NRO NRS – Documents deposited through the Norfolk Record Society

NRO PCP – Microfilm of manuscripts *penes* Mr P.C. Pearson in 1965, now NRO MF 4/1

NRO PM xerox – Photocopies of manuscripts formerly owned by the late P. Millican, now NRO FX 245

NRO RAY – Temporary deposit by the Marquess Townshend

NRO SOTH – Purchase from Sotheby & Co: SOTH 11/01/74 now NRO MC 1083

NRO Townshend Additional – Additional temporary deposit by the Marquess Townshend: Townshend, Bacon Project

NRO TSB – Deposit by T. S. Blakeney. Now NRO MC 934

NRS – Norfolk Record Society

ob. – obolus (halfpenny)

ODNB – Oxford Dictionary of National Biography (http://www.oxforddnb.com index.jsp)

OED – Oxford English Dictionary. Most definitions taken from the *OED* are not referenced

Owens, 'Local Government' – G. L. Owens, 'Norfolk 1620–1641: Local Government and Central Authority in an East Anglian County' (University of Wisconsin, PhD thesis, 1970)

Pitman, 'Stiffkey' – Jan Pitman, 'Social Relations in a North Norfolk Parish: Stiffkey *c.*1550–1650' (University of East Anglia, MA thesis, 1989)

PCC – Prerogative Court of Canterbury (now TNA PRO prob)

PCP – Manuscript collection *penes* Mr. P. C. Pearson (now NRO MF 4/1)

PML – Pierpont Morgan Library, New York, manuscript collection

PRO – Public Record Office

PRO C 2 & 3 – PRO Chancery Proceedings, Series I & II

PRO prob – Prerogative Court of Canterbury (formerly PCC)

PRO STAC – Star Chamber

PRO SP – State Papers

Prouty, *Gascoigne* – C.T. Prouty, *George Gascoigne: Elizabethan Courtier, Soldier and Poet* (New York, 1966)

qr – quarter

Reynolds, *Godly Reformers* – Matthew Reynolds, *Godly Reformers and their Opponents in early modern England: Religion in Norwich, c.1560–1643* (Woodbridge, 2005)

RH – Manuscripts *penes* the Marquess Townshend

r.h.s. – right-hand side

RUL – University of Reading Library, manuscript collection

Rye, *Musters* – *State Papers Relating to Musters, Beacons, Shipmoney etc. in Norfolk from 1626 Chiefly to the Beginning of the Civil War*, ed. Walter Rye (Norwich, 1907)

Rye, *Norfolk Families* – Walter Rye, *Norfolk Families* (Norwich, 1915)

Rye, *Visitation of Norfolk* – *The Visitation of Norfolk 1563 and 1613*, ed. Walter Rye (Harleian Society, xxxii, 1891)

s. – shilling/*solidus* (= 12*d*.; 20*s*. = £1)

Shaw, *Knights* – W. A. Shaw, *The Knights of England* (2 vols, London, 1906)

Smith, *County and Court* – A. Hassell Smith, *County and Court: Government and Politics in Norfolk, 1558–1603* (Oxford, 1974)

Smith, 'Labourers' – A. Hassell Smith, 'Labourers in late sixteenth-century England: a case study from North Norfolk', *Continuity and Change*, 4 (1989) pp.11–52, 367–394

Smith, 'Militia Rates' – A. Hassell Smith, 'Militia Rates and Militia Statutes 1558–1663', in *The English Commonwealth 1547–1640. Essays in Politics and Society presented to Joel Hurstfield*, ed. Peter Clark, Alan G.R. Smith, Nicholas Tyacke (Leicester, 1979) pp.93–110

Smith, 'Norf. Gentry' – A. Hassell Smith, 'The Elizabethan Gentry of Norfolk: Office-Holding and Faction' (London, PhD thesis, 1957)

Smith, 'Stiffkey Hall' – A. Hassell Smith, 'Concept and Compromise: Sir Nicholas Bacon and the Building of Stiffkey Hall' in *East Anglian History. Studies in Honour of Norman Scarfe*, ed. C. Harper-Bill *et al.* (Woodbridge, 2002) pp.159–188

Somerville, *Duchy of Lancaster* – Sir Robert Somerville, *History of the Duchy of Lancaster* (London, 1953)

Somerville, *Lancaster Office Holders* – Sir Robert Somerville, *Office-holders in the Duchy and County Palatine of Lancaster from 1603* (Chichester, 1972)

Sotheby – Catalogues of printed books, autograph letters and historical documents offered for sale by Sotheby & Co

SP Foreign, Lists – *List and Analysis of State Papers, Foreign Series, Elizabeth I*, ed. R. B. Wernham (3 vols, 1964–1980)

SR – *The Statutes of the Realm*, vol.iv, pt.2 (1899).

SRO (B) – Suffolk Record Office, Bury St Edmunds Branch

SRO (I) – Suffolk Record Office, Ipswich Branch

Stiffkey Database – University of East Anglia, computerised database of account books in the Bacon archive 1576–1598. (In volumes I- III referred to as 'UEA Bacon DATABASE'. In order to avoid confusion with the Bacon editorial project of which this volume forms a part, from volume IV the appellation used is 'Stiffkey Database'.)

Stiffkey Papers – *The Official Papers of Sir Nathaniel Bacon of Stiffkey, Norfolk, 1580–1620*, ed. H. W. Saunders (Camden Society, 3rd series, xxvi, 1915)

Supplementary Stiffkey Papers – 'Supplementary Stiffkey Papers' ed. F. W. Brooks in *Camden Miscellany XVI* (Camden Society, 3rd series lii, 1936)

Thirsk, *Agricultural Regions* – Joan Thirsk, *Agricultural Regions and Agrarian History in England, 1500–1750* (Basingstoke, 1987)

Tittler, *Bacon* – Robert Tittler, *The Making of a Tudor Statesman* (London, 1976)

TNA – The National Archives

Tregaskis – Catalogues of manuscripts offered for sale by James Tregaskis

TRHS – *Transactions of the Royal Historical Society*

TSB – Manuscript collection formerly owned by the late T. S. Blakeney. Now BL MSS Add. 63079–63141. Earlier TSB references were to document number rather than to folio

UEA Bacon Database – University of East Anglia, computerised database of account books in the Stiffkey archive 1576–1598. (From volume IV referred to as 'Stiffkey Database' in order to avoid confusion with the Bacon editorial project of which this volume forms a part.)

ULL – University of London Library, manuscript collection

Venn, *Al. Cant.* – John Venn and J. A. Venn, *Alumni Cantabrigienses: A Biographical Register of all known Students, Graduates and Holders of Office at the University of Cambridge, from the Earliest Times to 1900. Part I: From the Earliest Times to 1751* (4 vols; Cambridge, 1922–27)

VHS – Virginia Historical Society, manuscript collection

viz. – *videlicet*: namely

vol. – volume

Visit. of Norf. 1563 – *The Visitation of Norfolk in the Year 1563*, ed. G. H. Dashwood and W. E. G. L. Bulwer (2 vols; Norwich, 1878–95)

Wernham, *After the Armada* – R. B. Wernham, *After the Armada: Elizabeth, England and the Struggle for Western Europe 1585–1595* (Oxford, 1984)

Yale (Beinecke) – James Marshall and Marie-Louise Osborn Collection, Beinecke Rare Book and Manuscript Library, Yale University

Yaxley, *Glossary* – David Yaxley, *A Researcher's Glossary of Words Found in Historical Documents of East Anglia* (Dereham, 2003)

Youngs, *Administrative Units* – Frederic A. Youngs, Jr, *Guide to the Local Administrative Units of England, I: Southern England* (Royal Historical Society Guides and Handbooks No. 10; London, 1979)

EDITORIAL PRACTICE

What follows is a slightly modified version of the 'Editorial practice' section in Volume IV. This volume has retained the editorial changes first introduced in Volume IV (see *BP*, iv, pp. xx-xxii), which are covered by the information given below. Editorial changes first introduced in this volume are described under *Arrangement of the manuscripts* (2c and f) and under *Rules of transcription* (Latin quotations, Forenames, Holographs and signatures and Suspensions and contractions). To further benefit the reader, this volume also includes two maps and a Glossary.

A defining feature of the Nathaniel Bacon papers is that as a result of the vicissitudes of sales, re-sale, migration and illicit 'leakage' what formerly constituted a reasonably coherent archive has been widely scattered.[1] At the most recent count, papers that we believe were once in the archive in Stiffkey Hall have been dispersed to upwards of forty main deposits in over a dozen repositories on three continents. As a result, and as is evident in the case of some of the themes that can be traced through this volume, papers that form a sequence dealing with one issue may now be lodged in two or more manuscript collections thousands of miles apart. In practical terms, thus isolated and lacking a context, they are of relatively little use. Therefore, one purpose of this edition is to bring these documentary fragments back into a coherent and accessible relationship which will make them useful to scholars. Looked at from another angle, the reconstitution of the archive allows us once more to take a view of the multifarious and simultaneous activities of a local gentleman and J.P. in a period when these activities are of considerable interest to historians. In this respect the *Bacon Papers* are one among many groups of family-based provincial archives which proliferated in the second half of the sixteenth century. However, as has recently been said, probably it is 'pre-eminent' among such collections and therefore there is all the more reason for attempting to make it accessible.[2]

This has entailed an attempt to reconstitute the Stiffkey archive as it existed at the time of Nathaniel Bacon's death in 1622. In its turn the pursuit of this aim has called for the resolution of a series of problems.

1. *Definition of the archive*

Because the collection has become so scattered the editors have had to decide which of the many papers relating to Nathaniel Bacon were in his evidence room when its chests were carted off to Raynham Hall. The letters he wrote, if still extant, were likely to have been preserved in the muniment rooms of their recipients and have, by definition, been excluded. Draft letters, which can be identified

---

[1] For a fuller exposition of the process of dispersal see *BP*, i, pp.xx-xxxiv.
[2] Penry Williams, *The Later Tudors: England 1547–1603* (Clarendon Press; Oxford, 1995) p.20.

easily from the handwriting or endorsement, would have remained in the Stiffkey evidence room and have, therefore, been included. It is also reasonable to assume that substantial groups of late-medieval manorial and estate records relating to properties purchased by Nathaniel and his father belong or belonged to this archive, especially since Sir Nicholas was punctilious about requiring the surrender of records at the time of purchase. These have not been included in this edition.

Nonetheless, it is not possible to define the collection entirely by *a priori* reasoning. Sometimes documents not immediately ascribable to this collection (for example papers sent to Nathaniel Bacon for information or documents relating to a dispute in which he mediated) have been identified as papers that once were in the collection at Stiffkey Hall. Often they can be identified from the handwriting of the clerk in the endorsements. When this is the case they have been included in this edition. In other cases manuscripts can be identified from internal evidence. As we become familiar with the contents of this collection the problems of identification diminish. Like the pieces of a gigantic partially-completed jigsaw puzzle, increasingly manuscripts otherwise unidentifiable can be recognised through the gaps they fill in a known sequence. Even so, some documents defy firm identification, and when in doubt our policy has been to include them with due acknowledgement of our sense of their dubiety.

Despite strenuous efforts over many years we believe that between 20% and 30% of the original archive still remains untraced.[3]

Material that can be tracked quite recently to the sale rooms has not all re-surfaced in public collections. On the basis of past experience we suspect that in particular two types of documents may remain unlocated or unidentified. One type is the individual letter which has been acquired by private individuals who are postal historians or who derive satisfaction from owning an old document that bears the names of famous individuals or their own family cognomen. Usually the material only comes to light when the owner's own papers are being sorted *post mortem*. The second type is material which is likely to have found its way into the specialist collections of legal or agricultural documents, or materials gathered to teach palaeography. Such collections were actively in formation in the inter-war years when much of the Stiffkey archive was being dispersed. Again, we know from experience that provenance was often unrecorded, and only direct examination of the document will reveal its origins. As a result of the publication of earlier volumes of this edition a number of academics and archivists have been prompted to draw our attention to small caches of material that had escaped our earlier trawls. The reconstitution of the archive remains an active process and we would be pleased to hear of any new identifications, however tentative these may be. It is intended to produce an addendum to cover such finds as part of the last volume of this edition.

2. *Arrangement of the manuscripts*

In order to reconstitute the archive in its original form it would be necessary to re-sort the documents into their original bundles. One or two unbroken bundles

---

[3] *BP*, i, p.xxxvi.

have survived and a few more undoubtedly form the basis of 'lots' in Sotheby's catalogues. Others could be re-created with the aid of Bacon's secretary, Martin Man's, precise endorsements. But there would remain many documents the original location of which within the archive would remain unascertainable. This is mainly as a consequence of the deliberate breaking up of the original bundles by earlier editors, the attempts to optimise the attractiveness of the material by the making up of lots in the sale room, the subsequent separate sale of individual items, and in some instances the re-agglomeration for commercial purposes of materials that had earlier been sold as separate lots.[4]

In these circumstances the most rational approach has been to order the material on a chronological basis. The only exception to this rule is that the pre-1559 court rolls and estate papers will appear as an appendix to the final volume.

The following conventions govern exact placement within the chronological sequence.

(a) Documents which have been compiled sequentially over a period of time (e.g. account books) have been placed at the first dated entry.

(b) In those infrequent cases in which it can be determined that a sequential document has been compiled retrospectively it has been placed under the last dated entry.

(c) In a few cases several unrelated items, each bearing a different date, occur on the same sheet. In these cases each item has normally been presented under its date (or if undated, under an ascribed date). It has also been cross-referenced to all other items on the same sheet in order to reconcile archival integrity with the chronological presentation. Very rarely it has been felt most satisfactory to print the manuscript as a single document. One exception occurs in the case of (usually) undated petitions followed by a referral. Here it was felt to be artificial to separate the two items and these documents are treated simply as referrals and given the date of the referral.

(d) Partially-dated documents (i.e. dated only by year or by year and month) have been entered at the earliest possible point. Thus a document dated '1580' precedes that dated '25 March 1580'; one dated 'September 1580' precedes that dated '1 September 1580'.

(e) Undated documents have been dated as precisely as possible from internal evidence and, in some instances, external evidence. Such documents have been located according to the principles set out in (d) above. Thus a document ascribed to [*c.1588*] appears before one entered at 1 January 1588/9. In some cases where it has been possible to determine only the dates between which a document was written, e.g. [*1588, March 26 <-Θ-> 1589, March 2*] such a document appears in sequence at the earliest date on which it could have been written, with the use of the *inter* sign as employed in this edition and illustrated in this example.

---

[4] *BP*, i, pp.xxii-xxv.

(f) Copies are generally given the date of the document from which they are copied, not of the date of copying. However, in a few cases in the current volume where a much earlier document has been copied, the date given is that of the copy. In these instances the document is described as a copy in the heading.

(g) Documents which cannot be even approximately dated will be printed at the end of the edition.

(h) The only unequivocal way of representing the dates between 1 January and 25 March is the double dating convention (e.g. 8 February 1598/9) and this is used throughout.

3. *Transcripts, calendar entries and listings*

Both the scattered nature of the collection and our ambition to achieve total reconstruction have influenced our decision to produce an edition which, in today's climate, might be regarded as extravagant. Whenever possible the entire manuscript or a comprehensive calendar entry has been printed. While treating each document on its own merits, we have in most cases presented the different classes of documents as follows:

(a) Full transcripts have been produced for:
- (i)   most private correspondence (since the subject matter is normally disparate);
- (ii) most official correspondence which contains little common-form;
- (iii) memoranda and short documents such as single sheets of accounts.

(b) Transcripts with linking summaries have been produced for:
- (i)   official correspondence which contains extensive common-form;
- (ii) private letters relating to a single subject.

(c) Calendar entries, giving all personal names (original spelling) and place-names (modernised) have been produced for:
- (i)   deeds;
- (ii) commissions and other lists;
- (iii) depositions, petitions and miscellaneous legal and administrative papers.

(d) Brief entries have been used for documents which cannot be treated comprehensively. These include:
- (i)   court rolls;
- (ii) account books;
- (iii) field books and other substantial estate records;
- (iv) justice's memoranda books.

To avoid any possible misunderstanding, in this volume the entries for groups (b) and (c) are preceded by '*Calendar*' and those for group (d) by '*Summary*'.

4. *Entries from auctioneers' and booksellers' catalogues*

In pursuit of our ambition to reconstitute the Stiffkey archive we have included in this edition entries from auctioneers' and booksellers' catalogues about manuscripts which have so far not been located. These entries range from the briefest of listings to substantial descriptions, which occasionally even include short extracts. They also vary in quality: some, especially in the early catalogues, are inaccurately dated; others identify persons incorrectly; many, and in particular the more recent ones, provide full and accurate information. All entries from sale catalogues have been printed in italics in order to indicate their different status.

5. *Replication of documents already in print*

About 7% of the extant collection has already been printed in a variety of publications, not all of which are readily available. We have, therefore, had to balance the seeming extravagance of reprinting these manuscripts against the inconvenience to the reader of being referred to a variety of rather obscure sources, which in some cases provide an inaccurate text. We have opted for comprehensiveness, taking the opportunity to re-edit any text for which the original manuscript is extant.

6. *Transcription and the form of the manuscripts*

As has been noted, many of the documents in the Bacon archive are in the form of drafts. This presents both a problem and an opportunity. It is a problem because the palaeography is often difficult, and there are frequent emendations in the form of insertions and deletions by more than one hand. These are often accompanied by what initially appear to be random jottings and miscellaneous endorsements. Sometimes rough drafts have been made in blank space on documents of an earlier date. In these circumstances, if one was working from the manuscript directly it would be necessary to make a transcript simply in order to be able to work out what the import of the document really was. In editing these papers we have attempted to provide this service for readers.

But the draft form of many of the documents is also an opportunity. Sometimes, especially in the legal or quasi-legal documents, the emendations might be considered simply as technical corrections. But even this is a reflection of the legalistic precision which informed this society: words lacked power unless they were the right words and appeared in the correct collocation. One also sees a grasping for exact and unequivocal factual precision.[5]

The significance of the attitude of mind recorded in the scorings through and insertions in these documents contrasts sharply with our own too-often slap-dash habits and gestural prose. In some other instances a careful scrutiny of the process of excision and insertion reveals the thinking of the mind or minds at work behind the drafting. For example, how did one couch the most cogent and persuasive of arguments to a Council in London uncomprehending of the specific complexities of life in a particular region of England? Some among those who have

---

[5] On the methodical attention to detail and its association with the legally trained mind as manifested within the Bacon family see *BP*, i, p.xvii.

worked on these papers even claim to be able to detect at work within them the tug of mutual influence between Nathaniel Bacon and his leading secretary, Martin Man.[6]

Others also may care to pursue the analysis of this intriguing form of relationship through the vehicle provided by these volumes. Therefore, in the technical apparatus employed in the presentation of this edition there is a purpose beyond the mere formality of representing in a systematic manner in print what are often rather untidy manuscripts. The hope is that on occasion we can catch a glimpse of minds at work, formulating their thinking in response to the practicalities of their experience. Sometimes, in the process of editing a document a realisation is borne in on one beyond the practicalities of trying to tease out the words or characters on a messy leaf. It is that the physically disordered object in one's hand itself has no one single and unproblematic meaning. Rather, it is a territory of contested possible meanings. It is something of this that we have tried to capture through the use of our editorial conventions, especially those representing insertions and deletions.

7. *Biographical information and cross-referencing*

Biographical information may be found in one of two places. Firstly, it is often provided in a footnote at the first point at which mention of an individual occurs (though possibly in a later footnote, where more appropriate). Secondly, in volumes I to III the limitations imposed by the means of production led to the index being used as, in effect, a supplementary source of biographical information. For the sake of consistency and the convenience of users the established practice has been maintained, with supplementary information sometimes being given in the notes.

Probably most users of a volume such as this are not going to sit down and read it from cover to cover. Many will be seeking out specific individuals or topics. The index remains the main means of doing this. However, Volume IV also introduced a modest amount of cross-referencing within the footnotes. This is designed to provide an additional means of linking topics which occur at different points within the chronological sequence of the documents. For example, the third document in a sequence to do with a subject will have a note referring both back to the second and forward to the fourth document in what we have identified as the sequence. The second document will have a cross-reference to the first and the third.

[6] *BP*, i, pp.xix-xx.

RULES OF TRANSCRIPTION

ORIGINAL SPELLING has been retained in all full transcripts, with the following exceptions: the modern use of 'i' and 'j' has been adopted, and the final 'j' in Roman numerals and in occasional words has been transcribed 'i'; the modern use of 'u' and 'v' has been adopted; 'yᵉ' has been transcribed 'the'; and 'lettre' has been transcribed 'letter'.

CAPITALISATION has been modernised. Initial 'ff' has been transcribed 'F', or in mid-sentence 'f', and in certain abbreviations, e.g. 'Norff', 'ff' has been transcribed 'f' and the abbreviation extended. (Note: in specific cases where the sense could be in doubt, upper case has been used, e.g. 'Act', 'Court', 'Bench', 'Hundred' etc.)

PUNCTUATION has been added or deleted where the sense of the text would otherwise be in doubt but such silent emendation has been done only sparingly. However, in some texts excessive and inappropriate use of the comma has been corrected, while misplaced colons and semi-colons have been altered to commas or full stops as appropriate.

DOCUMENTS IN FOREIGN LANGUAGES have either been calendared, and the original language indicated, or given in full in the original language with an English full calendar or translation.

LATIN QUOTATIONS AND FOREIGN WORDS have been shown in italics. Words and phrases in common usage appear in the Glossary. Less common phrases and quotations have either been glossed or translated in the footnotes.

FORENAMES AND SURNAMES have been transcribed 'as is' in all cases and have not been modernised, including occurrences in calendared documents. Latin christian names have been translated. Abbreviated christian names have been extended except in cases where the abbreviation is ambiguous (e.g. 'Ed.' could be 'Edward' or 'Edmund'; 'Jo.', 'John', 'Jonathan' or 'Joseph')[7] and the identification of the person is in doubt. Initials have been retained in all cases.

PLACE-NAMES have been transcribed 'as is' in all full transcripts and in passages quoted from documents which have been summarised. If necessary, the modern equivalent has been placed in square brackets after the name and where required an explanation for the interpretation has been provided in a footnote. Place-names have been modernised in calendars.

ARABIC NUMERALS have been used in all cases, with Roman numerals being converted to Arabic. The exception is in dates where Roman numerals have been retained, e.g. 'ix June'. (Note: in dates 'th' has been omitted as has the superior 'o' denoting a Latin case-ending.)

---

[7] In the previous volumes 'Jo.' was usually extended as 'John'.

HOLOGRAPHS AND SIGNATURES. The description 'holograph' has been applied conservatively and only where the signature is clearly in the same hand as the text.

A change in this volume has been to make clearer what is actually written by the signatory. Valedictory phrases, such as 'Your very loveinge frind', have previously been put with the signature. Here they are given with the text and are only put with the signature where i.) they are in the same hand as the signature, and ii.) they are not in the same hand as the rest of the text.

Similarly, this volume aims to show the exact form of the signature. Whereas previously an abbreviation such as 'Na.' would have been silently expanded to 'Nathaniel', it will now be shown as 'Na[*thaniel*]'. 'Xpo' is rendered as '[*Christofer*]' and 'Xpofer' as [*Christ*]ofer'. For obvious reasons, this does not apply to copied or draft signatures, attestations by mark or signatures given in sale catalogues.

As in the previous volumes, the note [*by mark:*] precedes the signature to which it relates.

ADDRESSES have been abbreviated to omit such common phrases as 'give these with speed' or to omit 'Norfolk' when a more specific place-name is also given. Omission marks have not been used in these cases.

SUSPENSIONS AND CONTRACTIONS have normally been expanded and modernised, with the following exceptions: where the extension is in doubt; where the abbreviation is continued into modern usage, for example 'etc'., 'gent', '&' (except at the beginning of a sentence where '&' has been transcribed as 'and'); the superior letters denoting amounts of money been transcribed £. *s. d.* and placed on the line; residual and apparently meaningless abbreviation signs, usually associated with 'll', 'm' or 'n' at the end of words, have been disregarded. '&c' has been rendered 'etc' and 'gentl', 'gentleman'. It has not always proved possible, however, to avoid inconsistencies in the expansion of suspensions and contractions. In general the principle has been followed that where the addition of a letter (or letters) will help the reader (i.e. if it conforms to modern usage or will not distort the sense or pronunciation of a word), it has been added; if the addition of a letter will serve only to confuse the reader the abbreviation has been disregarded.

e.g.   'Com̄ission' has been transcribed 'commission'
       BUT
    'com̄pany' has been transcribed 'company'

    'cañe' has been transcribed 'canne'
       BUT
    'fam̄e' has been transcribed 'fame'

    'hono^r' has been transcribed 'honour'
       BUT
    'cont^{r}y' has been transcribed 'contry', i.e. country

However, there has been a change in this volume in the treatment of the super-script 'r' and 'a' in favour of inserting 'u'. For example: whereas previously 'wor-shippe' would have been given as 'worshippe', 'manor' as 'manor' and 'tenᵃnt' as 'tenant', in this volume they appear as 'wourshippe', 'manour' and 'tenaunt' respectively.

'Mr' has been transcribed 'Mr' (as the point in time at which 'Mr' becomes a title in its own right as opposed to 'Master' seems to lie somewhere in the reign of Queen Elizabeth I)
          BUT
     'Mrs' and 'Mres' have been transcribed 'Mistres'.

LENGTH The information given on length refers to the area covered by the main text, not to the size of the whole document of which it is a part.

SYMBOLS AND EDITORIAL CONVENTIONS

« »	Indicates words which have been inserted. Volumes I-III, * *.
«« »»	Indicates words which have been inserted within an insertion. Volumes I-III, ** **.
< >	Indicates words which have been deleted. Volumes I-III, I. .I.
<< >>	Indicates a deletion within a deletion. (A rare occurrence, but it is sometimes possible to discern the process of double excision.) This is distinct from a deleted insertion.
⇨ ⇦	Indicates words underlined, often for deletion. (This is an innovation in this volume.)
/	Termination of marginalia in the manuscript, here incorporated into the body of the printed text.
<-Θ->	Indicates period within which an undated MS must fall, and the date range of serial documents e.g. [1590, May 2 <-Θ-> 25].
***	Indicates the relocation of a MS already included in the text and subsequently redated. (Used in volumes I–III, not used from volume IV onwards.)
" "	Indicates transcription of a passage within a document which is summarised.
italics	Indicates editorial comment outside the text, or entries which have been derived from sale catalogues.
[*italics*]	Indicates editorial comment within the text.
[?]statute	Indicates doubt about the transcription of a word.
[*word illegible*]	Indicates word that cannot be read.
[*word inserted*]	Indicates inserted word that cannot be read.
[*word deleted*]	Indicates deleted word that cannot be read.
[the other]	Indicates missing words (through damage to the MS) which have been supplied, or the elucidation of doubtful words.
[?the other]	As above, but there is doubt about the first word (no space between question mark and following word).
[? the other]	As above, but there is doubt about both words (space between question mark and following words).

[*? two words*]	Indicates missing words that cannot be supplied.
[*and*] the lo[*r*]ds	Indicates words or letters omitted in MS which have been supplied.
Undated	Indicates undated MS or MS dated to the day only.

INTRODUCTION

As with previous volumes in this series the purpose of this Introduction simply is to draw attention to some salient themes to be found among the documents printed here. It is our hope that the considerable labour involved in reconstituting the Bacon archive and preparing it for publication will be recompensed by other scholars finding within the edition as a whole grist for their particular mills. At the same time the two general editors and their research students continue to work on the exposition of various aspects of early-modern life as revealed—along with other sources—in the *Bacon Papers*. Some indication of the fruits of that work will be found in the footnotes to this Introduction and in the explicatory notes to the documents themselves.

The initial section of the Introduction provides a view on the progress of the edition thus far now that we are more than half-way through and sets out a prospectus for its conclusion. This is followed by a brief review of the wider historiographical context with regard to both the significance of an edition of documents such as this and its possible ramifications for current interpretations of important aspects of the period. Matters to do with actors and with fairs are then used to illustrate some of the miscellaneous types of evidence to be found here. Finally, as in earlier Introductions, this is followed in turn by sections detailing what we consider to be some especially pertinent themes within this particular volume. It should be noted that the exigencies of an Introduction such as this is means that not all the points that are made along the way can be expounded to the full. The intention has been to provide only indicative pointers to the secondary literature and to some of the documents in both this and earlier volumes.

*   *   *

At this juncture in the edition it may be helpful to take stock and to provide an overview of where we have got to and what yet needs to be done. The first volume covered some seventeen years in around 300 pages. Thereafter succeeding volumes have each run to between 300 to 350 pages of documents, together with around fifty pages of preliminaries and editorial introduction. However, the trend has been for the number of years covered in each volume to decrease: volume I covered seventeen years in full (with a few earlier documents); volume II, eight years; volume III, ten years; volume IV, seven years; and this volume encompasses five years. This is against a background in which the general principles governing editorial policy have remained largely the same since the inception of the project back in the 1970s. Therefore, this pattern is to be accounted for by two things. First, there is the simple survival rate of documents in particular years. Second, and somewhat more complicatedly, there is the type of document that has survived.

As reference to the editorial principles will indicate, some types of documents are fully transcribed; others are calendared either summarily, or in somewhat fuller 'linked transcripts' with embedded quotation designed to pinpoint key phrases and to impart a flavour of the document as a whole but omitting or summarising much common form; others are simply listed.[1] An innovation was introduced in volume IV whereby single samples of lengthy types of documents were provided while the remainder were simply listed.[2] Paradoxical as it might seem, some of the most substantial individual documents, such as the court rolls, account books, and Bacon's memoranda books as a justice, are only listed. Full publication of these types of documents in conventional form simply is not practicable. However, as need requires, material from the listed documents has been used in the explication of the documents transcribed in full.

The intention always has been to terminate the edition at the date of Nathaniel Bacon's death in 1622. Given the variables outlined above, our present estimate is that it will be possible to complete the edition in another two volumes covering the years 1608–1622. This may bring relief to those who wait with bated breath for the next episode in this Norfolk soap opera and who, along with the General Editors, may have been ageing somewhat and along with them wish to see the denouement. Indeed, it might be considered that at the present rate, latterly Nathaniel has been winning, as it has taken us twice the number of years to edit aspects of his life than it took him to live it!

The last volume will include an addendum of documents that have come to light subsequent to the publication of what would have been the relevant volume. It will also contain corrections to the dating of documents already printed where subsequent editing and research has made such corrections possible. We would be pleased to hear from others of any corrections or elucidations that they may be able to offer. Similarly, we would be pleased to hear from anyone who thinks that they may have identified an errant manuscript from the Bacon archive now in a repository that we have failed to reach.[3]

It may be helpful to point out that a number of bulkier documents that cannot be printed in full have been the subject of systematic analysis by means other than conventional publication. This is the case, for example, with the account books. These have been computerised. To this core of material has been added information from outside the Bacon archive, such as parish register entries for Stiffkey and the adjacent parishes. It is this that is referred to as the 'Stiffkey Database' at various points in this and the preceding volume. This has made possible the nominal data linkage that has permitted the reconstruction of the lives of the numerous 'little people' who inhabited the neighbourhood of Stiffkey. For example, the nature of service, a dominant institution of the period, has been scrutinised.[4] Similarly, it has been possible to examine the relationship between local office-holding, wealth, marriage and household formation.[5]

---

[1] Above, p.xxii.   [2] Changes to previous editorial practice are indicated on p.xix.

[3] In which case please email victor.morgan@uea.ac.uk.

[4] Linda Campbell, 'The Women of Stiffkey' (UEA, MA thesis, 1985); Michael Hinman, 'Some Issues in Day Labouring with Reference to the Day Labourers of Stiffkey, 1582–1598' (UEA, MA thesis, 1988); Smith, 'Labourers'.

[5] Jan Pitman, 'Status and Participation in Early Modern England: A Case Study from North Norfolk'

* * *

Not least the specific importance of the work on the neighbourhood of Stiffkey is twofold. First, it provides new insights by using types of sources such as the household account books that have not been used for this purpose in other studies. Second, it may serve to correct what is, perhaps, a prevailing approach within studies of small communities. This is the concern to examine the most 'peasant-like' communities where 'the lord' is only a shadowy presence. But, of course, during the second half of the sixteenth century and on into the seventeenth, most local communities were becoming more like the community to be found at Stiffkey, as the number of gentry-dominated localities proliferated. Great houses were built, as at Stiffkey, and they transformed economic and social relationships in the neighbourhood. In this volume we see the beginnings of a further round of this process as Bacon puts together the estate and begins to build a second house at Irmingland.[6] Also, through the employments that they offered houses such as these changed the experiences and the mental horizons of those that they drew into the complex and far-reaching nexus of their activities.[7] Moreover, two other social and administrative mechanisms brought the rulers into closer proximity with the ruled.

One of these was the way in which a new educated, articulate and proselytising clergy spread out into the parishes.[8] In some areas an alliance was formed between ministry and magistracy. As we see throughout the *Bacon Papers* indubitably this was the case in north Norfolk. Both minister and magistrate subscribed to a doctrine of predestinarianism in which there had already been a divine winnowing of the wheat from the chaff. The social consequence of this was the increasing distinction that came to be drawn between the godly and the reprobate. The former became associated with and looked to the patronage of local J.P.s such as Bacon, while the latter were subjected to regulation and punishment not only for practical but also for moral reasons. We need to recognise this as a motivation when we observe Bacon spending many hours conducting detailed investigations into the background to cases of bastardy.[9]

Furthermore, the increasingly intrusive presence of the owning classes was felt

(UEA, PhD, 1999); *idem*, 'Tradition and Exclusion: Parochial Officeholding in Early Modern England, A Case Study from North Norfolk, 1580–1640', *Rural History*, 15 (2004), pp.27–45.

  [6] Below, p.172.

  [7] Jill R. Taylor, 'Nathaniel Bacon: an Elizabethan Squire, His Family and Household and their Impact upon the Local Community', (UEA, PhD, 1990); Linda Campbell, 'Sir Roger Townshend and His Family: A Study of Gentry Life in Early Seventeenth Century Norfolk' (UEA, PhD, 1990); A. Hassell Smith, 'North Norfolk Coastal Settlements, 1550–1650: a Case Study of Stiffkey', *Medieval Settlement Research Group Annual Report*, 16 (2001), pp.9–12; Richard T. Spence and A. Hassell Smith, *Londesborough House and its Community, 1590–1643* (East Yorkshire Local History Society series, 53; York, 2005); Victor Morgan, 'Reprise and Prospect: The "Great House" in Norfolk, *Circa* 1450–1750', *Journal of the Norfolk Historic Buildings Group*, 1 (2002–2003), pp.35–52.

  [8] Victor Morgan, *A History of the University of Cambridge: Vol. 2: 1546–1750* (Cambridge, 2004), pp.234–7.

  [9] See under Bacon, Nathaniel, in the index. For evidence in earlier volumes see the relevant entries in the indices.

even where they might not be resident. This occurred through their presence-by-proxy in the shape of the numerous bailiffs and stewards who worked at their behest. It is these members of the middling sort who served either the Crown or private landowners and who identified with the interests of their masters. Not least this was because in the structure of circumstances in which they operated they often needed to invoke the authority of their masters in order to overcome the recalcitrance of the locals.[10] Conversely, we see that when the issue of parliamentary elections arose, the support of locally influential individuals such as these was important to candidates among the gentry.[11] Instances of such social types populate the pages of the *Bacon Papers*, along with technical specialists such as the land surveyors.[12] The former are a neglected group and require more detailed investigation. It was they who were responsible at the grass roots for passing on detailed local knowledge to their masters and then for turning the screw in order to extract more profits from assets.

Examples of this process include the drainage of the fens, the early stages of which are documented here.[13] In the disputes that invariably arose in these circumstances—as they did in the fens—what we see is a clash of beliefs between, on the one hand, a commitment to an older sense of the moral economy and, on the other, a more instrumental view geared towards the maximisation of return on economic resources. This is evident in both private and public contexts. For example, there is the efficiency with which Bacon puts together the landholding in the vicinity of what was to become Irmingland Hall.[14] There is also the way that as steward of the Duchy of Lancaster in Norfolk and in similar capacities he facilitated the moves to increase the return from Crown lands that had been initiated by Lord Treasurer Buckhurst in 1598.[15] Moreover, what we also see here is a reflexive action. For the insistent demands of a new economic imperative among the owning elites actually contributed to the process of economic dislocation and social displacement that from another perspective prompted disquiet among those elites about the maintenance of social order. All facets of these interconnected processes are to be seen in the specifics of the wide range of individual documents to be found in the *Bacon Papers*.

Recent work has drawn attention to the increasing number of intersections between state and society in response—not least—to the economic dislocations of this period; the social displacements to which these economic changes gave rise; and the political and administrative response of the ruling elites to what they perceived to be the dangers inherent in those social displacements.[16] We concur with

---

[10] For example, *BP*, iv, pp.271–2.   [11] Below, p.67.

[12] See, for example, *BP*, iv, pp.122–3, 212; below, pp.80, 239.

[13] Below, pp.80, 187–191. The term 'fen' has been used because it is the generic term now widely employed. However, a distinction needs to be drawn between the Fenland peats and the Marshland silts, together with different modes of traditional exploitation. Locals would have recognised this distinction and it may have been one of the sources for the dissention that arose as the early-modern process of drainage was initiated.   [14] Below, p.172.

[15] Below, pp.72–3. See also *BP*, iv, p. xlvii and references thereat.

[16] Steve Hindle, *The State and Social Change in Early Modern England* (Basingstoke, 2000); Michael J. Braddick, *State Formation in Early Modern England, c.1550–1700* (Cambridge, 2000).

this view. Indeed, in the Introduction to volume IV, written over ten years ago, we were at some pains to place the evidence gathered there in the wider context of two earlier historiographical phases of discussion of what has become known as 'state formation'.[17]

Of course, in the particularities of the documents published in this edition what we are seeing is one aspect of state formation as, for example, in the remarkable series of poor law accounts. In themselves these document a new form of provision that had been created in the 1570s and that from the outset had come under the scrutiny of the justices.[18] But the evidence provided by the *Bacon Papers* suggests that this was only part of what changed the relationship between the rulers and the ruled, and indeed, changed the nature of who the rulers were at the lower levels of the governing hierarchy.

It is evident from the papers in this edition and the work that has been done around them, that in addition to the increasing intrusiveness of the state we also need to give substantial weight to the three other factors evidenced here in bringing about these changes. First, as we have indicated, there is the extent to which an expanding number of members of the middling sort such as stewards, bailiffs and clergy identified with and served as the willing instruments of the owning elites rather than as representatives of or mediators on behalf of the communities in which, often, they resided. There is both irony and paradox in this.

The rulers of the time were ever anxious about the likelihood of various sources of social unrest. We see it here in the instructions sent down to Norfolk by the near-paranoid Chief Justice Popham.[19] But the irony is that in this period the successful members of the middling sort such as the bailiffs, stewards and parochial clergy were largely recruited from relatively humble backgrounds. Their own social marginality may have encouraged them to affiliate upwards and to attempt to distance themselves from the taint of both the social groups and the values of the groups in which they had originated. The paradox is that this social mobility for individuals largely denuded the commons of their potential leaders, making a sustained challenge to the governors such as had occurred in the first half of the sixteenth century—as in Kett's rebellion—that much more unlikely.

Second, as we have noted, there is the proliferation of the gentry, their building activities—as with Nathaniel at Stiffkey and then at Irmingland—and the way that their presence transformed their neighbourhoods by creating new patterns of demand through their kitchens and new experiences for those recruited into the service of the great house and sent on errands out from there to experience a wider world. New administrative arrangements also contributed to the enhancement of the power and status within their neighbourhoods of those gentry who were also J.P.s. Thus the development of petty sessions and the limit tended to create exclusive bailiwicks.[20]

[17] *BP*, iv, pp.xxxii–xxxiv and references thereat.
[18] Below pp.28–33, 160–5, 177–8, 203, 234–5, 237, 276 281–2; *BP*, iv, p.xxix. See Tim Wales, 'Poverty, Poor Relief and the Life-Cycle: Some Evidence from Seventeenth-century Norfolk', in: *Land, Kinship and Life-Cycle*, ed. Richard M. Smith (Cambridge, 1984), pp.351–404.   [19] For example, below, pp.36–7.
[20] See below, pp.xliv–v.

Combined with this was the near-parallel spread of a new type of clergy who were also representatives of 'the great tradition' in a way that their predecessors the pre-Reformation catholic priests rarely had been. Both processes brought the rulers closer to the ruled and both processes can be seen in train within the particularities of these documents. Finally, there are the ideological changes that took place, both in terms of a new, more pressing economic motivation and in terms of the consequences for the social valuation of individuals that followed from the acceptance of the theology of Calvinist predestination. These motivations as such are not directly discussed in these documents. Not least this is because the change in economic motivation in particular could occur as an historical phenomenon while at the time there was not the conceptual vocabulary available to objectify it: that would have to wait for the emergence of sociological and psychological insights in the centuries to come and to which we are heir. Nonetheless, within the documents it is possible to divine these new motivations through the actions that they record, if not through any explicit record of cogitation and reflection on the part of the agents of change.

*   *   *

More broadly, we are assertive of the fact that from its inception this edition and the research done on its periphery runs counter to what has become a *de facto* convention of the period. This is the division between 'high' and 'low' history, between the study of what the anthropologists call the great and the little traditions. We well understand the largely extra-historical demands that have encouraged this division and its inherent economy of effort over the last thirty years. But immersion in the editing of the multifarious sources brought together in this edition, and engagement in the on-going research associated with it, enforces a realisation of how misleading that division is. For example, in the preceding volume we drew attention to the importance of the social mechanisms of mediation and arbitration.[21] Associated with this was the equally important mechanism of petitioning. Later in this Introduction we focus on petitioning as a process illuminatingly evidenced in this volume. All these interconnected processes presume on the part of the individuals involved a set of assumptions shared across the social order. Moreover, they reveal a familiarity with both the formal and informal procedures, even the conventions of language, that were to be used in the situations from which petitions arose. The same is true with regard to ideas of 'credit', briefly discussed below.

Furthermore, it may be that we are at a specific historiographical juncture. There are more historians alive and working in the world today than ever lived in the history of the world before: it is becoming crowded and ever-more competitive out there. Moreover, as historians we have elaborated our interpretative arguments to a degree that those newly embarking on research are induced to locate themselves within the argumentative preoccupations of the present rather than with no certitude of safe harbour to launch themselves upon the continuing sea of

---

[21] *BP*, iv, pp.xli-xliii.

unknowing that is the past. In these circumstances the discipline imposed by editing, piece after piece, what is there in the archives enforces a due humility in the face of another reality. On occasion it enlightens us to what were their preoccupations as distinct from what are ours. It is out of these realisations no less than the elaboration and criticism of existing interpretations that we may come to a better understanding of the ever-intriguing territory that is the past.

Clearly, then, what has just been said is a pitch for claiming that a project such as the Bacon edition, and others like it, serves an important purpose over-and-above the particularities of the evidence that it makes accessible through its publication. Quite simply, and taken as a whole, it is one way to make us think afresh and look anew.

*   *   *

We will turn now to a review of selected major themes to be found running through the contents of this volume. In doing so, we will attempt to set those themes within an understanding of the broader context. But at the same time, and as need requires, we will also indicate where we think that the evidence to be derived from the *Bacon Papers* amplifies, refines, or calls into question the established understanding on certain issues. Indeed, in one or two instances we will suggest that the *Bacon Papers* prompt consideration of issues that clearly were important to contemporaries but which have not been accorded an equal consideration by historians: petitioning is a case in point.

The *Bacon Papers* offer considerable insights into the nature of the family and of households in this period, both amongst the gentry and—usually as the result of the recording of crimes and disputes—further down the social scale. When looked at from the viewpoint of the history of the gentry family as a whole in this period, earlier volumes have provided evidence of the somewhat oppressive oversight of his sons exercised by Sir Nicholas Bacon, Elizabeth's Lord Keeper.[22] After his father's death in 1579, Nathaniel seems to have come into his own as a patriarch in his own right in his adopted locality. However, it is evident that he did not get everything his own way, especially in his relationship with his second wife, Dorothy, whom he had married in 1597.

Frustratingly, the archive as a whole contains very little *direct* evidence of the more intimate personal relationships within the Bacon family. This contrasts markedly with the archives of near-contemporaneous families such as the Knyvetts of Ashwellthorpe and the Pastons of Oxnead. We suspect that there are two main reasons for this. First, there is some evidence that after Nathaniel's death someone weeded the accumulated papers. This is likely to have been done in order to preserve the more public papers and those relating to family concerns such as land ownership. Probably it was Nathaniel's long-time factotum and *éminence grise*, Martin Man, who undertook this task.

---

[22] For a review and discussion of this theme see *BP*, iv, pp.xxvii–xxix. For the wider background see, for example, Felicity Heal and Clive Holmes, *The Gentry in England and Wales, 1500–1700* (Basingstoke, 1994) and Ralph A. Houlbrooke, *The English Family 1450–1700* (London and New York, 1984).

Second, there is the issue of individual personality and the wider social forces that helped to shape it. But even given the paucity of direct documentation of Bacon the man, and when due caution is exercised, something can be done to infer the personality behind the busy administrator and conscientious politician. Indeed, over time it may be that it was his life in the public domain and the language there used to address him that helped to form his persona.[23] But even when these psychological speculations are put aside it is evident that Nathaniel was not the most outgoing of individuals. If anything he was driven by an austere morality that certainly can be seen to characterise his public life and that is unlikely to have been switched off when he passed through the gatehouse at Stiffkey. He cannot have been the most joyous person with whom to live. (Editors may be grateful for the archives bequeathed them, but they are not obliged to like the individuals whom they document.) In the background we can divine the stoic reserve inherited from his father that proved to be a philosophy of the ancients that was remarkably sympathetic to the experiences of those in public life in this period. At the same time there is abundant evidence for the driving force of predestinarian Calvinism and a life lived under the harsh guiding oversight of an omniscient magisterial god. Nathaniel was a man who could neither understand nor tolerate his second wife's perceived frivolity evident in her penchant for pearls.[24]

An ongoing cause of friction between Nathaniel and his wife was the management of what was intended to be the patrimony of her two sons by her previous marriage, Owen and William. In the period covered by this volume the inherent complexities of family relationships among the gentry are implicit rather than explicit. But they are evident in the oversight at a distance of the manors in Suffolk that had come into Bacon's orbit through his marriage to Dorothy.[25] More importantly, Nathaniel can be seen using his connections to search out a suitable location in which to establish his stepson. After a tentative start in the west of the county he can be seen putting together the estate and purchasing the site of what was to become Irmingland Hall, near Aylsham: Nathaniel was building again.[26]

Work began immediately and was completed in 1609. It was said to have cost £3,391.[27] The plan was 'E' shaped and it was somewhat larger than the unfinished Stiffkey Hall. One much modified wing survives, together with traces of the foundations. Because the intention was that it should pass to her son it was very much Lady Bacon's house. The inscription over the door said it all: "*Nathanael Bacon Miles, Anno Ætatis suæ 63, pro Dorothea Uxore, et Gulielmo-Roberds Smith, Filio ejusdem Dorotheæ, has Ædes erexit Ano 1609*".[28] But from a family viewpoint this was all to come to nought. The intended heir, Dorothy's son William, died aged

---

[23] Below, pp.lvii–viii.

[24] For a sympathetic view of Nathaniel's second wife, but a view not necessarily shared by all of the editorial team, see Key, 'Dorothy Bacon'. There is a more fully documented and illustrated version of the text and an extended introduction in Jane Key, 'The Letters and Will of Lady Dorothy Bacon 1597–1629' (UEA, MA thesis, 1986).   [25] Below, pp. 182, 191, 242, 257.

[26] Below, p.172. Blomefield states that the estate as such cost £2,886 19s 10d (Blomefield, vi, p.325,n.10).   [27] NRO NAS Frere K (3A) Irmingland Bundle.

[28] Blomefield, vi, p.324.

around 17 in the year that the hall was completed. Thereafter Nathaniel and Dorothy lived, rather uneasily, at Stiffkey during the summer and at Irmingland during the winter. This transhumance suggests that Inrmingland may have been conceived as a lodge despite being slightly larger than Stiffkey Hall as it stood in 1604.

The work at Irmingland was not the limit of Nathaniel's building activities for the gatehouse and curtain walls at Stiffkey were completed in these years, in part using recycled monastic stone.[29] However, this represented a compromise because the initial plan had called for a long gallery wing on this, the southern aspect of the house.[30] Coming as this work does following the initiation of the Irmingland project it signifies that Nathaniel had abandoned any aspirations to complete the house which his father, the Lord Keeper, had intended to symbolise the family's hegemony in north Norfolk. If it had been completed it would have been one of the finest exemplars of a mid-Tudor great house.

* * *

Any collection of papers such as this throws light on a diverse range of topics likely to be of interest to many different types of scholars and to anyone interested in the history of the county as a whole. It is not possible in this Introduction to identify and to discuss all these topics and to place them in the broader contexts that they illuminate. What follows in this particular section of the Introduction is but one example among many of the range of material that may be found here: it is the apparently worrying prospect of touring players. Until recently historians of the drama in this period have been obsessed with the relatively well-documented activities of the commercial theatre companies in London, newly established from the mid-1570s onwards.[31] However, the systematic exploration mainly of provincial archives in search of evidence for performance is beginning to correct this anachronistic perspective.[32] Albeit, the primary concern is still with the touring companies rather than with the numerous other forms of performance that prevailed in the provinces, as, for example, in Norwich, or more broadly with a society that in many ways was becoming more 'performative' in its social and political

[29] Below, p.105. The gatehouse is well illustrated in a print by Humphry Repton, published in 1760, and reproduced on the jacket of *BP*, iv. The series editors gratefully acknowledge the access to the hall and gardens at Stiffkey for the purposes of research during the extensive conservation work by its current owners. Readers should note that the hall is a private home and is not generally open to the public.

[30] Smith, 'Stiffkey Hall', especially pp.184–6. See also A. Hassell Smith, 'The Gardens of Sir Nicholas and Sir Francis Bacon: an Enigma Resolved and a Mind Explored' in: *Religion, Culture and Society in Early Modern Britain : Essays in Honour of Patrick Collinson*, ed. Anthony J. Fletcher and Peter Roberts (Cambridge, 1994), pp.125–60; *idem*, 'The Making of the Garden at Stiffkey Hall, 1574–1596', *Norfolk Gardens Trust Journal* (Spring 2006), pp.6–17. See also Mark Girouard, *Elizabethan Architecture: Its Rise and Fall, 1540–1640* (New Haven, Conn. and London, 2009), pp.76–7.

[31] For a useful recent summary of much of this work, and one that does take cognizance of the more formal aspects of provincial performance, see Jane Milling and Peter Thomson, eds, *The Cambridge History of British Theatre, Volume 1: Origins to 1660* (Cambridge and New York, 2004).

[32] Peter H. Greenfield, 'Drama outside London after 1540', in Milling and Thomson, *Cambridge History of British Theatre, 1*, pp.178–99. Provincial 'performances' other than those of the touring companies are usefully summarised on pp.178–186. For a gathering of local evidence see in particular David Galloway, ed., *Records of Early English Drama: Norwich 1540–1642* (Toronto, Buffalo and London, 1984).

behaviour.[33] Certainly, the later decades of Elizabeth's reign had seen the touring companies in Norfolk—most notoriously on the well-documented occasion in 1583 when a fracas occurred during a performance at the Red Lion in Norwich, culminating in the murder of a bystander by one of the actors: in this performance the stage props had included real swords.[34]

The Vagrancy Act of 1572 had created the need for noble patronage of the then emergent professional acting companies. It had permitted members of the nobility to licence companies of players thereby excusing them from the restrictions on movement imposed by the Act on those that it treated as rogues, vagabonds and sturdy beggars. It is this that led to the creation of appellations such as 'The Lord Admiral's Men'. From a social and political viewpoint the main service provided by these companies was the advertising of the patronage of those whose name they bore. In a society the sinews of which consisted of patron-client relations this was no small matter.[35] However, shortly after his accession James I—in effect—dynastised the acting companies. New patents were issued transforming the company of the Lord Chamberlain into the King's Men, that of the Lord Admiral into Prince Henry's Men and that of the Earl of Worcester into Queen Anne's Men. Around the same time the re-enactment of vagrancy legislation omitted provision for the licensing of companies of actors by members of the nobility. However, it is evident from Popham's letter of 8 June 1605 that this had not entirely suppressed "certeyn players of comon enterludes, belonging to some noble men, that travell up & downe those partes".[36] This raises two intriguing possibilities.

The first is that there was an expectation that players would venture to parts such as north Norfolk which were distant from major concentrations of population such as Norwich.[37] This might suggest that the company in prospect was a small group of provincial players of what Popham does indeed refer to as "comon enterludes" rather than being a subset of one of the major London com-

[33] For some preliminary perspectives on performance in Norwich in particular, and the wider argument that early-modern England was a 'performative' society, see Victor Morgan, 'Civic Memory and Material Culture in Early Modern Norwich', in: *Material Memories: Design and Evocation*, ed. Marius Kwint, Christopher Breward, and Jeremy Aynsley (Oxford and New York, 1999), pp.183–97; *idem*, 'Perambulating and Consumable Emblems: The Norwich Evidence', in: *Deviceful Settings: The English Renaissance Emblem and Its Contexts: Selected Papers from the Third International Emblem Conference, Pittsburgh, 1993*, ed. Michael Bath, and Daniel Russell (jointly, AMS Studies in the Emblem, no.13, and Occasional Studies Series sponsored by the Medieval and Renaissance Studies Program of the University of Pittsburgh, no.6; New York, 1999), pp.167–206; *idem*, 'A Ceremonious Society: An Aspect of Institutional Power in Early Modern Norwich', in: *Institutional Culture in Early Modern Society*, ed. Anne Goldgar and Robert I. Frost (Cultures, Beliefs, and Traditions, 20; Brill; Leiden and Boston, MA, 2004), pp.133–63; Douglas Ezzy, Gary Easthope and Victor Morgan, 'Ritual Dynamics: Mayor Making in Early Modern Norwich', *Journal of Historical Sociology* 22 (2009), pp.396–419.

[34] This was documented in the 19th century in J.O. Halliwell-Phillipps, *Contemporary Depositions Respecting an Affray at Norwich in the Year 1583* (London, 1864) and more recently in Galloway, *Early English Drama: Norwich 1540–1642*, pp.70–6. For an exposition of the event see Siobhan Keenan, *Travelling Players in Shakespeare's England* (Houndmills and New York, 2002), pp.99–106.

[35] Victor Morgan, 'Some Types of Patronage, Mainly in Sixteenth- and Seventeenth-Century England', in *Klientelsysteme Im Europa der Fruhen Neuzeit*, ed. Antoni M czak (Schriften des Historischen Kollegs, Kolloquien 9; Munchen, 1988), pp.91–116.

[36] Below, pp.183–4.

[37] However, see the map in Greenfield, 'Drama Outside London After 1540', p.188.

panies porting the best bits of plays that we might now recognise. However, excessive weight should not be attached to the word "enterludes" in the context of this letter. One has the impression that Popham was not an aficionado of dramatic productions of any kind but, rather, that the phrase is used as a dismissive condemnation of the activities of these players. Interestingly, the letter was addressed specifically to Bacon and his fellow J.P., William Yelverton, and its phrasing suggests that it had been prompted by intelligence provided to Popham that players might be in the vicinity. In turn this might indicate that such a group was looking to play in the houses of at least some of the gentry as a source of income, or at least expenditure reduction on food and lodging. This suggests that such venues were as rewarding financially as performances in the larger towns. However, the historians of the drama have given scant consideration to another possibility, largely because it is not documented by records of payments.

Elsewhere in this volume formal legal investigations reveal the importance of local annual fairs as magnets that attracted visitors from considerable distances, including a company of cutpurses and highwaymen. It was just such rumbustious occasions that were likely to be as attractive to the players of interludes as to cutpurses: the sense of festivity, the liberal imbibition of drink as described in the depositions, and the availability of the ready money required for purchases and payments—again referred to in the interrogations—were conducive to the remunerative activities of players no less than cutpurses. Nor was it simply their attraction to similar events for similar reasons that may have led to the equation of players with the criminal element at fairs. In one instance among those associated with this particular criminal fraternity was the daughter of a musician from Ware: itinerant entertainers and itinerant criminals may not have seemed all that distinct in the eyes of the governing class.[38]

* * *

In turning from a consideration of social and family matters and some of the miscellaneous material to be found in this volume to a review of the evidence for public life as documented here, we are turning to what is at the core of this, the preceding volume and the volume that is to follow. Certain key features stand out in these pages. First, there are technical issues to do with the availability of sources and administrative practice that need to be considered briefly. Second, there is evidence of the changing administrative practices with regard to petty sessions and the use of the limit as a sub-unit of administration. Third, there is material that reveals much about the circumstances surrounding one of the most critical events that could occur in the public sphere in this period: regime change in the early-modern dynastic state. Fourth, there are matters to do with elections and parliament. Fifth, there is a range of evidence that illustrates some fundamental characteristics of the prevailing political culture. This includes the constraints imposed by the pervasive honour culture and substantial evidence to be found in

---

[38] Below pp.277–81, examination of suspected criminals as Walsingham and Hempton fairs. For more legitimate activities at fairs see p.286 (Stourbridge) and p.303 (Ely).

this volume of the scale and significance of the process of petitioning. Running through all these strands are the insights that are to be gained into the workings of patronage, the royal Court and the relationship of these to the locality.

                                    *   *   *

From the viewpoint of documentation of government, and especially the relationship between the centre and the localities, it is possible to argue that the *Bacon Papers* take on a new significance in the period covered by this and the succeeding volume. This is because of the loss of the Privy Council Registers for the early years of the Jacobean regime. True, there are some contemporary extracts from the registers[39] and use has been made of the extracts as part of the background of research in preparing this volume. Also, there are the three parallel series of Cecil papers in the first hundred and twenty volumes of the British Library Lansdowne manuscripts; in the manuscripts still at Hatfield (and also available on microfilm in the British Library), calendared in the twenty-four volumes of the Historical Manuscripts Commission Series 9; and among the Cecil and other papers in the State Papers Domestic. However, the *Bacon Papers* for this period are likely to convey a very good idea of what was being demanded of local government by the centre during the early years of the new regime. For example, in the preceding volume we saw how, under the aegis of Lord Treasurer Buckhurst, this included renewed attempts to exploit Crown lands more efficiently.[40] Because of the various local Crown offices held by Bacon, for example as the steward of royal manors, this campaign is evident again among his papers in this volume.[41]

Moreover, as will emerge from the more detailed discussion of petitioning,[42] the perspective from any one central institution such as the Court of Requests can be misleading with regard to both the incidence and the range of business transacted. The recent publication of contemporary indices to business in the Court of Requests has been most welcome.[43] But the papers published here make it clear that this view from the centre is by no means comprehensive, even with regard to the specific institution that the index does document.[44] But beyond that the *Bacon Papers* make it evident from the local perspective that petitioning, and the consequent mediation or arbitration to which normally it gave rise, was a pervasive practice employed in connection with many government and judicial bodies and officials, and even solicited informally by private individuals.

                                    *   *   *

Bacon's substantial involvement in local government means that his papers provide significant insights into local administrative procedures. This is valuable because in the case of Norfolk there is only piecemeal survival of the relevant Quarter Sessions records before the 1640s. A similar situation exists in the case of Assize

---

[39] BL MS Add. 11402.   [40] *BP*, iv, pp.121–5.
[41] Below, pp.9–10, 18–19, 21–2, 42–3, 66, 76, 79–80, 136, 138, 144–5, 166, 211, 218, 232–4, 246–7, 265, 268, 289–93, 304, 306, and especially pp.71–3.
[42] Below, pp.lx–xiii.   [43] Hoyle *et al.*, *Heard Before the King*.
[44] See the index to the present volume under 'Requests, Court of'.

records. Moreover, even if these archives had survived they would not necessarily have documented aspects of administration that are revealed here, especially with regard to the earlier stages of complaint or investigation, further examples of which are to be found scattered throughout this volume. But it is not just that records have been lost over the centuries: they were also mislaid and lost at the time. One zealous J.P., John Richers, had advocated the keeping of a proper record of liability to rates "putt into a booke and kepte with the recordes of the peace, there to be alwaies extant". Instead of which, he complained, it had been "delivered aboute in papers, and soe came to private handes & is now lost".[45] Moreover, military affairs were outside the purview of the Quarter Sessions and the Assizes as such and in the main their archives do not record business relating to military matters. Sometimes this is compensated for by the way in which some gentry who served as commissioners for musters or deputy lieutenants kept distinct 'lieutenancy books'.[46] Bacon seems not to have done this, and the papers relating to military affairs are distributed generally among his other papers. This may tell us something about how he conceived of these activities as part of the broad spectrum of his wider judicial and other administrative engagements. As with the issue of militia rates he may have conceived of military matters at least as much in constitutional as in strictly military terms.[47]

As a local archive the *Bacon Papers* also allow us to assess the extent to which the adoption of particular administrative procedures were the outcome of central government fiat or the result of local initiatives evolved in response to local circumstances. For example, on 23 June 1605 the Privy Council issued orders to "diverse Justices of the Peace" enclosing orders that they were to implement "within their severall precincts".[48] This was part of a wider campaign at this time to energise and to enforce greater responsiveness from local government generally. Thus a week later the Council wrote to the Lords Lieutenant of the counties about the need to maintain the expensively acquired equipment of the trained bands. But as with the periodic efforts of the Elizabethan Council to enforce efficiency in local government, this outburst of energy was as likely to have caused resentment as it did sustained improvement.[49] In Norfolk, one response to this particular order was the warrant to chief constables of August 1605.[50]

Among other things the Orders required the adoption of what effectively were petty sessions, to meet every six weeks in the intervals between full meetings of Quarter Sessions. This might be read as central government systematically imposing a new procedure on local government. In some parts of the country, such as the Borders, this may indeed have been the case.[51] But elsewhere, in advanced counties such as Norfolk, in effect the pressure of business had already led to the adoption

---

[45] Below, p.284. [46] For example, BL MS King's 265.

[47] Below, pp.117, 220–1, 298–9, and more broadly see Smith, 'Militia Rates', pp.93–110.

[48] BL MS 11042, f.101. There is a copy of the Orders in NRO AYL 304.

[49] Views differ somewhat on this. See Anthony Fletcher, *Reform in the Provinces: the Government of Stuart England* (New Haven and London, 1986), pp.52–3 and Diana Newton, *The Making of the Jacobean Regime: James VI and I and the Government of England, 1603–1605* (Woodbridge, 2005), pp.133–5.

[50] Below, p.203. [51] *HMC Salisbury*, xvii, pp.382–3, 427–8.

of something like petty sessions and the concomitant, sub-administrative geo-graphical entity of the division or "lymitt".[52]

Some aspects of the Orders of 1605 that touched upon the supervision of the justices themselves may have arisen from a high-handed ignorance on the part of the new Jacobean government of the complex relationship between the J.P.s in the counties and the Council.[53] There are other indications, in the fiscal area, that the new Scottish members of the Council may have ridden roughshod over English sensitivities.[54] However, in the case of the attempt to impose petty sessions across the country it is possible that practices already in place in some counties may have been observed by members of central government such as Chief Justice Popham, and Coke as Attorney General. They had come to appreciate the merits of these arrangements and then attempted to have them adopted elsewhere.

Certainly, in April 1605, before the issuing of the Orders, one of Martin Man's correspondents refers quite casually to "your master or some other justice of peace in the lymittes".[55] Even before then, at the time of proclamation of James' acces-sion, the county had been divided into limits or double limits for the purpose of proclaiming James' accession.[56] That said, the detailed evidence suggests that there may be more reference to the use of limits after the issuing of the Order, as in the allusions in the letter of John Palgrave in November 1607.[57] The evidence consist-ing of entries in Bacon's recognizance book makes it clear that the double limit was used as the basis for gatherings of petty sessions.[58]

The limit provided a more convenient area within which obligations could be enforced. Thus, John Richers, in his rôle as treasurer of the various county funds, sought the support of the justices within their respective limits as a means of jolly-ing up slack chief constables into collecting the rates that had been imposed.[59] As Richers appreciated, by invoking the limit it was possible to make specific justices responsible for what happened within a clearly defined area. Similarly, a testy letter from the judges of assize in Norfolk reported that they had been informed of "diverse robberyes burglaryes & other notorious fellonyes lately don" and attributed this to, among other things, "remisse pursuite of the offendours". The J.P.s were to make "diligent & carefull examinacions & sifting of all others, within your severall lymittes, which by reason of their idle course of life may give cause of suspicion."[60] Nevertheless, some energetic J.P.s such as Bacon on occasion acted on matters that fell outside their usual limit.[61] On the other hand, the corollary of enforcing responsibility of J.P.s for a specific limit was that some became unwilling

---

[52] Indeed, the origins of the limit can be traced back to the 1530s when the justices were required to divide their counties into four, six or eight areas and to meet to deal with business in these areas every six weeks. The Norfolk justices had responded by creating eight limits. These consisted of groupings of the older administrative unit of the Hundred. Flexibility was maintained by re-grouping the Hundreds within partic-ular limits as occasion required.

[53] Fletcher, *Reform*, p.53.   [54] Below, pp.47–8, 59.   [55] Below, p.171.
[56] Below, pp.25–6.   [57] Below, pp.300–1.   [58] Below, pp.281–2.
[59] Below, p.215. When he handed over this thankless job to Bacon he was still advocating the use of the limit as the unit for collecting information (below, p.284.)
[60] Below, p.302. The letter was addressed to the J.P.s "for the lymittes & Hundredes" there specified, to be delivered "from one to another with all speede".   [61] Below, p.177n. See also p.26n.

to deal within a limit that was not theirs.[62] Sometimes the implication seems to be that effectively the limit became an exclusive bailiwick. One reason for this was to avoid one justice being played off against another, as when John Rooke tried to have his alehouse licence renewed and the clerk of the peace told him that "it must be granted by thosse justices of the same limit that did grant yt the last yeare".[63] But another must have been that a justice would not act within another's limit for risk of offending a fellow gentleman in this status-conscious society.[64] The unforeseen sociological consequence of the widespread adoption of the limit and petty sessions must have been to enhance the status and authority of individual gentry within their own immediate neighbourhood as a result of the increasingly exclusive power that they exercised there.

Familiarity with the limit meant that it was also adopted for other purposes such as the assessment of the subsidy.[65] On occasion, such as an inquiry into the lands and goods of recusants, it was deemed appropriate to combine two limits for the purposes of the activity, as had been done in proclaiming James' accession.[66] This use of the double limit added to the authority of the occasion by increasing the number of justices present at the event while still holding them responsible for the specific area under their oversight, in addition to coinciding with the area encompassed by the familiar regular meetings of petty sessions.[67] At the most the Privy Council Order in the summer of 1605 merely gave further impetus and precision to arrangements that already were present in more than protean form in Norfolk.

* * *

A further major issue evident in this volume concerns the local ramifications of the death of Elizabeth and the accession of James I. During the late-fifteenth and sixteenth century throughout Europe there emerged a new type of politics based around the royal court. This curial politics replaced the household politics that preceded it and—in England—preceded the party-based parliamentary politics that emerged during the course of the late-seventeenth century. The focal component of this politics was a new type of personalised, charismatic dynastic monarchy. Within this structure of curial politics one of the most critical occasions was the transition of power from one monarch to another. After James' arrival in England, the Venetian ambassador recorded a conversation that he had had with Lord Kinloss, a Scots confidante of the new king of England. Kinloss alluded to the uncertainty about the situation as felt by James prior to his accession. His comment to the ambassador was that "by a Divine miracle all has gone well".[68] Both men shared a Continent-wide perspective and the comment is a measure of how far both men would have been aware of the potential volatility surrounding such events.

The uncertainties inherent in these occasions were that much greater when what

---

[62] Below, p.247.   [63] Below, p.283.   [64] Below, pp.lviii–x.

[65] Below, pp.270–1.   [66] Below, pp.201–2, pp.25–6.

[67] For limits and by implication the petty-sessional areas in Norfolk in this period see Map 1, p.lxiv.

[68] Quoted at <http://www.history.ac.uk/ihr/Focus/Elizabeth/index.html>.

was in prospect was not only a change of monarch but also a change of dynasty: something that in the English context had become inevitable as the childless Elizabeth aged and the consequences of her death were contemplated. In the days immediately following his proclamation James was to refer to the process as "the translation of a monarchy" and praised the smoothness with which this had been effected by his supporters in London.[69]

In so far as these occasions have been studied what has been looked at has been the centre of power.[70] What we have in this volume of the *Bacon Papers* is a perspective from the viewpoint of the periphery—albeit what is demonstrated in this matter as in others is the dialogue-like character of the relationship between these two parts of the polis.[71] What emerges is a sense of the understandable nervousness of those at the centre in handling what for them was an unprecedented circumstance, but one for which there were too many ill-precedents in recent European history, most immediately in the case of the disputes surrounding Henri IV's accession in France. What we see in the documents set out here is a real anxiety about what might happen.

In examining the texts of the documents disseminated to the county what we also see is a paradox. During this process of dynastic transition in the personalised monarchical state there is a necessary groping towards a rather more abstract view of the state.[72] Even before the Queen's death the concern is with "the preservacion of the state", with a distinction tacitly being acknowledged between "hir Majestie & the state".[73]

Moreover, in these circumstances the central elite implicitly invited the provincial elites to concur in the overarching imperative: to maintain stability and to maintain the state. The latter are characterised by the former as "being persons of chiefe authority & reputacion in that contrey, & of entire affection to the preservacion of the state".[74] The council affected to be "assured that the better & wiser sort of men will governe themselves, with such discretion & judgment, as is meete",[75] and in so opining no doubt hoped to ensure that this would be the case.

Interestingly, one might have expected that the main problem at such a point of transition would be the danger of factionalism within the inner circles of the central elite, or the danger of challenges from within the provincial elites over the line of succession. That had been the case in the past at both the inception and at points of transition within the Tudor dynasty. Ironically, in the first respect the ill-judged attempted coup by the earl of Essex in 1601 probably had removed this threat by permitting the consolidation of the so-called *regnum Cecilianum*.[76] It also

---

[69] Quoted in Pauline Croft, *King James* (Basingstoke, 2003), p.49.

[70] However, see Diana Newton, *The Making of the Jacobean Regime: James VI and I and the Government of England, 1603–1605* (Woodbridge, 2005), pp.133–140.

[71] As a specific example of this dialogue see the discussion of the documents in this volume concerned with the export of grain.

[72] Similarly, earlier volumes of this edition provide evidence of the way in which pressing military and financial circumstances, or the perceived catholic threat, led to the invocation of the notion of 'reason of state' which—it was implied—overrode the constraints imposed by practice, custom or law.

[73] Below, p.15.   [74] Below, p.15.   [75] Below, p.14.

[76] See in particular the as always insightful paper by Mervyn James, 'At a Crossroads of the Political

seems to have prompted Cecil to establish secret lines of communication with James in order to avoid any similar disturbances on the Queen's death. But of equal interest is the fact that by this stage in the evolution of the Tudor state the provincial gentry elites were so heavily implicated in it that they could be relied upon to concur with the management of the dynastic transition by their central confrères acting in their joint interests. As the Council recognised, "everie good subject is interested «in»" the prevention of "disorders, or anie the least disturbance of the comon quiet".[77] There was a verbal—and by implication, real-world—subsumation of the local elites within a shared community of interest among those who governed at whatever level and a rhetoric of invited recruitment by the central elite of their local compariots, that "wee & you, & all others, that truly love the state, maie in unitye & comon amity joyne togither in all such corses as may preserve both in publick & private the peace & tranquillity of the same".[78] There was good reason for the anxiety evident here.

Although in the outcome it never happened, at the time there was concern that alternative internal or external contenders might make a pitch for the throne. These included James' cousin, Arabella Stuart, who was also a descendant of Henry VII, and as a consequence she was kept under close observation at Hardwick Hall. Just across the North Sea, in Brussels, from 1599 onwards the Spanish Netherlands was governed by the Infanta, Isabella, and her cousin, Albert. In 1588 her father, Philip II of Spain, had claimed that her descent from Edward III justified her claim to the English throne. In the latter context there was also the added dimension of the possibility of support from dissident English catholics.[79] If either of these contenders had intervened it could have resulted in substantial and long-running upheavals. Catholic priests were to be implicated in the Bye and Main plots[80] and in the summer of 1603 there were suspects in Norfolk.[81] There was also a general background of anxiety about the supposed subversiveness of English catholics.[82] Interestingly, Chief Justice Popham required a census of recusants in the summer of 1605[83] and it may be that it was this that finally confirmed to catholic dissidents that there would be no relief for their condition from the new monarch.[84] In turn this may have helped to precipitate what was to become known as the Gunpowder Plot at the opening of Parliament in November of that year.

However, the main concern as articulated in the documents printed here appears to have been with the threat of popular unrest. In itself this offers a rather different perspective on the politics of dynastic transition as something of concern to more than the elites, both central and provincial. It suggests two things. First,

Culture: The Essex Revolt, 1601', in his *Society, Politics and Culture: Studies in Early Modern England* (Past and Present Publications; Cambridge, 1986), pp.416–65.

[77] Below, pp.14–15.   [78] Below, p.15.

[79] In the days prior to Elizabeth's death an order was issued for the restraint of recusants (BL MS Add. 11402 f.85v).

[80] Below, p.60.   [81] Below, pp.43–4.   [82] *BP*, iv, pp.xlviv–xlvi.

[83] Below, pp.185, 192–3, 200–206, 210.

[84] This was despite early signs of favour to some known catholics (below, p.213n).

there is the earth-moving nature of the prospect of a change of monarch at *all* levels of society. Second, it demonstrates the extent to which on such occasions the populace at large felt themselves to have an interest and engagement, even if this was not entirely approved of by their governors. The main concern appears to have been that news of the Queen's illness had given occasion to "the multitude, & especially to those that are of evil & unquiet disposicion, to raise & disperse manie bruites & rumours, everie man according to his humour & affection".[85] As we see below, a copy of the letter from the Council of mid-March 1603 was made by Bacon's factotum, Martin Man. In effect Man's endorsement for the purposes of filing reflects not only the main import of the letters themselves but also a tacit recognition of what might be expected in the circumstances of the time: for an experienced observer of the local scene they were, necessarily, "Letters concerning repressing rumors". Those of "place & quality" were encouraged to suppress rumours of the Queen's ill-health and to prevent what was contemplated might be "unlawfull assemblies, actions, & disorderly attemptes that such rumours maie breede there in the contrey about you".[86]

In the outcome what is worth remarking is how little local evidence there is of popular unrest as a result of the dynastic transition of 1603. Once again, this serves to demonstrate an important point about the thinking of the elites in this period. This is the degree to which the fear of popular unrest had been implanted by the experience of large-scale popular upheavals during the first half of the sixteenth century. Thereafter their avoidance became a prime directing aim of government. But the environing circumstances had changed. As we have suggested, many 'parish notables', who, like Kett, might have led revolts in earlier days, had been co-opted into dependence on and emulation of their social superiors by, among other things, their absorption within the lower reaches of office-holding in the expanding Tudor state. To this degree by the late sixteenth century contemporary fears of unrest were out of proportion to the prevailing sociological realities. Nonetheless, misjudged as it may have been, the fear of popular unrest remained intense. As such, as on this occasion, it constituted a prime concern and first anxiety among the nation's governors both central and local.

Therefore, whatever the fixity of what actually happened may appear to be in hindsight, perhaps we need to recognise that at the time James' peaceful accession was not so much a foregone conclusion as a nervous achievement. As we have indicated, some elements of that contemporary anxiety are evident in these papers.

* * *

Another feature of the period that is revealed by the documents surrounding James' accession is the punctiliousness with which legal and constitutional niceties were handled. To us, in a post-modern world, the law and the constitution are working rules and fictions of convenience that are designed to embody our prevailing norms. Recently, it is this underlying presupposition no less than issues of personality that gave us Blairite 'sofa government'. But in this earlier period the law

---

[85] Below, p.14.   [86] Below, p.15.

and the constitution were 'factitious', real things 'out there' that had, as it were, a life of their own. It is this which justifies describing the Tudor-Stuart state and much contemporary thinking as 'juridical'.[87]

As a consequence both those in the centre and in the localities displayed a marked sensitivity to the basis of their power and the propriety of their behaviour as a result of the death of the Queen. For example, today, the Council of Accession has become part of the constitution. But in the period with which we are concerned the precise status of any such Council was less clear. Moreover, the very length of Elizabeth's reign meant that there was little direct past experience of similar circumstances on which to rely. Also, because today monarchs may still reign but they have long since ceased to govern or to rule, a Council of Accession is largely a quaint formality. But in a world in which monarchs still ruled, and in which some such as Phillip II of Spain did, and—howbeit intermittently—the new English king would indeed attempt to, govern, the status and the actions of the residual Privy Council were hedged about with uncertainty. The death of the Queen had also dissolved what had become the central institution of the state— the Privy Council—local government's chief interlocutor. Certainly, that seems to have been the view of the Council itself according to which the death of the Queen meant that "ther remayneth unto us no further authoritie then by provisionall care to applye our uttermoste helpe and indeavours for the preservacion of peace & tranquilitie and to make the better accompt and representacion of the state unto the Kinge our Sovereigne that nowe is".[88]

It was in these circumstances, and at least in part it is for this reason, that the Council strove to legitimate its actions by seeking the concurrence of, and joining with it, the representatives of the wider social order.[89] At various stages this had involved the engagement of as many of the nobility as were available in London: "all persons of the nobilitie of this realme that at this tyme and place could presently be assembled" for the proclamation of the King's accession. Implied here is the notion of the aristocratic *respublica* and the need for its approbation. But at this latter juncture there was added what is the implicit further legitimation inherent in "the generall and firme consent of the Cittie of London the cheife place of resorte of this kingdome and all other good subjectes therabout eyther of greater or meaner qualitie".[90] Here is an echo of a medieval constitutionalism that was still to be heard in the forthcoming coronation in which one source of monarchical legitimacy, evident in the acclamation, derived from below. But already on hearing the proclamation of the new King the London crowds had given their spontaneous "joyfull acclamacions".[91]

At the level of the locality also there was evident uncertainty as to the legitimacy with which those in authority might act. Some five days after the Queen's death

---

[87] *BP*, iv, p.xlix. [88] Below, p.24.

[89] On the 19th of March the nobility in and around London were asked to come to Court the following day attended by their retinues "for the avoidinge of rumor". On the following day the Council wrote to the nobility assuring them that it would respect their interests in the state that arose from their pre-eminency of birth and place. (BL MS Add. 11402, ff.86, 87.)

[90] Below, p.24. [91] Below, p.24.

the subsidy commissioners in Norfolk had written to Sir Edward Coke asking if they might proceed. As always, Coke had a legal *aperçu* to hand: "though the glasse of tyme runneth out, yet *nullum tempus* (as is comonly said) *occurrit Regi* ['Time does not run against the Crown']. Nonetheless, the Lord Keeper, the Lord Treasurer, the Lord Chief Justice and the Attorney General as commissioners for the subsidy in London "have spared to proceede therin, untill further warrant & direcion be obteyned".[92]

There is a sense in all this of a strand of thought in which the death of the monarch was seen to dissolve the state and to invalidate its actions to an extent that we would find it impossible to comprehend today. At the same time there is a contrary thought that derives in part from the quotidian experience over preceding decades of those increasing numbers of individuals enrolled as the instruments of rule. This was something that an educated clergyman such as John Percival recognised in the person of his patron, Nathaniel Bacon, a man in *"gravissimis reipublicae curis"*.[93] Those such as Bacon had experienced the pressing demands for men and money to meet the continual threats from the Hapsburgs and from recent rebellion in Ireland. Increasingly, in these circumstances desperate politicians and administrators in Whitehall had invoked 'reason of state'.[94] Concurrently, during Elizabeth's reign one way of dealing with the incongruous reality of a female monarch was to elaborate long-standing theories of the monarch's two bodies.[95] Thus experience, necessity and the recent elaboration of theory had imparted to 'the state' an existence beyond the person of any individual monarch. In very practical ways 'the state' was becoming an abstraction of itself. Something of this is evident too in the language used by those in London when they communicated with those in the localities in the period surrounding the death of Elizabeth and the accession of James. As we have seen, in anticipation of Elizabeth's death those "persons of chiefe authority & reputacion in that contrey [Norfolk]" are assumed to be "of entire affection to the preservacion of the state".[96] Further, this distinction between state and monarch is explicit in the accession council's desire "to make the better accompt and representacion of the state unto the Kinge our Sovereigne that nowe is".[97] Linguistically, "the good of the state" is distinguished from the good of "the rightfull Sovereigne".[98] All this is enunciated by the central elite to their compatriots in the localities under the pressure of the exceptional circumstances of dynastic change in which they found themselves.

---

[92] Below, pp.26–7. The legal doctrine of *nullum tempus occurrit regi* dates back to Bracton's *De Legibus et Consuetudinibus Angliae* in the 13th century. Essentially, it maintains that, unlike private plaintiffs, the Crown is not subject to limitations of time, and today is mainly concerned with the Crown's exemption from statutes of limitations. Characteristically, here, Coke seems to construe it in a rather different way in order to meet the immediate circumstances arising from the Queen's death.   [93] Below, p.97.

[94] These developments and this language can be traced in earlier volumes of this edition.

[95] The classic statement is, of course, Ernst Kantorowicz, *The Kings's Two Bodies* (1957). See also Marie Axton, *The Queen's Two Bodies: Drama and the Elizabethan Succession* (Royal Historical Society Studies in History; London, 1977) and Albert Rolls, *The Theory of the King's Two Bodies in the Age of Shakespeare* (Studies in Renaissance Literature, 19; Lampeter, 2000).

[96] Below, p.15.   [97] Below, p.24.

[98] Below, p.24. See also pp.35–6 for a formulation in another context by Chief Justice Popham.

Nonetheless, in what they have to say we may be seeing a development in the evolution of the concept of the state in this period as it becomes more of an abstraction. Ironically, the distinction between the person of the monarch and the abstraction of the state was progressed at this, one of the most critical junctures in the structure of any early-modern state, as one monarch and one dynasty succeeded another.

*   *   *

The contents of this edition as a whole gives the lie to now outmoded view that the differences between the centre and the periphery, between what contemporaries would have called the 'court' and the 'country', were in any way a result of the isolation of the one from the other. This is true in general, but as we will see here, the upheaval occasioned by James' accession demonstrates the rapidity with which new lines of communication could be established. While there may have been differences of interest and to some extent different values associated with the Court and with the Country, in this period at least, what these dominant entities were depended largely on the one knowing about the other. As is evident here, the centre demanded information of the localities, as in the continual oversight of Norfolk exercised by Chief Justice Popham as an assize judge. Also documented here is the Lord Treasurer Buckhurst's strategy to boost royal income by a more thoroughgoing exploitation of Crown lands. As we see, this required detailed if rather piecemeal information about aspects of landscape and of tenures that previously had languished in convenient obscurity.

But the initiative to provide information about the county also came from the locality and took a variety of forms. For example, in this volume we have yet another round in the long-running saga in which representatives of the county— or, rather, representatives of an interest group within the county—continued to claim that the authorities in London did not understand the practicalities of the local agricultural economy and really should permit the export of grain.[99]

Another source of information about both persons and places was the stream of petitions from the locality with which a wide variety of central institutions were deluged.[100] Nor was it simply the persons within the petitions with which the centre became cognizant—sometimes tiresomely so if the terms of referral are read aright.[101] Most petitions were referred back for resolution to members of the gentry in the county. Implicit in this process is the fact that many officials in London must have had a considerable knowledge of who was who and who was where in the localities.[102] The number of petitions passed on to Nathaniel Bacon

---

[99] Below, pp.10–11, 47–9, 52–5, 59–62, 92–4, 153n., 158–160.

[100] For some discussion of petitioning in its own right see below, pp.lx–xiii.

[101] Also, there was an ongoing problem of suitors pestering the Court (BL MS Add. 11402, fo.82v).

[102] The *libri pacis*, listing the names of local J.P.s and still to be found in various parts of the central archives, were one source of information (see Thomas Garden Barnes and A. Hassell Smith, 'Justices of the Peace from 1558 to 1688: a Revised List of Sources', *Bulletin of the Institute of Historical Research*, 32, 1959, pp.221–42). From the 1570s this was augmented by the availability of printed maps compiled on a county basis (see Victor Morgan, 'The Cartographic Image of "the Country" in Early Modern England', *Transactions of the Royal Historical Society*, 5th ser., 29, 1979, pp.129–54). It should be noted that in some

by Sir Roger Wilbraham and Sir Julius Caesar, both Masters of Requests, suggest that he must have been very well known to these central government officials. Certainly, one of Julius Caesar's valedictions to Bacon and Sir Christopher Heydon is as "Your verie loving frend".[103]

From another viewpoint there is also the issue of how much individuals in the localities knew about who was who at Court and in the central administration, and to whom it would be appropriate to address a specific request. Related to this is the quasi-political issue of how much was known about who was in favour and who was not. One source of information of especial utility with regard to the latter type of intelligence was the manuscript newsletters that proliferate in this period. Given Bacon's evident public interests it is surprising that no coherent set of such letters survive in his archive. Again, there may have been post-mortem pruning. Allusions suggest that he was in receipt of information directly from the Court: "I knowe[,] it [is] written downe by a courtier ...".[104] Items of news also survive as adjuncts to letters of business and there are a number in this volume that detail events in and around the new Jacobean Court.[105] One such source of information was the Baker brothers of Lynn. Some of their activities on behalf of the interests of the county suggest a remarkable familiarity with circumstances in London, even extending to access to the Privy Council registers![106] An equally remarkable phenomenon documented here is the sheer rapidity with which agents of the locality and those in the locality latched on to who were the shining stars in the bright firmament of the new Jacobean Court. Conversely, the new Scots patrons at Court appear to have been equally adept at instantaneously developing a network of dependants in the English localities.[107] Evidently, Edinburgh had been a good training ground for how to operate in the lusher pastures to the south. This might suggest something that has not been remarked on before. The paradox is that the fundamentals of patron-client relations within the framework of a curial system of politics in early-modern Europe were more widely shared than the more varied experiences of the far more diverse national political structures that prevail in Europe today.

It was also the case that James' accession changed the fortunes of some of the Englishmen around the Court. For example, Sir Walter Raleigh was displaced by Sir Thomas Erskine as Captain of the Guards.[108] Under James the reinstatement of the Howards at Court also had ramifications for Norfolk. Up until the execution of the fourth Duke in 1572, Norfolk and parts of Suffolk had constituted one of the last surviving great magnatial 'countries' in England. The power of the Howards had emanated from their house at Kenninghall, the Castle at Framlingham, the family mausoleum in the priory at Thetford, the Duke's palace in Norwich and the Italianate villa of the mercurial Earl of Surrey that for a

instances the petitioners specifically requested that a named local dignitary be appointed to arbitrate their case. But even in these instances if the central official was to do his job properly he needed to know who the person proposed was.   [103] Below, p.38.

[104] Below, p.69. For an earlier period see *BP*, i, *passim*, and below, p.234n.

[105] Below, pp.68–9, 71–2. There is also the issue of how quickly information was exchanged between centre and localities, see, for example, below, p.25n.   [106] Below, pp.59–60.

[107] Below, pp.83–4.   [108] BL MS Add. 11402 f.88v.

time overlooked Norwich. This presence and monopolistic level of power was never to be regained. Nonetheless, they reappear as Lords Lieutenant of the county,[109] although the detailed manuscript evidence elsewhere suggests that they were never consistently effective in that rôle. These shifts in influence at Court as a result of James' accession also had ramifications for the local clients of courtiers. Thus, Bacon's campaign against James Pointer—in Bacon's view a wayward local clergyman—probably foundered on the rock of Pointer's patron, Henry Percy, Earl of Northumberland who for a time was back in favour at Court.[110]

A further feature revealed here is the fine tuning of local antennae to the changing fortunes of those at Court. With James' accession this meant learning the names and the standing of a lot of newly arrived Scotsmen. One such was George Home, Lord Treasurer of Scotland and in May 1603 appointed Chancellor and Under Treasurer of the English Exchequer. Not least awareness of him arose because he started to sign documents sent to the counties in tandem with Lord Treasurer Buckhurst, and as a member of the English Privy Council.[111] In pursuing the important issue to do with the constraints on the export of grain, Bacon's informant, one of the Baker brothers of Lynn, had tried to tweak the strings of patronage represented by courtiers with local connections such as the Attorney General, Edward Coke, and the secretary to the Lord Treasurer, who happened to be John Suckling, the son of a former mayor of Norwich. However, he was dismissive of the prevarication he received in those quarters: "I am to well acquaynted with those baytes <and so> «that I» refrayned" from pursuing the matter with them. Rather, the hot news was that the real influence now lay elsewhere: "Sir you shall understand that Sir George Howme is the onely man in favour with his Majestie at this day" and it was to him that the county should make their representations.[112] Following on from this recommendation the county's justices wrote acknowledging Home's "very good acceptance" of their petition "in this countreys behalf" and "beseeching the contynuance of your honours fartherance in this our sute for the good of the contrey".[113] Norfolk had acquired an influential Scottish patron. For his part, in this newly configured Court and surrounded by well-ensconced English courtier-patrons, Home had a vested interest in building up his own clientele. Consequently, he was very willing "to preferre the cause & to forward the same" on Norfolk's behalf. The county's agent in this matter found him "very redy & willing to accept thereof as a man much inclyning himselfe to do good to the cuntry, & he promised to further the sute at the Councell board".[114]

In sum, the documents in this volume provide a fascinating insight into some of the local ramifications of the upheavals at Court that resulted from James' accession. This is an important and under-explored facet of a critical moment in any early-modern state: that of monarchical, and in this instance, dynastic succession.

* * *

[109] Below, pp.207–8.
[110] Below, p.176n., and references thereat, and p.213.
[111] Below, pp.40–1, 47–8, 144, 166.
[112] Below, pp.59–60.
[113] Below, pp.61–2. See also pp.63–4.
[114] Below, p.59.

In the discussion of the documents in the preceding volume two points were made with regard to Parliament.[115] First, that when looked at from the viewpoint of the localities, many of the issues raised can be seen to be rooted to experiences at the grass roots. At the same time Parliament provided a forum in which what might have been experienced as a specific problem in a particular locality could come to be seen as part of a wider issue.

During a parliament the process of widening the purview of individuals could do two things. It could engender alliances between localities. For example, we see a proposed common response to the national environmental problem caused by flooding, as when the proposed "reliefe of Somersetshire, Monmothshire, of Wales, and some other partes of the West contrye, that hath sustayned losse by the late overflowing of waters" prompted residents of "this poore contrye of Marshland which is daylye distressed both with the raging of the sea, and fresh waters" to ask Bacon, "being selected to have care of the good estate of the whole contrye" to join Marshland in the request for relief.[116] Similarly, there appears to have been an alliance between Norwich and Gloucester in attempts to make provision for preachers in their respective cities.[117] But in addition we need to contemplate the possibility that, for at least some of those present, the crucible of Parliament melded an understanding of the general principles—both moral and constitutional—that underlay the specific complaints of which MPs were likely to be aware through the other roles that they occupied in their own localities. This does indeed seem to have been so in the case of Bacon and militia rates.[118]

Secondly, and again viewed from the local perspective, a parliament can be seen being treated as an intermittent occasion on which local and personal problems could be solved. In this respect it was one among many mechanisms for the achievement of ends—albeit probably the most authoritative and conclusive.[119] In this type of context the now conventional view of Parliament in this period as a brief and infrequent event—the so-called Russell orthodoxy—is a palpable exaggeration.[120] Rather, Parliament was an institution in expectation, as is evident throughout this edition.[121] This was the case even with the single-session parliaments such as that of 1593 in which Bacon had sat as junior member for the county.

[115] A fuller discussion of the import of the corpus of parliament-related documents in this edition as a whole has been reserved for the Introduction to the next volume. By that stage the great majority of the relevant documents will have been printed and a view will be possible overall. Only a few points relevant to this particular volume are made here.   [116] Below, p.276.   [117] Below, p.222n.

[118] Below, pp.117, 220 and note.

[119] Victor Morgan, 'Whose Prerogative in Late Sixteenth and Early Seventeenth Century England?', *Journal of Legal History*, 5 (1984), pp.39–64.

[120] It is also one to which in his more nuanced expositions he did not himself subscribe in any crude manner. See in particular Conrad Russell's seminal article, 'Parliamentary History in Perspective, 1604–1629', *History*, 61 (1976), pp.1–27 and his *Parliaments and English Politics, 1621–1629* (Oxford, 1979). There is a review of his work and scholarly influence in Thomas Cogswell, Richard P. Cust and Peter Lake, 'Revisionism and Its Legacies: the Work of Conrad Russell', in Thomas Cogswell, Richard P. Cust and Peter Lake, eds, *Politics, Religion and Popularity in Early Stuart Britain: Essays in Honour of Conrad Russell* (Cambridge, 2002), pp.1–17. Perhaps the most percipient assessment of Russell the man and the scholar is the recent addition to the *ODNB* by John Morrill (http://www.oxforddnb.com/view/article/94399).

[121] *BP*, iv, pp.xxxv–xxxvi.

However, this was to be even more the case because of the form that parliaments took in the early-Stuart period. In general the period between 1603 and 1640 was characterised by a succession of parliamentary and non-parliamentary decades. Indeed, as we shall see in succeeding volumes, the period between c.1610 and 1621 might be characterised as the 'Personal Rule' of James I. Second, there is a distinction to be drawn between the multiple parliaments—five in all—of the 1620s that consisted of one or two sessions, and the lengthy parliament consisting of five sessions over some six years that we see initiated during the course of this volume. The first Jacobean Parliament was most certainly an on-going event in further expectation even when it was in recess. This must have transformed for ever the experience not only of MPs such as Nathaniel Bacon as he trundled back and forth to London, but also the expectations of their importunate constituents. Moreover, this experience is likely to have been the more intense for Bacon because his fellow MP for the county, the courtier Sir Charles Cornwallis, was absent for the greater part of the parliament of 1604–10 as Ambassador in Spain, largely leaving to Nathaniel the burden of speaking for Norfolk—and beyond. This he certainly did through his contributions to debate, speeches in the House and service on committees.

Among the many other changes initiated by the death of Elizabeth and the accession of James was the expectation of a new parliament. To an extent the immediate expectation of a parliament was frustrated by the practicality of needing to avoid the spread of the plague.[122] But, if anything, in a locality like Norfolk this simply provided more time for preparation for the parliament in expectation. This included both a delicate jockeying for position among prospective candidates and the opportunity to prepare draft legislation for the resolution of both public and private ills.

For large parts of the population Parliament was not a distant and largely irrelevant abstraction. Not least this was because it reached into the lives of ordinary people through its sanction of taxation, and well beyond the span of its relatively short sittings: the session might end but the prosaic business of applying its decisions and collecting the money continued. The busy practicalities of assessment and collection are recorded here.[123] But also evident are the various forms of resistance that taxation provoked.[124] In turn this elicited an excoriating criticism from the Council.[125] One reason for this recalcitrance was that, increasingly, the assessment for the subsidy became the basis for other types of taxation, as, for example in the case of the payments for the militia: the issue was "Whither [to apply] the rule of the subsidy or what other rule".[126] Again, at a practical level the sitting of parliament required the absence from the county of leading figures such as Bacon. As a result there was a disruption of much of the multifarious other county business in which they were engaged.[127] Moreover, among at least the leaders of

---

[122] It disrupted normal patterns of activity in both the Court and London, and in Norfolk and more especially Norwich. See below, pp.34n., 44–5, 59, 71–2, 117–18, 183n.

[123] Below, pp.34–5, 47, 237–8, 270–1, 274, 286–9.   [124] Below, pp.26–7, 265–6.

[125] Below, pp.265–8.   [126] Below, pp.220–1.   [127] Below, pp.77–8, 79n.

county society there was a keen sense of parliamentary precedent and—evidently—a well-maintained record of earlier legislation relevant to their concerns, as over the export of grain and other matters.[128] Engaged individuals were equipped to cite the relevant folio in "the abridgment of the statutes".[129]

Today, we have grown accustomed to a near-monopoly by the executive of the initiation of legislation. But it was not like that in early-modern England. True, the Council might well have its own aims in view when a parliament was summoned. But in this period the prospect of a new parliament also prompted numerous local initiatives with proposals for legislation that it was hoped would resolve specific local problems. Thus, in the run-up to the meeting of the first Jacobean parliament, and following the election of Bacon and Cornwallis as MPs, the inhabitants of Wells penned an astutely persuasive petition to their new representatives. They entreated them "that nowe at the next Parlament some such course may be taken for the releife of the saied towne and other coast townes as also «for» the trade of fishingcraft, as in your good discretions shall seeme fitt and convenient".[130] Further, when earlier legislation failed to achieve its intended ends, as in the instance of outlawries, concerned individuals forwarded suggestions "For the avoyding of which mischeef & inconvenience" through the amendment of the existing Act.[131] Locally, individuals picked up on rankling issues such as feudal tenures that clearly were of the widest interest to the land-occupying classes and that were indeed to provide a *leitmotif* throughout the first Jacobean parliament.[132] There was an expectation that earlier legislation that had been found wanting would be repealed: "I have noe doubt but the late statute for triflinge [vexatious] actions shall be repealed, for that the same is soe generally misliked".[133] Moreover, the process of proposing legislation was that much more natural because, as in the case of the fishermen of Wells, it often involved the mechanism of petitioning: itself a procedure with which individuals and communities were entirely familiar in other contexts.

It is worth remarking on the apparently humble backgrounds from which some of this proposed legislation originated. We have already noted the petition from the poor fishermen of Wells. The bakers of Norfolk also complained about "abuses offered unto us in our trade or manuall occupation" because the Statute of Apprentices was not being observed. Similarly, the godly clergy looked to parliament for protection of their interests by the godly gentry such as Bacon "*in hoc honoratissimo senatu convenistis*".[134]

There is also evidence of what is an often neglected aspect of parliamentary activity but which clearly was of importance to the individuals concerned and which from the evidence reproduced here appears to have come to the attention of a wider circle of parliamentarians than might otherwise be suspected. This was

---

[128] Below, pp.53–5, 81.   [129] Below, p.82.

[130] Below, pp.78–9. See also the separate memorandum from Richard Stubbe for the correction of yet other ills, below, pp.81–3.   [131] Below, p.81.

[132] Below, p.82 and note.   [133] Below, p.83.

[134] Below, p.97. On a related matter see pp.222–3.

'private' legislation. For example, Sir Thomas Erskine petitioned Parliament for confirmation of letters patent granting him certain lands in Yorkshire. In this instance the assurance of statute was sought in order to trump competing claims by patent.[135] A not dissimilar case was that of Edward Seymour's attempt to confirm his residuary rights in the lands of the late Duke of Somerset.[136] Bacon was directly involved with legislation to resolve the debtor obligations of Edward Downes.[137] Kinship connections explain Bacon's involvement in the legislation to settle the problems of the Hopton family. His mother-in-law readily wrote that she fully appreciated his "speciall care in the Parliament house for this my buyssenes, but cannot acknowledge thannkefullnes ennoughe unto you for yt, for I perseave by my sonne your care hathe bine greate, or otherwise yt might have bine unto us greate hinderaunce".[138]

Personal obligations of kinship might be one of the drivers for the involvement of an MP such as Bacon in the promoting of certain legislation. But on a number of other issues the terms in which Bacon was addressed were in effect coercive because they manipulated his own self-image. In 1604, having just been elected, people like the bakers of Norfolk knew how to invoke terms in which he is likely recently to have appealed to the electorate. They remarked upon Bacon's punctillious constitutionalism, "knowinge your greate and provident care for thee good and dilligente observinge of every good Acte heretofore made"—a remark that must have been based on what they had seen of his assiduous administrative implementation of existing legislation. Alluding to his recent election they forsaw that they now had "soe good and wise a speaker as your good worshippe, consideringe yow beare justice in thee ballance of equitie" and therefore they were "nothinge doubtinge but that your good worshippe will see reformation" of the abuses of which they complained.[139] Others were "nothing doubt of your forwardnes in the cuntries good".[140] Among the godly, Bacon also had an image to maintain and an end to pursue on their behalf: "*Precor ut vos (ornatissimi viri) qui in hoc honoratissimo senatu convenistis, tuque prestatissime patrone, qui es inter ceteros religionis et ornamentum et decus, ecclesiae conlaboranti, ope vestra et consilio adesse voletis, neque nisi re perfecta conquiescatis*".[141]

If indeed this is the case, then we need to begin to think in a more subtle way about what interests were represented in Parliament. The middling sort in the form of the fishermen of Wells or the bakers of Norfolk may not have been directly present but middling sorts such as these were not innocent of the means by which they could get their social betters to articulate their interests. They did this in a variety of ways. The fishermen astutely alluded to the wider public interests that would be served by supporting their industry. The bakers and others directly appealed to Bacon's own self-image.

Looked at from another angle, that of the psychology of Bacon himself, his active engagement in the wider public domain resulted in his being addressed in terms such as we have just heard. This might well have echoed his own initial self

---

[135] Below, p.84–5.   [136] Below, pp.88–9.   [137] Below, pp.100–1.   [138] Below, p.111.
[139] Below, pp.87–8.   [140] Below, p.92.   [141] Below, p.97.

image but it must also have contributed to firming and shaping his own self perception. This type of language presented him with a public construction of his persona from which he is likely to have drawn gratification. But also he was constricted by the demands that its maintenance placed upon him. Here we may see in the making one of the ways in which a certain type of early-modern personality was constructed.

* * *

There is a further set of revealing concerns that are evident in these documents. At first glance they may look like separate matters but in fact they are components of and demonstrate much about an underlying cluster of values and practices in this society and its prevailing political culture.

Sometimes as historians it is good if we are pulled up short and have our anachronistic presuppositions shaken when we have too readily acted on the assumption that they were just like us. Sometimes a clutch of documents rubs our noses in the difference. And if there was one way in which the inhabitants of early-modern England were not like most of us it is in their concern for honour and public reputation. Moreover, recent work has demonstrated that this concern was shared across the social spectrum. Nor was this simply the investment of psychological energy in an abstraction, although it was that too. Rather, one's 'credit' or 'standing' was an essential means by which one exercised leverage and gained purchase in this relatively uninstitutionalised society.[142] 'Honour', 'credit', 'reputation' and 'friendship' were the essential specie of exchange in this world of patron-client relationships. There are a number of examples of this among the documents in this volume.[143]

For example, the humble prospective canniker or provider of liquid refreshment within a community depended upon the support of members of that community when he sought a licence from the justices. This was the case with the townsmen of Warham when they petitioned on behalf of William Halman. In turn the communal support that he enjoyed depended upon him having maintained a good reputation among his fellow residents. It is to be noted that the petition is supported by two clergymen.[144] Among the humble, without that support the sort of shifts and stratagems, such as operating as a canniker, that could make all the difference in terms of survival, would be closed off.

'Credit' implied more than money: it was reputation.[145] It endowed a person with standing. Crucial matters could be determined "by men of credit".[146] Different occupations imparted different levels of standing: one man "would gladly better his estate, and advance his creditt by leaving the place of an attorney, to become a steward".[147] When John Rooke was imprisoned in Ipswich he wrote:

---

[142] *BP*, iv, pp.xlviii-xlix.

[143] Further insights into the value system of the period can be gained from sources such as the essays of Sir Charles Cornwallis's son, Sir William Cornwallis the younger. Born in Norfolk, he, like his father, became a courtier as a member of James I's Household. See, for example, D.C. Allen, ed., *Essays by Sir William Cornwallis the Younger* (Baltimore, MD, and London, 1946).   [144] Below, p.183.

[145] See the usage below, p.20.   [146] Below, p.22.   [147] Below, p.102.

"Yt ys a great [?]discreted [discredit] to me bessides my losse of tyme in my procedinges".[148] Reputation was as important to women as it was to men and they
also tried to avoid "Reporte of evill shamles speches whirby the woman is touched
in creditt".[149] Even Nathaniel was not averse to building his stock in the locality:
"and if some litle creditt be gott thereby, where should I debarre my self herof".[150]

At this more elevated level, in the run-up to the parliamentary election we see a
tarantella-like dance around the niceties of the different sorts of standing that a
gentleman might enjoy. Who was to be the senior MP for the county? Bacon wrote
to Sir Henry Gawdy that, "having served twice already in the second place, I hope
that no man shall have just cause to judge amisse of me though now I seeke the
first. Judge not so meanly of my self but that I am able to discharge the place aswell
as some others and if some more creditt be gott by having the first then the second
I see not, whie I should debarre my self of it yf I can obteyne it."[151] As Nathaniel
remarks, he had served before as the junior member. However, his proposed
partner, Sir Charles Cornwallis, had just been knighted and self-evidently exercised
considerable influence in the new Jacobean Court. For his part, Bacon might enjoy
substantial local support as someone who would be "a speciall phisytion that will
put his best indevour to purge and cure those maladies" of his country.[152] But real-
ists knew that influence at Court also was essential to the achievement of the
county's ends. Indeed, the acuity of this awareness is evident in the rapidity with
which they latched on to which Scotsmen wielded influence as the new regime
ensconced itself in Whitehall.[153] In the new kaleidoscope of power that had been
ushered in by James' accession and was still resolving, Bacon could not be sure that
he would get the senior position that he felt he deserved, but not to do so would
be a public affront to his local standing.

On other occasions we gain an insight into the way in which individuals must
have harboured a finely tuned perception of their own standing relative to others.
One means by which this 'standing' was supported was through the articulation of
the network of family connections. As we saw in the preceding volumes, gift
exchange and the performance of mutual services between Nathaniel and his
thrice-married sister, Elizabeth, was one way in which these networks were maintained. Contrary to what often is said, the extended family was alive and well
among the gentry, not least because for many it was of immediate or prospective
utility.[154]

At a more unselfconscious level it is evident in the use of kinship terms of cousi-
nage and 'nevidom' (nephews and nieces) that are deployed far more broadly than
we would do today. Thus Bacon's mother-in-law refers to him as "Good sonne".[155]
It extended into the pseudo-kinship encompassed within a type of early-modern
'friendship'[156] which is—again—distant from our experience. This involved an
assertion of connection and status through association, and, as occasion might
require, of mutual obligation: "Your kynde care ... I wyll for my part ever indevor

---

[148] Below, p.282.   [149] Below, p.294.   [150] Below, p.68.   [151] Below, p.63.
[152] NRO RAY 252; below, pp.67–9.   [153] Above, pp.lii–iii.   [154] *BP*, iv, pp.xxviii-xxix.
[155] Below, p.109.   [156] Below, p.84.

to deserve in any offyce of frendshypp that I can".[157] Thus in soliciting the support
of Sir Christopher Heydon in the forthcoming parliamentary election Sir Charles
Cornwallis must have thought it useful and persuasive to sign himself in his vale-
diction as "Your very assured lovyng kynsman & frend."[158]

Albeit, in circumstances such as these that sensitivity could the more readily be
affronted when individuals failed to maintain their expected rôle, or when their
own economic position or quirks of personality meant that they experienced a perceived social derogation relative to the standing of their ancestors. In a society in
which these things really mattered, these must have been excruciatingly painful
experiences for the individuals concerned. Sometimes this must be inferred from
the structure of circumstances. So, for example, Nathaniel's stormy relationship
with his second wife can in part be explained by the very evident imputation as to
his virility in failing to produce a male heir for his branch of the lineage that his
domineering father had created.

And sometimes that pain is captured explicitly in the disgruntled terms that are
employed when standing is felt to have been affronted. This is the case with the
irascible and ill-judged Thomas Farmer. He claimed to have been demeaned by his
neighbour, Philip Russell of North Barsham. While Farmer's political and economic fortunes were in decline those of Russell appear to have been in the ascen-
dant and "nowe having gotten a lyttell pelfe [he] muste be an esquier". The distaste
that Farmer felt for Russell is evident in his allusion to the past circumstances of
their respective fathers. Farmer claimed that Russell's father "hathe bin glade to
take manye a dinner att Barsham amongst [my father's] ... sarving menne, wher he
fowend many his betters boathe in lyvinge and gentrye, beinge a poore bliwecoated
fellowe". Farmer now sought "suche a satisfaccion as the lawe of armes dothe
requier".[159] Others blustered and expostulated rather less but also sought public
redress for public insult. Christopher Grimston appealed to Bacon that "in regard
I seeke to redress and not [to] revenge wronges you would the rather right me from
those base terms of cowardly boy and rascall where with he hath soyled me, and
that it would please you to make his acknowledgement of his wronge to me as
notorius as the injury. You see how I forbear with temper, thow I cannot bear his
distemper".[160]

*   *   *

The Introduction to the preceding volume drew attention to the substantial rôle
that mediation and arbitration played in the society depicted by the *Bacon
Papers*.[161] These activities were deeply embedded within the wider political culture
of patron-client relations.[162] The fundamental means for initiating the mediatory
and arbitratory process was the petition. It was also the accustomed means by
which other grievances or needs might be addressed. In this volume we have even
more evidence for the centrality of the petition both formal and informal to the
regular social interactions of the time. Until recently petitioning has been a neg-

---

157 Below, p.67.   158 Below, p.67.   159 Below, pp.75–6.   160 Below, p.247.
161 *BP*, iv, pp.xli–xliii.   162 Morgan, 'Some Types of Patronage'.

lected topic. There are welcome signs that this situation is in the process of changing.[163] One of the intriguing things about petitioning is the longevity of the practice, and in itself that can be misleading. Petitioning may be one of those things
that retain an outward consistency but the inner meaning of which changes over
time. It is unlikely that its medieval incarnation is quite the same as the recent
(2006) revival in the days of the internet and the opportunity that that has
provided to address the Prime Minster's Office *en masse*.[164] The word is that the
new Coalition government will introduce for Westminster a requirement akin to
that already operative at Holyrood to ensure that large petitions will need to be
debated in the House. Evidently, petitions are back in fashion. Therefore, all the
more reason for us to be careful to 'read' the process of petitioning within the contexts of particular periods. The corpus of petitions provided by a source such as the
Bacon Papers is one way of doing this. Indeed, the accumulating volume of
petitions to be found in this edition requires a more detailed analysis than can be
provided in this Introduction.

While the *Bacon Papers* are by no means comprehensive, even for all the
petitions likely to have been dealt with by Bacon, they do demonstrate a key point.
This is the very wide range of persons and institutions that were caught up in the
process of petitioning and the wide range of issues both public and personal that
petitions addressed. Through petition debtors sought respite from their creditors.[165] A poor inhabitant of Aldborough petitioned the county's J.P.s when his
neighbours threw him out of his house.[166] Similarly, the townsmen of Alethorpe
directed their petition straight to Bacon, as on other occasions did the townsmen
of Eccles and Warham.[167] On other occasions Bacon was petitioned as the named
J.P. among others.[168] Some of these petitions to Bacon arose because of his interest
in the locality, either as a landowner or as in some way a deputy of the Crown.
Clearly this was the case when he was petitioned as high steward of the King's
manor of Walpole.[169]

One step up as a target for petitions were the judges of assize who in turn might
refer the cause back to their trusted workhorses among the J.P.s.[170] The process of

---

[163] See, for example, the essays in W. Mark Ormrod, Gwilym Dodd, and Anthony Musson, eds,
Medieval Petitions: Grace and Grievance (Woodbridge, Suffolk, 2009); R.W. Hoyle, 'Agrarian Agitation in
Mid-Sixteenth Century Norfolk: a Petition of 1553', *The Historical Journal*, 44 (2001), pp.223–38; R.W.
Hoyle, 'Petitioning as Popular Politics in the Early Sixteenth Century', *Historical Research*, 75 (2002),
pp.365–89; Hoyle *et al.*, *Heard Before the King*; B.A. Kumin and A. Wurgler, 'Petitions, *Gravamina* and the
Early Modern State: Local Influence on Central Legislation: England and Germany (Hesse)', *Parliaments,
Estates and Representation*, 17 (1977), pp.38–60; B. Weiser, 'Access and Petitioning During the Reign of
Charles II', in: *The Stuart Courts*, ed. Evelyn Cruickshanks (2000), pp.203–13; Joanna Innes, '"Legislation"
and Public Participation, 1760–1830', in: *The British and their Laws in the Eighteenth Century*, ed. D.
Lemmings (Woodbridge, 2005), pp.102–32. Petitioning has also engaged the interest of political scientists:
see Daniel Zaret, *Origins of Democratic Culture: Printing, Petitions, and the Public Sphere in Early-Modern
England* (Princeton, 2000). I am indebted to my research student, Peter Smith, for numerous conversations
on this topic. His work on petitioning in 17th century Norfolk will further enlarge our understanding of this
topic.   [164] http://petitions.pm.gov.uk, for those who feel the need.
[165] *BP*, iv, pp.296–7; below, pp.2–3, 100–101.
[166] Below, pp.17–18. For another petition directly to the county's J.P.s see pp.304–5.
[167] Below, pp.112–3, 115, 183.   [168] Below, pp.286–7.   [169] Below, p.136. See also p.141.
[170] Below, pp.111–12, 131, 166.

petitioning could intersect with stages in the legal process and on occasion a cause might be referred back to a gentleman in the county from Chancery to be decided "in law and conscience" or, in another instance, "to make some quiett and freindly ende between them accordinge to equity and goode conscience".[171] From Common Pleas a case was referred to Bacon, "he to end or certifie".[172] A frequent form of referral from Requests was that the matter was to be decided only if it was not already subject to legal process.[173]

Ultimately, the solution to both 'public' and 'private' ills might reside in the *larges* of the monarch. Thus the county petitioned successively the Queen and then the new King over the recurring issue of the export of grain.[174] The monarch might refer policy-related petitions such as this to the Council.[175] In turn this could generate a further petition to a prospective patron who might undertake to promote the cause in Council.[176] At a more humble level, individuals such as the Ringalls sought redress from the King over the complex financial entanglements in which they found themselves.[177] The seeking of relief from creditors was a regular source of petitioning.[178] Petitions from individuals to the monarch were likely to be referred to one of the Masters of Requests, who in turn were likely to refer them to the consideration of one or more gentlemen in the locality.[179] If they failed to resolve the issue they had to refer the case back to King.[180] Sometimes the petitioner named proposed arbitrators, usually local gentlemen of the likes of Bacon, and provision was made for the opposing party to name their representatives in the arbitration.[181] On occasion a cause would give rise to a series of petitions to different parties when satisfaction was not achieved in the first instance. This is what happened in the case of Ralph Jermyn who progressed from Chief Justice Popham, who had referred the matter to two local gentlemen, Heydon and Bacon, to the King who referred the matter to the Court of Requests.[182]

On occasion we catch a glimpse of the considerable amount of work that could arise for those to whom petitions were referred. As with the case of the decayed pier at Cromer this might require not only hearing parties but also observation in situ.[183]

There are some indications that James' accession may have encouraged more petitions to the Crown arising from the notion that a new monarch would have an enlarged beneficence to bestow. This may have given rise to attempts to regularise the process of petitioning at Court. The crowds of ordinary supplicants around the Court clearly were an irritation.[184] Bacon was asked to sort out one case so that "his Highnes maye bee no further troubled with suite in that behalf".[185]

Another target of petitioners was the Privy Council.[186] Again, these petitions were irritants that were felt to distract the Council from more pressing business of

[171] Below, pp.142, 154. For another referral from Chancery see p.152.   [172] Below, pp.244–5.
[173] Below, p.153.   [174] Below, p.11n., 52–5.   [175] Below, p.59.   [176] Below, pp.61–2.
[177] Below, pp.37–8.   [178] For example, below, pp.49–52, 55–6, 136–7.
[179] These can be traced through the Index under 'Requests, Court of', and see, for example, below, p.132.
[180] Below, p.107.   [181] Below, pp. 108–9, 135.   [182] Below, p.135.   [183] Below, pp.291–8.
[184] For example, the Knight Marshal was instructed to forbid certain suitors that had received their answer from further troubling the Court (BL MS Add. 11402, f.82v.).
[185] Below, p.38.   [186] Below, p.39.

state. With a parliament in prospect the county's MPs became the obvious inter-
mediaries chosen to promote the interests of a community such as Wells and the
bakers of the county, and to seek the relief sought as a result of the flooding of
Marshland.[187] Individuals also petitioned Parliament in pursuit of 'private' legislation.[188]

What has been summarised here regarding petitions should provide some indication of not only the diversity but also the bulk of such documents among Bacon's
papers. It becomes evident that work arising from petitioning must have occupied
a great deal of his time and energy. The petitions in this volume also demonstrate
a larger point. It is that petitioning was a pervasive practice, familiar to all across
the social spectrum. As such it is something about which we need to know more.
It is also the case that an awareness of the now evident importance of petitioning
is something that has been forced upon us by the discipline of needing to explain
what the process of editing has thrown up.

Victor Morgan

[187] Below, pp.78, 87, 276–7.   [188] Below, pp.84, 88–9.

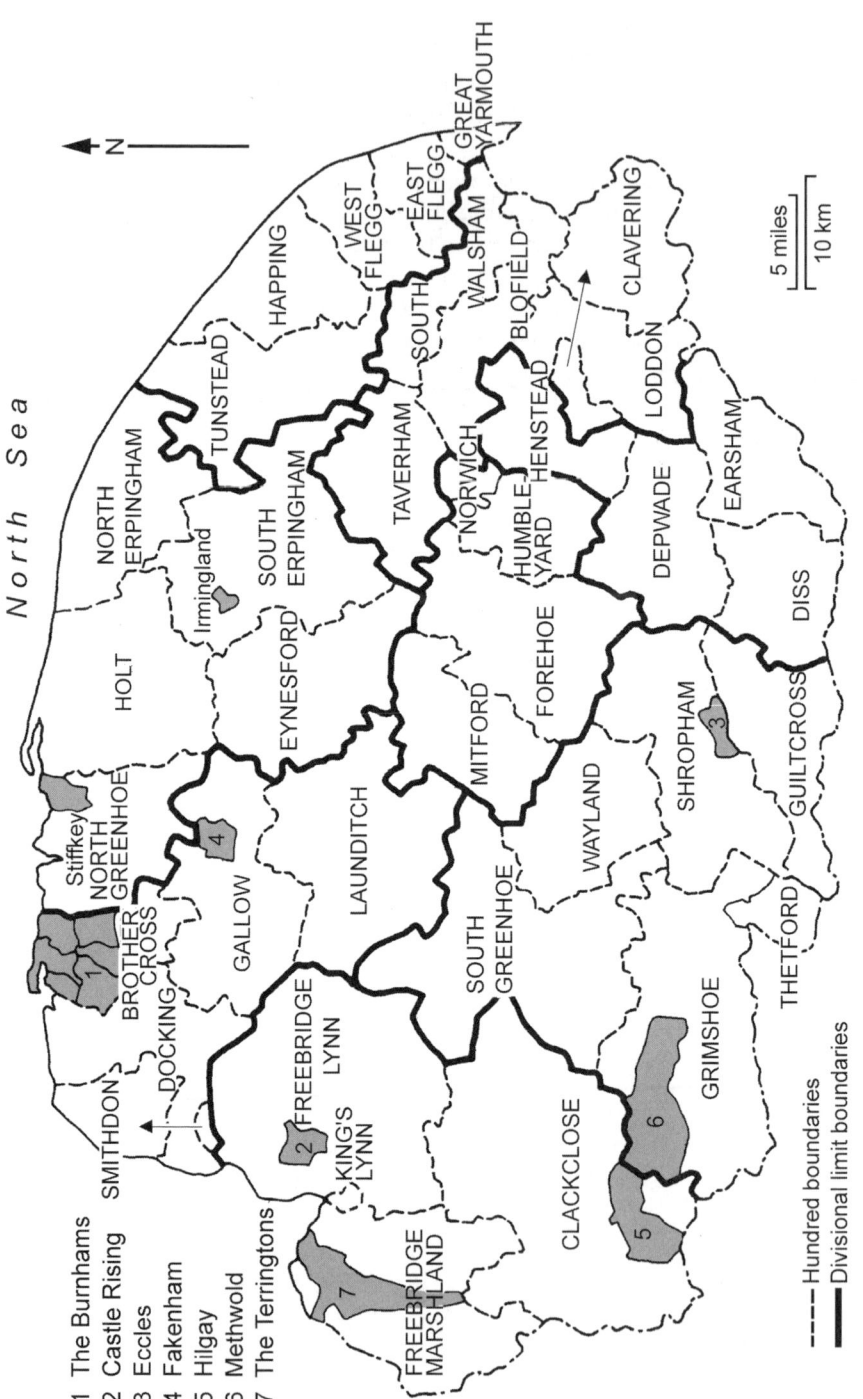

Map 1. Norfolk hundreds and divisional limits (with significant parishes outside the north-Norfolk limit)

North Sea

N

1 The Burnhams
2 Castle Rising
3 Eccles
4 Fakenham
5 Hilgay
6 Methwold
7 The Terringtons

5 miles
10 km

—·—·— Hundred boundaries
———— Divisional limit boundaries

GREAT YARMOUTH
HAPPING
WEST FLEGG
EAST FLEGG
WALSHAM
BLOFIELD
CLAVERING
LODDON
TUNSTEAD
SOUTH
TAVERHAM
NORWICH
HENSTEAD
HUMBLE YARD
EARSHAM
NORTH ERPINGHAM
SOUTH ERPINGHAM
FOREHOE
DEPWADE
DISS
HOLT
Irmingland
EYNESFORD
MITFORD
SHROPHAM
GUILTCROSS
NORTH GREENHOE
Stiffkey
GALLOW
LAUNDITCH
WAYLAND
THETFORD
BROTHER CROSS
1
4
SOUTH GREENHOE
GRIMSHOE
6
SMITHDON
DOCKING
FREEBRIDGE LYNN
2
KING'S LYNN
CLACKCLOSE
5
FREEBRIDGE MARSHLAND
7
3

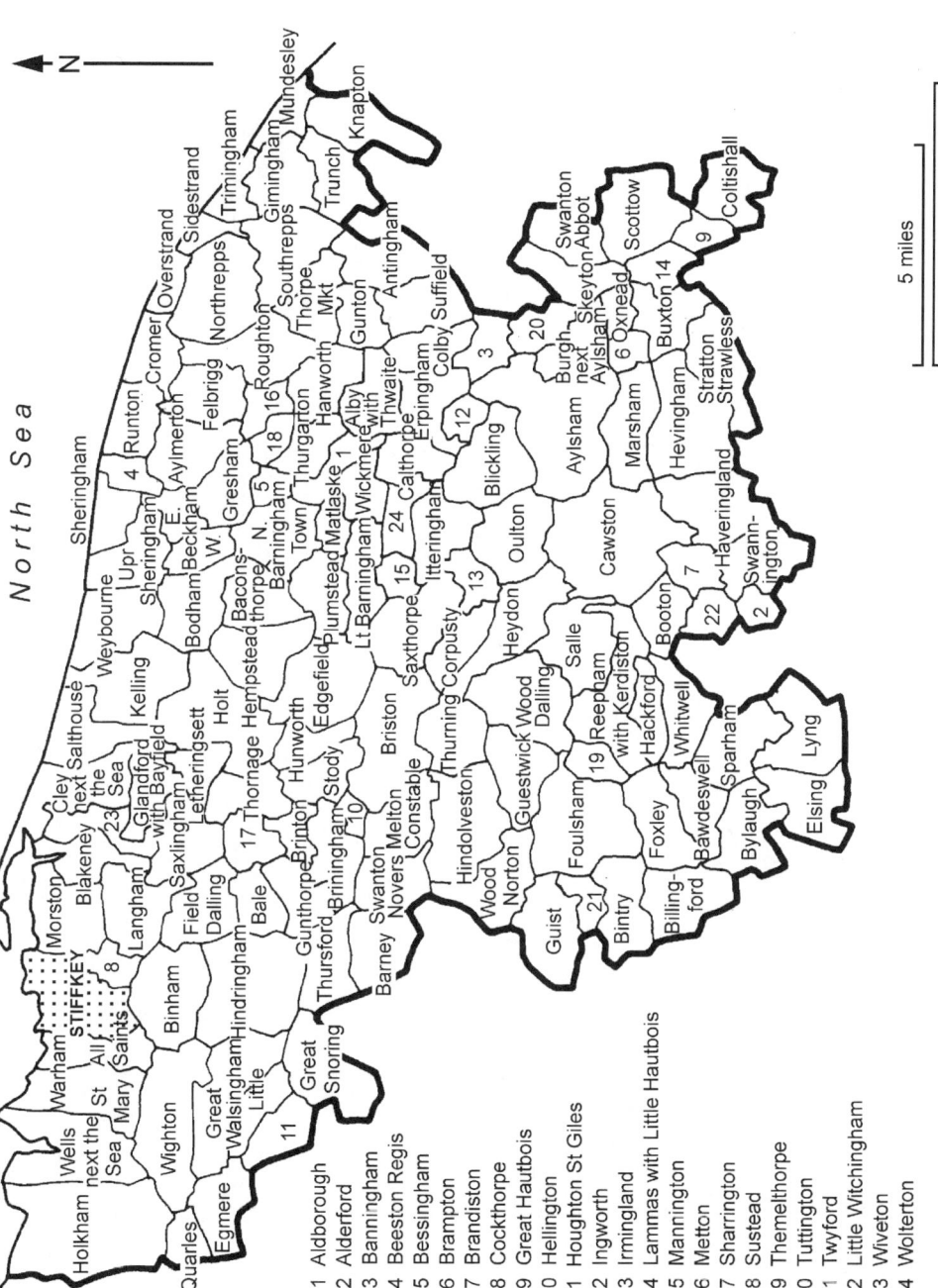

North Sea

Map 2. Parishes within the north-Norfolk limit

1 Aldborough
2 Alderford
3 Banningham
4 Beeston Regis
5 Bessingham
6 Brampton
7 Brandiston
8 Cockthorpe
9 Great Hautbois
10 Hellington
11 Houghton St Giles
12 Ingworth
13 Irmingland
14 Lammas with Little Hautbois
15 Mannington
16 Metton
17 Sharrington
18 Sustead
19 Themelthorpe
20 Tuttington
21 Twyford
22 Little Witchingham
23 Wiveton
24 Wolterton

5 miles

10 kilometres

BACON PAPERS 1603–1607

Agreement between William Armiger and Thomas Franklin

[*1602/3, January 3*].[1] The order and agreement made between Mr Armiger and Mr Francklyn for the parcells followinge.

First Mr Armiger is to pay unto Mr Francklyn for the tythe hay – 15*s*.

Item the said Mr Armiger is to pay him for tythe rackinges[2] – fyve cumbe barly.

Item the said Mr Armiger is to pay him for the tythe of tenn scor cooples of ewes and lambes sould to Mr Buggyn – 52*s*.

Item for grasses occupyde by Mr Armiger of the parsonedge glebbe for every acre – 16*d*.

The day of payment of the sayd somes of money and barly to be sett down by Mr Bacon his wourshippe.

Wytnes.

Undated.

Signed: Wylliam Holland, Harbert Warde.

Endorsed in William Sanders' hand: Inter Armiger & Franckling.

½ p. RH Box 71.

Privy Council to the Sheriff and Commissioners for Musters in Norfolk

1602/3, January 19. After our hartye commendations. Wheras certeyne of her Majesties shiepes are appointed to be sett out to the seas with expedicion,[3] her Heignes pleasure & commandment is that calling unto you the mayours of the porte townes within the county of Norfolk & by theire assistance within theire libertyes you cause a generall muster to be taken of all marryners & seafareing men fitt for service from the age of 16 to 60 yeres which be in the porte townes or elles where within the said countye, out of which you shall make choise of 150 of the most able & sufficient men without all partiall respecte and giveing them 12*d*. a pece for imprest mony and after the rate of *ob*. the myle for theire conducte from thence to Chatham in Kente, shall charge them uppon payne of death to presente them selves there before the officers of the navie before the viii daye of Februarye to be disposed into such shippes as they shall thinke meete giveing to everye man a tickett when he was impressed and when he was commanded to appere. And

---

[1] Dating: dated by reference to a memorandum of 27 December 1602 (*BP*, iv, pp.302–3) giving the substance of the dispute and stating that the case is to be judged by Mr Holland and Mr Ward (rectors of North Creake and Burnham Thorpe respectively) on the following Monday, i.e. 3 January. For Armiger and Franklin see *BP*, iv, p.302.

[2] Mr Franklin had claimed tithe rakings for 108 acres of barley (*BP*, iv, p.303).

[3] For the ongoing local problem with marauding Dunkirkers (pirates operating out of Dunkirk), see *BP*, iv, *passim*, and especially pp.lxvi, 276–7. They had been particularly active during the preceding spring and summer. Also at this time pinnaces were being deployed in order to picket the approaches to the English Channel and provide early warning of any approaching Spanish fleet and there was a maritime interdiction of trade with the Hapsburg Low Countries. Consequently, experienced seamen were much in demand to man naval vessels.

bycause many of these impressed men use to come upp both unarmed and naked without any convenient clothes which is an occasion (by reason of theire uncleanesse) of diseases in them selves and infection to others you must for redresse hereof provide that those which have meanes shall furnish them selves and that the rest be furnished by theire parentes masters or frindes with swordes & daggers and with necessarye apparel so that none be sent without reasonable provision aswell fitt to doe service when neede requireth as allso to maynetayne them both warme & cleane. And further bycause we meane to take more stricte accounte of these impressed men then hath beene heretofore you shall cause a roll to be made of theire names describeng everye man by his yeres stature or other directe note of his person the place whence he was impressed what he hath rec[*eived*] for impreste & conducte & when he is appointed to appere to the ende that if any defalte be made we <maie> «maye» take order for the service & exemplarye punishment of those which shalbe founde faltye herein. Requiring allso all justices of peace mayours shreives baleifes cunstables & other officers to be ayding and assisting you by theire best meanes in thexecucion of the premisses and in apprehending & imprisoning all such as shall disobaye or neglecte this service as they tender her Majesties good pleasure & this her Heignes speciall & important service. And what you shall disburse in this behalf shall duly be repaid to you or your assignes by the officers of the navye when you shall require it uppon your billes of demandes. So we bidd you hartelie farewell from the courte at Whitehall the 19 of Januarye 1602. Your very loving frindes. [*Signed:*] Thomas Egerton c.s., T. Buckhurst, Gilbert Shrewsbury, Notingham, E. Worcester, W. Knowles, Ed. Wotton, J. Fortescue, J. Stanope, Robert Cecill, John Popham.[4]

Copy.

Addressed: To our very loving frendes <Her Heighnes> the heighe shreive [*Sir Arthur Heveningham*] and the rest of the Comissioners for the Musters in the counteye of Norfolk.

Endorsed: Copy of the Councelles letters for 150 marineres January 1602.

Enclosed with letter of 27 January 1602/3 from Sir Arthur Heveningham and Sir Philip Wodehouse to Nathaniel Bacon, below, pp.4–5.

1 p. BL Add. 38508 f.60.

Agreement between Ralph Dade and his creditors

1602/3, January 21. *Calendar:* Raph Dade compounds for his debts before Nathaniel Bacon esquire and John Fountaine gent[5] as follows:

John Deane of Felbrigg. Debt £10. Will accept £9 at £1 a year from

---

[4] Sir John Popham (?1531–1607), chief justice of the Queen's/King's Bench, 1592–1607. Popham played an important rôle in local affairs because of his position as assize judge on the Norfolk circuit, 1592–1606. Unusually in this period for a judge, he was also a member of the Privy Council (*DNB*; Cockburn, *Assizes*, pp.267–8; *BP* iv, *passim*).

[5] John Fountaine of Salle (see *BP*, iv, p.297). The petition of Ralph Dade of Overstrand for respite from his creditors had been referred to four arbitrators, including Bacon and Fountaine, on 29 November 1602 (*BP*, iv, pp.296–7). Fountaine also worked in conjunction with Bacon in the resolution of other disputes referred for arbitration (*BP*, iv, p.301).

"Michaelmas come twelvemoneth". Security: a bond from Richard Johnson fermor to Raph Dade.

Thomas Ediman of Sal[t]house to be paid when due.

John Catlock of Northrepps. According to Thomas Edimont will accept £1 a year.

Nicholas Bacon of Cromer. Debt £8. Will accept £6 at £1 a year from All Saints next. Security: bond from Richard Johnson. Remaining 40s. at 10s. a year on Dade's bond.

Roberte Evered of Felmingham. Debt: £5 10s. due at Our Lady last on bond from Dade, Mote and Woodhouse. Has received 10s. from Botte ("Mote" deleted) for stopping action, with the promise of the £5 by Easter next. Demands charges and Dade's offer of half the debt at Lady Day and half at Michaelmas next has been refused. Accepts £3 at Lady Day and £4 at Michaelmas for debt, interest and charges. If £4 cannot be paid, to continue on good assurance.

John Mottes of Sheringham. Debt: £12 due January 1 last on bond from William Woodhouse, Raph Dade and Burrowes, of which 40s. is interest; £5 5s. by bond, of which 5s. represents interest for about five months. Dade claims to have given five bushels of wheat in addition to "the intereste of the fortie shillinges". If proved, both bonds will be void at law. Further debt: 24s. for two cades of herrings, 20s. for two warps of ling and 5s. lent to Dade's wife. Dade claims he has paid 40s. of the £5 5s. to Mottes' wife (admitted by Mottes) and paid for the fish in various ways and offers proof. Agreed that John Deane of Felbrigg and Richard Cooke of Sheringham should look into the whole debt and the amount established as due is to be paid by three equal annual instalments starting at Lady Day twelvemonth. Dade and Richard Johnson to be bound for payment.

Dated 21 January 1602.

Unsigned. In William Sanders' hand.

Endorsed: Dades debts compounded.

1½ pp. NRO MC 1872/29, 866X2. Calendared, *Supplementary Stiffkey Papers*, p.14.

Theodore Tomlinson to Nathaniel Bacon

1602/3, January 26. Right wourshipfull maye it please you to understand that in the tyme of [*your*] shrevalty[6] I delivered unto your undershreve Mr Spratt[7] an execution to be served on Anthony Burrough dwelling neer unto Yarmouth for £21 10s. which accordingly was served and the money received by the bayliffes and delivered to Mr Spratt which as yet I cannot (though sondry tymes I have bene with him my selfe and demaunded it) get out of his handes, but still contrary to his oathes promises and protestations detaines it from me. My humble request unto your wourship is that I may by your good meanes be satisfyed. <At> From

---

6 1599, when Bacon served as High Sheriff of Norfolk.

7 Richard Spratt of Barney, Bacon's long-serving under-steward of the Duchy of Lancaster estates in Norfolk. Bacon had chosen his trusted underling as his deputy during his shrievalty (see *BP*, iv, pp.104n., 297).

Sturbridge fayer last I rid purposely to Mr Spratt for my money and after I had attended at Walsingham a daye to speake with him he gave me no good wordes and protested that at the beginning of the next terme he wold appoynt his brother John Shovell to paye it me at London. But he hath not performed with me at all. I beseech your wourship let me not be so dealt withall for it lyeth in your handes to redresse it. I am perswaded that if it were made knowen unto you the maner of the cariage of the bayliffe and undershreve in this busines and how I was dealt withall or if I shold complaine unto my Lord Chiefe Justice [*Sir John Popham*], <of> to whom I must flye for reliefe except I be by your wourship relieved, their dealinges wold appeare very bad and not by lawe justifiable. For after they had arrested the partye they tooke a pawne and let him go home with one of his neighbors, and the next daye being come to them againe they went with him to a gentlemans howse where they willingly let him make an escape and afterwardes tooke £11 10*s*. of him for £21 10*s*. which I cannot have. But I told Mr Spratt that I wold complaine to your wourshipp who desired me to forbeare my complaint and for forbearance of my money I shold have in all £12. At his request I did forbeare but never the neerer am I. I beseech your wourship that the money may be paid to my frend Mr Ambrose Money of Welles[8] <and> whom [*sic*] will I am sure undertake that I will send downe a release the money being once paid. So I committ your wourship to the Lordes protection. London 26 January 1602. Your wourshipps to command.

Signed: Joseph Tomlynson for my brother Theodor Tomlynson.
Addressed: To the right wourshipfull Mr Nathaniell Bacon.
Endorsed in Martin Man's hand: Tomlynson concerning Mr Spratt.
1 p. Folger L.d.590.

Sir Arthur Heveningham and Sir Philip Wodehouse to Nathaniel Bacon

1602/3, January 27. Sur we have receivid letters from the Lords of the [*Privy*] Councell[9] a coppie whereof we sende you herein closed, we have also sent you warrantes to subscribe desiringe you thay may be sent with all expedition. The tyme is verie shorte that the marriners are appoynted to be at Chattam, therfor we have considered Twesdaye next [*1 February*] to be the longest daye for the sendinge them awaye. I praye have a care that the marriners in Welles, Blakneye and other towens aboute you may be sent well appoynted and we will likewise have a care that those from Yarmouth and the coaste towens thereaboute be well appoynted, and we wilbe glad to have your companye on the same daye at Norwich where we have appoynted our mettinge for the sendinge them awaye. Thus with our hartye comendations we comytt you to God. Norwich the 27 of *Januarii* 1602. Your very loveinge frindes.

[*Postscript*]: You may if you plese commande the justices there aboute to assiste you therein.

8 Ambrose Money was a merchant of some substance in Wells (Metters, 'Rulers and Merchants', p.159), and also involved in the Iceland fishing ventures.
9 For letters dated 19 January 1602/3 see above, pp.1–2. For the consequences, see the two documents of 29–30 January, immediately below.

Signed: Arthur Hevenyngham, Phillip Woodehouse.

Addressed: To the wourshippfull and our very loveinge frind Nathanyell Bacon esquire at Stukque these.

On verso of address in William Sanders' hand: 60 to be taken out of South Erpingham, North Erpingham, Tunsted, Holt and North Grenhoe, to make a perfect rowle [*roll*] afor the muster of the names and surnames, to be at Chappell le Feild [*Norwich*][10] on Tewsdaie by viii of the clock. That the men have good swordes and daggers, and be well apperrelled at their owne chardge or their masters or freindes.

Endorsed: [*1*] Sir Arthur Heveningham and Sir Phillip Woodhouse. [*2. in Martin Man's hand*] Proceeding in execution of the letters 1602.

Enclosure: the Council's letter of 19 January 1602/3, above, pp. 1–2.

½ p. BL Add. 41140 ff.48–9.

Schedule of men eligible for naval service

1602/3, January [*29–*]30.[11] *Summary*: Lists of mariners eligible for service, noting in most cases whether they appeared at the muster.[12] Comprising: 19 from Salthouse (9 appearing); 27 from Cley (aged 16 to 60 and "now at home"); 13 appearing, of whom 9 received imprest and conduct money); 98 from Wells (49 appearing, including a ship's carpenter; 13 others noted as masters). The Wells section is dated 30 January 1602.

Endorsed in Martin Man's hand: Sailors & seafaring men in Holt & North Grenho Hundredes.

3 pp. NRO MC 1868/19, 865X2.

Schedule of men impressed for naval service in Holt and North Greenhoe Hundreds

1602/3, January 29–30. The names of the mariners with the notes of their persons imprest out of Holt Hundred by Nathanael Bacon esq the xxix of Januarie 1602 <th> to serve in her Majesties Navie.

Holt Hundred.

Cley.

1.[13] Robert Annet of the age of 36 yeares of meane stature with a browne bearde.

2. Robert Wimprell of the age of 20 yeares of a lowe stature & without a beard.

3. <Arthur Dowell of 25 yeares of a good stature with a browne bearde> «dischardged at Norwich impreste, repayed *per* William Kinge».[14]

---

[10] The open area of Chapel Field had long since become the usual place of mustering in Norwich.

[11] Dating: dated from Schedule of men impressed, 29–30 January 1602/3, immediately below.

[12] The speed with which these schedules were produced (ordered 19 January 1602/3, above, p.1), suggests that lists of available seamen were kept in readiness, for use as required.

[13] The numbers 1–40 appear in the original.

[14] William King (d.1635) of Wiveton, chief constable of Holt Hundred (*BP*, iv, p.225). This is one of several entries that have been deleted, sometimes with a note of discharge, presumably at the muster held at Norwich on 1 February 1602/3 (see above, p.4).

4. William Trace of the age of 21 yeares of a lowe stature without a bearde.

5. Raph Heyton of the age of 23 yeares of a middle stature without a bearde.

6. John Dawson of 26 yeares of age of a lowe stature with a shorte bearde.
<Robert Lyston of 28 yeares of age of a meane stature with a browne beard.>

7. Robert Wallys of the age of 20 yeares of a middle stature without a bearde.

8. Henry Palmer of the age of 20 years of a middle stature without a beard.

Wiveton

9. Alexander Shortin of 20 yeares of age of a meane stature without a bearde.

10. John Miller of 20 yeares of age of meane stature without a bearde.

11. <John Pigeon of 35 yeares of age of a middle stature with a browne beard> «dischardged at Norwich impreste, repaid *per* William Kinge».

Blakeney

12. Richard Well of 20 yeares of age of a tall stature without a bearde. William Grene of Matsell [*Mattishall*] impreste in Welles place.

Salthouse

<James Howsego of the age of 20 yeares of a reasonable stature with a short black bearde.>

<Thomas Parre of the age of 40 yeares of a middle stature with a black heade and bearde.>

13. <George Clarke of the age of 30 yeares of a meane stature with a leane face and without a bearde.>
«Dischardged at Norwich their impreste repaid *per* William Kinge.»

14. John Stanforth of the age of 23 yeares of a middle stature with a smalle thinne bearde «dischardged at Norwich, impreste repaid *per* W. K.».

Waborne

15. William Bunne of the age of 30 yeares of a meane stature with a browne bearde.

16. Richard More shipcarpenter of the age of 28 yeares of a middle stature with a smalle bearde.

Morston

17. Robert Hilders of the age of the age [*sic*] of 20 yeares of a tall stature without a bearde.

Bodham

18. <Henry Tucke of the age of 20 yeares of a meane stature, a sanguine complexion without a bearde> «dischard[g]ed at Norwich impreste repaid *per* William Kinge».

19. <Henry Tinker of the age of 18 yeares of a meane stature without a beard> «dischardged at Norwich imprese repaid *per* William Kinge».

«Received of William Kinge for 6 impreste & conduct money of 6 mariners dischardged at Norwich at 12*d.* impreste & 10*d.* conduct to Norwich – 11*s.*»

Mariners imprest out of North Grenhoe Hundred the xxx of Januarie 1602 for her Majesties Navie.

Walsingham Magna

20. Richard Willson of the age of 25 yeares of meane stature with a black bearde.

Hindringham

21. Arthur Buntinge of the age of 33 yeares of a tall stature with a red beard.

Stifkey

22. Edmond Coe of the age of 21 yeares of middle stature without a bearde.

23. Dennis Wightman of the age of 21 yeare of a tall stature without a bearde.

Warham

24. Edmond Eccles of the age of 30 yeares of a meane stature with a black bearde.

25. William Yaxley of the age of 24 yeares of reasonable stature with a small bearde.

26. <Edmond Percivell of the age of 33 yeares of lowe stature with a browne bearde> «dischardged at Norwich and impreste ««& conduct»» repaid».

Holkham

27. Robert Ogle of the age of 26 yeares of tall stature without a bearde.

28. James Kendall of the age of 22 yeares of a lowe thick stature & a yellowish bearde.

29. Richarde Curtice of the age of 24 yeares of meane stature with a yellowe head & bearde.

30. Thomas Hastinges of 27 yeares of reasonable stature with a black beard.

31. <Roger Lawson of 26 yeares of reasonable stature without a beard> «dischardged at Norwich and him imprest & conduct repaid».

Binham

32. Henry Chapman of the age of 34 yeares of lowe stature with a black bearde.

Welles

33. <32.> Fraucis Clarke of the age of 24 yeares of lowe stature, a blacke head without a beard.

34. <33.> John Peerson of the age of 22 yeares of meane stature with a black bearde.

35. <34.> John Denmarke of 22 yeares of lowe stature, a black head without a bearde.

36. <35.> John Sharpe of the age of 22 yeares of lowe stature with a small bearde and <and> blacke heade.

37. <36.> Thomas Chandler of the age of 20 yeares of reasonable stature without a bearde.

38. <37.> John Dickson of the age of 17 yeares of reasonable stature with a black heade.

39. <38.> Nicholas Purdie of the age of 34 yeares of reasonable stature with a browne bearde and a curled heade.

40. <Robert Lewsie of 24 yeares of a reasonable stature with a browne bearde> «dischardged at Norwich and his imprest ««& conduct»» repaid by Thomas Bullock chief constable».

<Memorandum that ther was geven to every of thes «40» persons 12*d.* for

<<conduct>> «impreste» money and 10*d.* for conduct money unto Norwich which cometh unto £3 13*s.* 4*d.*>

Received by Goodman Bullock for the impreste and conduct money of thre dischardged at Norwich beinge parcell of £3 13*s.* 4*d.* – 5*s.* 6*d.*

Of thes 40 persons impreste out of both Hundredes 9 were dischardged at Norwich, 6 out of Holt, and 3 out of Northgrenhoe, and so ther went forth <13> 13 out of Holt and 18 out of Northgrenhoe, in both Hundreds 31. For which is to be demaunded of the high sheriffe for impreste and conduct money at 5*s.* a man £7 15*s.*, wherof 56*s.* 10*d.* was laid out by my master and the reste by the chief constables.

Unsigned. In William Sanders' hand.

Endorsed in a different hand: Mariners imprest out of Holte & North Grenhoe Hundreds for her Majesties navie the xxx Januarie 1602.

3 pp. NRO RAY 216. Printed, *Stiffkey Papers,* pp.69–72.

Report and order in a suit in Chancery. John and Jane Bridges against Nicholas Seafowle, Fermor Pepys and Nathaniel Bacon

1602/3, February 12. *Calendar:* The report[15] dated 9 February in the case between John Bridges, professor of theology,[16] and Jane his wife, lately wife of John Davy, plaintiffs, and Nicholas Seffolde, Fermor Pepes[17] and Nathaniel Bacon, defendants, explains that the case was referred to the reporter on 26 October last. In view of its difficulty he has decided to relate the case and leave it to the resolution of the court. In January 1567/8 John Davy gent, then married to Jane, one of the plaintiffs, paid £300 to obtain a rent-charge of £40 per annum, for the term of their joint lives and the life of the survivor, on all the lands of Thomas Seffolde, Thomas Peapes, and John Baynard. Jane had previously levied a fine of the lands that she held in jointure from a former husband. Soon afterwards, the three compounded with Davy to be discharged of the rent, and made ten separate bonds with him, each for £60. Davy intended to keep the deed of rent-charge as security until payment was made, but while he was out of the room Thomas Peapes cut it up into six pieces, so it is no longer pleadable at common law. Davy obtained some of the money due to him during his lifetime, and secured judgement at common law for another part of it. Since his death Jane, as his administratix, has sought execution, but because of the defacement of the deed the plaintiffs have no remedy at common law and must sue in equity for payment of the rent-charge and its arrears from the defendants, who now hold the land in question. The defendants claim that there is no equity constraining them to pay the rent, since they had no part in defacing the deed and the land was discharged at law by its cancellation. Nicholas Seffolde claims that his land

---

[15] This is the report by John Tyndall required to be made by an Order in Chancery of the preceding June (see *BP,* iv, p.263).

[16] Dr Bridges (1535/6–1618) had been Dean of Salisbury since 1577 and was soon to be appointed Bishop of Oxford (1603). His lengthy *Defence of the Government Established in the Church of England,* published in 1587, was a target of the Marprelate pamphleteer. He had married Jane Davy in 1592 (*ODNB*).

[17] "Fermor Pepes": either Jerome Pepys gent (1548–1633) of South Creake and Mileham, who was also known as Fermor Pepys, or his fifth son Fermor Pepys (1581–1660) of Mileham and Toftrees. "Thomas Peapes" is probably Thomas Pepys (d.1569) the father of Jerome. (*Visit. of Norf. 1563*, i, p.381).

was entailed to him before the rent was granted; Fermor Peapes that he received his land from a person to whom Thomas Peapes had forfeited it before the grant; and Nathaniel Bacon that his title is from a person who owned the land before John Baynard had any rights in it. The reporter has seen conveyances to this effect. He therefore urged the defendants to plead at common law, admitting the deed of rent-charge but using the conveyances to clear their lands; but both they and the plaintiffs are unwilling to go to this expense.

Following the appearance on 12 February by Mr Phillips for the plaintiffs and Mr Houghton[18] for the defendants, the case was ordered to be heard some day the next term.

Signed: Tothill *pro def*[*orciantibus*]. *Copy.*
Endorsed: [*1. in Martin Man's hand*] Copie of the order of Mr Tyndall *inter Bridges Sefoule & alios.* [*2.*] February 1602.
2½ pp. NRO RAY 217.

Richard Spratt to Nathaniel Bacon

1602/3, February 22. Right worshipful, concerninge a debt dewe to one Tomlynson of London[19] wherof you lately writt to me, it is trewe ther is dewe to hym eyther £10 or £11 which I will see aunswerd er it be long, thoughe it cam not to my handes as it should have done, but for eny other thinge dewe abought your shrevalty unpaid, I do not knowe eny penney. Henry Gibson[20] hath writt to me that he shall bringe downe your *quietus* which hath bene paid for longe past, and if it hadd not pleased God to lay upon me such an infurmytye as I have, then thinges hadd bene dispatched er this tyme, <wher> and so I hope your worship will consider. For Mr Badgecroftes debt[21] of £100 I have sett over a £110 to be paid to hym the third of *Maii* next in discharge both of the debt & use when no doubt you shall have your bond delivered <of> «over». Mr Spenlowe & 2 other sufficient men ar bounde to pay the money. I hadd come to your worship er this tyme but that the wether hathe bene so daungerouse for me, [*word illegible*] aswell abought thes busynes as towchinge Mr Taverner[22] in settinge his goodes over to his daughter[23] wherby the baliffes ar afraydd to distrayne, he beinge so troblesume a man except

---

[18] Probably Robert Houghton (1548–1624) of Gunthorpe and Lincoln's Inn, J.P. from 1593, knighted and appointed justice of the King's Bench in 1613 (Smith, *County and Court*, pp.353, 383; *Judges of England*, p.31).

[19] See Tomlinson's letter to Bacon of 26 January 1602/3, above, pp.3–4.

[20] Henry Gibson was a long-time associate of the Gawdy family (cf. *HMC Gawdy*, pp.50, 82). He had served as under-sheriff during Sir Bassingbourne Gawdy's shrievalty, 1601–2 (*BP*, iv, pp.291–2).

[21] Richard Badgecroft of Bexwell (Blomefield, vii, p.308). For the progress of the debt, see also Spendlove to Man, 12 June 1604, below, p.110.

[22] James Taverner gent (d.1604) was of North Elmham but had settled at Wighton by the 1570s (Clarke and Campling, *Visitation*, ii, p.216). He was a lawyer and initially did legal work for Bacon (see *BP*, iii, p.423), and acted as the latter's deputy steward of the Duchy of Lancaster property in Warham and Egmere. By 1599, however, they were at loggerheads, with Taverner resigning from his "elvish office" (MacCulloch, *Redgrave Hall*, p.72) and Spratt feeling free in this letter to describe him as "so troblesume a man".

[23] Here Spratt is turning from business arising from his office as under-sheriff to Bacon to matters arising from his other office as under-bailiff to Bacon as steward of the Duchy of Lancaster lands in Norfolk. Bacon was also high steward of the royal manors in Marshland. For more on Bacon's multiple office-holding, and by extension, as here, that of his underlings, see *BP*, iv, p.xxxv.

they may have assistaunce of you, if it pleased you to be advised at the Assisses you shalbe the more hable to direct them at your return. I am informed he kepeth howse & occupyeth his landes and yet <the go[*ods*]> all his catell ar his daughters, if ther be eny fraude methinke this should be one, she hath broken the pounde and rescued the catell from the baliffe who is a pore man and not hable to defend the wronnge. This would sewerly be ponished in the Duchy Chamber if eny man would take upon hym the folowinge the cause but the want therof spoyleth all. After the Assisses I will wayght upon your worship when I hope you will direct summe corse thereyn and in the meane I do pray to God for your worships pros-peryty longe to indeure. I humbly take my leave. Barney this 22 of February 1602. Your worships at commandment.

Signed: Rich[*ard*] Spratt. *Holograph*.
Addressed: To the right worshipful Nathanael Bacon esquier at Stifkey.
Endorsed in Martin Man's hand: Mr Spratt.
1 p. Folger L.d.557.

Thomas Shouldham to Nathaniel Bacon

1602/3, February 25. Yf yt please yow, wher as I stonde bounde unto your late undersherife Mr Spratt in <20> 60 poundes for payment of £30 13s. upon a distres taken of my goodes for a recusauntes debt, the cause being harde before my Lordes in the Exchequer Chambre they ordered ther «in court» that my bounde shoulde be redelyvered me which I beseche yow maybe executed accordingly. And I will be ryddye alwayes at your comaundement. Thetford this xxv of Februarye 1602. Your wourshippes too comaunde.

Signed: Thomas Schuldham. *Holograph*.
Endorsed in Martin Man's hand: Mr Shouldhams note concerning Mr Spratt.
½ p. NRO RAY 218.

The J.P.s in Norfolk to the Privy Council

1602/3, March [*1–14*].[24] Our humble duties remembred <unto your Lordships>. The transportacion beyonde the seas to places in amity with her Majestie, being the onely markett for our somer corne in this tyme of plentie, doth so much import the state of our contrey here in Norfolk, as wee are bolde to crave your honours favours, that it would please you to give direccion, wherby warrantes maie be sent to the officers of our portes for libertie to shippe away barley malt & peas «& beanes & also beere» payeing her Majesties custome according to the Statute. The reasons which move us to be suitors herin, be especially these. First our expe-rience letteth us see, that our contrey is so emptied of money as a number of persons within the same, when thei are demaunded to make payment towardes sondrie charges of her Majesties service & the realme, are to seeke, and do praie a staye, untill thei maie see that wherwith thei maie gett money. Now the sale of corne by vent of the same over sea, hath ben alwaies allowed, when plentie hath

---

[24] Dating: dated with reference to the reply of the Privy Council on 15 March 1602/3, below, pp.12–13.

ben, as an ordinary meanes in this parte of the realme, wherby their wantes have ben supplyed with money. And manie marryners, men worthie the cherishing, are also sett a worke by crossing the seas to & fro. Besides the prises of barly is all along the coast at 10*s.* the quarter, which price being so farre under the Statute, the subject humbly desireth the benefitt therof. Further her Majesties custome wilbe increased therby, because the greater quantity will be caryd out, when as every person shalbe at liberty to passe according to the Statute. And the poore fermors & husbondmen, having the more choice of buyers, shall reape good therby. For private men, dealing by particuler license,[25] make open therby the way (when none buyeth besides themselves) to contrive their owne gayne, by buyeng at such prises as is to the greate hindrance of the fermors & occupiers. And this is apparantly seen, and the subject therwithall not a litle grieved. Thus beseeching your honours good allowance of this our suite in our contryes behalf, wee humbly take our leave. March 1602.[26]

Copy in Martin Man's hand. Unsigned.

Endorsed: Letters *de trans*[*portacione*] from the justices. March 1602.

1½ pp. NRO RAY 221. Printed, *Stiffkey Papers*, pp.143–4. Calendared, *HMC Townshend*, p.12.

Henry Warner to Sir Miles Corbett

[*1602/3*], **March 2.**[27] Sir ther is a cause in contraversye at Flitcham[28] between Mr Atturny[29] and Mr Edward Paston.[30] They have bothe agreed to referre the cause unto you, and to Mr Nathanyell Bacon, and Mr Atturny ys desirous that you would appointe some tyme of meetinge for that purpose this Lent. I praye you therfore, that you would write to Mr Paston, what tyme you thinke fittest for it. Mr Bacon dothe thinke that Thursdaye the fift weeke in Cleane Lent the 14 daye of Aprill ys a fitt tyme for it. Yf you do thinke the same tyme fitt <for it>, or otherwise, I praye you appointe some other <tyme> daye, and I will be ready to attend

[25] For these unpopular licences granted to individuals by special commission under the royal prerogative, see Smith, *County and Court*, especially Chapters XI and XII.

[26] This letter is to be seen as part of an ongoing argument between some parts of the county and central government over the regulation of the export of grain, in which a repeated theme is that the Council and others do not properly understand the circumstances in Norfolk. For example, see *BP*, iv, pp.213–7, when the Queen was petitioned on the subject in 1601.

[27] Dating: the year is established from the reference to Thursday 14 April in the fifth week of Clean Lent. The only years after 1552 in which a Thursday 14 April fell before Easter were 1603 and 1614 (Cheney and Jones, *passim*). The letter with which this was enclosed (Edward Paston to Bacon, 23 March 1602/3, below, pp.15–16) was written before Bacon was knighted in 1604, making the year 1603. Clean Lent refers to the days in Lent reckoned from Ash Wednesday. Though, strictly speaking, 14 April was the sixth Thursday in Clean Lent in 1603, it was the Thursday falling in the fifth whole week since Ash Wednesday.

[28] Possibly a reference to Poinings Manor in Flitcham, acquired by Coke around this time (Blomefield, viii, p.413). It could also refer to the former prior's manor in Flitcham which extended into Appleton, the seat of one of the branches of the Paston family (Blomefield, viii, p.329). Flitcham and Appleton are adjacent parishes.

[29] The attorney general, Edward Coke.

[30] Edward Paston (1550–1630) of Appleton, son of Sir Thomas Paston. A recusant, who married as his second wife Margaret, the daughter of Henry Berney of Reedham, he was both litigious and an assiduous collector of music. (*ODNB*; *BP*, iv, *passim*).

uppon you at such tyme, as you shall appointe. Thus I committ you to God. From Culford this second daye of March.

Signed: Your very loving frend, Henry <Warner> Warner.[31]
Addressed: To the right worshippfull Sir Myles Corbett knight.[32]
On same page as letter of 5 March from Sir Miles Corbett, immediately below.
Enclosed with Edward Paston's letter to Nathaniel Bacon of 23 March 1602/3, below, pp.15–16.
½ p. NRO RAY (4) 32.

Sir Miles Corbett to Edward Paston

[*1602/3*], March 5.[33] Sir I am bowld to answer you in this letter for that this berar [*bearer*] cold nott well tarrye & my selfe came newe home. I shalle verey wyllynglye attende the busynes at the daye sett downe in this letter, & so I praye you sertye [*certify*] Mr Warner, & yf you come into these partes «as you[r] man sayd you wyll» lett me see you at my pore howse & we wyll conferre of the matter. And thus commendyng me hartelye to your selfe & my cozen your wyfe[34] I betake you to God. Sprowston this v of March. Your assured to his power.

Signed: Myles Corbett. *Holograph.*
Addressed: To the worshipfull Edward Paston esquire.
At the foot in Henry Warner's hand: Sir I praye you send this letter to Mr Nathaniell Bacon & God willing I will be ther at the daye appoynted. [*Signed*:] Henry Warner.[35]
Endorsed in Martin Man's hand: Letters concerning Mr Attorny & Mr Edward Paston.
On same page as letter of 2 March from Henry Warner to Sir Miles Corbett, immediately above.
Enclosed with Edward Paston's letter to Nathaniel Bacon dated 23 March 1602/3, below, pp.15–16.
½ p. NRO RAY (4) 32.

Privy Council to the Sheriff and J.P.s in Norfolk

1602/3, March 15. After our hartie comendacions. Whereas you have signified

[31] Henry Warner of Mildenhall (knighted July 1603), son of Robert Warner of Norwich and Attleborough (*Visit. of Norf. 1565*, i, p.18). Based in West Suffolk, and deeply involved in its local government and politics, Warner seems an unlikely figure to have undertaken this rôle. Socially, however, all these gentry were well integrated. Warner was a close friend of Edward Coke, had been a neighbour of Miles Corbett as a young man, and had rented much of his Mildenhall estate from Nathaniel's father, Sir Nicholas Bacon (MacCulloch, *Suffolk*, pp.247n., 328, 336).
[32] Sir Miles Corbett (d.1607) of Sprowston, J.P., knighted 1596 (*BP*, iv, p.325).
[33] Dating: the year is established by the letter from Henry Warner to Corbett of 2 March 1602/3, immediately above.
[34] Miles Corbett was the son of Jane the daughter of Robert Barney of Gunton (Rye, *Visitation of Norfolk*, p.84).
[35] This note may have been written at the same time as the letter of 2 March, immediately above, but it is also possible that both letters were returned to Warner for his agreement before being sent on to Bacon on 23 March.

unto us by your late letters[36] that there is so good store of graine in that cownty of
Norfolk and especially of somer corne and that the prices thereof ar so lowe as the
husbondmen of the cuntry doe susteyne great inconvenyence for want of meanes
to vent and utter the same att any such rate as may be agreable unto their trade of
husbondry, and thereupon have by your said letters made request for licence of
transportacion of grayne beyond the seas out of that cuntry and the rather in
respect that the prices (as you informe us) of some sortes of the said grayne ar
within compasse of the rates allowed by the statute for transportacion and allso for
transportacion of beare with payment of her Majesties custome for itt; although
(notwithstandinge the reasons alledged by you as allso by like letters of suit from
the towne of Lynne) we fynde itt not convenyent in regard of the comon estate of
this realme that lycense should be graunted to that cowntye in so large and generall
manner as is desired, neverthelesse we would be willinge that some good course
were taken for the ventinge and utteringe of some reasonable quantety of beare and
grayne from thence by transportacion over the seas for the better releif of the
cuntry and especiallie for the supplie of the husbondmen with money for their
grayne (which is the greatest want that you make knowne unto us). And therefore
yf you will upon good consideracion and advertisement (with the privitie of the
towne of Lynne) certefie to me the Lord Treasurer what proporcion of grayne and
beare you would desier att this tyme to be lycensed and likewise advertize me the
Lord Treasurer of the merchauntes or owners of shippes that shall transport the
same itt shall be considered of and we will take order that for some competent
quantetie lycense may be graunted. And so we bidd you hartely farewell. From the
court at Richmond the xv of Marche 1602. Your very lovinge frendes. [*Signed*:]
Lord Keeper [*Thomas Egerton*], Lord Treasorer [*Thomas Sackville, Lord Buckhurst*
], Lord Admirall [*Charles Howard, Earl of Nottingham*], Earl of Shrewsbrey, Earl of
Worcester, Mr Treasurer [*?William Knollys or John Stanhope*], Mr S[*ecretary*] Cecyll
[*Robert Cecil*].

Copy.
Addressed: To our very lovinge freindes Sir Arthur Hevennyngham knight highe
shreif of the cownty of Norfolk, Sir Phillipp Woodhowse, Sir Bassingbourne
Gawdy, knightes, Nathaniell Bacon esquire and other the justices of peace of the
cowntye and to all and any of them.
Endorsed in Martin Man's hand: The Councelles letters in aunswer *de trans*[*portacione*].

1 p. *slightly torn bottom r.h.s.* NRO RAY 220. Printed, *Stiffkey Papers*, pp.144–5.
Calendared, *HMC Townshend*, p.12.

J.P.s in Norfolk to Thomas Sackville, Lord Buckhurst, Lord Treasurer

1602/3, March [*post 15*].[37] Our humble duties remembred. Wee have receavid
letters from the right [?honourable] the lordes of the Privie Councell wherin wee
are directed to certefye your [Lordship] what proportion of grayne & beere to be

---

[36] Dated 1–14 March 1602/3, above, pp.10–11.
[37] Dating: this is a response to the Privy Council letters of 15 March 1602/3, immediately above.

transported beyonde the seas «out of Norfolk» [we] would desire at this present to be allowed. And wee, upon consideracion had that sondrie other counties do by their rivers bringe downe their corne to Lynne port, do estimate that there maie be spared to be shipped awaie out of that port with the members therof and Yarmouth «together»[38] the somme of 18,000 quarters, wherof <12,000> 10,000 of malt & barley & 8,000 of peas otes & beanes, «& 1000 tunne of beare». And this wee «do» sett down without conference had with the towne of Lynne bicause wee knowe the plentie greate, and the season of the yeare asketh no delaye, yf anie good be intended hereby to be don. Wee have no particuler persons either merchantes or owners of shippes whome wee seeke to preferre in this action «neither can we make certificat therin without longer [*word missing*]». Onely wee desire that it might stande with your Lordships pleasure «(the contrey being at this tyme burthened with a great quantity of ill inned [*poorly stored*] corne, which wilbe [?lost] if it be not presently vented)» to allowe ech man that will to passe according to the statute and <herwith the subject wilbe best <<pleased>> contented> «so» the common wealth shalbe best served and her Majesties custome « <wilbe> shalbe» most advaunced. Wee have made inquiry and cannot learne of anie merchant who hath shipped «latly» anie corne from hence, either into Ireland or the west parte of the realme, and if thei should shippe anie yt is not thought that thei will shippe anie of our somer corne, in regarde of their adventure by the length of the jorney, which will not be recompensed in their gayne, and when that faileth, then the merchant sitteth still, so as the onely hope for the vent of our somer corne doth rest upon transportacion. Thus beseching your Lordship that this which wee have so often moved for the good of our contrey maie have some respect had unto it, wee humbly take our leave. From Norwich this [*blank*] of Marche 1602. Your L[*ordship*] at commaundement.

Unsigned. Draft in Martin Man's hand, with amendments by Nathaniel Bacon.
Endorsed: The justices letters to the Lord [Treasurer] *de trans[portacione]*. March 1602.
1½ pp. *First page slightly damaged r.h.s.* NRO RAY 222.

Privy Council to the Sheriff, Commissioners for Musters, and J.P.s in Norfolk

1602/3, March 16. After our verie hartie comendacions.[39] Because it is not to be doubted, but that this contynuaunce of her Majesties indisposicion of health hath given occasion to the multitude, & especially to those that are of evil & unquiet disposicion, to raise & disperse manie bruites & rumours, everie man according to his humour & affection, although wee are assured that the better & wiser sort of men will governe themselves, with such discretion & judgment, as is meete, yet, for that there cannot be too much care had in such case to prevent disorders, or

---

[38] "That port with the members therof": the Customs House at King's Lynn covered all the smaller ports along the North Norfolk coast as far as, and including, Wells; Blakeney and the ports to the east fell within the jurisdiction of the Customs at Great Yarmouth.

[39] For discussion of the dynastic transition as seen from the local perspective, of which this letter is a harbinger, see above, "Introduction", pp.xlv–viii.

anie the least disturbance of the comon quiet, the which everie good subject is interested «in», wee have thought it verie expedient, by thes our letters, as councellours (according to the dutie wee owe to God, hir Majestie & the state) to advise & premonishe you, being persons of chiefe authority & reputacion in that contrey, & of entire affection to the preservacion of the state, and to require you, to take some extraordinary care at this tyme (so farre fourth as maie appertayne to your place & quality[)] both for the suppressing of all uncertayn & evil rumours, concerning the state of her Majesties health, or of ought elles thereto appertayning, & for the prevencion & redresse of all unlawfull assemblies, actions, & disorderly attemptes that such rumours maie breede there in the contrey about you. Assuring you, that as her Majestie (by whose authority wee do this) liveth with good sence & memory, & (thanckes be to God) with good hope of perfect recovery & amendment, so, yf it shall please God to afflict this state with such an inestimable losse & cause of griefe, you shalbe truly & tymely advertised therof from us, to the ende that wee & you, & all others, that truly love the state, maie in unitye & comon amity joyne togither in all such corses as may preserve both in publick & private the peace & tranquillity of the same. And in the meane while, whatsoever contrary reportes or rumours you shall heare divulged, you maie assuredly holde to proceede either from ignoraunce, levity, or evil affection. And so persuading ourselves, that in the performance of this our letter & direccion, you will carrie yourselves with such moderation & wisdome, as it is meete, wee bidd you hartely farewell. From the Cort at Richmond this 16 of Marche 1602. Your verie lovinge fryndes. [*Signed:*] John Cant[*uar*], Thomas Egerton c.s., Nottyngham, T. Buckhurst, G. Shrewsbury, E. Worcester, W. Knollys, Robert Cecyll, W. Knollys [*sic*], J. Fortescue, J. Stannope, Edward Wotton.

Copy in Martin Man's hand.
Addressed: To our very loving fryndes the High Sheriff & Commissioners for the Musters of the countie of Norfolk & to the rest of the justices of peace of the said countie.
Endorsed: Letters concerning repressing rumors.
1 p. BL Add. 63101 ff.24–5.

Edward Paston to Nathaniel Bacon

[*1602/3*], **March 23.**[40] Sir I send you by this bearer a letter sent unto me from Mr Henry Warner consernyng Sir Myles Corbet & your meting here at Appleton, the xiiii daye of Aprill next about a contoversie betwyn Mr Attorny[41] & me for landes in Appleton and Flytcham, since the receiveing of the which Mr Payne my steward of courtes sent me worde that you tolde him that you would not travell about the said cause except you had a letter from Mr Attornye (which I thought you had had long agoe) for without his warrant I am very lothe that the matter should be harde, and if you continue in mynde that you will not here the sayd cause without

---

[40] Dating. The year is established by the letter of 2 March 1602/3 from Henry Warner to Sir Miles Corbett, above, p.11.
[41] The attorney general, Edward Coke.

warrant by his letter, I praye you signifie so much unto Mr Warner by your letter and I will send the same to him that he may understand your mynde. Thus haveing no other thing to wright I comyt you to the Allmightie. Appleton this xxiii of Marche. Your very loving frend.[42]

Signed: Edward Paston.

Addressed: To the worshipfull his loving frend Nathanyell Bacon esquire geve these at Stewkye.

Endorsed: Mr Pastons letter.

Enclosure: letters from Henry Warner to Sir Miles Corbett, and from Corbett to Edward Paston, dated 2 and 5 March 1602/3, above, pp.11–12.
1 p. BL Add. 63081 ff.46–7.

Affidavits and memoranda concerning the sale of gunpowder by Thomas Gooch and related expenses

[*Post 1602/3, March 24*].[43] Mr Gooche[44] being in London in August 1599 did fill too vessells with ould gun poulder which dyd waye 7 skore & 18 pownd. The caske dyd waye 16 *li.* & *di.* So the pouder dyd waye 7 skore on[*e*] pound & a halfe at 6*d.* the pound. £3 10*s.* 9*d.* This was sould to a gunpowder maker in St Gylles, who would not have yt except Mr Gooch would pay for the caryadg of yt to his house which cost 4*d.* <too this I will take [*word illegible*] before>. [*Signed*] *Per me* Robert Jaye [*word illegible*]. *Holograph.*

Mr Jaie offereth to be sworne to that which he hath written above with his owne hand. [*Signed*] Will[*i*]am Thurlebye.

I went unto the gunpowder maker above mencioned and talked with him aboute the same gunpowder sold unto him by Mr Gooche «who affirmed» boath the quantytye and price in such sorte as is above sett downe and offered at anie time to be sworne to the same yf nead should be, & besydes said that yf yt had not bene at that present time he wold not have «geven» 4*d.* the pownde for yt the same was soe badd. He hath at this present above 40 *li.* of the same styll in his handes and offered me yt for 7*d.* the pownde, and yet yt cost him 2*d.* the pownde the newe workeinge <of the same>. He saieth he lost neare 20*s.* in <the same> «that bargaine» for within one daie after he bought the same the musters at London broake up, and he hath some of yt styll etc. [*Signed*] *Per me* Will[*i*]am Thurlebye.

[*On the verso:*] Memorandum that when the souldiers went to London in *anno* 1599 I did also travell up with them & I sent up two vessells of powder decayed which was the Hundredds & bought by Mr Beckham in *anno* 1588. I sent it by Norwich cartes and I layd out about the same cariage as followeth
1. The cariage from my house to Norwich – 12*d.*
2. The hooping of the vessels at Norwich – 6*d.*

---

[42] See also letters from Coke to Corbett and Bacon of 1–2 September 1604, below, pp.128–9.
[43] Dating: the reference in Gooch's memorandum to his service for Queen and King means that it must date from after the accession of James I on 24 March 1602/3.
[44] Thomas Gooch of Hoe, chief constable of the hundred of Launditch (*BP*, iii, p.383, iv, p.224).

3. The caryage by carte to London – 8s.

4. For cariage from the cartes at London to the powder mans house – 4d.

The two vessels wayed 158 waighte [lbs], the ferkins wayed therof 16 pound. The rest is powder 141 li. & di. which was sould at 6d. a pound, [?]summa [?]received by me £3 10s. 9d. and of this mony the fowre charges above sayd are to be deducted which are 10s. Resteth therof – £3 9d.

Memorandum that I bought at that tyme before I did come out of the city of London so muche pouder which was good to have still in store to the Hundreds use which cost me 9½d. the pounde besyds the caryage home of it agayne into Norfolk which cost [blank].

This powder was not good for service & I turned it away and I had never penny of the cuntry toward it, so the cuntry had no wrong.

I have 6 mattocks by me.

I have 9 bills in store by me.

And 248 waight of powder.

And 200 108 waight[45] of matche.

Thear was never any leade bought.

I understand that thear are fyve bills more then I have that are to be had in Northelmham.

I bought a new barrell of oake of Howell 3s. 4d. to putt in the powder.

I payd over to Mr Jewell 40s. when I went of my office of the powder mony which I sould at London. Rest – [?]17s. 5d.

[On the opposite page:] My humble desyre is for your worship & the rest of the worshipfull deputy leiftenantes to enquyre of the inhabiters within the Hundred of Laundiche whether they weare at any tyme heretofore charged to collect within their severall towneships any mony towards the common provision of pioners tooles powder leade match or any other <any other> thinges perteining too martiall services sithens 1588 that the Spaniards fleete was upon our seas.

Debet 17s. 5d.

I had never penny towards my charges & service for the Quene King & cuntry for 38 yeres, neverthelesse I payd to all charges. I lost by the decay of lyng for the Kings dyet 10s. for Godwick for which I crave favor to be alowed it [? by the] Hundred.

Undated. The three affidavits and the memoranda are in four different hands.
Endorsed: For Mr Gooche for the powder.
3 pp. Folger L.d.939.

Petition. John Platten to J.P.s in Norfolk

[Post 1602/3, March 24].[46] To the righte worshippfull his Majesties Justices of Peace for the countye of Norfolk.

In all humble manner sheweth & complayneth unto your good worshippes,

---

[45] Presumably 2 cwt 108 lbs. Written "200. 5ˣˣ. 8".

[46] Dating: dated from the accession of James I on 24 March 1602/3.

your poore & daylye suppliant John Platten of Al[d]boroughe in the countye of
Norfolk.[47] That whereas your poore suppliant haveinge dwelt and inhabited in the
seid towne, by the space of this thirtye yeres, & hath taken paynes by his honest
labour and industrye to maynteyne himself & his famylie, without molestinge or
in any way chargeinge the towne, yett one Thomas Parker gent[48] Valentyne
Croggate & Thomas Pye of the same towne invyeinge your poore suppliant caste
him in prison & dispossste him of his dwellinge, & hath constrayned him so to
contynewe without a dwellinge house ever since Our Ladye last, yett promised
your suppliant to builde him upp a lyttell house, for which your suppliant offred
to gyve towardes the buildinge 20s., & after to pay an anuall rent, yett through the
meanes of his foremencioned adversaryes his request cannot be graunted, so as he
beinge aged & lame, & his wyef lykewise aged, are constrayned to lyve in extreeme
penurye, & to waste & consume that lyttell which he had. The premisses considered, may it please your good worshippes to be a meanes that your poore suppliant
& his wyef (accordinge to the statute in that case provided)[49] may be placed in
some convenient place in the seid towne & to be releifed in this there owld age.
And they as in dutye they are bounden, will contynually pray to God for the prosperous estate of your good worshippes (in all felicitie) longe to contynewe.

Undated. Unsigned.
Endorsed: The humble peticion of John Plattyn of Al[d]borough.
Reprinted from *Stiffkey Papers*, pp.59–60.

Robert Plandon's answer to Jerome Alexander

[*1602/3, March 24 <-Θ-> 1603/4, February 16*].[50] Brother Alexander you wer
wont to sett doune thought [*sic*] untruly what somes & when yo<o>«u» p[ai]d
them as in your note of the 16 of Aprell 1601. Now your paymentes wante tyme,
& your wrightinges date. The same you d[e]lyvered unto <y> my father Lane[51] the
xx of September when we disagreed at Fackenham & I toulde you, as I cann prove,

[47] One of a number of parishes of this name in East Anglia. This one is some eight miles south of
Cromer.
[48] Presumably Thomas, the second son of Thomas Parker esq. His father was lord of the manor of
Aldborough. (Rye, *Visitation of Norfolk*, p.213; Blomefield, viii, p.73).
[49] The 1601 Act for the Relief of the Poor (43 Eliz.c.2), which included a right of appeal to Quarter
Sessions. An interesting example of paupers claiming their right to be relieved.
[50] Dating: despite Martin Man's endorsement, "Mr Blandes aunsuer", this document concerns a dispute
between the attorney Jerome Alexander and his brother-in-law Robert Plandon. Alexander was married to
Frances the sister of Henry Plandon of Thorpland gent (NRO NCC 1599 Force ff.155–6). On 27 March
1601, at the manorial court for the manor of Fakenham on the part of the Duchy of Lancaster, Robert
Plandon gent surrendered to the use of Jerome Alysander gent (the normal method for the conveyance of
copyhold property) a capital messuage in Thorpland late of Thomas Oxwicke gent together with its lands in
Thorpland, Fakenham, Alethorpe and Great Snoring. The surrender was subject to the condition that
Alexander pay the purchase price of £1,450 in instalments, namely £800 at Michaelmas (29 September)
1601, £200 on 1 November 1601, £200 on 1 November 1602, £100 on 1 November 1603, and the final
£150 on 1 November 1604 (NRO NRS 20745, 41D4). With its reference to "*43 Elizabethe nuper regine*" this
document post-dates James I's accession. On the other hand, it appears to be part of an earlier attempt by
Bacon to settle this dispute and so pre-dates the letter from Coke to Bacon of 16 February 1603/4, below,
p.74.
[51] Probably "Lane" rather than "Laue", as "law" is spelt later in this document with either a "v" or a "w".

that thence forthe I woulde pd [*sic*] my debtes my selfe. I spake all so thes wordes (which you quarrelled at) & sayd you should pd [*sic*] no debt of myne but I would have an honester man to pd [*sic*] my debtes. Yf this be no countermaunde me thincke that your not paymentes of £800 then should have given you ocasion then to stayed your pdes [*sic*] as well as [*a*]fter.

This nott of the <daye> date of 16 of Aprill I examinede & founde all to gither false excepte in £36.

And it was after you ought to have p[*ai*]d me, & at my appoyntment to others, £800 & failed in that payment payinge only therof £36. I thinke therby you broke the condicon in the surrender & forfited your estate.

Yf you have synce then serchede out such as have affirmed I am indebtede unto them & so performed that after with cunnynge which you should have done before with monye I & my councell ar decived.

I praye you anser me.

Did you owe me nothinge but for my lande at Michelmas *43 Elizabethe nuper regine.*

Did I apointe yow to pd [*sic*] any other somes with the monye which should be deue to me for my lande thene the somes in the not sett doune before the steward.

Yf you have ever hertofore sett downe or cann truly sett downe doe noue sett doune that the gentell men maye see it howe & to whome when & where you p[*ai*]d the eyght hundreth poundes which was due to me for Thorplond at Michelmas 1601, at which tyme by your oune hand wrightinge as well as by the surrender you ought to have p[*ai*]d that some wherof £722 3*s.* 4*d.* was to have bine p[*ai*]d by my consent & acknowled to others & £77 16*s.* 8*d.* to make up the £800 to my selfe. And I will inquier onces more of the truthe therof yf you regarde not the tyme when you p[*ai*]d the monye nor to whom so you p[*ai*]d it firste or laste saye sooe & I will aquainte the wardes men and yf they thinke it not to be regarded I will obaye ther direction.

I cannott learne of any howe I shoulde answere this your last settinge downe otherwies then I have allredye done excepte I shoulde make an other bargynge with you <with> for my land.

All men tell me that yf you p[*ai*]d not £800 at Michelmas 1601 eyther to my selfe acordinge to the surrender or to thos others my creditors for my use acordinge to my apoyntment you forfited the estate you hadd by my surrender <eyther> both in laue & equitye.

If I be herein miscounselled I praye you lett me knowe the advyse of betere councell to the contrarye.

Yf you cane prove that you p[*ai*]d anye more monye to me before or at that Michalmas 1601 for my land then the £20 I recyved upon that Michalmas daye or yf you did make anye secrett tendrye of monye which you hertofore never talked on I praye you lett me knowe of it. Yf you p[*ai*]d any othere by my ordere in that note besydes to Sheringam £6 & to Bullen £10 at or before that Michelmas I praye you lett me knoowe to whom and when.

I cannott beleve that you have sythence the forfitur of your estate having then p[ai]d but £36 payd more then £1000 of my debt with ought my further order.

Bit [sic] yf you have, saye playnely so & aquaint the wardesmen there withe or I my selfe will and all so ther upon be ordered by ther worshippes.

Mr Bacon charged me that I should not intermingel the matter of the lande with any of our other reckoninges ther for I ame determed [sic] to folowe his derection.

You mencyone the paiment of £390 17s. 8d. more than in my notte but that proveth not the payment of the monyes in the not acordingly. I hope your con-cyence hath moved yow to recompence the wronges you have formerlye done me for I protest I am £500 the worse for your harde dealynge with me heretofore.

Yf you have p[ai]d anye of my true & juste debtes I have cause to thanke you, but yf I hadd hadd monye to have p[ai]d th[e]m my selfe I coulde have satisfied them with lesse monye and more to my creditt. But I cannott yet assuer my selfe of any such <cuces> kyndenes, for yf I coulde I would acknouledge it.

You reherse many bandes forfited. It is materiall to expresse when and where you receyved them.

You brought to my father Lanes <ser> certeyne wrightinges which you delivered in August 1602 unasked.

But you toke from thence then dyverse thinges secretly which you myght with more honestye have lett lye wher they were.

I thanke you that you would putt «downe» that you lefte £64 3s. 4d. unpayde which you should & ought to have p[ai]d. I loste no littel for wante of there payment.

It is reason you should saye what you p[ai]d before or at Micheles in steade of them or else playnlye to confese for wante of payment of them & others you forfyted your estate at Michles 1601. At that tyme you might have departed with the lande with lesse losse then, then now you would willingely doe, for I here you will now willingly lose £150 to be rydd of it <ues> use playne dealinge or you may be redd of it when I cannott helpe it.

You sayd in your nott you p[ai]d all thes somes in this maner and you shoue no time no maner.

I answere they nor eany of them more then £36 to my knowledge wer paid in any manere before your estate was forfyted. Yf you will not lett me knowe at what tyme n[o]r in what maner the monyes were p[ai]d yett lett the wardesmen knowe.

So as you will not have me untrulye confesse that they were trulye p[ai]d ayther acordinge to the surrender or to my warrant I hadd raythere give you thankes for payinge of then [sic] then with much charges to inquier the trothe, & to affirme they be not now p[ai]d is more then I knowe. But yf they be p[ai]d it is not with or by my warrante sythence the forfytere of your estate.

Yf you cann make it verie playnlye appere to ther worshipes or wardes men that you have done me no wronge sythene my fathers deth or yf you cann not yett yf you will recompence thos wronges & the losses & hindrances I have hadd & sus-tayned by your dealynges as you & your wyfe have forrmerlye pronysed [sic].

It hath bene made knowne to you & to Mr Bacon howe I intende towardes you but yf you still indevour in this as in former thinges to make all good with wordes you may be deceyvede.

You saye you cann prove many somes confessed.

I did nevere see nor here that any somes were p[ai]d more then I have herein acknowledged otherewyse then of your affirmacon & <that yf> what yf I shoulde confesse or «saye» I beleve they be payde as you reporte, did I evere appoynte you to paye of the monye deue to me for Thorplond anye othere somes then those sett downe in the notte made indiferently betwine us by Mr Godwyn St[e]war[d] of Fakenhan [sic] court.

And did you paye thos somes at or before the tyme they ought to <be p[ai]d> have bene p[ai]d wherby the condicone was in equitye <pro> performed.

Or have you (I praye you saye troth) sythence the forfyture of your estate bothe in lawe & equitye goten into your handes by payinge of monyes, dyverse bondes of myne which you thought to wronge me with all, & therby to compell me to doe what you pleased (as I cann shewe to there worships the arbitrators you formerlye <you> practysed againste me) and fyndinge my crediturs not willinge to yelde to your iniuryous pretence now woulde saye you payde thos monyes of the purches, when in troth when that you entred into that your practyse your estate was uterlye voyd by your former breache of the condicion at the firste tyme.

Truly this is the faireste of your pretense how so ever you would now colore <an> & cover it.

Therefore yf you will have favour leve & be playn in your dealynges hereafteer and practyse not to over throwe <ne> me lest you overthrowe yourselfe by forceinge me to dispose so of Thorplond that it be to late for me to helpe you when you would <c> crave helpe and it is out of my pouere. I praye you when you have answered this sende it to Mr Bacon or to me with the answere.[52]

Undated. Unsigned.
Endorsed in Martin Man's hand: Mr Blandes [sic] aunsuer.
4 pp. BL Add. 63081 ff.77–8.

Nathaniel Bacon to the Lord Chief Baron of the Exchequer

[*1602/3, March 24 <-Θ-> 1611, June 29*].[53] It may please your Lordship[54] to be

[52] Jerome Alexander was an attorney practising in King's Bench and a member of Furnivall's Inn, one of the inns of Chancery (see BP, iv, p.174n.). He was still present in Thorpland by Fakenham in 1611, when he occupied the former chapel there, by then a barn (Blomefield, vii, p.98).

[53] Dating: the limits are set by the accession of James I ("his Majestie"), and Lestrange Mordaunt's baronetcy (*Visit. of Norf. 1563*, ii, p.273).

[54] Possibly William Peryam (d. 9 October 1604, *ODNB*), who had become Chief Baron on 7 February 1593. Around 1593 he had married as his third wife the twice-widowed Elizabeth Neville, Nathaniel Bacon's sister. Peryam had also acted as an arbiter in a family dispute within the Bacon family (*BP,* iv, pp.1, 3). In this respect, Clarke's appeal to Bacon to intervene on his, Clarke's, behalf was an astute move. Bacon was an interested party as steward of royal manors in Marshland and Clarke was his understeward there. As the case involved Crown lands, proceedings would be in the Exchequer, and the family connection with its chief judge was an advantage. However, the formal tone and the failure explicitly to mention family matters might suggest that the letter dates from after Peryam's death and is to one of his successors, Sir Thomas Fleming (from 27 October 1604) or Sir Lawrence Tanfield (from 25 June 1607) (*Judges of England*, p.95). Either way, in effect Bacon is here acting as a broker or intermediary in a patron-client relationship with Clarke.

advertised, that a comission out of the Exchequour hath ben graunted fourth against one Mathew Clerk gent of Lynne,[55] at the suite of one Purvys of Marshland,[56] for the examining of some abuses supposed by the said Purvyse to be comytted by the said Clerk <to the defrauding of his Majestie>, in the execution of his place as an understeward to my self for Terrington & other his Majesties manours in Marshland. And this comission hath ben set upon by <Mr> Stra[nge] Mordant[57] & <Mr> «R[ichard]» Stubbes[58] «esquires» comissioners. And what <thei> retorne thei will make of the comission, I knowe not. But the said Purvys, suying *in forma pauperis* (and yet by men of credit is affirmed to be worth £500) geveth it fourrth, that he will sue out a new comission, and so will contynue his molestacion which <I suppose> is «thought to be» without cause. For the said Ma[thew] Clerk is accompted a verie honest man, and this Purvys is said to be «used as an instrument &» set on to prose-cute this complaint, at the instigacion of <some> a rich man in Lynne, <where there is a faction between them> «who is the author of a lat faction ther». I beseech your Lordships favour herin, that this comission may not be renewed, unles some more cause to your Lordships satisfaccion be <to your> by Purvys shewed, and that he being so able may follow the suite at his owne charge. Thus resting to ack[nowledge] my self beholding to your Lordship for your favour herin and comytting you to the proteccion of Al[mighty] God I take my leave. From St[iffkey] this [blank].

Undated. Unsigned.
Draft in Martin Man's hand, with emendations in Nathaniel Bacon's hand.

[55] Matthew Clarke of King's Lynn gent (d.1623, son of Richard Clarke), deputy steward to Bacon of the royal manors in Marshland, mayor and MP for Lynn (*BP*, iii, pp.116–17, 336 n.137). (The index to the pre-ceding volume, *BP*, iv, incorrectly treats this Matthew Clarke as two separate persons.) For his career as a merchant, customs officer and civic leader see Metters, 'Rulers and Merchants', pp.351–362, 413. Unlike his fellow civic leaders he attended university (Venn, *Al. Cant.*, i, p.344) and he appears to have been a protegé of Nathaniel Bacon, who appointed him as his deputy steward in 1591, brushing aside the candida-ture of a client who was backed by none other than William Cecil, the Lord Treasurer (*BP*, iii, pp.116, 121). Metters describes him as "tenacious in defending what he saw as his legal rights", "acrimonious" and as "a hard man".

[56] Almost certainly Thomas Purvis of Terrington, who deposed before the Commissioners for Sewers in January 1600/01 (*BP*, iv, p.171).

[57] Lestrange Mordaunt (1572–1627) of King's Lynn and Little Massingham, J.P. The Mordaunts were an Essex family, but early in the sixteenth century Robert Mordaunt settled in Norfolk, marrying Barbara the daughter of John Le Strange of Little Massingham. It is not known whether Lestrange Mordaunt was a son or grandson of Robert (Smith, 'Norf. Gentry', pp.22–3 and App.III). However his Christian name, reflecting the contemporary practice of adopting as such the paternal surname of a family heiress, leaves little doubt that he was a direct descendant. He was ranked, perhaps surprisingly, as high as 14th among a peer group of 37 esquires when first named on the Norfolk commission of the peace in 1602, and became a con-siderable county figure. He served as sheriff of Norfolk in 1607 and 1624 and by 1614, having acquired a baronetcy in the first round of appointments in 1611 (an expensive titile to acquire at that time), he was placed 4th in the commission out of 66 local gentry. (Blomefield, ix, p.17; *Norf. Official Lists*, p.21; Smith, *County and Court*, pp.354, 387).

[58] Richard Stubbe esq (d.1619) of Sedgeford. Stubbe sat as MP for Castle Rising in 1588 and subse-quently on a number of commissions, including those for concealed lands and of sewers (see, for example, *BP*, iv, p.157). He came late to the commission of the peace (1609–16) and remained consistently low in the order of precedence. Bacon attributes the action here against his understeward to "faction" in Lynn, but on other occasions Richard Stubbe appears to have been moved by general issues of principle, as when he pro-moted a series of Parliamentary Bills dealing in part with abuses by local administrators (Smith, *County and Court*, p.331; 11 March 1604, below, pp.80–3).

Endorsed in Martin Man's hand: Copy lettere [?]*al* Lord Chiefe Baron *ex parte* Ma[*thew*] Clerk.
1 p. NRO RAY 532.

William Hunt to Nathaniel Bacon

1603, March 25 <-Θ-> 1603/4, March 24.[59] Worshipful sir, havyng receved your letter for the rent you challenge, for answere wherof I never promised your late bailif payment therof but I sayed yf upon the view of your evidence it were dew I would «put» you in possession of the sayd rent, & havyng sene your evidence I finde, yf the worest faule out that maye, that it is holden of you by fealtye in socage & so no cause of any tenure *in capite*. The rent I ferre not but loath I am to charge my land with more rent then it ought to pay. And perusing the evidence I find in H[*enry*] the 7 tyme one Langwod was owner of this close & other land & then it came to Barber & Barber sold this close onlye to Shortyng & so I nead to be satisfied what rent was pyed [*sic*] when the other land went with it & how it was apportioned when it came to Shortyng for I wright confidentlye that in that case there must be an apportionment. And as for any payment of rent to you I thinke never any was payed by either Man, Kyng or Lawes owner of the same, but only by Shorting which was your tenant of Langham. Yet yf any rent be dew to you & so long deteyned I hope you will not challenge any more arrerages of me then you did of the other of whome I had it. Thus had I sett downe the truth of the case that by your courte rolls this doubt maye be decided, & when you had serched the truth you wil offer me suche mesure as you will offer an other in that case. But yf I maye know when your next Michalas [*Michaelmas*] corte is kept I wilbe ther, & yf your styward can satisfie me of the rent, & for the apportionment, I will put you then in possession therof, which I hope will satisfie you, & in the meane while you will urge me no more then you had don others this fortie yeres. Thus fering to be to troblesome I take my leave. [?]Hild[*erston: for Hindolveston*] this present Sattedaye 1603. Your lovyng frend.

Signed: Will[*ia*]m Hunt.[60]

Addressed: To his wor[*shipful*] & verye good frend Nathaniel Bacon esquire at Stiffkeye.

Endorsed in Martin Man's hand: Mr Hunt.
2 pp. Folger L.d.366.

Expenses incurred by Ellen Howes

1603, March 25 <-Θ-> 1603/4, March 24.[61] *Anno Domini* 1603. A true and perfect note of the charges that hath bene bestowed upon the teneme[*n*]te sence Ester last.[62] /Ellen Howse./

[59] Dating: from the reference to "1603".

[60] William Hunt of Hindolveston, son of Sir Thomas Hunt of the London Fishmongers' Company (d. 1616), and husband of Margaret Briggs of Letheringsett, who brought him a number of properties in north- and mid-Norfolk (Blomefield, viii, pp.205, 214; ix, p.437).

[61] Dating: from the reference to "1603".

[62] Depending on the date of this document, the Easter referred to could be either 4 April 1602 or 24 April 1603. An allusion in a subsequent document in Ellen Howes' dispute with John and Edmund Girdleston of King's Lynn (September 1604) takes their relationship back to 1602 (below, p.126).

Item laid out for strawe – 2s. 8d.

Item laid out to the workman for his wage for layinge of the saied strawe – 2s. 8d.

For prickwode and byndinge and for one <[?]eust [used]> dassborde – 12d.[63]

For makinge of the buttrye and mendinge of the gathowse with tymber and workmanshippe – 4s.

Laid out for the taxe at two severall times – 8d.

Sum 11s.

½ p. NRO RAY 250.

Council of Accession to the Sheriff and J.P.s in Norfolk

1603, March 25. After our hartie commendacions. Forasmuch as it hath pleased God to call out of this life to His mercie our late dearest Sovereigne Quene Elizabeth by meanes wherof ther remayneth unto us no further authoritie then by provisionall care to applye our uttermoste helpe and indeavours for the preservacion of peace & tranquilitie and to make the better accompt and representacion of the state unto the Kinge our Sovereigne that nowe is, we doe therfore geve you advertisment therof, as we have done to others of the like place and qualitie to the ende that all and every one accordinge «to their severall degrees maie as dutifull subjectes joyne in» the like care and indeavour for the wellfare of the same. And because ther is nothinge that can more suerly & strongly binde and mainteyne the safety of the realme and of other dominions therto apperteyninge both againste the provicions and designes of forraine and common enemies of this whole state and againste anie domesticall and inwarde trobles then a spedie resolucion with a firme unitie in the acknowledgment & profession of our present Sovereigne & Kinge namely James the 6, Kinge of Scotlande, and nowe allso James the firste Kinge of England Fraunce and Ireland, we doe herwith send unto you a proclamacion[64] the which as all persons of the nobilitie of this realme that at this tyme and place could presently be assembled, and the generall and firme consent of the Cittie of London the cheife place of resorte of this kingdome and all other good subjectes therabout eyther of greater or meaner qualitie out of an assured conscience both for the good of the state & of the rightfull Sovereigne, have received and published with joyfull acclamacions. So it is very necessarie that the effect and substance therof be forthwith published and proclaymed in that countie, which we praie you that you <will> would cause instantly to be done, as you tender your duetie to the Kinge our Sovereigne and to the state. And so we bid you hertily farewell. From the pallace of Whitehalle in Westminster this xxv of March 1603. Your very lovinge freindes [*Signed:*] John Cant[*uar*], Thomas Egerton, Thomas Buckhurste, Notingham,

---

[63] "Prickwode and byndinge": materials for thatching (Yaxley, *Glossary*, p.163). "Dassborde": presumably for "dashboard", a sloping board to carry off rain-water from the face of a wall, although the *OED* gives this usage only from 1881.

[64] The proclamation referred to here had been prepared beforehand by Robert Cecil and sent to Scotland for James' approval (Pauline Croft, *King James*, Basingstoke and New York, 2003, p.49; Larkin & Hughes, *Stuart Proclamations*, pp.1–4). For a discussion of the accession as seen from the local perspective see above, "Introduction", p.xlv–viii.

Northumberland, Gilbert Shrewsburie, William Darbie, Edward Worecester, Georg Cumberland, Robert Sussex, Pembroke, Jo. [*sic*] Lincolne, Gab. [*sic*] Kildare, Thomas Howard, Richard London, Anthony Chichester, John Norwich, Thomas Laware, John [*sic*] Morley, Edward Cromwell, Robert Rich, Gilb. [*sic*] Chandois, William Crompton [*sic*], William Knowles, Edward Wotton, John Stanhope, Robert Cecill, John Fortescue, John Popham.

Copy.
Addressed: To our lovinge freindes the Sheriffe & justices of peace of the countie of Norfolk and to every of them.
Endorsed in Martin Man's hand: Proclamation.
1 p. RH Box 69.

Council of Accession to the Sheriff and J.P.s in Norfolk

1603, March 25. *Summary:* Another version of the letter printed above, with minor variations, repeating most of the apparent scribal errors in the witness list.

Copy.
Endorsed: Letters from the nobilitie to proclaime the Kinge.
1 p. BL Add. 63082 f.19.

Memorandum concerning the proclamation in Norfolk of James I as king

[*1603, March 25 <-Θ-> April 6*].[65] For Walsingham Frydaie at 9 clock. Mr [*Nathaniel*] Bacon, Mr [*John*] Pagrave, Mr [*Anthony*] Browne,[66] Mr [*Henry*] Windham.[67]

At Lytcham Thursdaie. Mr [*William*] Yelverton, Mr [*Henry*] Windham.

At Snetsham Satterd[*ay*]. 11 of the clock. Mr [*William*] Yelverton, Mr Henry Spelman,[68] Mr [*Wimond*] Carie.

At Downham [*Market*] Sat. 11 clock. Mr Justice [*Francis*] Gawdie, Mr [*Wimond*] Carie, Mr [*John*] Repps, Mr [*Gregory*] Pratt, Mr [*Thomas*] Hewar.

At Harleston Wedensdaie 11 clock. Sir Clement Heigham, Mr Lettes,[69] Mr Clipsbie Gawdie, Mr [*Robert*] Kempe of Gissinge.

The proclamacions [*?*]delivered unto Mr Justice [*Francis*] Gawdie, Mr High Sheriffe [*Sir Arthur Heveningham*], Sir William Paston, Sir Miles Corbett, Sir Bassingborne Gawdie, Sir Phillip Woodhouse, Mr [*Anthony*] Browne.

[65] Dating: the Council's letter, immediately above, instigating these arrangements was drafted on Friday 25 March. Given both the practicalities and the urgency of the situation, it is likely to have been discussed by the justices as soon as possible after its arrival in Norfolk. The arrangements for the muster of seamen (above, p.4) and the letter from Edward Coke, immediately below, both suggest that this would have taken approximately seven days, thus suggesting a *terminus ante quem* of 2 April. Therefore, the probability is that the "Wednesday next" referred to in the arrangements was 6 April. These inferred circumstances provide an insight into how quickly urgent information from the Court could be disseminated in the localities.

[66] Anthony Browne of Elson (Elsing) was knighted 23 July 1603 (Shaw, *Knights*, ii, p.119).

[67] The details of all the justices listed in this document are given in the Index.

[68] Henry Spelman, the historian and antiquary, lived at Hunstanton and served as a J.P. until 1616 and as sheriff of Norfolk 1604–1606 (*ODNB*).

[69] Mr Lettes does not appear on any other surviving lists of J.P.s for Norfolk. The transcription has been checked and he is not identifiable in any other capacity.

For the doble lymett[70] wherin Mr Henry Gawdie serveth & others. Est Flegge, West Flegge, Hap[ping], Tunstede, Taverham, Loddon, Claveringe, Blawfeild, Walsham. The proclamacions to be made at North Walsham upon Thursdaie next at 11 of the clock. To be attendinge upon it, Sir Miles Corbett, Mr [Henry] Holdeich, Mr [Anthony] Death, Mr Kempe,[71] Mr [James] Scamler.

For the doble lymett of Forehoe etc, wher Sir Phillip Woodhouse. Att Windham upon Wedensdaie next 11 of the clock. Mr Sheriff, Sir Phillip Woodhouse, Sir Bassingborne Gawdie.

For the doble lymett of South Grenhoe. At Watton on Wedensdaie. Sir Bassingbourne Gawdie & Sir Thomas Lovell, Mr [Edward] Bartlet. At S[w]affham on Satrdaie 11 clock. Mr [Edmund] Montford, Mr [Henry] Holdeich, Mr Clement Spelman.

For North Erpingam the doble lymett. At Cawston Wedensdaie. Sir Edward Cleare, Mr [Anthony] Browne, Mr [John] Kempe. For Holt, Mr [Nathaniel] Bacon, Mr [John] Pagrave, Mr [Anthony] Browne. Satterday 12 clock. For Cromer on Satterdaie 9 clock. Mr [John] Pagrave, Mr [Anthony] Death, Mr [John] Kempe.

Undated. Unsigned.
Endorsed in Martin Man's hand: Touching the proclamation.
2 pp. RH Box 69.

Edward Coke, Attorney-General, to Sir Arthur Heveningham and other gentlemen in Norfolk

1603, April 4. Your letter of the 29 of Marche I received this present daie the 4 of Aprill and do much commende your care & forwardnes in the service of his most excellent Majestie concerning the subsidy. You well knowe that a dutie or interest being once vested in the Crowne by act of Parliament, though the glasse of tyme runneth out, yet *nullum tempus* (as is comonly said) *occurrit Regi*.[72] But for your direction (which you desire) herin you cannot have better president [*precedent*] then of the Lord Keeper, the Lord Treasurer, the Lord Chief Justice, and amongst others myself, late comissioners for this subsidy within the cittie of London, who have spared to proceede therin, untill further warrant & direcion be obteyned in that behalf, which as sone as it shall come (being daily expected) you shall be advertised therof. And so with my right hartie comendacions to you all, I comytt you to

---

[70] For "limit" and "double limit" see the Glossary and Map 1. For a discussion of the administrative units in Norfolk see the "Introduction", p.xliii–v. For a general overview see Victor Morgan, "Local Government" in: *Tudor England: an Encyclopedia*, ed. Arthur F. Kinney, David W. Swain, Euguene D. Hill and William B. Long (New York and London, 2001) pp.298–300. The use of the double limit involved combining two of the usual limit divisions. It was a way of ensuring a substantial presence of leading J.P.s. It also allowed them more easily to be present at different places on different days. Clearly, this was appropriate on an occasion such as this: the proclamation of the new king.

[71] There were two Mr Kemps in the Commission of the Peace at this date, John Kemp of Antingham and Robert Kemp of Gissing (Smith, *County and Court*, p.353; John is given in the index as of Gissing, *ibid.*, p.385). Neither of these parishes lay within this double limit, although Antingham borders upon it (see Map 2).

[72] "Time does not run against the Crown". For a discussion of the implications of this exchange, see the "Introduction", p.1.

the blessed protecion of the Almighty. From Holborne 4 April 1603. Your assured loving frynd, [*Signed:*] Edward Coke.[73]

Copy in Martin Man's hand.

Addressed: To the right worshipfull his verie loving fryndes Sir Arthur Heveningham, Sir Edward Clere, Sir Clement Heigham, Sir Phillip Woodhouse & Sir Bassingbourne Gawdy knightes give thes.

Endorsed: Copy of Mr Attorneys letter.

½ p. NRO RAY 224. Printed, *Stiffkey Papers*, p.78.

Privy Council to the J.P.s in Norfolk

1603, April 24. After our very harty commendacions. Whereas wee are informed[74] that there is in that countie of Norfolke great quantitie of graine, and especially of barley and rye, of suche sorte as cannot be uttered in the country, and if it be kept [*until*] the sommer following is in danger to perishe and be loste, and in that respect, and because also it is certified that country doth otherwise abounde of great plenty of graine and of the easy prices that the same doth there beare, humble suyte hath ben made unto us for lycence to be graunted for the transportation of some good quantitie thereof, namely by the porte of Lynne, the which tolleration wee thincke fitt to be graunted if the suggestions which have ben made in that behalf, shall appeare to be true. Wee have therfore thought good to pray you to examen whether there be any such quantitie as may be spared, and of suche sorte as is above mentioned; and if you shall fynde that it will not be inconvenient to graunte libertie for the transportacion of some convenyent proportion of the said sortes of grayne, then wee pray and requier you to signifie to the officers of the said porte of Lynne, what quantitie you thincke may be spared of the said sortes of grayne which wee have required them upon the receipt of your letters to suffer to passe, so as the same doe not exceed the quantitie of fower thowsand quarters. And so wee bid you hartily farewell. From the pallace of Whitehall the xxiiii of Aprill 1603. Your very loving freindes.

At the foot: Justices of peace of Norffolk.

Signed: Tho[*mas*] Egerton c.s., T. Buchurst, E. Worcester, W. Knollys, Ed[*ward*] Wotton, J. Stanhope, J. Popham.

Addressed: To our loving freindes Nathaniell Bacon, Edward Bell, Humfrey Gwybon,[75] Clement Spilman, John Reppes and Thomas Heward esqrs, justices of the peace in the county of Norfolk, or to any twoe of them.[76]

---

[73] Bacon was appointed to be at Fakenham on the Thursday before Easter (21 April) "to receive the subsidie bookes" (Bacon memoranda book 1602–7, NRO BL/BC/5/22, p.22).

[74] See letter from the J.P.s to the Lord Treasurer, 1–14 March 1602/3, above, pp.10–11.

[75] "Edward Bell" is presumably Edmund Bell of South Acre, knighted 13 May 1603 (Shaw, *Knights*, ii, p.109). Humfrey Guybon had died in 1601 and had been succeeded by his son, Thomas (Smith, *County and Court*, p.364). The clerk drafting this letter may have been working with an out-of-date entrybook listing J.P.s.

[76] Apart from Bacon all the justices named here came from the immediate hinterland of King's Lynn (ten or twelve miles radius) and may be taken to represent the interests of those engaged in the heavily capitalised and commercialised sheep-corn husbandry on the light soils of this area of the county. However, the majority

Endorsed in Martin Man's hand: Letters for transporting 4000 quarters barlie.
1 p. NRO MS 21508/4, 368X5.

Accounts for the relief of the poor

[*1603, post April 24*]. *Summary*. Accounts for the year 1602–1603 submitted by
churchwardens and/or overseers of the following parishes, which are given under
their modern spelling.[77] The normal accounting year ran from Easter (4 April in
1602) to Easter (24 April in 1603). All accounts are dated to the year, but not all
accounts give the day that they were drawn up. "Carried over" indicates money
brought over from a preceding year. "In hand" is money left over at the end of the
account. "Expenditure" covers both regular weekly and one-off payments. "House
farm" is rent paid on behalf of individual paupers. The rate was often assessed by
the month (or even the week) and "rate uncollected" frequently represents instalments not yet gathered in from ratepayers previously named. "Stock" is a sum of
money kept separate from the main account to set the poor to work.
"Outdwellers" were those not resident in the parish who paid rates on the land that
they held there. "Annotated and/or endorsed by Martin Man" indicates minor
accounting memoranda in the body of the account and/or the name of the parish,
often followed by "examined", on the dorse, all in the hand of Martin Man.
Significant annotations and endorsements are given in full. "(*Martin Man*)" shows
that the accompanying statement is in his hand. Examples showing the form of
these accounts in full are given in *BP*, iv, pp.187–8.

Bale. 7 May. Rate collected by 14 April: £3 9s. 9d. Rate uncollected: £1 6s. 8d. 21
ratepayers named in total. Principal contributors: Mr James Armestead and daughter, Thomas Shaxton. Expenditure to April 14: £2 16s. 9d. including house farm.
9 poor named. In hand: nothing. Signed: *per me Rob[er]tum Bulleyn* gent and *per
me Rob[er]tum Lasbey*, churchwardens, with no overseers in office. Listed at the
bottom of the third page: William Jarvis gent, Thomas Shaxton, Arthure Sherting,
Robert Danyell. Annotated and endorsed by Martin Man.
2½ pp. NRO RAY 225.

Bayfield and Glandford. 4 May. Rate collected by the overseers: £2 19s. 13 ratepayers named. Principal contributors: Francis Fyske gent, Mrs Brigges. Expenditure
for 13 months: £2 11s. 2d., including 11s. hire for a house for the poor. 4 poor and
a child named. In hand: 7s. 10d. (*Martin Man*: "which is to be made up 30s.").
Signed by Thomas Erle, John Caster, Rob[er]t Crytaft. Annotated and endorsed
by Martin Man.
1 p. NRO RAY 232.

Bodham. Carried over: 10d. Rate collected: £1 1s. 9d. 40 ratepayers named.
Principal contributors: Sir Christopher Haydon knight, Mr Sydneye, John Buttell.

---

of justices in the county (50 to 60), from the heavy soils area, may be presumed not to have complained to
the Council about the grain situation. The division over this issue is evident on other occasions.

[77] These accounts cover twenty-four of the twenty-six parishes in Holt Hundred and five of the seventeen
parishes in North Greenhoe Hundred.

Expenditure: £1 1*s*. 4*d*. 9 poor named. In hand: 1*s*. 3*d*. Overseers: Henry Armiger, Robert Buttall, Jeffrye Ryches, Robert Baliston. Unsigned. Endorsed by Martin Man.

2 pp. NRO RAY 212.

Briningham. Rate assessed: £3 5*s*. 6*d* (no details). Rate uncollected: 13*s*. 5*d*. (changed to 11*d*., then 6*d*.). 6 late-payers named (*Martin Man*). Expenditure: £2 11*s*. 7*d*. (changed to £2 12*s*. 1*d*.). 7 poor named. Stock: 17*s*. in hands of William Caster and Thomas Carter (*Martin Man*). Unsigned. Heavily annotated, and endorsed, by Martin Man.

3 pp. NRO RAY 6 (37).

Brinton. Rate collected by the overseers: £1 6*s*. 3*d*. (no details). Expenditure: £1 3*s*. 2*d*. (no details). In hand: 3*s*. 1*d*., to be used for repair of a poor house. Signed by John Playford, Thomas Yaxly, Rychard Kendell, [*by mark:*] Richard Marret. Endorsed by Martin Man.

½ p. NRO RAY 213.

Briston. Rate assessed: £8 10*s*. 7*d*. 58 ratepayers named. Principal contributors: John Huntt doctor of law,[78] William Cattes, John Colfer. Expenditure: £8 15*s*. 5*d*. (*Martin Man*: £8 5*s*. 4*d*). 29 poor named, and weekly account to 26 September 1602. In hand: 5*s*. 3*d*. (*Martin Man*). Signed by Will[*ia*]m Toolye, [*by mark:*] William Yarham, churchwardens; Roberte Wyggot, [*by mark:*] Richard Tolke, [*by mark:*] Cutbeart James. Annotated and endorsed by Martin Man.

8 pp. NRO RAY 204.

Cley. 1 May. Rate collected: £15 0*s*. 7*d*. Rate uncollected: £1 19*s*. 2*d*. 30 ratepayers named in total. Principal contributors: Barnard Utber gent, John Kinge, John Rayley. Expenditure: £15 15*s*. 18 poor named, including 5 children. Deficit: 18*s*. 5*d*. [*sic*]. Signed by Chrystofer Newgate, John Raylie, overseers; Thomas Cooke, Tho[*mas*] Greve, churchwardens. Also named as overseers: Thomas Coo, John Parnell. Endorsed: "An accompt for the pore in Claie". Endorsed by Martin Man.

1 p. NRO RAY 231.

Edgefield. Account of the overseers for 8 April 1602 to 7 May 1603 made to Nathaniell Bacon esq and John Palgrave esq. Stock: £7 used for wool, hemp and yarn to put the poor to work but not increased. Rate collected: £4 1*s*. 9*d* (no details). Expenditure: £4 8*s*. 8*d*., including house farm. 19 poor named, including 6 children relieved "at our howses". Deficit: 7*s*. 1*d*. [*sic*]. Signed by Willya[*m*] Burwell, John Harstonge, churchwardens; Willya[*m*] Digbey, James Hamond, [*by mark:*] William Feake, overseers. Endorsed by Martin Man.

1½ pp. NRO RAY 233.

Field Dalling. 2 May. Carried over: 1*s*. 9*d*. (*Martin Man*: 3*s*. 5*d*.). Rate assessed: £3 11*s*. (no details). Rate uncollected: 3*s*. 9*d*. 5 late-payers named. Expenditure for 14 months: £2 16*s*. (no details). In hand: 13*s*. 2*d*. Stock: [*hole in ms*]. Signed by John

Knyghts, [*by mark:*] Rychard Housego, [*by mark:*] John Newman, overseers. Previous year's overseer: William Orrys. Endorsed: "We cam on the 8 daye of Aprell and go of the 8 day of May". Annotated and endorsed by Martin Man.
1 p. NRO MS 20523, 132X6.

Gunthorpe. Account of overseers and churchwardens. Rate assessed: £4 15*s.* (no details). Rate uncollected: 7*s.* 1*d.* 3 late-payers named. Expenditure: £3 11*s.* 9*d.* (no details) and 18*s.* house farm for Richard Morris for 18 months, of which 1*s.* 10*d.* not yet paid. Deficit: 5*s.* 3*d.* Unsigned. Endorsed by Martin Man.
½ p. NRO RAY 215.

Hindringham. 2 May. Carried over: £1 18*s.* 5*d.* Rate assessed: £9 16*s.* 2½*d.* (no details). Expenditure: £9 13*s.* (no poor named). In hand: £2 1*s.* 7½*d.* less £1 5*s.* 5*æd.* uncollected. 41 late-payers named, including 12 out-dwellers. Principal debtors: Mr Hastinges gent, Thomas Reade. Signed by John Fletcher, [*by mark:*] John Basham, [*by mark:*] Robert Smirley, [*by mark:*] George Clarke. Annotated and endorsed by Martin Man.
2 pp. NRO MC 1017/1–2, 802X3.

Holkham. Account of churchwardens and overseers. Carried over: £1 18*s.* 8*d.* (*Martin Man:* 5*s.* 3*d.* omitted). Rate assessed: £6 0*s.* 4*d.* (no details). Expenditure: £5 13*s.* 10*d.* (no details). In hand: £2 5*s.* 2*d.* New overseers: Robert Cocke, William Mason at Stathe, William Mason junior at Town, Robert Segon. Signed by Will[*ia*]m Armiger, Edward Stone, Richard Mansier, [*by mark:*] Thomas Lawson, [*by mark:*] William Clarke, [*by mark:*] Edmond Clarke. Annotated and endorsed by Martin Man.
1 p. NRO MS 20524, 132X6.

Holt. Account of overseers 11 April 1602 to 7 May 1603 made to Nathaniell Bacon esq and John Palgrave esq. Stock: £3 2*s.* 10*d.* used for wool, hemp and other things to put the poor to work but not increased. Rate collected: £6 16*s.* 10*d.* 10 ratepayers named. Expenditure: £6 16*s.* 10*d.* plus 14*s.* 4*d.* (incorrectly totalled as £7 13*s.* 10*d.*). No poor named. Deficit: 17*s.*, to be gathered from late ratepayers. Signed by Rob[*er*]t Bevis, [*Christ*]ofer Ryngold, [*Christ*]ofer Seman, Nycholas Loveday. Endorsed by Martin Man.
1½ p. NRO Townshend Additional Box 32.

Hunworth. 7 May. Account 4 April 1602 to 1 May 1603 made to Nathaniell Bacon esq and others by overseers and churchwardens. Stock: £2 11*s.* Carried over: 4*s.* 4*d.* Rate collected: £2 13*s.* 9*d.* (no details). Expenditure: £3 2*s.* 6*d.* 5 poor named. Deficit: 4*s.* 5*d.* (*Martin Man*). Signed by Thomas Peckett, Ed. Britiff, [*by mark:*] Thomas Fytte, [*by mark:*] Robert Smethe. Annotated and endorsed by Martin Man.
1 p. Folger L.d. 720.

Kelling. 7 May. Account by churchwardens and overseers to Easter. Rate collected: £2 17*s.* Rate uncollected: 9*s.* 6*d.* 29 ratepayers named altogether. Principal contributors: Thomas Gilberd, Peter Tompson, Robert Styleman. Expenditure, including house farm and apprenticeship: £2 13s. 4d. (*Martin Man:* £2 12s. 11d.). In hand: 3s. 8d. (*Martin Man:* 4s. 1d.). 8 poor named. Signed by Edward Stanton, Thomas Borne, churchwardens; Thomas Gilberd, Peter Tompson, John Clarke. Annotated and endorsed by Martin Man.

1 p. NRO RAY 6 (38).

Langham, Great. Account made to Nathaniell Bacon esq and others by overseers and churchwardens to Easter. Rate collected for 12 months: £5 7s. 3d. 27 ratepayers named including 4 out-dwellers. Principal contributor: Robert Barnard. Expenditure for 13 months, including house farm: £4 16s. 11d. 11 poor named. In hand: 10s. 4d. Stock: £4 12s. in hands of John Grix the younger. Signed by Rob[er]t Barnard, John Greyx, John Sheringham, John Tayler. Annotated and endorsed by Martin Man.

1 p. NRO RAY 226.

Letheringsett. 10 May. Account to Easter. Rate collected: £3 13s. 6d. 18 ratepayers named, including 8 out-dwellers. Principal contributors: Richard Fitt gent, Robert Beales. Expenditure, including house farm: £3 4s. 2d. 3 poor named, one unnamed. In hand: 9s. 4d. Signed by [*by mark:*] Richard Albrowe, churchwarden; Robert Beales, Will[ia]m Corchever, overseers. Also named: William Barker, churchwarden; Richard Fitt gent, Richard Flemin, overseers. Annotated and endorsed by Martin Man.

2 pp. NRO RAY 6 (39).

Morston. 25 April. Rate collected: £3 5s. 5d. 18 ratepayers named, including 5 out-dwellers. Principal contributor: Thomas Kinges gent. Expenditure: £3 6s. 6 poor named. Stock: £1 4s. Signed by John Wym[er], [*by mark:*] William Palmer, overseers; John Podiche, Tho[mas] Barker, churchwardens. Endorsed by Martin Man.

1 p. NRO RAY 229.

Salthouse. 7 May. Account to Easter. Rate collected: £7 1s. 10d., including £1 14s. 8d. of previous year's arrears. Principal contributors: Nathaniell Bacon esq, John Curby (in arrears), Robert Hetherington clerk. Rate uncollected: £1 4s. 10d. 35 ratepayers named altogether. Expenditure: £7 14s. 1d. 23 poor named and additional arrangements for children. Signed by Peter Tucke, Robert Stanforthe, churchwardens; Robert Tucke, G[e]orge Tucke, [*Christ*]ofer Tucke, Raff Bloome, overseers. (*Martin Man:*) "Ther is to be levied for a stock 20s." Endorsed by Martin Man.

1 p. NRO RAY 237.

Saxlingham. Account to Easter. Rate collected: £3 5s. (no details). Expenditure: £3 0s. 4d., including house farm. 5 poor named. In hand: 4s. 8d. to be added to the town stock. Stock: with addition, £2 10d. Signed by [*by mark:*] Robert Chevelie, Thomas Shaxton, overseers. Annotated and endorsed by Martin Man.

1 p. NRO RAY 227.

Sharrington. Rate collected: £1 19s. 11d. (no details). Rate uncollected: £1 3s. 10d.

(no details). Expenditure: £3 3s. 9d. (no details). Signed by [by mark:] John Cootes, Nicholas Ringold the elder. Endorsed by Martin Man.
½ p. NRO RAY 214.

Stody. 25 April. Carried over: 1s. 9d. Rate assessed: £1 9s. 4d. 12 ratepayers named, including 6 out-dwellers. Principal contributor: Thomas Sherwood gent. Expenditure: £1 11s. 1d., including house farm. Poor family of William Teasdell named. Stock: £1. Signed by John Cooke, churchwarden; John Tubbynge, [by mark:] William Cooke, [by mark:] Thomas Athowe, overseers. Endorsed by Martin Man.
1½ pp. NRO RAY 228.

Swanton Novers. 7 May. Account made to Nathaniell Bacon esq and John Palgrave esq. Rate collected: £1 4s. less 5s. 4d. unpaid. 15 ratepayers named in total. Expenditure: £1 2s. 3 poor named. Signed by [?by mark:] Henry Pond, churchwarden; [?by mark:] Lawrance Webster, George Fysher, Edmond Lawes, overseers. Overseer named: Nicholas Ranshame. Endorsed by Martin Man.
1 p. NRO RAY 6 (40).

Thornage. Rate collected: £2 6s. 10d. 23 ratepayers named. Principal contributors: Sir Nicholas Bacon, "the farmers of the heath" (assessed at £44), Christopher Burlingham. Expenditure: £2 8s. 3d., including house farm. 15 poor named. Deficit: 1s. 5d. Stock: £2. Signed by W[illia]m Maxwell, churchwarden; [by mark:] Richard Kendall, [by mark:] William Kendall, Robart Stemes, overseers. Endorsed by Martin Man.
1 p. NRO RAY 6 (36).

Warham. Easter 1602 to Easter 1603. Rate collected for 13½ months: £10 12s. 9d. No ratepayers named. Rate uncollected: 3s. 3 late payers named. Expenditure: £9 6s., including house farm and purchase of wool. 6 adult poor named and arrangements for care of 5 children. In hand: £1 6s. 9d. Unpaid: £2 from Edmund Framingham, imposed at Walsingham Sessions for neglecting his office as overseer. Signed by Richard Uttinge, John Greve, churchwardens; [by mark:] Richard Fuller, [by mark:] John Younger, overseers. Also named as overseer: Richard Curby. Annotated and endorsed by Martin Man.
3 pp. NRO MS 20526, 132X6.

Weybourne. 7 May. Rate collected: £2 0s. 6d. 19 ratepayers named. Principal contributors: Mr Justice Kyngesmyle,[79] John Rooke, Thomas Moore. From the profit of the town stock: 5s. 10d. Expenditure: £2 6s. 4d. 7 poor named. Signed by Martin Money, Thomas Moore, [by mark:] Gogfry [sic] Hemblyne, overseers; James Bull, [by mark:] Anthony Bound, churchwardens. Endorsed by Martin Man.
1 p. NRO RAY 234.

Wighton. Account to Easter. Carried over: £1 8s. Rate collected: £6 15s. (no details). Expenditure: £6 (no details). In hand: £2 3s. Additional expenditure

---

[79] A member of a long-standing legal and staunchly Protestant family, George Kingsmill (c.1539 - 1606) was appointed a judge of the Common Pleas in 1599 (ODNB under 'Kingsmill family'; Judges of England, p.74).

weekly on bread: 1*s*. 10*d*. Stock: £10. Signed by [*?*]Ja[*mes*] Taverner, George Feke clerk,[80] Barnab Brown, [*by mark:*] William Masson, overseers. Annotated and endorsed by Martin Man.
1 p. NRO RAY 223.

Wiveton. 7 May. Account by churchwardens and overseers Easter 1602 to 7 May. Rate assessed for 14 months: £9 6*s*. 8*d*. (no details). Rate uncollected: £1 13*s*. 5*d*. (changed to 11*d*.). 12 late ratepayers named. Expenditure: £7 9*s*. 11*d*. 24 poor named. In hand: 3*s*. 4*d*., and 7*s*. of uncollected rate since paid. (*Martin Man:*) "An accompt of the last yeares stock to be required". Signed by Solomon Lech, [*by mark:*] Richard Blome. Annotated and endorsed by Martin Man.
2 pp. NRO RAY 235.

Oath of allegiance taken by J.P.s in Norfolk

1603, April 26. I AB doe utterlie testifie & declare in my conscience that the Kinges Highenes ys the onlye supreame governor of this realme & of all other his Highenes domynions & countries aswell in all spirituall or ecclesiasticall thinges or causes as temporall, and that no forrayne prince person prelate state or potentate hathe or oughte to have any jurisdiction power superioritie preheminence or authoritie ecclesiasticall or spirituall within this realme. And thefore I doe utterlye renounce & forsake all forraine jurisdictions powers superiorities & authorities and doe promise that from henceforthe I shall beare faithe & true alledgeaunce to the Kinges Highenes his heires and lawfull successours, and to my power shall assiste & defende all jurisdictions priviledges preheminences & authorities graunted or belonginge to the Kinges Highnes his heires & successours or united & annexed to the imperiall Crowne of this realme.[81] Soe helpe me God and by the contentes of this booke.

Ye shall sweare that as justice of peace in the countie of Norfolk on all articles in the Kinges commission to you directed, ye shall doo equall righte to the poore and to the ritche, after your cunnynge wyll and power and after the lawes & customes of this realme and statutes therof made, and ye shall not be of counsell withe any person in any quarrell hanginge afore you and that ye houlde your sessions after the forme of statutes therof made. And the yssues fynes and amerciamentes whiche shall happen to be made & all forfeitures whiche shall fall before you, ye shall trulie cause to be entred withoute any concealemente or ymbeaselinge & trulie send them to the Kinges Exchequer. Ye shall not lett for guifte or other cause, butt well & trulie yee shall do your office of justice of the peace in that behalfe, and that ye take nothinge for your office of justice of the peace to be done but of the Kinge and fees accustomed and costes limitted by the statute, and ye shall not directe or cause to be directed any warrante by you to be made to the parties, butt ye shall directe

[80] George Feake (d.1607) vicar of Wighton from 1576 (Barton, *Anthony Harison*, i, p.208). In early 1593 also rector of Warham St Mary Magdalene and St Mary the Virgin (*BP*, iii, p.237) but by June 1605 this benefice had been taken over by Henry Feake (below, p.183). Not in Venn, *Al. Cant.*

[81] This oath contains some interesting echoes of the terminology employed in the preamble to the Statute in Restraint of Appeal to Rome (1533: 24 Henry VIII, c.12). See also the preamble to the Elizabethan Act of Supremacy (1559: 1 Eliz I, c.1).

them to the bayliefes of the saide countie, or other the Kinges officers & ministers or other indifferente persons to doe execucion therof. Soe healpe ye God and by the contentes of this booke.

Unsigned.
Endorsed in Martin Man's hand: A coppy of the oathes taken by the justices at East Dirham[82] 26 April 1603.
1 p. BL Add. 63101 f.28.

Memoranda of arbitration between Mr Bland and Jerome Alexander

1603, April 28. Remembrances upon hearing the cause between Mr Bland[83] & Mr Alexander.

Ex parte Bland.

In primis to take order for £200 to Mr Sherinam [*Sheringham*] for delivery out of Mr Blandes bonde.

Item for Thomas Plandons £44.

Item the exception for the interest demanded for Raynoldes dett to Mr Barsham. £8 demaunded. £4 onely w[*as*] asessed.

Exception to the surplus of Bullyns dett. Bicause the fault said to be Mr Alexanders. Costes of suite 30s. (but 10s. due for half a yeaur interest).

Denyell to allowe £5 paid to Mrs Mary Blande, & £5 to Thomas Blande, alledging he owed not the same to them, & £5 to Mr Bettes.

Exception to 25s. 8d. parte of Waltons dett.

Denyell £10 to Mr Mabbes.

To examine whithir Mr Mowntny & Sherinam saw a booke of the suite charges when thei did order the matter. Or whither Mr Alexander did at that tyme kepe a booke of suite charges.

Ex parte Alexander.

That Mistress Bland release.

To heare Mistress Blande touching her husbandes spache before his death for the dett.

Unsigned. In Martin Man's hand.
Endorsed: Remembrances concerning Mr Bland & Alexander cause. [*In another hand:*] Mr Martyn Mans note. [*In Man's hand:*] A copy of Mr [?]Attorneys letter.[84]
½ p. NRO RAY 230.

Subsidy assessment for the Hundred of North Greenhoe

1603, April 29. *Summary:* Assessment for the first part of the third subsidy granted at the last Parliament. 173 names, of which 1 deleted. Including 2 aliens: Ester

---

[82] East Dereham. A conveniently central location for the entire county, but also a means of avoiding the plague current in Norwich.

[83] Probably not the dispute between Alexander and Plandon (above, pp.18–21), where the similarity of surname may have led to Martin Man's misendorsement.

[84] This may refer to the letter from Edward Coke, attorney general, of 16 February 1603/4 (below, p.74), showing possible further confusion on the part of Martin Man.

Halle "a dane" from Wells and John Rogers "duchman" from Little Walsingham. Assessors: James Callthorpe, Christofer Bedingfeild, Thomas Hastinges, Richarde Sprate, gents; Henrye Boulte, Thomas Bullocke, constables of the Hundred.

Signed: [*Christofer*] Bedingfeild, Rychard Spratt, Henrye Boulte, Thomas Bullocke.

Endorsed: 3 subs[idium] 1 pars. N. Grenho.

On the dorse: [*1*] Names of a few taxpayers who have moved. [*2*] "At Holt the 19 of Julye for alehouses".

6 pp. RH Box 47. Listed, *Stiffkey Papers*, p.85.

Subsidy assessment for the Hundred of South Erpingham

[*1603, late April*].[85] *Summary*: Assessment for the first part of the third subsidy granted by the Parliament in 43 Elizabeth. 375 names, including 1 deleted.

Signed: *Per scessores hic subscriptos* [*by the assessors here underwritten*] Tho[*mas*] Thetford, Rob[*er*]t Kempe, Henrye Norgate, Cle[*ment*] Rolf, Anthony Page, John Rayner.

Endorsed: 3 subs[*idium*] *1 pars* S. Erpingham.

15 pp. RH Box 47.

Memorandum concerning a dispute between Richard Neave and Edmund Catton

1603, May 17. A remembraunce of the proceeding & order of Nathaniel Bacon esq upon the hearing of the varyaunce betwen Richard Neave & Edmond Catton set downe 17 May 1603.

It appeared by some profe shewed by R Neave that he had hired of one Jo. Neave certayn landes in W[*ood*] Dalling, wherof one closse called the Horseclosse is part. And that the said Catton held the same by [?]agreement from R Neave & not from Jo. Neave as he pretended. And that the said Catton having barganyed with Jo. Neave for certayn wood growing upon the closse did (for more conveniency to either partie for having away the wood) hire the closse of R. Neave & entred it about Hall[*owm*]as 1601. And helde till on May even last.

The said Nathanael helde it just & reasonable that Catton should contynue the occupacion of the closse untill Hall[*owm*]as next, seing he gave not warning for the leaving therof, and should paie (according to their former agrement) 20*s*. a yeare more then R. Neave doth paie to J. Neave.

In Martin Man's hand.

Endorsed: Copy order *inter* Neave & Catton.

½ p. *slightly damaged on r.h.s.* Folger L.d.728.

Sir John Popham, Lord Chief Justice, to Nathaniel Bacon

1603, May 27. With my very hartey commendacions. I have receaved your letter, whereby I understande youe have commytted one Thomas Irelande to the goale,

---

[85] Dating: dated by reference to the parallel assessment for North Greenhoe, immediately above.

whose wandringe course of lyfe, I make no doubt of, will dyscover him to be ill affected to the State.[86] Therefore I doe holde youe have done verye good servyce in commyttynge him and doe requyre youe to geve order for his staye there untyll the next Assizes to be holden in that countye in which meane tyme he maye happely be dyscovered what he ys. And even [*sic*] I byd youe verye hartely farewell. Att Sergeauntes Inn this 27 of Maye 1603. Your verie lovinge freind.

Signed: Jo[*hn*] Popham.

Addressed: To the worshipful my verie lovinge freinde Nathaniell Bacon esquier att Stifkey.

Endorsed in William Sanders' hand: My Lord Chief Justice touchinge Irelande.

½ p. BL Stowe 150 ff.184–5.

Sir John Popham, Lord Chief Justice, to Nathaniel Bacon

1603, June 3. With my hartie commendacions. Wheare uppon complaint heretofore made unto you as I have benne let to understand of the riotous pulling downe <of certeine> of certeine the inclosures of Rice Gwynn[87] esquire in Fakenham you bound some of them to the Quarter Sessions thinckting that would have benne a sufficient warning unto them which as it should seme hath not wrought that effect in them as was expected for divers of them being for the most parte <being> very <disor> insolent & disorderly people have (as I have benn informed) neverthelesse even of late assembled themselves in tumultuous sorte and threwne downe the same inclosuris againe using their owne wills for a lawe and making them selves the execucioners thereof. To the end a matter of this qualety maie not passe away without dewe examinacion and that some ensample may be made therof least others of their condicions should take encouradgment thereby <to> and committ the lyke hereafter, I have thought good to pray you to send for these malefactours and to examyn the matter and thereuppon (the same appearing to be true) to bynde some of the principall actours or stirrers of this mutenous disorder with good sewerties to make their personall appearance at the next Assises for the county of Norfolk to answere the same, which if they shall refuse to doe then to committ them untill they shall find sewerties as aforesaid, whereby they maie be forthcoming to be proceeded on and dealt with as shalbe fitt in justice. And hereof <*word illegible*> «and of» the true estate of the cause to certefie me at the same Assizes.[88] And eaven soe not doubting you will have dewe regard to doe what

---

[86] This demonstrates yet again Popham's near paranoid concern with subversion in its various forms. It also articulates in a workaday document an emergent notion of the state and its imperatives.

[87] Rhys Gwynn esq (c.1552–1629) of Bedfeddan, Anglesey, and Fakenham. (Described as "Richard" in Smith, *County and Court*, and *BP* iv.) A Welshman and a distinguished lawyer from the Inner Temple, Rhys became a Norfolk J.P. in 1601 and from 1612 served simultaneously as recorder of Great Yarmouth, Norwich and Thetford (but not, apparently, of King's Lynn). He represented Norwich in Parliament in 1614 and was closely associated with Bacon, who appointed him as second supervisor to his will (Smith, *County and Court*, p.55; *BP*, iv, p.338; *Norf. Official Lists*, pp.127, 170, 200, 235; *CSPD Add. 1580–1625*, p.543).

[88] On 18 May 1603 John Chaddock, tailor, Henry Thurston, grocer, Thomas Cornwell, husbandman, and James Myller, carpenter, all of Fakenham, had been bound over to appear at the next sessions for Gallow Hundred. On 8 June Thurston, together with Jerome Hunt, yeoman, Thomas Allen, shoemaker, and Edmond Sheltram, was ordered to appear at the Assizes (Bacon memoranda book 1602–7, NRO

shalbe convenient herein I betake you to the Lordes proteccion. From my chamber at Sergeantes Inne this third of June 1603. Your loving frind.

Postscript in Popham's hand: Such mutynous corses are not to be surpassed.

Signed: Jo[*hn*] Popham.

Addressed: to the right worshipfull and my very loving frind Nathaniell Bacon esq geve these.

Endorsed in William Sanders' hand: My Lord Chief Justice touching Mr Gwynne. 1 p. BL Stowe 150 ff.186–7.

Nathaniel Bacon to Sir John Popham, Lord Chief Justice

[*1603, post June 3*].[89] Your Lordship comaunded me to bynde certeyn men of Fa[*kenham*] for their riotous plucking downe a dyke made by Mr Gwynne. And thes men will be persuaded to no order and are meete for examples sake to be bridled. For even lately the like <ha> attempt hath been made in a towne nere unto Fa[*kenham*] by manie persons togither upon a piece of grounde of Mr Godfrys the councellour[90] in carreing away his whynnes [*furze*].

Unsigned. Draft in Martin Man's hand.
½ p. NRO RAY 243.

Petition of Nicholas Ringall to the King

1603, June 23. *Calendar*: Headed: "23 *Junii* 1603. To the Kinges moste excelent Majestie. The humble peticion of Nicholas Ringolde the father and Nicholas Ringolde his sonne". About three years ago the petitioner [*sic*] secured an execution against Thomas Chambers for a debt of over £80, and, while Chambers was in prison, laid an action against him for a further £160. But Chambers escaped without settling any part of the debts, and the petitioner sought relief from Richard Buntinge, bailiff of the liberty,[91] who was in charge of the prisoners. Buntinge promised before witnesses to make satisfaction for the execution, and also lent him about £40. Soon afterwards Chambers was taken prisoner again, and

BL/BC/5/22, pp.26, 28–9). Though the men's offences were not specified on either occasion, these summonses tally with Popham's account and with his instructions. Bonds entered on 9 July by Thomas and Walter Toll, yeomen, and Edward Hutchen, tailor, also of Fakenham, to appear at the Assizes may also be linked to this affair (*ibid.* f.31).

   89 Dating: dated by reference to Popham's letter of 3 June 1603, immediately above.

   90 Richard Godfrey esq (d. 1618), of Hindringham and Chancery Lane, London, counsellor-at-law (TNA PRO prob/11/131; *BP*, iv, p.140n.).

   91 Richard Bunting gent of South Creake, who married Elizabeth Walpole, the sister of Calibut Walpole of Houghton, in 1591. A wealthy merchant and shipowner, he joined with others in the 1580s to export 20,000 quarters of barley by special licence. In his will proved 1 February 1601/2 he left £4 a year from the profits of "my Duchy" to be distributed to the poor of the Hundreds of Smithdon, Gallow, Brothercross, North and South Erpingham, Holt and North Greenhoe, at the discretion of Nathaniel Bacon (*Visit. of Norfolk 1563*, ii. 47, 55–6). This is presumably the area over which his Duchy of Lancaster bailiffship was exercised; except for Holt, the same Hundreds were under a single Duchy bailiff in 1605 (see Sir Henry Spelman to the bailiff of the Duchy, 5 August 1605, below, p.205). Bunting had also sold various Duchy posts at Methwold to Richard Spratt in 1597 (see assignment, 10 January 1603/4, below, p.66), as well as acting as High Constable of Brothercross. (*BP*, iii, pp.17, 144; iv, p.259).

is understood to have made a full settlement of the debts before being released, but Buntinge died before he had paid the money to the petitioner. Buntinge left his wife worth at least £10,000 clear, but she refuses to pay anything, knowing the petitioner has no means to go to law and thinking to deter him with the £40 debt. The petitioner is impoverished by sureties of £500 and deprived of various sums by his grandfather and uncle, Nicholas and Henry Ringold(e), so that "he is utterly disabled to satisfie his poore creditours or to relieve himselfe his poore wife & childerin". He asks that his complaint be referred to "some indifferent gentlemen" in Norfolk who may examine the petitioner and witnesses, and also persuade his creditors and those of his father to agree to reasonable payment by instalments.

Unsigned.

Endorsed in Martin Man's hand: N. Ringoles peticion to the Kinges Majesty.

Enclosed with letter from Dr Julius Caesar dated 24 June 1603, immediately below.

1 p. Folger X.d.502 (16).

Dr Julius Caesar, Master of Requests, to Sir Christopher Heydon and Nathaniel Bacon

1603, June 24. After my very hartie commendations. This petitioner Nicholas Ringold hath by his suplication here inclosed, informed his Majestie of some hard dealing shewed unto him, by the widowe of one Richard Bunting, and of the unkynd usage of his owne grandfather, & uncle, in deteyning his due from him. With the one, hee sayeth, that hee wanteth meanes to contend in lawe, and with the other, hee is unwilling. Unto these his sufferaunces, the rigorous dealing of some of his creditours doth add further cause of affliction unto him. In consyderacion of all which, his Highnes good pleasure is, that yow should call both him, & his adverse parties before yow, & examine the differences betweene them, and thereupon mediate such good end & order betwene them, as you shall fynd to be agreeable to good conscience & degnitie, that his Highnes maye bee no further troubled with suite in that behalf.[92] And so I committ yow to God. From the court at Greenwich this xxiiii of June 1603. Your verie loving frend.

Signed: Jul[*ius*] Caesar.[93]

Addressed: To the right worshipfull my very loving frendes Sir Christofer Heydon, knight, and Mr Nathaniel Bacon esq.

Endorsed in Martin Man's hand: Dr Caesars letters *ex* [?]*parte* N. Ringoll.

Enclosure: Nicholas Ringall's petition of 23 June 1603, immediately above.

½ p. Folger X.d.502 (17).

---

[92] See Memoranda of 12 July 1603, below, pp.41–2.

[93] The two Masters of Requests in ordinary usually served turn and turn about at Court on a monthly basis. For petitions referred by the other Master, Roger Wilbraham, see for example, *BP*, iv, pp.296–7, and below, *passim*. It is a matter of interest to know how they might be aware of to whom they might most appropriately refer specific petitions. See above, "Introduction", pp.li–ii.

Award in an arbitration of a dispute at South Creake

1603, June 28. *Calendar.* Award made on 28 June 1603 by Harbert Warde[94] and Peter Stewardson,[95] clerks, chosen as arbitrators to settle all suits between Rychard Boulter of South Creake, gent, on the one hand, and Gyles Mychell and Thomas Grene of South Creake on the other.

Grene and Mychell and others having a lawful interest in the impropriation[96] of the rectory of South Creake have begun a suit in the Consistory Court of Norwich against Boulter for withholding tithes. The suit is to cease and Boulter is to bear his own charges and half those of the plaintiffs.

In consideration of 54 sheaves of rye withheld from the impropriators at harvest 1602 Boulter is to pay two bushels of rye before Michaelmas next.

Boulter and Mychell both have suits of trespass pending against each other. Two of the actions shall be held to countervail each other and not proceed, but as regards Boulter's action for damages done by Mychell's swine, he is to have compensation of 2s., but not his charges, since Mychell had in the past offered reasonable payment for use of the premises as judged by their neighbours.

Concerning covenants in a pair of indentures for land lately bargained and sold to Boulter by Mychell, Boulter may reasonably require Mychell's son Mardocheus, at his coming of age, to release to him all title and interest in the premises.

Whereas Boulter has attempted suit in law against Grene for various matters and trespasses, and Grene has just cause to take Boulter to law as appears by his bill, Grene is to pay 3s. 4d. to Boulter and remit his bill, and all suits between them are to cease.

Unsigned.

Endorsed in Martin Man's hand: The awarde between Mr Bolter & Michelles etc. 2 pp. NRO MC 571/8, 778X4.

Sir Henry Sidney to Nathaniel Bacon

1603, July 4. Sir I am requested by Nycholas Ryngall to signifie my knowledg unto you towching a cause betwyxt Mrs Buntyng and hym.[97] So yt is that in Mychelmas terme *anno* [15]91 Nicholas Ryngall being at London would have complayned to the Cowncell of the hard dealyng of Mr Richard Buntyng, for suffrynge one Chambers to breake pryson being layd in upon his ex[e]cution and other accomptes betwyxt hym and the sayd Chambers, and as he informed me, he had used all the best meanes he could to move Mr Buntyng to satysfie hym, but he could not prevayle. At my request at that «[?]tyme» he stayed his complaynt, being persuaded by me that Mr Buntyng upon my letter would have a better consyder-

---

[94] The rector of Burnham Thorpe.

[95] Peter Stewardson (d.1612), a non-graduate but a licensed preacher, vicar of Binham (1578–92), rector of Warham All Saints (1592–1612) (*BP*, iii, p.237; Crossley Evans, 'The Anglican and Nonconformist clergy of Cheshire and Norfolk', Bristol PhD, 1989, p.548). Bacon commended him as a Puritan preacher in 1585 (*BP*, ii, pp.316–18).

[96] "Impropriation": the process whereby lay owners became entitled to rectorial tithes. See also Glossary.

[97] For the petition dated 23 June 1603 of Nicholas Ringall, father and son, to the King, see above, pp.37–8. For subsequent proceedings see the memorandum of 12 July 1603, below, pp.41–2.

ation of hym, wherof I much presumed, and wrot unto hym, sygnyfyng unto hym that I had stayed the sayde Nycholas complaynt and withall desyryng «hym» as well in regard of his own creadytt as in regard of the povertie of the pore man, that he would not offer hym so manyfest a wrong. Uppon the receypt of my letter he did lett hym have som mony uppon band [*sic*], and at my first metyng with hym, which was at your howse at Styfkey he gave me thanckes for staying the complaynt, saying that he should fare the better for yt, yett he towld me that he could over-throw both hym and me by a wrytt of error as he was informed by Chrystofer Reve.[98] <At h> When Chambers broke pryson he was in ex[e]cution at my sute which Mr Richard Buntyng paid me. Chambers was «further» indebted unto Nycholas Ryngall uppon an accompt betwyxt them in a good some of mony, out of the which the sayd Chambers promysed to pay me with Ryngalls consent £41, wherof he paid by Wymer unto Thomas Whytyng £9, the rest as yett is unpaid. This is all that I can say in the cause betwyxt Mrs Buntyng Ryngall and Chambers. And all this of my honestie and creadytt is most true. Thus leavyng you to the pro-tection of the Hyghest I end. Walsyngham this 4 of July 1603. Your assured lovyng frend.

Signed: Henr[y] Sydney.[99] *Holograph.*

Addressed: To the right worshipful his verry lovyng frend Nathaniell Bacon esquier at Styfkie.

Endorsed in Martin Man's hand: Sir H. Sydneys letter concerning N. Ringold.
2 pp. Folger X.d.502 (18).

Thomas Sackville, Lord Buckhurst, Lord Treasurer, and Sir George Home, Chancellor of the Exchequer, to the officers of the port of Lynn

1603, July 5. After our hartie commendacions. Wheras by letters sent unto you from me the Lord Treasurer in Februarie laste, you were then streightly required for divers momentarie reasons and consideracions therin expressed tendinge to the publique good of this realme, not to permit or suffer anie kinde of corne or beere to be shipped or transported beyond the seas untill other order and direccion should be geven you in that behalfe.[100] Forasmuch as we are informed that manie persons as well English and Scottes as straungers have since that tyme (*viz*) presently upon the Queens late death and before and since the cominge of the Kinges Majestie into <th> his kingdome with your privitie and connivance trans-ported from that porte out of this realme great quantities of graine and beere

[98] Christopher Reve, deputy to Richard Bunting. After the latter's death he was appointed Duchy of Lancaster bailiff for the Hundreds of Gallow and Brothercross in early1603 and by 11 January 1603/4 he is mentioned as steward of the manor of Methwold. (*BP*, iv, 229; below, p.66).

[99] Sir Henry Sidney (1553–1612) of Little Walsingham, knighted 11 May 1603, a major landowner who succeeded his father, Thomas Sidney, as receiver of the Duchy of Lancaster in Norfolk, Suffolk and Cambridgeshire in 1585; merchant and shipowner. Although a fellow J.P. from ?1603 and a near neighbour to Bacon, their relationship was affected by Sidney's irascible behaviour (see below, 16 April 1605, 17 and 24 May 1606, pp.170, 229–32). (Venn, *Al. Cant.*, iv, p.294; Somerville, *Duchy of Lancaster*, p.597; TNA PRO PROB 11/120/103.)

[100] This evidently ran counter to the interests of leading figures in north-west Norfolk. See above, p.27, and below, 16 October 1603, pp.47–8.

without warrant, wherby the prises of corne are allreadie in some partes within that
sheire and other borderinge counties theraboutes very much as we heare increased,
and likely to increase more and more, unles a spedie strict course be taken to
prevent the same. In regarde wherof thes are specially to require you not to permit
or suffer anie sorte of corne or beere to be shipped or transported from that porte
or anie the members therof out of this realme beyonde the seas, unles you shall
receive speciall & sufficient warrant and direccion for the same. Nor are you in
your sufferinge of corne or beere to passe from porte to porte (which is not
restreyned) to repute or account the kingdome of Scotland as in the nature of a
porte of this realme, and looke what dueties they hertofore were wont to paie,
eyther for corne or beere, or anie other kinde of marchandiz[e] they are still to continue the like paiment therof untill the Kinges Majestie shall be pleased to take
other order therin. Herof you are not to faile as you will aunswere the contrarie
doinge at your uttermoste perilles. Geving you nevertheles to understand, that our
meaninge is not to prejudice or recall such warrantes as are allreadie directed unto
you for transportacion of corne or beere into Scotland or otherwise, so as their
tyme for the doinge therof be not yet ronne and expired. From the courte at
Windsor this fifte of July 1603. Your lovinge freindes. [*Signed*:] T. Buchurst, G.
Howme.[101]

Copy.

Addressed: To our lovinge freindes His Majesties officers of the porte of Lynne and
the members therof.

Endorsed in Martin Man's hand: Letters of restraynt of transportation, 5 July 1603.
1 p. NRO RAY 236. Printed, *Stiffkey Papers*, pp.145–6. Calendared, *HMC
Townshend*, p.13.

Memoranda concerning the dispute between Nicholas Ringall and the widow Bunting

1603, July 12. Remembrances touching the cause between N. Ringoll & the
widdow Mistres Bunting.[102]

The question is whither the satisfaction given by Thomas Chambers to
Christopher Reve maie be taken in lawe to be a satisfaction to Mr Bunting in
regard that Reve was deputie unto Mr Bunting. Which being so, then yt is thought
that Mr Buntinges executors maie be charged by law to satisfie Chambers
execution mony to Ringold.

N. Ringoll his dett from Chambers upon the execution besides charges of suite
about £46 as appered by an accompte received of Mr Bunting & the widdow
sythence Chambers escape. £45 in cons[*ideration*] of the escape yet delivered but
by way of loane & Ringolles bonds remayne for the same. A reckoning under
Chambers hande set downe during his imprisonment wherin he acknowledged to

---

[101] Sir George Home, Lord Treasurer of Scotland, was appointed Chancellor and Under Treasurer of the
English Exchequer in May 1603 (*ODNB*; Fryde *et al.*, p.109).

[102] See Ringall's petition of 23 June 1603, and Henry Sydney's letter of 4 July 1603, above, pp.37–40,
and the evidence of Richard Ringall of 28 July 1603, below, p.43.

be in his handes of N. Ringolles mony received for corne, £46 odde mony.

Sir Henry Sydny testefied a kynde of promise to satisfie N. Ringoll for Chambers dett. And Ringoll offereth to prove a promise of satisfaction by Mr Bunting in his life. Mr Banckes testimony. Mr Buntinges promise that Ringoll should not loose anie parte of his due dett.

A new daie to be appoynted when as Reve may be before the commissioners & then to proceede to hearing.

Mr Walpoles offer: iff the commissioners would judge it either by law or in conscience due from Mistres Bunting yt should be satisfied, & would give some £4 besides the due dett which is agreed to be about £46.

Touching the other dett wherupon Chambers had ben arrested & a *cepi* retorned by Mr Bunting, yt was thought not to be charged by lawe.

Unsigned. In Martin Man's hand.
Endorsed: Remembrances touching N. Ringoldes matters.
1 p. Folger X.d.502 (19).

Memorandum concerning fens at Methwold

[*1603, July 23 <-Θ-> 1617, 6 May*].[103] The fennes within the towne of Methwold.[104]

Firste there is one fenne called the Severall which Sir Edmunde Mondford enjoyeth by vertue of his lease and conteyneth by estimacion 1200 acres. And is fedd with cattall of his owne, and with cattall taken into joystement [*agistment*] of the cuntry and with his owne shepe called the Kynges flocke.

Allso there is one other fenne called the Broade Fenne which conteyneth abowte 200 acres which is fedde by the tenantes withowte any cattall taken into joystement.

Allso there is one other fenne called Southmore conteyning abowte 400 acres which is fedde by the tenantes of Methwolde. And some part thereof is fedde by the inhabitauntes of Southery in entercomonage. And with 1700 shepe, whereof the Earle of Arundell 300, Sir Edmunde Mondford 500, the maister and fellowes of Christe Colledge in Cambridge 500, Rycharde Bachecrofte esquire 400. All these are fedde there at theire pleasures.

Fennes Ende and the Whynnes.

Allso there is one fenne called Pottesford More which conteyneth abowte 100 «acres» which is the comon pasture of the tenauntes, and the greater part therof hathe ben fedde by the manor flocke unto a place called Willford whereof there is a mencion of an olde bancke yet remayninge. And the tenauntes doe affirme that they have hearde the saide flocke <on> in former tyme have used to feade <but>

---

[103] Dating: the covering dates are provided by the reference to Sir Edmund Moundford as a current tenant. Moundford was knighted on 23 July 1603 and was buried at Feltwell 6 May 1617 (Shaw, *Knights*, ii, p.117; *Visit. of Norf. 1563*, ii, p.280).

[104] We do not know the purpose for which this document was prepared, but it provides a vivid picture of Fenland farming and topography within this huge parish of 13,370 acres. It reveals a sense of dilapidation and chaos; a world ripe for reclamation such as was already being undertaken within its even larger neighbour, Mildenhall, at some 16,767 acres (MacCulloch, *Suffolk*, p.328).

noe further but to the saide Wyllford. And nowe the saide flocke dothe feade over all the saide comon all the yeare to the hinderaunce of the tenauntes.

Allso there are two dykes <by belon> which shoulde be kepte by Sir Edmunde Mondford belongynge to the severall which are nowe soe growen up that the water can have noe passage to the overflowynge of the comon used by the tenauntes, whereof one dyke is called the easte dyke and the other the southe dyke.

For the libertie of fyshinge and fowlynge the profighte theerof is soe smalle that it is not worthe anye thinge, none of the tenauntes wille gyve 3*s*. 4*d*. by yeare for it.

Undated. Unsigned.
Endorsed in Martin Mans hand: A note of the fennes at Methwold.
1 p. NRO MC 1872/16, 866X2. Calendared, *Supplementary Stiffkey Papers*, p.38.

Evidence of Richard Ringall

1603, July 28. 28 July 1603. Richard Ryngall saith that at the tyme mencioned in an acquittaunce shewed by him & remayning with Nathanael Bacon esq younge Nicholas Ryngall his nephew paid him £30 at London at one Mr Cromptons house. And tolde him that it was mony due from his <fa> grandfather to the said Richard.

And after this his nephew meeting him upon the waie towardes London paid him £3 more. And said that his <fa.> grandfather sent it to the said Richard for interest of his mony, being £30 remayning.[105]

Signed: By me Richard Ringall. *In Martin Mans hand.*
Endorsed: Richard Ringalles informacion.
½ p. Folger X.d.502 (20).

Memorandum on a dispute between Gilbert and Rooke

1603, August 16. 16 August 1603. *Inter* Gilbert & Rooke.[106]

Ordered that Rooke shall paie £20 being the dett & 20*s.* for use since Our Lady last. At which tyme it was due. And to paie all the costes of suite for the plaintiff.

Memorandum the mony being tendred accordingly, & offer made to discharge the costes in presence of Mr Clowdesley[107] the plaintiffs attorny, the plaintiff refused. *Test[ibus]* M. Man & Ambrose Mony.

Unsigned. In Martin Mans hand.
Endorsed: Inter Gilbert & Rooke.
½ p. NRO RAY 238.

Nathaniel Bacon to Sir John Popham, Lord Chief Justice

1603, September. My humble dutie remembred unto your Lordship. There <are> hath lately dyed a servant of myne. And though it be uncertayn whether he dyed

---

[105] For the previous document in this case, see Memoranda of 12 July 1603, above, pp.41–2.
[106] Possibly the Thomas Gilbert and John Rooke listed as householders in Kelling in 1595 (*BP*, iii, p.297).
[107] Thomas Cloudsley gent, of Cley.

of the infection or upon another infirmity which he had, yet I have thought it more fitt for me «to» forbeare my attendaunce at thes Assizes upon your Lordship then to repaier thither «and in regard herof praie to be excused». There be sondrie persons whome I have bounde to appeare at the Assizes wherof some were bounde by your Lordships commandment and others upon such causes as shalbe related unto your Lordship by the bearer my servant who was not at all in company with the other after he fell sick, for the man dyed in Suffolk «farre» from my house in a jorny which I made thither. There is one Basill Man whome I have bounde for wordes spoken betwen Easter terme & midsomer. And his wordes gave strong suspicion as if he or some other of whome he heard <it> «them» had ben acquaynted with those conspiracyes which sone after brake out against the Kinges Majestie.[108] And his master being one Mr Fytt[109] hath his wife & his wifes father one Mr [Francis] Kempe (a man likely to be knowen to your Lordship) recusantes in his house. And this fellow attended upon his master Mr Fytt in Easter terme at London being his clark. Thus beseeching God to graunt your Lordship longe life to his glory, I humbly take my leave. From St[iffkey] this [blank] of September 1603. Your L[ordships] at comandment.

Unsigned. Draft in Martin Man's hand.
Endorsed: Copy letters Lord Chief Justice.
1½ pp. NRO RAY 242. Printed, *HTM* v. 25.

Orders of the J.P.s in Norfolk concerning beacons, muster masters, and plague precautions

1603, September 12. Orders agreed upon at the session holden at Wymondam[110] for the said countie by the justices ther assembled the xii of September 1603.

For the beacon watch and such as have watched

Imprimis it is ordered that a note be taken by the justices of peace within their severall lymettes of the beacons within the countie of Norfolk, what chardge is or hath bene levied or bestowed upon the watch of the said severall beacons, and what will defraye in truth the chardge of them, whether the money have bene levied or not, and by whome, and what hath bene receyved by every severall watchman, and whether, and in what sorte, they have performed the service, and what particuler Hundred are chardgable to every beacon.

For the muster masteres[111]

It is ordered, that for the tyme passed, they shalbe paid as hertofore, accordinge

---

[108] Conspiracies to seize James I and to "persuade" him to repeal the penal laws (the Bye Plot) or, with Spanish help, to depose him in favour of Arabella Stuart (the Main Plot) had been uncovered by the government in the summer.

[109] Probably Thomas Fitt or Fitch of Letheringsett, clerk in Chancery (*BP*, iii, pp.284–5, 296 and n.362). His wife Barbara was presented as a non-communicant in 1598 (J.F. Williams ed., *Diocese of Norwich: Bishop Redman's Visitation 1597*, NRS, xviii, 1946, p.56). The visitation return noted that she had conformed, but in 1604 both she and her father were listed as a recusants (Barton, *Anthony Harison*, i, p.178).

[110] The sessions were held in Wymondham because of fear of the plague in Norwich at this time.

[111] In Norfolk as elsewhere the Privy Council's insistence on the payment of professionally qualified muster masters and their consequent cost was a source of ongoing resentment. For details of recent appointments and resignations of muster masters see *BP*, iv, pp.20n., 30n.

to the order of colleccion heretofore used. And that we shall joyne in a letter to the lordes of the Councell, signifienge the discontent <of> the countrye taketh to be chardged with the money yearly gathered for the said muster masteres, and signifienge that the service, consideringe the new devision of the bandes within the countie maie be well performed without them, and prayinge favour for the ease of the countie in that behalfe.

Concerninge the infeccion

That the justices shall meete and <take such order therin> procede in takinge such order therin, as are set downe in a booke, lately printed and remembred unto us by the Kinges Majestie.[112]

That before the tyme of the Assizes houlden at Thetforde,[113] and likewise before St Faithes faire,[114] the justices of every lymet shall take order that all such particuler townes within their severall lymettes, as shall have anie sicke, or that have bene at anie tyme, within one moneth laste paste sicke or dead of the infeccion, shall kepe watchmen duringe the said tymes of the Assizes and the faire at every severall house infected, to the ende that none within the said houses shall, or maie, duringe the said tymes come forth of their owne houses.

Unsigned. ?In William Sanders' hand.
Endorsed: Orders at the sessions for beacon watch and muster masters 1603.
1 p. NRO BRA 833/8, 669X1.

Memorandum of arrears due to Captain Herbert Bozom muster master

[*Post 1603, September 29*].[115] Gallow. Dewe to me from <Will> Thomas Hallmane & his partnar[116] for there [*three*] quartares at thurtiefife shillinges the quartar. Fife pound fife shillinges dew at the feast of Sent Mikle [*Michael*] in *ano* 1603.

Brothercros. Dew to me from the Hundard of Brothercros from Mr Lane but ten shill[*ings*] & from his partnar Mr Thurlo there quartars at ten shillinges the quartar and from Mr Norton for one quartar before Mr Thurlose comene one.

Northe Grenehoo. Rew [*sic*] to me in areragis from Mr Bullock but ten shillinges 3d.

Houlte. Dew to me from the Hundard of Hoult for one quartar but 30*s*.

Northerpinghame. Dew to me in areragis but ten shillinges.

Southe Erpinghame. From Mr Page in areragis 15*s*. & hise partnar Mr Raynar 25*s*. – 40*s*.

[112] *Orders, thought meete by his Majestie, and his Privie Counsell, to be executed throughout the counties of this realme, in such townes, villages, and other places, as are, or may be hereafter infected with the plague, for the stay of further increase of the same* [30 July 1603], STC 9209. In itself this is likely to have been a a reprint of similar orders of ?1578.

[113] This is an allusion to the winter Assizes which customarily were held at Thetford in February or March each year.

[114] The cattle fair held at Horsham St Faiths, just to the north of Norwich, and lasting several days from 6 October (Blomefield, x, p.441).

[115] Dating: dated from internal evidence. See also Orders of the J.P.s immediately above and Order of 17 July 1604, below, pp.117–18.

[116] The men named here are all the chief constables of their Hundreds. There were two chief constables in each Hundred, who served for an indeterminate number of years. The use of the term "partner" may indicate seniority of service.

Taverhame. Mr Langford and Mr [*?*]Winsdone for one hole yeare there pound there shillinges fowr pence.

Eynsford. Mr Outlawe in areragis 32*s*. 6*d*. & his partnar Mr Tomsone 9*s*. or theraboutes.

[*Word illegible*]. Dew from Mr Norton [*blank*].

Undated. Unsigned.

Endorsed in Martin Man's hand: Arr[*erages*] due to Mr Bosome.[117]

½ p. *slightly damaged r.h.s.* NRO RAY 241.

Memorandum of arrears due to Captain Herbert Bozom muster master

[*Post 1603, September 29*].[118] Due to Capteyn Bosome in Gallow Hundred for three quarters at 30*s*.[119] a quarter at Michaelmas 1603 (*viz.* from Thomas Halman & his partenor) in all, £5 5*s*.

Undated. Unsigned. In Martin Man's hand.

Endorsed: Gallow arr[*erages*] to Captain Bosome.

½ p. NRO RAY 540.

Arrangements for the payment of Mr Rokesby's debts

[*1603, September 30 <-Θ-> 1604, March 25*].[120] *Calendar*: "Remembrances upon the hearing the causes concerning Mr Roksby".[121] Orders were made involving the following parties. Although the situation is not generally spelled out, Rokesby is presumably the debtor unless otherwise specified.

W. Browne.[122] The case involves Jasper Roper's debt of £160, compounded for £100. £20 has been paid in money, £40 by two bonds of £20 each, £8 by land and £28 for a ship. Roper, Railton and Rokesby were bound to Browne. The first bond was paid and £8 of the second. 10*s*. is to be recovered against Railton. Subsequent notes query some of these figures. The whole section, apart from "*Inter Rookesby & Browne*" in the margin, is deleted up to this point.

To pay £5 a year from Michaelmas 1604. Browne to deliver all the bonds and Rookesby to enter into new ones to him.

Christopher Page of Corpusty. To pay Page 20*s*. at Christmas for the debt.

Frances Brayve. A claim by Rookesby for a debt is dismissed because Brayve produced a general acquittance. The matter had been ordered by Sir Christopher [*Heydon*] and Mr Ordwell.

---

[117] For Herbert Bozom, appointed as one of the two muster masters for Norfolk in December 1596, see *BP*, iv, pp.20n.

[118] Dating: dated from internal evidence.

[119] This sum, as is clear from the total and from the preceding document, should be 35*s*.

[120] Dating: mention of payments beginning at Michaelmas 1604 suggest that this postdates Michaelmas 1603, while Dockett accepts payment at Our Lady 1604.

[121] "Mr Roksby." Nicholas Rokesby, the non-graduate rector of Sharrington, died before January 1602/3 when Samuel Stallon was instituted to the benefice (*BP*, iii, p.237; NRO DN/REG 14, f.297). A clergy list of 8 October 1608 gives Stallon as the rector of Sharrington and another of 18 October 1608 naming Rokesby as still rector there must be either misdated or incorrect (Barton, *Anthony Harison*, ii, pp.226, 254). The "Mr Roksby" here might be the curate of Wiveton of that name, mentioned on 16 May 1605 (below, p.181).

[122] Probably William Brown, grocer of Holt (*BP*, iii, p.343 n.252).

Wolsey. Claim for £100 due on a bargain where £40 and £140 in land had been received. Dismissed because the case had gone to arbitration and been followed by an acquittance.

Richard Mony. Debt of 40*s.* to be paid at 10*s.* a year from Michaelmas next.

Robert Bullen senior. Debt of 40s. for [?]furze to be paid at 6*s.* 8*d.* a year as before.

John Sheringham. Debt of 40*s.* to be paid at 6*s.* 8*d.* as before.

Thomas Greve. Debt of £3 to be paid at 10*s.* a year as before.

Walter Rummynges. Debt of £7 involving Mr Barrick. To be paid at 20*s.* a year from Michaelmas 1604 and Barrick to enter into a bond.

Henry Whoode. Debt of £3. Accepts 30*s.* at 7*s.* 6*d.* a year, starting as before.

Mr Burlingham.[123] Debt of £4. Accepts 40*s.* to be paid at 10*s.* a year as before.

Thomas Shaxton.[124] Debt of 35*s.* Accepts 5*s.* a year.

Michael Mowlton. No entry.

Dockett. Accepts £4 at Our Lady 1604 and £4 the following Lady Day.

Shene and Beeston (Newby deleted). Claim on a bond said to be discharged. Debt of £4 to be paid at 13*s.* 4*d.* a year from Michaelmas 1604. Rokesby and Shene to enter into bonds.

Undated. Unsigned. In Martin Man's hand.

Endorsed: Concerning Rokesby.

2½ pp. NRO RAY 525.

Subsidy assessment for the Hundred of South Erpingham

[*1603, c.October*].[125] *Summary*: Assessment for the second part of the third subsidy granted by the Parliament in 43 Elizabeth. 363 names, including 5 deleted.

Signed: Jo[*hn*] Dyx *alias* Ramsey, Rob[*er*]t Kempe, Henrye Norgate, Cle[*ment*] Rolf, Anthony Page, John Rayner.

10 pp. RH Box 47.

Order of the Privy Council concerning the export of grain

1603, October 16. 16 October 1603. Present the Lord Chancellor [*Sir Thomas Egerton*], Lord Treasorer [*Lord Buckhurst*], Duke of Lenox, Lord Admirall [*Charles Howard, Earl of Nottingham*], Lord Chamberlaine (*Thomas Howard, Earl of Suffolk*), Earl of Northumberland, Earl of Worcester, Earl of Devon, Earl of Marr, Lord H. Howard, Lord Cecill, Lord Knollis, Lord Wotton, Mr Chancellor of thexchequer [*Sir George Home*], Master of the Rolles [*Edward Bruce, Lord Kinloss*].

---

[123] Probably Christopher Burlingham, rector of Brinton and Thornage (Blomefield, ix, p.371).

[124] Thomas Shaxton of Bale (*BP*, iii, p.301).

[125] Dating: on the dating of the instalments of the four subsidies voted by Elizabeth's last Parliament see *BP* iv, p.222, n.485. The assessment for the first payment of the third subsidy was made in April 1603 (see pp.$$), and as payments fell due at six-monthly intervals the next assessment was probably made sometime in October. Presumably the assessments were complete by 27 October 1603, when Bacon noted: "To be at Holt v November to retorne the subsidy bookes" (Bacon memoranda book 1602–7, NRO BL/BC/5/22, p.38).

This day in full councell consultacion was had of the generall prejudice and inconvenience like to growe to the fermors and such others his Majesties subjectes of this realme, whose livinges did specially consist one [*sic*] husbandry and tilladge,[126] and consequentlie to the whole realme, for that tillage would therby be gyven over yf the aboundant stoare of corne and grayne (continewing nowe at base & lowe prises) should not be permitted to be vented by transportacion overseas, as in like case of Godes great blessing in former tymes, aswell by the advancement of the Kinges Majesties customes as allso to the great benefitt of the whole realme. Wheruppon it was moved by the Lord Treasurer of England, and so after much deliberacions concluded, that all persons whatsoever shalbe suffered to transport ther corne & grayne to foreyne partes in amity with the Kinges Majestie untill by other dyrection the same be altered or revoked, paying to his Majestie for every quarter that shalbe so transported the soom [*sic*] of 3*s.* for wheat and 14*d.* for barley and mault over and above the rates sett downe by the statute, as long as wheat shall continewe at or under the prises of 20*s.*, and so in like manner of all the other graynes conteyned in that statute respectively. Which sooms of money so imposed was then declared by his Majesties learned councell then attendant to be lawfull & agreable with the opinion of all the judges of the realme, whoe heretofore by a generall meting consulted & resolved uppon the same pointe. Which ther Lordships resolucion was recomended to the Lord Treasurers care to cause duely to be putt in present execution as a matter properly belonging to the charge of his Lordshipps office, and comaunded to be entered into the register of Councell. [*Signed:*] *Ex parte* Thomas Smith.

Copy.
Enclosed with letter of Thomas and John Baker to Nathaniel Bacon, 18 December 1603, below, pp.59–61.
1 p. NRO MC 571/7, 778X4. Printed, *Stiffkey Papers,* pp.146–7.

J.P.s in Norfolk to the Privy Council

1603, October 18.[127] Our humble duties remembred. The libertie of transportacion of corne beyonde the seas to places in amity with his Majestie according to the statute, is of so great importance to this our countie here in Norfolk, which hath in the tyme of plentie no other markett, as «the same being restrayned» wee cannot (with due regard of our duties) but use the meanes to have helpe therin. And therefore wee humbly beseech your honours for your furtherance, that liberty in this behalf maie be freely given by his Majesties proclamacion. The prises of wheate is under 20*s.* the quarter, & barley & malt under 10*s.* the quarter, & rye peas & beanes under the prises lymitted by the statute. Wee assure your Lordships that no private respect hath moved us to <write so often> «importune your honours» in this cause, but a just regard «both of the Kinges profit by his custome & also» of the common good of the contrey, upon our knowledges of the wantes &

---

[126] See 5 July 1603, above, pp.40–1, and the letter immediately following.
[127] This letter must have crossed with news of the Privy Council order which immediately precedes it above.

necessityes therof, occasioned principally by this restraynte. Thus craving your honours favourable acceptance of this our suite, wee humbly take our leave. From Wymondham this 18 of October 1603. Your honours at commandement.

Unsigned. Draft in Martin Man's hand.
Endorsed: Letters to the Lordes *de trans[portatione].* Copy.
1 p. NRO RAY 244.

J.P.s in Norfolk to the Privy Council

1603, October 18. *Summary:* Fair copy of letter printed immediately above.

Unsigned. In Martin Man's hand.
½ p. BL Add. 63081 f.84. Printed, *Stiffkey Papers*, p.149.

Rent due from Richard Maidston

1603, October 27. A reck[*oning*] with Richard Maideston.

Due from him to my master[128] for a yeares ferme of Wymondham landes at Michaelmas last £18. *Unde* paid this daie £5.

Rest £13, which he is bounde to paie in this maner, *viz.* at Christmas next £5 & the rest at Midsomer.

In Martin Man's hand.
Endorsed: R. Maidstons reck[*oning*]. 27 October 1603.
½ p. Folger L.d.730.

Edward Breese to Ralph Furness, Rector of Morston

[*1603*], **October 28.**[129] Sir I ame bould to intreat eyther my sister or your self,[130] to bestowe a jorney with my man the bearer herof unto Mr Bacon, who hath by vertue of the letter herinclosed sent for him, wherin he is sent for as a creditor of the partye greved, which indeed he is not, neyther hath he had any thinge to doe with him since Hillari tearme was a twelmonnthe. Yet for as muche as Newbye[131] hathe certefied unto the comissioners that he is one of his creditors he is enforced to make his defence by his apparance, least a contempte should be returned. First he is not within the compase of the Kinges commission as I gather by this warrant because he is no c[r]editor of Newbye at all. He had execution aginst him at Hillari tearme afforsaid for twelf poundes which is at last with muche adoe come to his handes,

---

[128] The nature of Nathaniel Bacon's interest in Wymondham is not clear, but he appears to have had a connection with the manor of Stanfield Hall there (Blomefield, ii, p.503).

[129] Dating: dated from the Memoranda on Newby's disputes, immediately below.

[130] Ralph Furness (c.1559 - 1639), who came from Yorkshire, was rector of Morston, 1596–1606. One of several radical ministers whom Nathaniel Bacon recruited in an effort to establish "forward protestantism" in North Norfolk, he began his somewhat stormy career by succeeding John More "the apostle of Norwich" as public preacher at St Andrew's church in 1591 (Venn, *Al. Cant.*, ii, p.186; Collinson, *Puritan Movement*, esp. pp.186–7; Reynolds, *Godly Reformers*, pp.192–3).

[131] Edmund Newby of Warham and Horstead. This appears to be the Newby who is given as Edmund in *BP*, iv, p.140, and in error as Edward in *BP*, iv, p.94. Despite living for some years at Horstead "in good estate", he had returned to Warham by 1595 where he figured as a man of some substance, being occasionally styled "yeoman" (Stiffkey Database).

but the one half spent in recoveringe of it. First it was all the pore fellowe had left him by his frendes, and about 16 yeers past it was paid him, at which time this Newby was in good estat dweling in Horstead and became seuerty for one Sams bond in £10 for payment of £5 10s. at the end of a yere to this Flecher. Flecher at that time dwelt with Shreve oue [sic] whome I bowght my howse. The bond beinge sealled Flecher havinge no frend dothe deliver the bond to his dame Shreve to keepe, the party principall was hir sonne in lawe. This Newby was hir frend very welcom as well in hir husbondes absence as in his presence, so that for love of the one and the other Flecher could get neyther money use nor bond, by the space of 11 or 12 yeres, for it was lost, and in the meane tyme, the principall was decaid and the suerty cleane gone, we of Horstead did not knowe wher to find him. At last the bond being found was delivered to Flecher, and then hering Newby to be in good estate, sent him word by his sonne in lawe «that he would accept his dett» wherunto he gave no regard, then proces was had aginst him, first 2 writes were lost and upon the third write he was arested, he put in bond to answer the lawe, at length execution was had aginst him at Hillari tearme abovsaid and being arested upon the execution, presently paid the money to Mabes who was for the balye of the Duchye, since which tyme Flecher never had to doe with him, and therfor I think is offered great wrong to be called aboute this bussines. Nowe the money being in Mr Mabes his handes would not come out by the space of thre tearmes after, then Flecher was forsed to sue the baly of the Duchye, then order was taken by one Wilson of Aylsham and bond entered. Wilson fayled, then he sued Wilson, then Wilson put in a good suerty to be paid at St Bartholomew [24 August] last, who paid honestlye. Nowe in my conseit Flecher hathe nothinge but that he hathe good right unto if it «had» bene more then it was, being driven 16 yeres out of money, and at last to get it by suche extreame chardg. Brother I pray you once agin helpe him to get dischardged, for he is as you [word deleted] se very simple and poore and like to come to muche misery if yeers come one, and it is all he hathe to helpe himself withall in the world, and thus makinge an end of a longe tale with harty commendations to my sister and your self, from my mothers my wief and my self I commit you to the Lord, Horsted October this 28. Your loving brother in lawe.

Signed: Edward Breese.[132] *Holograph.*

Addressed: To his lovinge brother in lawe Mr Raph Furnes at Morston.

Endorsed in Martin Man's hand: Mr Breese his letter touching Fletcher.

1 p. Folger L.d.193

Memorandum concerning proceedings on a petition to the King by Edmund Newby for relief from his creditors

1603, October 29. *Calendar*: Memorandum on Newby(e)'s disputes with the following parties, made 29 October 1603, with many abbreviations and corrections.[133]

---

[132] Thought to be the builder of Horstead Hall (B. Cozens-Hardy, 'Some Norfolk Halls', *NA* xxxii, 1961, p.186).

[133] The claim made by Fletcher in the letter from Edward Breese (immediately above) that "he is not

Mr Alexander: Newby admits 40s. remaining of an execution. Also £8 due a year and a half ago for which Jo. Allen is bound, plus a consideration of 24s. Also £23 due on 10 October on Newby's own bond. Newby claims he is unable to pay. Order: no cause for relief.

Fletcher: Newby owed £10 and 40s. for legal costs. Being in execution, he assigned a lease of lands in Warham to Mr Thomas Mabbes to discharge the £12. Newby claims a consideration as the lease outweighed the debt. Order: no cause for relief.

Edmund Framyngham: Newby was bound with Henry Corker for £5 of which 50s. is in arrears. Order: Framyngham will accept the 50s. in 2 years' time.

Henry Greve and Jo. Framyngham: Greve claims £60 on a bond for which Newby was surety with Mr Stompe. Newby says that Stompe, to save himself harmless, assigned to Greve a lease of corn and cattle for £48. £36 of this was to be paid to Jo. Framyngham. Greve claims that he had paid out £48 by paying £13 arrears of Stompe's rent together with £5 to Stompe demanded for a house and £30 to Jo. Framyngham. Greve also claims that the assignment was by Mr [?] Douty rather than by Stompe but he apparently entered and occupied the premises. Framyngham acknowledges the payment of £30 of his debt but claims interest for the £6 from January 1600. No order is to be made until Stompe and Christopher Reve can be present and heard.

The same parties: Newby took on a debt of £7 owed by Peters of Attlebridge to Greve and entered into a bond on the understanding that Peters' bond should be turned over to him. He claims not to have received this, and that Peters says that it is discharged. A claim that the bond is in Jo. Pynchin's[134] hands is denied. Order: the matter is left open.

Framyngham: A debt of £12 15s. 5d. is admitted. Newby claims to have paid £7 14s. 1d. Jo. Pynchin is vouched a witness for a debt of 53s. 4d. for grinding malt.

Jo. Driver against Newby and Diker: Alleged that Driver lent G. Diker £18 13s. 4d. a week before Michaelmas upon a bond for £40 to pay £20 at Lammas, (?)warranted by Newby. Diker claims that only £10 was paid in money and that he was to have 17 combs of barley at 10s. a comb delivered at Candlemas but he did not receive this. Driver agrees that £4 10s. was repaid at Candlemas and entered on the bond. Goldsmith affirms that barley was not mentioned when the bond was sealed.

Greve: Newby claims disbursements on clothing for Greve's wife and other sums lent.

within the compass of the Kinges commission" because "he is no creditor of Newbye" suggests that these proceedings were initiated by a petition from Newby to the King. This is confirmed by an entry in the entry book of Sir Roger Wilbraham, a Master of Requests: "Edmond Newby that his creditors may deale well with him. Referred to Sir Edmond Bell, Nathaniell Bacon et al[ius] to end or certifie" (Hoyle *et al., Heard Before the King*, p.24, no. 337). The meeting to consider Newby's debts was held at Wells (Bacon memoranda book 1602–7, NRO BL/BC/5/22, p.38). Newby was frequently in dispute over financial matters (*BP*, iv, pp.94, 130).

134 John Pinchin of Stiffkey (1561–1618). In the 1580s and 1590s Pinchin served Bacon as falconer and huntsman but by March 1602/3 is described as an innkeeper (Stiffkey Database; Bacon memoranda book, NRO BL/BC/5/22, p.22).

Henry Curson s[*enior*]: A debt of £25 12*s*. 8*d*. admitted. Newby assigned him all his corn at Stanhoe, namely 140 combs of barley and 60 combs of peas and oats, thought worth £50. Witnessed by Jo. Congham.

Unsigned. In Martin Man's hand.
Endorsed: Remembrances concerning Ed. Newby & his creditors.
2½ pp. NRO RAY 245.

Nathaniel Bacon to Robert Clarke, Baron of the Exchequer

1603, November. Sir, it was ordered by my Lord Chiefe Justice[135] at the Assis last holden in Norfolk that <2 const> Jo. Danyell & Thomas Browne constables of Walsingham should be bounde to appeere in the Exchequer upon some complaint made against them by an under collector of the taske, whome I had bounde to thass[*izes*] & did judge him in the fault, and not the constables. And if my self might have ben at thas[*sizes*][136] to have opened [*opined*] at the cariadg of the collector I make no doubt but my Lord would so have judged of him for he had proceeded in the collecting of the taske of that towne without all manner of discretion & sought «as I was ledd to judge» but his owne gayne. Synce the Assizes Mr Gwynne hath had both the constables & the collector before him and hath hearde the allegacions on both sides and he judgeth the collector in fault. And yet because the tyme is dangaris to travell & the jorny verie longe «the men have presumed not to come up and have intreated me to beseche» <I beseech> your lawfull favour that their recognisances may be discharged for both the collector & undercollector & constables are all drawn to an agreement by Mr Gwynnes travell and the Kinges dutie is wholly aunswered. And thus both Mr Gwynne & I do hope that you will be pleased to shew the constables this your favour, the cause being thus brought to an ende as it is. Thus comitting you to the keping of Almightie God I take my leave.[137]

Unsigned. Draft in Martin Man's hand.
Endorsed: Dra[*ft*] of a letter to Baron Clerk.[138] November 1603.
1 p. NRO BL/BC/6/1.

Petition. J.P.s and others in Norfolk to the King concerning the export of grain

[*1603, November*].[139] *Summary*: Possibly a draft version of the document printed below, mentioning previous petitions made to the Lord Treasurer and requesting a

---

[135] Sir John Popham, chief justice of the Queen's/King's Bench, 1592–1607, senior assize judge on the Norfolk circuit.

[136] Bacon had absented himself from the Assizes because of the death of a servant, possibly from plague (Bacon to Popham, September 1603, above, pp.43–4.)

[137] This is an example of mediation by a third party to avert or abort a formal process (in this case, in the Exchequer). Entries in Bacon's recognizance books, 1585–1623, (FBL MS.31; Folger V.a.273; NRO BL/BC/5/22; NRO BL/BC/6/24; MC 1872/8, 866X1; RAY (6) 31), suggest that this procedure was widely used but rarely figures in the formal records, beyond a note that the case was dropped (see also *BP*, iv, pp.xlii–xliii).

[138] Robert Clarke, Baron of the Exchequer and judge of assize for the Norfolk circuit (Cockburn, *Assizes*, pp.267–8).

[139] Dating: dated from the petition immediately below.

general licence to export corn from Norfolk. It contains variations in phrasing, and lacks the summary compiled for endorsement.[140]

Undated. Unsigned.
Endorsed: Draught of a peticion to the Kinge for transporte.
Printed, *Stiffkey Papers*, p.151.

Petition. J.P.s and others in Norfolk to the King concerning the export of grain

1603, November. November 1603. To the Kinges most excellent Majestie.

Humbly sheweth unto your Majestie your peticioners the justices of the peace & others your Hyghnes sujectes within the county of Norfolk. That whereas at a Parliament houlden in *anno* 35 of our late Quene it was enacted for the mayntenaunce of the navy and increase of tylladg, that a generall transportacion of corne should bee made from such places within this land where the same was bought at these prysses followeing *viz*. wheat at 25[*s*.][141] the quarter, pease beanes & rey at 13*s*. 4*d*. the quarter & barlie and mault at 12*s*. the quarter, which act standeth styll in force and the due execucion thereof is not only benificiall unto his Majestie, but allsoe very necessary for all your Majesties subjectes, which our experience leadeth us unto, first for the great encrease of your Majesties customes by transportacion of corne from the portes of this county within one yeare last past more then in many former yeares, secondly the great benyfyt we find the husbandmen do recyve by ventyng of there corne, without which dyverse of them are dysabled to pay such serviceable dutyes as belonge unto your Majestie, lastly the navie will thereby be encreased and the marriners and seafaring men cherished and set on work. And yet we find that the transportacion of corne uppon particuler lysences (nowe usuall) are very prejudiciall unto your Majestie and your subjectes, and the said statut is thereby utterly frustrated, and the generall good thereby intended is turned <unto> to the generall hurt of all, unlesse some fewe persons. Your Majestie in your princcly <pleas> care may at your pleasure restrayne transportacion of corne aswell uppon generall as particuler lysences when neede requireth, and we should shewe our selfes very necligent & undutyfull yf we dyd not certyfie and become sutors to your Majestie aswell for the restraynt as lybertie of transportacion, when occasion serveth. We have presumed at this tyme aswell in regard that our former certyficates to the lyke purpose [*have*] taken noe effect, as alsoe for many important cawses tending to the generall good of this county & places in amytie with your Majestie by your Highnes proclamacion or other direccion, and for the prohibyting of all partyculer lysences the prises of corne contyneweing under the rate sett downe in the said statut, as nowe they doe. And herein not only we but the whole county of Norfolk and dyverse other shyers thereunto adjoyning shall according to our bounden dutyes acknowledg your Majesties godly care over us

---

[140] These characteristics suggest that, as with the document immediately following, it may have been drawn up at a somewhat later date as part of a retrospective process of documenting precedents for such petitions.

[141] There may be a scribal error here. The endorsement below puts the price at 20*s*., which is that specified in the statute of 1593.

and wyll alsoe daylie pray to God for the contynewance of your Majesties most happy and long raigne over us.

Indorcement.

Humbly sheweth that in *anno* xxxv of our late Quene it was enacted for the mayntenaunce of the navie and encrease of <tyllag> tylladg, that a generall transportacion of corne should be made in Inglyshe vessells from such places where the pryces weare as followeth, *viz.* wheate at 20s. the quarter, rey pease and beanes at 13s. 4d. the quarter, and barlie or mault at 12s. the quarter, reserving to your Majestie for the custome of every quarter of wheate 2s. and for every quarter of the other kindes of corne 16d.

That the due execution of the sayd statutes is very benificiall to your Majestie & generally good for all your Highnes subjectes for sundry reasons herein expressed.

That with very good consyderacion both the prises of corne & the custome thereuppon was establyshed for mayntenance of the husbandry and that aswell the husbandman as the engrossers of corne are barred of all unlawefull meanes to rayse the pryses above the said statut bycause they shall then have noe vent.

And that almost noe corne hath ben transported of late tyme but uppon particuler lycences etc.[142]

Unsigned. Copy.
1½ pp. NRO RAY 246. Printed, *Stiffkey Papers*, pp.147–8.

Petition of the J.P.s and others in Norfolk to the King concerning the export of grain

[*? 1603, November*].[143] To the Kinges most excellent Majestie.

Humblie shew unto your Highnes your suppliants & subjects undernamed justices of peace in your Majesties countie of Norfolk in the name of the poore husbandmen there. That wheras upon grave & necessary consideracions & chiefly for the increase & mayntenance of husbandry & tilledge, by sondrie actes in Parliament, transportacion of corne in tyme of plentie hath ben allowed to places in amity with the realme, and lastly in the 35th yeare of the raigne of our soveragn lady Queene Elizabeth the said transportacion was permitted when as wheate should not exceed the rate of 20s. the quarter, rye peas & beanes 13s. 4d. the quarter & barly & mault 12s. the quarter. This notwithstanding of late yeares, & now especially corne being at much lower rates then the statute lymiteth and the plenty (by Gods blessing) verie greate at this tyme, the libertie of transportacion hath ben & is at this present restrayned and the subject denyed to passe (saving except some small quantities) by license. Wherby our contry & especially the husbandmen are sore weakened & impoverished. Our contry (gracious Soveraign)

---

[142] This is not in Bacon's hand or that of one of his secretaries. It reads more like the work of the Baker brothers of King's Lynn, whose identifiable correspondence makes frequent reference to statutes (see letter of 18 December 1603, below, pp.59–60).

[143] Dating: this petition has been assigned tentatively to November 1603 because of its general similarities to the documents printed immediately above. The earlier certificates referred to in the first petition were directed to the Lord Treasurer and this petition must pre-date the act of 1604 (1 James I c.25), when prices were increased to 26s. 8d. for wheat, 15s. for rye, peas and beans, and 14s. for barley and malt.

being large dependeth principally upon tilledge & husbandry and hath no other vent or markett for their corne in tyme of plentie but the parts beyond the seas, so as transportacions being denyed & restrayned tilledge must necessarily decaye. Wee have presumed in love & compassion of our contrys grievaunce (bound also in dutie so to do) to present this cause to your Majesties consideracions humbly craving relief herin, that your Majesties poore subjectes maie have the benefitt of this lawe by the libertie of transportacions and the same being permitted in such sort as the statute provideth, your Majesties custome wilbe much advanced therby & your subjectes in this county receive singuler good and the realme in no other parts indamaged.

Undated. Unsigned.
Reprinted from *Stiffkey Papers*, pp.138–9.

Referral of petition. Symion Martindale and Giles Maye to the King

1603, November. *Petition of Symion Martindale and Giles Maye to the King, November 1603, to recover the petitioner's [sic] farm, etc., which have been taken by their creditors, as they failed to pay the rent, with a note signed by Roger Wilbraham,*[144] *stating that the King has required Sir Henrie Sidney, Sir Charles Cornwallis*[145] *and Nathaniel Bacon esquire, to take note of the petitioner's grievance.*[146]
Dobell, 63 (1941), p.16.

Examination in a case of paternity

1603, November 7. The examinacion of Cicely Kymer widdow taken 7 November 1603 before Nathanael Bacon esquire.

She saith that Robert Englishe of Bodham is the father of her childe wherof shee hath ben lately delivered. And that he had the use of her «about» a moneth before Christmas last. And the same was don in her owne house. And saith that shee laid it to her husband by the procurement of olde Englishe.

She saith that shee hath not seen her husband since his going over sea.

At the foot: Apparrell of the widdow Kymers in Edmund Englishes handes. *Viz.* a doblett & hose of hir husband, 2 pillowberes, 1 neckerchief, an apron, 2 pewter platters, a pair of pepper quernes.

Signed: Na[*thaniel*] Bacon. *In Martin Man's hand.*
Endorsed: Examination of Cicely Kymer.
½ p. NRO MC 1370/4, 810X1.

---

[144] Master of Requests. There appears to be no record of this referral in Wilbraham's entry book (Hoyle *et al.*, *Heard Before the King*).

[145] Sir Charles Cornwallis (*c.*1555–1629), courtier and diplomat, knighted 11 July 1603. A member of a leading Suffolk family, Cornwallis became a substantial local figure, owning property in north Norfolk and serving as J.P. from 1601. In 1604 he represented Norfolk in Parliament alongside Nathaniel Bacon. (*ODNB*; Smith, *County and Court*, p.352.)

[146] Sidney and Bacon examined the case at Wells on 26 November 1603. See below, p.57.

Referral of petition. Walter Sheltram to the King

1603, November 12. *Calendar*: Walter Sheltram of Walsingham states that, because of losses due to sureties undertaken and other problems, he is unable to satisfy his various creditors unless given time and allowed to follow his profession.[147] Some creditors have agreed, but the rest "being of an unconscionable mynde" seek to recover their debts by law, to the undoing of himself, his wife and children.

He claims to be very poor, aged and weak, and requests that Sir Henrie Sidney and Nathaniel Bacon esquire be commissioned to call the creditors before them and to seek a reasonable settlement period or to certify the King of those who remain obstinate. *Undated. Unsigned.*

At the foot: Order from the King to Sidney and Bacon to arrange a composition with the creditors. Should this not be possible they are to certify the names of the obstinate parties so that, if appropriate, the King may be moved again for speedier relief. 12 November 1603 from the court at Wilton. [*Signed*:] Rog[er] Wilbraham.[148]

Endorsed ?in Martin Man's hand: Sheltrams November.
1 p. Folger L.d.731.

Examination in a case of paternity

1603, November 17. The examinacion of Elizabeth Howard taken the xvii of November 1603 before Nathanael Bacon esquire.

Shee saith that about half a yeare synce one Robert Barwick began to have the unlawfull use of her bodie, & some tymes since he used her, and the last tyme was about a moneth past, and all was comytted in her owne bedd chamber in Sir Henry Sydneys house in Saxlingham.

And shee saith that shee is with childe by him and so hath found her self to be about 6 or 7 weekes.

Shee saith that about a moneth past shee did tell Goodwife Chestney and Bashams wife that shee was with childe by the said Barwick.

Signed: Na[thaniel] Bacon. *In Martin Man's hand.*
Endorsed: Examination of Elizabeth Howard.
½ p. NRO MC 1083/4, 803X1.

Robert Wood to Nathaniel Bacon

1603, November 22. May it please your good worshipp to be advertized, whereas Mr Spratt[149] owe me £80 for which you stand bound as suerty, and doth paye in neyther principall dett nor interest, contrarie to his faithfull promise wheron I did

---

[147] Sheltram was an innkeeper in Little Walsingham. His petition to the King was successful despite his age and debts; by 1615 his widow was being licensed in his stead (Folger V.a.273, p.102; NRO BL/BC/5/22, p.102).

[148] This is another instance of a petition signed by Wilbraham that does not appear in his register (Hoyle *et al., Heard Before the King*). Bacon examined the case on 12 December 1603. See below, p.58.

[149] The gist of Spratt's response is presented in the sale catalogue entry for December 1603, below, p.57.

rely at Mihelmas last and was disappointed, these are to desire your worships resolucion how your pleasure is to paie me, for I verely thinke he meaneth nothing
lesse. I holde it convenient to <knowe your> acquaint you herewith that so by your
direction I may have my dett, or some good meanes to your likeing to come to the
same. I know your meaning is not to be holden in that sort contrary to your will
neyther is it my desire so to doe. So resting uppon your worships answere, I take
my leave. Tharston 22 November 1603. Your in any thing he may.

Signed: Robert Woode. *Holograph.*
Addressed: To the worshipfull Nathanaell Bacon esquire at his house at Stifkye.
Endorsed in Martin Man's hand: Mr Woodes letter.
½ p. Folger L.d.625.

Orders made by Sir Henry Sidney and Nathaniel Bacon

1603, November 26. A remembrance of proceedinges at Welles 26 November
1603 by Sir Henry Sydney & Mr Nathaniel Bacon.

Ordered between Wylbore & others: that Wylbore shall discharge suite charges
before the iiii of December, *viz.* a *latitat* «5s.», the warrant 4s., a *cepi* 2s.,
thatt[*orneys*] fee 3s. 4d., yf Mr Burredge have sent up.

Ordered between James Tidde and Jo. Curson: Jo. Curson to paie 2s. for the
warrant of the peace, & to discharge the proces fee, if Mr Burredge have sent for it.

Memorandum

Inter Martyndale & May *ac* W. Tailor:[150] Martyndale sold unto Tailour 100
combes of barley for £24 & 40 combs rye for £16. Some [*sum*] disb[*ursed*] is £40.
Unde confessd to be satisfied in barley 40s., in money £13 & in sheepe £8. Some
£23. Some rem[*aining*] £17.

Order: the commissioners for composition did sett downe that the £17 should
be made up £25 in regard the bargayn was not performed, and in regard of the
suertie his ability etc. But Tailour refused it.

Mr Christofer Smith & Christofer Reade, 2 of the creditors, being required and
warned to be before the commissioners by George Esty, made default.

Unsigned. In Martin Man's hand.
Endorsed: Proceedinges at Welles 26 November. Concerning Martendale, Curson,
Wylbore.
½ p. NRO RAY 247.

Richard Spratt to Nathaniel Bacon

1603, December. *Signed letter asking for further time to pay a debt and proposing
terms.*[151]

1 p. Dobell, 46 (1925), no.194.

---

[150] See petition dated November 1603, above, p.55. Bacon noted on 9 November 1603 that Smith,
Tailor, Rade, May and a John Davy were required to attend Martyndale's hearing (Bacon memoranda book,
NRO BL/BC/5/22, p.40).
[151] See above, 22 November 1603, p.56.

Memorandum concerning Walter Sheltram's debts

1603, December 12. Remembrances upon hearing the cause of Walter Sheltram, 12 December 1603, before Nathaniel Bacon esquire.[152]

Inter Edw. Bevys & Sheltram. The dett £10 5*s.* for 20 combs wheate due 3 yeares past. Deliverd about a moneth before Sheltram brake upon his worde. Composition at 6*s.* 8*d.* the £.

		Dette		Composition
	Robert Lane	50*s.*		16*s.* 8*d.*
/Reade/[153]	Jo. Monforth	£6 16*s.*		45*s.*
/Reade/	Lawrence Royston	<£11 10*s.*> «£7»		<43*s.*>«46*s.* 8*d.*»
	Robert Cock	£7 10*s.*		50*s.*
	Thomas Bullock	55*s.*		18*s.* 4*d.*
/Defalt/	Halman	55*s.* defalt		18*s.* 4*d.*[154]
	G. Walpole	£6 5*s.*		41*s.* 8*d.*
	Barsham	50*s.*		20*s.*
/Reade/	Mr Sabbe	£3		20*s.*
/Read/	Mr Nicholas Browne	£4		26*s.* 8*d.*
/Read/	Henry Myles	£6 10*s.*		43*s.* 4*d.*
	Clark	40*s.*		13*s.* 4*d.*
/Reade/	Edw. Bevys	£10 5*s.*	£3	<6*s.* 8*d.*> «8*s.* 4*d.*»
	Ma. Dey	26*s.* 8*d.*		5*s.*
	John Hirthe	£11		10*s.*
/Defaltes/	{Francis Pilche	18*s. mort.*		6*s.*
	{Thomas Woodes	40*s. egrot.*		13*s.* 4*d.*
	{Newton	£5 15*s.*		38*s.* 4*d.*

Total /23. [£]25   1[*s.*] 0[*d.*]/[155]

Memorandum. £12 10*s.* due to Monforth, Roiston, Sabbe, Browne, Myles & Bevys is undertaken by Francis Reade to be paid <before Whitsonday> «the Wednesday in Whitte weeke». And billes to be entred by Reade & upon sealing therof ther olde bondes or acquittes to be delivered.

The rest is to be paid then by Sheltram. And such as have bondes to take the benefitt of them if he faile. And <to> the other <he is to seale new billes> to take ther bargaynes if he faile.[156]

Unsigned. In Martin Man's hand.

Endorsed: Compositions made with the creditors of Walter Sheltram. December 1603.

1 p. NRO MS 2674, 3A4.

[152] Sheltram's petition had been referred to Nathaniel Bacon and Sir Henry Sidney on 12 November 1603, above, p.56.

[153] The "Reade" noted against Monforth and Royston's names is repeated in the right hand margin.

[154] The "18*s.* 4*d.*" has been added later.

[155] The figures are given in the left hand margin.

[156] The evidence suggests that of the 18 creditors listed above, 12 lived within a 3 mile radius of Walsingham; Bevis probably came from Holt; 5 have not been identified (Stiffkey Database).

Thomas and John Baker to Nathaniel Bacon

1603, December 18. Sir in regard of your forwardnes for the generall good of the cuntry I have thought mete to lett your worship understand of my procedinges. First I delyvered the peticion[157] to the Kinges Majestie whoe referred me for answeare & redresse therein to the Councell table and afterwardes the same peticion coming agayne to my handes I thought it very fytt to use the meanes of Sir George Howme[158] to preferre the cause & to forward the same, whom I found very redy & willing to accept thereof as a man much inclyning himselfe to do good to the cuntry, & he promissed to further the sute at the Councell board & that I should be called therunto. But after long stay I found the Councell dispersed uppon the remove of the court & not likely to sett in Councell untill a setled court.[159] I toke my leave of Sir George Howme and at my departure promissed to returne so sone as convenientlie I could to knowe his honours pleasure therein, which he liked well of and kept the peticion promising to deale therein in the meanetyme yf occassion served. I allso tooke a coppie of the order sett downe in the Councells book for transportacion[160] uppon the last letter sent from the justices to the Lords of the Councell[161] by <Mr> Sir Clement Spelman his man, wishing that letter had bene sent by some other whoe could have sayd something in the behallffe of the cuntry, the coppie wheareof I send your wourship herein-clossed, but by whose occassion the same great imposition is layd uppon corne & the purpose therof may easely be discerned. The imperfections which I fynd in that warrant is, first ther is no exception of shipping corne in strangers vessells for the mayntenance of the navy acording to the same statute of transportacion, then ther is libertie gyvne to the stranger to transport corne paying no more custome then his Majesties subjectes which is contrary to dyvers lawes & statutes of the realme, lastlie ther is no exception of particuller lisences formerly granted or hereafter to be granted, neyther is it declared by whom other dyrection shalbe gyvne & the same warrant revoked. I acquaynted Mr Atturney Generall [*Edward Coke*] with the same warrant whoe utterly disclaymeth that ever he consented therunto, and I was earnestlie moved by Mr Sucklyn[162] to goe & speake with my Lord Treasurer [*Lord*

---

[157] Presumably one of the petitions of November 1603, above, pp.52–5.

[158] The newly appointed Chancellor of the Exchequer, a Scotsman and favourite of James in both Scotland and then England. See the discussion, above, in the "Introduction", pp.lii–iii.

[159] By this time the severity of the plague in London, which had driven the court to spend the late summer and autumn of 1603 at Woodstock, Winchester and Wilton, had lessened but after a brief return to Whitehall in mid-December the King moved to Hampton Court and remained there until the end of January 1603/4 (G. B. Harrison, *A Jacobean Journal, 1603–1606*, 1941, pp.49–103).

[160] The Bakers' complaints make it clear that they are referring to the order of 16 October 1603, above, pp.47–8.

[161] The meaning here is unclear. Baker may mean that he physically wrote the order of 16 October on the same sheet of paper as the J.P.s' letter of 18 October 1603 (above, p.48–9), but there is no archival evidence to support this interpretation. Alternatively, he may be referring to an earlier letter to the Privy Council that has not come to light.

[162] John Suckling (1569–1627), son of Robert Suckling formerly mayor of Norwich, was at this time secretary to the Lord Treasurer. Knighted in 1616, he was appointed a Master of Requests in 1619 and secretary of state in 1622. His elder brother Edmund became Dean of Norwich Cathedral in 1614 (*ODNB*). John's splendid monument is in St. Andrew's church, Norwich. Its presence there indicates his continuing involvement with his home city and the county that it served. Here, as a courtier, he provides advice to a provincial supplicant.

Buckhurst], but I am to well acquaynted with those baytes <and so> «that I» refrayned. Sir you shall understand that Sir George Howme is the onely man in favour with his Majestie at this day and yf you please to drawe some peticion or letter to his honour signiffying therby that I have made knowen unto the justices aswell of the leaving of the peticion with him, as allso of his forwardnes to further your sute with some other groundes which your worship canne better sett downe then I canne certifie <I think> ther is no question but such a letter or peticion from the justices would compasse the sute & cause me the rather to prevayle which I will bestowe my traveyle to effect, & therffore yf you please to send me word by this bearer when the next meting wilbe of the justices I will resort thether, & will attend your pleasures.[163] For newes at the court ther is none, the King is removed from Willton to Hampton Court and ther is thought will continewe with the Quenes Majestie, and the Prince he kepeth at Oatlandes, <my> the Lord Cobham, Lord Grey and Sir Griffin Markam being sevrally brought to the skaffold at Wynchester on Fryday was a sevenight last & ther redy to be executed weare one after another stayed & caryed apart by the sheriffe & then by the Kinges warrant weare reprived, & the Monday following Sir Walter Rawleigh had warning to be in a redynes for his execution. What is become of him I cannot learne for I came from Wynchester ymediately after the frist [*sic*] three weare so reprived. Ther hath suffered Sir George Brooke, Watson & Clarke, what shalbe done with the rest I knowe not but of all others it is thought Sir Walter Rauleigh shall not escape.[164] Ther be very many embassadors at this present at the court & in London, the French & Spanishe embassadors, the Venetian & Florentyne embassadors, the Savoy embassador & the Poolishe embassador. My brother hath subscribed this letter with me to your wourship as thinking well & liking of the proceding for the ease of the cuntry and of the towne. I will God willing at my coming to your wourship bring a coppie of the peticion with me according to your request. And so we leave you to God. From Kinges Lynne this xviii of December 1603.

Your wourships assured to ther powers.

Signed: Thomas Baker, John Baker.[165] *In John Baker's hand.*

Addressed: To the worshippfull Nathaniel Bacon esquier at his house at Stukey.

---

[163] This letter probably prompted the letter to Sir George Home, immediately below.

[164] The principal conspirators in the Bye Plot and the Main Plot were tried at Winchester in mid-November. Henry Brooke, Lord Cobham, was the most highly connected of the accused: implicated by his younger brother, George, he in turn implicated Raleigh. George Brooke was executed along with William Watson and William Clarke, two Catholic secular priests who had previously advocated non-resistance. Cobham, Raleigh, and Thomas, Lord Grey of Wilton, were confined to the Tower following their reprieves. Sir Griffin Markham and two other conspirators were exiled. (See S. R. Gardiner, *History of England, 1603–1642*, 1887, i. pp.108–39). On attitudes to rebellion among English Catholics see Peter Holmes, *Resistance and Compromise: the Political Thought of Elizabethan Catholics* (Cambridge, 1982).

[165] Thomas Baker (d.1626) was a leading merchant of King's Lynn. He became notorious for his homosexual interests and underhand business transactions (see *BP*, iv, p.264). His brother John never became a freeman of Lynn and was probably based at Wells, while another brother, Walter, lived in London. This combination helped the Baker brothers in their efforts—as shown here—to orchestrate the local justices to protect the interests of the town of King's Lynn and its hinterland. The "I" of the letter is presumably John Baker, who was responsible for writing it.

Endorsed in Martin Man's hand: Mr Baker *de peticione, [?]scilicet peticio pro transportatione.*

Enclosure: Order of the Privy Council concerning the export of grain, 16 October 1603, above, pp.47–8.

2 pp. NRO RAY 248. Printed, *Stiffkey Papers*, pp.157–9.

Draft Petition from the J.P.s in Norfolk to Sir George Home, Chancellor of the Exchequer

[*1603, post December 18*].[166] Right honorable. We understand by this bearer of your honours furtherance in our suite at the Councell board for a generall lycense to transport corne according to our peticion lately sent unto the Kinges Majestie by this bearer, which peticion (he enformeth us) is left with your honour with very good acceptance therof in this countreys behalf. And foresmuch as we doe lykewyse understand that there is an order set downe in the Councell booke uppon the mocion of my Lord Treasurer for a generall libertie to transport corne in paying 3*s.* for the custome of every quarter of wheate & 14*d.* for the custome of every quarter of barley and mault over and above the rates sett downe by statute, we have presumed to sett downe our opinions therin which is that a generall libertie according to the statute would be more beneficiall to his Majestie in his customes by transportacion of the greater quantyties and that by meanes of soe great an ymposicion eyther the husbandman shall be dryvne to abate the same in the price of his corne which he selleth to the merchant, or els the merchant will seeke to defraud his Majestie of soe much of his custome as he is overchardged withall, for that in payeing the full due according to the same order the King in fower voyages shall reap the whole stock of the merchantes adventure, which chardge the marketts in Holland (wheare the most parte of the corne is adventured from these partes) will not beare as we are creadiblie geven to understand, and yf the merchant fayle in the former meanes then he shalbe dryvne agayne to seake for particuler lycenses, as heretofore hath been usuall. Wee have thought meete (by your honours good favour) to sett downe such matter of substance as we find to be omytted in the same order, which are these: *viz.* there is noe excepcion of transportacion of corne in strangers vessels, notwithstanding the same statut is especially made, and provyded for the mayntenance of the navie of this land, but an alien hath therby free lybertie to transport corne in paying no more custome then his Majesties subjectes doth which is contrary to dyverse lawes and statutes of this land, nether is there any excepcion or barring of transportacion of corne uppon particuler lycenses obteyned at a lower rate, nor any expresse order by whom the same order shalbe altered or revoked. This great ymposicion uppon corne will neither make plenty nor skersety therof, but yf yt standyeth with his Majesties good pleasure, transportacion therof may be offered aswell in payeing according to the statut as in posing soe great a chardge thereuppon, and the subjectes generally receyve a great contentment and satysfaccion when they shall enjoye the benifitt of the lawes and statutes of this realme.

[166] Dating: this document is the draft letter or petition which the Baker brothers suggested in their letter immediately above, some of whose arguments it reproduces almost verbatim.

Sett downe the prises of corne at this present[167] and that yf any occasion serve they wyll become sutors for a restraynt and soe beseeching the contynuance of your honours fartherance in this our sute for the good of the contrey, we humbly take our leves.

Undated. Unsigned. Draft.
Reprinted from *Stiffkey Papers*, pp.139–40.

Richard Spratt to Martin Man

1603, December 25. Frynde Marten I pray you by this berer send me the coppyes if they be made otherwise [*than in*] the assignment of the Lord North[168] for I am in much care to discharge Mr Bacon both of his debt & anger toward me. I am now in goinge thoroughe [?]with those leasses upon Tewsday next and do hope to send Mr Bacon some money upon Weddensday or Thursday next, and for the debt of Mr Woddes[169] he shall have the money before he doth deliver the grade indenture[170] which I hope shalbe presently. Thus prayinge your favor to helpe my necessyty wherby I may hould Mr Bacon his love toward me I betake you to Godes mercy. Barney this present Sonday 25 of December 1603. Your lovinge frynde.

[*Postscript*]: My wiffe is sick and in daunger of death. God be her comfort.

Signed: Rychard Spratt. *Holograph.*
Addressed: To my lovinge f[r]ynd Mr Marten Man at Stifky.
Endorsed in Martin Man's hand: Mr Spratt.
On same sheet as memorandum concerning Fakenham and Methwold rents, immediately below.
1 p. Folger L.d.558.

Memorandum concerning Fakenham and Methwold rents

[*Post 1603, December 25*].[171] *Calendar*: Fakenham rents: £53 5s. 11d. a year, of which £15 paid at Our Lady and £38 5s. 11d. at Michaelmas.

Methwold rents: £21 8s. 6d. paid at the feasts of the Annunciation and Michaelmas in equal parts.

Latin. Undated. Unsigned. In Martin Man's hand.
On same sheet as Richard Spratt's letter to Martin Man, immediately above.
½p. Folger L.d.558.

---

[167] At this point the Bakers are leaving the J.P.s to fill in the details.
[168] This refers to the terms and conditions on which various offices of the Duchy of Lancaster estates in Norfolk were granted or sold on by the previous holder. Bacon had originally become deputy steward in 1588 under Sir Roger North, Lord North; he became steward in 1599 (Somerville, *Duchy of Lancaster*, pp.595/6).
[169] See letter of Wood to Bacon of 22 November 1603, above, pp.56–7.
[170] "Grade indenture": precise meaning not known. Possibly connected with Spratt's sale of his Duchy offices (see 6 and 10 January 1603/4, below, pp.64–6).
[171] Dating: this memorandum post-dates the letter immediately above.

Nathaniel Bacon to Sir Henry Gawdy

1603, December 29. Brother Gawdy,[172] I understande by my wife who was lately at Plumsted & there spake with my sonne Gawdy that you expected an aunswer of a letter which should have ben sent lately to me from you. There came no such letter to my handes so as it semeth yf anie such were sent the same is either lost or kept back in the cariadge. And therefore I pray you bethinke your self by whome it was sent and so perhappes it may be founde out who hath don some ill office therwith.

Touching the eleccion of the knightes of the shire about which your sonne had speeche with my wife, I am in some sort tyed to leane to Sir Charles Cornwallis yf you relinquishe your suite for the place.[173] And ther it is like that wee shall fall asonder, for he was content when as I yealded to joyne with him yf you gave over your labour for the place to accept of the second voyce and now I am tolde by severall persons that he will stande with me for the first voyce. And therin I purpose neither to give him nor anie other the place unles it be given away from me by the contrey.[174] For my labour hath ben for the first <place> voyce and many who did promise me the first did denye me the second. And I am not like to serve often hereafter in anie Parliament and having served twice already in the second place, I hope that no man shall have just cause to judge amisse of me though now I seeke the first. Judge not so meanly of my self but that I am able to discharge the place aswell as some others and if some more creditt be gott by having the first then the second I see not, whie I should debarre my self of it yf I can obteyne it. I knowe that both care trouble & charge must be undergon by having the place which I am willing to take upon me that I may do some such service as I am able both to God, the Kyng, & the contry. I wryte playnly to you that you may knowe my hearte, and I desire that it may be secrett to your self. Thus with my commendations etc. Stifky. 29 December 1603. Your verie assured. [*Signed:*] Natha[*niel*] Bacon.

Copy in Martin Man's hand.
Endorsed: Copy letter to Sir Henry Gawdy. December 1603.
1 p. Folger L.d.102.

John Baker to Nathaniel Bacon

1603/4, January 1. Sir your letter is receyved and I must countermaunde one thinge which I spake unto your wourship concerning my Lord Cheiffe Justice [*Sir John Popham*] his being in Northamptonshire at the cristning of my Lord of Kynlosse his child,[175] ther is no such matter, but a dronken fellowe a Skottishman

---

[172] Sir Henry Gawdy of Claxton, whose son Robert had married Bacon's third daughter, Winifred, in 1597 (Key, 'Dorothy Bacon', pp.101–2).

[173] This election campaign had started early since Parliament was not summoned until 31 January 1603/4. For an account of the campaign see Smith, *County and Court*, pp.329–30. Clearly, expectation of it had been aroused by the accession of the new monarch.

[174] "Country" is being used here in the sense of the county electorate. It appears again later in the letter referring to the county as a social and administrative unit.

[175] Edward Bruce, Baron Kinloss (1548/9–1611), accompanied James I to England in 1603, was appointed privy councillor, and was made Master of the Rolls on 18 May (*ODNB*).

came first to Mr Justice Gawdy,[176] & so hether to this towne whoe gave out the report & made himselfe to be one of my Lordes pages, and nowe being gone from hence we heare contrary newes and would fayne fynd out the author to have him punished yf he might be layd hould of. Heare is other news of my Lord Cheiff Justice but I love not to meddle or wright of more then I knowe to be certyne. Good sir I pray you be a meanes to procure eyther Mr [*Henry*] Spelman or Mr [*Richard*] Stubbe to goe with me with the letter[177] to London for I knowe they ar men very sufficient to forward that busynes & I have written a letter to Sir Charles Cornwallis[178] which I would desyre your <good> wourship to send with the noates & coppies I lefte with you, for I have intreated his wourships furtherance therein. And so resting yours undoubtedly to my severall power, I leave you to God. Lynne the first of *Januarii* 1603. Your wourships in what he may.[179]

Signed: John Baker. *Holograph*.
Addressed: To the worshippful Nathaniell Bacon esquier at his house in Stifky.
Endorsed in Martin Man's hand: Mr Baker 1 January.
½ p. Folger L.d.151.

Richard Spratt to Nathaniel Bacon

1603/4, January 6. Right worshiful [?]withyn two day past Mr Bullen of Bathelye[180] hath bene with me for my part of Fakenham & Methould to bi them for his master the Attorney Generall [*Sir Edward Coke*]. And doth offer me a good prisse. Synce that tyme John Alleyn[181] hath bene with me and doth desier «to by» them both. Whether Allyans request be for his master I knowe nott but he sayeth it is for hym selfe. I signifyed to them I hadd talked with your worship and what so ever your pleasure for them «wilbe» that will I do. Allen offereth for both £160 which money he shall pay over to you in so much as shalbe agreed of. His meanyng is not to meddell with them if your worship myndeth otherwise for which cause he this day or to moroughe purposeth to attend upon you. I have gyven Bullen my word whether he <will> shall have eny further talke with me abought this busynes or not upon Monday next therfore I do intreate your worship what you purpose heryn. I make no doubt to have £80 for Methould for ther is ther serten gayne. I have sent to Mr Sutterton[182] for the writinges and thus praying your worship to make of them as much as you cann I do desier your favorable aunswere and do praye to God for your worships increase of prosperyte. I humbly take my leave this <9 of> vi of January 1603. Your worships at commandment.

---

[176] Francis Gawdy (d.1605), chief justice of the Common Pleas, of Wallington, Norfolk.

[177] Possibly the letter from the J.P.s to Sir George Home of *post* 18 December 1603 (above, pp.61–2).

[178] For the significance of Cornwallis in the context of the county's connections at Court see below, p.65n.

[179] For Nathaniel Bacon's response, see letter to Cornwallis of 8 January 1603/4 (below, pp.65–6).

[180] "Bathelye": namely, Bale. Probably Robert Bullen, later in dispute with Robert Laseby (see below, 5 November 1606 and 2 November 1607, pp.263, 300).

[181] Probably John Allen of Fakenham (*BP*, iv, p.30).

[182] Possibly Nowell Sotherton, clerk of estreats in the Exchequer, who succeeded his father John as Baron there in 1606 (*CSPD 1598–1601*, p.458; B. Cozens-Hardy, 'Norfolk lawyers', *NA* xxxiii, 1965, p.281).

Signed: Rychard Spratt. *Holograph.*
Addressed: To the right worshipful Nathanael Bacon esquier at Stifkey.
Endorsed in Martin Mans hand: [*? words missing*; Spra]tt 6 January 1603.
1 p. Folger L.d.559.

Nathaniel Bacon to Richard Spratt

1603/4, January 7. Mr Spratt. Though by a former letter of yours you sett the price of both your leases at £130, which I did accept of, & did agree to see the same go towardes the payment of thos dettes which you owe unto me, & the overplus towardes thos dettes paying for which I am bounde, yet I am loath to hinder you, so as I may do it with my honest creditt. Touching the parte of Fakenham, which you had put over to me, I have given my worde for the same to Mr [*Rhys*] Gwyn at the price of £70, at which rate he might have had it before this tyme at your handes. But for the lease of Methould, which you have put over to me, I was purposed to have given & allowed you upon the reck[*oning*] the price of £60, & have kept it in myne owne handes, and yet seing you are offered more, I will not hinder you, so as whatsoever is taken for the same be satisfyed unto me towardes the discharge of myne owne dett, & then towardes the discharge of such other dettes as I am bounde for you. This must then be don out of hande, that I may not rest upon thes uncerteynties. For otherwise I will seke by the sale therof, or by myne owne enjoyeng therof, to make the best profitt. 7 January 1603.[183]

At the foot: Copy letter to Mr R. Spratt.
Unsigned. Copy in Martin Mans hand.
Endorsed: Copy letter *al* Mr Spratt.
½ p. NRO NNAS S2/17/12.

Nathaniel Bacon to Sir Charles Cornwallis

1603/4, January 8. Sir I give you manie thanckes for your kynde offer in inviting me to lodge at your house in Norwich,[184] but I must pray you to holde me excusd, for I understande that the state of the sicknes within the city is so dangerous as it appereth by the increase therof, as my purpose is not to come at the Sessions unles some occasion of greater importance then hitherto I take knowledge of should be offered. Thus etc. 8 January 1603. [*Signed:*] N. Bacon.

[183] See assignment of 10 January 1603/4, and Rhys Gwynn to Bacon, 27 February 1603/4, below, pp.66, 76.
[184] Sir Thomas Cornwallis of Suffolk, a man of recusant leanings and father of the Sir Charles Cornwallis addressed in this letter, purchased the former college of priests, called the Chapel in the Fields (now the Assembly House) in Norwich in 1571. After extensive renovation, he resided there for long periods during the struggle between his friend Bishop Freake and the Norfolk puritans—one of the foremost of the latter being Nathaniel Bacon (Smith, *County and Court*, p.215). For the Cornwallises in Suffolk see MacCulloch, *Suffolk*, *infra*. At this time Charles Cornwallis was already set on a career at Court under the sponsorship of Robert Cecil. In 1604 he was appointed ambassador to Spain and later became Treasurer of the Household to Prince Henry (*ODNB*). Quite evidently his Court connections were well known in the county and we have seen them being invoked in the letter from Baker to Bacon of 1 January 1603/4, above, p.64. Later, he can be shown to have had connections with George Hume, Earl of Dunbar (BL Add. MS 39853, f.148v).

Postscript. I sende you a letter left with me by Mr Baker of Lynne.[185] I thinke it fitt that a letter be written by us the justices of peace or some of us to Sir G. Hume for his favor in furtherance of the peticion, and no maner of hurte can come of it. I would wishe that a letter were written to Mr R. Stubbes or to Mr Henry Spelman to followe the cause with Baker in the contryes behalf[186] and that 20 markes or £20 were allowd by the contrey to one of them towardes his charges. And there is mony in some of our handes to defray the same.

At the foot: Copy letter to Sir Charles Cornwalleys. *In Martin Man's hand.*
Endorsed: Copy letter to Sir Charles Cornwaleys. 8 January 1603.
Enclosure: Letter from Baker of 1 January 1603/4, above, pp.63–4.
½ p. Folger L.d.103.

Assignment of Duchy of Lancaster offices in the manor of Methwold

1603/4, January 10. *Calendar.* Richard Spratt of Barney, gent, grants to Nathanael Bacon of Stiffkey, esq, in consideration of £40, the offices of feodary, coroner, escheator, and clerk of the market of the Duchy of Lancaster within the King's manor of Methwold and the parishes of Methwold and Hilgay, and receipt of goods forfeit and execution of writs within the same manor and parishes, which he had of Richard Bunting of South Creake, gent, deceased, by indenture of 20 January 1597, for remainder of the term of years specified under Bunting's assignment.[187]

Signed and sealed: Per me Ricardum Spratt. Witness: Rice Gwynne.
In Martin Man's hand.
Endorsed: Assignment *del* roialties in Methould.
1 p. NRO MC 1872/16, 866X2. Calendared, *Supplementary Stiffkey Papers*, p.38.

Richard Spratt to Nathaniel Bacon

1603/4, January 11. Right worshipful I have sent this berer to Mr Payne[188] who aunswereth that he is so plyed with busynes as he cannot be at eny leysure before Monday come senyt[189] and then he will be at Fakenham if so it shall please you. I do send to hym to moroughe, he desier to have your worships letter to knowe your pleasure hereyn and I shall deliver hym the same to moroughe, he is at Catton. Mr Reave is steward of Methould, it were good for you to kepe present courtes in them both. Sir Henry Sidney was very willing to make the acquitaunces[190] and sayeth he «hath» done so to many. He goeth to London presently and if eny question be made (as he sayeth ther cannot) he will aunswere it hym selfe. And so prayinge to

---

[185] See letter from Baker of 1 January 1603/4 (above, pp.63–4).
[186] Here Bacon appears to be following the tactics proposed by Baker in his letter to Bacon of 1 January 1603/4.
[187] See above, letter of 7 January 1603/4, above, p.65.
[188] "Mr Payne": probably the "Mr Payne" mentioned by Edward Paston as steward of his courts. See Paston to Nathaniel Bacon, 23 March 1602/3, above, p.15; see also p.238n.
[189] "Senyt": seven-night, a week.
[190] In his capacity as Duchy of Lancaster Receiver for Norfolk, Suffolk and Cambridgeshire.

God for your worships prosperyty I humbly take my leave. 11 of January 1603. Your worships at commandment.

Signed: Rychard Spratt. *Holograph.*
Addressed: To the right worshipful Nathanael Bacon esquier at Stifkey.
Endorsed in Martin Man's hand: Mr Spratt. 11 January 1603.
1 p. NRO SOTH 28/12/67.

Sir Charles Cornwallis to Sir Christopher Heydon

1603/4, January 13. Sir, I pray gyve me leave to contynew my clayme to your promysed assystance at the electyon of the knyghtes for the shyre[191] for which places Mr Bacon & I have now fully agreed to joyne & therfore in hys behalf as well as myn own I requyre your best furtherance.

Your kynde care of us bothe herin I wyll for my part ever indevor to deserve in any offyce of frendshypp that I can. And so with my most harty commendatyon to your self & your lady I wyshe unto you all the good fortunes you wold & end hastely. Thys 13 of January 1603. Your very assured lovyng kynsman & frend.

Signed: Charles Cornwaleys. *Holograph.*
Addressed: To my very lovinge cosen and freind Sir Christofer Haydon.
Endorsed in Martin Man's hand: Sir Charles Cornwalleys to Sir Christopher Heydon *de electione.*
½ p. Folger L.d.241.

Nathaniel Bacon to Sir Charles Cornwallis

1603/4, January 17. Sir I have ben made acquaynted by Mr Christopher Reve with a letter lately written by you, touching the eleccion,[192] which is shortly expected for knightes to the Parliament, and I am willing, as heretofore I have sig-nifyed unto you, to have you joyned with me in the service, so as you will be content not to strive with me for the precedency of the place. And this is agreeing to that, which was intended betwen us, when you did in the beginning of the sommer write unto me therabout, and though you have synce obteyned a better place, then you had,[193] yet I hope, that neither you nor anie other shall have just cause herin to thinke amisse of me, seing I have served twice in the other place before, and am doubtfull whether ever I shall serve agayne to have the first place, if I have it not now. Besides I have tyed my self to sondrie gent[*lemen*] by my

---

[191] For earlier correspondence related to this topic see above, letter of 29 December 1603, p.63.

[192] Reve was Duchy of Lancaster bailiff in the hundreds of Gallow and Brothercross (BP, iv, p.229) and by virtue of his Duchy offices a factotum of Bacon. He was also the type of man that parliamentary candidates needed to win over to their side. Possibly also related to this issue is the letter from Cornwallis to Heydon, the original of which found its way into the Bacon archive (immediately above). The delicate edging for position over first and second place in the prospective election is evident here. This arose because English shire consitutencies returned two members. For the resolution of the issue of who should be the first and second candidates see below, 25 January 1603/4, p.68.

[193] The "better place" probably relates to the relative ranking of Bacon and Cornwallis in the Commission of the Peace. Cornwallis was placed in a higher position because he had been knighted in July 1603.

worde, to stand for the first place, and if some litle creditt be gott thereby, where should I debarre my self herof, when as I am put in comfort by most of my fryndes, that I shall not fayle of the place? I was resolved to have stoode therin, even with my brother Gawdy, yf he had not given over.[194] Therefore I pray you let me herin be excused, and as I write now unto you, and signifye under my hande, that I desire in this sort to joyne with you, so I wishe that you will signifie back agayne to me under your hande, that you will in this sort joyne with me, and then I will labour the eleccion so much as in me lieth accordingly. Thus I hartely commende both you & my Lady to the favour of almighty God. From Stifky this 17 of January 1603.

Unsigned. Copy in Martin Man's hand.
Endorsed: Copy of a letter to Sir Charles Cornwalleys *per* Reve.
1 p. Folger L.d.105.

Information concerning felling of timber at Morston

1603/4, January 24. John Kempe[195] informeth that within thes 6 weekes ther hath «ben» felled in Morston park 10 trees of oke & ashe.

That on Christmas even John Dallyday «of Morston» was taken there felling of a tree «an oke» by John Kempe the yonger & Jo. Loades.

That there was a stulpe of a faldgate[196] belonging to Mr Furnes[197] founde in a busshe there yesternight.

Unsigned. In Martin Man's hand.
Endorsed: John Kempes information 24 January 1603.
½ p. NRO BL/BC/6/2.

Nathaniel Bacon to Sir Charles Cornwallis

1603/4, January 25. Sir I have this daie received your letter of the xxiii of this present, in aunswere of a letter of myne, which I sent by Christofer Reve, and accordinge to my former letters so now againe I certifie you that I will wholy apply my selfe for the futherance of your eleccion to the second place of the knightes of the shere, seing my brother Gawdie hath geven over his labour, and I assure my selfe that you will performe the like for laboringe my eleccion to the firste place.[198] I can aime at no nomber of voices, but I am put in comforte by gent[*lemen*], and others, out of manie partes of the countie, that I shall have their helpe, so as I am in comforte to prevaile, and though I be stodde against and doe loose the place yet

---

[194] See Bacon to Sir Henry Gawdy, 29 December 1603, above, p.63.

[195] "John Kempe": not the parish constable, but a labourer from Langham, who made a living from cutting and bundling furze and working as a day labourer looking after Morston Park and Langham pond, both secluded outlying areas of Bacon's garden/pleasure grounds. (Stiffkey Database). Either this John Kempe or John Kempe the younger continued to carry out similar work after Bacon's death (NRO RAY 442, 446, 459).

[196] "A stulpe of a faldgate": the post of a fall-gate, a type of gate or fence often used for a sheepfold. This suggests vandalism, possibly night-walking.

[197] Ralph Furness, rector of Morston.

[198] For Bacon's earlier letter in this sequence concerning the election see above, 17 January 1603/4, pp.67–8.

be you assured, that I will doe my best indeavour, to have you obteyne that which you stand for. God graunt that the sicknes maie be better staied at Norwich or if it should not, I would thinke that the sheriffe should doe best to have it at Dearham, wher I was once chosen before when as the sicknes in Norwich was lesse then (I thinke) now it is. I judge that Mondaie come thre weekes wilbe the daie because I knowe it written downe by a courtier, that the Parliament should beginn the xi of March, and upon the xxiiii the solempnitie of the coronation holdeth in London. Thus with my wives commendacions remembred to my Lady and your selfe, I commit you to the kepinge of Allmightie God. From Stifkey this xxv of Januarie 1603.

[*Postscript*]: I have tould the undersheriffe and have allso caused it to be spoken to the high sheriffe that if the sicknes holde at Norwich then Dearham is moste indifferent for the ease of the people, and moste free from infeccion for I heare of none touched there but only in an owtshifte of the towne, some halfe mile from the towne. Yours very assured.

Unsigned. Copy in William Sanders' hand.
Endorsed: Copy of a letter to Sir Charles *pro electione militum* [*for the election of the knights*]. 25 January 1603.
1 p. Folger L.d.107.

Valuation of lands in Alethorpe

1603/4, **January 27.** A valuacion of the landes in Althorp[199] set downe before Nathanael Bacon esquire 27 January 1603.

William Day for 100 acres at	£24
Roger Grene for 25 acres at	£4
Henry Greve for a tenement & 25 acres	£5
George Blackborne for a tenement & <25> «9» acres	50*s.*
William Ellys for a tenement & 2 acres	20*s.*
Edmund Ellys for 3 acres	10*s.*
Summa totalis of the value of landes in Althorp	£37 00*s.*

At the foot: Vera copia ex[*aminata*] *per* Martyn Man.
Unsigned. In Martin Man's hand.
Endorsed: A valuacion of the landes in Althorpe.
½ p. NRO MC 1872/19, 866X2. Printed, *Supplementary Stiffkey Papers*, p.19.

Evidence in a case of paternity

1603/4, **January 28.** A remembraunce of the proceedinges before Nathaniel Bacon, Strange Mordant, Henry Spelman esquires justices of peace at Burnham 28 January 1603 concerning Marye the bastard childe of Alice Welland.

The substaunce of the evidence in the cause.

Contra Thomas Chapman.

[199] About 2 miles north-east of Fakenham.

The midwife affirmed her constant accusacions in her travell [*labour*], & others present.

The childe gotten a forthnight before Our Lady 1603 & borne a forthnight after Christmas last. Gotten in Growtes house.

Welland affirmed shee came from the house on Shrove Sonday.[200]

Pro Chapman.

<2 women & R. Warren *jurati* testifye> «Agnes Rust & [*forename deleted*] Last of Walsingham test[*ified*]» that Alice Welland laye with <a yonge man> «a brewer of Welles» in the beginning of Lent, & confessd it to Agnes Rust the next morning & lodged <her> a mayde her bedfellow within the said Rustes chamber.

R. Warren test[*ified*] that the mayde «one Awdry Gogney» which <had> used to lye with Alice Welland confessd to him that <the> «one Jo. Gunder a» brewer lay with Alice on the night aforsaid.

Agnes Rust affirmed «to» Gunder to his face that he was in the chamber with the woman at 6 «or 7» a clock at night in one Hilles house wher supped Gunder Alice Welland Widow Rust & Audry Gogney.

Katheryne Lewys of Walsingham affir[*med*] upon report of the mayde & Alice Welland that Gunder lay with Alice.

Contra Chapman.

Ro. Hutchinson infor[*med*] that Alice Welland kept in his house from midsummer till Our Lady & wroght out a dores.

Rememb[*ered*] the brewers [?]coming but denyeth to know of lodging.

Alice Welland denieth shee went to bedd that night. Confesseth that he supped with her & the rest but went away an hour after supper. Confess[*eth*] he had too much drynke, & lay downe after the company was gon.

Pro Chapman.

Jo. Ponde «*juratus.*» That Alice Welland asked Henry Halman whether his man the brewer were a batchelor or maryed. And he aunswering he was maryed shee blushed.

She confesseth shee asked the question, on the Fryday after ther meeting at supper *ut ante.*

Henry Halman: *juratus.* About Hall[*owm*]as Alice Welland asked if Gunder was maryed or not, & he affir[*med*] him «to be» maryed, shee said he was a [?]brealer.

The said Alice charged of infamous «living & of» leudnes with a servant of «Mr [?]Dereham at» E. Growtes <& one Alliardes> 16 yeares since. Sate up all night with him.

Alice Parton *jurata* hearde it by a servant then dwelling in the house the next day & being charged for it did not deny it but A[*lice*] sayd that shee would go to London to <the> him if shee fell with childe.[201]

[200] The Sunday before Shrove Tuesday.

[201] It is noted *c.* 29 July 1603 that a constable had arrested Chapman, singleman of North Creake, for fathering a bastard with Alice, but had allowed him to escape. Alice had hired a house at Wells at Our Lady last but was refused entry after her landlord's death at Midsummer and was owed £3 by the widow. On 26–27 September Alice was granted a warrant for the peace against Chapman and Mary Growte, and Chapman was bound over to appear at the next sessions for Brothercross Hundred (Bacon memoranda book 1602–7,

Unsigned. In Martin Man's hand.
Endorsed: Proceedings upon the cause *inter* Chapman & Wellond.
1 p. Folger L.d.732.

Thomas Oxborough to Nathaniel Bacon

1603/4, January 31. Good Mr Bacon I commend my selfe to you and unto good Mistres Bacon, geving you both very harty thankes for your kynd intertaynement.[202] Sir concernyng a parte of the speche that you had with me in your garden att my being with you that is concernynge the directing of you to a purchase wher you myght bestowe your mony profytably «and wher you myght mak a seate».[203] I have bethought my selfe of a thing which I thinke will well befytt you. The value will come to about £4000 and yt is three mens estates. I thinke I canne within a yeare compasse them all for «you» yf you shall lyke of them. They be in the towne of Norwould [*Northwold*][204] in Norfolk neare Sir Edmond Mountfordes and the fyrst of the three persons is one Roger Hobart «a gent[*leman*]» who hath bene often tymes in hand with me to by his landes ther «& of late hath geven me tyme to be advised for two monthes». His is a maner & hath sundry copyholdes & he hath lately bestowed in bylding as he hath tould me £300 & more. He maketh of yt by letting about £100 by the yeare. He doth aske £2000 but it will come for lesse. The second is the land of one Pearse who is not yett out of his wardshipp but as I take yt more then 20 years old and I know him to be incombred by one Boulton, who is dead, with a statute[205] which I canne buy. I knowe he wilbe inforced and willing to sell. And the third parte is a maner of the Kynges in the fearme of one Mr Croftes. Yt was parcell of the Bisshopp of Elye his possessions and hath bene in lease many years and ther is about 18 years to come. I could buy the lease and ther is good to be done in that the rent to the Kyng is about £8 by yeare of the [?]demeans and £5 of the royaltyes. That is a good thing as yt is valued. Yf you shall lyke to proceed herein then wright your letter to Lynne after the tearme and then I will proceed accordingly but yf thys «devise» come to be publickly knowne I doubt that the thinges will growe the dearer. I reffer yt to your wisdome & take my leave this last of January 1603 Lincolns Inn. Your to his powar.

On the dorse: The Parliament is appointed the xix of March[206] and the shewes in

NRO BL/BC/5/22, pp.36–7). There were further repercussions in 1606: on 29 May Alice Wellon secured another warrant for the peace against Chapman and Christofer Growte, and the latter was summoned to appear at the sessions for Gallow (*ibid.*, pp.76–7).

[202] At this time Thomas Oxborough was Recorder of King's Lynn and a J.P. (*BP*, iv, p.14n).

[203] This is the first indication that Bacon was contemplating building a new house, in part in response to pressure from his wife. He finally settled on a property at Irmingland near Aylsham (see Indenture of 20 April 1605, below, p.172).

[204] Located roughly equidistant between Thetford and Lynn. A move here would have substantially shifted Bacon's neighbourhood basis of power in the county.

[205] "Statute": a bond entered into under Statutes Merchant or Staple.

[206] This was hot news: the date of summons was 31 January, the date of this letter. However, as can be seen from the discussion of prospective M.P.s for Norfolk in the correspondence over the preceding months, the new Parliament had been long in expectation. It had been postponed because of the prevalence of the plague, especially in London. A proclamation of 11 January 1604 had referred to the expectation of the imminent abatement of the plague in London and announced the King's resolve to hold a Parliament "as

London be appointed upon the xv of the same monnthe.[207] Ther is a newe commission for selling some of the Kynges landes and for manumitting of copyholdes holden of his manors and for making of leases & for other purposes.[208] Yf you lyke <or lyke not> to deale in this purchase <be [?]most secrett, and> make no shewe to desyre yt, I will cause yt to be putt upon you. And yf you lyke it not kepe yt very secrett. And yf yt please you «then» wrighte your mynd therin. Ther is no man that will desyre to buy any of these thinges except he be such ane one as may & shalbe procured to buy all and <ther> «that being understood» I am persuaded that the thinges wilbe much desired. *Postscriptum per Tho*[*mam*] *Oxburgh.*

Signed: Thom[*a*]s Oxburgh. *Holograph.*

Addressed: To the righte worshipfull my very good frend Nathaniell Bacon esquire be these delivered att his house at Stukeye.

Endorsed in Martin Man's hand: Mr Oxburgh touching a purchase.

1½ pp. Folger L.d.451.

Examination in a case of paternity

1603/4, February 13. The examinacion of Prudence Wise taken before Nathanael Bacon esquire the 13 of February 1603.

Shee saith that shee is with childe, and that one Thomas Flawe is the father therof.

Shee saith that he laie first with her sone after he came out of Iselan[d] [*Iceland*] being a sevenight afore Lammas last, and the next tyme he lay with her was a sevenight afore Michaelmas last «(at which tyme his wife lay in childbedd)», and that he never had the use of her bodye at anie other tyme before or after, except at one tyme about a twelvemoneth since.

Shee saith that the 2 last tymes he lay with her at a place called Moises Busshes in the fieldes, & in the evening at both tymes.

Signed: Na[*thaniel*] Bacon. *In Martin Man's hand.*

Endorsed: [?Examination] of Prudence Wise for a bastard.

½ p. *slightly damaged on l.h.s.* NRO MC 1370/5, 810X1.

Thomas Sackville, Baron Buckhurst, Lord Treasurer, to Nathaniel Bacon

1603/4, February 15. After my hartie commendacions.[209] Whereas by vertue of your office of the stewardship of the mannours of West Walton Walsoken &

---

soone as we shall finde, that the same may be done without the perill aforesaid" (Larkin & Hughes, *Stuart Proclamations*, pp.66–70, quotation at p.67).

[207] This refers to the civic entry into London put on for James by the City. The allusion to both the Parliament and the entry—in one breath as it were—supports the recent contention that in the eyes of contemporaries they were perceived to be integrated events (see David M. Bergeron, 'King James's Civic Pageant and Parliamentary Speech in March 1604', *Albion: A Quarterly Journal Concerned with British Studies*, 34, 2002, pp.213–231; see also Stephen Harrison, *The Arches of Triumph*, London, 1604).

[208] See further the Lord Treasurer to Bacon, 15 February 1603/4, below, this page.

[209] This letter and the two following it need to be read in the context of the Court gossip passed on to Bacon by Thomas Oxborough in his letter of 31 January 1603/4, this page.

Emeth & Tylney in the countye of Norfolk you have heretofore from tyme to tyme graunted estates of the copiehold or customarye landes and tenementes within the said mannors as they continuallie have happened or fallen, forasmuch as the Kinges Majesties pleasure is otherwise to dispose of the same landes and tenementes, these are therefore in his Majesties name to will & require you from henceforth to forbeare to graunte any estate or admit any tenaunte to any the copiehold or customarye landes or tenementes of the said mannours whereof the fyne is arbitrable, until his Majesties pleasure be by me further signifyed unto you, and that you further send me a true certificate of the totall summe of the yerelie rentes of all the copiehold landes of the said mannours, and whether the tenauntes there have estates of inheritaunce or for terme of lief or lives or at will, and what fyne heriot or other proffit is due to the King upon everye alteracion discent or graunte, and a true estimate what an acre of meadowe an acre of pasture and an acre of arable land there is worth «by yere» upon improvement by common reputacion. And what store of woodes underwoodes and tymber trees are upon the same copiehold premisses, and whether there be any myne or mynes of mettall cole or other thinges on them or any of them or any other matter of proffit whatsoever appertyning to the Kinges Majestye. And withall to certifie unto me the name or names of all and everye the justices of peace dwelling within or nere the said mannours. Of all which I doubt not you will have especiall regard as you tender his Majestie service. And so do wish you hartily well. At the court this xv of February 1603. Your loving freind. [*Signed:*] T. Buchurst.

Copy.

Addressed: To my lovinge frend Nathaniell Bacon *generosus* steward of the Kinges Majesties mannors of Westwalton Walsoken Emeth & Tylney.

Endorsed in Martin Man's hand: Concerning Walton etc.

1 p. BL Add. 41140 ff.52–3. Calendared, *HMC Townshend*, pp.12–13.

Thomas Sackville, Baron Buckhurst, Lord Treasurer, to Nathaniel Bacon

1603/4, February 15. Letter as immediately above, with minor alterations, relating to the manors of Terrington and Walpole.[210]

Copy.

Endorsed in Martin Man's hand: Letters concerning Terrington.

1 p. NRO NNAS S/2/17/13.

Thomas Sackville, Baron Buckhurst, Lord Treasurer, to Matthew Clarke

1603/4, February 15. Letter as immediately above, with minor alterations, addressed to Clarke as steward of the manor of East Dereham.

Copy.

Endorsed in Martin Man's hand: My Lord Treasurers letter concerning the manor of Est Dereham.

1 p. NRO NNAS S2/17/14.

---

[210] Bacon replied for both Terrington and East Dereham on 10 March 1603/4, below, p.79–80.

Edward Coke, Attorney General, to Nathaniel Bacon

1603/4, February 16. After my verie hartie comendacions. I have receaved knowledge, that there are verie manie suites betwixt this bearer my servant[211] & one Plandon his wifes brother.[212] And that there are commissions awarded to you & others directed to examyne witnessis & to ende & determyne the same sutes. And forsomuch as I hartelie wish a peace betwen them, least thone should consume thestate of the other, & in the ende feele the sharpenes of their owne faultes to their great hinderaunces. Therefore I hartely praie you in the behalf of both their goodes to take the more paynes at my request to reconcile all questions betwixt them, so shall you do a worke of much pyetie betwixt them, & give me occasion to be hartelie thanckfull to you for your travell therin to be taken. And even so I comytt you to Almightie God. In hast this 16 of February 1603. Your verie loving frynde. [*Signed:*] Edward Coke.[213]

At the foot: Vera copia.
Copy in Martin Man's hand.
Endorsed: A copy of Mr Attorneys letter to Nathaniel Bacon esqr.
½ p. NRO MS 21508/5, 368X5.

Robert Plandon to Nathaniel Bacon

1603/4, February 23. Right worshipfull I am bounden and yt is my dutie first to give you verie humble & hartie thankes emongest many other your kyndnesses, for the last paynes you toke to heare with purpose to ende the controversie betwein my adverse stepp brother Alexaunder and me.[214] In which no doubt you hadd prevayled if hee hadd condiscended to answeare the truth as you appoynted to my objections, as I was and ame willynge to dooe to his. Next I most humblie beseech you (allthough my adversarie importune you not heerin) once agayne to take some further paynes in that busynes for in trothe at the tyme of nomynatynge commissioners, my adversarie with more than ordynarie termes, importuned me to name your worshipp for my self but his overmuch pressinge me therewith (protestynge that if I refused you he woulde have you) made me, betweyn feare that your oportunitie woulde not serve to that purpose & desire to have so just a comissioner chosen agaynest me, suffer him to have you nomynated on his parte. [?]But twoe dayes passed not before he bewrayed his polleysie therein which was to have berefte me of a comissioner for hee delivered that he knewe that your determynacion was with your famylie to come to London so shorteley as there was little hoope of the frute of <the frute> your presentes at the speedynge our comission, and theiruppon required that Mr Strandge Mordant might be added to supplie in your absence to the which I condiscended. But Sir if your oportunitie will afforde you any tyme to

---

[211] The attorney, Jerome Alexander.

[212] For possible previous and subsequent documents concerning the dispute between Robert Plandon and Jerome Alexander see 24 March 1602/3 on and 28 April 1603, above, pp.18–21, 34, and Plandon to Bacon, immediately below.

[213] An example of recourse to mediation as a process of peacekeeping, especially within families or between social equals. Sadly, on this occasion it appears to have failed.

[214] See the letter immediately above, and 27 February 1603/4, below, p.77.

spende heerin at my humble intreatie you shall fynde me as willynge to be censured by your good self as by any other meanes whatsoever not doubtynge but you will eyther bee informed trewlie in the state of the cause by confession or by profe. For my parte I will deliver the bare treuth of everie matter, accydent, & circumstaunce, that concerneth the cause, that shalbe demaunded of mee, that you seeinge the same may proceede accordynglie. If my adversarie will dooe the like their is no question but an honest ende maye speedielie bee hadd in the cause. If hee will not deale treulie, and playnelie, but doubtfully, & subtellye, I cannott hoope that a good ende cann bee hadd in the matter without examinacion of wittnesses. I have therfore put downe unto you in wrytynge the trew state of the cause as yt standeth betweyn us. I beesech you lett my brother Alexaunder have a coppie therof and lett him putt downe in wrytynge wheirin I have erred and I will answeare theirunto and lett us bee at a perfecte hedd before we trouble you to travayle in the busines. So shall your paynes bee to good purpose and wee both, but espetially my self, be allwayes bounden to praye for your worshipp of whom I humblie take my leave. Gateley this 23 of Februarie 1603. Att your service and commandement.

Signed: Robert Plandon.
Addressed: To the right worshipfull Nathanyell Bacon esquire at Stukye.
Endorsed in Martin Man's hand: Mr Plandon letter.
1 p. Folger L.d.472.

Thomas Farmer to Nathaniel Bacon

[*? 1603/4*], **February 25.**[215] Sir to deale triwlye with you, I did not bynde my selfe to the peace att London, neyther am I willinge to be bowende, consideringe the base abuse Mr Russell[216] offered me to whom I gave no cawse to accompte me base, whose father hathe bin glade to take manye a dinner att Barsham amongst Sir William Fermors sarving menne, wher he fowend many his betters boathe in lyvinge and gentrye, beinge a poore bliwecoated fellowe[217] him selfe not many yeers since Sir Phillippe Parkers[218] manne. And yet nowe having gotten a lyttell pelfe muste be an esquier. Sir he shall make me suche a satisfaccion as the lawe of armes dothe requier

[215] Dating: the references to Sir Philip Wodehouse, who was knighted in 1596 (Shaw, *Knights*, ii, p.92), and to Nathaniel Bacon as esquire (i.e. before July 1604), set the limits for this letter. On 2 March 1603/4 Farmer wrote to Bacon again about his quarrel with Mr Russell (below, pp.77–8), mentioning Bacon's absence at Parliament, which suggests that the year in question is 1603/4.

[216] It seems likely that the Russell in question was Thomas Farmer's neighbour Philip Russell of North Barsham (c.1551–1617). His father, disdainfully referred to here, was Edward Russell of Burnham Thorpe (*Visit. of Norf. 1563*, i, pp.399–400). Possibly in connection with this quarrel Philip Russell esq had been bound in £40 to appear at the next sessions for North Greenhoe on 8 January 1603/4 (Bacon memoranda book 1602–7, NRO BL/BC/5/22, p.44).

[217] An allusion to the dress of servants and generally of the lower orders. It is likely that this reference is meant to be especially disparaging as it implies that Russell's father had not even merited a livery, a step up from the ubiquitous blue coat. The term was also used dismissively of urban dwellers when compared with the rural elite. There is a certain irony in its use by Farmer here, given his own grandfather's origins as London merchant. The entire letter is richly informative of attitudes towards status.

[218] Philip Parker was a prominent J.P. and Deputy Lieutenant in Suffolk (McCulloch, *Suffolk, passim*). He may also have held lands in Norfolk where he appears as a J.P. for one year in 1585 (Smith, *County & Court*, p.354).

by the judgment of Sir Arthur Heveningham, Sir Phillipp Woodhowse, and your selfe. Or otherwise iff you can not compownde itt, I will take suche remedy as I maye by the lawes of the lande. In the meane tyme, I protest unto you neyther my selfe nor any by my prokurement shall deale with him nor any of his and this shallbe more secure for him then any bande you can binde me in. I have taken suche a cowlde as I dare not ryde a myle. Thus with my harty commendacions I committe you to God his proteccion. Barsham this 25 of February. Your asiwered loving frend.

[*Postscript*:] Sir iff this will not satisfye you so soone as I am well able to travell I will come over to Styfkey and enter a recognisaunce for the peace.

Signed: Thomas Fermor.[219] *Holograph*.
Addressed: To the worshippfull my very lovinge frend Nathaniell Bacon esquier.
Endorsed in Martin Man's hand: Mr Fermor concerning Mr Russill.
1 p. Folger L.d.289.

Rhys Gwynn to Nathaniel Bacon

1603/4, February 27. Sir, Mr Spratt[220] could furnishe me with nothinge for a serche not so much as the chest key which he saieth remayneth in the handes of Goodwyn the last steward.[221] I fynde him willinge to joyne in an assignement, and to covenaunt for himself, but uncertayne whether his sonne wilbe drawne to it or noe, that aswell as some <ease> discharge of the fyve powndes I have undertaken for him to Sir Henry Sydney must be effected by your good meanes or not at all, yet hath «he» made greate protestacions to me it should be paid this next weeke, wherein nothwithstandinge I praye you to cary such a hand with him as you maie secure me therof. I could not receave soe much direccion of him as to set me downe the certaynty of the rent nor manner of payement, therefore, receavinge £40 by this bearer, and the interest in the lease restinge still in you, I must desire you to send by him the originall lease, wherof I shall have greate use. And yf it please you I shalbe bownde besides for the paiement of the rest of your money in Easter terme. So with my very harty comendacions to your self & Mistres Bacon, and restinge much bownde unto you I committ you to God. My house in Fakenham this xxvii of February 1603. Your very assured to his power.

Signed: Rice Gwynne.
Addressed: To the right worshipfull my very good frend Nathaniell Bacon esquier at Stifkey.
1 p. NRO BCH 27/9/74 I (94).

---

[219] Thomas Farmer (*c*.1546–1621) of East Barsham. His grandfather, Sir Henry, was a rich London merchant who became one of the greatest early-Tudor sheep-masters, and his father, Sir William, ranked amongst the foremost Norfolk gentry when he died in 1558. Thomas, however, squandered his inheritance and succeeded at nothing. Vituperative by nature (as his correspondence shows), he was thrice appointed as J.P. and thrice dropped from the commission, was defeated when he stood as knight of the shire in 1586 and never served as sheriff. (Smith, *County and Court, passim*).

[220] See Bacon to Richard Spratt 7 January 1603/4, above, p.65.

[221] The reference here is to the steward of the Duchy manor of Fakenham (see Robert Plandon's answer of 24 March 1602/3, above, p.21). "Goodwyn" is most likely Christopher Goodwin, steward of Methwold in 1607, but might be his brother John, the surveyor (see note to 22 August 1607, below, p.286).

Jerome Alexander to Nathaniel Bacon

1603/4, February 27. Accordynge to your worshipps direccion I sent my brother Plandon your letter unto whome I wrote wisshing hym to write his mynde for answere, but he denyed to write & to com sayenge he was lame. But all his lamenes was the want of Wolverston[222] the onlye makebate [*issue*] betwixt us. Thus I humbly take my leave of your worship. Thorpland this xxvii of Februarye 1603. Your worships to commaunde.[223]

[*Postscript:*] Your worships letter was delyvered hym on Saterday mornynge by eight of the clock.

Signed: Jerrom Alexander. *Holograph*.
Addressed: To the right worshipfull Nathaniel Bacon esquyer.
Endorsed in Martin Man's hand: Mr Alexander.
½ p. Folger L.d.2.

Robert Campe to Nathaniel Bacon

[*?1603/4*],[224] **March.** Right woorshipful, had I not taken my leave of you, I would have mad bould word to intreate your favour for our old allehouse keper this bearer, and the rayther in that Wynter who you allowed of and Dalyman who soughte to be allowed of have bothe surceased and lefte our towne to be provided for by more sufficent persons. I thought good therfor by these few lynnes not only to aqaynt you ther with, but allso to requeste your favour to allow of him, but untyll you heare juste complaynt of him, which beinge, I proteste I will never after usse aneye meanes for him. I assure you two is moste fytt for our towne, now our shippes are to be rigged one house will hardly lodge them, besyd it is moste unfytt that men shalbe inforcd to one only house. Thuse reffaringe all to your good consideracion and yet requestinge your favour herin, I humbly take my leave. Blakney in haste this present morninge the [*blank*] Marche. Your to comaund.

Signed: Rob[er]t Campe.[225] *Holograph*.
Addressed: To the right woorshipful Mr Nathaniell Bacon esq at Stifky in haste these.
Endorsed in Martin Man's hand: Mr Campe.
½ p. NRO RAY 473.

Thomas Farmer to Nathaniel Bacon

[*1603/4*],[226] **March 2.** Sir, accordinge to my promise I wolde willingly come to Styffkey to satisfye your request but since I wrote my laste letters unto you beinge

---

[222] Possibly Woolverstone, near Ipswich, Suffolk, or Wolverton Place, 2 miles north-east of Swaffham and about 9 miles from Brisley where Alexander may have lived (*BP*, iv, p.174). Neither is close to Thorpland.

[223] For the previous document in this dispute see 23 February 1603/4, above, pp.74–5.

[224] Dating: this letter must post-date an entry in Bacon's memoranda book (1602–7) of 31 December 1603, recording that Hugh Dallymond had been "enjoyned to forbeare victualling", and Thomas Wynter had been asked to provide surety that he would "sell onely to the poore & not within doores" (NRO BL/BC/5/22, p.44).

[225] Robert Campe of Blakeney, gent (*BP*, iii, p.294).

[226] Dating: dated from Farmer's letter of 25 February 1603/4, above, pp.75–6.

entreated by Mr Tirrell and my cosen Greene to ryde in to the feildes to take the ayer I have had two fitts of an agiwe [*ague*]. I proteste unto you, my selfe nor any by my meanes shall deale with Mr Russell befor your retourne from the Parliament otherwise iff «I» were bowend to the peace I thincke my sonne is not so veary a cowarde but he and the reste of my kinsmen and frends wolde revendge this villanye offered by so base a fellowe to me spedely. Sir I protest your love hathe made me forbear «and» to staye for his submission more then all the bandes that can be exacted of me and I pray you soe take itt. So soone as the horse ryder cometh over to me I will send him to Styfkey. Thus with my harty commendacions I committe you to God his proteccion. Barsham this 2 of Marche. Your asiwered lovinge frend.

Signed: Thomas Fermor. *Holograph.*
Addressed: To the worshippfull my very loving frend Nathaniell Bacon esquier att Stifkey.
Endorsed in Martin Man's hand: Mr Thomas Fermor touching Mr Russell.
1 p. Folger L.d.290.

Petition. Inhabitants of Wells to the knights of the shire for Norfolk

1603/4, March 4. Humbly sheweth unto your good worshipps the inhabitantes of the towne of Wells with in the saied county, that whereas the estate of the saied towne doth cheifly stand by the trade of fishincraft (being a sea coast towne) whereby not onely her «late» Majestie hath yearely received freely a good portion of fish for the provision of her houshould (to the value of one hundreth poundes), but also divers pore men as well of the same inhabitauntes as others of divers townes nere adjoyninge are sett on worke and trayned upp for the better maintenaunce of navigacion, and whereas through the exceeding cheapnes of fish (which we doe persuade our selves cometh by the not duely observinge of the daies appointed for the onely eatinge of fishe (especially in all manner of vittaling houses[)]) the saied towne is not onely much impoverished, but also divers owners are constrayned to keepe their shipps at home not being able through the cheapnes of fish to receive so much of their adventures as will discharge the provision of their voyages whereby not onely his Majesties provision is greatly abated & diminished, but also many pore men are not so sett on worke as other wise might be. In consideracion whereof we of the saied inhabitauntes whose names be underwritten doe humbly entreate of your worships that nowe at the next Parlament some such course may be taken for the releife of the saied towne and other coast townes as also «for» the trade of fishingcraft, as in your good discretions shall seeme fitt and convenient.[227] And so we most humbly take our leaves. From Wells this fourth of March *anno* 1603.

Signed: John Greene, Rob[er]t Mony, [*by mark:*] Clement Bollt, Wyll[*ia*]m Tydd, Will[*ia*]m Starking, John Yates, Richard Mettarson, William Gouldsmith, W[*illia*]m

---

[227] For Bacon's engagement with the progress in Parliament of this petition see above, "Introduction", p.lvi.

Tydd, Thomas Grogon, Thomas Halman, Symon Metterson, Robert Sampsonn, George Hutcheson, John Housegoe, Thomas Bunting, Richard Barnye, Richard Manne, Will[*ia*]m Todd, Robarte Todd, John Kynge, John Perce, James Mettersone, Henrye Boulte, [*by mark:*] John Congham, Rob[*er*]te Leech, John Elvye, Henry Congham, John Chamberlin, Rob[*er*]t Mangles, Nicholas Tydd, Rob[*er*]te King, Nicholas Wasselbee, Rob[*er*]t Knapp, James Tydd, Will[*ia*]m Tyd, [*Christ*]ofer Bunten, Fraunces Congham, Henry Armstrong, Fraunces Tod, Hewe Dye.
1 p. NRO BL/BC/6/3.

John Palgrave to Nathaniel Bacon

1603/4, March 6. Sir. At theise last Assizes houlden at Thetford[228] my Lord Cheife Justice of England [*Sir John Popham*] gave order to me & others, that theire should be no more alehowses allowed to have contynuaunce in any Hundred, but the just number heretofore allowed by his Lordshipp.[229] Whereof his Lordship ment (as he sayd) to have accoumpt of. And therefore so many as be above the number allowed by his Lordship, I & others that be justices dwellinge within the Hundred of Northerpingham intend to cause them there to be suppressed. Whereof for good will I beare you I thought good to advertise you of, least hereafter fault be found with you by his Lordship for not observinge the same order within the Hundredes of Northgreenhoo & Holt. Northwood Barningham the vi of March 1603. Your very assured frend to his power.

Signed: J[*ohn*] Pagrave.
Addressed: To the worshipfull my assured good frend Nathaniell Bacon esquier at Stifkey.
Endorsed in Martin Man's hand: Mr Pagrave.
½ p. NRO RAY 251.

Nathaniel Bacon to Thomas Sackville, Lord Buckhurst, Lord Treasurer

1603/4, March 10. <Maie it please your Lordship to be advertised> «My humble duty etc. In aunswer of [*your*] Lordship's letter of the xv of February last»[230] concerning <the> «sondry his Majesties» manours <of Estderham> ⇨ Terrington Walpole West Walton Walsoken Emneth & Tilney⇐ in the countie of Norfolk wherof I am Steward. <And by your Lordships letters of the 15 of> Maie it please your Lordship to be advertised first concerning the manours of Terrington etc <which be within Marshland>

The fynes of copy«holdes» within these manours are certayn, 4*s.* the acre.

The tenantes within the said manours have estates of inheritance in their copyholdes.

---

[228] Invariably the winter Assizes for Norfolk were held at Thetford in order to shorten the journey required of the justices of assize in what was often a season of adverse weather. Only the much better attended summer Assizes were held in Norwich. Although the first session of the new Parliament did not convene until 19 March 1603/4, Bacon seems to have been in London earlier than this and therefore would not have been able to attend the Assizes.
[229] See further below, 1 September 1604, pp.127–8.
[230] Above, pp.72–3.

There are neither mynes of metall nor coale & verie little woodde within the said manours.

The cop[*yhold*] landes are solde for £3 & £4 the acre & in some of the manours for £5 & £6 as thei are more or lesse in charge. And accordingly thei are rented.

The cop[*yhold*] rentes cannot justly be sett downe by reason that Raphe Agas[231] who was joyned with G. Waking in a comission of survey hath gotten the ancyent rentalles & bookes into his handes which should sett out the said rentes, neither do the tenantes knowe how to come by the same agayne.

And concerning the manour of Estderham. The fynes have not ben «heretofore» above 12*d.* the acre. The tenantes have estates of inheritance in their copieholdes. There are no mynes of mettall or coale within the manour. Meadow there is worth to be lett by the yeare 8*s.* the acre, pasture 6*s.* 8*d.* & arable 6*s.* Where wood & tymber is upon the copyholdes cannot be discerned <because> «because» for want of a survay there of long tyme, the copieholdes cannot be [?]severed <or sett out> from other fees, amongst which thei lye intermixt.

There are no hariottes paid by the tenantes of this manour.

The rentes cannot <well> be sett downe by the Steward but <is to be certifyed> by the Bailiff, in whose custody all the rentalles do remayne.

/Justices of peace/.

b. There are resiaunt nigh unto Estderham thes justices of peace,[232] *viz.* Sir Philip Woodhouse knight, Sir Anthony Brown, Sir [?]R[*ober*]t Wynde,[233] Rice Gwynn esq.

a. And nere unto the other manours thes, *viz.* Jo. Reppes esq, Thomas Hewer esq, Thomas Oxburgh esq.

From St[*iffkey*] 10 *Martii* 1603.

Unsigned. Draft in Martin Man's hand.
On same sheet and with same endorsement as Notes on correspondence between Nathaniel Bacon and Thomas Sackville dated 20 December 1604, below, pp.144–5.
1 p. NRO NNAS S2/17/16.

Richard Stubbe to Nathaniel Bacon

1603/4, March 11. Sir, I am verie sory that your sudden going out of Norfolk was such as I could not speake with you before, but forasmuch as I know not what advertisementes or motions have ben made unto you for the amending and curing

[231] Ralph Agas (?1545–1621), land surveyor; he had worked on other royal manors, as at Pulham in 1600, and had been patronised by Lord Burghley and by his successor as Lord Treasurer, Lord Buckhurst (Peter Eden, 'Land Surveyors in Norfolk 1550–1850, pt.2', *NA*, xxxvi, 1971, p.128; *BP*, iv, pp.121–5, and note 266). This was not the first instance of his overbearing behaviour (*BP*, iv, p.122).

[232] An interesting sidelight as to the attention given by the Council to ensure that the patronage system did not distort a sensible distribution of J.Ps and an instance of why such a distribution was of practical value.

[233] Sir Robert Wynde came from a somewhat elusive gentry family, based at South Wootton. Robert succeeded his father, Sir Thomas, in 1603, and was knighted the same year. The period of his service as a J.P. is uncertain. Presumably it is Robert listed here, although he is not named in the *Liber Pacis*, dated July-October 1604 (BL Add. 38139, ff.144v-146). In 1627/8 he sold his South Wootton estate and presumably left the area. (Blomefield, ix, p.199; N. Pevsner & B. Wilson, *Norfolk 2: North-West and South Norfolk*, 1999, p.666; Shaw, *Knights*, ii, p.123).

of divers disseases here in Norfolk, whereof the countrie is now sicke of, I thought good to commend unto you, by this inclosed, 3 thinges (roughlie hewen) as to a speciall phisytion, that will put his best indevour to purge and cure those maladies.[234] Soe not doubting of your good endevour herein (according to your late speech, to the bodie of this sheire) wherein you shall bynd the whole countie, to be tied in love & affection towardes you, I commytt you to God, and shall ever rest. Sedgford, xi *Marcii* 1603.

Postscript in Richard Stubbe's hand: Not forgettinge my verye hartye commendacions to your selff & Mistres Bacon. Yf you knew how wellcom the understanding of the succes of the seid 3 thinges shoulde be here, I shoulde somtyme hear of the same.

Signed: Your lovinge & assured frend to my poure [*power*] Rich[*ard*] Stubbe.[235]
Endorsed in Martin Man's hand: Mr Stubbe.
Enclosure: Memoranda immediately below.
½ p. NRO RAY 252.

Memoranda by Richard Stubbe of matters to be considered by the Parliament

[*1603/4, c. March 11*].[236] 1. That where an act was made in the xxxi yeare of our late Quene Elizabethes raigne, intituled an act for the avoyding of secrett outlawries,[237] in which is declared that in every action personall when any writt of *exegent* shalbe awarded, that the shreive shall make 3 proclamacions, one in the open countie court, 2. at the generall quarter sessions, 3. to be made one moneth at the least before the *quintus exactus*, at or nere the most usuall dore of the church or chapple of that towne or parishe, where the defendant shalbe dwelling, (as by the same amongst other thinges appeareth), and that all outlawries had and pronounced, and retourned, contrary to this statute shalbe utterly voyd. Which law was then made & intended, that yf the said proclamacions were not hadd and made as aforesaid, what retourne soever the shreive should make, the outlawrie should be voyd. And yet now contrary to the meaning of the makers of the same, the shreive commonly retourne that the defendant had all his said proclamacions, according to the said statute, where in truth he never soe had, and especially at or nere the most usuall dore of the church <of> «or» chapple, where he dwelt, according to the said statute. Against which said false retourne, the defendant cannot now by the common law of this realme make any averrment, whereby many of his Majesties subjectes have of late receyved greate losse, and detriment, to their utter undooinge, by seasing, selling & taking away of their goodes and leases, without any notice of their outlawry. For the avoyding of which mischeef & inconvenience, it may be enacted that this may be added unto the said act, that all outlawries had contrary to this act shalbe avoyded by averment, without suing of any writt of

---

[234] For discussion of Bacon's representation of the county in Parliament see above, "Introduction", pp.liv–viii.

[235] For Stubbe see above, 24 March 1602/3, p.22n. He had been recommended by Baker as one of those qualified to represent the interests of the county at Court (above, 8 January 1603/4, p.66).

[236] Dating: dated with reference to the letter from Stubbe to Bacon immediately above.

[237] For discussion of business in Parliament see above, "Introduction", pp.liv–vii.

error. And the very like addicion was in an act made in 6 H.8 for proclamacions for outlawries in a forraine countrie, as in the abridgment of the statutes, in the title of *exigent* & outlawries fol.102 appeareth.

2. That where, upon & after the death of any of his Majesties subjectes, the exchetour [*escheator*] and feodary procure offices to be found for the tenure of their landes, and that yf they cannot prove how every particuler parcell is houlden and of whome (which is impossible for many of them to doe, for that their landes are dispersed in many places, and their rentes are generall, and many tymes the lord is unwilling to shew what he can, for the benefitt of the tenaunt) then upon two *ignoramus* found & certified, by the said exchetor and feodarie, the tenure must be *in capite*, to the greate prejudice, & undoing of the most part of his Majesties subjectes.[238] For remedie whereof, an act to be made, that his Majesties subjectes shall not any waie be compelled to make any such proffe, but the proffe shall rest onely on the behalf of the King, his heires & successors, & that the King shallnot [*sic*] be intituled to any such tenures, without good proffe on the behalf of his said Majestie & upon the inquisycions taken before the said exchetor & feodary.

3. That where upon his Majesties generall pardon, every man supposeth by the preample of the said statute, that every man should be pardoned for such offences as are pardoned therein, yet all penalties & forfaytures of goodes, recognizaunces, yssues, amerciamentes, and other thinges, are to be levied & paid, by & to the grauntees or <patentes> pattententes [*sic*] of the libertie of the dutchie of Lancaster, and other liberties graunted «by» his Majesties progenitors for life or yeares. Soe that all his Majesties subjectes within the said liberties, receyve not ben-efitt or proffitt by the same, contrary to all equitie & reason.[239] For remedie whereof be it enacted, that all his Majesties subjectes, aswell within any liberties as without, shall have, receive & take the benefitt & advauntage of his Majesties gen-erall pardon, in as ample and large manner to every intent & purpose, as yf the said liberties were in his Majesties handes & possession. Any graunt or letters pattentes of the said liberties to the contrary notwithstanding. Provided alwaies that this act extend not to any person or persons, or citie or towne corporate, which have had any graunt or letters pattentes heretofore graunted, by his Majestie or by his pro-genitors, of any liberties or priviledges, wherein they or any of them have any estate of inheritaunce.

---

[238] The uncertainties arising from feudal tenures were to be a constant subject of complaint and negoti-ation throughout the Parliament, culminating in the abortive Great Contract of 1610. The abuses of wardship were immediately raised as a grievance in 1604, and Sir Edwin Sandys broadened the question in a speech of 26 May: "Our desire is, the taking away the tenures *in capite* and knight service, and the burdens depending on them" (*CJ*, i, p.227). The justice of Richard Stubbe's points about escheators and feodaries can be seen in the government's later anxiety that the Aid for Prince Henry's knighthood in 1609 should proceed by composition rather than inquisition (*BP*, vi, forthcoming).

[239] There is no evidence that this specific problem was raised during the Parliament. Liberties and franchises are not mentioned in the 1605/6 Act of general pardon (3 James I, c.27). The issue here seems to have been not so much liberties as such, as that this prerogative of the Crown had been sold to patentees.

I have noe doubt but the late statute for triflinge [*vexatious*] actions[240] shall be repealed, for that the same is soe generally misliked.

Undated. Unsigned.
Endorsed in Martin Man's hand: Touching utlaryes & the escheator.
Enclosed with letter from Stubbe of 11 March 1603/4, immediately above.
1½ pp. NRO BL/BC/6/4.

Edmund Pooley to Nathaniel Bacon

1603/4, March 19. Sir I thinke yow maie call to remembraunce one John Waller who is longe sithence deade, who was an earnest sutor to Sir Nicholas Bacon your brother & your self, to extende a recognizaunce of 2000 poundes, acknowledged by one William Waller to my lord your father.[241] But the matter, concerning one Mr Kyrbie & one Thomas Waller, who were plaintiffes in the Chauncery uppon that extente it appeared uppon the hearing of the matter, that theire was noe cause to extende the recognizaunce, & their decreed accordinglie, for thintencion of the recognizaunce, as by the condicion appeared, was to restrayne the said William Waller from the alienacion of a mannour in Suffolk called Peyton Hall. But he having a purpose afterwardes to enlardge a lease which he had made to the said Kyrby of the said mannour for divers yeares, did suffer a recoverie of the same, for the making good the lease, but to the verie same uses he stoode seazed before. Besides John Waller who soughte the benefite of the said recognizaunce if their had beene any cause, thoughe he were one to whom the remaynder was limited, yet theire were divers before hym & still are, who nowe take the benefite of the rente that is reserved uppon the lease *viz.* £40 per annum, and his remaynder was noe whitt empayred, but lefte in the same degree it was before the recovery, and all this appeareth by the decree.

Nowe sir the cause of my writing to yow in this matter is this. Thinterest of the lease is in my neice Kyrbie nowe the weddowe of one Mr Thomas Kerby sonne to Mr Kyrbie above mencioned, who died shrodely[242] indebted, and hathe lefte the weddow 3 young chilldren & small meanes to maynteyne hir self & chilldren & to paie his debtes, besides the benefit of that lease, against whom one John Waller, sonne of the said John Waller, seeketh to rayse upp newe troubles by pretence of that recognizaunce, & hathe beene with one Sir John Lephinstone a Scott,[243] to

---

[240] 43 Eliz., c.6. The Act penalised sheriffs and other officers who summoned or arrested parties to suits without having the original writ or process authorising their action. It was not repealed: on the contrary, it was among those renewed in the 1604 statute for continuance or repeal of legislation (1 James I, c.25 §1).

[241] The original recognizance was dated 12 July 1569 and John Waller the father bound himself to the executors of Sir Nicholas Bacon on the same conditions on 5 February 1580/1 (*BP*, ii, p.157). See further, 4 December 1604, below, pp.143–4.

[242] Shrewdly, i.e. heavily.

[243] John Elphinstone, brother of James I's Secretary of State for Scotland, Sir James Elphinstone, the latter of whom was created Baron Balmerino on 20 February 1603/4 (*GEC*). Balmerino was in Edinburgh at this time (12 April 1604 *sub* Sir James, *CSPD, 1603–10*, p.94). John had served as Gentleman Usher to James I's wife, Queen Anne, since the 1590s, and was granted free denization in 1605 (*CSPD, 1603–10*, pp.218, 408, 479, 509). Although he wielded little political power, it is evident that this did not stop him from attempting to profit from his position of influence in the new Jacobean Court.

procure favour by his meanes for he hath written to me about it, for he was alto-gether misinformed by the said Waller, but I hope uppon my answer he will rest satisfied, but yet I cannot assure my self of that, and therfore am bolde to imparte this much to yow, with whom it maie be & with Sir Nicholas Bacon they will deale agayne, beseeching yow bothe, nowe yow knowe thequitie of the case, that yow will stande the poore weddows frinde, whose name before she marryed was Ann Brewster, that served the Lady Wentworthe[244] [(]a gentlewoman well knowne to your wife) and to protecte & keepe hir what yow maie from the trowbles & wronges that by such courses without your frindshipp mighte be broughte upon hir, for suerly sir yow shall find that she hathe bothe lawe & equity of hir side. And so assuring my self of all the favour that Sir Nicholas & yow maie lawfully afforde in this case, I do betake yow to Godes most mercifull proteccion. Written from Myleend the 19 of Marche 1603.

Signed: Your very lovinge frynd, Edmund Polly.
Addressed: To the worshipful and my verie loving frinde Nathaniell Bacon esqr.
Endorsed in Martin Man's hand: Mr Poley.
1½ pp. Folger L.d.475.

Petition. Sir Thomas Erskine to Parliament concerning a Bill to confirm letters patent for land in Yorkshire

[*1603/4, March 19 <-Θ-> 1604, May 26*].[245] *Calendar*: By his letters patent dated at Wilton, 10 November 1603, the King granted the petitioner and his heirs the late priory of Watton in Yorkshire, with all its appurtenances including the precinct and the church, together with the manors of Watton, Hooton, Cranswick, Kilnwick, Huggate, Barnby Dun, Sancton and Hessle, Yorkshire, to hold in free socage as of the manor of East Greenwich at the rent specified. The petitioner requests that Parliament enact that the letters patent shall stand and that the petitioner, his heirs and assigns, may enjoy and have possession of the said lands against the King, his heirs and successors, notwithstanding any entail, Act of Parliament or fine to the contrary; but saving to all persons or corporate bodies (except the Crown) any title or claim they may lawfully have to the estate or any part of it.

Undated. Unsigned. Incomplete copy.
1 p. NRO BL/BC/6/5.

[244] Dorothy Bacon's aunt, Anne Hopton, widow of Henry, third Baron Wentworth (d. 1593) (see genealogy of the Hoptons in Key, 'Dorothy Bacon', p.110). Actually, by this date she was no longer Lady Wentworth, having married Sir William Pope in 1595 (*GEC*).

[245] Dating: this petition has been placed at the beginning of the session to bring it together with various other undated documents relating to Parliamentary business in 1604. Sir Thomas Erskine's Bill for naturalization and for confirmation of letters patent made to him was read in the Lords on 29 March 1604, and after amendments there was sent to the Commons on 28 April. On 2 May the Commons ordered that "all such tenants of the lands contained in the same [patent], as desire to be heard by their Counsel, be admitted accordingly, and have two days warning before the second reading". The Bill was passed on 24 May, and read again in the Lords on 26 May (*LJ* ii. pp.269, 272, 279, 280, 286, 305, 306; *CJ* i. pp.189, 194, 196, 213, 222, 224).

Valuation of Watton priory lands

[*1603/4, March 19 <-Θ-> 1604, May 26*].[246] *Comitatus Ebor. Parcella posses-sionum nuper monesterii de Watton.*
Graing de Hesall Skiugh et pastura ovila in Sancton et Etton per annum £13 6s. 8d.
Rectoria de Watton 50s.[247]

These landes aboveseid were purchased of our late soveraigne lady Queen Elizabethe the xxii daye of Marche in the twoe and fortithe yere of here Majesties raigne by Richard Burrell of London grocer at 40 yeres purches for redy mony.

Thes landes are in Sir Thomas Arsking patentes.

Undated. Unsigned.
½ p. NRO BL/BC/6/6.

Objections of former patentees to Sir Thomas Erskine's Bill

[*1603/4, March 19 <-Θ-> 1604, May 26*].[248] *Calendar.* The late Queen sold lands of Watton priory to various persons. The King has granted Sir Thomas Areskin the same lands, some expressly named, others in general terms. Some leases are mentioned in the grant, including that to Sir Thomas Henneage. These are not mentioned in the Bill and as originally drafted the Bill would have con-firmed all the lands and leases of former beneficiaries under letters patent to Areskin. The Bill has been amended so that it does not include lands sold, but Areskin would have left in the named lease to Henneage, although it was granted for service and money, and estates, annuities and interests and many tenants depend upon it "in a place not fitt to get new farmes, nor they able to pay newe fynes". A proviso is sought that not only Sir Thomas Areskin's, but all former patents be confirmed equally, both to lessees (with reversion only to Areskin) and to purchasers. This is the only way to make the Bill safe for the former beneficiaries and to avoid doubts in interpretation, which "daily arise in making of lawes and may sooner do in private billes where lesse care is commonly used". A general saving to all persons of their lawful rights applies only to Common Law and not to rights in Equity.

Undated. Unsigned. Copy.
Endorsed in Martin Man's hand: Sir Thomas Erskyn.
1 p. NRO BL/BC/6/7.

Proposal for an Act of Parliament to restrain abuses of undersheriffs and pleaders

[*1603/4, March 19 <-Θ-> 1604, July 7*].[249] For that there is a generall complaint in the Star Chamber & all other courtes in Englande of the injustice & cruell

---

[246] Dating: as petition immediately above.

[247] "County of Yorkshire. Part of the possessions formerly of the monastery of Watton. Grange of Hesselkew and sheep pasture in Sancton and Etton for the year £13 6s. 8d. Rectory of Watton 50s."

[248] Dating: as petition above, p.84.

[249] Dating: dated from the first session of the 1604–10 Parliament, before Nathaniel Bacon was knighted in mid-July 1604. These grievances were not among those put forward on behalf of the Commons by Sir

dealinge of the under sheriffes which is knowne to most of the Kings subjects for when they and their lawyers with their paines and great charges hath brought their causes of true dep[*ositions*] and the like to execution then this writt shallbe carried to the ballance of the under [*sheriff*] which must be waied downe by the plant[*iff*] one vacation & then waied up by the defendant another vacacion so that by this briberie ympietie & corruption the[*y*] are never or seldome served nor any other writts to the great greife and hinderance of the subject. For this my self tasts of. I have sent upon an <execution> «statute» 10 executions 11 *lattitattes* and five *cappies* upon an outlare to the sheriffes of Sommersetshire against one Mr Duke Brook and can get non served & likewise upon the return of a *ceepie* by the sheriffes of Nottinghamshire I could get no apparance nor agrement untill I had procured 15 *distringashes* which, when the sheriffe had returned, he would againe convey them of[*f*] the file. Therfore in remedye wherof <that it would please> for these & many of the like slippery & vile ymperfections of the under sheriffes, that it would please this honarable Howse to give by acte authorytie by oathe to all constables or the like officers appointed for that purpose to serve all writts & executions as now the sheriffes bailiffes doe & this done to returne them againe to the under sheriffe and for their service to be paid their fees as the bailiffes now are. And againe wheras theras ther is not now above some 40 or 50 bailiffes in a shire that havinge this service in their hands will serve no writts but what they list to their owne likinge, wheraras to the contrary if these officers be authorised as aforesaid then shall there be some thowsand so that no offender shall live in any parishe but by this meanes ther shall be likewise officers to attache him to eschew *non est inventus* which will breed great certaintie to the lawe & saftie to the subject in preservinge the good & suppressinge the badd. And if this shall not be liked then to add a greter punishment for their offences then now there is.

There is in handlinge of the lawe a great ymperfection by the covetous humors «& greedy desires» of the takinge lawyier, which is knowne to all men that hath had to doe therin in losinge their fees given & many times their cause, & the reson is that you shall have a counsellor will take 10 fees for the hearinge of 10 causes in one day when indeed in honestie & truth they can heare but one or twoo at the most, & in like manner for mocions when they can performe truly but one or twoo as aforesaid. And againe takinge so many fees they have no true leasure to stand out the pledinge of his clientes cause so that by this ymperfection the client doth not only lose his fees given but he loseth his whole cause whether it be landes or deptes & therfore to prevent this great inormity & generall hinderance to all such as hath suites in the lawe, that it would please this honorable Howse to erect an Acte that no lawyer, of what degre soever he is, shall take above one or twoo fees for the hearinge of one or two cawses with the like for motions & to be there & give his attendance accordinge to his fee taken. So shall the subject have his counsell at the hearinge of his cawse certaine which is now cleane contrary as is usuall in experience for by reson of the lawyers many fees taken they now stand to

Robert Wroth and Sir Edward Montague on 23 March 1603/4 (*CJ* i, pp.150–1), nor do they appear to have formed the basis for any proposed legislation.

heare no cause out but by peece meales from bar to bar & wheras now the hearinge of causes are but in few mens handes it will be then as well to the generall as to the particular being honestly ymploied. And that all lawyers may be orderly and indifferently h[e]ard one after another, for wheras now there be but a few hard & they undertake more causes then they can dispache their clientes are enforced to strive which of their causes he shall first move by outbiddinge of their fellowes with greater fees.

At the foot: Sir I have set downe 2 great faultes in the commonwelth but without method [*word deleted*] but if you shall please to like my intent then I entreat your protection & preferment of them otherwise I pray you hold me excused for «my» attempt.

Undated. Unsigned.

Addressed: To the worshipfull Nathaniell Bacon esquier at West Minister or els where.

Endorsed in Martin Man's hand: Touching abuses in sheriffes & councellors.

1 p. NRO SOTH 28/12/67.

Petition of the bakers in Norfolk

[*?1603/4, March 19 <-Θ-> 1604, July 17*].[250] To thee righte worshippfull Nathaniell Bacon esquior onne of his Majesties justices of peace and *coram* [*quorum*] and one of thee knightes elected and chosen for this county.

Whereas righte worshippful having juste cause to move yow with certayne abuses offered unto us in our trade or manuall occupation and knowinge your greate and provident care for thee good and dilligente observinge of every good Acte heretofore made and established we therefore whose names are hereunder written, havinge soe fitte opportunity offered as to have soe good and wise a speaker as your good worshippe, consideringe yow beare justice in thee ballance of equitie, in regard whereof we your pore suppliants have made boulde to incense your good worshippe with parte of thee abuses which are contrary unto thee Statute made in thee fifth yeare of thee reigne of our late soveraigne Queene Elizabeth of famous memory, which is provided that noe man oughte to enter into any trade not beinge apprentised seaven yeares, which is greately and by many abused to thee great prejudice and hurte of moste of our facullty within this county, and especially of such pore men and younge begynners «as» not knoweinge where to seate themselves, but are urged to leave their saide occupations and to betake themselves unto such labour, as not beinge therewith acquainted, whereby they are not able to provide for their families and to paie such charges as are daiely imposed uppon them. Therefore nothinge doubtinge but that your good worshippe will see reformation hereof, which otherwise will turne to our utter undooeinge and overthrowe of our trade, and divers other if this abuse shoulde still continewe, we shalbe bound to praie to God for your good worshipps lonnge and

---

[250] Dating: unless this petition dates from Bacon's previous tenures as knight of the shire (1584–93), it must date from between the opening of the Parliamentary session on 19 March 1603/4 and Bacon's knighthood in mid July 1604. For discussion of this see above, "Introduction", pp.lvi–ii.

prosperous dayes in this worlde, and in thee worlde «to come» everlastinge feliciety both of bodie & soule. Yours assured to our powers to command.

Undated.

Signed: [251] John Hiethe, Willyem Nicolas, John Worship,[252] Walter Sheltrom, John Bassin, Thomas Cooper thelder, Robart Grave, Thomas Sheltrom, John Sheltrem, Frances Dicker, Thomas Wrinch, Abraham Hubbard, Thomas Nwegate [*sic*], Andrew Call, John Leverinton, John Watkins, Thomas Sherwine, Cristofer Lee, Wilyam Emms, Thomas Cooper the yonger, Robart Corker, Willyam Noris, Roger Eache, Stevin Mitchell, John Clarke.

Endorsed in Martin Man's hand: The bakers peticion.

1 p. NRO SOTH 28/12/67.

Breviat for a Bill in Parliament to confirm Edward Seymour's rights of remainder in the lands of the late Duke of Somerset

[*1603/4, March 19 <-Θ-> 1604, July 7*].[253] *Calendar.* Points supporting the claims of Edward the son of Sir Edward,[254] second son of the Duke of Somerset by his first wife Katherine, as follows:

That the bad relationship between Somerset and John, his eldest son by his first wife, was the result of John's closeness to his father's enemy the Duke of Northumberland, whose son had married his sister. There was no intention to disinherit him until long after Somerset's second marriage and the birth of the present Earl of Hertford.

That this only affected John. Although Somerset preferred the heirs male of his second wife in the Act of 32 Henry VIII, the remainder was reserved by name to Sir Edward and his right heirs. This remainder should be preserved.

That it appears from an Act of 5 Edward VI that the Act of 32 Henry VIII was corruptly obtained and authenticated by neither "the Kinges signe nor stampe".

That Sir Edward was restored as son and right heir of Somerset by the Act of 7 Edward VI and, John having died without issue, Edward Seymour is thus entitled to claim compensation for Katherine's lands alienated by Somerset without her consent. These should have descended to the heirs of the first wife in default of the Act of 32 Henry VIII, they were "but a triffle to thinheritaunce of the dukes aincestors the Seymours", and John was given inadequate compensation.

"A fyne levied by tenaunt in taile is but only a barr to the yssue in taile, and the

---

[251] Not all these names are necessarily autograph.

[252] John Worship of Little Walsingham, baker (*BP*, iv, p.208n.).

[253] Dating: dated from a Bill "for the establishment of certain manors, lands, and tenements belonging to the late Duke of Somerset", which was introduced in the Commons on 26 April 1604 and had a second reading on 15 May. Counsel for the Earl of Hertford and for Seymour argued the case over several days, and on 12 June the Bill was committed to all the privy councillors in the House, all serjeants at law and 36 MPs. Bacon was not one of those named. Parliament was prorogued before the committee had reported (*CJ*, i, pp.185, 210, 233, 237, 975). According to rumours, Somerset had divorced his first wife, Katherine Fillol, on grounds of misconduct. The inheritance, including the earldom of Hertford, was settled on the issue of Somerset's second marriage to Anne Stanhope, a situation briefly reversed by an Act of 1553 but restored under Mary (*Letters and Papers, Foreign and Domestic, of the Reign of Henry VIII*, xv, p.219; *DNB*; *ODNB*, which casts doubt on the divorce).

[254] Edward Seymour esquire (c.1563–1613) of Berry Pomeroy, Devon.

cause why a recoverie is a barr to him in the remainder is because of a supposed recompence which is entended to be given therby to him in the remainder, but although for the better assuraunce of landes to purchasors this fiction of law is permitted betwene party and party upon conveyaunces made by themselves, yet that is noe cause why this peticioner should not be releived by this high court of Parliament and the rather because thestate upon which the remainder doth depend was created by Act of Parliament."

That the petitioner asks only to have the remainder preserved as in both former Acts, so that the land should come to him if Lord Hertford, Lord Henry and other heirs male of Somerset's second wife and of Lord Hertford's present wife fail. By the Act of 32 Henry VIII no lease by the tenant in tail is valid unless made in possession for 3 lives and 21 years and any lease will be void against the remainderman if the tenant in tail dies without issue. However there is a special proviso in this Bill that leases shall hold good against the petitioner. The committees can alter anything that seems too strict on this point.

That it is unfair for Lord Hertford to benefit by the disinheritance of Sir Edward "contrarie to the lawe of God and nature" in the Act of 32 Henry VIII, and yet to seek to cut off the remainder contrary to the meaning of the Acts of 32 Henry VIII and of 5 Edward VI, the "only recompence for all the Seymours landes".

Undated. Unsigned.
Endorsed in Martin Man's hand: A briefe concerning the Seymours landes.
1 p. Folger L.d.1022.

Breviate for a Bill in Parliament concerning woollen cloths

[*1603/4, March 19 <-Θ-> 1606, March 31*].[255] A breviat for the Byll of the clothworkers.

The Bill is thus in effect.

That whereas in the time of King Edward the fourth, of King Henry the 7th & also of King Henrye the eight, & also in the time of Queene Elizabeth diverse Acts & statutes have bene made to this effect, that all wollen clothes both white & died should be dressed and fullye wroughte in England with certaine exceptions of lowe prise clothes (as by the name of white clothes of the price of £4 & coloured clothes of the price of £3) before they were transported, els all such clothes should bee forfeited that were transported undrest in England.

And that notwithstanding the same statutes, diverse licenses have bene graunted with *non obstante* of anye statutes, to transporte English clothes undressed.

That it would please the Kinges Majestie with th'assent of the Lords &

---

[255] Dating: a Bill "against transporting of woollen cloths undressed and for setting on work the poor commons of this realm" had its first reading on 31 March 1604. On 4 April it was sent to a huge committee, including all knights of the shire, of whom Bacon was one. It was reported on, with three other clothing Bills, on 5 July; all "were thought fit to sleep till the next session" (*CJ*, i, pp.160, 165, 252). It was duly introduced again on 1 February 1606, though now restricted to coloured cloths; sent to committee on 24 February (Bacon was not a member); and passed on 31 March (*CJ*, i, pp.262, 273, 288, 291). Following pressure from the Merchant Adventurers' Company it was eventually rejected by the Lords (*LJ*, ii, pp.406, 408–10, 432–4). See Brentnall, 'Regional Influences', pp.206–8.

Commons in this Parliament (for the releif & maintenance of the clothworkers of this realme whose living & needye sustenacion dependeth onely on the workmanship of cloth) that all manner of clothes white & coloured made in England maye be dressed & wrought in England before they bee transported or els that the same clothes so transported maye be forfeited, & that the forfeitures thereof maye bee, thone halfe to our souvereigne lorde the King & th'other halfe to such person as shall seize or sue for the same.

The motives or reasons for the passing of this Byll are theise.

The infinite multitude of poore workmen in England dressers of cloth, sheremen & clothworkers which have bene brought up in that trade & are multiplied by the long peace of the lande & doo for the most parte either want worke altogeather, or els are so slenderlye sett a worke & that at such hard salaries as their worke will not finde them sufficient maintenance for their families.

That the benefitt of the licenses do extend onelye to some one or verye fewe, & that those that have benefitt of such licenses are persons some of great honour, & others of great abilitye to live in great estate otherwise, without the benefit of such licenses, whereas the licenses «that» doo increase their superfluitye «doo» diminish the supplye of the great necessities of infinite multitudes, whereas in all Christian policye there is no question but that the miserye of multitudes ought to be releived rather then the excesse of some one or a verye fewe to be increased.

It maye be objected that clothworkers have the workmanship of the draperye of this realme. But the people of this lande doo now for the most parte in their apparell were grograines, rasshes, & other stuffs & little wollen cloth in respect of that they have done heretofore, whereby the drapers (by whose worke great releif hath bene to the sayd handicraftes men) have nothing so much vent of their cloth as in former times they have had, so that they have no certentye of worke to trust to.

The Netherlander & Hamburgher bring from their countries no commoditye that yealdeth labor or maintenance to this nacion of our realme of England yet doo their merchantes vent all our clothes undrest to sett their countrimen a work, when the workmen of this lande are readye to perish for want of labor.

Also the merchauntes adventurer bring no commoditye from Germanye or the Lowe Countries but it is fullye wrought & brought to perfection before it cometh hither, which the straunger doth in policye to mainteine their poore & employe men in labor to bee fitt for the service of their prince. Which maye give us example to have the like regard both for the service of our King & good of our nation. And thereby our poore might be sett on worke to avoide begging & the punishment thereof as the handicraftes men in Flaunders & Germanye now are, who have great parte of their maintenance by the dressing of our English cloth.

In like manner in Dansk & Elvin under the King of Polon[256] the people desire our English cloth undrest, to th'intent to sett their poore on worke, which maye likewise moove us to bee as carefull (for the strengthning of our land) to sett our poore on worke with the labor which both the lawes of this lande & our native countrey doth yeald them.

[256] Danzig (now Gdansk) and Elbing, Poland.

The compassion which the Kinges most famous progenitors have had of the poore commons & which in this verye case the said handycraftes men desire that the Kinges Majestie would imitate, & also that his Majestie would shew the same severetye in censuring such offenders in this same particular greivance to his commons, which his most noble predecessors have done, that is, of King Edward the fourth & King Henry the 7th of both which Kinges his Majestie is lineallye descended, who made the lawes in this case for the releif & maintenance of those that were then their poore commons, as by the preambles of their lawes maye appeare. And therefore to that purpose are to bee urged the statutes made by the sayd Kinges in their time, and all the other statutes before & since to that purpose ordeined, & therefore looke:

11 Ed.3 cap.5. The statute inviting all straungers & forreiners that were clothworkers to come into England, & a promise made by the King to give them franchises, & that was, that the clothworkers of England (which were then but a few) might be instructed by the forreiners which were then more skilfull then Englishmen. But the King then would not suffer clothes undrest to bee transported for he would rather suffer forreiners to come into England to dresse them.

4 Ed.4 cap.1. A penall lawe made against clothworkers & sheremen that yf they should not doo well their worke they should yealde double domaiges to the partie greived. Whereby one objection to this Byll is answered, that yf the clothworkers doo not dresse their clothes so well as they maye bee done beyond the sea, that then they shall yeald double domaiges to the partye greived.

7 Ed.4 cap.12. All clothes not fullye wrought yf they were transported, were forfeited, & dressing is a cheife parte of the working of clothes for there upon are they called clothworkers that dresse them, & therefore by that lawe clothes not drest being transported are forfeited.

3 Hen.7 cap.11. All clothes being transported undrest are forfeited, except clothes of 11s. price or under. But out of this statute were exceptions made after of clothes of a litle higher price.

3 H.8 cap.7. Clothes of 4 markes price excepted.

5 H.8 cap.3. Clothes of 5 markes & under excepted.

27 H.8 cap.13. White clothes £4 price excepted. And coloured of £3 price excepted.

33 H.8 cap.19. The same exception.

Undated. Unsigned.

Endorsed: A breviate for the clothworkers Byll.

1½ pp. NRO SOTH 28/12/67.

Notes concerning Parliamentary business

1603/4, March 20. "*Remembrances during Parliament business, 20 March 1603.*"[257]

2½ pp. Dobell, 38, item 42.

---

[257] This is dated to the second day of the session. Could it have been a summary of all the various Bills and breviats submitted to Bacon? The use of the term "Remembrances", used elsewhere by Martin Man, Bacon's secretary, suggests that this is may have been drawn up by him. Despite the apparent coincidence of

Thomas Baker to Sir Charles Cornwallis and Nathaniel Bacon

1603/4, March 20. Right worshipfull. Although I nothing doubt of your for-wardnes in the cuntries good, and that you cannot but remember the great hin-drances which this countie hath susteyned for want of a generall libertie to transport corne, yett I have thought good to send herewith the coppies of two statutes granted for that purpose, whereby you may perceyve the cause & collour for barring of transportacion, and may (yf you please) move in Parlament to have the same redressed & amended.[258] The confirming of a generall lisence this Parlament, I thinke will be more requisite then in former tymes, for that (thankes be to God) the peace & tranquility of this realme & of our neighbours adjoyning, is likelie to bring great plenty and in lieu of furnishing of Barwick [*Berwick-on-Tweed*] and Ireland with vyctuall from hence, ther is nowe great aparance of a suplie from those places, and we shall I doubt be to seek of marketts wheare to vent our corne yf tillage doth continewe with the like plenty that hath bene <the last> «of late» yeares. I send allso here inclossed a coppie of the last generall libertie graunted by the Lords of the Councell for transportacion,[259] which I think to be nothing so ample as the former, which was granted in consideracion of the payment of 5*s.* uppon a quarter of wheat and 2*s.* 6*d.* uppon a quarter of other kindes of corne, for ther is a clause in this graunt that such persons shall have libertie to transport wheat, which desyre the same of my Lord Treasurer [*Lord Buckhurst*] which (in my opinion) doth savour both of restraintes & setting forward of particuller lisenses when this Parlament is past, and the transportacion of corne being so uncerteyne as now it is, fewe men will adventure to buy any, wherffore it may please you to be mindfull of this speciall busynes so much importing the generall good of the whole countie, wherewith I have acquaynted Mr Oxburgh Recorder of this towne & one of our burgesses this Parlament, whoe hath promissed to joyne with your worships therein, and to further the same as much as in him lyeth. And so I take my leave, from Kinges Lynne this xx of March *anno domini* 1603. Your wourships to his small power.

Signed: Thomas Baker.

Addressed: To the right worshippfull Sir Charles Cornwallis knight & Mr Nathaniell Bacon esquire.[260]

Endorsed in Martin Man's hand: Mr Thomas Baker.

Enclosed: extracts from statutes and proposed amendments, immediately below; and a copy of the last general liberty.

1 p. NRO RAY 253.

---

date and length, it seems unlikely to be the memorandum concerning liberty for the grain trade sent by Thomas Baker to Nathaniel Bacon and Sir Charles Cornwallis (below, p.$) which is itself undated and in which the word "remembrances" does not appear.

[258] The very real economic interests of both the local merchants, such as Baker, and the landowners, such as Bacon, were at issue here. For earlier complaints about the restraint on export and the misuse of licences see above, 16 October 1603 p.48, and document following.

[259] Perhaps a reference to the order of 16 October 1603 (above, pp.47–8), although the Bakers had apparently already sent a copy to Bacon on 18 December 1603 (above, p.59).

[260] Bacon and Cornwallis had been elected to Parliament as MPs for Norfolk on 20 February 1603/4 (*Norf. Official Lists*, p.49).

Extracts from statutes regulating the transportation of grain together with proposed amendments

[*1603/4, March 20*].[261]

Anno v Regine Elizabethe.[262]

An Act touchinge certeyne politick constitutions made for the mayntenance of the navy, *viz.*

And be it enacted by the authoritie of this presente parliament that from and after the feast of Saint Mychaell tharkangell next coming, it shall be lawfull to all & every person & persons being subiectes of the Quenes Majestie her heires & successors, ⇨ onelie out of such portes & creekes as by the Quenes Majesties proclimation hereafter shall be published and apointed & not elswheare, ⇦ [263] to lade carry or transport any wheat rye barley mault pease or beanes unto any partes beyond the seas to sell as a merchandisse in shippes crayers[264] or other vessells wheareof any Englisheborne subiect <the> then shall be the onelie owner, so that the price of the sayd corne or grayne so caryed or transported, excead not the prisses hereafter following, at the tymes havens & places wheare & when the same corne or grayne shall be shipped or laden *viz* the quarter of wheat at 10*s.*, the quarter <of> of rye peaze or beanes at 8*s.*, the quarter of barley or mault at <8*s.*> 6*s.* 8*d.* currant money of England, any lawe usage or estatute heretoffore made to the contrary hereof, in any wisse not withstandinge.

Anno xxxv Regine Elizabethe.[265]

An Act intituled the reviving contineruance explanation & perfecting of divers statutes, *Cap. 7 viz.*

Provided allso and be it further enacted by the aucthoritie of this presente parlament, that when the price of cornes or <gay> graynes excedeth not the rates hereafter following at the tymes havens & places wheare & when the same corne or grayne shall be shipped or laden, *viz.* the quarter of wheat at 20*s.*, the quarter of rye peaze & beanes at 13*s.* 4*d.*, the quarter of barley or mault at 12*s.* of currant Englishe money. That then it shall be lawfull for all & every person & persons, being subiectes of her Majestie her heires or successors to loade carry or transport any of the sayd cornes or graynes in such manner & fourme as in the sayd Act made for the mayntenance of the navy is limited & apointed, and that the Quenes Majestie her heires & successors shall have & receyve by the customers & officers of her portes for the custome or pondage of every quarter of wheat to be transported by force of this statute 2*s.* and of every quarter of any other grayne 16*d.*, which sayd severall sooms so to be had or levied as custome or poundage to be in full satisfaction of all manner of custome or pondage for the sayd corne or grayne by any constitution order statute lawe or custome heretoffore made used or taken, for transporting of any such manner of corne or grayne.

---

[261] Dating: dated from the letter from Thomas Baker, immediately above.
[262] 5 Eliz. c.5, §17.
[263] Underlining has been used here for emphasis.
[264] Crayer: a small trading vessel.
[265] 35 Eliz. c.7, §§5 and 14.

And in the end of the same Act it followeth *viz.*

Provided allwayes & be it enacted by the aucthority of this presente parlament, that the Quenes Majestie her heires & successors may at all tymes, by her & ther writt of proclimation to be published generally in the whole realme or in any the counties of the realme wheare any port townes ar, comaund that no person shall by vertue of this Act transport or carry any manner of grayne out of her Highnes dominions generallie, or out of any speciall portes to be in the same proclimation particularly named, for such tyme as shall be therein limited & apointed.

And that it shall not be lawfull for any person to carry out any such grayne contrary to the tenour of the same proclimation uppon such paynes & forfeytures as by the lawes & statutes of this realme ar & have bene provided & ordeyned in that behallffe, this Act or any thing therein conteyned to the contrary notwithstandinge.

To be a meanes that this <Ac> latter Act may be sett downe as followeth, *viz.*

Provided allso & be it further enacted by the aucthority of this present parlament, that when the price of cornes or grayne excedeth not the rates hereafter following at the tymes & havens & places wheare & when the same corne or grayne shalbe shipped or loaden *viz.* the quarter of wheat at 20*s.*, the quarter of rye peaze & beanes at 13*s.* 4*d.*, the quarter of barley or mault at 12*s.* of currant Englishe money, that then it shalbe lawfull for all & every person & persons being subiectes of her Majestie her heires <&> «or» successors to loade carry or transport any of the sayd cornes or graynes unto any partes beyond the seas to sell as a marchaundisse in shippes crayers or other vessells, whereof any Englishe borne subiect then shall be the onelie ownere, <And th> any lawe usage or estatute heretoffore made to the contrary hereof in any wisse notwithstanding. And that the Quenes Majestie her heires & successors shall have & receyve by the customers etc.

The wordes which ar here inserted out of the former Act made for the mayntenance of the navy ar to be added to this latter Act, and the reference in this latter Act unto the former Act to be lefte out, bycause the statute is ells to small purpose & gyveth no libertie at all as you may perceyve.

And yf your worshippes could procure that when wheat did rise in price to be worth 26*s.* 8*d.* that then the libertie of <restraynt > «transportacion» should continewe paying the Kinges Majestie for the custome of every quarter thereof 3*s.* and so according to the rate for all other kindes of corne & grayne, as in the latter warrant granted by the Lords of the Councell (whereof I send herewith a coppie) is mencyoned & expressed, I think this latter clause will be very benefficiall to his Majestie in his customes, & a great mayntenanc to the husbandman.[266]

Undated. Unsigned.
In the same hand as, and enclosed with, Thomas Baker's letter of 20 March 1603/4, immediately above.
Endorsed: [*1*] Coppies of a statutes [*sic*] made in *anno v Regine Elizabethe* and in *anno xxxv.* [*2. In Martin Man's hand:*] Concerning the navy.
2½ pp. NRO BL/BC/6/8.

---

[266] By the statute 1 James I c. 25 §2, the price at which export of wheat was restricted was raised to 26*s.* 8*d.*, the customs duty remaining at 2*s.* a quarter.

Papers relating to the proposed union of England and Scotland under James I

[*1603/4, March 22 <-Θ-> 1607, March 30*].[267] "*Eight documents relative to the Union of England and Scotland in 1604, including Abstract of the articles agreed upon by the Commissioners for the Union, Inconveniences by admitting the Scottish Nation to free commerce with England, Objections against the Union, Answer to Objections against the Union, Speech of James I to the Commons, etc.*"[268]

16 pp. Dobell, 3 (March 1912), item 1377.

Evidence of John Holmes

[*1604, March 25 <-Θ-> 1604/5, March 24*]. *Anno Domini 1604.*[269]

Memorandum that my brother Nicholas Holmes <my brother> «abought» [*blank*] last past arrested one Roger Towneshend gentilman[270] uppon an execucyon. Which my mynde <John Holme> was that the sayd Roger Towneshend should never be arested for the same nor never knewe of the sayd execucyon untill the sayd Mr Roger Towneshend was arrested of the sayd execucyon. And after he beinge arrested of the execucyon I the sayd John Holmes was to afferme enything for my brother, for he <vou> vowed secretlye that if I would «not» stande to justefye the sayd execucyon, he would make me paye serten detes that I was bounde for him & for parte of which debt I am nowe in execucyon for.

Item where as he challendge a letter of attorny from me to sue the sayd Roger Towneshend, he never had eny, nor I did never consent to the suite of the sayd bond or bill. But dyd always forbyd the same unto Mr Wolmer.

Signed: Wytnes me John Holme the wryter hereof. *Holograph.*

Endorsed in Martin Man's hand: John Holmes disavowing the suite upon a bond in his name against Roger Tounshend. 1604.

½ p. RH Box 66.

---

[267] Dating: most of these documents probably date from the beginning of the 1606–7 Parliamentary session. The *Inconveniences* and the *Objections*—the latter drawn up by the merchants of London, with an *Answer* by the Earl of Salisbury—are assigned to 4 December 1606 in *CSPD 1603–10*, p.336. Articles of Union had been agreed by the commissioners for both kingdoms as early as December 1604 (*CSPD 1603–10*, p.173), but were formally reported to Parliament only on 21 November 1606 (Gardiner, i, p.329). The King's speech is more problematic. Urging the advantages of the union took up a good part of his address on 18 November at the opening of the session (*CJ*, i, pp.314–15); and on 30 March 1607 he returned to Parliament to answer at length some of the objections that had been raised during the debates, a speech that was soon afterwards printed (J.P. Sommerville ed., *King James VI and I: Political Writings*, Cambridge 1994, pp.159–78). However, James' desire for the union had also been a principal theme of his opening and closing speeches at the 1604 session (Sommerville, *King James*, pp.132–46; *CSPD 1603–10*, p.130). The final item mentioned here is a speech to the Commons. All those cited so far were made to both Houses, but in March 1604 the same oration was given separately to the Lords on 19 March and, (because by error the lower house had not been invited), to the Commons on 22 March (Gardiner, i, pp.165–6).

[268] These documents are not explicitly connected with Nathaniel Bacon, but they do occur in a sale catalogue among a collection of Bacon/Townshend manuscripts.

[269] This is the first in a long series of documents relating to this dispute, which Nathaniel Bacon was probably attempting to mediate (see Evidence of *post* 2 April 1605, below, p.167)

[270] Roger Townshend of Twyford. He was presumably a substantial landholder in the parish as in 1572 he alone qualified to pay the fines for failing to sow his quota of flax and hemp (*BP*, iii, p.196).

Evidence of John Holmes

[*1604, March 25 <-Θ-> 1604/5, March 24*].[271] Memorandum there was a bill put in suite abought twoe yeres past and more by Nicholas Holme agaynst Roger Towneshend gent in the name of John Holme without his consent. After the saide bill beinge in suite the saide John Holme & Nicholas Holme havinge communica-cyon together, the saide John <demande> demanded of the saide Nicholas Holme howe he shoulde recover the saide debt against the saide Roger Towneshend for that he was a wytnes to the bill him selfe and howe he could be a wytnes in his owne cause. Where upon he answered he would wryght his letter to Mr Vynyor whoe was Mr Towneshendes his attornye that he should pleate such a plea that the saide Mr Towneshend should be dryven to prove the issue, althoughe he dyd give the saide Vynyor 10*s*. or 20*s*. for his paynes. Where upon the saide Vynyor pleated to the saide bill *nil debet* and so the saide Mr Towneshend was overthrowne in the accion.[272] After this abought Trynytye Terme last past the saide Thomas Vynyor beinge attornye for the saide John Holme for diverse causes & demandinge of the saide John monye for his fees with other speches then he the said Vynyor told the saide John Holme he could gyt noe monye of his brother Nicholas which he dyde owe him and he ferther saide that he had deserved better use at his brother Nicholas his handes for <the plesiering> he pleasiered him in the plea for Mr Towneshend for to serve his brother Nicholas turne. And for that he should so doe my brother Nicholas promysed him 10*s*. But he coulde neyther get a pennye of that nor for fees otherwise which was due to him. But further saide that if he had thought to have ben no better rewarded at his brothers handes he should never have recovered against Mr Towneshend the bill which he dyd put in suite against the said Mr Towneshend in your name, for that he never <bought> had eny letter of attornye from you. But should have recovered agaynst you in that accion for that he never bought nor soulde nor borrowed of you a pennye and you confessed to me so muche your selfe.

Undated. Unsigned. ? in John Holmes' hand.
Endorsed: (1.*in Martin Man's hand*) John Holmes concerning Vyniour & his brother Nicholas Holme; (2.) Mr John Homes hys note *inter* Tounesh[*end*] & Vynyer.
1 p. RH Box 66.

Evidence of John Holmes

[*1604, March 25 <-Θ-> 1604/5, March 24*]. *Summary:* Copy of the Evidence of John Holmes, immediately above, with minor variations. Dated 1604 and signed: *Teste Johanne Holme.*[273]

Copy.
On the same sheet and with the same endorsements as Evidence of John Holmes 29 March 1605 <-Θ-> 24 March 1605/6, below, p.160.
1 p. RH Box 66.

---

[271]　Dating: dated from copy of the Evidence of John Holmes, immediately below.
[272]　*Nil debet* (he owes nothing) was a good plea to a simple action of debt, but not to a suit (as in this case) based on a written document.
[273]　The next document in this dispute is dated 2 January 1604/5, below, p.148.

John Percival to Nathaniel Bacon

1604, March 26. *Invitius feci (ornatissime vir) post tam insperatam «rerum» muta-tionem ut te a gravissimis reipublicae curis, literis meis revocarem. Sed tamen subductis mecum omnibus rationibus, et fretus anime tue candore, id in me recepi ut hoc ad te scriberem. Regis edictum contra quam opinabantur multi, quinto martii editum, plurimis ministris merorem summum et animi tristitiam attulit. Si enim res in eum locum adducta sit, cogentur aut levitatis aut ignorantiae crimen subire. Levitatis quod unam rem tam constanter exorsi, alio se traduci sinant. Ignorantiae quod in publico ecclesiae negotio subeundo, id in se susceperunt, cuius non satis firmam rationem ex Dei verbo reddere non possunt. Sustinebant magnam et pietatis et doctrinae opinionem, et [?]inanes redire turpissimum esset, dedecorantes autoritatem causae et fratrum suorum. Sed ego neminem unquam tam felicem esse exestimavi, qui non sit subiectus errori, et hoc proprium non esse demonis verum hominis. Cancellarius Norvicensis civitatis min-istros, et ecclesiarum gardianos convocavit, ex regis mandato precipiens, ut curarent publicam liturgiam, quae [?] similiter est typis excusa, in suis ecclesiis coli et observari. Idem quoque infra biduum apud nos fiet. Suspicantur multi, fore ut nonnulli eorum qui hanc publicarum precum formam subire recusant, in Hiberniam aut extremas regni insulas deportentur. Deus suorum suspiria et gemitus exaudiet, et suis in periculo probationis adsit. Multi suis fratribus insultant acsi magnam victoriam reportassent. Arma nostra sunt preces et lacgrimae. Deus det nobis suum spiritum ut quid optimum factu sit, opportune indicemus et constanter et ut chrestiana panoplia instructi omnem adversum casum forti animo feramus. Precor ut vos (ornatissimi viri) qui in hoc hono-ratissimo senatu convenistis, tuque prestatissime patrone, qui es inter ceteros religionis et ornamentum et decus, ecclesiae conlaboranti, ope vestra et consilio adesse voletis, neque nisi re perfecta conquiescatis. Et ne quid per episcopos probare cogantur ministri, nisi quod secundum formam statuti cautum sit et confirmatum. Idem erit illis verbi Dei ministris et levamen magnum et solatium. Tum ut poena quae est lege illis impo-nenda qui ceremonias violant remittatur, aut ad non ita grave periculum reducatur. Tibi ornatissime vir tuisque liberis et prestatissimae uxori tuae prout oficii ratio postulat omnem in domino salutem precor, ut cum hinc migraveritis in celum venti, aeterna in Christo vita fruamini. Res tuae domesticae salvae sunt et incolumes. Stiffkey Marcii 26 1064 [sic]. Tuae amplitudini in domino devotissimus.*

[*Modern translation:*[274] Most distinguished Sir,

I have somewhat unwillingly, after such an unexpected alteration of circum-stances, come to the conclusion that I should recall your attention from the very serious affairs of state by writing this letter. However, it is only after turning over all the arguments in my own mind, and because I can rely upon the impartiality of your spirit, that I have taken it upon myself to write this to you.

The King's proclamation, published on 5 March,[275] in opposition to the opin-ions of many, has brought the deepest sorrow and dejection to very many

[274] Translation by Dr Sheila Adam.

[275] The edict was the proclamation "for the Authorizing and Uniformitie of the Booke of Common Prayer to be used throughout the Realme" issued, as Percival states, on 5 March 1603/4 (text in Larkin & Hughes, *Stuart Proclamations*, pp.74–7).

ministers. For if matters be brought to that point, they will be compelled to endure an accusation either of inconsistency or of ignorance. Of inconsistency, because after initially maintaining one position so constantly they would be allowing themselves to be brought over to another. Of ignorance, because in undertaking the public business of the church they have taken upon themselves something which they cannot sufficiently firmly justify from the word of God. They have always maintained a great reputation for piety and learning and it would be most base to retreat from that empty-handed, bringing shame on the authority both of their cause and of their own brethren.

But I have not ever thought anyone so fortunate as not to be subject to error, and this is a characteristic not of the devil but of a human being.

The Chancellor has called together the ministers of the Norwich diocese and the guardians of the churches, bidding them, according to the King's command, to ensure that the public liturgy, which has been printed in a standard form, is honoured and practised in their own churches. And what is more, this very thing will be upon us in two days.

Many have suspicions that the outcome will be that some of those who refuse to submit to this form of public prayers will be deported to Ireland or to islands on the boundaries of the kingdom. God will hear the sighs and groans of his people, and may He stand beside his own in the peril of their trial.

Many are taunting their own brethren as though they had won a great victory. Prayers and tears are our weapons. May God grant us His spirit, so that we may both declare appropriately and consistently what is best to be done, and bear every adverse fortune with a courageous spirit, armed with our Christian panoply.

I pray that you (most distinguished gentlemen), who have come together in this most honourable council, and you (most excellent patron, who are an ornament and embellishment of religious belief in this company), may be willing to attend to the unity of the Church with your strength and counsel, and not rest until the matter has been resolved. And may ministers not be forced by their bishops to approve of anything which has not been stipulated and confirmed according to the form of the statute.[276] This will be a great relief and comfort to those ministers of the word of God. Then may the penalty which is to be imposed by law on those who transgress against the observances be remitted or reduced to a less serious danger.

For you, most distinguished sir, and for your children and your most excellent wife, I pray for all health in the Lord, just as the duty of my office demands, and that when you pass from here to God's heaven you will enjoy eternal life in Christ.

---

[276] Presumably a reference to the Act of Uniformity of 1559, 1 Eliz. I, c.2, which, with certain alterations and amendments, had re-adopted the Edwardian book of Common Prayer. Albeit, that Act had reserved a right of amendment to the Crown (§13). Given the contemporary concern for the maintenance of statute on non-religious issues, evident elsewhere in these documents, this was an astute tweaking of the constitutional and legal concerns that Percival must have observed among his gentry patrons quite apart from his appeal to the religious proclivities that they shared with him.

Your domestic affairs are safe and sound.[277] Stiffkey March 26 1064 [*sic*].
I remain most devoted to your welfare in the Lord.]

Latin. Signed: Joannes Percevallus.[278]
Addressed: To the right worshippfull Mr Nathaniel Bacon esquier.
Endorsed in Martin Man's hand: Mr Percivall.
1 p. NRO RAY (4) 36.

Sir Francis Bacon to Nathaniel Bacon

[*1603/4, March 29 <-Θ-> 1604, April 18*].[279] Notes of myne own I wanted tyme
to sett down. I send you copies of both the Kinges projectes and of the Act of
Recognition. Yors.

Undated. Signed: Fr[*ancis*] Bacon.
Endorsed in Martin Man's hand: Sir Fra[*ncis*] Bacon.[280]
½ p. BL Stowe 150 ff. 228–9.

---

[277] A somewhat bathetic conclusion, alluding to circumstances at Stiffkey, Bacon being at this time in London attending Parliament.

[278] John Percival (d.1622) MA, BD, fellow of Queens' College, Cambridge, 1566–74, rector of Stiffkey 1574–1622 (Venn, *Al. Cant.*, iv, p.294). Presented to the benefice by Nathaniel Bacon and very much of his puritan persuasion, being regularly mentioned as a preacher and referring to himself as such in his will (see *BP*, i, p.296 n.140, ii, p.316, iv, p.17; Barton, *Anthony Harison*, i, p.100; NRO NCC 1622 Bradstritt ff.138v–139v).

[279] Dating: the "Act of Recognition" is presumably that recognising James I's hereditary right to the English throne ("A moste joyfull and juste recognition of the immediate lawfull and undoubted succession descent and righte of the Crowne", 1 Jas. I c.1). The Bill was introduced in the Lords on 26 March, brought to the Commons on 29 March and passed the same day (*LJ*, ii, pp.266–9; *CJ*, i, p.158). As Francis Bacon refers to it as an "Act" we may presume that this note and its enclosures dates at least from after the legislation's passage of both houses. This is somewhat anomalous as presumably it still required the royal assent although already in its final form. The most important of the King's "projectes" was undoubtedly his desire for the formal union of his two kingdoms. In a message of 13 April he intimated that this should be the Parliament's main business, and at a conference between Lords and Commons the next day it was proposed that he should immediately assume the title 'King of Great Britain'. That proposal was abandoned after negative reaction in the Commons. Nathaniel Bacon was among those who spoke in the debate of 18 April, though his view is not recorded (*CJ*, i, pp.176–7). On 21 April Lord Cecil and Francis Bacon reported to their respective Houses "a draught or form (which had been conceived by the King's Majesty himself, and the same written out as his Majesty did dictate), being thought fit by his Highness to be the substance of such a Bill as might be framed for that matter of the Union" (*LJ*, ii, p.284; *CJ*, i, p.180). The King was suggesting that English and Scottish commissioners should meet to give substance to his model and report to their respective next Parliaments.

[280] This was one of those rarely recorded occasions when there is evidence of contact between Nathaniel and his more famous half-brother. Their apparent cold and distant relationship may date back to the dispute between the two sets of brothers over their father's will. Albeit, at least for a time, they shared a similar forward protestant perspective and antipathy to the ecclesiastical hierarchy. At this time Francis had no substantial permanent official state office save as a learned counsel intermittently engaged on legal work for the government. In 1594 he had been thwarted in his desire for the attorney-generalship by Edward Coke, as he was to be again in 1606 by Henry Hobart—from a local perspective very Norfolk affairs. The former rebuff may largely have been a result of his disastrously free-speaking performance in the Parliament of 1593. He had been active in the Parliaments of 1597–8 and 1601. Now, in 1604, under a new monarch who might be thought to share Francis' scholarly perspective, in general he was immensely active in Parliament and specifically engaged in support of the union of the two kingdoms. This topic dominated the business of this first session. For these reasons it was to be expected that Francis would have copies of these documents.

Sir James Calthorpe to Nathaniel Bacon

[*1604*], **March 31.**[281] Sir whereas my sonne in lawe Sir William Grey[282] is advysed to putt a Bill into the Parlament howse for the explanation of the statutes made in the 23 and 28 yeares of the rayne of Queen Elizabeth for recusansy,[283] and I having moved you at your last being at Norwich concerning the same, it pleasing you at that time to promyse me your furtherance in such behulfe, presumyng to veryfy unto you that the matter of the Bill (when his cause shalbe layd open touching the burden hee indureth, and in what mannor sondry others in the like have bene formerly discharged by ordinary course of justice) requireth favorable interpretation to conceyve the lawe by which meanes the extremyty of his case may be redressed, trusting in the end that equity will censure the cause one [*sic*] his syde. So (sir) having wished my sonne in lawe to expostulate with you concerning your approving his course, by preferring his Bill as afore sayd, I agayne rejoine my sute, for intreating your especiall frendshipp, and advyse towardes him, according as it semeth good in your wisdome, with the remeamberance of my commendations & do remayne. Your coosen and frend to command.
31 of March.

Signed: James Calthorpe. *Holograph.*
Addressed: Too the right worshipfull Mr Nathaniell Bacon esquire.
Endorsed in Martin Man's hand: Sir James Calthorp.
1 p. NRO RAY 62.

Abstract of petitions from the creditors of Edward Downes

[*1604, April 1 <-Θ-> 1605, August 26*].[284] An abstracte of the peticiones of the creditors of Edward Downes gent[285] <bein> the number of the creditors are 24.

1. He ys becom indebted to diverse of them, and diverse others of them he hath procured to stand ingaged for him as his suerties, for which they stand indaungered & must paye in his defalte in all to the some of £3000.

---

[281] Dating: Sir William de Grey introduced a Bill to explain the proviso on arrears in the Recusancy Act of 29 Eliz. c.6 on 4 April 1604. It was rejected on second reading, one argument being that approval would take £100,000 out of the King's purse (*CJ*, i, pp.166, 175, 948).

[282] Sir William de Grey of Merton (knighted July 1603) was married to Calthorpe's daughter, Anne (Clarke and Campling, *Visitation*, i, p.65). Despite the failure of his Bill, he was granted a release (20 July 1604) from all debts with which he was charged for the recusancy of his late father, Robert (*CSPD 1603–10*, p.135).

[283] Actually 23 Eliz. c.1 and 29 Eliz. c.6.

[284] Dating: a Bill to sanction the sale of land for payment of Edward Downes' debts was introduced in the Commons on 1 April 1604; Nathaniel Bacon was a member of the committee to which it was referred on 2 May. The committee reported on 18 May, but when the Bill passed on 16 June a proviso on behalf of the creditors (presumably calling for payment by Michaelmas, as specified in this abstract) was entered and accepted with it (*CJ*, i, pp.171, 195, 213, 240). For unspecified reasons the Lords rejected the measure (*LJ*, ii, pp.321, 331, 333, 338) and a similar Bill went through all its stages again in the 1605/6 session, to be finally enacted, with proviso, on 8 May 1606 (*LJ*, ii, p.428). The end date derives from Sir Francis Gawdy's appointment as Chief Justice of the Common Pleas on 26 August 1605 (*Judges of England*, p.49).

[285] Edward, son of Robert Downes esq of Great Melton, married Katherine Lovell, widow of both Sir Thomas Knyvett of Buckenham and of Edward Spring, and daughter of Sir Thomas Lovell of East Harling (Blomefield, v, pp.16, 21). His father Robert appears in a list of recusants in 1585 (*BP*, iii, p.10).

2. Beinge seised of landes to the value of £300 *per annum*, he hath other landes in the right of his wiffe to the value of £500 *per annum*, he hath fedd them with promises to sell his seid landes to paye dettes these 7 yeres, & more.

3. In the late quenes tyme about fower yeres since the then lordes of her councell graunted letters to the creditors to spare ther suites against him for fower monthes at his instance, in which tyme he promised them to sell his landes.

4. The late quene aboute two yeres since freed a great parte of his landes of a charge lyinge uppon yt for the recusancy of Robert Downes his father, to the intent the same should be sould to paye his dettes.

5. By reason of not sellinge thereof not <oly> only those his creditors are still delayed of ther dettes, but also diverse of those his suerties have & yet do indure imprisonment, some of them these fower yeres & more, and diverse other to eschewe imprisonment have for his dett payed so much, <for his dett> that yt hath ben the utter overthrowe of them ther wyves & children.

6. By course of Lawe they have no remedye against him for he standeth outlawed at many of ther suites, and kepeth himselfe in a castle stronge by seate [*sic*], and he ther accompanyed with manye desperate persones who professe that they will yeild to no processe that com against him, but defend him against shreiffe and all other ministreres of justice, with the hazard of ther lyves, & any that shall attempte him.

They disier therfore, that if he shall not himselfe before Michealmas next make payment to his seid creditors of ther principall due dettes & discharge his seid suerties of such dettes as they have undertaken for him, that then certene comissioners named in ther Bill may stand authorished by Acte of Parliament by all wayes & meanes at ther discretiones to inquire out the certentye of the seid creditors due dettes or by them undertaken as suerties for him, and theruppon shall have power to <hi> sell his seid landes, to satisfye the seid dettes & to discharge his seid suerties.

/Comissioners/. 1. The Lord Bishop of the diocesse of Norwich for the time beinge.

2. Sir Fraunces Gawdy knight one of the justices of his Majesties court of Kinges Bench.

3. Sir Henry Hobart knight seriante at lawe.

4. Sir Phillip Woodhouse knight.

5. Sir Anthony Browne knighte.

6. Robert Houghton esquire seriante at lawe.

/or any two of them whereof the Lord Bishop, Sir Fraunces Gawdy or Sir Henry Hobarte to be one/.

Undated. Unsigned.
1 p. Folger L.d.896.

William Yelverton to Nathaniel Bacon

1604, April 9. Sir, Mr Edward Sybsey, my brother in lawe, would so farr be beholding unto yow, as to have the deputation of a stuardshipp (which is now soly exercised by Mr Spratt) to be granted by yow to Mr Spratt and himselfe.[286] The former of these is unable in regard of sicknes, and unwilling besides in respect of other incumbrances, to medle any more therwith. The other (Mr Sybsey I meane) would gladly better his estate, and advance his creditt by leaving the place of an attorney, to become a steward. This change maye happily be made, if yow be pleased to grace him so much. Besides the certenty of having your accustomed rent, I dare promis all thankefulnes of his part, and for myne <selfe> I will acknowledge a beholdingnes for your undeserved love, and tie mye selfe to the requitall of so exceeding a favour, if the small meanes I have maye any tyme herafter effect it. Thus hoping of your kyndest furtherance herin, with my harty commendations I committ yow to Gods most holy protection. Sedgeford this 9 of Aprill 1604. Your loving frend.

Signed: Will[*ia*]m Yelverton.[287]

Addressed: To the worshipfull his verie loving frend Nathaniell Bacon esquire at London.

Endorsed in Martin Man's hand: Yelverton *ex parte* Sybsey.

½ p. Folger L.d.636.

Memoranda concerning agreements between Nathaniel Bacon and Edward Sibsey and Ralph Symonds

1604, April 13 – May. Memorandum. 13 April 1604 Nathaniel Bacon esquire sealed a deputacion to Edward Sybsey (*durante beneplacito*) [*during pleasure*] to kepe the duchie cortes assigned before to Mr Spratt. And Sybsey promised to see discharged the fee paiable by Mr Spratt quarterly to my master being about £20 per annum. *Teste* M. Man.

Memorandum. *Maii* 1604. Yt was agreed betwen Nathaniel Bacon esquire & Raffe Symondes[288] esquire as followeth: *viz.* the said Nathaniel should assigne & passe over his interest in the okes in Hilderston [*Hindolveston*] woodes. And Mr Symondes is to paie in consideration therof £200 wherof £100 at Michaelmas next & £100 at Our Lady following, and to give security for the same by suerties.

Nota respitt given for a weekes space after Mr Symondes going downe to refuse or accept of the bargayn. *Teste* M. Man.[289]

Unsigned. In Martin Man's hand.

Endorsed: Remembrance of the agreements with Mr Sybsey & Mr Symondes.

½ p. Folger L.d.736.

[286] Spratt's role as a steward and his service in other capacities to Bacon can be traced through this and preceding volumes. See in particular, above, pp.4n., 66.

[287] William Yelverton, junior, of Bayfield, a fellow J.P.

[288] Ralph Symonds of Hindolveston. The family was numerous in both Norfolk and Norwich in this period. A spirited portrait of a "Symonds", c.1595–1600, currently hangs in the Elizabethan House, Thetford (*see* Andrew Moore with Charlotte Crawley, *Family & Friends: a Regional Survey of British Portraiture*, Norfolk Museums Service & HMSO, London, 1992, pp.77, 81–2, colour plate 3).

[289] See further 24 July 1604, below, p.119.

Thomas Barsham to Nathaniel Bacon

1604, April 22. In humble maner my dutie presuppo[*se*]d (right worshipful) I thought good, havinge so fytt opportunytie to wrytt these few scribled lynes unto you, partly to signifye in what estate your affaires remayneth with us, and partly to understand from you what shalbe done concerninge the same. For the first the losse your worship susteyneth by your sheepe in our towne is greater then I expected or thought of, many ar deade we have all[*r*]eady above an hundred skynns, smale renew [*small renewal*] in lambes, and yet those that we have, what by reason of the weakenes of the ewes, as also by the hard and could weather we had in daminge [*lambing*] tyme, we have had, and I feare me shall have more losse hereafter in them, many beinge quenchlinges [*weaklings*] already. Much losse also in wool, for all that ar scabbed and infected will lose most of their wooll, I doubt befor the sheerers. No flock that I heare of in all our country is in the same plighte that ours is in, and no flock in all our heathe groundes this tyme twelmonth was in better case then ours in sight semed to be, the negligence of the shepehard the last sommer every man suspect to be the undoubted & mediate cause therof, but the immediate cause is from God who gyveth and taketh as yt pleseth him &c. I have accordinge to your commaundement gyven your shepeheard warning to departe his service at midsomer next. I think yt good (if yt so standeth with your good likinge), that those shepe that shewed tokens of infection (as many did) be noted by some by [*sic*] mark that they may be done away, for though they escape now, yet by the judgment of old heard [*herd*] men they will dey the next yeare. And for the supplyinge the want of those decayed, yt wer good your worship would direct some course to be taken, whether yt pleaseth you that any hogges or yonge sheepe be bought at Thettford fayr or els where, at that fayer for the most part ther is plenty and choise to be had and more reasonable then afterwardes.[290] Wheras your rentes and firmes for the last halfe yeare remayne still in your balieys handes (for he knoweth not where or to whome to make payment therof) if yt pleaseth you that that be bestowed uppon sheepe for store, we will do our best, or what other course you shall direct. Other thinges I omytt tyll such tyme as your worship cometh into the county, at which tyme I will wayte uppon you if yt please God to make me stronge and able, beinge now and have bene these 6 weekes visited with sicknes so as I was not able no not to get from my house to my churche. Thus leaving you and your affairs to God his blessing. Eccles in hast this 22 of Aprill 1604. Your worshipps in all duty to comaunde.[291]

Signed: Thomas Barsham.[292]

Addressed: To the right worshippfull and his very good patron Mr Nathanael Bacon.
Endorsed in Martin Man's hand: Mr Barsham.
1 p. BL Add. 63081 ff.89–90.

---

[290] Probably the fair held on 3 May originally granted to the priory of the Holy Sepulchre, Thetford. The priory was also granted a fair to be held there on 14 September. (William Page, *A History of the County of Suffolk*, VCH, 1975, p.109.)

[291] For more on Bacon's farm and sheep at Eccles see 13 February 1604/5 and 26 June 1605, below, pp.152, 194–5.

[292] Thomas Barsham, rector of Eccles (1586–1639), "clerk, overseer and dealer for the lordes shepe" there (*BP*, iv, pp.87n., 88; Blomefield, i, p.410).

Sir Thomas Knyvett to Nathaniel Bacon

1604, April 25. My verye good brother, I am most glad to understand of the good health of your self and my good syster,[293] the convenyancie of this bearer have made me fynde owt some tyme to remember you with thes few lynes, & as your Parlyament affayers will geve you leive requit your poore countrie frend with some of your fresshest newes. Sir my daye of payement unto you approcheth att hande I woott not as yet whether I shalbe able to kepe touche with you att the tyme or no, by reasone that my brother Hollond[294] have hastened me more quicker then I expected, & have called all my daughters porcion owt of my hande. He hath lent unto my Lord William[295] a great somme of monye upon a mortgage of lande here in Norfolk. Yf you can forebeare yt you shall much pleasure me att this tyme for in all truth monnye was never so deade in thes parts att all hands, I can not gett in my owne rents & farmes, I maye verye safelye protest unto you that it is not yett fullye three weekes past synce my wyfe receyved a good parte of Myheltyde [*Michaelmas*] rente, such is the generall want of monye amongst us. God brother if you have any spare tyme let me heare from you. And with my verye hartie commendacions sent you & my good syster I commytt you both to God, in all hast this 25 of April 1604. Your brother and verye assured frend.

Signed: Thomas Knyvett.[296] *Holograph.*
Addressed: To the right worshipfull my verye good brother Nathaniel Bacon esquier.
Endorsed in Martin Man's hand: Sir Thomas Knyvett.
1 p. *faded in parts.* Folger L.d.389.

Richard Stubbe to Nathaniel Bacon

1604, April 29. Sir «as» I am very sorry you could not fynd the fourmer Bill of the outlawry,[297] soe I am very gladd to se you well inclyned to further the same, to the greate good (as I thinke) of your country and the whole realme. But to further your good intent therein, I have sent you a copy thereof, which although I sought diligently for, yet I could not fynd it at my late writing unto you, but now by greate chaunce I <fould> «found» the same. In my simple opynion, the other 2 Actes, which I commended unto you (& specially the Act for <tenures> «the generall pardon») might be very well effected, & have had an easie passage, without any prejudice to the King his fearmers of liberties. For as they should lose somewhat

---

[293] Thomas, the son of Sir Thomas Knyvett, was married to Bacon's second daughter, Elizabeth. The "good syster" here is presumably Lady Dorothy Bacon.

[294] Thomas Holland, son of John Holland of Kenninghall, was married to Knyvett's sister, Mary (Rye, *Visitation of Norfolk*, p.158).

[295] Probably Lord William Howard (1563–1640), a younger son of the 4th Duke of Norfolk. His wife, Elizabeth Dacre, was co-heiress to large estates in the north, long sequestrated because of a legal challenge, but released in 1601. It was around the time of this letter that Naworth Castle, in Cumberland, became their chief residence (*ODNB*).

[296] Sir Thomas Knyvett (c.1539–1617) of Ashwellthorpe. His own family's papers–now in various repositories— evidence his continual and considerable appetite for news from London.

[297] See letter and memoranda of 11 March 1603/4, above, pp.80–3.

thereby, soe «they and» their frendes were like to gayne more by the saffetie of their bodies and goodes. But «for the tenures» yf the two writtes of *ignoramus* might worke but a tenure in soccage, yt would suffice. Mr Carie[298] is like to purchase the fearme of Snetisham. I hartely thanke you for your late frendly advertisementes, and for your favour and kyndnes to Sipsey who I have noe doubt will behave himself in all respectes to your good liking. Soe being desyrous to heare of the good successe of your Parliament busynes, & specially for the union, & likelyhood of subsedie & taske I rest ever. Sedgford, xxix April 1604.

Signed: Yours well assurd, Rich[*ard*] Stubbe.

Addressed: To the wourshippfull his very good frend Nathaniell Bacon esquire at London.

Endorsed in Martin Man's hand: Mr Stubbe.

½ p. NRO RAY 254.

Henry Armiger to Nathaniel Bacon

1604, April 29. Sir accordynge to your worshypps dyrectyon by your letter, I cawsed Goodwyn[299] presentlie to goe over to Wallsyngham[300] to se the freestone there to be solde, which he lyked & bowght at for 18*s*. beinge 3 lodes of verie good hard stone as he saythe fytt for steppynges at the gate & suche lyke purposes. Your buyldynge[301] goethe forward as fast as tyme & wether hytherto wolde permytt, beinge verie dylygently followed of all handes. Brett & his companye beinge 8 in numbre besydes Sparke & Moore 2 morter [*mortar*] men, began the woorke the Mondaye next before Easter daye, & wrought 6 dayes the weeke & 3 dayes the next weeke followinge upon the same, & 5 dayes this last weeke, in which 14 dayes thei have raysd the walles in some place 4 foote in some 3 foote & some lesse then 2 foote accordynge to the grownde, yet all at one levell. The mayne wall with the crosses [*cross walls*] dothe conteyne at the least 16 skore foote so mesured. Yt hath taken up a verie great deale of stuffe allredye. Brett sayeth it will take at least fyftie challdres of lyme & neere twoe hundrethe loades of stone[302] to fynyshe it. Lyme I hope we shall want none for the kyll is at work withowte intermyssyon, but the stone is so harde to dygge, at every pytt, as a man can scarce dygg a loade in a daye, so as we are constrayned for fyllynge some tymes to gather the landes & cleare every place abowte the yardes for supplye therof. The free mason hathe begun to

---

[298] Wimond Carey of Snetisham, J.P.

[299] Thomas Goodwin, stonemason from Norwich (Stiffkey Database), not in Millican, *Freemen*.

[300] Almost certainly an allusion to the recycling of building materials from the former priory of the Austin Canons there. From this letter it would appear that this material found its way into the still extant gatehouse.

[301] This letter records the completion of the building of Stiffkey Hall, begun in 1576, by the addition of a gatehouse and curtain walls. The timing is significant, as work began immediately after Nathaniel and his wife had decided to build a new seat elsewhere (see Oxborough to Bacon, 31 January 1603/4, above, pp.71–2) and shows that Bacon had abandoned any aspirations to complete the great courtyard house as planned by his father, Sir Nicholas Bacon. For the terms used herein and an exposition of the building process see Smith, 'Stiffkey Hall'.

[302] "Stone" here refers to flint quarried locally, not freestone. Flint was used widely for building in North Norfolk. At Stiffkey it was plastered with mortar and used together with moulded brick facings for the doors and windows.

sett up the gate & the dores of bothe lodges, but of suche heyght, as the gate will requyer 3 steppes to awnswer the levell of the grownde towardes the halle dore. Barnye kyll [*kiln*] hangeth so in ballance who shall occupie it, as we can gett no tablynge bryck at all there nor cantes,[303] neyther yett any other bryck good to make cantes of but are enforced to buye of William Kynge at Hemptsted. The tablyn the free mason sayethe he will supplie with the stone from Wallsyngham & yet spare ynowghe for the rest of the woorke. James «Lynne»[304] hathe latelye seen your fatt bullockes & sett downe his opynyon whatt he thinkethe best to be done with them, which is that they showlde be sowlde nowe whylest they are in best plyght and the tyme for best pryce. For he saythe when the wether waxethe whett, they will falle, besydes some other dawnger to be feared, & so prove less profytable eyther to be sowlde or kept for your owne use. Thus muche I thowght good to sygnyfie unto your woorshypp, that receyvinge advertysment of your pleasure herin I myght lett him understand the same. He saythe he dare undertake to sell them for £5 a peece one with another. Your yonge companye[305] & whole howsh-olde are in perfect good healthe God be thanked, and all thinges elles of yours are well. Onelie Thomas[306] hathe yeilded your fee & carryed your charytie to the grave. He was syck afortnyghte before but wolde neyther keepe his bedd nor the howse untyll he was fownde deade in his yarde the xiii daye of this monthe Aprile. I have «sent» your woorshypp herinclosed Wattes his bandd, the rest I have receyved & delyvered ther bandes.[307] Mr William[308] his trunke with all the rest of the thynges sent by sea ar come home safe. Thus with remembrance of my humble dutie to your woorshypp & my verie good mistres I commytt yow bothe to the tuycion of the Allmyghtie, who send «yow» all healthe & happynes. Styfkie the xxix of Aprile 1604. Your woorshypps at commandment to his best power.

Signed: Henry Armiger.[309] *Holograph.*

Addressed: To the ryght woorshypfull his verie good mayster Mr Nathanyell Bacon esquyer.

Endorsed in Martin Man's hand: Henry Armiger.

1 p. NRO RAY 255.

---

[303] "Tabling": a horizontal projecting course or moulding. "Cantes": corner or side pieces.

[304] James Lynn of Stody; farming in his own right in the 1590s (Stiffkey Database) but here apparently acting as Bacon's bailiff of husbandry.

[305] Probably six in total. Bacon's eldest daughter, Anne, had returned to Stiffkey with her three children (Roger, Stanhope and Anne) following the death of her husband, Sir John Townshend, in 1603. Lady Dorothy, Nathaniel's second wife, had had three children by her first marriage (William, Owen and Mary), the eldest of whom was still only about 13.

[306] Thomas Batha (?Bartholomew) joined Bacon's household in the late 1570s, rising to serve as butler. Latterly, having married the kitchen maid, he lived in the village, but remained a liveried servant, often in attendance on his master and clearly a much revered figure (Stiffkey Database).

[307] In the context, possibly mourning bands for the household servants, rather than the usual meaning of 'bond'. Unfortunately, however, we have no full details of Bacon's household servants after 1600 and Wattes is unidentified, so this may refer to a completely unrelated transaction.

[308] William Smith (c.1591–1609), the eldest son of Lady Dorothy.

[309] Armiger is writing here as a senior household servant, probably the steward. There were several local families of this name.

Report in an arbitration between Jo. Johnson and Thomas Oxborough

1604, May 1. *Calendar.* A report concerning a dispute as follows:

Jo. Jonson presented a petition to the King against Thomas Oxborough esq, guardian to the heir of William Fenne deceased, and Jo. Bussell, attorney, concerning a messuage and 103 acres of land, meadow, pasture and wood in Briston, which Jonson claims in right of his wife Elizabeth. By a letter of 21 August 1603 the writers of this report were directed to examine the parties complained of (the latter naming equal commissioners to join them), and have had several meetings.[310] The property originally belonged to Thomas Appleton the grandfather and the position of the claimants is as follows: Jonson's wife claims as aunt and next heir of Thomas Appleton, grandchild of the first Thomas; Thomas Oxborough claims in right of William Fenne, son and heir of William Fenne, deceased;[311] Jo. Bussell claims as heir to Thomas Allen, attorney, deceased. The facts are that Thomas Appleton the grandfather conveyed the property to his wife Agnes, who was seised of it for life after his death, with reversion to their son, Thomas Appleton. By a conveyance of 20 March 1577 the latter sold his reversion for £120 to Agnes' second husband, St[ephen] Flowerdew;[312] but on 6 July of the same year he also sold it to William Fenne and his heirs by another conveyance. Several suits ensued between Fenne, a rich merchant of Lynn, and Flowerdew who was a poor man but "verie honest in his dealinges". In Star Chamber it was claimed that Flowerdew's conveyance was forged, but the case was dismissed with costs. Suits at common law became so onerous for Flowerdew that he was persuaded to sell his rights to his attorney Allen by bargain and sale. But there was no delivery of seisin, enrolment or any consideration proved, and Flowerdew affirmed at his death before witnesses that if any title passed it was in trust. Flowerdew remained seised during his lifetime, and by his will of 28 April 1588 left the property to Thomas Appleton the grandson. Agnes survived Flowerdew, but sold her life interest to William Fenne. Before her death, Thomas Appleton the grandson died without issue. Agnes has since died and in the writers' opinion the coheirs at law to the reversion are the aunt of Thomas Appleton the grandson, namely Elizabeth Jonson, and the child of one of his sisters. The property is kept from Jonson on the grounds that William Fenne is under age and in ward to the King for other lands. Bussell's claim, inherited by marriage to the heir of Allen, can be disregarded. The writers have been unable to persuade the parties to a settlement, and now refer the petitioner back to the King.[313]

Unsigned. Copy in Martin Man's hand.
4 pp. NRO RAY 256.

[310] Clearly Nathaniel Bacon was one of the arbitrators whose report is summarised here, but there is nothing to indicate who his associate(s) were, nor the signatory of the letter of 21 August to whom they were replying.

[311] The will of William Fenne the elder of King's Lynn, yeoman, was proved and confirmed in 1598 (TNA PRO prob/11/91, Lewyn ff.177–179; ff.442–3. The latter entry appears incorrectly in the online catalogue under William Fenn of Lyme Regis, Dorset). Thomas Oxborough, recorder of King's Lynn, was one of the executors.

[312] Stephen Flowerdew of Briston, yeoman (d.1588). By his will he left all his property in Norfolk to Thomas Apleton, son of Jone Apleton kinswoman (NRO ANW 1588/9 ff.31v-32v).

[313] The concluding remark referring the issue back to the King suggests that the initial referral to Bacon and others had come from one of the Masters of Requests. However, there is no entry relating to Johnson or Oxborough in Roger Wilbraham's entry book (Hoyle *et al.*, *Heard Before the King*).

Referral of petition. Martin Hambleton to the King

1604, May 16 *Calendar.* In his petition Martin Hambleton of Heydon states that, having sustained great losses by suretyship, fire and other causes, he was forced to mortgage a tenement and land worth £150 to John Mingay, gent, and his son Henry, in return for a loan of £60 with £6 interest over one year. He was granted longer when he could not pay by the named day. But Mingay and his son combined with Edward Murton, then in possession as farmer of the land, to seize the premises and turn the petitioner's wife and small children out of doors, although Hambleton had shortly before offered them all their money. They retain the land without compensation for the surplus value and without allowing him to sell it for the best price in order to pay them. As he is too poor to go to law, he requests that Sir Edward Cleer and Sir Christopher Heydon, knights, and Nathaniell Bacon, John Pagrave and Henry Sidney, esquires, or two or three of them, be authorised to examine his case. *Undated. Unsigned.*

At the foot: Order from the King that if the case is not being dealt with or decided judicially, then the "comitties desired", or some of them, with two more chosen by the other parties, should settle it equitably. 16 May 1604 from the court at Whitehall. [*Signed:*] Roger Wilbraham.[314]

Endorsed in Martin Man's hand: Martyn Hambletons peticion.
1 p. NRO MC 571/10, 778X4.

Articles submitted by Martin Hambleton in the arbitration of a dispute with Mr Mingay

[*1604, post May 16*].[315] *Calendar.* The information given is as follows. Hambleton borrowed £60 from Mingaye for one year, with interest of £6, on security of a tenement and lands worth £150. Before the year was up he sought a renewal at Mingaye's house, and Mistress Mingaye promised that her husband would renew. When Hambleton raised the cost of new conveyances, she said that Mingaye would act in good conscience. Nevertheless at the expiry Mingaye called for his money, which Hambleton could not pay unless Mingaye would transfer the land to a buyer. He was offered £150 by Mr Thomas [*blank*], but could not proceed because he had promised Mingaye first refusal for his nephew Mr Kempe. One Dewen offered to pay off the debt, but Mingaye would not agree unless Hambleton also paid £40 for the debt of one Middleton. Mr Easton then offered £136 for the property, but declined when Mingaye would not show the evidence unless £20 of Middleton's debt was paid. Mingaye then got possession of the house, and although he agreed to give a month's respite and Hambleton managed to procure the money, he came with company before the month was up, and evicted Hambleton and his wife and small children in very cold weather and seized his goods. If Mr Kempe had not harboured the children that night they would

---

[314] Reference to this petition is entered in Roger Wilbraham's register of petitions (Hoyle *et al.*, *Heard Before the King*, p.48, no.684).
[315] Dating: dated from the referral immediately above.

have perished. Hambleton and his friends offered £71 and the costs of a fine to redeem the land, and Mr John [*blank*] further offered two milk cows. Mingaye refused all this, but would not specify what more he wanted.

Undated. Unsigned.
Endorsed: Hambletons articles against Mr Mingay.
1½ pp. Calendared from transcript by H. W. Saunders, NRO MC 934/1, 800X5.

Duchy of Lancaster rental

1604, June 1. *Summary*: List of rents and reliefs in Upwell, Outwell and Waterwell for two years ended at Michaelmas 1603. 65 persons named. Made 1 June 1604.

Signed: *Per me Johannem Watson.*
Endorsed in Martin Man's hand: Upwell. Rentall 2 Jac.
2 pp. NRO MS 1621, 1C9.

Act of Parliament appointing commissioners to treat about a union of England and Scotland

[*1604, post 2 June*].[316] "*An act authorising certain Commissioners of the realm of England to treate with Commissioners of Scotland for the weale of both Kingdoms.*"

Undated.
15 lines, folio. Dobell, 3 (March 1912), item 1376.

Rachel Hopton to Nathaniel Bacon

1604, June 4. Good sir I ame verry hartely glade to heare of your good healthe, which I becetche God in his mercye to contineue longe and mannye yeres, to the comforte of your pore wieff and frindes, amongeste home Mr Hopton and my selfe, dothe much desire yt. Good sonne I have writen unto you [*word deleted*] thankes for your speciall care in the Parliament house for this my buyssenes, but cannot acknowledge thannkefullnes ennoughe unto you for yt, for I perseave by my sonne your care hathe bine greate, or otherwise yt might have bine unto us greate hinderaunce. Sir I doe acknoweledge this my buyssenes which yt had not prospered, I muste have bine the author of Mr Hoptons evell, but I truste God will blise yt to his good which yt dothe nowe appeare is envyed by some whoe will not be sene in yt, I leave ther malissiouse humor to God to requite, and soe resteinge ever thannkefull unto you for this and other your greate love showed unto us, and ours, which in some sorte you are evell requited, which dothe much greve me thate frome anye of ours there should be soe litle discretione. I wishe yt otherwise. With Mr Hoptonns «and my» lovinge comendaciones unto you, hopeinge that we shall see you and my daughter here at Withame[317] which would be excedeinge greate comforte to Mr Hopton and my selfe. Withame this iiii of June 1604. Your verry lovinge mother.

[316] Dating: the Act (1 Jas.I c.2) was passed by the Commons on 2 June, having been brought down from the Lords on 30 May and considered by a committee of both Houses on 1 June (*CJ*, i, pp.228, 230–1).
[317] Witham Priory, Somerset, the Hopton family seat since at least 1596 (Key, 'Dorothy Bacon', p.78).

Signed: Rachell Hopton.[318]

Addressed: To the right worshipful and my verry lovinge sonne Mr Nathaniell Bacon esquier.

Endorsed in Martin Man's hand: Mistres Hopton.

1 p. Folger L.d.363.

Henry Spendlove to Martin Man

1604, June 12. Mr Martine Man I have enquired of your sister of Norwiche[319] for you many tymes of late to understand when I might speak with you there or in Norfolk to lett you knowe the just reconning for the mony due to my cozen Mr Richard Bachcrofte from Mr Spratt,[320] for which your master is bounde with him to my cozen Bachcroftes wiffe, and hath undertaken to dischardge the same as Mr Spratt sayth, but I can not yet heare the certaine tyme of your cominge home. And my cosen hath written to me very latelie that he shall have speciall occasion to use the said mony or £20 therof at the least at London this terme, and ernestlie desyereth to have it payd him at his brother Mr Ambrose Gennyes howse nigh Charinge Crosse if your master maye convenientlie spare it. Therefore these are to certifie you that the 14 of March *anno* 1602 there was due from the said Mr Spratt to my cozen Bachcrofte upon the said bond £110 the use wherof till the iii of Maye followinge *anno* 1603 which is half a quarter of a yeere & 4 dayes & a half cometh to 30s. 3d. & so the wholle some to him then due (*viz*) the said iii of last Maye was £111 10s. 3d. wherof Mr Spratt payd then £85, soe rested £26 10s. 3d. which for a yeere cometh to 53s. 3d., *somma totalis* due the iii of Maye last *anno* 1604 is £29 3s. 3d., the use wherof for every moneth since accomptinge 30 dayes & a thirde parte of a daye for the moneth is 4s. 10d. Thus desyringe you to acquainte your master herewith prayinge the eternall God to blesse him in his busynes with my very harty commendacions to your self, I leave you to the tuition of the Almightie. Wymondham this xii of June 1604.[321]

Signed: Yours assuredly to use, Henry Spendlove.[322]

Addressed: To his assured frend Mr Martyne Man servaunt to the right worshipfull Nathaniel Bacon esquier.

Endorsed in Martin Man's hand: Mr Spendlove. Mr Sprattes dett to Mistres Badiscroft.

½ p. Folger L.d.554.

---

[318] The mother of Nathaniel's second wife, Dorothy. It is not clear which Mr Hopton is referred to here, or the nature of the service. Rachel's husband, Arthur, might seem to be ruled out as he was knighted in July 1603 (Shaw, *Knights*, i, p.155), but Man's endorsement refers to Rachel as Mistress rather than Lady Hopton, leaving the question open.

[319] Cecily Man, who married Edmund Peckover, a Norwich tailor who was also involved in the transfer of money to London and acted as a general agent for Bacon (*BP*, iv, p.33n.; Stiffkey Database).

[320] For previous and subsequent references to this debt, see Spratt to Bacon, 22 February 1602/3, above, p.9, and Reckoning between Bacon and Spratt, 18 July 1604, below, p.118.

[321] See further 18 August 1604, below, pp.124–5.

[322] For Henry Spendlove's family connections see P. Millican, 'The Rebuilding of Wroxham Bridge in 1576', *NA* xxvi (1938), p.284.

Sir Nicholas Bacon to Nathaniel Bacon

1604, June 16. Brother sens yow sente yowr man to me I have called to remembrance the matter betwene my cosen Stanhoppe[323] and me and in this sorte yt was. <He desyred> He dyd aske me if I hadde not an indenture that conserned Sir Jhonn Townsend dettes betwene hys mother and hym. I tolde hym I hadde sutche a wonne wheare upon he tolde me that the cownterpart was with my Lady Bartelet [*Berkeley*] and she was in the cowntrye and he cowlde not come by yt and so desyred me that he myght have myne to sette off the fyndynge of an offyce which otherwyse the bysynes cowelde not goe on, wheare upon I delyvyred yt unto hym. I doe verye well remember besydes that there ys a seduall annexed to the indentur of all hys detes that my Ladye Bartelet was to paye which cann not be severed from the indentur. What the dette was I have forgotte but there ys not above w[*onne*] or towe names «to yt» my cosen Stanhope [*2 words deleted*] «affyrmyde» unto and that yt was all payed savynge wonne or ells toe wheare of the wonne was as suertie to Medlycote the tayeler and as I take yt abought £50. Thys «ys» all that I remember at thys tyeme.

Postscript on dorse. I praye you keepe thys letter for I have no copye.

Signed: Nycholas Baco[*n*]. *Holograph.*
Addressed: To my lovynge brother Nathanyell Bacon esquyer.
Endorsed in Martin Man's hand: Sir Nicholas Bacon 16 June 1604.
1 p. BL Add. 41140 ff.54–5.

Memorandum of a debt

[*1604, July 3 <-Θ-> mid July*].[324] To Mr Nathaniell Bakcon.
Pro bond dew the 3 January 1601	£63
For use their of to the 3 July 1604	£15
	£78

Unsigned. Undated.
Endorsed in Martin Man's hand: Mr Farringtons dett. £78.
½ p. Folger L.d.735.

Referral of petition of John Braddock

1604, July 5. "*Petition from John Braddock,*[325] *who complains of having been drawn to a place 'distant 100 myles from both their dwellinges' owing to the malicious action*

---

[323] Presumably one of the brothers of Jane, née Stanhope, the mother of Sir John Townshend, who by this date had married Henry, Lord Berkeley. The brothers still living were John (c.1545–1621), privy councillor and vice-chamberlain; Edward (c.1547–1608), master in Chancery and chancellor for the diocese of London and known as "rich doctor Stanhope"; and Michael (c.1549–1621), of Sudbourne, Suffolk, MP for Orford in the Parliament of 1604–10 (for all three see *H of C, 1558–1603*; *ODNB*).

[324] Dating: limited by Bacon's knighthood. Shaw, referring to Bacon as 'Nathaniel (Francis) Bacon junior of Norfolk' ascribes this as likely to have been after 21 July 1604 (Shaw, *Knights*, ii, p.134). However, Bacon is referred to as "Sir Nathaniel" in the Order of 17 July 1604, below, p.117.

[325] John Braddock, gent, of Wiveton, Searcher of the port of Blakeney and fish merchant (*BP*, iv, p.294).

of a neighbour.[326] *Endorsed with instructions to Nathaniel Bacon for the next Assizes in the handwriting of Sir John Popham, with his signature."*

Tregaskis, 720, p.60; 923, p.81.

Petition. Townsmen of Alethorpe to the J.P.s in Norfolk

[*Post 1604, mid July*].[327] The complaint of the poore inhabitantes of Althroppe, for refformation of divers injuries, and wronges, which course they were directed by the right worshipfull Sir Nathaniel Bacon knight.

In most humble manner complayneing unto your good worshipps we the poore inhabitantes of Althrope [Alethorpe] doe praye a redresse of these manifold open injuries and wronges done unto us, whose names are hereunder written, by one Wylliam Dye of the same towne. First the unjust detayneing of an order set downe in writeing by the right worshipfull Sir Nathaniell Bacon knight for the equall and indifferent rayteinge of all bills and taxations, which should be att any tyme layde amongest us, which wryteinge he now flattlye denyeth to have, seekeing to suppresse the same, so as for want of the good direction therin contayned we are by the said Dye continually oppressed in the collectinge and gathering of all town charges. Secondly the abuse in surcharging of our small common with his sheepe, to the extreame starving of all our great cattell, against all coullour of law equitye or reason. Thirdly he keepeth up fences against our common, butt purposelye layeth open his home yardes and other groundes so as our cattell going upon our common doe daylye against our wills run into his daunger, and that only through his owne default, when they are so hunthed and beaten, bayted and otherwise abused, as is incredible that any Christian should offer the like unto dum beastes, and intollerable for us to endure. Fourthly whereas many of his groundes lay open heretofore, for the maintenance of his fold course, he hath now inclosed the moste part of them, and keepeth them severall to him selfe all the yeare, and yett notwithstanding doth mantayne his full number of sheepe as ever he did before to our utter undoeing yf it be not redressed. Fiftlye he breaketh up other mens severall groundes for the more freer passage and ease of his sheepe, and as it is well to be proved, even att this tyme doth drive over their new sowen winter corne and into their home yardes and orchardes, eatinge spoylinge and breaking downe their new sett griftes [*grafts*] and plantes and saith he will doe it, for that he knoweth we, your poore orators, wante abillitye to contend with him att the common lawe, and further doth animate and incourage his soones and servauntes to beate and abuse us his poore neighbours affirming openly in threatninge and menacing sort, that he shall, and will breake our hart stringes whereof wee as poore subjectes doe by your worships good meanes crave redresse before any further inconvenience doe ensue, and we your poore injured neighbours will not faille to praye for the prosperous continuance of our gratious Soveraigne his good

[326] It seems likely that the action was that of James Pointer, rector of Blakeney and Wiveton, who cited a number of his parishioners, including Braddock, in the ecclesiastical courts for alleged slander: see The Commission for Causes Ecclesiastical to Norfolk J.P.s, 15 June 1605, below, pp.185–6.

[327] Dating: dated from Nathaniel Bacon's knighthood.

and wholesome lawes, and the good health and wellfare of all yow his Majesties justices longe to continew.

Undated.

Signed: Henry Greene, Wyll[*ia*]m Ellis and George Blackburne and Edmunde Ellis.

Endorsed in Martin Man's hand: Information of the inhabitauntes of Althorp against W. Dye.

1 p. SRO (I) HA411/1/11/2/1/3. Printed, *NA* x, 1888, pp.150–51.

John Hunt and William Bulwer to Sir Nathaniel Bacon

[*Post 1604, mid July*].[328] Good Sir Nathaniell Bacon, mortall men shoulde not have immortall suites, & suites commenced by fathers, & continewed by ther children in an uncristian & uncharitable succession, doe often tymes ravall up, & undermyne the fathers estates, before they dye, & in the ende, doe utterlie undoe ther heires by discent, when they be deade, a crosse, & a curse, that contention by Godes wrathfull ordinaunce bringe with yt, which you in your wisdom & experi-ence, hath sene to fall upon diverse families. Not far of, *Sic obduruit cor Pharaonis* [329] through the which, by excessive fees disbursed upon exceding lawiers, both Mr Bulwers familie & myne, shall hereafter fare the worse, for pre-vention wherof at the first, before eny suite was sett on foote betwin him & me, I for my parte, made an overture of peace unto him, above 10 yeares since, to submitt all entended controversies, to eny men of worth & wisdom in all Norfolk, to decyde & censure the same. But Mr Bulwer then, before the walking spiritt of the landes in question was eny wise conjured, utterlie refused that my peace offer-ing, saying, he would not putt his coate to daying [*?dyeing*],[330] to never a man in England. Butt now of late (& sum whatt to late for us both) he hath chaunged his mynde, & out of his owen voluntarie, (the pleasingest motive that maie be) yt hath pleased him, to come walking unto me in the path waie of peace, protesting to embrace that peace now, which longe since was offered unto him, before eny money was spent, or rather spoyled at law. Requesting at my handes a submission & a compromise of all matters in difference betwixt us, to sume men of worship in the cuntre (lawiers excepted, the mynters of other mens coyne, out of the true owners purses, into ther owen). Gladlie I condescended to this his motion, as pro-ceding from God, & did putt upon him first, to chose one for him self, & I would seconde yt, suite & sorte an other of like qualitie & condicion. He, for him, chose Sir Nathaniell Bacon, a knight in his opinion without exception. And I purposing to chose one, that was *omni exceptione maior* & in all respectes sutable & sorteable that never would dissente in judgment, nor jar in the proceding, chose for me your worship, to be the judge, the justicer, & *honorarius arbiter*, of all our contro-versies. Att which my seconding choise Mr Bulwer was so well pleased, that

---

[328] Dating: dated from Nathaniel Bacon's knighthood.

[329] "Thus the heart of Pharoah was hardened". A reference to the Book of Exodus chaps 7–10.

[330] For the possible significance of the colour of a coat see note to letter from Farmer to Bacon, 25 February 1603/4, above, p.75.

presentlie of[f] went our hattes, on went our handes & hartes to a pacification, which was the first tyme, that ever we twoe shooke eyther handes or hartes together, making you by mutual & reciprocall consent, our judg, yf you please to assume that office upon you, *beati pacifici, exuenda est persona amici, et induenda judicis*, to ende as in a moment 10 yeares tedious & costlie suites, therby to geve better satisfaction to Mr Bulwer, concerning his supposed right & tytle to the landes in question by delivering your opinion therin, then eyther the Lord Chauncclor & the hiegh court of the Chauncery, by decre, inju[n]ction, & comission, <would> «could» doe, or then I cann doe, by payinge 200 markes out of the said landes, to his sister for hir mariag portion, & by spending in suite & otherwise, 400 markes more, *in toto* paid & spent out of my poor purse, twice as much money as the recovered landes be worth. Thus stand I, *de damno vitando*, a looser at the close, although I <have> gott sumwhat at the crushe. Thus contendeth he, *de irreparabili damno*, for lawiers have irrevocably gott his money. *Omnia vestigia antrorsum, nulla retrorsum, opera et impensa periit.*[331] Fearing tediousnes I submitt my self to your censure, & you & yours I doe recomend to the protection of th'Almightie, together with my duety remembred to the good Lady Bacon. Yours at comaunde.

Undated. Signed: John Hunt, Will[ia]m Bulwer.[332]
Addressed: To the right worshipfull Sir Nathaniell Bacon knight.
Endorsed in Martin Man's hand: de Hunt.
1½ pp. Folger L.d. 365.

Dr John Hunt and John Browne to Sir Nathaniel Bacon

[*Post 1604, mid July*].[333] Right worshipfull sir. So it is John Colffer of Briston[334] beinge yesterday at a courte leete there houlden for that mannor, chosen by generall consent of all the leeters twelve in number for one of the cunstables there this yeare, and being required and charged in his Majesties name to take his othe accordinglye, the said Colffer in contempt of that jurisdiccon and in evill example of all the then and there tennantes more then thirtye, did not only depart that courte disdainefully without licence, but utterlye refused to beare that office, so imposed uppon him. And bycause inferior authorities ought not to be made contemptible and elusorye in publique affayres, but hath been supported and assisted alwaies by superiour powers, they in their grave wisdomes and censures reprovinge suche scorners and forcinge them to conformitie, we your dutifull suppliantes lord

---

[331] *Omni exceptione maior*: without exception greater. *Honorarius arbiter*: honourable arbiter. *Beati pacifici, exuenda est persona amici, et induenda judicis*: of the blessed peacemaker, laying aside the character of a friend and taking on that of a judge. *De damno vitando*: for the avoidance of harm. *De irreparabile damno*: irreparably harmed. *Omnia vestigia antrorsum, nulla retrorsum, opera et impensa periit*: all the effort is behind us, none in front, trouble and expense have passed away.

[332] The parties involved are almost certainly Dr John Hunt of Briston, master in Chancery, and William Bulwer, lord of the manor of Wood Dalling (Blomefield, viii, p.321). Briston and Wood Dalling are neighbouring parishes south of Holt.

[333] Dating: dated from Nathaniel Bacon's knighthood.

[334] A principal ratepayer in the parish in 1601 (*BP*, iv, p.188).

and steward of the jurisdiccon aforesaide do beseeche *vestrum brachium implorando*[335] your assistance to compell by your superior power the said Colffer to take uppon him the seid office and to be sworn thereunto. This our humble request we comend and comit to your grave consyderaccon and yours and your good ladies helthe and happines to the Almightyes proteccon. Your dutifull suppliantes.

Undated. Signed: Jo. Hunt, John Browne.

Addressed: To the right worshipfull Sir Nathaniell Bacon knight att Stifkey.

Reprinted from *Stiffkey Papers*, p.50; printed *NA*, x, 1888, pp.162–3.

Petition. Townsmen of Eccles to Sir Nathaniel Bacon

[*Post 1604, mid July*].[336] The humble peticion for the poor towneshipp of Eccles.

Shewinge unto you the right worshippfull the wronges and injuries we are offerid by your farmours John James and Robert James in breakeing and plowed upp the heath groundes wheare not only we but our predecessors from tyme to tyme <out> «with»out mynd of man have had our common feed according to our aunceent use & custome. We most humble beseche your good worshipp that we may have a spedie reformacion of theise wronges without the which it is lyke to be to the utter undoinge of <we> «us» your poore tenauntes & our children forever. If it be your good worshippes pleasuer <shall go on in this sort> & mynde that your farmours shall go on in this sort then we most humble beseche your favour & kyndnes without any offence that we your poore tenauntes may trie that which we hope is our right.

Undated.

Signed: By me Jeames Plowman, by me Robert Jolly, Stephen Carlton; [*by marks:*] Thomas Cooe, Robart Barnerd, Henery Wright, Willeam Taylor, Rychard Elcey, John Younges, John Leder, Thomas Nele, John Coulson.

Addressed: To the right worshipfull Sir Nathaniell Bacon knyght.

Endorsed in Martin Man's hand: A peticion by the inhabitantes of Eccles.

1 p. NRO MC 571/15 778X4. Printed, *Stiffkey Papers*, pp.50–1.

George Feake, vicar of Wighton, to Sir Nathaniel Bacon

[*1604, mid July <-Θ-> 1606/7, March 7*].[337] Right worshipfull , I receyved your letter, which intimateth your purpose to my Lord Bishoppe for Mr Burward[338] to serve at Wighton under me, which thing needed not, for he might have done if he

---

[335] "Imploring your support".

[336] Dating: dated from Nathaniel Bacon's knighthood. The petition may relate to the 104 acres in Eccles leased to Stephen Smith of Botesdale on 26 June 1605 for 10 years (below, pp.194–5), in which case it would date from before June 1605 or after June 1615.

[337] Dating: these limits are set by Nathaniel Bacon's knighthood and the burial of George Feake at Wighton on 7 March 1606/7 (NRO PD 553/1). However, the letter may well date from after Robert Burward's ordination, see note immediately below.

[338] A John Burward was the long-standing rector of Baconsthorpe, but it seems more likely from the context that this is his son, Robert Burward (aged 18 in 1593), curate of Wells, ordained priest in September 1604, later rector of Caldecote and vicar of Hunstanton (Barton, *Anthony Harison*, i, p.189; Venn, *Al. Cant.*, i, p.269).

would, but refused & would not, but upon such condicions as was not fitt for me
to condisend unto as shalbe proved upon dyvers oathes, if there were cause that any
prevented him, but himself, is not true, and that Mr Same[339] his carriadge in that
respect is censured, I doe protest the truthe, & wilbe sworne & others that knowe
it, that it was honest, justifiable, & such as no indifferent man can disalowe, never
prejudicing him, nor any other, but only himself howsoever your worship hath
bene informed by some, of whome Sct Hierome [*St Jerome*] spake well *Vilium est*
hominum alios viles facere etc. & Seneca *Quid interest an Deum neges an infames.*[340]
But it is well knowen you worship would not willingly receyve a false tale, as
Exodus 23.1.[341] much lesse beleeve it, which in Deuteronomy 13.12. by those
wordes, 'Seeke search & inquire diligently',[342] we are admonished that it is a fault
to condemn before we knowe, & to beleeve what ever we heare by & by, Syrach
11.7.[343] Blame no man before the matter be inquired etc, & Cicero *Nervus est sapi-*
entie non temere redere.[344] That the towen hath had no preacher a great while, it
<is> cannot be trulie sayd, but that we have had many sermons, & every moneth a
great while, by on man, if there were no other, & at this present have on[e] alowed
to helpe me that preacheth every Sabaothe, but none will serve except he be at the
disposicion of such as shall not prevaile with me further then I like well of & I have
faithfully past my promise to Mr Same, & I must & will honestly according to a
good conscience perfourme itt & leave the burthen to his conscience to provyde
when I am gone, & for makeing marchandyse of itt, I have to do that which none
shall have any just cause to disalowe & so with my dutie remembered, I humbly
take my leave. Wighton.

Undated. Signed: Your wurships olde poore neighbour George Feke.
Addressed: To the right worshipfull Sir Nathaniel Bacon knight.
Endorsed in Martin Man's hand: Mr Feake.
1 p. NRO RAY (4) 34.

John Buck, vicar of Langham, to Sir Nathaniel Bacon

[*1604, mid July* <-Θ-> *1610, September 8*].[345] Right worshipful Sir Nathanyel
Bacon my humble dutie remembered unto you. The cause of my writing unto you
is to let you onarstand that one Clarke[346] maketh chalenes [*challenge*] to my house

---

[339] Probaby Ralph Sayme, rector of Cockthorpe, licensed to preach in January 1602/3, formerly vicar of
Binham (*BP*, iv, p.16n.; Venn, *Al. Cant.*, iv, p.11).

[340] In the King James version: "It is customary for worthless men to vilify others"; "What is the
difference, whether you deny God or denigrate him?"

[341] In the King James version: "Thou shalt not raise a false report: put not thine hand with the wicked to
be an unrighteous witness."

[342] In the King James version these words come in Deuteronomy 13.14.

[343] From the book known as "The Wisdom of Jesus the son of Sirach", more familiarly known as
"Ecclesiasticus", one of the books of the Biblical Apocrypha. The verse alluded to here is rendered in the
King James version as "Blame not before thou has examined the truth: understand first, and then rebuke".

[344] "It is the strength of wisdom, not to respond blindly."

[345] Dating: these limits are set by Nathaniel Bacon's knighthood and the institution of the new vicar of
Langham Regis, James Pearson, on 8 September 1610 (NRO DN/REG 16, ff.15, 20).

[346] Possibly a son of the Mr Clark of Cockthorpe who had grain stored at Langham in 1595 (*BP*, iii,
p.295).

in Langhame which house I bought of his father and as I understand he make reporte that his father was not payde for the house and also that I should detaine and kepe backe those thinges due then to his father but as I shall answer before God at the dreadful day of Judgment when the secretes of ale hartes shalbe dicclosed that he was paide his ful due with advantage, for the prise of his house was £30. He was to have ale my tythes at Langhame with a vicrage and ale other profhetes belonging to it for 3 yeares which he had for the ful and I did not kepe backe any of thenges and at the thre yeares end I demanded of him what he did make the liveng worth and he tould me his owne self that he made it worth £12 a yeare so by his own speach he made it worth £6 bettare then his house. This I hope your good worshipe shale ondarstand how I ame wronged in this accones. I desire your god worshipe that you woulde be so frindly to me as to let your stuard of your corte undarstand the truth and move him to eus favarably justes [*justice*] and both my self wife and children shalbe bonde to pray God for your good prosperitie heare upon earth and after this lif ended to bring your soule to everlasting lif [*word smudged*] kingdome.

Undated. Signed: By me John Bucke clarke. *Holograph.*
Addressed: To his right worshipful Sir Nathanyel Bacon.
Endorsed in Martin Man's hand: Mr Buck.
½ p. NRO Townshend Additional Box 113.

Order. Muster Commisioners and J.P.s to the chief constables of the Hundred of North Greenhoe to pay arrears to the muster master, Captain Herbert Bozom

1604, July 17. Wheras we have formanly sent forth our warantes for the speedy collectinge of all arerages[347] dew to <Mr> Captain Bozonne one of the muster masters for this county and as it semeth you have littell regarded the same he beinge still unpaid wher upon complaynt hath bene made by him unto the Lords of his Majesties most honorable Privey Counsell of your gret necligence herein, insomuch that they have derected ther letters unto us the commissioners & the rest of the justices here assembled proportinge, that in regard of dismisinge him of his place & disburdeninge <him> of the conttery of that chardge wee should see him speedely satisfyed of all the arrerages dew to him for his formar service. These are therfore by vertue thereof straightly to charge & command you presently upon receypt hereof all excuses sett appart to collect & gather within your Hundered of Northgrenhoo all such arrerages as are & were dew to him at or before the feast of St Michell tharchangell last past & the same so gathered to pay it over unto the said Har[*bert*] Bozonne at Sir Nathanyell Bacon[348] his house the 14 of August next by tenne of the clock in the fore noone & we are further to signefy unto you that the Lord Chefe Justice [*Sir John Popham*] at this last Assizes did <openly> publikly pronounce that yf aney should refuse to make rates or to contrebut unto this

---

347 For objections to paying for the muster masters, see Orders of 12 September 1603, and for the arrears, see Memorandum of arrears due, *Post* 29 September 1603, above, pp.44–6. For the controversy over the payment of military rates see Smith, "Militia Rates", pp.93–110, especially pp.93–100.
348 This is the first precisely dated reference to Nathaniel Bacon as a knight.

service that forthwith you bring them before us the commissioners & justices of the peace & upon ther refusall to be committed or otherwyse to lay in bond to answer the same before his Lordship at the next Assizes houlden for this county & hereof have you a speciall care as you will avoyd the danger that thereof may insew. From Thetfor the 17 of July 1604. Your loving frendes. [*Signed*:] Arthur Heningham, Henrye Gaudy, Bassingborne Gaudey, Phillip Woodhouse, Clemant Spilman, Le Strange Mordant, William Yelverton.[349]

Copy.
Endorsed in Martin Man's hand: Captain Bosome.
1 p. BL Add. 63101 f.32.

Reckoning between Sir Nathaniel Bacon and Richard Spratt

1604, July 18. A reckoning betwen Sir Nathaniel Bacon knight and Richard Spratt gent set downe 18 July 1604.
Sir Nathaniel Bacons demandes:

Re[*maining*] due of £30 lent Mr Spratt 29 *Junii* 1603 & paiable 1 August 1603 £10

Re[*maining*] more due of £40 lent 9 January & paiable *ultimo* February 1603 £20

Paid to Mr Bolton for fynes & amerciamentes due in my masters shrievalty to be allowed by Mr Spratt £6

Paid to Sir Myles Corbett being mony recieved by Mr Spratt for an execution £3 6s. 6d.

Paiable to Mr Holland upon an execution which my master hath undertaken to satisfie £9

Paiable for the recusantes money by my master £25

<Paiable> «Paid» for Mr Sprattes dett to Mistres Badiscrofte £29 3s. 3d.[350]

Due from Mr Spratt for the stewardship at Michaelmas 1603 £23 6s. 8d., at Christmas £5, at Our Lady £5, & at midsummer 1604 £5. In all £38 6s. 8d.

Paiable to Mr Mapes for the shrievalty 40s.

Summa £142 16s. 5d.

Mr Sprattes demandes
To be allowed for Fakenham lease £70
To be allowed for Metholde lease £60

Summa £130
Rest   £12 16s. 5d.

[*Inserted at the foot.*] More for 3 monthes
Use of the £29 3s. 3d. to Mr Badiscrofte *viz. a* 3 May *usque* 3 August at 4s. 10d., 14s. 6d.

---

[349] The first four signatories were commissioners for musters as well as J.P.s. Presumably with their colleagues they had gathered at Thetford for the Assizes, which may have been held at Thetford this summer because of plague in Norwich.

[350] For this debt see Henry Spendlove to Bacon and to Martin Man, 12 June and 18 August 1604, above, p.110, below, p.124.

[*On the dorse:*] Paiable to Mr Farrington for which my master standeth surety £78
And to Mr Robert Wood likewise, besides charges in suite £80

                              Summa £170 16*s*. 5*d*.

More for use to Mr Farrington of £78 from the 3 of July 1604 «till the 3 January 1604» £3 18*s*.
Paid more to Mr Woodes £25 17*s*.
<More to Mr Mapes 40*s*.>
More to Mr Funsten £11 10*s*.
More charges of suite in Mr Woodes cause disbursed to Mr Franckling & Mr Kynge 15*s*. 2*d*.

                        Summa totalis £213 11*s*. 1*d*. *inde*

To be allowed for the roialties of Methold £20
More assured by Webster & paiable at Our Lady 1605 £90
Paid by «Mr» Sybsey for the stewardship £3

                              Summa £113
                        Rem[*aining*] £100 11*s*. 1*d*.

In Martin Man's hand.
Endorsed: Mr Spratt dett.
2 pp. Folger L.d.753.

Counterpart of assignment of lease of oak woods at Hindolveston

1604, July 24. *Calendar*: Sir Nathaniell Bacon of Stiffkey, knight, assigns to Raphe Symondes[351] of Hindolveston, esquire, for £200 the remainder of a lease of the right to cut and cart oak timber in the greater and lesser woods of Hindolveston (otherwise known as the east and west woods) for a period of 21 years at a yearly rent of £4, granted to Bacon by the Dean (Thomas Dove) and Chapter of Norwich Cathedral on 26 November 1595.

Signed and sealed: Radulphus Symonds.
Witnesses: Thomas Utber, Martyn Man, Robert Styleman.
Endorsed in Martin Man's hand: The assignment of Hildoveston woodes to Mr Raffe Symondes 24 *Julii* 1604.
1 parchment. NRO RAY (6) 19.

List of Thomas Haylock's debts

[*1604, August*].[352] A note of such sommes of mony as Thomas Haylocke oweth unto those men hereunder named:
    Item I owe unto William Tidd of Welles which I stand in a bond of £10 for the payment of £5.
    Item I was constrayned for to take up thirtie poundes more into which some he forced me to take 40 combes of mault the price at 10*s*. the combe, which came to the some of <twen> £20, and £10 I receyved which some came to £30 and then I

---

[351] See 13 April - May 1604, above, p.120.
[352] Dating: dated from Certificate to Sir Roger Wilbraham, 23 August 1604, below, pp.125–6.

entred into a bond of £60 for the payment of £30.

Item I stand bound in another of £16 for the payment of £8.

Item I ought unto Hew Dike ever since our last Ladie Daye was a twelvmonthe 4 score poundes.

Item I ought unto Henery at St Gregorie last past was a twelvemonthe £20.

Item I ought unto Mr Whitinge in *anno domini* 1601 £40 whereof I have payd £16 by ten poundes at one time and £6 at another time so rest unto Mr Whitinge «with the use» the some of £32 10*s*.

Item I oughe unto Thomas Fresson of Norwiche the some of £22.

Item I ought unto John Hunter ever since our last Ladie past £10.

Item I oughe unto Richard Gouldsmithe the some of £20.

Item I oughe unto my brother John Haylocke the some of £25.

At the foot in Martin Man's hand: £252 10*s*.
His lease worth 200 markes.

Undated.
Endorsed in Martin Man's hand: Thomas Hailockes dettes.
1 p. NRO MS 20521, 132X6.

Complaints of Thomas Clarke in a mediation involving Robert Barnard

[*1604, c. August*].[353] A not of certayne wronges offred by Mr Barnard[354] to me.

First he locked «me» my wife & servantes out of my mawlthowse contrary to his promise. To my «great» losse as it shall appeare.

More he locked me out of my barnes and wowld not suffer me to make the best of my strawe wheras I was to take bowllokes to winter to the valwe of £5.

More he tooke from me my horsses & kept them three weekes & more & plowed his owne landes and sent them home all, only the beste which he kepeth still untill this day which is a great part of the cawse that my landes lye unsowne to my great losse contrary to his promise.

More he tooke from me my <net> neette[355] in the begining of Maye when they wear at the best and kept them 25 dayes which he mad of them very near £5 as it shall apperre.

More he did take frome me threschor [*three score*] [*word deleted*] «combes» of barly which he had promised me I showld have had for my seeds and by that meanes I was driven to leave my landes unsowne to my great losse.

Neyther was he to sell any barly at all but showld have bene towrned into mawlt which was to my losse.

More he sent fower horsses to my stable & ther they remayned for the space of three weekes and weer fedd with such horsemett as I had to my losse.

More he did sett a false man who had the kepinge of his corne that did sell away part therof as I will prove to my losse.

---

[353] Dating: dated with reference to Memoranda and Agreement of 7 August - 6 September 1604, below, pp.123–4.

[354] Robert Barnard of Langham (*BP*, iv, p.2n.).

[355] Cattle. This implies that in this season they were most productively in milk.

More diverse wronges as I will lett your worshipp[356] understand.

Undated. Unsigned.
Endorsed in Martin Man's hand: Thomas Clarke.
1 p. NRO BL/BC/6/9.

The case between Mrs Bosome and George Gardiner

[*1604, August*].[357] Remembrances upon the cause betwen Mistress Bosome & G. Gardyner.[358]

That Gardyner was trusted by Mistress Bosome to take a bond from Mr Banckes for £40 to thuse of her sonne Christopher Hall, and the bond to be taken in the name of Mr Drury <& himself> «& Mr Gryme», but taken to him self alone, & delivered Mr Banckes bond.

Thus appeared to be in Mr Banckes his handes of the dett with interest £57 15s. And in Gardyners handes £11 10s.

Mr Grymes witnesse: that Gardyner had consented to this agrement: *viz.* to repaie the childes mony upon delivery to him of the bondes entred to Mr Davy with Mr Bosome. After desired the mony to remain upon good security which being yealded by Mr Drury, Gardyer failed of security.

Gardyner confessed he had power over the bond entred by Mr Banckes to D. Tonge to govane it.

For order: the bondes of Mr Davyes to be delivered out to Gardyner and security to be given by Gardyner for his part & Mr Banckes for the rest.

Mr Banckes to be discharged of danger by his bonde, bicause the gentlewoman, & others in the childes behalf, required him to retayne the mony in his handes.

Gardener gave the letter to Mr Bedingfeld upon his delivery of his informacion before the commissioners. And departed without leave.

Gardener pretended to holde the mony for his indempnity in regard of the bond to Mr Davy. And had besides a mortgage of Mr Bosomes lande for his security.

/G. £11 10. R. £57 15./

Undated. Unsigned. In Martin Man's hand.
Endorsed in Martin Man's hand: Inter Gardiner & Hall.
1 p. L.d.653.

Depositions in an arbitration between Christopher Hall, plaintiff, and Luke Banks and Daniel Tonge, defendants

1604, August 3. *Calendar:* Depositions taken at Wells before Sir Nathaniel Bacon, knight, and Richard Backham (Beckham), gent, by virtue of a commission out of

---

[356] Presumably Nathaniel Bacon, given his involvement with arbitration and mediation.

[357] Dating: dated with reference to the Depositions of 3 August 1604 between Hall, Banks and Tonge, immediately below.

[358] George Gardiner, gent, of Heydon, an attorney. Bacon opposed his ordination in 1609 on the grounds that he had "lived verie contentiously with his neighbours", had "sondry tymes ben called in question for his miscariage in his suites" and was likely to "prove a scandalous minister" (NRO BL/BC/7/23). Again, this appears to be a document arising from Bacon's role as an arbitrator.

the Court of Requests between Christofer Hall, gent, plaintiff, and Luke Banckes and Danyell Tonge, defendants, as follows:[359]

Depositions for the plaintiff are made by George Gryme of Foulsham, gent, aged about 47; Margaret Bozome, wife of Adam Bozome of Wendling, gent; Christofer Bedingfeld of Walsingham Magna, gent, aged about 43; and Robert Drury of Docking, gent, aged about 47.

Depositions for the defendants are made by William Bacon of Corpusty, gent, aged about 40; Margaret Bozome (re-examined); John Coates of Sharington, yeoman, aged 50; and Arthur Funteyn of W[ood] Dalling, gent, aged 35.

Evidence for the plaintiff suggests that about six years since, with the help of Margaret Bozome, his mother, Hall lent £40 to Luke Banckes, who entered a bond to Robert Drury and possibly George Gryme to Hall's use. The bond remained in Margaret's hands and Drury did not know the details. About three years ago George Gardener, who was married to Margaret's niece, persuaded her that Drury needed the bond in order to take better assurances; but instead he delivered it to Banckes in exchange for a new bond in his own name for £50 (£2 being remitted), claiming falsely that he had Margaret's consent to this. Gardener later got Banckes to transfer the bond again to Daniel Tonge (the debt, with interest, now amounting to £55), without assurance of repayment to the plaintiff. Tonge was bound to Christofer Bedingfeld, as surety for Gardener, for sums of £20 and £45; he and an associate, Rayner, had Gardener arrested in Norwich for failing to provide assurances for their indemnity.

Robert Drury further testifies that Gardener had also entered a bond to pay him or Gryme £60 within three years of the decease of Adam Bozome, with proviso that he be discharged of three other bonds to William Davy of Stanfield, gent, relating to £50 to be paid in three instalments over the same period. He was also bound in £20 to pay Margaret Bozome £6 a year for three years after Adam's death. Meeting Gardener in Norwich, Drury had agreed not to press for payment on condition of good assurances.

Evidence from the defendants' witnesses includes the fact that Christofer Bedingfeld had two executions against Tonge for Gardener's debts, secured by two bonds for payment of £65. Tonge paid £40 on execution, and borrowed £25 from John Coates, which he said was also to meet Gardener's obligations. Gardener set over the bond for £52 10s. from Banckes to Tonge in consideration for the bonds to Bedingfeld. Long before this Gardener had agreed to cancel a bond by which Banckes was bound to him for £50 owed to Charles Suckling, gent, for a land purchase; a new long-dated bond was to be substituted, but the agreement was not carried out, because Banckes failed to provide sufficient security.

Signed: [1] *By witnesses after their depositions: Per me Georgium Gryme,* [*by mark:*] Margaret Bozome, [*Christofer*] Bedingfeild, Rob[*er*]t Drury, *per me Will*[*elmu*]*m*

---

[359] A referral for toleration—extension of time—for the payment of the debts of Daniel Tonge is recorded as having been made in Requests in March 1603/4 (Hoyle *et al., Heard Before the King*, p.35, no.493). However, Bacon and Beckham are not named as the commisioners and Tonge is the plaintiff, not the defendant.

Bacon, [*by mark.*] Jo[*hn*] Coates, *per Arthurum Founteyn;* [2] *At the bottom of each page.* Rich[*ard*] Beckham.
In Martin Man's hand.
9½ pp. SRO (B) E3/43/3.

Memorandum concerning the mediation of a dispute between Robert Barnard and Thomas Clark

1604, August 7 - September 6. Remembrances 7 August 1604.[360]

Inter Robert Barnard & Thomas Clark.

Memorandum that Mr Clerk offreth to prove that Grixe of Alborough[361] offered 5*s.* 8*d.* for the barley. And Mr Barnard solde it for 5*s.* 6*d. viz.* 60 combes. And Mr Clerk rode to Alborough & procured the chapman to come over.

The dett £250.

80 combes wheate rem[*aining*]. A chapman (Thomas Speller) procured by R. Barnard to buy it at 12*s.* but refused by Thomas Clark to lett him see the corne.

15 combes messlyn rem[*aining*].

The corne by estimation at £229 4*s.* 2*d.*

A horse at £4. A bull at 40*s.*

Strawe 21*s.* 2 calves 21*s.*

Otes 13 combes, 80 combes, 4 combes, 4 combes 2 bushels, 1 combe, 5 combes 1 bushel, 8 combes 1 bushel *di.* – 116 combes *di.* bushel, *inde* deduct 5 combes for measure.[362] Rem[*ainder*] 111 combes *di.* bushel.

All the peas rem[*ain*].

220[363] malt rem[*ain*].

R[*emembrance*] 6 September

R[*eceived*] £87 2*s.* 2*d.* for corne solde.

Unsigned. In Martin Man's hand.

Endorsed: Remembrances upon hearing the cause betwen R. Barnard & Thomas Clarke.

1 p. NRO RAY 257.

Agreement in a mediation between Thomas Clarke and Robert Barnard

1604, August 7 – September 6. 7 August 1604. Mr Clarkes demaundes.

For 340 combs malt at 6*s.*	£102
For 111 combs otes *di.* bushel at 4*s. le* comb	£22 4*s.* 6*d.*
For 95 combes 2 bushels wheate at 12*s.* a comb	£57 6*s.*
For messlyn 20 combs at 7*s.* 6*d.* a comb	£7 10*s.*
For peas 87 combs at 6*s.* a comb	£26 2*s.*
For 60 combs barly at [*blank*]	£16 10*s.*
For a horse	£4

---

360 See also Complaints of Thomas Clarke of *c.*August 1604, above, pp.120–1.
361 Probably Aldborough near Aylsham, Norfolk.
362 To allow for differences in measurement.
363 In the original 'Cv^{xx}', i.e. a long hundred (=120) and five score.

For a bull	40s.
For 2 calves	21s.
For strawe	21s.

For horsemeate.[364]
For the use of his kyne [*cattle*]for 20 dayes.
For the use of his maulting house.
For the use of the barne & want of strawe.
For the use of horses 3 weekes.

/£239 14s. 6d./

[*Postscript*]: It is agreed 6 September 1604 betwen Robert Barnard gent & Thomas Clarke as followeth *viz.* the said Robert Barnard doth accept in full discharge of a debt of £250 due unto him from the said Thomas Clerk the £239 14s. 6d. demaunded as above by Thomas Clerk. And in discharge therof, as also of all other demaundes agreeth to seale him a speciall acquittance. And the said Thomas Clarke agreeth to seale the like acquittance unto the said Robert Barnard.

In Martin Man's hand.
Witnesses. Tho[*mas*] Kinges,[365] Martyn Man.
1 p. NRO BL/BC/6/10.

Henry Spendlove to Martin Man

1604, August 18. I received a letter from my cozin Mr Richard Bachecrofte of late,[366] whereby I perceive that he hath intelligence from your maister, that the money due to my cozin by Mr Sprattes bande [*bond*], (wherein also your master is bounde) is readie for him if he woulde sende for it to Stukie [*Stiffkey*]. And for that the bonde is in my custodie, woulde have me to come thether for [the] said money, which desire because I can not yet accomplishe by reason of urgent busines, & I see that he hath gret occation to use his money, I praye you therefore good Mr Mann entreate Sir Nathaniell Bacon that I maye receive the saide money at your sister Peckafordes house in Norwiche,[367] or at some other place in Norwiche where he shall thinke fitt, & upon the receipte of the money I will deliver his saide bande God willinge. The residue of the some due upon the said obligation the iii daye of this instante moneth, with the interest for the same, amounteth unto £29 17s. 9d., & I did certefie you the laste terme at London by

---

364 No sums are given for the final five entries.

365 The Thomas Kinges appearing throughout this volume is generally Thomas Kinges, gent (d.1618, formerly yeoman), of Morston, who named one of his sons Nathaniel. From as early as 1577 he can probably best be regarded as one of Nathaniel's 'extraordinary' servants: never resident at the Hall, but always about its owner's business and often at his side, even in London. Socially he was widely rooted in the community: uncle to Martin Man, witness to the wills of at least six of his more substantial neighbours and acting as surety for others, he held the normal gamut of parish offices. (Stiffkey Database; *BP*, iii, pp.82, 272; NRO ANW 1618 f.34.) He may be the Thomas King who carried out surveys for Bacon (*BP*, iii, pp.290, 322) but should probably be distinguished from Thomas Kinges of Binham, gent, who was appointed attorney to deliver seisin in 1600 (*BP*, iv, pp.125–6). Either may be Bacon's "understeward", domestic or manorial, mentioned on p.145.

366 For Spendlove's previous letter of 12 June 1604 concerning this debt see above, p.110.

367 Cecily Man, who married Edmund Peckover of Norwich.

my letter howe it groweth to be thus muche (excepte onlye for the laste quarter betweine the iii of Maye & the iii of this Auguste). Thus prayinge you to remember my dutie to your master, with my right hartie commendation to your self, I leave you to the gratious protection of God Almightie. Wimondham this xviii of Auguste 1604. Yours assuredly to use.

[*Postscript*]: I purpose to enquire of your sister Peckaforde for aunswere of this my letter therfore good Mr Man let me heere from you touchinge this busines as soone as you can.

Signed: Henry Spendlove. *Holograph.*

Addressed: To my good freinde Mr Martin Man, servante to the right worshipfull Sir Nathaniell Bacon knight.

Endorsed in Martin Man's hand: Mr Spendlove.

1 p. Folger L.d.555.

Certificate to Sir Roger Wilbraham, Master of Requests, concerning Thomas Haylock's debts

1604, August [*23*].[368] Sir, wee receyved your direccion, signifieing his Majesties pleasure, that wee should call before us the creditors of one Thomas Hailock, & treate & persuade with them, to accept such reasonable satisfaccion «for their debtes», as his estate may be anie wayes able to performe. And to certefye if wee founde anie obstinate in so charitable a corse. It maie please you to understande, that wee have proceded accordingly. And amongst other the creditors <whome wee founde tractable>, there is one William Tidd, with whome wee could not prevaile, to accept of such a satisfaccion, as wee do judge to be both just & reasonable. And the state of the matter thus standeth. The due dett from Hailock fell out to be in all £43, wherof there was lent by Tidd in money £23.[369] And £20 <he> «Hailock» was forced for the supplie of his want to take «in ««20 quarters of »»malt» <15s.> at 20s. the quarter <at Tiddes handes>, when by the report of honest witnesses the ordinary price was «but» 13d. 4d. «the quarter» and by Tiddes owne confession before us but 16s. the quarter. Wee persuaded Tidd to content him self with his due dett (<allowing him> «without abatment of» his extraordinary gayne upon <«bargayne of»> the mault <bargayne>) and <which> «allowed him» interest (according to the lawe) for the forbearing «of» his dett, from the tyme it was due, & <with> such costes of suite, as he hath ben at for the recovery of the same. But he refused to yealde unto it unles one John Hailock (the brother of this peticioner) would release the said Tidd of a bargayne passed betwen the said Tidde and John Hailock, wherin the peticioner had nothing to do, and the matter besides is of more value & importance unto John Hailock, then the wholle dett of the peticioner to Tidd. And thus referring the poore man to receive your <good> <«further»> advice & furtherance for relief in this case, wee hartely commende you to Gods protection. From Stifky this [*blank*] of August 1604. Your verie loving fryndes.

[368] Dating: dated from the final version, immediately below, and see further, c. 24 July 1605, below, p.198.

[369] See List of Thomas Haylock's debts, August 1604, above, pp.119–20.

[Postscript]: The <extremity> «some» which the said Tidd «now» offereth to take of the said Hailock & his suertyes ariseth by forfytures & charges in lawe to £93 10*s*. And the dett being £43 was due about May was twelvemoneth.

Unsigned draft in Martin Man's hand.

Endorsed: Tidde and Hailock. A certificate to Sir R. Wylb[*raham*].

1 p. NRO NRS 24660, 125X3.

Certificate to Sir Roger Wilbraham concerning Thomas Haylock's debts

1604, August 23. *Summary:* Final version of the above letter with minor variations in spelling and dated 23 August 1604.

Signed: Chris[*tofer*] Heydon, Henry Sydney, Na[*thaniel*] Bacon. *In Martin Man's hand.*

Addressed: To the right worshipfull Sir Roger Wylbraham knight one of the masters of his Highnes Cort of Requestes.

Endorsed: Certificate *pro* Thomas Hailock.

1 p. NRO MC 1370/8, 810X1.

Evidence of John Girdlestone against Ellen Howes

[*?1604, September*].[370] A condiscion betwix John Gyrdlelston and Ellyn Hous widowe for on cotteges hous in Salthous that the sayd Ellyn House showld give John Gyrdelston £11 5*s*. to be payd thirtie shillyng down and 30 shillyng a yeare begining at Michalmas in the yeare of Our Lord God 1603 and so 30 shilling a yeare till the som of a 11 pownes and 5 shillyng be payd wherupon shee bownd hur slif [*self*] [? *two words deleted*] by condiscion to repayer the hous in part of payment wittnes Robard Jarves gentleman stuward in the lord cort and Mr Par[371] hearin the condiscion and the full agrement betwix them, wherupon shee fle from hur bargany with thes word saying that shee will not paye for hur own. I cam according to my condiscion and to parforme my agrement I unshipted my slif and lost a vieng [*voyage*] of 19 shilling, for a hors hier 5*s*., for a «man» coming to [?]Lyn to bryng hym bod [*?back*] tow shilling. This was in the yeare of Our Lord God 1603 morover I come agayn the next yeare foling [*following*] for to see if shee wold com to hur bargany and parform hur condistion and shee would not wherupon I entred, wherof my charges comes to fifte shilling and my hors hier 5*s*. which I have lost by unplasen of my slif of a Bareck viog and so bak to the Sheldes[372] this have I lost by coming to hur for to hould my bargany whe[*r*]upon shee will stand to non. I payd in *anno* 1602 the full some of twinte shilling in Ruchard Making hous in Slatthous [*Salthouse*] wittnes Ruchard Making and Robard Making. Morover shee owes me for 3 yeares fearm wanting on[*e*] quarter at tirtten shilling and fower pence the yeare.

---

[370] Dating: dated from agreement between Howes and Girdleston of 25 September 1604, below, p.130. See also above, 25 March 1603, pp.23–4.

[371] Almost certainly Christopher Parr, gent, of Salthouse, aged 65 in 1631 (TNA PRO DL4/80/1), referred to in 1611 as attorney in the Court of Common Pleas (Maggs, 471, item 2644), and a kinsman of Martin Man (BL Add. 63081, ff.94–95).

[372] A voyage to Berwick-on-Tweed and back to Shields.

Undated. Unsigned.
Endorsed in Martin Man's hand: Writinges betwen Girdleston & Howse.
1 p. NRO RAY 249.

Articles concerning inns and alehouses

1604, September 1.[373] Articles to be inquired of by the constables churchwardens and overseers for the poore in everie towne, where innes, alehouses, and cannykers[374] be. Wherof certificat is to be made, when thei shall be required, from tyme to tyme.[375]

1. *Imprimis* whither anie person do sell beere or ale without license there.

2. Item whither anie inkeeper, alehouse keper or cannyker there, do suffer anie person, dwelling in the towne, to remayne & contynue drinking or tipling in their houses. Except such as the statute doth permytt namely 1) Such as are invited by travailers, & shall accompany them onely during their necessary abode there. 2) Also, labouring & handicraftes men, in markett townes, that upon the usuall working daies, for an houre at dynner tyme, shall take their dyet in an alehouse. 3) Also, labourers & workmen, who having taken worke by the daie, or by the greate[376] in the said townes, shall during their contynuing in worke, sojorne, lodge, & victuell in the said houses. 4) And also, upon other urgent & necessary occasions to be allowed by two justices of peace.

3. Item whither anie inkeper, alehousekeper or cannyker, shall utter, or sell lesse, then one quarte of the best beere or ale, for a pennye, or lesse then two quartes of small bere or ale for a pennye. And to be informed herof, to view the pottes whither thei be of the assise or not.

4. Item whither the beere or ale solde in the said houses do not exceede the assise enjoyned to the brewers, which is, stronge beere at 6*s.* the barrell, and small beere at 4*s.* the barrell.

5. Item whither anie person dwelling in anie other townes adjoyning do resort to the said houses, & contynue tipling & drinking there, and whither anie of the towne shall sende for bere & ale to their houses from the innes or alehouses, to tipple & contynue drinking. Thereby to defeate the intent & good meaning of the lawe.

6. Item to certefie the names of some persons that maie testefye the offences comitted against anie of thes <assi> articles.

---

[373] Although the endorsement has been crossed through, there seems no reason to question the date.

[374] Canniker: in this volume a person licensed to supply beer or ale without keeping an alehouse or providing food, rather than the premises where this was done. The term seems to have derived from association with the "cannikin", the name for a small can or drinking vessel. The implication is that consumers had to take their own cannakins along to be filled, as there was no provision for drinking on the premises. A sense of the clinking pots being carried to the canniker is reinforced by a contemporary reference in Shakespeare, "And let me the cannakin clinke, clinke", "Othello", II, iii, 71 (*OED sub* "cannikin"). Godly magistrates and ministers are likely to have preferred cannikers to alehouses. They met a practical need but they also avoided the opportunity for alcohol-induced socialisation in gatherings that challenged godly culture with the alternative culture of the alehouse.

[375] This order arises from the instructions issued by Lord Chief Justice Popham at the Assizes. See 6 March 1603/4, above, p.79.

[376] For the whole piece of work.

Unsigned. In Martin Man's hand.
Endorsed: <The justices proceeding concerning innes & alehouses at Holt 1 September 1604> Copy of the articles to be delivered to the constables.
1 p. NRO RAY 259. Printed, *Stiffkey Papers*, pp.55–6.

Evidence of Cicely Bangey concerning her excommunication

1604, September 1. *Anno domini 1604, 1 Septembris.* Cicelie Bangeye widowe of Holt saythe that about Lent last past John Downing of the same towne cam unto her house dwelling then alone in the towne house about 9 of the clock at night and would have had to doo with her, continewinge theare about the space of fouer howers, and did <force> wrestell with her to the same ende untill she was out of breathe, so as she was constrayned to runn away into the towne to her sisters house for her safetie.

Item she saythe that about the monthe of Julie last past the said John Downing hearing that the «sayd» Cicelie Bangeye had complayned unto her frendes and diverse of the towne of his misbehavour, then the said John Downing by the meanes of one Samper belonging to the Consistorie Court, procured a citation against the said Cicely to appeare at Norwich, which for that she did not, he procured an excommunication against her, and so was excommunicated, and so by reason of her povertie not hable to procuer her absolution remaynethe still excommunicate.

Signed: George Ledys,[377] Ric[*hard*] Snoden,[378] W[*illia*]m Dobson,[379] W[*illia*]m Broun;[380] [*by mark:*] Cicelie Bangey.
Endorsed in Martin Man's hand: Cicely Bangeys confession touching John Downing.[381]
1 p. BL Add. 63081 f.91.

Sir Edward Coke, Attorney-General, to Sir Miles Corbett and Sir Nathaniel Bacon

1604, September 1. "*After my verie hartie comendations, whereas before I had any-thing in Flitcham ... there was a sute moved and depending betwen my very good cosin & friend Mr Edward Paston and Mr Savel tuchinge certen matters contoverted betwen them concerning the same. I being very desirous not only of quietnes betwen ourselves (whereof I made no doubt) but also betwen our posterities afterwards, and that sute (that commonly are mothers of unkindnes) might staye, desired you (as likewise my cosin Paston did) to informe yourselves of the true state of the matter in variance; and by your good mediation to end the same. Whereuppon (as I ame informed) you have taken the paynes to viewe the grounde, and to heare the allegations & proffe of eyther*

---

[377] George Leeds, MA, rector of Holt 1583–1630. A man of puritan leanings who regularly preached at the exercises at Wiveton (*BP*, iv, p.155; Venn *Al. Cant.*, iii, p.68).
[378] Richard Snoden. By 1597 apparently tutor at Stiffkey Hall to Lady Dorothy Bacon's children, when he buys an "accidence [*grammar*] and horn book", and master at Holt School 1602–3. Probably ordained 1604 and rector of Irmingland and vicar of Corpusty in 1615. (Stiffkey Database; Venn, *Al. Cant*, iv, p.119).
[379] William Dobson. Possibly a baker at Holt (*BP*, iii, pp.269, 302–3).
[380] Bacon regularly made substantial purchases of grocery and drapery from William Browne, junior and senior, of Holt (*BP*, iii, p.101, iv, p.294; Stiffkey Database).
[381] On 9 September 1604 a warrant for good behaviour pending the next sessions at Holt was issued against Downing on the information of G[*eorge*] L[*eeds*] (Bacon memoranda book 1602–7, NRO BL/BC/5/22, p.49*bis*).

partie. These are to desire you to procede in so good a work, and to the ende your labours alredy taken may not be lost, & that eyther partie may receive the better satisfaction, that you would be pleased to meete againe at Flitcham sometyme this next weke, & to sett down the prooffe & matters tending to the maintenance of the claymes by either partie, & to the manifestation of the right touching these matters in variance, wherein as you shall doe a charitable and friendly work, so shall you make us both much beholding to you for your paynes and indifferecy herein. And so I committ you to the blessed protection of the Almighty.'"[382]

Pearson, (undated), item 91.

Sir Edward Coke, Attorney-General, to Sir Nathaniel Bacon

1604, September 2. Sir, you shall perceive by these inclosed what a desire I have of quietnes, and howe bould I ame to desire your further travaile. Sir Miles[383] sent me word by the messenger that any day after to morowe he would give meetinge about the finishing of your former travailes. Wherof I ame the more desirous, because I would have « it» driven to an ysue before I depart. What day it please you to appoint, this bearer shall give notice therof to Sir Miles. It was my cosin Pastons resolute request that the reasons & prooffes of eyther side should be sett downe or els he would no further proceade. And so with my verie hartie commendations to you & your good lady I committe you to the blissed proteccion of the Almightie and ever rest, your very assured freinde.

In the margin in Coke's hand: Godwike 2 September 1604.

Signed: Edw[ard] Coke.

Addressed: To the right worshipfull my especiall good freinde Sir Nathaniell Bacon knight.

Endorsement in Martin Man's hand illegible.

1 p. BL Stowe 743 f.18.

Richard Foster, rector of Burgh Parva, to Sir Nathaniel Bacon

[1604 <-Θ-> 1617],[384] **September 7.** Sir my humble dutie remembred unto your worship. These are to intreate your favour in the behalfe of this poore mann one John Balden of Sharringeston who is trobled by John Bacon of Thornage. He hath arrested him upon Friday last by writ for some [*word deleted*] tresspas done to him in his pease about Whitsontyde last, which this bearer utterly denieth and I thinke he will not speake an untruth willingly. He was my servant five yeares together in the which time he behaved himselfe honestly both in word and deede neither have I hard since he came into that towne that he hath behaved himselfe amisse workeing faithfully and truly that he might provide maintenance for himselfe his «wife» and children, as I suppose he may have the testimonie of the townesmen there. It

---

[382] See previous correspondence relating to Paston's dispute with Coke, 2–23 March 1602/3, above, pp.11–12, 15–16.

[383] Corbett: see letter from Coke, immediately above.

[384] Dating: the year is limited by Nathaniel Bacon's knighthood, and the institution of Richard Asteley at Burgh Parva in 1617 (Blomefield, ix, p.372).

is probable that some enviuos man, for some sinister respect hath exasperated this Bacon against him as yow in your wisdome by examination of the matter betwene them may peradventure finde out. May it please your worship therfore to send for this John Bacon by your letter and to make an end betwene them of this suite, which otherwaise is like utterly to undoe this poore man, he protesteth earnestly that he is cleare & guilt[l]esse of that accusation he layeth against him, for if he were not I thinke he would have compounded with him before he was arrested. I humbly beseech your worship to doe your endevour to succour and to free [*2 words deleted*] this poore man that no further law be prosecuted against him, he hath litle neede of it in regard of his povertie. So shall I as ever heretofore «be» beholding unto yow and this poore man shall «have» occasion continually to pray for yow. Thus with the remembrance of my dutie to the good Ladie Bacon I humblie take my leave, commendeing yow both and your affines [*relations*] to the protection & blesseing of the highest. Burrough Parva this 7 of September. Your worshipps to command ever in the Lord.

Signed: Richard Foster.[385] *Holograph.*
Addressed: To the right worshipfull Sir Nathaniell Bacon att Styfkey.
Endorsed in Martin Man's hand: Mr Forster.
1 p. Folger L.d.293.

Agreement in a mediation between Ellen Howes and John and Edmund Girdleston

1604, September 25. A note of an agreement set downe 25 September 1604 before Sir Nathanael Bacon knight betwen Ellen Howse widdow of thone parte and John Girdleston of Lynne and Edmond his brother on the other parte.[386]

Inprimis John Girdleston <& his brother are> is to deliver out «a» certayn bonde which <thei> «he» hath of the said Ellen.

Item eche partie to seale and deliver to other generall acquittances.

Item the said John & Edmund to enter bonde to paie unto the said Ellen 42*s.* at Michaelmas 1605.

Item the said John to paie more in hande 22*s.* 4*d.*

And all reck[oning] cleer.

And the said Ellen «is» to seale a bonde of £10 to John Girdleston that shee shall suffer him to use the coppiehold grounde till William Howse her sonne come to 14 yeares.

Unsigned. In Martin Man's hand.
Endorsed: Order & agreement *inter* Ellen Howse & John Girdleston.
½ p. NRO RAY 258.

---

[385] Foster was part of the circle of forward protestant clergy sponsored by similarly-minded laymen such as Bacon (*BP*, iv, p.17n.). The practical benefits of of being accounted one of the godly are evident here.
[386] For the previous document relating to this dispute see John Girdleston's evidence, September 1604, above, p.126.

Certificate concerning Ralph Jermyn's petition against Thomas Moore and William Taylor

[*1604*],[387] **September 25.** *Calendar.* The writers[388] have heard the case of Raphe Jermyn, petitioner, against Thomas Moore and William Taylor referred to them by Sir John Popham, the Lord Chief Justice, and find as follows:

Jermyn being in debt to Moore made him a bill of sale of his goods as security. He remained in possession and also leased a tenement and lands[389] from Moore for nine years at £60 a year. Interest on the debt was £24 a year. After two years Moore urged Jermyn to approach a friend to bind himself for the debt, suggesting their neighbour William Taylor.

Taylor agreed, the total debt, with interest, then being £240. For Taylor's security the lease was renewed in his name at the former rent for twelve years and the goods assigned to him, though Jermyn remained in possession of both.

One William Reache denounced Moore to the Exchequer for exacting more interest than allowed by statute, and in alarm Moore urged Taylor "to turne Jermyn out of his coate, into his shirte and so to begger hym", as Taylor told Reache and Robert Bayes.

John Hawes and Robert Rickes (one of whom was brother-in-law to Jermyn) offered to discharge the obligation to Moore, but Taylor professed good will and refused.

However, Taylor was accused of being in league with two loose companions, Greene and [*letter missing*]eaman, to defraud Lady Bucke of Lincolnshire[390] of a great quantity of wool that she was selling, and was called into Star Chamber. Fearing Moore would testify against him, Taylor tricked Jermyn into a journey and seized his property, expelling his wife and household. He then surrendered the lease and goods to Moore. This was within a year and a half of the new lease. All due payments had been made, as Taylor had confessed to Hawes and Rickes.

Thus Jermyn, although he had not defaulted in payment, was deprived not only of lease and goods but also of crops in the barn and in the ground and of cattle. The question of redress for him the writers refer wholly to his Lordship, Jermyn being too poor to pursue a remedy at law.

Copy. Unsigned.

Addressed: To the right honourable our verey good lord Sir John Popham knight Lord Chiefe Justice of England and one of his Majesties most honourable Pryvie Counsell.

Endorsed in Martin Man's hand: Copie of the certi[*ficat*]e to my Lord Chiefe Justice of England.

1½ pp. Folger L.d.701.

---

[387] Dating: dated with reference to Jermyn's further petition of 23 October 1604, below, p.135.

[388] The case had been referred to Sir Christopher Heydon and Sir Nathaniel Bacon. See Jermyn's further petition of 23 October 1604, below, p.135.

[389] In Hingham and Hardingham; see Memorandum of 27 December 1604, below, p.145.

[390] Probably Eleanor, widow of Sir John Bucke of Hamby Grange (d. 1596), although she had contracted another marriage to Sir William Rigdon before April 1600 (A.R. Maddison, *Lincolnshire Pedigrees, i*, Harleian Soc. 50, 1902, p.199).

Sir Henry Spelman to Sir Nathaniel Bacon

1604, September 26. *Autograph letter dated 26 September 1604, "relative to a petition of Henry Young addressed to King James, accompanied by the original petition, endorsed 'At the Court at Greenewich the 4th of Julie 1604,' signed by Roger Wilbraham (Master of the Court of Requests)";* [391] *also two autograph letters of Austin Young concerning the matter.*

4 docs. Ellis, 157 (c.1914), p.26.

Order for the maintenance of an injured workman

1604, October 2. *Calendar.* Order made at the Quarter Sessions held at Norwich Castle on Tuesday 2 October 1604 before Sir Henry Gawdie, Sir Miles Corbett, and other J.P.s.

A complaint had been made to the justices at the Sessions held at Holt on Friday 8 June last by the inhabitants of Al[d]borough, concerning Henry Nickerson, who was retained in service at Saxlingham and injured by a fall in climbing there, and who had since been removed to Alborough at the charge of the town. At that time it was ordered that the churchwardens and overseers of Saxlingham should pay those of Alborough 2s. a week for his maintenance until Alborough was discharged of him. It is now thought that 2s. is too much, since Nickerson has recovered, and the court orders that Saxlingham shall pay 2s. for the ten weeks since 1 May, and 1s. a week thereafter until the discharge. The inhabitants of Alborough claim that the order made at Holt has been ignored, and the court therefore further orders that if the said sums are not paid, the inhabitants should complain to Sir Nathaniel Bacon, who will bind over the churchwardens and overseers of Saxlingham to the next Assizes.[392]

Unsigned copy.
Endorsed: Copy of the order betwene the townes of Alborough & Saxlingham for Nickerson.
Calendared from transcript in *Stiffkey Papers*, pp.58–9.

Account for malt sold in Holland

1604, October 12. Recconing of 22 last of malt sould by Roger Dickenson of Amsterdam 12 of October 1604 as followeth:

First the 22 last sould in Hollond for 1507 gilders[393] which is unexchanged of sterling moonye £150 14s. 9d.

Ought of which ther was taken of for charges in Hollond first for a pylott upp to Amsterdam 8 gilders 5 stivers which is 16s. 6d.

---

[391] Not in Wilbraham's register of petitions (Hoyle *et al.*, *Heard Before the King*).

[392] Nathaniel Bacon's memoranda book notes under 1 November 1604 that John Crockley, churchwarden of Saxlingham, had been bound in £20 to appear at the next Assizes for not performing the order of the sessions regarding Nickerson. Andrew Howsegoe, the other churchwarden, and Thomas Whiting and Robert Cheveley, the overseers, were to be bound for the same offence (NRO BL/BC/5/22, p.55).

[393] 20 stuivers = 1 gulden of account (Peter Spufford, *Handbook of Medieval Exchange*, Royal Historical Society Guides and Handbooks no. 13; London, 1986, p.xxiv). As is apparent from this account, the rate of exchange at this time meant that a gulden was worth about 2s.

More for the custome of the malt in Hollond at 1 gilder per last, for 20 last £2

More for litters for to put the malt into in Hollond at 50 stivers *per* day for 9 dayes di. £2 7s. 6d.

For turning of the malt being hott 8s.

For metting [*measuring*] of the same at 6 stivers ½ *per* last 13s. 3d.

For brogerage [*brokerage*] to the brogers man 4s.

Paid for excize for the malt at 8 stivers *per* last 16s. 3d.

Paid for the brogers going abord at sundry tymes 1s. 3d.

Paid the broger for his fee at £2 per 100 for selling the corne for £150, £3

For a wine cope [*cup*] uppon the sale 8s. 6d.

For a passe in Hollond 1s. 5d.

For mattes and primage[394] to the marriners 10s. 6d.

Some [*sum*] of the charges in Hollond £11 8s. 2d.

Which some of £11 8s. 2d. being abated from the somme of the malt sould for rest £139 8s. 7d. [*sic*][395]

Which some being exchanged at £10 per C [*100*] ther remayne exchanged the just some of £126 15s.[396]

Ought of which some take of for fraight and custome of 22 last £29 14s.

So rest to be devided into 22 last of malt the some of £97 1s.

Which maketh just in the somme for every last some £4 8s. 3d.

Signed: John Greene.[397]

Addressed: To his frind Mr Martin Man.

Endorsed in Martin Man's hand: Greens reckoning for malt in Holland.

1 p. Folger L.d.737.

Memorandum concerning stock held by the parish of Langham

1604, October 16. A note of what monie is remayning in sondry mens handes in the towne dwelling as followeth the xvi of October 1604.

Item in Allin Lampkin handes for the fearme of one cow for 6 yeares at 3s. 4d. the yeare, 20s. /[*In Martin Man's hand*:] Promiseth bitwen this & Whitso[n]tyde./

Item in Mary Mans[398] handes 13s. 4d. and use for fower yeares wich comith to five shillinges.

Item in John Gryx junior handes for one cowe given by John Gryx the elder deceased 40s. and for the fearm of hir for 4 yeares, 13s. 4d.

Item in John Gryx junior handes 52s. ever since the yeare of our Lord God 1598, the use of it doth amount to the some of 30s.

Item in Richard Lodes handes since he was constable 6s. 6d. /[*In Martin Man's hand*:] Promised./

---

[394] "Primage": a customary allowance to the master and crew for the loading and care of the cargo.

[395] The calculation £150 14s. 9d. minus £11 8s. 2d. is worked in the margin, giving a correct total of £139 6s. 7d.

[396] This sum is calculated in the margin by taking £10 from £139 8s. 7d., £2 from the total, and 13s. 7d. from that total, giving a final total of £126 15s.

[397] John Green of Wells (see *BP*, iv, p.289).

[398] Mary Man: widow of Richard Man, yeoman, of Langham, and sister-in-law of Martin Man.

Item owing from the widdow Massingham since the vii day of May 1598, 10s.

On the dorse in Martin Man's hand: In Mr Barnardes handes paid by John Pinchyn £3. [?] *Fatetur* [*he admits*] 40s.

Inde 20s. in Lampkyns handes.

More due by Mr Gassingtons will £7.[399]

Unsigned.

Endorsed in Martin Man's hand: A note of the stock for Langham par[*ish*].
1 p. RH Box 50.

Edmund Wythipoll and Sir Charles Cornwallis to Sir Nathaniel Bacon

1604, October 20. Sir, I came hyther with full purpose to have seene yow my sellfe and intreated your frindlie travill unto my howse at Ipswige for the determininge and fynishinge of that busines for poore Penninge and his wyfe which soe charitablie and kyndlie yow travyled in at London.[400] But myne uncle Sir Charles Cornwaleys assuring me that my letter would prevayle sufficientlye with yow to that purpose I have adventured the same, earnestlie intreating yow soe fare to favour me as to take the payne to be at my howse the xvii of this moneth next wher I doubte not but your frindlie paynes and myne unckles shall sawlter[401] to the desired effecte <of the desired> «in making» peace betwen the brethren. The poore man and his wyfe for so charitable a worke shall have cause to praye for yow and my sellfe will rest behoulding unto yow for <that> «your» kyndenes and redy to requyte yow in the like <kindnes>. Soe commending me very hartilie unto yow I leave yow. Norwich this xx daye of October 1604. Your very loving frinde. *Signed*: Edm[*und*] Wythypoll.[402]

At the foot: Sir I must needes putt to some few lynes in favor of the dystressed & pray yow also on my part not to fayle at that day of meetyng & withall to dyrect your letters wherin I wyll joyn with yow to Mr Anthony Pennyng desyring hym to be prepared with hys arbytrators agaynst the tyme to thend wee may upon the Monday folowyng attend the cawse & bryng yt to end «by [?]agreement». Wryght yt in bothe our names & send yt by thys bearer that I may also subscrybe yt & lett me know by hym how yow determyne your jornays & so in hast I commend me most hartely to yow & your good lady & leave yow. Your assured. *Signed*: Cha[*rles*] Cornwalis. *Holograph.*

In the margin, in William Sanders' hand: A promise by letter in aunswere to avowe

[399] William Gassington (d.1595) of Great Langham, gent. His will suggests that he was unmarried and he may have moved with his widowed mother from Botesdale (Suffolk) to Baconsthorpe in 1567. A keen huntsman, his dogs on one occasion killed 23 of Bacon's ewes. He served as high constable of Holt Hundred in 1592. Among other more substantial bequests he left 20s. a year for 7 years to the poor of Great and Little Langham. (Stiffkey Database; *BP*, iv, p.2n.; NRO NCC 1595 Hinde ff.185–189v.)

[400] A Bill had been introduced in the Commons on 6 June "for the frustration of a release unduly procured by Anthony Penning from Edmund Penning his brother"; on 8 June 1604 it was sent to a committee which included Sir John and Sir Henry Hobart, Sir Francis Bacon and Thomas Oxborough (*CJ*, i, pp.233–4). The committee recommended arbitration, and Nathaniel Bacon and Sir Charles Cornwallis were appointed to act for Edmund Penning (see Court order of 11 February 1605/6, below, pp.221–2).

[401] "Sawlter": perhaps from the Middle English *sault*, a leap, for 'assault'.

[402] Edmund Wythypoll of Topcroft and Ipswich. Bacon's connection with the family is likely to have been through his father's marriage to Jane Ferneley, the daughter of an Ipswich merchant (*BP*, iii, p.348 n.349).

the laboure of the younger brothers behalfe, and no laboure in the behalfe of the elder for the metinge.

Addressed: To the righte worshipful and my very lovinge frinde Sir Nathaniell Bacon knight at his howse in Stewkey.

Endorsed in William Sanders' hand: Mr Withypolls letter for Pennings cause.

1 p. Folger L.d.635.

Referral of petition. Ralph Jermyn to the King

1604, October 23. *Calendar*: Ralfe Jermyn petitions the King that on an unspecified date he made Thomas Moore and others, as his special friends, trustees of his whole estate, but contrary to the trust reposed in them they have entered into his farm and goods in Norfolk and wrongfully withheld them from him. Upon his complaint to the Lord Chief Justice, Sir John Popham, his Lordship referred the matter to Sir Christofer Heydon and Sir Nathaniell Bacon, who examined the case and tried to persuade Moore to make restitution, which he utterly refused to do.[403]

The petitioner claims to be "a very poore man chardged with wyfe and many children" and unable to proceed at law. He requests the King to refer the case again to Heydon and Bacon to end it if they can, or else upon their certification to direct such further order for his relief as the King thinks most fit. *Undated. Unsigned.*

At the foot: If the cause is not currently being or has not been dealt with in any court of justice, the King agrees that it should be decided by Heydon and Bacon so that his Majesty be troubled no further. The other party may name an equal number of commissioners.[404] 23 October 1604 from the court at Whitehall. [*Signed*:] Jul[*ius*] Caesar.[405]

Endorsed in Martin Man's hand: Jermyns peticion.

1 p. Folger L.d.738.

Inquest on the death of Gregory Martin

1604, October 27. An inquisicion taken at Methwold the xxvii daye of October *anno regni regis Jacobi etc. <primo> secundo et Scotie xxxviii* upon the oathes of Thomas Baker senior, Robert Shingfeild senior, William Russell, Robert Tuddenham, Richard Yonge alias Sporle, John Yong, Thomas Watson, William Rolf, Simon Fuller, William Rumbold, John Addams, Thomas Olyet and Robert Baker, who say upon ther oathes that the 3 day of May 1603 one Gregory Martyne of thage of 17 yeires or ther aboutes was slayne in the wynd myll of Methwold, and that upon the viewe and sight of his body before he was buryed they perceyved that one of his fyngers of his right hand and his arme in two places wounded and torne, his brest was wounded, and his neck broken, upon which he dyed, and thei further say that the seyd Gregory being negligently playing about the mill whele, was caught by the cogges of the same whele, and so thorowe the same & by vyolence

---

[403] See Certificate of 25 September 1604, above, p.131.

[404] See Memorandum and Valuation of 27 December 1604, below, pp.145–8.

[405] The matter and the form of words in the endorsement at the foot leave no doubt that here Caesar is acting in his capacity as one of the two main Masters of Requests.

therof (the mill being then under sayle) he <was> then & ther receyved his «mortall» woundes and hurtes aforeseyd wherof he instantly dyed. And thei further say that the day & yeere aforeseyd one John Auger of Methwold aforeseyd was owner of the same myll, and the same day & yeire the seyd myll had two myll stones and that the sales of the same myll wer clothed with sayle cloathes, and that the stones, myll whele, and sayles of the same myll that wer in the same myll the daye & yere aforeseyd wer movinge at the tyme of the <death> casuall death of the seyd Gregory, and be nowe at the day of this inquisicion in yt and belonging to the seyd myll.

And they further say that the seyd Gregory so being slayne as aforeseyd was afterward buryed (by Christofer Constable then being vicarr of Methwold) in the church yard of Methwold aforeseyd. In wytnes wherof etc.

Unsigned.
Endorsed: Inquisicio de morte [*inquest concerning the death*] Gregory Martyn.
1 p. NRO RAY 260. Printed, *Stiffkey Papers*, pp.17–18.

Petition. Thomas Edwards to Sir Nathaniel Bacon

[*1604, early November*].[406] *Calendar*: Thomas Edwardes of Wisbech, mercer, petitions Sir Nathanaell Bacon, high steward of the King's manor of Walpole, on the grounds that for many years he was seised of a copyhold messuage and seven acres of land in the manor, but recently Edward and [*blank*] Gregges began a suit of formedon in the remainder in the manor court and thereby obtained a writ of summons against him. When he made default after the writ was returned, a grand *cape* was awarded against him, and because he did not excuse his default, judgement was given against him. As many errors were made in the judgement, he prays that it may be annulled, and the profits taken by the Gregges since they obtained seisin restored to him.

Undated. Unsigned.
Endorsed in Martin Man's hand: Edwardes peticion.
1 p. Folger L.d.734.

Sir Nathaniel Bacon and Sir Christopher Heydon to Sir Roger Wilbraham

1604, November 1. Sir upon a peticion put up by this poore man Thomas Croget[407] unto the Kinges Majestie wee receaved <comaundment by your letter> «direccion from you in his Majesties [*?*]name» of the 6 of July 1603 to call the poore mans creditors before us and to persuade them to a charitable composicion for his dettes.[408] And divers of them were founde verie trattable [*sic*]. But one Robert Bright a citizen of L [*?London*] unto whome this peticioner was most indetted wee could not by anie intreatie drawe before us, <for> «though» wee wrote &

---

[406] Dating: dated with reference to Chancery order of 14 November 1604, below, p.141.
[407] Possibly the Thomas Crogatt who was overseer of Holt in 1600 (*BP*, iv, p.190). The petition and referral is not recorded in Wilbraham's register of petitions (Hoyle *et al.*, *Heard Before the King*).
[408] See Bacon's recognisance book 1602–7 for 23 July 1603, "to give knowledge to Tho. Grogans wife of Welles of the daie for the compoundinge of Crogates debtes"; and 26 August 1603, "Sir Christofer [*Heydon*] and my master are to mette at Holte the xv of September for Crogate" (NRO BL/BC/5/22, pp.33, 36).

sent unto him severall tymes. Upon the receipt of our first letter he refused in effect to come before us alledging matter of excuse merely frivolous. Upon a second letter he came to the place appointed and then by <good> «just» occasion wee could not meete. And therupon wee appointed another day and wrote unto him but he falled to come before us. And therby the peticioner is hitherto without that relief which by his Majesties pleasure was intended him. Thus much wee have thought good to certefy unto you, and withall do intreate your good helpe for the poore mans further relief. And so wee hartely commende you to Gods proteccion. Stifky 1 November 1604. Your very loving fryndes.

Unsigned draft in Martin Man's hand.
Endorsed: Copy letter *pro* Croget *al* Sir R. Wilbraham.
1 p. NRO RAY 261.

Privy Council to Sir Miles Corbett and other J.P.s in Norfolk

1604, November 12. After our hartie commendacions. Whereas our verie good lord the Earle of Northampton being seized in fee of the castle, chase, and warren of Risinge in that countie of Norfolke, and of diverse mannours, auncient roialties, liberties, and priviledges thereunto belonging, findeth (as it is supposed) that diverse persons in the tyme of the late Earle of Arundell deceased, have greatelie encroched upon the said liberties, amonge whome Sir Henry Spilman knight is saied to be a cheefe and principall person therein. And whereas there have bin and are diverse suites in law depending betwixt the saide Sir Henry Spilman, and Richard Howell the younger gent,[409] tenaunt unto the Earle of Northampton, by occasion whereof, and of the evidence produced in those suites, some juste matter by waie of testimony hath bin opened & discovered neerelie towching the inheritance of the Earle of Northampton. Forasmuch as the Earle in a juste and honorable disposition, is desirous that without any farther troble or charges of law, the state of the cause may be well understoode, and that all parties may have the right that appertayneth unto them, which might be the more readilie effected upon a true acknowledgement, & shew of such proofes and evidence as may be produced by them. Wee do therefore praie and require yow, by authoritie of these our letteres, at some convenient place and tyme, to call before yow the saide Sir Henry Spilman «Thomas Athowe esquire»[410] and Richard Howell, and also John Wright of Northwotton, and John Baxter of Castle Risinge «and any other persons whome the matter may concerne». And upon examination and perusall of suche proofes and matters of evidence as they have severallie, towching the matters in controversie betwixt them, to consider how farr foorth the same may concerne the said right of the Earle of Northampton. As also to call before yow suche other witnesses as yow shall thincke needefull to be examyned for the setting foorth of the truth of the premisses, and them to examyne, and thereupon to ende the controversie if yow can, or otherwise

---

[409] For the Hovell family of Hillington see Blomefield, viii, pp.465–6.

[410] Thomas Athow of Beachamwell, sergeant-at-law (Blomefield, vii, pp.288, 293), who held property in the parish of Grimston, next to Castle Rising (see 10 January 1604/5, below, p.150). His special expertise is referred to in the Agreement of 1 December 1604, below, p.143.

to certifie us of your whole proceedinges in the cause. Whereof wishing yow not to faile, wee bidd yow hartelie farewell. From the Court at Whitehall the 12 of November 1604. Your verie loving freendes. [*Signed:*] T. Ellesmere *cancellarius*, J. [*sic*] Dorset, Notingham, Suffolke, E. Zouche, Cranborne.

At the foot: Sir Miles Corbett, Sir Nathaniell Bacon, knightes, Thomas Crumwell, Owen Sheppard,[411] esquires, or to any 3 or 2 of them.

Copy.
Addressed: To our verie lovinge freendes Sir Miles Corbett, Sir Nathaniell Bacon, knightes, Thomas Crumwell & Owen Shepheard esquires, or to any 3 or 2 of them.
Endorsed in Martin Man's hand: Letters concerning Rising.
1 p. NRO RAY (4) 37.

Privy Council to Sir Miles Corbett and other J.P.s in Norfolk

1604, November 12. *Summary:* Copy of the above letter.
Copy in Martin Man's hand.
Endorsed: Copy of the letters concerning the Erle of Northampton, Sir Henry Spelman & Mr Howell.
1 p. NRO RAY (6) 20i.

Evidence for the manor of Roydon against the fermors of Castle Rising warren

[*Post 1604, November 12*].[412] *Calendar:* "A tru particular of the proper demeane landes & evidences belongeng to the mannour of Roydon & the warren thereunto apperteyneng where nowe of late the farmors of the Ryseng warren doe challendge a right." The points made are as follows:

The witnesses of the plaintiff Wright are suborned and self contradictory.

The inquisition *post mortem* of Robert, the father of Roger de Monte Alto, included a warren worth 3*s.* per annum. But the inquisition held after the death of the late Earl Philip reported 27,000 conies killed in one year, worth £340 at 4*d.* the rabbit [*sic*] "besydes a treble veiw [*three times as many*] left uppon the ground", which was all by encroachment on other men's ground, since the lord of Rising neither held nor purchased land in Roydon or Grimston.

Dominus Roger de Monte Alto had to pay damages "to law [*lay*] a dogg" (put a dog on the scent) in Congham, which the jury found to be outside the limits of Rising Chase.

The same Roger claimed free chase and free warren from Gaywood bridge to Wood bridge and so to the sea and from Bawsey bridge to Babingley water mill, far from the townships and including much of other men's lands. The plaintiffs now claim the same over seven townships, to the destruction of corn and grain and the undoing of the inhabitants, whereas the plaintiff Wright's own evidence shows it was never so before Bull became warrener there under a lease of 13 Elizabeth.

---

[411] Owen Shepherd esquire of Kirby Bedon, the Earl of Northampton's receiver-general in Norfolk (Linda Levy Peck, *Northampton, Patronage and Policy at the Court of James I* (London and Boston, 1982), p.66).
[412] Dating: this must result from the Privy Council letters of 12 November 1604, immediately above.

The charter to Thomas Daniell, esquire of the body to Henry VI, and its confirmation show that free warren of Roydon and Congham belongs to their lords; likewise the patent to Henry Woodhouse for free warren in his Norfolk demesnes and
the confirmation of the same to Sir Henry Collett. That the fields of Roydon and
Congham have always been arable is shown by Lawes's book of 14 Edward IV, which
includes 300 acres belonging to the writer. Numerous deeds from Thursby and
others dated 25 Henry VI to 7 Henry VII confirm this. Also the accounts of Pury
and Hamond, bailiffs of Roydon in 12 and 13 Henry VI, show amounts of sheep
and tillage that would be impossible given a tenth as many deer and rabbits as now.

For evidence that conies have always been killed in Roydon and Congham, but
the plaintiffs and their fermors excluded, reference is made to depositions given to
three sittings of the commission.

For evidence of conveyances and fines, see the depositions of Mr Dewhurst,
clerk, and others on tillage in Goalworth/Gouldworth Field in Roydon and elsewhere.

Undated. Unsigned.
Endorsed in Martin Man's hand: Profes concerning Roydon.
1½ pp. NRO RAY (6) 20iii.

Memoranda concerning the rights and boundaries of Castle Rising warren

[*Post 1604, November 12*].[413] *Calendar*: Memoranda relating to the dispute over
Castle Rising warren between Richard Hovell gent and Sir Henry Spelman and
others, concerning how far it extended into the neighbouring parishes. The notes
are fragmentary, making it difficult at times to distinguish past from current testimony and the names of contemporary witnesses from those merely referred to in
evidence. The information given is based upon depositions taken between 1588/9
and 1596/7, on undated depositions and on documentary evidence and is roughly
arranged by parish.

Roydon. Testimony is given for Hovell on the foldcourse. Hovell's counsel
discredits Mr Spelman's depositions. There is documentary evidence from 1432/3
for a flock of over 1,000 sheep, leading to the query as to how this was possible at
Roydon without the heath. Other information given is: that in 1518/19 Thomas
Woodes knight leased the manor etc in Roydon and Congham to Thuresby for 10
years at £16 a year; that land in Rompes Wonge and 44 acres in le Westfeld were
leased as arable; that 40 acres called Johns Landes were leased in 1518/19; that a
charter of Edward VI granted liberty of free warren in all the manor in Roydon and
Congham, in Wethall and in Hollwood, with the right to fortify and impale 600
acres of marsh; that "Mr Hovelles grounde is wett and clay and the conyes cannot
burrogh in it" (Baxter, warrener). Other witnesses: Robert Mendham.

Wootton. Mr Marshall the fermor claims for Sir Arthur Capell that the lord of
Rising has granted Capell all liberties in North Wootton except royal fishes. He
promises to write to Capell to produce the conveyance next term for Sir Nathaniel

---

[413] Dating: dated with reference to the Privy Council letters of 12 November 1604, above, pp.137–8.

Bacon. Baxter claims that he has paid rent to Marshall for the right to the conies but without licence from the Lord of Arrundell.

Grimston. Mr Athowe denies the claim that Grimston is part of Rising warren. The grounds in question amount to 400 or 500 acres, with specific reference to Wyveling grounds and Wyveling Hill. The fermor of Rising, Ed. Chartresse, had complained to Sir N. Strang[414] that W. Heydon fermor of Wyveling had killed conies there and was told that Grimston was not in his lease. 300 sheep had been kept in the past but the grounds were not sufficient for 100 without the land claimed as warren. Evidence is given: of ferm conies (rabbits paid as rent) paid by warreners but not by owners; of a grant by Sir Ro. Woodhouse to H. Jordan; and of the warreners being forbidden to dig for conies in 1549/50.

Congham. An exemplification of a recovery excluded the liberty of warren and chase in Congham. Information is given for and against Spelman on whether Rompes Wong/9 acres and the 3 acres were part of the warren. Evidence relates to the payment of tithe conies to the parson of Congham and on the payment of ferm conies and money as rent. The warrener killed 1,000 conies in Rompes Wong/9 acres using traps ("falles") and nets ("hayed").

Grimston and Congham. In an extent of Rising of 1274/5 the value of the rabbit warren was given as 3*s.* a year. According to a presentment taken before Simon Rolf and others the chase and warren extended "from Gaiwood bridge to Woodbridge and from Woodbridge to the sea. And from Bawsey bridge to the watercourse of Baburgh Mill", which excludes Congham and Grimston with Wyverley grounds. Frankpledge extends to Rising, North Wootton, South Wootton and Roydon. According to the priviledges of Rising stated 1461/2 (*temp.* Jo. Hamond mayor) and repeated 1588/9 they could attach for their debts within the town of Rising and without as far as the warren extended. As no arrests were made in Congham or Grimston there was no warren. Richard Weston and Jo. Pond, mayors of Rising, extend this to Roydon.

Witnesses and additional persons mentioned in connection with Grimston and Congham: Humfrey Bastard, Francis Bastard, Ed. Bastard, Henry Bastard, Thomas Salter (warrener), Jo. Norrys (fermor of the warren), Leonard Baxter, Jo. Jonson (servant of Sego or of Francis Bastard), Sego, W. Swanton, John Furnes (warrener of Rising), Russell (fermor of Wyverley), Ratcliff, Jo. More, W. Yonges, R. Umfrey (warrener), Ralph Waller (fermor), Thomas Gall, Jo. Pond (80, keeper), [*illegible*] Bull (68), Jo. Jefferyes, Alice Swanton (servant of Jo. Norrys), Might (servant), Laurence Bell (servant of Spelman), James Rutledge, Thomas Tymperly (fermor), Gurlington (fermor of Congham), Robert Davy, W. Goll, Agnes Hines and Thomas Bennett (both 80, servants of Thomas Canne in 1589/90), Thomas Canne (fermor of Congham for Thuresby), Mr Cobbe (lessee of the 3 acres), Sir Henry father of Henry Spelman.

English and Latin. Undated. Unsigned. In Martin Man's hand.

---

[414] Presumably Sir Nicholas L'Estrange (1550–1580).

Endorsed: A note of the evidence & proofe concerning Rising & other townes adjoyning for the warren and chase.
4 pp. NRO RAY (6) 20iv.

Memoranda concerning Castle Rising warren

[*Post 1604, November 12*].[415] *Calendar:* "Concerninge Mr Hovells fouldcourse against Sir Henry Spelmans tytle". Evidence produced includes accounts dated 11–14 Henry VI, showing between 744 and 1,318 sheep on Roydon foldcourse and what quantities of corn were sold. Also extents and deeds showing that lands in the West Field of Congham and Roydon were let in 14 Edward IV for 6*d.* and 8*d.* an acre and regarded as arable. Nine witnesses in their interrogatories testify that owners of the manor of Rustings (Thomas and Francis Thursby and Henry Spylman) and their fermors never occupied the foldcourse in Congham West Field during the last 50 or 60 years, that in 10 Henry VIII Mr Thomas Thursby leased it from Woodhouse for 10 years at £16 a year and that Woodhowse and Waller occupied it. Witnesses: Pond, Turnor, Tompson, Thursby, Mendham, Swanton, William Howse, John Howse, Thomas Barcham.

"Towchinge the warran in Roydon". Evidence produced includes: grants under the Broad Seal of Henry VI to Thomas Danyel and Henry Woodhouse of free warren for the manor of Roydon; ancient deeds showing much of the land claimed for warren to be arable; depositions proving that the warreners of Rising paid rent conies when they took conies on land now Mr Hovell's, that the lands were often sown with corn, and that Waller and his fermors and other owners of Roydon manor took conies.[416]

Undated. Unsigned.
1½ pp. NRO RAY (6) 20iv.

Order in Chancery referring a case to Sir Nathaniel Bacon

1604, November 14. *Calendar:* Chancery order in the case between Thomas Edwardes gent, plaintiff, and Thomas Griggs *et al.*, defendants, the Lord Chancellor [*Sir Thomas Egerton, Baron Ellesmere*] being present. According to examination of the matter by Mr Gawsell, counsel for the plaintiff, and Mr Athowe, counsel for the defendants, and the reading of an order of 11 October last, a recovery in the formedon in the remainder suffered by the plaintiff in a manor court passed by default and the plaintiff has put in an exception to the steward.[417] The case is to be referred to Sir Nathaniell Bacon as high steward of the manor court concerned to decide in law and conscience. The Lord Chancellor is to write to Bacon for his better proceeding.

Signed: Per Ric[ard]um Edwards, deputatum Regis.
Endorsed in Martin Man's hand: Order *inter* Edwardes & Grigges.
Enclosed with Lord Chancellor's letter of 18 November 1604, below, p.142.
1½ pp. Folger L.d.739.

[415] Dating: dated with reference to the Privy Council letters of 12 November 1604, above, pp.137–8.
[416] For the subsequent Agreement arising from these inquiries see below, 1 December 1604, p.143.
[417] For Edwards' petition of early November 1604, see above, p.136.

John Percival to Lady Bacon

1604, November [*17 or 22*].[418] My good Lady[419] my honourable duty remembred. I suppose hit best your wolle be sente to Norwyche. The charge is 10*d.* for
the carriage of eight stone att a tyme. The price here is not so good [as] there and
money is more scant with us. I have commenced with Robarte Hogges[420] of our
towne for the carriage of the whole summe but not concluded untill your aunswere
be come. He requireth but 10*d.* for the carriage of an hundreth [*word deleted*]
weight which is eight stone and some odde poundes. Yf youe «please» to appoynte
the place where, the tyme when it shalbe sent I will loocke unto hit. Packinge
clothes wolde be sent to <[?]wrappe> packe hit in. Hit will quite spoyle any shetes.
My good Lady I rest still bounde to your worshippe for many [?]respectes. God
further your Ladyshippe in the best reckoning of the lyfe to come that the good
thinges in youe may encrease and abounde [*word illegible*] ever untill the cominge
of Christ. The gentlemen your sonnes are in good healthe and thus I rest alwayes
att your commaund in the Lord. From Stifkey this xvii [*or xxii*] of November
1604. Your Ladyshippes to commaunde in the Lorde.

Signed: John Percevall. *Holograph.*
1 p. *faded and damaged in parts.* NRO BCH 27/9/74 I (97).

Thomas Egerton, Lord Chancellor, to Sir Nathaniel Bacon

1604, November 18. After my verie hartye commendacions. I send yow hereinclosed an order latelye made in the Court of Chauncerye, upon perusall whereof
yow may more particulerlye understand the partyes whom it concernes, the nature
of the differences between them, and what is hereupon ordered. I praye yow to
take consideracion hereof, and (since the court hath made choyce of yow, (being
highe steward of the manour) as the fittest person to decyde this controversye) to
call the partyes before yow, and then to doe your endevour to make a quiett and
frendlye ende betweene them, according to lawe and conscyence, for the pre-
ventinge any further charge and trouble in suyte. Wherein not doubtinge of your
willinge travaille, I bid yow hartelye farewell. At Yorkhouse 18 *Novembris* 1604.
Your verie loving frend.[421]

At the foot: Sir <Nicholas> «Nathanyell» Bacon, knight.
Signed: T Ellesmere, *Cancellarius.*
Addressed: To my verie loving frend Sir Nathanyell Bacon knight.

---

[418] Dating: there is a hole in the MS where there could have been either a 'v' or an 'x'.
[419] Almost certainly Lady Dorothy, Bacon's second wife. The relationship between them was not an easy
one, and this may be why she was using as her factor the relatively inexperienced John Percival, the rector of
Stiffkey, rather than either Martin Man (Bacon's clerk) or William Sanders (her own clerk from her first marriage). On the other hand, Thomas Barsham, rector of Eccles, had reported recently to Nathaniel on the state
of his flock there (22 April 1604, above, p.103) and Percival had on occasion written to Bacon about estate
business in the past (*BP*, i, p.187, ii, pp.301/2, iii, p.46). Dorothy may have been running her own small
flock, or this could represent her share of the Stiffkey clip.
[420] Robert the son of Edward Hodge of Stiffkey. The latter ran a regular carrier service from Stiffkey to
Norwich via Dereham, which presumably was continued by his son (Stiffkey Database).
[421] For Bacon's report of 23 April 1605, see below, p.175.

Endorsed in Martin Man's hand: My Lord Chancelors letter *pro* Edwardes.
Enclosure: order of 14 November 1604, above, p.141.
½ p. Folger L.d.284.

Agreement between Sir Henry Spelman and Richard Hovell

1604, December 1. An agrement sett downe betwene Sir Henry Spilman knight and Richard Hovell gent by the mediation of Sir Miles Corbett, Sir Nathaniell Bacon knightes and Owen Sheppard gentleman by vertue of their letters *primo Decembris* 1604.[422]

Inprimis yt ys agred that Mr Hovell shall assure unto Sir Henrye Spilman knight all those his landes lying in Congham Westfeld lying on the north side of a waie called Longthorne Waye within Sir Henry Spilmans shepecorse, leading to Short Trees, and a pece of 7 roodes called Calke Pittes, paying £5 reserving calke [*chalk*] to Mr Hovell.

In consideracion therof Sir Henry Spilman ys to assure to Mr Hovell all his landes lying within Reydon, and one cotage nowe in the occupacion of Oliver Handle, permitting the tenaunt to hold yt by coppie for liefe of him & his wiefe or by lease for 21 yeres att the tenauntes choice. And «he» the said Sir Henry to paye unto Mr Hovell £85 *viz.* att Candlemas £40 and the rest att Candlemas 1605.

The conveyaunces on eyther parte to be referred to counsell for the drawing of them, *viz.* Thomas Athow esquire.

Item Sir Henry Spilman ys to have Mr Hovelles landes lying in the Estfeld in Congham in the Outweie by like assurance paying 40*s.* an acre being about 4 acres.

Item Mr Hovell ys to allowe unto Sir Henry Spilman £3 for the frehold of a coppiehold pece of ground in Reydon parcell of the premisses.

Memorandum eche partie ys to enter the landes presentlie.

All <the> trespasses remitted on eyther partes.

Unsigned. Copy [*? in William Sanders' hand*].
Endorsed in Martin Man's hand: Coppie of thagreement betwen Sir Henry Spelman & Mr Hovell.
1 p. NRO RAY (6) 20ii.

Sir Edward Coke to Sir Nicholas Bacon and Sir Nathaniel Bacon

1604, December 4. After my very hartie comendacions. Wheras I understand that you are willing that this bearer John Waller shall have the benefytt of the extent uppon the recognisaunce acknowledge by William Waller deceased unto the Lord Keeper your father,[423] so as you maie doe the same with saffetie and without impeachement of the former order in the Chauncerie, I have thertofore (for the saffetie of you the executors, and the good of the said John Waller) advised him (being of councell with him in the said cawse) to exhibit a newe bill into the Chauncerie, being the most apte and ready meanes to procure unto him the

---

[422] For documents concerning the dispute over Castle Rising warren, *c*.12 November 1604, see above, pp.137–41.
[423] Sir Nicholas Bacon. See Edmund Pooley to Bacon, 19 March 1603/4, above, pp.83–4.

benefytt of the said extent, without daunger unto the executors, which course I thought good to acquaint you withall. And so doe very hartily committ you to Godes blessed keeping. At the Temple this 4 of December 1604. Your assured loving frende.

Signed: Edw[*ard*] Coke.

Addressed: To the right worshippfull my assured good frendes Sir Nicholas Bacon, and Sir Nathaniell Bacon knightes.

Endorsed in Martin Man's hand: Mr Attorneys letter touching John Waller.

½ p. Boston (Richards).

Order of Thomas Sackville, Earl of Dorset, Lord Treasurer, and George, Lord Home of Berwick, Chancellor of the Exchequer, to Nathaniel Bacon as steward of the manor of East Dereham

1604, December 20. *Calendar*: The Lord Treasurer about February last[424] directed the stewards of the King's manors of Snettisham Ferdar, Burnham Overy, East Dereham and Pulham to suspend all fines and admittances to copyhold lands in these manors where the fine was arbitrable until further notice, and to send him a certificate of copyhold rents and estates, fines and heriots, and of the true value of arable, meadow and pasture, and of woods and mines, and of the names of the justices of the peace dwelling in or nearest the manor. As the stewards have neglected to return any certificates, this letter is to require the unnamed recipient(s) to enforce the previous orders. The stewards are to send their certificates by him, or to appear with him to answer for their contempt. Even if they have returned certificates, each steward is also to deliver to the auditor of their county all court rolls, rentals, surveys or court books and entries of copies made up to the 40th year of the late Queen, with an indented inventory. They are also to certify the names of any who hold such documents. From the court 20 December 1604. [*Signed*:] "by the Erle of Dorsett and the Lord of Berwick".

At the foot: Norfolk.

Copy. On same sheet and with same endorsement as Bacon's draft reply of 1 April 1605, below, pp.166–7.

1 p. NRO NNAS S2/17/17.

Notes for a certificate from Nathaniel Bacon to Thomas Sackville, Lord Treasurer

1604, December 20. Notes for cert[*ifying*] to my Lord Treasurers last letters. 20 December 1604.

1. That since his last letter the admitt[*ance*] of cop[*yholders*] be stayed. And that there was a stay upon the first letters for a tyme.

2. To deliver presently. That the cort rolles & evidences in the Stewardes custody shall be sent up presently. And that the ancyent cort rolles remayne at [?]Ely.

3. A letter to be sent to Mr Arthure Futter to bringe all the cort rolles rentalles

---

[424] On 15 February 1603/4, above, pp.72–3.

& custumaryes concerning Est Dereham[425] in his handes to Norwich uppon Weddensdy come sennet next to Mr Rychard Briges[426] leyte scolemaster of the fre scole dwelling right over against St Martyns <ho> churche of the Pallace in Norwych to be del[*ivered*]to my understeward Thomas Kinges to send to London accordinge to the Lord Treasurers letter.

The abstract of the letters.

1. To forbeare to <admitt> assesse fynes grant estates admitt tenantes till his Majesties pleasure be further knowen.

2. To make cert[*ificate*] of the thinges cont[*ained*] in the former letter.

3. To deliver <the rolles> into the Auditors handes of this county «all» rentalles cort rolles surveys cort bookes & entries of coppies till the 40th of the Queen by inventory indented betwen the Auditor & understeward.

4. To certifie their names in whose handes anie cort rolles rentalles surveys or cort bookes.

Undated. Unsigned. Date and abstract in Martin Man's hand.
On same sheet and with same endorsement as Nathaniel Bacon to Thomas Sackville, 10 March 1603/4, above, pp.79–80.
Endorsed: Copy of the «first» certificate to my Lord Treasurer *de maneriis* [*manors*] in Norfolk. With remembrances upon the 2 letters 20 December.
1 p. NRO NNAS S2/17/16.

Memorandum concerning the case of Jermyn versus Moore and Taylor

1604, December 27. *Calendar.* Notes made after the hearing of witnesses at Blakeney before Sir Christopher Heydon and Sir Nathaniel Bacon as follows.[427]

Raphe Jermyn leased lands in Hingham and Hardingham from Thomas More for 9 years. About March 1598, Jermyn being indebted to More in £240, More agreed to renew the lease for 12 years from Michaelmas on better security. Accordingly Jermyn arranged to become bound to Tailor for both debt and rent and took the lease in Tailor's name, while also making over his goods to Tailor as security. After more than a year, during which Jermyn spent £100 in "retting"[428] the ground, he was evicted without cause. The goods seized from him were worth £500, including 220 combs of threshed winter corn grown in one close worth 20*s.* the comb. Other goods of value are listed in an inventory. Witnesses: Mistress Dannock, Jo. Hawes, Robert Rickes, Robert Bayes, Steven Parke, Thomas Kydde, Walter Carman, W. Beasly, George Wenne.

Abstract of the information.

Robert Boyes and Steven Parke: Tailor confessed he had no interest in lands or goods except as surety for Jermyn.

Boyes: about Hallowmas 1600, Tailor told him and Jermyn that More had

---

[425] See 1 April 1605, below, pp.166–7.
[426] On Richard Briggs, master at the Norwich Grammar School, 1599–1636, see H.W. Saunders, *A History of the Norwich Grammar School* (Norwich, 1932), pp.270–78. "Thomas Kinges," see p.124n.
[427] This hearing follows Jermyn's further petition of 23 October 1604. See above, p.135.
[428] "Retting": usually to soften with water. Here perhaps generally to improve.

urged him to turn Jermyn out as soon as his winter corn was sown, but said he would not do so as he had suffered no loss.

John Hawes and Robert Rickes: Tailor refused further security, saying that Jermyn had discharged everything.

Thomas Kydde and Walter Carman: 100 acres of the ground were so overgrown when Jermyn entered that they were scarcely worth 2s. an acre. By good husbandry he made it worth 8s. and spent over £100 on it. The lease is worth 20 marks above the rent.

George Wenne: the lease was worth £200.

Unsigned. In Martin Man's hand.
Endorsed: Remembrances concerning Raphe Jermyn.
2 pp. Folger L.d.754.

Valuation of Ralph Jermyn's goods

[*1604, c. December 27*].[429] A note of all such gooddes of Raphe Jermyn being priced by thos whose names are underwritten.

	By the pricers	In true worth[430]
Inprimis 80 coomes of pease viewed and priced at 6s. the coome	£24	at 10s. – £40
Item 10 coomes barlye & 10 coomes fetches [*vetch*] at 5s. the coome	£5	at 6s. 8d. – £6 13s. 4d.
Item twoe shodde cartes[431] with the furniture	£7 13s. 4d.	£8
Item «2» ploughes furnished & a paire of iron barres	20s.	£1 10s.
Item in the stable 3 mares, 1 geldinge & one stoned horse [*stallion*]	£20	£30
Item 2 loadinges of haye over the stable	20s.	£1 10s.
Item 1 sorelled <bealed> mare coult	30s.	£1 10s.
Item 7 yerlings bullocks	£6 13s. 4d.	£7
Item 5 milch neate, 10 hefkers & a bull	£32	£37 6s. 8d.
Item 1 mare & a foale 1 horse colt & a mare colt	£10	£12
Item 1 stacke of haye & 2 closes of grasse	£9	£10 13s. 4d.
Item 1 close of winter corne of 46 acres	£78	£176
Item 1 close with hole grasse	£6	£6
Summa	£201 16s. 8d.	£338 3s. 4d.

---

[429] Dating: dated with reference to the Memoranda of 27 December 1604, immediately above.
[430] This column appears in the left-hand margin of the original.
[431] A cart with iron-tyred wheels (Yaxley, *Glossary*, p.34).

A note of certeine gooddes not put into inventarye nor priced.

Inprimis one posted bedd with a seeled tester	40s.
Item one framed table & a benche & a skreen	13s. 4d.
Item one saltinge trowe [*trough*]	10s.
Item one cheese presse	10s.
Item one cheese tubbe	6s. 8d.
Item one cherne	6s. 8d.
Item 2 cheese fattes with the breddes[432]	6s. 8d.
Item 6 milkinge bolles	3s.
Item 2 great killers[433]	3s. 4d.
Item one fleshe tubbe	2s.
Item 6 <combe> sackes	6s.
Item 2 fannes	3s. 4d.
Item one new sadloppe[434]	10d.
Item one riddle & a chaffe syve & a new pannell[435]	3s. 4d.
Item one «ould» chest of <old> iron	10s.
Item one gristone with a crank of iron	2s.
Item one shodd skeppett & one spade	2s. 6d.
Item 3 longe pikeforkes	2s.
The lease worth £13 6s. 8d. *per annum* above the rente reserved & so in 11 yeares	£146 13s. 4d.
Summa	£153 5s.[436]
/ In toto	£491 8s. 4d./[437]

Summa utraque [*total of both*]   £355 20d.[438]

But Jermyns debt to Moore was but £220. And so in surplusage £135 1s. 8d.

A note of certeine gooddes accrued to Raphe Jermyn after the date of the byle of sale made by him to Taylour, and which were taken awaye by Taylour.

White pease 80 coome at 10s.	£40
Barlye 10 coome and fytches [*vetch*] 10 coome at 5s.	£5
Haye in the stable 2 loades at 13s. 4d.	£1 6s. 8d.
A stacke of hey & 2 closes of grasse	£10 13s. 4d.
Wheate and myxtelyn in the grounde which yealded 220 coome at 16s.	£176
A stoned horse	£6
A newe shodde carte	£4
A foale	£1
Yearling bullockes 7 at 20s.	£7
One cloase of wholle grasse	£6
	£247

---

[432] The cover to the cheese-vat, of sufficient weight to act as a press (Yaxley, *Glossary*, p.40).
[433] Wide shallow bowl (Yaxley, *Glossary*, p.113).
[434] Basket used for broadcasting seed (Yaxley, *Glossary*, p.183).
[435] Either a saddle cloth or a large wicker basket (Yaxley, *Glossary*, p.146).
[436] Total repeated in the left-hand margin.
[437] £153 5s. plus £338 3s. 4d.   [438] £153 5s. plus £201 16s. 8d.

The yeare that Jermyn was dispossessed of his lease the prices of grayne were as followeth: wheate the coome 20*s.*, mestlyn 16*s.*, barlye 10*s.*, white peas 13*s.* 4*d.*

[*Signed.*] Steven Parke, George Wenne, Thomas Kydd, Robert Boyes.
Undated. Copy.
Endorsed in Martin Man's hand: The prisement of the goodes.
3 pp. Folger L.d.733.

Petition. John Williamson to J.P.s in Norfolk

[*Late 1604*].[439] *Calendar:* John Williamson of Norwich, clothier,[440] complains to Sir Nathaniel Bacon, Justice Palgrave, and the rest of the J.P.s in Norfolk that he is possessed of a house at Cley and of goods there and at Glandford, and also of a pack of Jersey ("Jarsey") stockings sent beyond the seas, and of certain bonds and bills, to the value in all of £260 or thereabouts. By dishonest practices Thomas Chambers of Cley and his confederates have secured possession of this property, on what grounds he does not know. He requests their worships to call Chambers before them and take order to punish the offenders and restore his goods. He will pray for their prosperity in this life and "itternall felicetie in the worlde to come".

Undated. Unsigned.
On the same sheet as letter from Thomas Hyrne of 3 January 1604/5, two documents below.
Endorsed in Martin Man's hand: Concerning Chambers & Willinson.
½ p. BL Add. 41140 ff.203–4.

Evidence of George Oldman

1604/5, January 2. *Calendar:* Declaration made by George Oldeman gent before Sir Nathanaell Bacon that he did not act as witness to a bond for £5 claimed by John Holmes from Mr Roger Tounshend. About the beginning of "this laste sommer" he was asked to do so by Nicholas Holmes, the brother of John. John confessed that the bond was of his own making and George Oldeman refused. With a postscript that the original signed by George Oldeman "remayneth with my master".[441]

Unsigned. Copy in William Sanders' hand.
Endorsed: George Oldmans declaration.
1 p. RH Box 66.

Thomas Hyrne to Sir Nathaniel Bacon

1604/5, January 3. Sir my humble dutye remembred to yower worship. Soe yt is that wheras one John Williamson stranger[442] hath bene divers times verye impor-

[439] Dating: dated by reference to the letter from Thomas Hyrne to Nathaniel Bacon, 3 January 1604/5, below, this page.

[440] Not recorded as a freeman of Norwich (Millican, *Freemen*). In Hyrne to Bacon, 3 January 1604/5, he is specifically referred to as a "stranger". This is one of many instances when a foreign name has been anglicised.

[441] For earlier and later documents in this dispute, see Evidence of John Holmes, *Post* 25 March 1604, above, p.96, and Holmes to Townshend, 8 March 1604/5, below, p.157.

[442] "Stranger": this term was used specifically for a Dutch or Walloon immigrant.

tunate with «me» to certyfye unto yower worship my knowledge in certayne matter betwixt him & Thomas Chambers of Cley & nowe at this instant in most urgent maner charged me before the prissoners to certyfie yower worship my knowledge herin as I will answer yt before God at the last daye of judgement. This is therfore to signifie unto yower good worship that about fyve yeres since the seyd Williamson had certayne corne lying in a howse of mine at Cley which he had as I suppose of Chambers, which corne the seyd Chambers wold have replevied for certayne moonie he demanded from John Williamson where uppon my request the seyd Williamson browght in his acount in wrighting what was due to him from Chambers & what Chambers had put over to him for the satisfaction of his acount amonge which yt appered he had putt over a certayne bond of one Julyer to the said Williamson which was due to Chambers from Julyer now. Williamson seyd he wold use what meanes possible he could for the obteyning of that moonie, & uppon the obteyning therof to satisfie Chambers what showld growe due to him by the seyd acount, & thereupon the seyd Chambers for that time surceased his sute & the seyd Williamson injoyed the corne & yf their be anye other matter out of my memorie by reason of my great opression & longe imprissonment I protest before God to certifie the truth herin before what judge or justice soever I shalbe lawfullye called to the uttermost of my remembrance & soe with my hertye prayer to God for yower worships happye preservation with yower good ladye & all yower I humbly take my leave. From Norwich Castle this 3 of Januarye 1604. Yower to comand in what I maye to the glory of God.

Signed: Thom[*a*]s Hyrne.[443]
On the same sheet as the petition from John Williamson (late 1604), above, p.148.
1 p. BL Add. 41140, f.202.

Sir Nathaniel Bacon and others to Henry Howard, Earl of Northampton

1604/5, January 10. Our duties in humble wise remembred. Sone after our receipt of the letters from the Lordes of the Privie Counsell of the 12 of November past,[444] for the calling of Sir Henry Spelman knight, Thomas Athow esquire, & Richard Hovell gent, together with Jo. Wright of Northwootton & Jo. Baxter of Castle Rising, before us, touching the incrochmentes supposed to be made by some of them upon the liberties of the chase & warren of Castle Rising in the countie of Norfolk, being parcell of your Lordships inheritaunce, wee did meete therabout at Lynne neere unto Rising, and according to their Lordships direccions did examyne the state of the same cause, by perusing both evidence, and deposicions of verie many persons. And though wee were not so prescribed in their Lordships letters,

[443] The most obvious candidate as signatory of this letter is Thomas Hyrne, ironmonger and mayor of Norwich on three occasions, including at the time of this letter. The reference to imprisonment is puzzling. However, it may be ironic. Hyrne was well established as a country gentleman resident at Haveringland. Unusually, he was to become sheriff of Norfolk in 1621. He had tried to evade the considerable expense and effort involved in being mayor (Cozens-Hardy, *Mayors*, p.68). The references to "Norwich Castle" (the County prison) and "before the prissoners" are unexpected, but given the contents of the letter, Williamson may at this time have been imprisoned there for debt.
[444] See above, p.137, and the documents following.

yet wee thought it more fitt, & agreeing to our duties, to signifie unto your Lordship in particuler, and not unto their honours in our aunswer to their letters, how our judgmentes be guided, in regard of those liberties, which is as followeth.

First, yt appeareth by ancient evidence (parte wherof hath ben had & coppied, as it seemeth, out of the evidence of Castle Rising) that the towne of Grymston, where the landes called Wyvelinges do lye, parte of the inheritance of the said Athow, and also the towne of Congham, where the inheritance of Sir Henry Spelman doth lye «& Roydon where the inheritance of Howell doth lye», bc not within the boundes of the warren of Rising. And though conyes have burrowed upon sondrie parcelles of grounde within the said townes, bordering upon the same warren «wherby the warryners of Rising in tymes past have usually taken the conyes there as appeared unto us by diverse deposicions already taken & retorned in the Chauncery». Yet by testimony of manie witnesses, concurring in a sort with the truths of the auncyent evidence, the owners of the groundes have usually taken the profitt of the conyes, or rent by money, or conyes for the same at the warreners handes, so as for anie thinge hitherto that hath ben produced before us, our opynion is, that the warreners of Rising ought to give recompence for the conyes burrowing & killed upon those groundes, unles it be upon some parcelles of grounde, which are the inheritaunce of Rising. Though the wordes of the auncient evidence do leave out thes townes last named, as no parcell of the chase for the deere, as well as for the warren, yet «by sondry deposicions it appeereth that the landes called Wyvelinges parte of the inheritaunce of the said Athow, & Roydon the inheritaunce of Mr Hovell, & parte of Congham the inheritaunce of the said Sir Henry Spelman, do lye within the circuite of the chase. And» the gentlemen before named <do everie one of them> who are owners of the inheritaunce there, <in> do everie one of them not stande so much upon the feeding of the deere, though thei come sometymes upon their groundes, and do promise so to carrie themselves in regard of the deere, as neither your Lordship nor the Lady of Arundell shall have cause to be grieved.

Touching South Wootton, which appeareth by the evidence to have ben both parcell of the chase & warren, Sir Arthur Capell lord of the same manor doth by his fermor promise to give satisfaccion to your Lordship that by a graunt from the lord of Castle Rising his manor of South Wootton is freed of chase & warren and hath also all other liberties graunted from Rising except wreck of the sea.

Touching North Wootton, wee have seen evidence, which doth laie the same towne within the libertie & chase of Castle Rising, and nothing was produced before us to impugne the same.

Wee have thought it our duties, though our opynions be carryed, as is before set downe, yet not to resolve upon anie thinge herin before your Lordship be made therwith acquaynted, that your Lordship maie as it shall seme good unto you here-after give direction. And wee take it to be the best corse for your Lordships inher-itance & mayntenance of the royalties of dere, that the warreners should kepe a farre lesse nomber of conyes. ⇨ And therby become not so harde borderers upon other mens groundes. ⇦ [445] <And> For the multitude of the conyes causeth <also>

---

[445] The underlined section has "*stet*" written above.

that the game of the dere cannot be faire, bicause for want of meate thei seeke their feed out of the chase, and there are often kylled up, and the game seldome or not at all farre within the chase, and the flock of weathers is also impayred thereby.

Concerning the contencion betwen Sir Henry Spelman knight & Richard Howell gent wee have hearde at large their allegacions on both sides, and have ended the contencion to both their contentmentes. And wheras ten acres of the demeanes of Rising doe lye in the Westfelde of Congham, and did lye there inter-mingled amongst the landes of the said Richard Howell, for which the contencion was, and were subject to the like quarrell, yet it was shewed unto us by Sir Henry Spelman, and not denyed by Baxter of Castle Rising, that the weatherflock of Rising had, in regard of Sir Henry Spelmans feede of the said ten acres, «the shack» from Michaelmas till Hallowmas yearly over the said Westfeld, as a recompence for Sir Henry Spelmans feede of the ten acres. And weras there was besides a parcell of ten acres, being the demeanes also of Rising, lieing in the same fielde, yt appeared by Baxters owne confession, that the same was burrowed with conyes, and that he tooke the profitt therof in the right of the warren.

Thus referring the consideracion hereof to your Lordships wisdome, wee wishe your Lordship much increase of honour to the glorie of Almightie God. From Norwich this 10 of January 1604. Your Lordships at comandement.

Unsigned. Draft in Martin Man's hand.
Endorsed: Copy of the letter to the Erle of North[*ampton*] concerning Rising.
4 pp. NRO RAY (6) 20vi.

Sir Nathaniel Bacon and others to the Privy Council

1604/5, January 10. Our humble duties remembred. According to the direccion given by your Lordships letters of the xii of November past,[446] wee have called before us Sir Henry Spelman knight, Thomas Athow esquire, & Richard Hovell gent, togither with Jo. Wright of North Wotton & Jo. Baxter of Castle Rising, touching the incrochmentes supposed to be made by some of them upon the lib-erties of the chase & warren of Castle Rising in the countie of Norfolk, being parcell of the inheritance of the right honorable the Erle of Northampton. And at this our meeting wee did peruse both evidence & deposicions of sondrie persons and hearde also the allegacions of both sides touching the suites in lawe depending betwixt the said Sir Henry Spelman & the said Richard Howell, and have to both their contentmentes ended their contencion. But concerning the incrochementes upon the liberties of Castle Rising, inasmuch as the same is the inheritaunce of our verie good lord the Erle of Northampton, wee have thought it our dutie, to certefie his Lordship at large how wee have proceeded therin, and what our judgement is touching the same cause. Thus wee humbly take our leave. From Norwich this 10 of January 1604. Your Lordships at comaundment.

Unsigned. Draft in Martin Man's hand.
Endorsed: Copy of the letter to the Lords of the Councell concerning Rising.
1 p. NRO RAY (6) 20v.

[446] Above, p.137, and documents following.

Thomas Barsham to Sir Nathaniel Bacon

[*1604/5*], **February 13.**[447] Right worshippfull my humble duty presupposed. These ar to signifye unto you, that diverse and sundry men hath bene with me about your fearme at Eccles which semed very desirous to deale with your worship for the same, unto whome I have imparted the particulers as they were sett downe to me &c., who hath promised to have come agayne, but as yet I have not heard of them. They all do generally much mislike the howses beinge neyther fyttinge for men of any worth to dwell in, nor yet able to receyve the commodities growinge upp[*on*] the groundes for want of bearne [*barn*] rome and other howses for necessary imployment, which I finde to be one of the greatest discoragmentes unto them, that otherwise would deale ther with. The valew lykewise of the rent they lykewise thinke to be very greate, so that both in respect of the one and the other I can not perswade any to come to any conclusion as yet, your howse stande still empty without a dweller which will if yt so continue growe into decay. One howse which was used to lay in beast meate standinge empty this winter is overthrone with the winde already so that if ther be not some other course taken thinges will rune into further decay, and your worships fearme lesse regarded. Your worships shepe ar (thankes be to God) in very good case, we dyd fodder them some three or 4 dayes this snowe which if that snowe had continued we did not knowe how to have done for hay for them, yt is so <scarce> harde to come by in our country the want is so greate, but I hope the worst is nowe past. I purposed to have come over to your worship before this tyme, but that yt pleased God this winter to visyte me with sicknes so that I am not yet able to travayle abrade, not [*sic*] to indewr the <the> ayre, but asone as I can I will wayte upon your worship. In the mean tyme cravinge pardon for this my rude scriblinge to your worship I humbly take my leave this xiii of February. Eccles in hast. Your worshipps to comaund in all duty to his power.

Signed: Tho[*mas*] Barsham.[448]
Addressed: To the right worshipfull Sir Nathanael Bacon knight at Stifkey.
Endorsed in Martin Man's hand: Mr Barsham.
1 p. NRO RAY 480.

Petition. John Rust to Thomas Egerton, Baron Ellesmere, Lord Chancellor

1604/5, February 15. *Petition to the Rt. Hon. the Lord Ellesmere, Lord Chancellor of England, to ask Sir Nathaniel Bacon to help the petitioner*[449] *in a dispute arising at the customs house in Lynn, 15 February 1604.*

Dobell, 68 (1941), item 246.

---

[447] Dating: the year has been deduced fron Nathaniel Bacon's status as knight (*post* July 1604) and the fact that his farm at Eccles was re-let on 26 June 1605, below, pp.194–5.

[448] Parson and sheep-reeve at Eccles. See 22 April 1604, above, p.103, and 26 June 1605, below, pp.194–5.

[449] John Rust: possibly a small boat owner in Holkham (*BP*, iii, pp.70, 72), one of the creeks under Lynn's jurisdiction. Although Rust is not mentioned by name in the catalogue entry, this appears to be the petition referred to in the Lord Chancellor's letter of 18 February 1604/5, below, p.154.

Referral of petition. Dr Julius Caesar, Master of Requests, to Sir Christopher Heydon, Sir Nathaniel Bacon and Sir Henry Sidney

1604/5, February 17. *Calendar.* The King refers the examination of the case concerned in the enclosed petition from John Barwicke to Heydon, Bacon and Sydney, provided it has not been nor is being dealt with in any of his Majesty's courts. The other party may name an equal number of commissioners. They are to call both parties before them and to mediate an equitable settlement so that his Majesty is no further troubled. From the Court at Whitehall.[450]

Signed: Jul[*ius*] Caesar.
Addressed: To the right wor[*shipful*] my verie lovinge freindes Sir Christopher Heydon, Sir Nathanaell Bacon and to Sir Henry Sydney knightes.
Endorsed in Martin Man's hand: Jo. Barwickes etc. peticion to his Majesty.
½ p. BL Stowe 150 ff.200–01.

Sir Edward Coke, Attorney General, to Sir Nathaniel Bacon

1604/5, February 17. After my very hartie comendacions. Whereas there is a matter of controversie betwene Thomas Fairfaxe gent,[451] and this poore man John Rust[452] the bearer herof, I have thought good to praie and desire your charitable & frendly paines to sende for both the said parties, and to heare & understand the cawses of the said controversie, and theruppon to doe your frendly endevour to ende and determine the same betwene them, that no further sute or charge maie growe therof. And if by your good perswasion & meanes you cannot bring them to accept of such order & agrement as you in your wisdome and conscience shall thinck fytt for them, then I praie you to certifie unto me the trewe state of the said controversie & in whome you finde the defalt to rest, that such further order maie be taken therein, as is according to justice & equitie. And so doe very hartilye committ you to God. At the Temple this xvii of Februarie 1604. Your very loving frende.

At the foot: Sir Nathaniell Bacon knight.
Signed: Edw[*ard*] Coke.
Addressed: To the right worshippfull my very loving frende Sir Nathaniell Bacon knight.
Endorsed in Martin Man's hand: The Kinges Attorny *pro* Rust.
½ p. BL Stowe 150 f.202.

---

[450] The petition has not been traced and the substance of the case is not known.

[451] Thomas Fairfax, gent, of Walsingham Parva, was a substantial landowner and merchant who traded in grain and malt, usually from Wells to London, Newcastle and Plymouth. He was a forceful character who was twice bound over to keep the peace. (Metters, 'Rulers and Merchants', p.217; Bacon memoranda books, 1597-1602 (FBL MS 31 *sub* 16 July 1598) and 1602–7 (NRO BL/BC/5/22 p.2.) In 1608 he was to represent the county's case at the Council Board for the unrestricted export of grain (*BP*, vi, forthcoming).

[452] See the documents dated 15 February 1604/5, above, p.152, and immediately below.

Referral of petition. Thomas Egerton, Baron Ellesmere, Lord Chancellor, to Sir Nathaniel Bacon

1604/5, February 18. *Calendar.* As John Rust, by his enclosed petition,[453] has desired the Lord Chancellor to refer to Bacon a suit depending in Chancery between Thomas Fayrfaxe, plaintiff, and the petitioner, defendant, the matter is accordingly recommended to Bacon "to make some quiett and freindly ende between them accordinge to equity and goode conscience", or otherwise to certify the truth of the matter and through whose default the matter cannot be settled. From York House.[454]

At the foot: Sir Nathaniell Bacon knight.
Signed: T. Ellesmere, *Canc[ellarius]*.
Addressed: To my verie loving freind Sir Nathaniell Bacon knight.
Endorsed in Martin Man's hand: Pro Rust.
½ p. BL Add. 63101 f.29.

Thomas Sackville, Earl of Dorset, Lord Treasurer, to the J.P.s in Norfolk

1604/5, February 22. After my verie harty commendacions. There have bin dyvers bruites and infourmacions brought aswell to the Lordes of the Councell as to my selfe, of huge quantities of corne passed and transported beyond the seas out of the portes within that county, and that thereby the price of corne is so enhaunsed, as that the same is farr above the Statute, and likely to growe higher and higher, whereby the poore people are ready to mutyne, and like to suffer great want and penury, and that which is moste of all, that a very greate quantity of corne hath bin of late by the permission of the officers of the portes transported beyond the seas, the price being above the rate lymited for transportacion by the Statute. Wherefore, to the end that the truth thereof may be examyned and knowne, and a present remedy given for the stay of further transportacion, if upon the matter there shall appeare juste cause to move the same, I am to requyre you or any two of you at the least next resyding to any porte where corne is transported within the said county, to call the officers of every suche porte before you and likewise all suche other as by any meanes can give you any good infourmacion touching transportacion of corne beyond the seas synce midsommer last even unto this present day, and by what warrant the same was transported, as namely whether by warrant of the Statute in respect of the price, or by warrant of speciall lycence from his Majestie or by any other warrant whatsoever, and lastly what is the price of every severall sorte of corne in the markett at this present, and what store of corne by your conjecturall estimate doth nowe remayne in surplusage within that shire, which may be transported both for encouragement of the farmer and the publique good of the shire, by venting that surplusage which the shire itselfe cannott spende, or whether at this present, in respect of the highe price of corne and likelyhood of want of corne to serve for the shire itself, and for releife of the poore, it be not fitt

---

[453] Of 15 February 1604/5, above, p.152.
[454] Bacon took evidence in this dispute on 5 March 1604/5, below, p.156.

that a present stay be made from henceforth of all transportacion beyond the seas, yea though the same be warranted by the Kinges license unto them. This service being of so greate importence both to <the whole> his Majestie and the whole realme in generall and to yourselves cheifly in pariculer, I requyre you in his Majesties name that you execute the same with all speed possible, and to send me a certificate of your proceedinges therein accordingly, and in the meanwhile to have vigilant care that neither the officers by their permission, nor any other by their unlawfull transportacion do passe away any corne, and likewise, if the present urgent necessity, and the publique good, and preservacion of the poore from myserie shall so requyre, even to make stay aswell of all corne already embarqued and not yet passed away, as also of all corne from henceforth to be transported, yea though by license from the Kinges Majestie. And so I commend you to God, this xxii of February 1604. Your very loving freind.

At the foot: Justices of peace in Norfolk.
Signed: T. Dorset.
Addressed: To my very lovinge freindes his Majesties justices of the peace within the county of Norfolk.
Endorsed in Martin Man's hand: Lord Treasurers letter *de transp*[*ortatione*].
1½ pp. BL Stowe 150 ff.204–5.

Thomas Sackville, Earl of Dorset, Lord Treasurer, to the J.P.s in Norfolk

1604/5, February 22. *Summary:* A copy of the above letter.
Copy in William Sanders' hand.

Endorsed: Copy of letters concerning transport[*ation*], 22 February 1604.
1½ pp. NRO RAY (6) 21.

Margaret Berney to Sir Nathaniel Bacon

1604/5, March 5. Sir wheras about twoe yeares past our steple came downe and ruinated the whole church, and wee now are enjoyned to repayre the same to our great charge, and wheras there is divers workmen boath of carpenters, «plumers» and masons, appoynted for the same work, and some of them alredy in work there, I have moved boath my uncle Rugg[455] and Mr Palgrave[456] that wee myght have a alhouse within our towne dureinge the tyme of the said work, for they cannot have any provision either of meat or drink nearer than North Walsham which is above twoe myles from this place, and I found them verie [*word deleted*] willinge therin. Mr Palgrave desires your assent unto it, to which effect I have written, desireing your certefycate under your hand unto Mr <Mr> Palgrave by this bearer, and the partie that I would have lycensed, whoe I knowe to be a verie honest man and of good behaviour amongst his neyghbours, and soe desyreinge your lawfull favoure herin I taike my leave. Gunton this v of Martch 1604. Your wourshipps to commaund.

---

[455] Probably William Rugg esq. (d.1616) of Felmingham. J.P. from 1577 (Smith, *County and Court,* p.354).
[456] Presumably John Palgrave of Barningham Northwood and an active J.P. in this period (*BP,* iv and v, *passim*).

[*Postscript*]: Yf it will pleas you to wryte this bearer will deliver it.

Signed: Margaret Berney.[457]

Addressed: To the right worshipful Sir Nathaniell Bacon knyght.

Endorsed in Martin Man's hand: Mistress Barny.

½ p. Folger L.d.173.

Memorandum concerning a dispute between Thomas Fairfax and Jo. Rust

1604/5, March 5. Memorandum 5 *Martii* 1604. Yt was thus proceeded betwen Mr Thomas Fairfaxe & Jo. Rust, before Sir Nathaniel Bacon knight.[458]

It appeared that the bonde shewed fourth was not the originall bonde which Jo. Rust had entred as suerty for Mr Fairfaxe in Lyn Custome House. And so much confessed by Mr Fairfaxe.

Jo. Rust objected, that the originall bond maie hereafter be brought in and put in suite. And that the certificat maketh him merchant & not Mr Fairfaxe, whereby hereafter he may be questioned upon the record.

It was moved that Mr Fairfaxe should enter a covenaunt agreeable with the condicion of his counterbond, and Rust to deliver out the counterbond. And both parties helde it reasonable & yealded to it.

It was thought reasonable that Mr Fairfaxe should beare Rustes charges in the Chauncery, which he refused. Wherupon Sir Nathaniel Bacon resolved to certefye.

Unsigned. In Martin Man's hand.

½ p. BL Stowe 150 f.203.

William Goldsmith and Simon Metterson to Martin Man

1604/5, March 7. Mr Man, I commend me unto you wishing your helth to the plesure of Almighty God. I have thought good at the request of the bearer heare of to certifie you, that whear as she having «the last year» a sonne dwelling with one Thomas Wildbloud of our towne, who being scalt [*scalded*] with trying [*purifying*] of oyle, and <laying> «being» so paynfull that the boye could not doo any thing, yet neverthe less his m[*aster*] and dame being more greedy of his work then forward to gitt him remydyd of that harme which he gott about his worke, sett him to bunche[459] when he had more need to have kept his bedd. And upon a tyme <Symo> I being at Symont Myttersonnes howse, he being then constabell, the boy cam to him, with his masters consent, to request that he would goe to his masters house to beare witness that his master would give him his indenture and so to be ryd of him. And after I hearde of it I was desirous that the constabell should goe

---

[457] Margaret Barney, née Flint, wife of Martin Barney of Gunton (Rye, *Visitation of Norfolk*, p.15). The date of Martin's death is uncertain, but the tone of the letter suggests that Margaret was now widowed and in charge of the estate. Martin Barney had been charged with celebrating mass in his house and described as "backward in religion", which probably led to his being twice dismissed from the Bench (Smith, *County and Court*, pp.214, 351). As such, he would not have been a natural ally for Bacon, hence, presumably, the formality of this letter from his widow.

[458] Rust's petition was referred to Bacon on 18 February 1604/5, above, p.154. For Bacon's report of 8 April 1605 see below, pp.169–70.

[459] "Bunch": to pound hemp or flax prior to retting (Yaxley, *Glossary*, p.26).

with me to Wildbloudes house to se [what] his intent was, & when we cam thir we found him so parromtory as his answer was yf we would have him better tended & kept we should doe it our sellfes. And thus I thought good to certifie to you, and no more then I will justifie before whome soever I shall be called. Thus committing you to God. From Welles this presant Thursday being the 7 of Marche 1604. Your frinds to the uttermost of <my> «our» poweres.

Signed: W[*illia*]m Gouldsmith[460] & Symon Metterson.
Addressed: To his approved good frind Mr Martin Man at Styfkye.
Endorsed in Martin Man's hand: Certificate concerning Wildbloude.
1 p. *some staining*. NRO MC 1872/19, 866X2. Calendared, *Supplementary Stiffkey Papers*, p.19.

John Holmes to Roger Townshend

1604/5, March 8. Mr Towneshend I have receyved youre kynde letter. As for the letters of Vynyors I have sent for them by my kynsman John Everarde to have them safelye kepet. And where as you wrytt to me that my brother should reporte that I should make the bill obligatorye betwen your father and him, yt ys more then I cann <de> remember for God I take to wytnes, I [*?4 words deleted*] was never acquaynted withall untill the matter was in sute & by chance goinge to Mr Wolmers he dyd shewe me the bill and then dyd I byd him in enye wyse he should not procede there with for that I would not stand to justefye the same. My brother ys full of pollecye, he havinge me att the advantage he thinkes he wyll make me confesse more then I knowe, but what I have before reported unto you I wyll stande to justefye my selfe to be an honest mann. And as for the notes for Vynyor I wyll make all sure or elles my frindes shall deceyve me. I wyll fullye be furnyshed for your fathers comynge & youres of those thinges you desire. This with my hartye comendacyons I leve you to thAlmyghtye. Norwich the viii of March 1604. Your frinde to command.[461]

Signed: John Holme.
Addressed: To his verye good frind Mr Roger Towneshend att Smalburroughe.
Endorsed in Martin Man's hand: Jo. Holme. 8 *Martii* 1604. Disavowing his making the bill oblig[*atory*] from R. Townshend to Nic. Holme.
½ p. RH Box 66.

Certificate of grain prices at King's Lynn

1604/5, March 12. Tewsdaye the xii of March 1604.[462]
[Price]s corne [a]t Kinges [Lynn].
    Wheate the quarter   26s.

---

[460] William Goldsmith was one of the overseers of the poor at Wells in 1600/01 (*BP*, iv, p.192), and, as such, may have been responsible for putting the boy out to Wildblood.

[461] For earlier and later documents in this case, see the Evidence of George Oldman, 2 January 1604/5, above, p.148, and that of John Holmes, *Post* 29 March 1605, below, p.160.

[462] This, and the document immediately below, are a response to the Lord Treasurer's letter of 22 February 1604/5, above, pp.154–5.

Rye the quarter	16s.
Mault the quarter	16s.
Barlye the quarter	15s.
Pease the quarter	14s.
Beanes the quarter	14s.
Oates the quarter	9s.

Signed: John Kerchere maior, Thom[a]s Oxburgh.
½ p. *l.h.s. torn.* NRO RAY (6) 21.

Certificate of grain transported from the port of Blakeney

1604/5, March 16. To the right worshipful Sir Nathanyell Bakon knight.

[These] are to certiffie your worship that ther hath been transported over the seas [out] of Blackeney haven from myd somer daie 1604 to the xxii of Februarie [acc]ording to his honores derection seven hundreth & fortie quarters of wheat, [of] rie fyve quarters, of barlie nyne hundreth thre score & eleven quarters, [of] moult [*malt*] two hundreth three score & tene quarters, the which severall [sortes] of graines hath all passed by vertu of the statut, and from portt [to] portt[463] eight quarters of wheat, of barlie eleven hundreth fyftie quarters, [of] moult two hundreth quarters & of ottes three hundreth & twenti [quar]ters. And as we are enformed the prices of merchauntable corne are this daie being the xvi daie of March to be sould in the markettes neare [u]nto this plac *viz.* wheat at fower & twenti shillinges eight pence the quarter, rie at fourten shillinges eight pence the quarter, barlie and moult at fourten shillinges the quarter. And thus with our duties remembred to your worship we humblie take our leaves. Blackny the 16 of March 1604. Your worshipes to comand.

Signed: Andrew Rug customer, Joh[n] Braddock surveyor, Tho[mas] Austen comptroller.

Endorsed in Martin Man's hand: Certificat of corne transported out of Blakeny port till the 22 February 1604.
½ p. *l.h.s. torn.* NRO RAY (6) 21.

J.P.s in Norfolk to Thomas Sackville, Earl of Dorset, Lord Treasurer

1604/5, March 19. Our duties humbly remembred. By your Lordships letters of the 22 of February last,[464] wee understand, that informacion hath ben given unto your Lordship & the rest of the Lords of the Councell, of exceeding quantityes of corne, shipped oversea, out of this countie of Norfolk, and much of it being above the rates lymited by the statute, whereby the prises be so enhaunsed & like to increase, as the poore are readie to mutyne. And withall your Lordship requireth us, to take informacion by the officers of the portes, & otherwise, both what corne hath ben so transported synce midsomer last, and by what warrant, as also what the prises be of corne at this present, with some further direccions therin given us.

---

[463] "Portt to portt": coastal trade.
[464] See above, pp.154–5, and the documents immediately preceding this one.

For aunswer therunto, yt may please your Lordship to be advertised, that wee have taken order for a certificat to be sett downe by the officers of the portes, what quantetyes have ben so transported, whereby yt shall «also» appeare <what hath passed, &> by what warrant the same was passed. Touching the prises of corne, being all of us mett at this tyme by occasion of the common service of the contrey, wee have conferred amongst ourselves, and inquired of the chiefe constables of the severall hundredes of the shire, who cannot be ignorant of the state of the contrey in this behalf, and wee fynde, that wheate hath not, since the late transportacion of grayne, exceeded the price of the statute, and to be at this tyme, at 24s. & 25s. the qr the best merchant, barley to be in most places under 14s. the qr, saving in the places about Lynne by reason of more vent there then in other partes of the shire yt hath a little risen above the price lymitted, other graynes are ⇨ under the rates⇦ «not transported». And for anie mutyne by occasion of transportacions, the people are so farre from it as wee cannot learne of anie ⇨ generall⇦ discontentment by that occasion. And where your Lordship requireth our estimate of the quantityes of corne that may be forborne by the contrey, wee cannot set downe a certificat therin as yet, but upon examinacions & conference wee do fynde that out of some small hundredes there may be spared 1000 qrs wheate & the <lik> «greater» quantityes of barly. So wee humbly take our leave. From Norwich 19 *Martii* 1604. [*Signed*.] Sir Arthur Heveningham, Sir Myles Corbett, Sir Philip Woodhouse, Sir Nathaniel Bacon, etc [*sic*].

Draft in Martin Man's hand.
Endorsed: Letter to the Lord Treasurer 19 *Martii de transp*[*ortatione*].
2½ pp. NRO RAY (6) 22.

J.P.s in Norfolk to officers of the port of Lynn

[*Post 1604/5, March 23*].[465] After our hartie comendacons. Wheras by a statute made in the 3 yeare of his Majesties rayne that now is it was ordayned that when barley and mault in anie port in this his kingdome should not exceed the price of 14s. the quarter that it should be lawfull for the subjects of this kingdome to transport the same grayne in Englishe shipping payeng his Majesties customes due for such corne so transported. And forasmuch as wee his Majesties justices of peace within the county of Norfolk whose names are herunder written are credibly informed that now at this present and likewise for the space of 6 monethes now last past barlie & mault within the port of Lynne & the members of the same hath stood at the same price of 14s. the quarter for which cause we have thought it

---

[465] Dating: dated from the final day of the regnal year 1 James I. The reference to 3 James is almost certainly an error, either in the original or, more likely, in the early 20th century transcription on which we have had to rely here. It was the statute of 1 James c.25 that gave permission to export when the maximum price of barley was 14s., while that of 3 James c.11 only allowed the export of cask beer when the price of barley and malt was under 16s. a quarter. Export of corn was a recurring issue, but this letter does not appear to be part of the discussion in early 1608 (*BP*, vi, forthcoming; *Stiffkey Papers*, pp.156–7). The grain in question then was any corn, while here the issue is limited to barley and malt. Furthermore, the price of barley in February 1608 was given as 12s. 8d. or 13s. while here it is said to have been 14s. the quarter for the past six months.

convenient to desire you his Majesties officers of the port of Lynne & the members of the same to take knowledge hereof. Hoping that withall you will labour by your best endeavours to be aiding to his Majestys subjectes in thes partes for the transporting of their said barlie or mault as the law in this case hath provided. Wherin wee think the husbondarey of this country shall find the better meanes for the sale of this corne, and the merchantes be encouraged to buy, when there may be hope of transportacon. In the furtheraunce wherof you shall do good service to his Majestie in regard of his customes and also much good to the countie for the exporting of such corne as the plenty of this yeare maie afford to be spared. And so not doubting of your care & due considiracon of the premises, wee bide you hartely farewell.

Undated. Unsigned. Copy.
Reprinted from *Stiffkey Papers*, pp.149–50.

Evidence of John Holmes

1605, March 29<-Θ->1605/6, March 24. *Calendar.* Dated *Anno domini 1605.* John Holmes declares that on Good Friday, 29 March last, Mr Tavener and Thomas Skott came to the gaol at Mr Worslyes house in Norwich to persuade John to write to his brother Nicholas saying that Nicholas had had a letter of attorney from John warranting the suit on a bond brought by Nicholas against Roger Towneshend gent. John, who had previously refused similar requests from his brother, refused to do this, despite Tavener and Skott's discontent with his answer to "so smalle a request". Signed: *Teste Johanne Holme.*[466]

Copy.
On same sheet and with same endorsements as Evidence of John Holmes 25 March 1604<-Θ->24 March 1606, above, p.96.
Endorsed: [1] Notes made by John Homes in testymony of a cawse for Roger Touns[en]d; [2 in Martin Man's hand] John Holmes declarations touching the bond & Vyniors & Nicholas Holmes pracetise.
½ p. RH Box 66.

Accounts for the relief of the poor

[*1605, post March 31*]. *Summary.* Accounts for the year 1604–1605 submitted by churchwardens and/or overseers of the following parishes. All accounts are dated to the year, but not all accounts give the day they were drawn up. The normal accounting year for these poor accounts ran from Easter to Easter, in this case from 8 April 1604 to 31 March 1605. For an explanation of terms used in this list see the introductory paragraph to the poor accounts for 1602–1603 on p.28.

Bale. Rate collected: £3 2s. 1d. Rate uncollected: 7s. 11½d. 32 ratepayers named altogether. Principal contributor: Thomas Shaxton. Expenditure: £3 9s. 6d.,

---

[466] For an earlier document in this case see above, 8 March 1604/5, p.157. For the next document relating to this case, see Evidence of *post* 2 April 1605, below, pp.167–8.

including 2*s*. for four briefs for fires. 7 poor named. Signed by Rob[er]t Bulleyn gent, Rob[er]t Lasbey, churchwardens; George Mason, [*by mark:*] Robert Smith, [*by mark:*] Robert Daniell. Endorsed by Martin Man: "Batheley. Order to have 40*s*. in stock."
1½ pp. NRO MC 1872/21, 866X2.

Bodham. Rate assessed 23 April 1604: 18*s*. 8*d*. Rate uncollected: 10*d*. 37 ratepayers named. Principal contributor: Sir Christopher Haydon. Expenditure: 17*s*. 10*d*. 5 poor named. Signed: [*all by mark:*] William Andrewes, Symon Francke, Anthony Tincker, Jhon Dawes. Endorsed by Martin Man.
1 p. NRO MC 1872/21, 866X2.

Brinton. Rate assessed (with valuation) 25 March 1604 and collected: 25*s*. 8*d*. 45 ratepayers named, including 29 non-residents. Principal contributors: Mr Birlingham, Mr Yonges, Mr William Playford. Expenditure: 24*s*. 5*d*. 14 poor named. In hand: 15*d*. Stock: 20*s*. Signed: William Playford, overseer, [*by mark:*] Thomas Yaxley, Chr[*ist*]opher Burlingham. Endorsed by Martin Man.
2 p. NRO MC 1872/21, 866X2.

Briston. Rate collected: £7 5*s*. 64 ratepayers named. Principal contributors: Dr Hunte, Mr Scamber, John Howmans. Expenditure: £7 3*s*. 11*d*. 32 poor named. Unsigned. Listed: Thomas Hubbart, Thomas Kinge, William Bauldinge, overseers; William Toleye, William Yarram, churchwardens. Endorsed by Martin Man.
2 pp. NRO MC 1872/21, 866X2.

Cley. April 6. Rate assessed: £16 18*s*. 6*d*. Rate uncollected: £2 16*s*. 1*d*. 33 ratepayers named. Principal contributor: Barnard Utber gent. Expenditure: £11 2*s*. 9*d*. 21 poor named. In hand: £2 19*s*. 8*d*. Signed: Thomas Grene, churchwarden; Chrystofer Newgate, John Raylie, Thomas Cook, overseers. Endorsed by Martin Man.
1 p. NRO MC 1872/21, 866X2.

Edgefield. Account from 22 April 1604, made 6 April 1605. Carried over: 14*d*. From increase in stock: 11*s*. Rate collected: £3 13*s*. 35 ratepayers named, including 9 non-residents. Principal contributors: Sir Nicholas Bacon, Thomas Lawes. Expenditure: £4 3*s*. 3*d*. 11 poor named. In hand: 23*d*. Signed: [*by mark:*] Thomas Lawes, Bryant Barker, [*by mark:*] William Overton, overseers; [*by mark:*] Robert Crogate, [*by mark:*] William Burwell, churchwardens. Endorsed by Martin Man.
1 p. NRO MC 1872/21, 866X2.

Glandford and Bayfield. 5 April. Rate collected: 55*s*. 3*d*. Rate uncollected: 5*s*. 7*d*. 13 ratepayers named. Principal contributors: Frauncis Fiske gent, Robert Beales, Richard Braye gent. Expenditure, including house farm, putting a boy out to service and 2*s*. 6*d*. for briefs: 51*s*. 3 poor named. In hand: 4*s*. [*sic*]. Stock: 11*s*. Signed: Rob[er]t Crytaft, John Caster. Endorsed by Martin Man.
1 p. NRO MC 1872/21, 866X2.

Gunthorpe. April 6. Carried over: 13*s*. 4*d*. Rate assessed 22 April 1604 (1*s*. for

every £5): £3 3s. Rate uncollected: 11s. 8d. 23 ratepayers named. Principal contributors: Mr Nicholas clerk, Giles Godfrey gent, Christofer Houghton gent,
Edmund Moine, Richard Duckett. Expenditure, including 7s. house farm: £3 4s.
10d. 2 poor named. Signed: Christofer Houghton, Edmund Moine, Thomas
Gannar [*Gardener*]. Endorsed by Martin Man.
1 p. NRO MC 1872/21, 866X2.

Holt. May 11. Account 22 April 1604 to 5 May 1605 made to Sir Nathaniell
Bacon and John Pagrave esq. Stock: 43s. 3d. used to put the poor to work but not
increased. Rate collected: £4 9s. 6d. (no details). Rate uncollected because of
refusal to pay: 9s. 10d. 10 men refusing to pay named and another crossed out.
Expenditure, including for a brief and for shipwreck: £4 4s. 8 poor named. In
hand: 5s. 6d. Signed: W[*illia*]m Brown, [*by mark:*] Thomas Donne, [*by mark:*]
Andrew Massie, overseers; Tho[*mas*] Gayton, churchwarden. Endorsed by Martin
Man: "Holt accompt at Easter 1605".
1 p. NRO MC 1872/21, 866X2.

Houghton. Rate assessed: 24s. 2d. 16 ratepayers named. Principal contributor: Sir
Hendrie Sidnie. 3 poor named. Signed: Nicholas Gaie, Will[*ia*]m Denmark,
Richard Fenne. Endorsed by Martin Man.
1 p. NRO MC 1872/22, 866X2.

Hunworth. Account 23 April 1604 to 6 April 1605. Rate collected: 16s. 4d. 12
ratepayers named. Principal contributors: William Armested clerk, Mistress
Chamberleigne, Robert Smyth, Thomas Peckett, Widow Newman, Edmond
Brightif. Expenditure: 15s. 4 poor named. In hand: 16d. Signed: Thomas
Newman, churchwarden; Thomas Peckett, [*by mark:*] Thomas Slatter, [*by mark:*]
John Broune, overseers. Endorsed by Martin Man.
1 p. NRO MC 1872/21, 866X2.

Kelling. Rate collected: 52s. 9d. Rate uncollected: 6s. 2d. 25 ratepayers named,
including the lord of the manor. Principal contributors: Thomas Gilberd, Peter
Thompson. Expenditure: 52s. 9 poor named. In hand: 9d. Signed: Thomas
Gilberd, Ed[*ward*] Stanton, churchwardens; Thom[*a*]s Bourne, Abraham
Waterson, overseers. Endorsed by Martin Man.
1 p. NRO MC 1872/21, 866X2.

Langham, Great. Account made to Sir Nathaniell Bacon and John Pagrave esq.,
"justeses of this lymett". Rate collected: £5 4s. 4d. 36 ratepayers named, including
13 non-residents. Principal contributors: John Newman, Robart Barnard.
Expenditure: £5 1s. 10d. 6 poor named. In hand: 2s. 6d. Parish officers named:
Allin Lampker, John Tayler, overseers; Edmund Knapes, John Parsons, churchwardens; John Gryx senior, Robert Tooly, Robert Barker, new overseers. Unsigned.
Endorsed by Martin Man.
1 p. NRO MC 1872/21, 866X2.

Letheringsett. Rate collected from 16 April 1604: 36s. 5d. 20 ratepayers named,
including 11 non-residents. Principal contributor: Sir Henry Sidney. Expenditure,
including house farm, not totalled. 6 poor named. In hand: 7d. Parish officers

named: Richard Lawson, Richard Fleming, overseers; William Corchever, John Boulton, churchwardens. Unsigned. Endorsed by Martin Man.
1 p. NRO MC 1872/21, 866X2.

Melton Constable. Rate assessed 4 May 1604: 12*s*. 8 ratepayers. Principal contributor: Thomas Asteley esq. Expenditure: 12*s*. 6 poor named and 2 children. Stock: 40*s*. Signed: Richarde Foster, Edward Nabbes, [*by mark:*] Ruben Nayles. Endorsed by Martin Man.
1 p. NRO MC 1872/21, 866X2.

Morston. Account of overseers and churchwardens made 6 April. Rate collected: £3 1*s*. 17 ratepayers named, including 5 non-residents. Principal contributor: Thomas Kinges gent. Expenditure: £3 3*s*. 2*d*. 5 poor named. Stock: 25*s*. Signed: Tho[*ma*]s Barker, [*by mark:*] Robart Powdich, [*by mark:*] William Paldinge. Endorsed by Martin Man.
1 p. NRO MC 1872/21, 866X2.

Salthouse. Account to 30 March 1605. Carried over: 6*s*. 2*d*. Rate collected: £3 18*s*. Rate uncollected: 9s. 10d. 25 ratepayers named altogether, including the lord of the manor. Principal contributors: the lord of the manor, Robert Hetherington and Christofer Tucke. Expenditure: £4 8*s*. 18 poor named and children. Deficit: 3*s*. 10*d*. Signed: Peter Tucke, Peter Abram, churchwardens; Robert Hetherington clerk, Robert Tucke, overseers. Endorsed by Martin Man.
1 p. NRO MC 1872/21, 866X2.

Saxlingham. Rate assessed: 11*d*. the week; 4*d*. the month. 12 ratepayers named. Principal contributor: Sir Henry Sidney. Expenditure: 8*d*. the week; 40*s*. charges, including house farm, part paid out of stock. 3 poor named, including a lame man from Alburgh. Signed: Tho[*mas*] Whyting, Rob[*er*]t Chevelie, overseers. Endorsed by Martin Man.
1 p. NRO MC 1872/21, 866X2.

Sharrington. Rate collected: 27*s*. 3*d*. 32 ratepayers named. Principal contributor: William Hunt esq. Expenditure: 30*s*. 2*d*. 14 poor named. Signed: [*by mark:*] John Whood, overseer; [*by mark:*] John Cootes, John Chestnie, churchwardens. Endorsed by Martin Man.
2 pp. NRO MC 1872/21, 866X2.

Snoring, Great. Monthly rate assessed: 6*s*. 8*d*. 13 ratepayers named. Principal contributors: Sir Henry Clare, Dr West. Monthly expenditure, including putting a child out to nurse: 7*s*. 8*d*. 8 poor named, with wives and children. Stock in the hands of Henry Mylls, Symon Newton and Gregory Plaford: £3. Signed: John Clarke, Symon Jello, Henery Millis. Endorsed by Martin Man: *"De novo* [*new*] Henry Mylles, Val. Yonges."
1 p. NRO MC 1872/21, 866X2.

Stiffkey. Account of overseers and churchwardens. Rate collected (no names given): £7 4*s*. 5*d*. Expenditure, detailed by month and including house farm, work on the town house/almshouse and payments to watchmen: £6 9*s*. 2*d*. 8 poor

named. In Edmond Mondefforde's hands for stock: 13*s*. 3*d*. New overseers: John Framyngham, Peter Smythe. Signed: Edmond Moundeford, Robert Framyngham, Thomas Speller, Jeoffry Stele. Endorsed by Martin Man.
2 pp. NRO MC 1872/22, 866X2.

Stody. Rate collected: 39*s*. 8*d*. 15 ratepayers named. Principal contributor: Thomas Sherwoode gent. Expenditure on one unnamed woman and her two children not totalled. In hand: 8*d*. Signed: [*by mark:*] William Cooke, churchwarden; Edmund Bond overseer. Endorsed by Martin Man.
1½ pp. NRO MC 1872/21, 866X2.

Thornage. Rate assessed 13 May 1604: 50*s*. 10*d*. 19 ratepayers named. Principal contributors: Sir Nicolas Bacon, Mr Bures, Mr Spilman, Christopher Burlingham. Expenditure, including house farm: 50*s*. 10*d*. 8 poor named. Stock: 20*s*. Churchwarden named: Thomas Bircham. Signed by overseers: Chr[*ist*]opher Burlingham, Henry Bures, John Parkins. Endorsed by Martin Man.
2 pp. NRO MC 1872/21, 866X2.

Thursford. April 10. Rate collected (no details): £4 10*s*. Expenditure, including house farm. No names are given, the 13 monthly amounts are reduced from 5*s*. to 4*s*. and the final total is altered by Martin Man to £3 18*s*. 6*d*. Overseers named: William Bonde, William Dey. Unsigned. Endorsed by Martin Man.
On separate sheet in the same hand: "We doe nomynate to be overseers *pro anno futuro* [*for the coming year*] Edmund Colles, John Framingham senior, Steaphen Lea, Richard Browne."
1 p. NRO MC 1872/22, 866X2.

Wells. Rate collected (no details): £21 19*s*. 4*d*. Stock carried over in the hands of John Greene: £2 3*s*. Expenditure, including maintenance of poor children (no details): £22 17*s*. 10*d*. Stock remaining in the hands of John Sabb and others: 24*s*. 6*d*. Overseers nominated for the coming year: Robert Mangles, Richard Gouldsmith, Richard Mitterson, Nicholas Wassellye. Signed: John Greene, Willyam Tyde, Hendrye Cowngham, [*by mark:*] William Tydd mariner, Henrie Halman. Endorsed by Martin Man.
1 p. NRO MC 1872/22, 866X2.

Weybourne. April 6. Given at Holt before Sir Nathaniell Bakon and John Pagrave esq. Rate collected: 47*s*. 6*d*. 21 ratepayers named. Principal contributors: Justyse Kyngmyle,[467] John Smyth, Thomas Moore. Used from the profit of the stock: 12*s*. Expenditure: 59*s*. 7*d*. 5 poor named. Signed: John Rooke, James Bull, Thomas Barrowe, overseers; Peter Tubbinge, [*by mark:*] John Cook, churchwardens. Endorsed by Martin Man.
1 p. NRO MC 1872/21, 866X2.

Wiveton. From 20 May 1604 to Easter 1605. Rate collected, including from Sir James Calthropp for the wind mill: £4 4*s*. 10*d*. 24 ratepayers named. Principal contributor: Mr John Kynge. Expenditure (no details): £4 4*s*. 10*d*. Thomas Neale,

[467] George Kingsmill (see poor accounts for 1602/3, above, p.32n.).

overseer; John Jenkinson, Peter Bishopp, churchwardens. Endorsed by Martin Man.
1 p. NRO MC 1872/21, 866X2.

All listed, *Supplementary Stiffkey Papers*, p.13.

List of overseers in Holt Hundred

1605, April.
Holt.[468] Churchwardes, Christofer Semondes, Laraunce Hagon. Overseers,
Samewell Browne, William Dobson, Roger Dybolde.
Letheringsett. Richard Fytt gent, William Couchefer.
Edgfyld. Thomas Coper the sone of John Coper, James Hamond, Thomas Abbes.
Byrston [*Briston*]. William Toley, William Crogatt, Thomas Crogatt, Thomas Mors.
Borrowe [*Burgh Parva*]. <Edmond West>, John Lodes, John Balye.
Melton [*Constable*]. Edward Nabbes, Ruben Nayles.
<Byrningham>
Stodye. Thomas Athowe, Robert Hunt, Petter Heythe.
Hunworthe. Robert Smith, Thomas Pockett, Edmond Brytofte, Thomas Fytt.
Salthouse. Churchwardens <Peter Tucke, Peter Abraham>.
<Kelling. Overseers> John Kydbalde, Edmond Gyrdleston, Christofer Tucke,
Steven Mone.[469]
Waborne. Thomas More, Godfrye Hemblinge, John Cade.
Bodham. Simond Frannke, <Anthoney Tyncker>, George Dixe.
Hempstead. Edmond Brettingham, Edmond Freeman.
Kellinge. Thomas Gylberte, John <Marke> Dyx.
Blackneye. Brimston Chadwicke gent, William Godskyrke, Edmond Graye.
Claye. John Fyshe senior, John Collens, Raphe Greve, Edwarde Leske.
Brunton [*Brinton*]. John Plesaunce, Richard Yonges, Christofer Playford.
Langham. John Grix senior, Robert Toleye, Robert Barker.
Swanton [*Novers*]. Edmond Baker, Thomas Blacke.
Bathley [*Bale*]. William Jervis gent, Thomas Shaxton, George Mason.
Wiveton. Steven Houssegoe, <John Braddock>, William Daynes, John Yaxleye.
Thornage. Robert Stembes, William <Kendall> Maxwell, John Parkinges.
Saxlingham. Andrewe Claxton, Robert Framingham.
Morston. John Mumforde, Robert Poudidge.
Gunthrop. Gregorye Daynes, Richard Mutton, Richard Moneye.
Sherington. John Whode, Gregorye Softleye.
Glamford & Bayfield. Robert Beales, John Caster, Simond Abbes.
Buringham [*Briningham*]. Jo. Bussell senior, Edward Bond, Thomas Bussell.[470]
Unsigned.
Endorsed in Martin Man's hand: Hoult Hundred overseers in Aprill 1605.
2 pp. NRO MC 1872/21, 866X2.

---

[468] All the place names are marked with a cross and "delivered". Holt, Letheringsett, Edgefield, Burgh,
Hempstead, Blakeney, Gunthorp and Briningham are also marked with a "C".
[469] It is not clear from the layout of the document whether these men should actually be attributed to
Salthouse.
[470] The entry for Briningham has been added in Martin Man's hand.

Petition. William Bennett to Sir Robert Clarke, Baron of the Exchequer

[*1605, April*].[471] To the right worshipfull, Sir Robert Clarke, knight, one of the Barons of Thexchecker,[472] the humble peticion of William Bennett.

Wheras your worships poore suppliantes wife, by name Katheren Bennett, was at the last Assise in Northfolke founde gillty before your worship of manslaughter, and uppon pittifull consideracion thereof reprived in gaole without judgement, there to abide that unhappie hazard most commanly falling uppon suche wofull accidentes, except God in his infinite mercy ordayne a speedy remedy.

I moste humbly beseeche your worshipp that forasmuch as your suppliantes crosse in this case is very heavie, & he being poore, & having a greate charge of chilldren, & feaw frendes, & no knowledge in matter of this importance, is at his wittes end, not knowing what to doe, it might now please your worship of your especiall commiseracion, to afforde your poore suppliant by some meanes the knowledge of the moste fitt & orderly course for redresse of this extremytie, and he will for ever pray to God for your blessed & happie prosperytie.

On the opposite page: Mr Baron woolde have a certificatt from the justisses of the pittifullnes of that cause & behaviour of the parte, & allso a coppie of the indictment, and then he will shew what favoure he may. [*Signed*:] [?]St. T.[473]

Undated. Unsigned.
1 p. NRO MC 1872/19, 866X2. Calendared, *Supplementary Stiffkey Papers*, p.19.

Sir Nathaniel Bacon to Thomas Sackville, Lord Treasurer, and Lord Home, Chancellor of the Exchequer

1605, April 1. My humble dutie remembred. In aunswer of your Lordships letters of the 20 of December last concerning his Majesties manour of Est Derham in the county of Norfolk wherof I am steward.[474] May yt please your Lordships to be advertised that upon the receipt of your Lordships <former> letters <of the xv of February last>[475] I caused my understeward to forbeare the admittaunce of anie tenantes <within the manour who accordingly <<perfor>> observed the same> or assessing of anie fynes within the said manour till his Majesties pleasure shall be further knowen therin. And further have taken order that the cort rolles rentalles and surveys, which be in the handes of the bailiff of that manour, shall forthwith be sent up and delivered into the handes of the Awditour of this county as your Lordships hath directed. Divers rolles and surveyes «belonging to the said manour» I <learne> «am informed» be remayning in the Bishop of Ely his officers possession, for Estdereham was somtyme parcell of the possession of that B[*ishop*]

---

[471] Dating: dated by reference to the justices' certificate to Sir Robert Clarke of 22 April 1605, below, p.175.

[472] Here addressed as one of the Justices of Assize on the Norfolk circuit.

[473] Not identified. The petition and the postscript are written out in the same rather elaborate hand, possibly by one of the Clerks of the Exchequer.

[474] See above, p.144.

[475] The Lord Treasurer to Matthew Clarke, steward of the manor of East Dereham, 15 February 1603/4, above, p.73.

<of Ely.> Touching the other poyntes <required by your letters of the xv February to be certefyed I have already <<sent>> retorned my certificat> «wherof your Lordships requireth to be certefyed according to your letters formerly written in February 1603, I did» upon the receipt of these <your honours> letters «retorne <a certificat> unto your Lordships a particular certificat.» So I humbly take my leave. From St[*iffkey*] this first of Aprill 1605. Your Lordships at commandment.

Unsigned. Draft. In Martin Man's hand.
On same sheet and with same endorsement as Order of 20 December 1604, above, p144.
Endorsed in Martin Man's hand: Letters concerning Est Derham 20 December 1604 with a copy of the aunser.
1 p. NRO NNAS S2/17/17.

Evidence of John Holmes concerning suit between Roger Townshend and Nicholas Holmes

[*1605, post April 2*].[476] A note made by John Holme for his remembrance as followeth.[477]

Memorandum the third day in Ester weke, there dyd come <unto> unto me, the sayd John Holme, one Miles Burton late of Foulsham one of my acquayntance, whoe delyvered unto me commendacyons from my brother Nicholas Holme. Whoe dyd send me worde that I «had» delt very hardlye by him, and he was heighelye displeased with me that I should opplish [*publish*] that which should be kepet secret betwene us. I demanded of <him> «Burton» wherein I had used him a mysse. He answered me he could not wright eny letter to me, but yt was knowne. And that he had wrytten a letter to me that he was like to be brought in question for, that should be to his greate troble and discredytt. I likewise demanded of him what letter yt should be, he answered a letter my brother dyd «send» to me that dyd [*word illegible*] Mr Towneshend whoe was my brothers great adversarye, and that I had declared that thereby Mr Towneshend myght prevayle againste [? him in] his matter in question before Sir Nathaniel Bacon. I answered I had delyvered no more before Sir Nathaniel Bacon but the trewth, and that I [?]would be sworne to. And that I delyvered the letter he sent me concerninge that matter unto Sir Nathaniel Bacon. And that he wrytt to me, that if I would I should shewe the letter unto Sir Nathaniel Bacon, for that he had promised unto Sir Nathaniel Bacon that he would wright «unto» me to that effect he had sett downe in his letter. The sayd Miles Burton [?]demanded of me to have a sight of the letter, or that I would send my brother a true coppye thereof, for that he was within fewe dayes to make his ferther answere unto Sir Nathaniel Bacon for the matter in contoversye betwene Mr Towneshend and him. I answered him I could not let him have eny coppye of the letter for that

---

[476] Dating: the year 1605 is established from the brief details of the visit by Miles Burton given in the letter of 7 April 1605 from Holmes to Roger Townshend (below, p.169). In 1605 Easter Day fell on 31 March, so the third day in Easter week referred to here was 2 April 1605 (taking Easter Day as the first, see Cheney and Jones, p.93).

[477] For the previous document relating to this case, see Evidence of Holmes , *post* 29 March 1605, above, p.160.

I delyvered the letter [?]as I had answered to the sayd Miles before, and that Sir Nathaniel Bacon had the letter in kepinge. Uppon further communicacyon betwene us at <that> that instant the sayd Myles sayde he was sorye to see me in prison. And and [*sic*] that I would not be ruled <ad> as he dyd advise me. My answere to him was, I was to much ruled by him that should wisshe me well, nameinge my brother Nicholas. But for him I had not ben arrested. And were yt not for his dettes which he have by his senister meanes and practeze unburdened uppon me, which ys his owne debt and I but suertye for him, I would by the grace of God have my inlargement agayne. The sayd Myles answered agayne that the sayd Nicholas Holme my brother was not to be trusted & that he dyd trust to have made an ende for Mr <Themyllh> Themylthorpe⁴⁷⁸ his matters. And the sayd Myles sayd that the sayd Nicholas should saye to him that if I would be ruled by him he had noe intent that I should be longe in pryson. I answered to the sayd Miles that I would hardelye bel[e]ve what my brother sayd for that if he had <ben> performed his promise & greate othes which before he had vowed to Mr Tompson William Hempsted & others, I had not a ben in durance. The sayd Myles sayd agayne that there was nothinge to be had or gotten at his hand, in not <bl> beleveinge him, for if Themylthorpe and he dyd not agree presentlye the sayd Nicholas Holme would take such a course that he would not care for eny matter that should be objected agaynst the sayd Nicholas Holme, by Mr Towneshend or by enye other whatsoever. The sayd Myles sayd that Mr Towneshend was in durance for <ever> his life tyme [*?two words illegible*]. I answered agayne that Mr Towneshend might come out of pryson <at> when he would at his plesure. And further if my brother dyd not care for Mr Towneshendes matters he had against him, and for other matters that were to be brought in question and against him, he [?]must then flee his cuntrye. The sayd Myles sayde he was so determyned to <doe> for to doe, and that presentlye. And with other wordes concerninge oure owne causes we departed.

Undated. Unsigned.
2 pp. RH Box 66.

John Holmes to Roger Townshend

1605, April 4. Mr Towneshende I have ben most ernestlye labored unto by especiall frindes <my> from my brother Nicholas Holme for to informe him of my exsaminacion, what I have delivered unto Sir Nathaniell Bacon. Here hath ben with me Mr Tavener and Thomas Skott of Twyforde for the purpose, offeringe me greate curtesye, conferringe with me about that matter thinckinge to have <prevau> prevayled with me to have wrytton to my brother. But I am not so simple for to <have > discredytt my selfe so shamefull in denyinge the trewthe which I have alredye spoken «before» a man of so greate worshipp. But I will juste-fye yt att eny tyme upon my othe what wronge have ben offered unto your father by my brother and Vynyor upon my knowledge. I have since my exsaminacion called to mynde, which att that tyme dyd forgett to informe Sir Nathaniell Bacon,

---

⁴⁷⁸ Thomas Themilthorpe gent, ?of Runcton (*BP*, iii, p.90).

howe that Vynyor & I havinge some conference together the sayd Vynyor delyvered him his mynde to me that he had shewed greate favor and kindnes to my brother, & that was for Mr Towneshendes matter in pleatin that he did pleate to the sayd bill. But he would not paye him what he ought him, <not> «nor» what he promised for the matter for Mr Towneshend which was 10s. And nowe they would have me to bere them out in ther false procedinges. But I will never agree to them, althoughe I mus bere the losse of yt. I meane in payment of my brothers dett which by ther falsenes together have imposed uppon me, thinckinge that this matter should « <have> » come in question to have me <sayd> «saye» what they would. This I comend me to you, Norwich the iiii of Aprill 1605. Yours in affirminge the truth.

Signed: Jo. Holme.

Addressed: To his frinde Mr Roger Towneshende the younger be this delivered att Smalleburrough or elles where.

Endorsed in Martin Man's hand: Jo. Holmes lettere 4 Aprill 1605. Affirming the truth of his declaracion to Sir Nathaniel Bacon, discovering some badd dealing in Vyniour the att[*orney*].

1 p. RH Box 66.

John Holmes to Roger Townshend

1605, April 7. Mr Townshend there was with me, after youre cominge from your father, Miles Burton of Foulsham, whoe dyd commend [*him*] to me from my brother, with greate circumstaunces beinge to tedius to resite, therfor I omytt them. But perswading with me for the cause in variance betwen your <father> father and my brother, that if the matter went against him I should be assured to paye well for yt and that <he> let yt fall out howe yt should my brother cared not, for he was providinge for him selfe and intendinge to flee his cuntrye, with many wordes with thretes to wright to him contrarye to truthe. Good Mr Towneshend use such meanes, as he maye be bounde to answere the same and other matters that wilbe objected against him at the next Assizes before my Lorde Cheiffe Justice, let him finde sufficient suertyes or elles he will never appere. This in hast I leve you to thAlmightye. Norwich the vii of Aprill 1605. Your frinde.

Signed: John Holme.

Addressed: To his frinde Mr Roger Towneshende the younger at Twyford or elles where.

Endorsed in Martin Man's hand: John Holme. 7 April. Concerning his brothers threates.

½ p. RH Box 66.

Sir Nathaniel Bacon to Thomas Egerton, Baron Ellesmere, Lord Chancellor

1605, April 8. My dutie in humble wise remembred. Yt pleased your Lordship by your letter of the 18 of February last[479] to require <me> that I should call before

---

[479] See 18 February 1604/5 and 5 March 1605, above, pp.154, 156, and 22 April 1605, below, pp.173–4.

me one Thomas Fairfaxe plaintiff in a suite depending in the Chauncery and Jo.
Rust the defendant, and should do my best indeavour to make some quiet ende
betwen them, wherin if I could not prevaile, then to certefie your Lordship the true
state of the cause, with my opynion through whose default I could not ende the
same. According to your Lordships direction I have had both the said parties
before me, and do fynde that Jo. Rust about 6 yeares past became bounde <at the
instance of the said Thomas Fairfaxe> together with the said Thomas Fairfaxe & at
his instance in the custome house of Lynne for retorning a cerrificat from
Alborough in Suffolk of the discharging of 200 qrs of barley «there». And in regard
thereof the said Fairfaxe gave the said Rust a counterbond to save him harmlesse,
for the delivery of which counterbond the said Fairfaxe complayneth by his bill
before your Lordship in the Chancery against Rust, and yet rendreth not to Rust
the bond, which by him & Fairfaxe was entred into the custome house, buth [*sic*]
giveth another bond, which by some ill cariadge seemeth to have ben contrived in
the custome house. For the said Fairfaxe confessed before me, that the said corne
was transported into the Lowe Contryes, and in regard therof he paid his fyne in
the Exchequer, and so there made his peace, & tooke out such a bond, as the customers had there certefied, and saith, that the customers do alledge, that the first
bond entred by <Rust &> Fairfaxe «& Rust» was lost, and the second sent up in
the lieu therof. Being satisfied of the truth of the cause thus farre, I moved them
both, that Fairfaxe should enter a covenant to [Rust] to save him harmlesse of the
first bond, and so doing Rust [should] deliver the counterbond being of some
valew, and herunto thei both agreed. But I further pressed, seing «Fairfaxe his suite
in the Chancery was (as my judgment ledd me to thinke) without just cause &»
Rust was knowen unto me to be a poore man, that Fairfaxe should beare his
charges which I did <avise betwen 3 &> «esteeme to» £4 «or more». <And Fairfaxe
obstinatly refused to allowe him anie maner of charges> «And to beare thes charges
I could by no meanes persuade the said Fairfaxe.» Thus submitting my judgment
to your Lordships wisdome & grave consideracion, I humbly take my leave. From
St[*iffkey*] this 8 of Aprill 1605. Your Lordships at comaundment.

Unsigned. Draft in Martin Man's hand.
Addressed: To the right honorable Thomas Lord Ellesmere, Lord Chancelour of
England.
Endorsed: Copy letter to the Lord Chanc[*ellor*] *inter* Fairfaxe & Rust.
2 pp. *tear on r.h.s. of second page.* NRO SOTH 28/12/67.

Sir Nathaniel Bacon to Sir Henry Sidney

1605, April 16. Sir there hath come unto me Thomas Bullock the late chiefe constable,[480] and hath craved the peace against you & one of your men alledging great
threates & some evil wordes to be given him upon occasion of some service don by
him in his office. I tolde him that I would speake with you and make tryall if I
could pacifye the offence. I thought good to signifie this much unto you that if

---

[480] Thomas Bullock of Great Walsingham can be found acting in his capacity as chief constable of Gallow
Hundred and in other administrative capacities during 1603 and earlier (above, *passim*; *BP*, iv, *passim*).

your leasure will serve to be at my house tomorowe in the afternone I will then sende him worde that he may attende. It seemeth by his speeche as if Mr Christopher Bedingfeld[481] had ben fitt to be present when this cause should be understoode. Thus desiring your aunswer herunto I commende both you & my Lady to Godes keping. 16 April 1605.

Unsigned. Copy in Martin Man's hand.
Endorsed: Copy of the letter to Sir Henry Sydney.
½ p. NRO MC 1872/19, 866X2. Calendared, *Supplementary Stiffkey Papers*, p.19.

Edward Thurlow to Martin Man

1605, April 19. Mr Man I greete you well. Sir, this bearer Mr Thomas Stevenson a merchaunte of London, importeth my letter unto you in his behalfe, beinge (as he saith) nowe uppon his shipp laden with wheate & barlye, bounden in the custome house of Lynne in £40 for the delyvery of 30 quarters of rye [at] 22*d*. the bosshill [*bushel*] at Burnham Markett unto the poore. I have delte with diverse of the townesmen, and we do all verely thincke (that in regard the countrie ys yet well stored with corne) that one markett daie will not carrie awaie two combes therof to the price, yf the same should be brought in, neither will any of the townesmen take yt upp their chamber to disburse present money and so delyver yt forth to the poore accordinglie. Wherefore the said Mr Stevenson (havinge longe bene in the countrye & nowe hasting homewardes) to withdrawe his said bonde, is content either to bringe in the said 30 quarters rye into the markett (thoughe to small purpoose, and great trouble) or otherwise, which we all desier (yf yt might stande with the right worshipfull your master his good lykinge) he is willinglie content to leave in the handes of William Browne one of the overseers of the poore in Burnham Markett 20 combes rye, to be sould out hearafter to the poore (at that price) as neede shall require (which we take wilbe sufficient for the markett towne & townes adjoyning neare untill harvist)[482] and better for the poore so to have yt delyvered then to be brought on the soddaine into the markett all in one daie to be bought upp by strangers «or otherwise carryed back unsould». Yt seemeth he cannot have out his bond without certificate of your master or some other justice of peace in the lymittes. I praye you (uppon consideracion herin) procure him the same yf you maye, and for your paynes he will ever rest behoulden, and my self wilbe thanckfull. And so with my hartie commendacions I bidd you farewell. Burnham *raptim* [*in haste*] 19 April 1605. Your verye lovinge frende.

Signed: Edw[*ard*] Thurlow.[483]
Addressed: To my very lovinge frende Mr Martyn Mann at Styfkye Hall.
½ p *slightly clipped on r.h.s.* Folger L.d.588.

---

[481] Of Great Walsingham.
[482] Annually prices were highest in the period, as here, in the months before the new harvest.
[483] Chief constable of Brothercross Hundred in 1602 (*BP*, iv, pp.224, 260). In the latter case the name has been mistranscribed as 'Thurton'.

Indenture of bargain and sale. Thomas Catelyn to Sir Nathaniel and Lady Dorothy Bacon

1605, April 20. *Calendar*: Indenture made between Thomas Catelyn of Lakenham in Norwich, gentleman,[484] of the one part, and Sir Nathanyell Bacon of Stiffkey and Dame Dorathie his wife on the other part.[485] In consideration of £2,800 paid by Sir Nathanyell, Catelyn bargains and sells the following properties:

1. The manors of Hastingshall and Whitefootshall lying in Irmingland, Corpusty, Saxthorpe, Heydon, Oulton, Itteringham, Mannington and Wickmere.[486]
2. The capital messuage where Andrew Wortlye dwells in Irmingland.
3. All the freehold properties mentioned in an attached schedule.
4. All Catelyn's other freehold possessions and rights in the said parishes.
5. A pightle of three roods of pasture in Corpusty, with the common north and next to Corstie close, bought of Edmond Batrome of Corpusty, husbandman, 25 December 1598.
6. One rood of land in Irmingland, abutting lands of Joane Allens, widow, on three sides, bought of Edmond Bell of Oulton, linen weaver, 25 November 1599.

Catelyn covenants to deliver by the feast of St James the Apostle next all deeds and evidences relating solely to the property conveyed. Nathanyell and Dorathie are to pay the rents and services due to the chief lords of the fee from Michaelmas next. A lease made to Andrew Wortley for £120 a year on 18 July 1601 and expiring at Michaelmas 1606 is to continue. For five years Catelyn is to agree to take reasonable action advised by counsel to extinguish any right of dower that might be claimed by his wife Judith and to assure the title, provided that neither Thomas nor Judith be obliged to travel further than Norwich.

At the foot: Examinatur per me Johannem Hull.
Witnesses to sealing and delivery: Robert Bendishe, Thomas Richmonde, Thomas Kinges, John Norfford, Martin Man.
Copy.[487]
Endorsed: A true coppie of Mr Catlyns bargaine and sale to Sir Nathaniel Bacon knighte and Dame Dorathye his wife.
4 pp. NRO BRA 926/60, 372X9.

---

[484] Probably either Thomas Catlyn, gent, described as being of Bracondale, or his father (Millican, *Freemen*, p.217).

[485] This purchase marks the culmination of Bacon's quest for a site on which to build a second "seate". For an earlier, abortive, stage in this quest see 31 January 1603/4, above, p.71. Work on what became Irmingland Hall began immediately (for discussion of this building activity see above, "Introduction", pp.xxxviii–ix). The completed Hall was H-shaped in plan and somewhat larger than the final stage of Stiffkey Hall. One wing still stands, together with traces of the foundations.

[486] These are all parishes centred around Irmingland. The church was early in ruins and the ecclesiastical parish of Irmingland itself was absorbed into Heydon, although residents of the new Hall appear to have used the more conveniently located church of Oulton. Significantly, the religious radicalism that Bacon brought to Irmingland was maintained by his successors as residents in the Hall and in the late 17th century a non-conformist chapel was built in the parish. It still survives.

[487] Probably made *post* 1622 in the course of the dispute over Nathaniel Bacon's will. See further below, *post* 1 May 1605, p.179, for Memorandum concerning title to the property in Irmingland.

Copy of lease. Sir Christopher Heydon to Thomas Page

[*Circa 1605, April 20<-Θ->May 1*].[488] *Calendar.* Copy of lease dated 20 January 1553/4 whereby Christofer Heydon, knight, leases for 10 years to Thomas Page of Saxthorpe, yeoman, 26 acres 1 rood of land and pasture in various pieces in Irmingland and Corpusty for 18s. 6d. a year. Part late Brownes. Others mentioned: Thomas Betts, John Betts, Edmond Betts, John Borne, Thomas Cappe. Placenames mentioned: Coppings Crofte, Goose Acre, the Rothe, Leyes Crofte, Rotheyeard, Dennes, Symnells Brigge, Camplions Crofte, the Crundell, Brakyland, the Marlepytts. Manors mentioned: the manor of Stinton, Loundhall in Saxthorpe. The lessors may resume the land on notice given. With marginal notes in a different hand including: "It should seem Sir Christofer Heydon was lord of this manor at this time."

Undated. Unsigned. Copy.
Endorsed in Martin Man's hand: Copie of a lease from Sir Christofer Heidon and Thomas Page of landes in Irmingland and Corpusty.
2 pp. NRO NAS 1/1/5/38.

Edward Thurlow to Sir Nathaniel Bacon

· **1605, April 22.** My humble duty remembred. Theis are to certifie unto your good worshipp, that according to your warraunt, I have given warninge unto the vynteners (which be Joseph Walker and Edward Boston of Burnham Markett) to appeare before your worship this morninge.[489] Which said Walker and Boston aunswered me that they this last weeke beinge called before Sir Henry Spelman knight highe shreife of this countie, for the entringe their bondes for their apperaunce at London by the end of this terme before the commissioners, have performed & entred to him their bondes accordinglie.[490] Other vynteners we have not any within our Hundred. The Almightie longe preserve your good worshipp in all helth and happines. Burnham 22 Aprill 1605. Your worshipps most humble in all dutye to be commaunded.

Signed: Edw[ard] Thurlow.
Addressed: To the right worshippfull Sir Nathaniell Bacon knight at Styfkie.
Endorsed in Martin Man's hand: Mr Edward Thurloes letter.
½ p. Folger L.d.587.

Sir Nathaniel Bacon to Sir Edward Coke, Attorney General

1605, April 22. Sir yt pleased you by your lettere of the 17 of February last[491] to <write> «to write unto» me to doo my endeavour to ende a controversie betwen

---

[488] Dating: a copy probably made in connection with the Irmingland bargain and sale from Thomas Catelyn immediately above or the later notes of *post* 1 May 1605, below, p.179. However, other memoranda on the title to Irmingland appear as late as 16 September 1608 (NRO RAY (6) 65).

[489] Under the statute of 1553 (7 Edw. VI c.5) sellers of wine had to be licensed by the justices. Thurlow was chief constable of Brothercross Hundred.

[490] Probably this is related to the exploitation of wine licences as a source of Court patronage and income generation (TNA PRO E.163/17/2). This was one aspect of the emergence of the 'concessionary interest', on which see *BP*, iv, p.xli, and references thereat.   [491] Above, p.153.

Mr Thomas Fairfaxe & one Jo[hn] Rust my neighbors. And in case I could not bring them to order & agreement, to certefye the state of the cause unto you. And accordingly I had the parties before me, and do fynde that Jo[hn] Rust (as in the certificat to my Lord Chancellor).[492] Thus referring the poore man to your further favour «for his» relief, and comending you to the grace of God I take my leave. From Stifky this 22 of Aprill 1605. Yours assured.

Unsigned. Draft in Martin Man's hand.
Endorsed: Copy letter to Mr Attorney. *Inter* Fairfaxe & Rust.
½ p. NRO MF 4/1.

Mathew Clarke to Sir Nathaniel Bacon

1605, April 22. Right wourshipfull I understand yow have appoynted to heare the matter in controversie betwene Grigges and Edwardes to morrow att your howse att Styffkye.[493] And therfore I have thought yt my dutie to signifie unto yow that the proceedinges in the copyhold court (howsoever I have bene traduced for them and unjustly chardged with corruption and indirect dealing) weare all honest and just, and such as I will mayntayne to be agreable to lawe, for I did nothing but by good advise and councell. And wheras the defendant uppon lawfull summons gyven to his owne person, did wilfully mak a defalt, yet yt was offered him in court (befoer judgment) that the defalt should be realeased, soe as he would beare the one halffe of the chardges past, and pleade an issuable plea that they might soe have an equall & indifferent tryall by the tenantes of the manor, which was likewise refused by them. So as they have noe cause to complayne but of theare owne obstynacie and follye. And for the title it is soe cleare in lawe agaynst Edwardes, that I thinke Grigges wilbe contented (soe as Edwardes beare the chardges) to come to a tryall with him att the common lawe, and to tak noe advantage of the former judgment, but to contynue the posession untill the matter be tryed, which yf they will not accept, yt may easily appeare to (your worship) what little cause they had to com-playne in Chauncerye against the steward, when as they distrust theare owne case, and know, yf yt come to tryall of lawe yt will goe against them.

I would have attended uppon (your worship) but my ship is lately come home and I have very much busines in getting her fitted for Iseland [*Iceland*]. Soe craving pardon, with humble remembrance of my dutie I rest. Lyn 22 April 1605. Your worships to commaund.

Signed: Mat[thew] Clarck.[494]
Addressed: To the right worshipfull Sir Nathaniell Bacon knight att Styffkye.
Endorsed in Martin Man's hand: Mathew [*Clark*] concerning Edw[*ards*] & Grigges.
1 p. *endorsement faded.* Folger L.d.221.

---

[492] This implies that this covering letter enclosed an additional copy of the "certificate" that Bacon had sent to Lord Ellesmere (8 April 1605, above, pp.169–70).

[493] The case had been referred to Bacon on 14 November 1604 (above, p.141). See also Bacon to Athowe and Gawsell, 23 April 1605, below, p.175.

[494] See note to letter of 24 March 1602/3<-θ->29 June 1611, above, p.22.

Certificate from the J.P.s in Norfolk to Sir Robert Clarke, Baron of the Exchequer

1605, April 22. Sir, this bearer William Bennett, the husband of Katheryne Bennett, who was convict of manslaughter at the late Assises «in Norfolk» & remayneth in the gaole <at Norwiche>, reprived, hath prayed our certificat in her behalf.[495] The woman (as wee learne by notable testimony) in the course of her life otherwise, hath ben of honest behaviour, and being moved with passion, on the sodayne fell into the offence, as appeared upon her tryall. The respect wherof did move you to have comisration of her. And shee is verie penitent for the fact. Our request & suite unto you is, that it will please you to contynue your favour towardes her, and to be a meanes unto his Majestie, for obteyning of his gracious pardon for her. And so comending you to the proteccion of Al[*mighty*] God, wee take our leave. This 22 of Aprill 1605. Yours verie assured.

Unsigned. Copy in Martin Man's hand.
Addressed: To the right worshipfull Sir Robert Clarke knight, one of the Barons of <the «his Majesties»> Exchequor.
Endorsed: Copy of a cert[*ificate*] unto Baron Clark for Bennettes wife.
½ p. NRO MC 1872/19, 866X2. Calendared, *Supplementary Stiffkey Papers*, p.18.

Sir Nathaniel Bacon to Thomas Athowe and Robert Gawsell

1605, April 23. *Calendar:* Bacon notifies Athowe and Gawsell of the day's proceedings held before him in the controversy between Thomas Edwardes and Edward Grigges and Thomas Grigges his brother. The case had been previously referred to Bacon by order of the Lord Chancellor.[496] Bacon had considered the state of the title and what could be alleged in equity for Edwards (without otherwise entering into points of law) and asked each party in turn whether they would pay a consideration to hold the land or relinquish it in return for such a consideration. Edwardes was willing to submit to direction, but the Grigges brothers refused either course. Bacon therefore advised, and will certify as his order to the Lord Chancellor, that a trial should be held at the next county Assizes to decide the title. Edwardes assented, but the Grigges brothers appeared to want further advice. He asks for the addressees' opinion as soon as possible.
/"I enclyne rather to have the cause mediated then referred to the lawe if Grigges would be ruled by me."/

Unsigned. Heavily amended draft. In Martin Man's hand.
Addressed: To Thomas Athowe & Robert Gawsell esquires.
Endorsed: Copy of the letter to Masters Athow & Gawsell. *Inter* Edwardes & Grigges.
1 p. NRO MC 1872/30, 866X2. Calendared, *Supplementary Stiffkey Papers*, pp.51–2.

---

[495] See April 1605, above, p.166.
[496] See Chancery order of 14 November 1604 (above, p.141). Athowe was counsel for the Griggs brothers and Gawsell counsel for Edwards.

Examinations in a case of paternity

1605, April 23. The examinacion of Ellen Reve of Wiveton widow taken before Sir Nathanael Bacon knight the xxiii of Aprill 1605.

She sayth that her daughter Elizabeth Reve, who lyveth in house with her, upon her beinge discovered to be with childe, was examined by women of the towne of Wiveton, who was the father therof. And at the firste she did name one Sander Dove, a comber, and since upon other examinacion by this exam[inate] and mother Thurlowe, she hath confessed, that Mr Poynter[497] the minister of Wiveton & Blakeney is the father of her child.

She confesseth that she sent Margaret Mason together with her daughter to Mr Smyth for some phisicke, and her daughter toke the drinke and caste it againe, and this examinate sent Mr Smyth 12*d.* for the same drinke.

Signed: [*by mark*] Ellen Reve, Na[*thaniel*] Bacon.

The examinacion of Elizabeth Reve taken the daie and yeare aforesaid.

She sayth that she is with childe by Mr Poynter the minister of Blakeney, and that she was firste defiled by him at Blakeney parsonage, before Mr Berrye, curate, came thither to dwell, and she gesseth the tyme to be somewhat before Hallowmas laste. And sayth allso that he hath defyled her sondry tymes since, and reckoneth 6 or 7 tymes. And sayth that he gave her money at severall tymes.

She allso confesseth that the said Mr Poynter when he knew her with childe, did advise her to lye with some other man, and named Sander Dove, and accordingly she sayth the said Sander Dove did once lye with her in her mothers house, and an other tyme in the feilde.

She further sayth, the said Mr Poynter did bid her saie that the said Sander Dove was the father of her childe.

She sayth that the places wher Mr Poynter did meete with her when he defyled her was sometymes at Blakeney parsonage and sometymes at Wiveton parsonage.

She sayth that her mother sent one Margaret Mason of Wiveton to Mr Smyth of Saxlingham, together with this examinate, to have a drinke of him, which she had, and toke it presently and fell sick therof in her cominge home, and so did caste it up againe. And the said Mason gave the said Mr Smyth 12*d.* for the drinke, and 2*d.* for shewing her water, and this money was sent by this examinates mother.[498]

Signed: [*by mark*] Elizabeth Reve, Na[*thaniel*] Bacon.

On another sheet: She sayth the daie and yeare aforesaid, upon a further examinacion, that the firste tyme when Sander Dove did abuse her, was about a fortnight before Christmas in the feilde amonge the furres [*furze*],[499] as he & she went

---

[497] This is the first of a series of documents relating to allegations concerning James Pointer (d.1621), vicar of Blakeney and Glandford and rector of Wiveton. Pointer was a man of some substance who employed two non-preaching curates. He was also chaplain to Henry Percy, 9th earl of Northumberland—the so-called 'Wizard earl'. Through the latter's influence at Court he managed to thwart Bacon's attempts to get him removed. (Barton, *Anthony Harison*, i, p.192; Venn, *Al. Cant.*, iii, p.390; NRO NCC INV 31/23; Bacon to Bishop Jegon, 1 May 1605, below, pp.178–9; Bacon to Commissioners for Causes Ecclesiastical, 30 September 1605, below, pp.211–13).

[498] For Margaret Mason's examination of 13 May 1605 see below, p.180.

[499] The implication is that furze, used as fuel, is being cultivated as a field crop. This was certainly the practice at Raynham, where great quantities of furze were required to fire the kilns during the building of the Hall in the 1620s.

towardes Holte from Cley upon a Sondaie. And the second tyme was lately, about five or sixe weekes since at her mothers house in Wiveton.

Signed: [by mark] Elizabeth Reve, Na[*thaniel*] Bacon.
In William Sanders' hand.
Endorsed: The examinacions of Ellen Reve & Elizabeth Reve of Wiveton.
2½ pp. NRO RAY 262. Printed, *Stiffkey Papers*, pp.18–19.

Examination in a case of paternity

1605, April 29. The exam[*ination*] of Marie English of Holme[500] taken before Sir Nathanael Bacon knight the xxix of Aprill 1605.

She sayth that she is unmarried, and of the age betwene 30 and 40 and that she is with childe by Robert Spooner of Holme.

She sayth that it is about a twelvemoneth and more, since he defiled her firste, and that he hath often come into her house in the night tyme, when he hath lefte his worke at Ringsteade.[501]

She sayth that she gesseth her selfe to be nyne weekes gone with childe.

Signed: Na[*thaniel*] Bacon. *In William Sanders' hand.*
Endorsed: Exam[*ination*] of Marie English of Holme [*?*]concerning bastardy.
½ p. NRO NRS 24659, 125X3.

Giles Godfrey to Sir Nathaniel Bacon

[*1605*],[502] **May 1.** Right worshipfull maye yt plese you to understand that my self and other of my naybores beinge contributurs for the relef of the poore inhabitantes havinge satisfied the overseares for the hole year paste notwithstandinge the poor doth find them selves not satisfied therewith for some weekes passed of the old yeare, desiering your woshipes assistance «in» ther behalf and that yt woulde please you to locke into ther accountes. For I and other of my naybores do find some bade delinge in ther colectinge which I hav charged them with, being confessed by my naybor Edmund Money that ther remayned 26s. 8d. over pluste colected for the poore, the holle some whiche the poore is to hav is £3 16s. 4d. and by account herin inclosed the some which hertofor thaye hav collected or at leste ought to colect is £4 9s. [0d.]. Thuse being bowld to troble you I humblye commit your worship to the tuition of the Almighty. Gunthorpe thise first of Mai. Yours alwayes to comand.

At the foot in William Sanders' hand: A warrant to Mr Holton Ed. Money Thomas Gardener and the reste of the churchwardens and overseers for the pore of Gunthorpe of the last yeare.
Signed: Giles Godfrey.[503]

500 Holme-next-the-Sea (near Hunstanton) is outside the double limit within which Nathaniel Bacon usually operated (see Map 2).
501 Presumably after walking down the Peddars Way that runs between the two parishes.
502 Dating: this letter postdates Nathaniel's knighthood in mid-July 1604. As the enclosed account (immediately below) presumably refers to 1603/4 it is unlikely to be much later. The officers named had accounted for the year 1604/5 on 6 April 1605 (above, pp.161–2), giving lower totals.
503 Probably of Sharrington. 'A survey of corn' in Holt Hundred in 1595 listed a Mr Godfrey with a substantial household (17 persons) and 20 acres of barley. It is quite possible that most of his land lay in the

Addressed: To the right worshipfull Sir Nathaniell Bacon knight at Steifkey.
Endorsed in William Sanders' hand: Mr Godfries letter against the overseers of Gunthorpe.
Enclosure: abstract immediately below.
1 p. BL Add. 63081 ff.108–109. Printed in *Stiffkey Papers*, p.62.

Abstract of Gunthorpe poor rate and expenditure 1603/4

[*1605, May 1*].[504] A colection 1603.

Christofer Holton *per annum*	12s.		
Henrey Nicholus	13s.		
Edmond Money	12s.		
Richard Duckit	12s.		
Giles Godfrey	17s.		
Gregorey Daynes	5s.	6d.	
Richard Money	3s.		
Johne Spooner		12d.	
Thomas Gardener		18d.	
Richard Frayday		16d.	
Richard Mutton	3s.		
Johne Plaford		18d.	
Alis Morise		4d.	
Gorge Jewell		4d.	
Thomas Bullinge		20d.	
Robert Lasby		18d.	
Robert Buling jun.		12d.	
Nicholus Ringhold		20d.	
Robert Carre		8d.	

Summa   £4   9s.   6d.
the pore   £3   16s.   4d.

Unsigned.
Endorsed: Of [?] Gunthorpe.
In same hand as and enclosed with letter from Giles Godfrey, immediately above.
1 p. NRO MS 20435, 126X6. Printed, *Stiffkey Papers*, p.62.

Sir Nathaniel Bacon to John Jegon, Bishop of Norwich

1605, May 1. My very good lorde. Ther is one Mr James Poynter, minister of Blakney and Wiveton with Glamforth [*Glandford*], thre distinct parishes, wherof two be united. And this man is accused by one Elizabeth Reve, lyvinge with her mother upon the almes of the towne, that she is gotten with child by Mr Poynter, as your Lordshipe shall see by her exam[*ination*] taken before me the coppie

adjacent parishes of Gunthorpe and Bale, where in 1602 he defaulted over highway repairs. (*BP*, iii, p.301; iv, p.266).
[504] Dating: dated with reference to the letter from Giles Godfrey to Bacon, immediately above.

wherof I send inclosed.[505] I hold my selfe in due respect to make the state of this cause knowne unto your Lordshipe because I knowe you have moste power to doe good in the cause. For this Poynter hath dwelt longe in this kinde of sinne, though he hath a wife of his owne, from whome he lyveth, and yet is no woman of evill reporte. And if your Lordshipe make inquirie of Mr Chauncellour,[506] you shall heare how in the late Bishops tyme, and allso (as I take it) in Scamlers tyme[507] he hath bene convented for this kinde of cryme, and was once allso openly arraigned for a rape. Ther was one Alice Whitbie a younge woman of Blakney, for whome he was sondry tymes in question, and she had severall children, wherof she was delivered of some in one place and some in another, and he suspected to be the father of them, and this woman is not longe since married and now he is fallne to this other. Your Lordshipe shall doe both God and the country good service if he might be removed, that some better man might be placed in his chardges, which are great, and the lyvinge therof good, and yet he spendeth all in this bad manner, and in passinge thorough his trobles, and is behinde hand, and as men suppose by thes «his» occacions. Thus referring it to your Lordships wisdome for redresse herin, I commit you to the kepinge of Allmighty God. Stifky. i Maye 1605. Your Lordships very loving frinde.

Unsigned. Copy in William Sanders' hand.
Endorsed: Copy letter to the Bishop touchinge Mr Poynter.
1 p. NRO RAY 263. Printed, *Stiffkey Papers*, pp.20–1.

Memorandum concerning title to land in Irmingland and elsewhere

[*Post 1605, May 1*].[508] A note of conveiaunces made of landes in Erminglondes sometyme Mr Bettes.

Primo Maii anno regni regis Jacobi 3. A feofment from Mr Thomas Catelyn to Sir Nathaniel Bacon knight & dame Dorothie his wife of the manors of Hastingshall & Whitefootehall and all other landes & hereditaments in Irminglond Corpsty Saxthorp Heidon Oulton Itteringham Manington & Wickmer.[509]

26 Aprilis anno Elizabethe 40. A feofment of the premisses made by Mr John Bettes & Margaret his wief & John Bettes the sonne to the said Thomas Catelyn.

3 Septembris 39 Elizabethe. Divers landes passed by Mr Bettes to Mr Pottes lieing in Erminglond & <Corpust.> Owlton for £860.

Undated. Unsigned. In Martin Man's hand.
1 p. NRO NAS 1/1/5/41.

[505] For Bacon's own file copy see 23 April 1605, above, p.176–7.
[506] Robert Redmayne, chancellor of the diocese of Norwich, 1589–1625 (*BP*, iv, p.370).
[507] "The late Bishops tyme": William Redman, bishop of Norwich 1594–1602; "Scamlers tyme": Edmund Scambler, bishop of Norwich 1584–94. (Fryde *et al.*, *British Chronology*, p.262)
[508] Dating: dated from internal evidence.
[509] For the bargain and sale preceding the feoffment see 20 April 1605, above, p.172.

Examination in a case of paternity

1605, May 13. The examinacion of Margaret Mason of Wyveton taken the 13 of May 1605 before Sir Nathanael Bacon knighte.[510]

Shee saith that about 7 weekes ago, shee went with Elizabeth Reve of Wyveton by the meanes of the said Reves mother to Mr Smith of Saxlingham of whome the said Elizabeth had 2 spoonefulles of drynke which shee cast up agayne in her retorne home. And after her comyng home shee was sick therof.

Shee saith that the said Elizabeth would at that tyme in no sort be aknowen that shee was with childe, saying that shee had never deserved for it.

Shee also saith that yesterday was forthnight one of Wyveton called William the Cripple came into the yarde where this ex[*amina*]t dwelleth and asked for the said Elizabeth Reve, who comyng fourth to him, thei two talked togither. And this was in the morning. And at noone he came agayne to her. And within a day or 2 after the said Elizabeth tolde this examinat that the said William had ben in hande with her to marry her and that he should have a cowe & £5. And the said William liveth of the almes of the towne.

At the foot: A warrant to Saxthorpe & Baconsthorpe *pro* Sander Dove.
Signed: Na[*thaniel*] Bacon. *In Martin Man's hand.*
Endorsed: Examinacion of Margaret Mason.
1 p. SRO(I) HA411/1/11/2/1/2. Printed, *Stiffkey Papers*, p.21.

Examination in a case of paternity

1605, May 15. The examinacion of Henry Drury of Baconsthorpe taken the xv of May 1605 before Sir Nathaniel Bacon knight.

He saith that since his servant Alexander Moye was accused by Elizabeth Reve to have ben lewde with her he hath made his repayer to Wyveton and there inquired of the women whose worke he there useth how often his said servant hath ben there the last wynter. And he findeth that the said servant was there three severall tymes & no more. And the first tyme was about a forthnight after Michaelmas last. The second tyme a weeke afore Christmas. And the third tyme a weeke after Christmas or thereaboutes. And no oftener.

He saith that in his opynion his servant is not faultie in the cryme wherwith he is charged.

Signed: Henrie Drewrie, Na[*thaniel*] Bacon. *In Martin Man's hand.*
Endorsed: Examinacion of Henry Drury.
½ p. NRO RAY 266. Printed, *Stiffkey Papers*, pp.21–2.

Examination in a case of paternity

1605, May 15. The examinacion of Alexander Moye of Baconsthorpe taken before Sir Nathanael Bacon knight the xv of May 1605.

He saith that his age is as he reckoneth 15 yeares or thereaboutes, & was borne

---

[510] For further documents in this case see 23 April and 1 May 1605, above, pp.176–9, and immediately below.

at Potter Heigham in Flegge.

He saith that he hath ben at Mother Reves house of Wyveton, & but once, which as he thinketh was since Christmas last.

He saith he knoweth Elizabeth Reve, the olde womans daughter, by sight & not otherwise.

He saith that sone after Christmas last he comyng to Wyveton about his masters busynes did retorne homewardes towardes <Baconsthorpe about noone> «Wickmer where his» master then dwelt. And the said Elizabeth Reve did put hir self into his company at Mother Wrightes house in Wyveton. And from thence shee went about with this examinat towardes Holt. And when thei came at the heathe shee did then leave this examinat, saying, that shee would never come so farre with him agayne, bicause he would not kisse her at their parting.

He being demaunded what cause drew the said Elizabeth to go in his company aunswereth, that he knoweth not, and saith also that by the waie, the said Elizabeth would have had of him a payer of gloves which he denyed her.

He saith that he did never defile the woman and doth offer his oath to avowe the same.

He saith that by the way as the said Elizabeth went with him from Wyveton, shee tolde him, that shee sholde be maryed, but tolde him not to whome, and said also that if he would come to her mariage shee would give him a silke poynt.

Signed: Na[*thaniel*] Bacon, [*by mark:*] Alexander Moye. *In Martin Man's hand.*
Endorsed: Examinacion of Alexander Moy.
1 p. NRO RAY 265. Printed, *Stiffkey Papers*, pp.22.

Examination in a case of paternity

1605, May 16. The examinacion of William Sayers of Wyveton taken the xvi of May 1605 before Sir Nathanael Bacon knight.

He saith that this daie three weekes Mr Rokesby the curate of Wyveton[511] did come to this examinat in Mr Leeches malthouse at Wyveton and there moved him to the mariage of Elizabeth Reve, telling him, that he should have two cowes with her & sommer meate & wynter meate for them and a piece of money besides and further his dwelling so longe as he lived.

He saith that the said Mr Rokesby came agayne after to this examinat asking him if he would go on with the mariage of the said woman. And his aunswer was that he would not marrie her without the consent of the towne.

He saith also that he spoke with the said Elizabeth Reve about maryeng of her after the said Mr Rokesby had spoken to him. And shee was willing to have gon on with the mariage.

Signed: Na[*thaniel*] Bacon. *In Martin Man's hand.*
Endorsed: Examinacion of W. Sayers.
½ p. NRO RAY 264. Printed, *Stiffkey Papers*, pp.22–3.

---

[511] According to Nathaniel Bacon's letter of 30 September 1605 (below, p.212), neither of Pointer's curates preached, and one was "scarse able to reade". Mr Rokesby was probably a non-graduate as he is not in Venn, *Al. Cant.*

John Maplesden, archdeacon of Suffolk, to Sir Nathaniel Bacon

1605, May 21. My dubty to your worship remembred etc. I am entreated by this bearer Mr Selby,[512] that wheras the benefice of Easton Bavent [*Suffolk*] is and hath bene long in lapse, uppon thacceptacion of a benefice which the last incumbent had in Kent, (as I am certefyed & also lately deceased) it wold please your worship to vouchsafe the presentacion one [*sic*] him, who hath a smale vicaridge adjoyning to the parishe of Easton called Raydon.[513] He ys a very sufficient man «to» discharge a plac of good accoumpt both for learning & discresion, a master of artes of 12 yeres & hath preched in the universyty, at the common plac of Norwich[514] & at our seane[515] at Ypswich with speciall liking. Againe your worship shall doe a great favoire to that poor towne to procure them «one» to teach them, & to bring the benefice in order, which is so fleiced by some indigent ministers, sequestrators etc. that beside that yt «is» in arrere to the King so to others, they reaping what they «can», & pay nothing at all which he wold cleere, yf your worship wilbe pleased to bestowe the same uppon him. I tak yt in the Kinges guift by lapse, but that it is highly valewed & much of the parishe eaten upp with the sea whereby I thinke the tythes hardly worth £10 the valuacion, I see none desirose of yt & lately I tok thaccomptes of a sequestrator by the Lord Buishops order & found them lesse then the valuacion. And so leaving this to your worships godly consideracion for the best of that poer people, I tak my leave. Oulton [*Suffolk*] xxi *Maii* 1605. Your worshipes to comaund.

Signed: J. Maplizden archdeacon Suffolk.[516]

Addressed: To the right worshipfull Sir Nathanaell Bacon knight at his lodging at Norwich.

Endorsed in Martin Man's hand: Mr Maplezden concerning Easton.

1 p. Folger L.d.413.

---

[512] Robert Selby, vicar of Reydon and Southwold 1596; rector of Easton Bavents 1608 (Venn, *Al. Cant.*, iv, p.41).

[513] Bacon's interest in this area of north-east Suffolk arose from his marriage to Dorothy Smith in 1597. His connection with Easton Bavents (together with Wissett, Burgh Castle, Kessingland and Holton) resulted mainly from his guardianship of William Smith (b.1591), Dorothy's eldest son, although Dorothy also enjoyed a life interest in the property (see Key, 'Dorothy Bacon', pp.78–9; *BP*, iv, p.211).

[514] By the end of the sixteenth century there were two open-air preaching yards in Norwich. The first, north-west of the cathedral nave and known as the Green Yard, had been established before the Reformation. The other was the open space on the south side of the former Blackfriars' church, acquired by the city together with its complex of buildings at the Dissolution. Here some of the puritan city fathers established and funded a form of open-air worship that was more radical than that offered at the Cathedral. Confusingly, this site was also known as the Green Yard. Given Bacon's own religious predilections, the use of the phrase "the common place" in this context suggests the latter venue. (Ian Atherton *et al.* eds, *Norwich Cathedral: Church, City and Diocese, 1096–1996*, London & Riō Grande, 1996, especially pp.247, 535–42, 557).

[515] Presumably the equivalent in Ipswich of the "common place" in Norwich, possibly from the French "seance".

[516] Maplesden had been a student at St. Johns, Cambridge, during its radical days in the 1560s, subsequently becoming University Preacher in 1575. He served as archdeacon of Suffolk, 1575–1613, and as rector of Oulton, Suffolk, 1582–1613 (Venn, *Al. Cant.*, iii, p.138).

Petition. Townsmen of Warham to Sir Nathaniel Bacon

[*1605, c. June*].[517] To the right worshippfull Sir Nathaniell Bacon knight.

Maie it please your good worshipp that wheareas this our towne of Warham hath no alehowse in it, and hath many pore that (for the moste part) doth buy theire beere. And that William Halman hath a small breweng howse in our said towne and therefore the meetest theare to serve our said pore of beere for theire money «oute att dores». Wherefore yt maye please your good worshipp that the man be allowed so to do, and we according to duety shall desire of God your worshipps felicitie. Your worshipps humble to comaund the inhabitauntes of Warham *viz.*

Undated.

Signed: Peter Stewardsoon minister there,[518] Edmond Framyngham, Henr[y] Feke rector Marie Magdalene,[519] Rob[er]t Purland, [*by marks:*] Richard Fuller, Henry Greve, Thomas Greve.

Endorsed in Martin Man's hand: Certificate for a canyker in Warham.

½ p. NRO RAY (4) 26. Printed, *Stiffkey Papers*, p.53.

Sir John Popham, Chief Justice of King's Bench, to Sir Nathaniel Bacon and William Yelverton

1605, June 8. With my hartie comendacions. Understanding that there are certeyn players of comon enterludes, belonging to some noble men, that travell up & downe those partes, usinge the same contrary to the lawe.[520] These are therefore to pray & require you, forthwith to take order that some of the chiefest of them be bounde to make their personall apperaunce at the next Assises for that county to aunswer the same. And if thei shall refuse to fynd suretyes as aforsaid to comytt them to the gayle, there to remayne till thei shall so do, whereby thei maie be forth-comyng to be proceeded with according to the lawe. And even so I bidd you

---

[517] Dating: William Halman was licensed (not as a canniker but to run an alehouse) on 24 June 1605 (Bacon memoranda book 1602–7, NRO BL/BC/5/22, p.67).

[518] Peter Stewardson, rector of Warham All Saints (see 4 July 1603, above, p.39n.). As rector of Warham he witnessed the wills of at least fourteen parishioners, which suggests his rootedness in the parish and is reflected in his lead position among the signatories here.

[519] Henry Feake, ordained in 1596, had succeeded George Feake, possibly his father, as rector of Warham St Mary Magdalene and St Margaret (Venn, *Al. Cant.*, ii, p.128; *BP*, iii, p.237).

[520] Once again Popham displays his obsession with suppressing any form of popular gathering, perhaps with some justification (see J. O. Halliwell-Phillipps, *Contemporary Depositions Respecting an Affray at Norwich in the Year 1583*, London, 1864). During the summer performers from within the London theatre companies went 'on tour', as they also did when plague closed the theatres in London. Usually their performances consisted not of entire plays but of selected scenes. Probably the comic scenes predominated. Certainly, the leading comic actor Richard Tarleton seems to have been known in Norwich. The London companies 'took the livery' of noble patrons such as the Lord Chamberlain and the Lord Admiral, in order to avoid the vagrancy laws—but apparently this was not enough to escape Popham's clutches. It may be that he had in mind the disturbances that could arise when performances coincided with the occasions of popular festivity: St. John's Eve, midsummer, was in prospect. For an introduction to the issue of provincial touring by theatrical companies see R. A. Foakes, 'Playhouses and Players' in *The Cambridge Companion to English Renaissance Drama*, ed. A. R. Braunmuller and Michael Hattaway (Cambridge, 1990), pp.39–43, 47 and quotation at p.58; Peter H. Greenfield, 'Touring' in *A New History of Early English Drama*, ed. John D. Cox and David Scott Kastan (New York, 1997), pp.251–68; Peter H. Greenfield, 'Drama outside London after 1540' in *The Cambridge History of British Theatre I: Origins to 1660*, ed. Jane Milling and Peter Thomson (Cambridge, 2004), pp.178–99.

hartely farewell. At Serjeantes Inn this 8 of June 1605. [*Signed:*] Your loving frynde Jo. Popham.

At the foot in Martin Man's hand: A warrant to the chief constables of N[*orth*] Grenho, Gallow, Brothercrosse, & Holt, to bring the chiefe of such players before Sir Nathaniel Bacon, to be bounde over, if anie come to play within their Hundredes. 14 *Junii* 1605.

Copy in Martin Man's hand.

Addressed: To the right worshipfull my loving fryndes Sir Nathaniel Bacon knight & William Yelverton esquire, or to either of them.

Endorsed: [My Lord] Chiefe Justices letter touching players.

½ p. *endorsement stained.* Yale (Beinecke) MS195.

John Richers to Sir Nathaniel Bacon

1605, June 13. Good sir. This bearer informeth me of a verie riotouse rescuse [*sic*] made from a deputie of his, whose informacion herinclosed I sende you. The matter seemes fowle, and they praye that the offendors maye be bounde to the Assises. But for my parte I knowe no reason why we should troble the judges with theise matters, that apperteigne to our dueties, but rather thinke they wyll be offended with us bothe for oure owne neglecte, and for trobling of them, with theise improper businesses, by which the Assises are drawen to a greate lengthe, & yet manye of those kinde of causes are not there proceeded in, eyther for wante of tyme <and> «or» because the parties are agreed betweene them selves, & so the malefactors goe home withowte punyshement (saving their fees in coorte) & make them selves merye with them that bownde them. I doubte not but the judges wylbe well pleased with our lawfull proceedinges, & bothe countenance the same, & thinke them selves well eased, unles it be some speciall misdemeanors, which eyther in respect of the haynowsnes [*heiniousness*] therof, or custome «or countenances» which hathe prevayled over strengthes, in which cases we are to praye their aydes, as allso wherin we doubte. Yf therfore it wyll please you somtymes to joyne in consent, & execucion, I doubte not, but we shall cincerely correct manye of theise common abuses, & ease the judges of muche troble, to their good lykinges. And for this present matter, (the motive of my writing) I howlde it a fowle riott in the ende, & therfore to be inquired of by a jurie, asswell for the punyshement of the offendors, as for our owne discharge, & doe verie hartely desyer your presence and assistance therat, which yf you doe, I praye you eyther to delyver this bearer a warrant to the sheryffe to retorne a jurie before us at what place, and daye, it shall please you to assigne, so it be within the monthe, & I wyll subscribe it. Or yf your leysure wyll not nowe permitt the present making therof, then uppon knowledge from you, of your daye, & place, I wyll send a warrant to you for your hand & seale. And so with all due salutacions I tak my leave. Swenington Hall this 13 of June 1605. Your commaundable freind.

[*Postscript*]: Yf it please you to use Sir Anthony Brownes name allso in the warrant, I wyll send it to him, and acquaynt him with the busines.

Signed: John Rychers.[521]. *Holograph.*
Addressed: To the right wourshipfull Sir Nathaniell Bacon, knight, at Stifkey.
Endorsed in Martin Man's hand: Mr Richers.
1½ pp. Folger L.d.496.

Sir John Popham, Chief Justice of King's Bench, to the J.P.s in Norfolk

1605, June 13. With my harty comendacions. I praie you in anie wise take care
that I maie be certefied of thes pointes by the next Assises for the county of
Norfolk. First, that it be truly certefyed who thei are that are recusantes at this
tyme that were conformable at the tyme of the late Queenes deathe.[522]

Then what recusantes being men of quallity there be within that countie. And
whose wyves or widdowes of quallity be also recusantes. And what nomber thei
have in their severall familyes that do not come to churche. And how manie of
them come to churche. And what tenantes such recusantes have which doe not
come to the churche.

Who thei be that be recusantes (not having 20 markes in landes or £40 in
goodes) that are curryers [*couriers*] from recusant to recusant or from contrey to
contrey[523] or that otherwise be holden dangerous in corrupting others. And even
so I bidde you hartely fare well. At Serjeantes Inne this 13 of June 1605. [*Signed*:]
Your loving frynde, Jo. Popham.

Copy in Martin Man's hand.
Addressed: To the right worshipfull my verie loving fryndes Sir Arthur
Heveningham & Sir Henry Gawdy knightes and to the rest of the justices of peace
for the county of Norfolk.
Endorsed: Copie of my Lord Chiefe Justices letter concerning recusantes.
½ p. NRO BL/BC/6/11.

The Commission for Causes Ecclesiastical to the J.P.s in Norfolk

1605, June 15. After our hearty comendations etc. Whereas certaine articles have
bene lately exhibited unto us of his Majesties Commission for Causes
Ecclesiasticall on the behalfe of Mr James Poynter clerke bachelour in divinity
parson of Bleekney and Wyveton in the county of Norfolk, against Alice
Thurlowe, Elizabeth Fenn, John Bradocke, & [*blank*] Bradocke his wiefe of
Wyveton, & Christopher Seaman of Holt Markett within the county aforesaid, in
which articles the said Mr Poynter chargeth the said severall partyes with a most
dishonest plott practise and combination against <first> him, first in procuring
the said Elizabeth Fenn to charge the said Mr Poynter to be the father of a child of

---

[521] John Richers esquire of Swannington. Richers had only recently been made a J.P. (1604–?1629:
Owens, 'Local Government', p.570). However it is probable that he was the son of Edmund and Bridget
Richers and through them his connection with Bacon may have been of longer standing (his mother had
been one of those lending Bacon money at the time of the Bacon/Townshend marriage in 1593: *BP*, iii,
pp.246–7), thus in some degree justifying his assertiveness towards his senior on the bench.

[522] For anxieties about Catholicism at this time, the reasons for it and the steps taken to contain it, see
BP, iv, pp.xlviv-xlvi.

[523] In this context "contrey" bears the meaning of "county".

her body, unlawfully begotten, (the said Elizabeth being as we are informed a woman of very light & lewd behaviour) and afterwardes by their owne slaunderous reportes in raising a fame or suspition thereof in the country as is likewise complayned, thereby to traduce the said Mr Poynter & to bring him into scandall & obloquy, & so to make him the reputed father of the said child, by meanes whereof the said Mr Poynter is drawen into question before yow as we have bene also informed.[524] And although we are not ignorant what power and authority is by the statute geven to the justices of peace to provide in cases of bastardy the keeping of the child. Yet forasmuch as that it is deduced in the articles objected by Mr Poynter against the said partyes, that the said Elizabeth Fenn did first charge one Alexander Dove to be the father of her said child, and was afterwardes drawen by the sinister practises of the said partyes <of> or some of them to accuse him the said Mr Poynter, as also for that we have taken bond of the said Mr Poynter in the some of one hundred markes to his Majesties use, that he shall prosecute the matters aforesaid with effect, & pay to the defendantes good charges, in case he faile in proofe of his articles objected against them. We therefore holding it very unmeete and neither agreable to lawe or equity that the said Mr Pointer being a bachelour in divinity, houshold chaplaine to an honourable person residing in these partes,[525] on whom he is now attending, well reputed of for his learning & conversation, should by such indirect meanes (in case hes objections be trewe) be traduced, & himselfe and his ministry therby brought into contempt, have thought good to pray wishe and advise yow for the causes abovesaid, that during the dependancy of the suite before us, and untill the same shall receave dewe examinacion according to order of lawe, yow would forbeare to proceede against him for or concerning any matter touching the premises, assuring yow that whomsoever uppon dewe examination of the cause (whereof we purpose to take speciall regard) we shall find any wayes faulty, whether yt be Mr Poynter the complaynaunt, or the said defendantes, we will not faile God willing to do our dewties by inflicting such condigne punishment uppon him or them as the quality of his or their offence shall deserve, and then further to certify yow what we find by our proceedinges therein, whereby yow may with an equitable course proceede in the cause of reputed father, as by lawe & your discretions yow shall find most meete. And so we bid yow right heartily farewell from Lambeheth this fyfteenth of June 1605. Your loving freindes.

Signed: R. Canterbury, Ric. London, John Overall, Tho[*mas*] Montforde, John Kinge, Edw[*ard*] Stanhope, Will[*ia*]m Ferrand.

Drafted by: *Robertus Christian deputatus Johannis Plomer et Georgii Paull reg*[*ist*]*rar*[*iorum*] *recordorum* [*registrars of the records*].

Addressed: To our loving freindes Sir Edward Cleare, & Sir Nathaniell Bacon knightes, Robert Redmayne doctor of the lawe chauncellour of the dioces of Norwich, John Pagrave esquier & others his Majesties justices of the peace within the county of Norfolk.

[524] See 1 May 1605, above, pp.178–9.
[525] The Duke of Northumberland. See Bacon to Robert Rich, *post* 30 September 1605, below p.213.

Endorsed in Martin Man's hand: High Commissioners letters *ex parte* Mr Poynter.
1 p. Chicago 4449–A; photocopy in NRO FX 245/12/2.

Order to the Sheriff of Norfolk to proclaim a session of the Commission of Sewers

1605, June 15. *Calendar:* The King to the Sheriff of Norfolk [*Sir Henry Spelman*] ordering that a session of Sewers be proclaimed to be held at Cambridge on Friday 28 June for the counties of Lincoln, Northampton, Huntington, Cambridge with the Isle of Ely, Norfolk and Suffolk, and to give notice to the commissioners named below. The Sheriff is also to attend.[526]

Given at Huntingdon under the seal and witnessed by Sir Olyver Croomewell, Sir Robert Bevell, Sir John Cuttes, Sir John Cotton, Sir Robert Wingfield, Sir Robert Cotton, Sir Thomas Lambert, Sir Simon Steward, Sir Richard Coper, Sir Anthonie Forest, Sir Henry Spillman, Robert Cromewell, Anthony Jollye, Thomas Ogle, Christofer Hodson, William Sturrin, John Fytcham and William Marshall, commissioners of sewers within the above counties.

List of commissioners to be notified given at the foot:[527] Sir Fraunces Gawdye, Sir Raphe Hare, Sir Robert Jarnine [*Jermin*], Sir Nicholas Bacon, Sir John Hiningham,[528] Sir John Payton senior, Sir Bassingborne Gawdy, Sir John Payton junior, Sir Edward Coke, Sir Edward Lewkner, Sir Edmund Bell, Sir Henry Warner, Sir Nathaniel Bacon, Sir Henry Spilman, Thomas Oxburgh esquire, Robert Mawe esquire.[529] *In the margin in another hand:* Sir Jhon ?Hyhame (Higham).

Dated 15 June 1605.

Unsigned. Copy. In William Sanders' hand.
Filed with, and with same endorsement as, the documents relating to the drainage of the fens, immediately below, and Letter to the Commissioners of 24 June 1605, below, p.193.
1 p. NRO BL/BC/6/12.

Documents relating to the drainage of the Fens
[*1605, June 15<-Θ->June 24*].[530]

[*Answers to objections to the drainage of the Fens*]
Answers to the objections made against the drayninge.

First wheras yt is objected that the fennes are so rotten and fownderous in

---

[526] See 24 June 1605, below, p.193, for what was discussed at this meeting.

[527] These include representatives from the counties of Norfolk and Suffolk and the borough of King's Lynn.

[528] Either John Heveningham the eldest son of Sir Arthur Heveningham or, as indicated by the marginal note, Sir John Higham.

[529] Sir Nicholas Bacon the younger's lawyer and an administrator in the extensive Liberty of St. Edmund (MacCulloch, *Suffolk*, pp.92, 330). Effectively the Liberty consisted of the entire western half of Suffolk and had riverine outfalls through Marshland.

[530] Dating: the undated documents taken together here are part of a contemporary file, as evidenced by the endorsement. They are dated with reference to the order of 15 June 1605, immediately above, and the letter

manye places, thorowgh which the new ryvers are to passe, as they will not endure banckinge, for the ryver of Owse the passadge alreadye hath been so searched and tried as yt will bothe beare banckinge and dikinge fitt to make the passadge parfitt. And for the passadge of the rest of the ryvers they shalbe made in suche places as upon tryall maye be founde firmest bothe for banckinge and dikinge. And soe that inconvenience avoyded. But yf anie such inconvenience showld be founde for the present, yet when in parte the waight of the water ys timelye taken awaye from the fennes those fownderous partes will every yeare growe fyrmer and firmer. And it is founde by experience within and against the fennes that banckes made of the verie soddes where the ground ys most rotten, beinge well looked unto for some fewe yeares togeather will growe very firme and sure. And so in shorte tyme the rottenes of the soyle wilbe soone avoyded and the banckes become perpetuallye firme.

Item wheras yt is objected that the passable ryver to Cambridge upon this dreyninge will become unpassable for botes. It is answered that the cheefest cause that nowe makes yt passable in somer ys the growing of weedes within the ryver which quarrs[531] the water so high as that therby the boates doe passe the better. But by that meanes the water being still kept so high as the banckes the fennes are continewallye made rotten by the water wherof more hurte growes to the commonweale then benefitt canne growe <by> «of» the <benifitt> «passadge» of the water.

But to helpe the one and the other that river beinge bancked in and drawen to a streighter passadge with the helpe of some few floodgates will make that ryver more passable for boates then ever it was.

And where it is objected that the drayninge of thes fennes may hazard both the losse of Holland and Marshlande, and so not fitt upon the dowbtfull hope of the one to endanger the knowne assuraunce of the other. Yt maye as welbe said lett not the drainning of the fenne be medled with lest Lincolne Minster showld be drowned, for Marshland is defended from the fennes lyeng muche lower then the fennes doe, by the bancke of Poe Dyke and sondrye other bancks betwen that and Wisbiche.[532]

And Holland beinge in like manner under the fenne ys defended by Sowthy

of 24 June 1605, below, p.193. The substance of this and the immediately following documents clearly were discussed at the meeting held at Huntingdon on 15 June but they may have been prepared and copied earlier as briefing papers. A report on the discussions had been sent to the King. All this is clear from the substance of the letter of 24 June 1605. For a window into the clash of views inherent in these documents between the farming and the navigational interests, see M. Chisholm, 'Re-assessing the navigation impact of draining the Fens in the seventeenth century', *Proceedings of the Cambridge Antiquarian Society*, xcvi (2007), pp.175–192. For earlier documents relating to the vexed question of the conditions in Marshland see *BP*, iv, *sub* 'Marshland'. Together, these documents constitute evidence for the earliest stage in this phase of fen drainage that was to run on into the 19th century. See also "Introduction", above, p.xxxiv.

531   "Quarrs": ? for 'queers', in the sense of putting out of its normal condition.

532   It is clear from this paragraph that there was a rift between the Fenland commissioners who represented the Marshland area of Norfolk and those representing the Holland interest in Lincolnshire. It is at its starkest in the contrast between the commissioners who attended the meeting in Huntingdon and those who were absent and had to be notified by the sheriff of Norfolk (immediately above, p.187). At that meeting only Sir Henry Spelman was present to represent the interests of Norfolk. He may have been the source of the originals of which these documents relating to drainage are copies.

Bancke & sondry other banckes betwen that and Deepinge fenne which banckes doe nowe onlye withstande the weight of the water of the fennes which otherwise would surrownd bothe those countryes of Holland & Marshland.

But the conveyinge awaie of the waters (as ys purposed by this drayninge) removes awaie the waight which formerlye laie upon the same banckes. And so takethe awaie all daunger & great chardge both from Holland & Marshland which otherwise might growe in respect of the fennes.

And wheare it is objected that this speedye conveyaunce of the waters from thorowgh the fennes to the sea, would endanger the haven of Lyn yt is an infayleable reason that the strength of the fresh watter ever preserveth the haven. Which thorough the weaknes of the fresh (as we finde by experience elce wheare) becomes barred. But the ryvers of Nean & Welland are to be taken cleane from Lynne and therfore that arguement faileth.

And to saie that the towne of Lynne may be loste or Marshland much impayred upon this draininge by the force of the sea cominge in more then before is but an imaginarye argument for that they cannot rec[eive] hurte therby but in respect of ther owne necligences or defaltes in not makinge there apte and usuall defences against the sea.

But yf happelie <ther> it might growe to a matter of some more chardge to make ther defences then in tymes past yet that is recompensed sufficientlie by the good & readye passage of all thinges att all tymes by thes newe ryvers from the upland countries for the one and by the ease of ther chardge for mayntenaunce of the banckes of the fennes & by the great benifitt that will growe hereby to sondry of the groundes within Marshland for the other.

[*Calculation of the cost of drainage of the Fens*]
A collection concerninge the matter of the fennes.

The chardges of drayninge the fennes besides the continuinge chardge to pre-serve the same will amount unto at the lest £100,000.

The one half of the landes beinge allotted to the undertakers in respect of the chardge, the whole beinge 230,000 acres, will amount unto in acres 115,000.

Oute of which ther must be deducted for the ryvers and common waies and pas-sadges of acres 6,000.

Thear must be deducted also for the maintenaunce & the continewinge chardge succedinge, of acres 8,000.

Suche as laie downe ther monye towardes this chardge are to have for every £1,000 put in a 1,000 acres. Which for the whole will after that rate amount unto £101,000.

But happelie ther will fall out much of the fenne grounde unrecoverable in any convenient tyme. And so the rest not able to supplie the charge.

In respect wherof the groundes without the precinctes of the fennes aforesaid which shalbe much bettered must be in some reasonable proporcion contributory unto the chardge.

[Matters relating to the draining of the Fens]
Articles concerninge the undertakinge of the drayninge of the fennes.

First that the landes within the fennes which are to passe to the undertakers of the chardge of the drayninge, be passed to suche as the undertakers shall name of trust in ther behalf.

Item in respecte of the greatnes of the worke and the charge of doinge therof yt were requisite that the undertakers should have allowed unto them seaven yeares tyme for the <drayninge> performaunce of the drayninge.

Item yf anie <use> parte of the same fennes to the quantytie of the fourthe parte of that of anie lordship which shalbe lefte to the lordes & commoners not beinge parcell of the meares [*small lakes*] within the same fennes shall not within the space of seaven yeares nowe next cominge to be drayned, then the said undertakers shall allowe out of the landes to be passed unto them within the same lordship, so manie acres as the same landes so drayned shall amownt unto.

Item that the undertakers shall perpetually maynteyne the newe ryvers to be made for the conveyinge of the water of Owse Nean Welland and Glean from thorowgh the fennes to the sea with all the sluces and bridges of the same ryvers and all the banckes in the fennes next towardes the uplandes with the watercourse to <the banckes> passe by those banckes <in the fennes next towardes the uplandes> unto any the ryvers aforesaid betwen Erith Bridge and the <fenne> Glenne.

Item yf thorowgh the defalt of the undertakers in not observing & performing what they are to doe as aforesaid, anie parte of that same fennes after the same seaven yeares shalbe surrownded and not reformed within the space of [*blank*] yeares that then so muche of the groundes to be passed to the undertakers within that lordship which so shalbe surrownded shall retorne againe to be enjoyed by the owners and commoners of the same lordship until the same surrownded growndes be againe recovered by the undertakers att the chardge of the same undertakers.

[Likely advantages of the drainage of the Fens]
The benifitt that maie growe by the generall drayninge of the same fennes.

First the fenney groundes betwen the ryver of Owse and the ryver of Glenne are upon the pointe of 230,000 acres which after the rate of 4*d.* the acre one with the other amowntethe yearely but to £3,833 6*s.* 8*d.*

Which being well drained and brought to manurance maye in five yeares after be browght to be worthe 6*s.* 8*d.* the acre one with the other att the least which amownteth yearelye unto £76,666 13*s.* 4*d.*

Besides where a multitude of poore cotagers dwellinge in & neare the fennes lyve nowe onlye in the somer tyme by gatheringes of reeds flaggs & sometimes by fishinge and fowlinge but most parte of the yeare idelye by reason ther is no other meanes ther to sett them aworke. By this dreyninge trenchinge devidinge plantinge and manuringe of thes drained growndes and by preserving the waies passadges & inclosures of the same ther wilbe worke enowgh founde for at least 2000 familyes thorowgh the yeare which will amount unto yearelie to be disposed amongst them for ther labours not so little as £13,666 13*s.* 4*d.*

Besides such winter worke as they maye have by meanes of hemp flax and suche like to be sowen in the said drayned groundes. And, for ther fishing in the common meares & dikes to be lefte to the lordes & commoners yt wilbe so good heareafter as before.

Besides with theis pore men havinge therby meanes to kepe them selves on worke thorowghout the yeare where nowe they have skarce <meate> meanes to put breade in there mouthes, they maie heareafter by ther labour be inabled to buy some kyne or other cattell to goe in the commons for ther better relief.

Undated. Unsigned. Copy. In William Sanders' hand.
Filed with, and with same endorsement as, the Order of 15 June 1605, immediately above, and Letter to the Commissioners of 24 June 1605, below, p.193.
4 pp. NRO BL/BC/6/12.

Clement Bacon to Sir Nathaniel Bacon

[*?1605*], **June 18.**[533] Right worshipfull my dutie remembred in most humble maner rendringe most harty thankes for your worshipps great favour and kindnes unto me (not beinge able to deserve any part thereof). So it was that about some eight yeares past you did give unto me the service of the cure of Wissett in Suffolk, but for that Ciprian Salluse then had a lease of it and had hired on Mr Swallowe[534] to serve it I was by him prevented and your worshipp willed me to attend upon «you» afterwardes if Salluse had hired any before, and that you would bestowe some other of me. So it is if it may please your worshipp that Wisset is voyde at this tyme, but it is not that I desire, but that I might stand in your favour for the parsonage of Easton Pavett [*Bavents*] which is next unto me. You gave it to on Mr Selusby of Sothold, who had two befor *viz.* Royden and Sothold [*Reydon and Southwold*] so that he dare not be instituted into Easton, for then he must loose his other, so he holds Easton now only by sequestration, and so it runs into lapse and you shall loose your title of presentinge. My humble suite is unto you, to crave the gift of it, to bestowe it on me, for it is more fitt for me then for him in regard of the service, and for that I have none but only a lease of an impropriation. Mr <Seal> Selusbye hath offerd to leave it (*sub conditione tacita*) [*under the tacit condition*] if you do not present it will be goten *per lapsum temporis.*[535] So cravinge and beseching your

[533] Dating: the archdeacon of Suffolk had recommended that Nathaniel Bacon present Mr Selby to the living of Easton Bavents on 21 May 1605 (above, p.182). Assigning this letter to 1605 assumes that the appointment was made at once and provoked a prompt reaction from this rival claimant. However, Selby was not instituted as rector until September 1607, the year before he died (NRO DN/REG 16, ff.15, 20; Venn has 1608, *Al. Cant.*, iv, p.41) so this letter might date from 1606 or 1607.

[534] George Swallow, ordained at Norwich in 1596 and curate at Wissett in 1604 (Venn, *Al. Cant.*, iv, p.189; NRO DN/REG 31, p.975).

[535] *"Per lapsum temporis"*: by lapse of time. A patron had to appoint to a vacant benefice within 6 months or risk losing his right to the bishop, the archbishop or (after 18 months) to the Lord Keeper acting on behalf of the Crown. During the vacancy the profits of the benefice went into sequestration. "Impropriation" relates to the situation where a benefice had a lay rector (see also the Glossary). The rules against pluralities generally limited clergy to two benefices, even with a dispensation. For the wider context see Rosemary O'Day, 'Ecclesiastical Patronage: Who Controlled the Church?' in *Church and Society in England, Henry VIII to James I*, ed. Felicity Heal and Rosemary O'Day (London, 1977), pp.137–55.

good favour in this my behalf, beinge bold to wright my mind, seinge I could not speak with you, and having not leysure to staye by reason of my place, the Lordes day drawinge <nig> nighe, entending by Gods grace to wayte uppon you agayne vere shortlye, when as for my liff and industrye in the churche your worshipp shalbe fully satisfied so remembringe my dutie I take my leave this 18 of June. Your worshipps to command.

Signed: Clement Bacon.[536]

Addressed: To the right worshipfull and my assured good maister and frend Sir Nathaniell Bacon knight.

Endorsed in Martin Man's hand: Mr Bacon.

1 p. Folger L.d.24.

Commission to enquire concerning recusants' goods and lands

[*1605, June 19*].[537] *Calendar:* The King greets the Bishop of Norwich, Sir Arthur Heveningham, Sir Henry Gawdy, Sir Ralph Hare, Sir Miles Corbett, Sir Nathaniel Bacon, Sir Henry Hubbard [*Hobart*] (serjeant at law), Sir Clippesby Gawdy, knights, Robert Houghton (serjeant at law), Jo. Pagrave, Thomas Richardson,[538] Thomas Oxborough and Rice Gwynne, esquires. They are to inquire and take sworn evidence concerning the goods of recusants and lands held by them at their conviction or subsequently acquired, their annual value and who holds them. Powers are given to seize the goods and to supervise two-third parts of these lands and also of land charged for non-payment of fines under the act of 28 Elizabeth.[539] One part of the indentures detailing the goods and two-third parts of land seized is to go to the sheriff, the other to the Exchequer by the quindene of Michaelmas.

Latin. Undated. Unsigned. Copy in Martin Man's hand.

On same sheet as the instructions immediately below.

Endorsed in Martin Man's hand: Abstract of the commission concerning the recu-santes goodes & landes. Inquiry. 1605.

1½ pp. NRO FX 245/7/5.

Directions to the Commissioners for Recusancy in Norfolk concerning recusants' goods and lands

[*1605, June 19*].[540] *Calendar:* Headed "Instruccions for the Commissioners".

---

[536] Clement Bacon: not a relative of Nathaniel Bacon, but probably the son of Edward Bacon (d.1591) of King's Lynn. The latter seems to have played upon the spurious association through their common name when he tried to obtain the under-stewardship of the Queen's manors in Marshland in 1587 (*BP*, iii, pp.30–1, 331n.47).

[537] Dating: the date of the commission is mentioned in instructions of 24 July 1605 to the Sheriff of Norfolk, below, p.200.

[538] Thomas Richardson of Hardwick (1569–1635), barrister; later Speaker of the House of Commons (1621) and Chief Justice of Common Pleas (1626); knighted 1621; J.P. 1604–1635 (*ODNB*; Owens, 'Local Government', p.570).

[539] Clause 4 of 28/9 Eliz. c.6 (1586/7) specified that where offenders had defaulted on their monthly fines of £20 for non-attendance at church, all their goods and two-thirds of their lands, tenements, leases and farms might be seized, leaving one third for maintenance of their families.

[540] Dating: as the commission immediately above.

The commissioners are to allow any lawful interests in a recusant's lands transferred for good consideration before his conviction, provided there is no power of revocation and that the profits have been taken. Only those rents or profits reserved to the recusant are to be included in the return. If there is suspicion of fraud in such cases, the issue shall be referred to the Exchequer for judgement and the lands included in the return. However, any estate granted or leased since the beginning of the late Queen's reign with power of revocation is liable to be seized according to the statute [*28 Elizabeth*] and should be included by the commissioners, as is any estate granted since that time upon trust to a recusant's use or for relief of himself and his family. No grant or lease made since the conviction of the recusant is to be allowed.

If the commissioners value the lands of any recusant more highly than when they were surveyed or seized under the late Queen and this is challenged, he is to be referred to the Exchequer to prove his case, "the same being justly to be suspected in respect of the former tolleracion".

Not every particular case can be covered, but the commissioners are to follow the reasoning prescribed above.

Undated. Unsigned. Copy in Martin Man's hand.
On same sheet and with same endorsement as the commission immediately above.
1½ pp. NRO FX 245/7/5.

The King to the Commissioners of Sewers for Norfolk and other counties

1605, June 24. *Calendar:* At their last assembly at Huntingdon the commissioners present endeavoured, in response to the King's letters, to satisfy his wishes concerning the draining of the fens.[541] Having answered all objections made, they wrote to the Council signifying that the work was feasible, could be done without damage to anyone and would be beneficial. The summer should not be allowed to pass without doing as much as possible. This year is suitable because of the long continuing drought, and the King recommends a more speedy prosecution of the work, his former letters notwithstanding, lest future wet years prove a hinderance. He has involved the Chief Justice,[542] despite wishing to spare his years. Given under the signet at Greenwich.[543]

Unsigned. Copy in William Sanders' hand.
Addressed: To our trustye and welbeloved the Commissioners of Sewars within the Ile of Elye & countyes of Norfolk Suffolk Cambridge Huntington Northampton & Lincolne.
Filed with and with same endorsement as Order of 15 June 1605 and the following

---

[541] See above, 15 June 1605, p.187.
[542] Sir John Popham, born *c.*1531.
[543] Attempts to secure an Act for the draining of 300,000 acres of fenland in the Isle of Ely and surrounding counties were defeated by fairly narrow majorities in both the 1605/6 and 1606/7 sessions of Parliament (*CJ*, i, pp.270, 277, 296, 298, 305–6, 308, 311, 340, 364, 371; Bowyer, *Parliamentary Diary*, pp.149–50, 157). Bacon was involved in the committees, along with fellow knights of the shire for Norfolk, Huntingdonshire, Cambridgeshire, Northamptonshire and Lincolnshire. Another drainage bill brought forward in March 1609/10 seems to have excluded Norfolk (*CJ*, i, pp.411, 414).

Documents relating to the drainage of the Fens, above, pp.187–191.
Endorsed in Martin Man's hand: Comission & direccions concerning the sewars & fennes in Lincolnshire etc. to be drayned. *Anno regni regis Jacobi 3.*
1 p. NRO BL/BC/6/12.

Memorandum concerning a distress by the bailiff of Gallow Hundred

1605, June 26. John Pond of North Creake bailiff of Gallow Hundred having taken a distresse *viz.* 2 neate of Thomas Dobson at the suite of Robert Pereson of Tattersett to appear at the Hundred cort, delivered back the distres underhande, compounding & giving an olde horse to Dobson for one of the cowes & delivered back thother. And tolde Pereson that hee could not retorne the distres for that one Mr Twaytes had interest in the cattell. And therby Pereson hath lost his cort, for the partie since is gon, & left nothing.

Memorandum. Pond is commaunded to appeare at thassises when he shall be called. 26 *Junii* 1605.

Unsigned. In Martin Man's hand.
½ p. NRO MC 1872/19, 866X2. Calendared, *Supplementary Stiffkey Papers*, pp.19–20.

Counterpart of lease. Sir Nathaniel Bacon to Stephen Smith of Botesdale

1605, June 26. *Calendar*: Sir Nathanaell Bacon of Stiffkey, knight, leases to Stephen Smithe of Botesdale ("Bowdesdale") in Suffolk, yeoman, the following property in Eccles, Norfolk. Namely: Norres Meadow (4 acres), Fangate Close (pasture, 3 acres), Wrightes Meadow (2 acres), Halleclosse (pasture, 12 acres), Whitegappe Close (arable, 8 acres), the tenement where James Canne dwells with a hempland opposite (1 acre), the Whittle (fen, 12 acres), 62 acres of arable given in a schedule annexed. Reserving all hawking, hunting, fishing and fowling, and all timber and underwood. Also the occupation and feed of Halleclosse from 3 September to 3 May every year for Bacon's sheep or other cattle, and the feed of any of the above premises which are "somerleyed or in somertyme tilled" in the fields of Eccles (these lands to lie mainly together). Also reserving shack in the same and pasturing of sheep on the same terms as George Nunne gent, deceased, or other occupiers of the foldcourse in the last 20 years. For 10 years from next Michaelmas, at £18 15s. a year. Smith is to maintain the property and to pay Sir Nathanaell's shepherd(s) every year in four instalments 6 combs 1 peck of good rye and the same of malt and 16s. (changed from 6 combs 2 bushels 3 pecks of rye and malt and 17s. 9d.), and also to see to the washing and shearing of 480 of Bacon's sheep, and to provide five dozen hurdles to the shepherd. Sir Nathanaell covenants that his sheep will tathe[544] within the hurdles for 73 nights yearly or pay 12d. for each night missed, and that he will give Smith free pasture for 27 ewes in the foldcourse and as many brakes[545] from the foldcourse as a mower can cut in 3 days.

[544] "Tathe": to manure the ground with their dung.
[545] "Brakes": probably used here for bracken or brushwood, rather than for "breck" (spasmodically cultivated land).

Smith is to yield up 14 acres to till for summer ley at the feast of the Purification of Our Lady before the end of the term. Sir Nathanaell is to discharge all feudal dues. Smith is to reside on the premises with his family and to use there all the dung produced, and to meet any church, town, or county charges, or charges for the King's diet. He is not to assign the lease without licence.

The annexed schedule lists 36 strips, totalling 62 acres and a half rood, in the fields of Eccles. Places mentioned: North, South and West Fields; Northmore and Southmore commons; Shamblegate Way; Buckenham Way; Shortbushe Furlong. Persons mentioned: Walter Tailor, Stephen Tailor, Thomas Canne, William Elsie (or Elcie), Thomas Nonne, John Karver, Stephen Galte, Thomas Barnes, Otwell Witewood clerk, John Nonne gent, Richard Carleton.

Signed and sealed: Steven Smith.

Witnesses to sealing and delivery: Thomas Kinges, Tho[*mas*] Barsham, Martyn Man.[546]

Endorsed in Martin Man's hand: Eccles. Steven Smithes counterpart.

4 pp. NRO BRA 926/61, 372X9.

Thomas Sackville, Earl of Dorset, Lord Treasurer, to the port officers of Great Yarmouth

1605, June 27. After my hartie comendacions. Although it hath pleased his Majestie by his letteres patentes under his great seale of England to graunt a large chartere unto his Highnes subjectes the meere merchantes of England trading into Spayne & Portugall, and thereby inhibiting all others to use anie trade to those two realmes, or either of them, other then such as maie lawfully clayme by vertue of the said chartere, or be admitted by the true meanyng thereof, and by the same letteres patentes hath graunted, that thei & such onely as shall be of the same corporation, shall have the wholle intire & sole trade to & from thence, straightly prohibiting all others from trading to those partes,[547] and also thereby requiring all customers[548] comptrollers & other officers, that neither thei, their clearkes or substitutes, shall take entry of anie merchandizes, to be transported into Spayne or Portugall, or make anie agreement for custome, but onely with such as are, or shall be free of that Companye, and thereby excluding all retaylers artificers inholders farmours common marryners & handicraftes men, out of the said Society, as by the said chartere may fully & at large appeare. Yet neverthelesse, I am informed, that divers persons, not being free of the said Societye, do presume and adventure to trade thither, contrary to the tenour & effect of the said chartere & to the manifest contempt thereof. Wherefore thes are to will & require you, to have due &

---

[546] Thomas Barsham was parson and sheep reeve at Eccles and therefore directly interested in this transaction.

[547] This restriction was soon to be lifted. The privileges of the chartered companies came under strong attack in the first two sessions of James I's first Parliament, and the right of all merchants to trade into Spain, Portugal and France was conceded by the statute 3 James I c.6. See Robert Ashton, 'The Parliamentary Agitation for Free Trade in the Opening Years of the Reign of James I, *Past & Present*, 38 (1967), pp.40–55 and Ashton, 'Jacobean Free Trade Again', *Past & Present*, 43 (1969), pp.151–7.

[548] The title given to the principal customs officer in each port town.

speciall care, for the true observance of his Majesties gracious pleasure in that behalf, and for the better performance thereof, I require you not to take dutie for anie merchandizes to be transported, as aforsaid nor make anie agreement for custome with anie person, other then of & with such as shall produce & have sufficient testimony under the hande of the president, or his deputie, that thei are of that fellowshipp, and are neither retaylours nor artificers, & by their orders allowed to use trade thither, as meere merchantes, inhibiting and restrayning all others, that shall attempt anie thinge to the contrary. And hereof faile you not. From Dorsett House this 27 of June 1605. Your loving frynde. [*Signed:*] Thomas Dorsett.

Copy in Martin Man's hand.
Addressed: To my loving freindes his Majesties officers & the fermours deputies, of the porte of Yarmouth & the members therof.
Endorsed: Copy of the Lord Treasorers letter to Yarmouth port to restrayne transp[*ortation*] into Spayne & Portugall.
1 p. NRO MS 2650, 3A2.

The King to the Sheriff and Commisioners for Musters in Norfolk

1605, July 1. Trusty and welbeloved wee greet yow well. Uppon information of the sufficiency of Thomas Balle gent[549] wee have ben moved to recommend him to you to bee admitted to the place of mustermayster of that countie in such manner as heretofore others have had yt, which, because it is for the necessary use of all our people there in their trayning, wee doubt not but your selves will fynde meet to be done, the contynuance of their trayning being so necessary as our councell have for that purpose recommended him to yow. Soe as wee do expect that hee shall have a speedy admission aswell to the office as to all other profittes and allowances usually given to it. Gyven under our signet at our pallace of Westm[inster] the first day of July in the third yere of our raigne of Grea[te] Brytaine France & Ireland. [*Signed:*] James R.

Copy.
Addressed: To our trusty and welbeloved the Sheriffe of our county of Norfolk, and to the rest of our Commyssioners for the musters there.
On same sheet as, and with same endorsement as, the Commissioners' reply of 11 July 1605 to the Privy Council, immediately below.
½ p. *r.h.s. damaged.* BL Add. 63081 f.87.

The Commissioners for Musters in Norfolk to the Privy Council

1605, July 11. Our dutyes in humble wise remembred unto your Lordships. Yt may pl[ease] you to be advertised that we have received the Kings most excell[ent] Majestie his letters for admittance of Thomas Balles gent to the place of muster maister within the county of Norfolk as a thing necessary for trayning the people there, and according to our dutyes have accepted of him. But we have thought it

---

[549] The Privy Council had expressed their approval to the Commissioners of their choice of Thomas Balle as muster master almost a year before, on 20 August 1604 (*CSPD 1603–10*, p.145). For his subsequent behaviour see 24 May 1606, below, p.231.

convenient to for beare [*sic*] from taxeing of the county towardes the charge hereby growing untill your honours shalbe pleased to have the people mustered & trayned, in regarde that uppon a generall conference had with the justices of peace of the county wee doe fynde that the people hath ben distasted with this kynd[e] of charge. And to putt them unto yt now before your wisdomes shall thinke it convenient to have the musters [were to] <more> dislyke «them» more then heretofore. In consideracion where[of we] trust that this our proceading shalbee approved by his [Majestie]. And the rather yf yt shalbe thought well of by [your honours to] whose wisdomes for further direction wee submitt [our selves] & so humbly take our leaves. From Norwich 11 July [1605]. Your honours at command[ment]. [*Signed:*] Henry Spelman, Henry [?Gawdy], Arthur Heveningham, Phillip [Woodhouse], Nathaniel Bacon.

Copy. On same sheet as, and with the same endorsement as, the King's order of 1 July 1605, immediately above.
Endorsed in Martin Man's hand: Coppies of the Kinges letter for Thomas Balles with the justices letter to the Counsell therein.
½ p. *r.h.s. damaged.* BL Add. 63081 f.88.

Robert Hayward to Sir Nathaniel Bacon

1605, July 11. My dutie in most humble manner remembred to your good woorshipp and to my good lady trustinge Allmightie God of your prosperowes healthes, the continewance whereof I wish to his good will & plesure. Yt hath pleased God to visitt me with extremitie of sicknes these three yeares and more, the paynes whereof beinge soe greate have not only taken parte of my strenth awaye, but allso have impayred and hindred my sences soe that I have not had that cariadge of my self as I have had in tymes paste as maye be proved by honest neighboures. Notwithstandinge my weekenes beinge thus perceaved, Rushmer have not ceased to practice to gett me out of my howse, he havinge gotten a farme at Elowe [*Ellough, Suffolk*], and nowe sayth he hath obtayned a promes from me in my extreme sicknes and my paynes beinge soe greate I knowe not now what was done then. These are therefore to entreat your woorshipp that you will not rest upon Rushmer but that I maye still stande your farmour and whether I live or dye you shalbe honestlie payed. Rushmer was to subtill for me, he delth with me closelie my poore wyfe not beinge acquainted with the matter, & therefore I hope these thinges beinge considered they shalbe frustrate. Thus hopinge of your woorshipps favour in this behalf I leave you to the protexion of the Almightie. Keshingland[550] the xi daye of Julie 1605. Your poore farmour to comaunde.

Signed: Robert Haywayrd. *Holograph.*
Addressed: To the right woorshipful Sir Nathaniell Bacon at his howse in [?]Stuky.
Endorsed in Martin Man's hand: R. Ha[yward] [*word faded*] Kesland.
1 p. Folger L.d.342.

---

[550] Kessingland was one of the Suffolk manors administered by Bacon on behalf of his step-son, William Smith.

Memorandum concerning a dispute between William Tydd and Thomas Haylock

[*1605, circa July 24*].[551] Righte worshipfull maye it please you to understande theffect of matters betwene William Tydd of Wells[552] and Thomas Haylocke of Branston [*Brandiston*]. Fyrst the saide Haylocke being constreyned to use monye tooke up of the same Tydd, one Knapp being suretye for the same, £5.

Item att another «tyme the said Haylock» being dryven to an hard straighte for the some of thirtye powndes the saide Tydd woolde nott graunte it him except he woold take fortye combe maulte at 10*s.* the combe (whereas the best prise through Norfolk at that tyme was but 6*s.* 8*d.* which for neede the saide Haylocke was compelled to accepte of) and tenn powndes in monye, the saide Hayllocke [?]laying twoe suretyes *videlicet* John Haylocke & Richard Goldsmith, £30.

Item at an other tyme the saide Thomas Halocke had of the same Tydd, John Haylock & Thomas Greene suretyes, £8.

May it please your good worshipp to understande the offers that hath «beene» profered <for> to the said Tydd for the satisfaccion of these debttes.

Inprimis the said William Tydd having hired a ferme of the «said» John Haylocke at Causton for 10 yers at £40 the yere to be paid halfe yere and half yere by evene portions the saide yeres to begyne at the feaste of Sct Michaell in *anno* 1603 the saide John Haylocke to thende «to» ease the saide Thomas Haylocke & to continue his credite sente unto the saide Tyd by one John Balye «to tell» him for the foresaid £43 to gyve him threskoare powndes to be paide to the saide Tydd in the thre firste yeres of his saide ferme to the which the saide Tydd answered yf the said John Haylocke woould allowe the saide threskore pondes for the aforesaid debtes the firste yere & halfe yere that then Tyd woold cease his sute & gyve backe his bondes wherupon the saide John Haylocke Thomas Haylocke John Balye and Henrye Yonges rod to Wells to the saide Tydd to make sure to him his requeste, at which tyme he refused that that before he desired. Forthermore the saide John Haylocke (to thende the suretyes of the said Thomas might be discharged) offered in the presentes of the saide Balye & Yonges fowre bondes of fowerskore powndes growing from a sufficient man to be paide in fower yers (for the sayd £43) and the saide Tyd refused that alsoe <onelye to uppon malice to> besides other [?]tow greate offers offered by the suretyes both before the dayes of paymentes, & since.

Undated. Unsigned.
Endorsed in Martin Man's hand: Thomas Hailockes dett to Tidd.
1 p. NRO NRS 24660, 125X3.

---

[551] Dating: Bacon had been involved in arbitrating between Tydd and Haylock the previous summer, together with Sir Christopher Heydon and Sir Henry Sidney (above, 23 August 1604, p.125). However, the fact that this memorandum is addressed to a single person suggests that it belongs with Martin Man's notes on the case dated 24 July 1605, immediately below. It may have been written by Christofer Reve, reporting to Bacon on his attempt to mediate (see the 24 July Memoranda immediately below), but could have been drawn up later.
[552] No fewer than three William Tydds signed the petition from the town of Wells on 4 March 1603/4 (above, pp.78–9); one of this name was a mariner (see Poor accounts, *post* 31 March 1605, above, p.164).

Memoranda on a dispute between William Tydd and Thomas Haylock

1605, July 24. Remembrances *inter* Hailock & Tidd. 24 July 1605.

Per Hailock.

Henry Yonges: present «when» Tidd badde £40 a yeare in his hearing. «Hailock» to make a fatt & nyle.[553]

Tidde gave 10*d.* for 10 yeares «to binde the matche» & concluded for it & «[?]pressed» to have a malthouse «at Swa[*nnington*]» into it. Jo. Baly, Hailock & their wyves also present. 13 *Martii ante* Michaelmas «1603» when etc.

The olde fermour in at that tyme & Hailock too.

The inv[*entory*] referred to writing only.

Mr Gury *ex relac*[*ione*] Baly. The office a matter given in in good will besides the [?]bargain.

Per Tidde.

A relacion in writing that Baly upon his retorne from thas[*sizes*] complained he was [?]forsworne.

Per Hailock.

Ro. Knapp: Tiddes offer to Knappe to joyne in the brewhouse & malthouse in the ferme. Jo. Balyes relacion to Knappe. Tidde confessed he had hired Baly to be his brewer a moneth afore Michaelmas.

Tiddes report in the towne & to Knapp that he had hired Baly.

Per Tidde.

Ex sua relacione. A senight after Michaelmas the house shutt up. The vesselles not made according to [?]agreement (when he came thither), nothing fitt founde by him.

Per Hailock.

Mr Gury. *Per artes serv. Ho*: He undertoke *pro salvatione grani*[554] & 10*s.* to reape & lay up the corne.

Per Tidde.

Mr Christofer Reve.[555] Moved to arb[*itrate*] *inter partes*. Tidde brake severall [?]pro[*mises*] wherupon Hailock grew discontent. Reves offer of £100 bonde *ex parte* Hailock to abide order «of Mr [?]Gyff.» Tiddes willingnes to peace in [?]disav[*owal*] elles untractable.

That H. Yonges brought [*word illegible*] «writ» as [?]seller *pro* Hailock, never mencioned the malthouse, instructed Reve for the [*word illegible*] drawing leaving out the malthouse.

H. Yonges denyeth to remember anie covenantes for the beere & affirm[*eth*] that Baly did the like.

Mr Funston. That Tidde had promised to lende him £10 & «that» he had 40*s.* already. *Ex relatione* Yonges to Mr Funston.

---

[553] "Fatt & nyle": a vat and possibly 'gyle', the wort for the beer.

[554] "*Per artes serv.*": ?by the professions of Hailock's servant/s; "*pro salvatione grani*": for the sake of the grain.

[555] For Christopher Reve see p.218n.

Mr Reve. Yonges <informed> coming with Hailock to instruct him for [*word illegible*] for the beere did approve it by his silence & consent. *Postea.*

Thomas Hailock. That Tidd confessed to him he had hired his brothers house & lande, tolde him he should take «his» corne & would use his help. Prayed him to carry his firing. This about 6 weekes afore Michaelmas. Offered to accept corne to shorten his dett. This [*?*]speche upon [*?*]occasion.

Ex parte Tidde.

[*Name illegible*]. Went with Tidde after Michaelmas to the house. Founde the doore shutt, but 14 vesselles of the nomber covenanted to be [*?*]received [*with*] the house.

R. Goulds[*mith*] & Thomas Hailock. Tendered £35 before suit «for the dett» but refused it unles in part of payment of the bond.

Memorandum on Tuesday 13 August the parties appointed to appeare agayne at Stifky *hora* [*hour*] 8.

Unsigned. In Martin Man's hand.
Endorsed: R[*emembrances*] *inter* Tidde & Hailock 24 *Julii* 1605.
1 p. NRO NRS 24660, 125X3.

Commissioners for Recusancy in Norfolk to the Sheriff

1605, July 24. *Calendar:* By virtue of his Majesty's commission of 19 June[556] touching inquisition to be made of the lands, leases and goods of recusants named in the annexed schedule, the commissioners require the Sheriff [*Sir Henry Spelman*] to summon 24 good and lawful men from the Hundreds afterwards mentioned to appear before them or any two of them at Norwich Castle on Friday 2 August by nine o'clock in the morning: *viz.* East Flegg, West Flegg, Happing, Tunstead, Blofield, Walsham, Taverham, Loddon and Clavering, and similarly from the Hundreds of Diss, Depwade, Earsham, Henstead, Mitford, Forehoe and Humbleyard. He is to return men well affected in religion. "Gyven under our seales" 24 July 1605. [*Signed:*] Henrye Gawdye, John [*Jegon, bishop of*] Norwich, Arthur Hevenyngham, Myles Corbett, Robert Houghton, H. [*?*]Huighbart [*Henry Hobart*].

Copy.
Addressed: To the Sheriffe of the said countie of Norfolk.
On same page as Memorandum 24 July <-Θ-> 2 August 1605, immediately below.
Endorsed in Martin Man's hand: Proc[*eedings*] upon the comission concerning recusantes for inquiry etc. A warrant *pro sum*[*monitione*] *jur*[*atorum*] [*for summoning the jurors*] *per* Serjeant Houghton.[557]
1 p. Brewer; photocopy in NRO FX 245/9/9.

---

[556] Above, p.192.
[557] Robert Houghton of Gunthorpe, one of those named in the recusancy commission of 19 June 1605. He was appointed sergeant-at-law in 1603 (*BP*, iii, p.336n.138).

Memorandum concerning proceedings against recusants

[*1605, July 24<-Θ->August 2*].[558] The comissioners in thes partes have made their
warrant for thes Hundredes being the half of the county according to this warrant
leaving thother Hundredes of this county to the comissioners nerer those partes
(but desyer) that the comission be sent backe to be here the said second of August
elles there can be no proceding here and after it be sett on here and a day given to
the jury for their verdit it is again to be sent to Sir Nathaniel Bacon to be sett on
for the other hundredes. And one retorne to be of all their <[*?*]> procedings but in
any case the comission is to be sent back to be <[*?*]said> here on the said second of
August next.

Undated. Unsigned. In ?Robert Houghton's hand.
At the foot of letter from the commissioners to the sheriff dated 24 July 1605, immedi-
ately above.
½ p. Brewer; photocopy in NRO FX 245/9/9.

Sir Henry Spelman, sheriff of Norfolk, to Sir Nathaniel Bacon

*1605, July 30. "30 July 1605. I sent unto you on Saturday laste ... the King's comission
touching recusante[s] to be safely delyvered to your owne handes, but (bycause I since
heare not of my mann) I am desirous to understande whether you received yet or not. Yf
you did, it is to be retourned to Norwich so early on the Fryday morning as my Lord
Bishopp (who sent you the c[o]mission) and the other comissioners for that partie may
have it then to execute it.' Etc." Signed.*
½ p. Maggs, 488 (1927), item 562.

Sir Nathaniel Bacon to Sir Ralph Hare and Thomas Oxborough

1605, July 31. After my verie hartie commendacions. There was <sent> «broght
unto» me yesterday the comission for inquiry of the landes & goodes of recusantes
<wherin>.[559] «And withall I was certefied that» the comissioners about Norwich
«namely the Bishop Sir H. Gawdy Sir Arthur Hevingham Sir Myles Corbett Sir H.
Hobart & Mr Serjeant Houghton» have begon therin providing for thes
Hundredes *viz.* Est Flegg W. Flegg Happing Tunsted Blofeld Walsham Loddon
Clavering Taverham Disse Ersham Depwade Hensted Mitford Forehoe &
Humbleyard. And the jury is to appeare before them at Norwich castle on
Satterday next being 3 August. And the other parte of the countie is left to us «the
rest of the commissioners» which conteyneth thes Hundredes *viz.* Landich
Smithdon Gallow Brothercrosse N. Erpingham S. Erpingham N. Grenho
Einsforth Holt (which 2 lymittes shalbe undertaken by Mr Pagrave Mr Gwyn &
my self) S. Grenho Grymshaw Wailond Shropham Gilcrosse Freebridge Lyn
Frebridge Marshland & Clacclosse, which Hundredes are aptest to be dealt in by
you.

[558] Dating: dated from letter of 24 July 1605 from the commissioners for recusancy, immediately above,
and internal evidence.
[559] See 19 June 1605, above, p.192.

I appende the retorne of the jury for <those> «our» 2 lymittes <before us> to be upon the 9 of August at Walsingham. And som <thre daies> after you maie appointe the same for your lymittes. And so sone as the jury be charged by us the comission shall be sent unto you. In the meane tyme you may proceede as wee do to sumoning the jury without it, for the comission remeyneth in the Bishops handes till their meeting on Satt[*urday*] next be past.

I sende you a coppie of the commissioners names, & of the warrant sent by us for the summons. And so comende you <verie> to Gods proteccion. From St[*iffkey*] 31 July 1605. Your verie loving frynde.

Unsigned. Draft in Martin Man's hand.
Enclosure: first list of jurors given immediately below.
On same sheet, and with same endorsement, as letter of 10 August 1605 to Hare and Oxborough, below, p.205.
1 p. NRO FX 245/9/10.

Lists of jurors to inquire into the goods and lands of recusants

[*1605, July 31 - August 9*].[560] *Calendar*: Two lists of jurors summoned and jurors serving for the inquiry. Three categories are indicated on the first list: those marked *jur*[*atus*]; those marked *pc* (?*parcitus*: excused); those marked *10s.*, presumably fined for non-appearance. The second list repeats the names of those marked *jur*[*atus*] and also marks some with a *d.* The significance of the *d.* is not clear, but it cannot be an abbreviation for any word indicating incapacity as the names of those so marked appear in the return of 25 September 1605 (below, p.210).

North Erpingham: Robert Miller of Matlaske *jur.*; Edmund Sheringham of Barningham *jur.*; Robert Elding of Plumstead *pc.*; Thomas Clarke of Trimingham 10s.; John Wortes of Trunch *jur.*

South Erpingham: William Ryse of Ingworth *jur.*, *d.*; Thomas Gilbert of Erpingham *jur.*, *d.*; Francis Crome of Tuttington 10s.; Roger Ormes of Banningham 10s.; Clement Poyte of Scottow 10s.

Smithdon: John Hamont of Brancaster 10s.; Roger Warner of Docking gent *jur.*; Nicholas Skey of Holme *jur.*; Ed. Cremer alias Skryne of Heacham 10s.; John Cowper of Snettisham *jur.*; William Banyaad (Baniard) of Snettisham *jur.*; John Elgar of Sedgford *pc.*

Brothercross: William Newarke of Burnham Westgate gent *jur.*; John Thurlowe of Burnham Sutton *jur.*; John Gaseley of Burnham Thorpe *jur.*; Edward Thurlowe of Burnham Ulp gent *pc.*

Gallow: Thomas Hallman, of Sherford *pc.*; Mathew Benseley of Snoring Parva *jur.*, *d.*; Thomas Gilbert of Barmer *jur.*; Ed. Dyke of Helvington (for Helhoughton) *jur.*; James (William deleted) Beckham of Sculthorpe *jur.*.

[560] Dating: the year is confirmed by the fact that 25 September fell on a Wednesday (Cheney and Jones, p.175). The original list of jurors nominated is probably that enclosed in Bacon's letter of 31 July 1605 (immediately above), but the annotations and amended list must date from the meeting on 9 August 1605 referred to in the same letter.

North Greenhoe: Thomas Bullocke of Great Walsingham *pc.*; Robert (Thomas in second list) Bucke of Great Walsingham gent *jur.*; Philip Browne of Little Walsingham *jur.*; William Leverington of Little Walsingham *pc.*; John Framingham of Stiffkey *jur.*

Launditch: Leonard Constabell of Weasenham gent *jur.*; Richard Burges of Brisley 10*s.*; William Hall of Brisley 10*s.*; Richard Doo of Wellingham *jur.*; Richard Thurrold of Mileham *jur.*.

Holt: Cristofer Parr of Kelling gent *jur.*; Ed. West of Burgh gent *jur.*, *d.*; Peter Byshope of Wiveton gent *egrotus*; Cristofer Newgate of Cley *pc.*; Allen Lampkyn of Langham *pc.*

At the foot of the first list in Martin Man's hand: Dies retorn[*i*] ar[*ticulorum*] *Walsingham Mercurii xxv Septembris.*
Latin. Undated. Unsigned.
Endorsed in Martin Man's hand: Nomina juratorum infra Hundreda de *Northerpingham etc. pro recusantibus.*[561]
2½ pp. NRO FX 245/7/18.

Warrant. J.P.s to the chief constables.

1605, August.[562] *Calendar:* A *pro forma* with the day of the week and dates left blank. By virtue of orders from the King and his Privy Council the justices require the chief constables, together with all petty constables of the towns in their Hundreds, to appear before them at Fakenham. They are to enquire of all persons in their Hundred keeping an alehouse or tippling house without licence, or if licensed those who allow play, drunkenness or other disorder or who have forfeited their recognisances; also of all persons living idly, of common drunkards, of tipplers, brewers and bakers who do not keep the assize of bread and drink, of recusants popish or sectarian, of poor children not bound apprentice, of churchwardens and overseers who do not provide for their poor by setting them to work or otherwise, of vagabonds, of disobedient servants, and of all felons, murderers and disturbers of the peace. The alehouse keepers, felons, drunkards, vagabonds, disobedient servants and murderers are to be brought before the J.P.s.

At the foot: [?]bacb.
Undated. Unsigned.
Endorsed in Martin Man's hand: Draught of a warrant to the chief constables *per* Mr Caryes.[563] August 1605.
1 p. NRO BL/BC/6/13.

---

[561] "*Dies retorni articulorum*": the day of the return of the articles; "*nomina juratorum ... pro recusantibus*": names of the jurors ... for recusants.
[562] Dating: dated from endorsement.
[563] Although he is here referred to as "Mr", this is probably Wimond Carey of Snettisham, knighted in 1604 (Shaw, *Knights*, ii, p.132).

Information concerning a recusant suspect at Wells

[*? post 1605, August*].[564] The wordes of [*blank*] which sould a shippes lading of coales to Roberte Jary.

He said he had ben at masse & would againe be att masse, & being reproved for so sayeng, he aunswered that the papistes do in theire masse serve God better or aswell as we the protestantes do in our service now, and that the semenaries & Jesuites which are executed here, suffer for religion & not for treason, & are martirs, but we replieng saied that the papistes are rather traitours because they mayntayne the supremacie of the Pope, then he said that the papistes are as good or better subjectes then we protestantes. Then he defended the setting upp & wur-shipping of images, said that they do not wurshipp the images but are put in remembraunce of God by them, and when I replied saieng that in theire masse & idolles they served not God but the Devill, alledging Ps.105 & 1 Cor.10, he said if he might have private conference with me, then I would be of his mynde. «These wordes he spake boldly in Partrickes house,[565] the same being then almost full of people.» And Patrick, as it semed, growing angry towardes Mr Feake «& me» for so contradicting his gheste said that we contended with him for a messe of mustard, & that he woold take no knowledge of such speches, but we advised him to have a regard to lodge none other ghestes then such as he would aunswer for, he aunswered that he might lodge any man for a night by his recognizaunce, & that he wold medle with no such matters but do as «he» shalbe taughte by the churche, & that he must be for all companies & all mens money & fell so rageing against us.

Undated. Unsigned.

Endorsed: The informacion of William Halman[566] against Owen Griffeth.
1 p. Folger L.d.980.

Sir Henry Spelman, Sheriff of Norfolk, to the bailiff of the Duchy of Lancaster

1605, August 5. By vertue of a precept touching the execucion of his Majesties commission bering date the xix of June[567] for inquisicion to be made of landes leases & goodes of divers recusants from Sir Nathaniell Bacon knight & Rice Gwynne esquire to me directed, theise are in his Majesties name to charge and command yow <& every of yow> to cause fyve good & lawfull men of every Hundred hereunderwriten to be before the commissionars aforenamed or any other the commissioners in that behalfe at the sherehouse in Litle Walsingham[568]

---

[564] Dating: this document, although undated, could well be a consequence of the warrant, immediately above, requiring chief constables to report, among other things, on popish recusants.

[565] Patrick Anderson kept an alehouse in Wells and Robert Jary regularly stood surety for him between 1603 and 1606 (Bacon memoranda book 1602–7, NRO BL/BC/5/22, pp.18, 45, 75).

[566] A William Halman was a man of some importance at Wells, either witnessing or supervising the wills of at least ten local testators (NRO ANW 1558–9, 1600–07, 1611–13), and was probably the William Halman who was constable there in 1614 (Folger V.a.273, p.95). It is not clear whether he was also the William Halman who was chief constable and subsidy assessor for Gallow Hundred in 1602 (*BP*, iv, pp.224, 259), or the William Halman who was suggested as a canniker at Warham in *c.*June 1605 (above, p.183).

[567] Above, p.192.

[568] A still-surviving two-storey 15th century building, largely of flint. It continued in use for Quarter Sessions until 1861.

on Friday the ix of August next by nine of the clocke in the morninge and for the better performance hereof to retourne none but those who are well affected in religion «together with their names & this precept». And hereof fayle yow not as yow will answere the contrary. Hunst[*ant*]on this 5 of August 1605.

At the foot: Duchy Hundreds *viz.* Smethdon Gallowe Brothercrosse Northerpingham Southerpingham Northgrenhoo.
Above the signature [*? in Spelman's hand*]: *Domini nostri Jacobi regis Anglie 3.* Let them be very sufficyent men.
Signed: Henry Spelman *vic*[*ecomitem*] [*sheriff*].
Addressed: to the baliff of the liberty of the Duchy of Lancaster.
Endorsed in Martin Man's hand: Mr sheriffes warrant to the bailiff of the Duchy to sumon the jury. 1605.
½ p. NRO MC 170/17, 643X3.

Sir Nathaniel Bacon to Sir Ralph Hare and Thomas Oxborough

1605, August 10. Sir, I have thought good to give you knowledge of our proceeding upon the comission concerning recusants for which wee had the jury yesterdey before us, and thei are to retorne their inquisition upon the xxv of September before us at Walsingham.[569] In the meane while our desire is that you will take order to cause the commission to be sent so as wee may have it at that day, bicause some of us do make question of proceeding without it. The commission was sent to be delivered you by Mr Warner of Dock[*ing*] who undertooke to convey it. So I hartely commend you to Gods prot[*ection*]. St[*iffkey*] 10 August 1605.

Unsigned. Draft in Martin Man's hand.
On same sheet and with same endorsement as letter of 31 July 1605, above, p.$.
Endorsed: Letters to Sir Ralph Hare & Mr Oxburgh.
½ p. NRO FX 245/9/10.

Sir Augustine Pagrave to Sir Nathaniel Bacon

1605, August 18. Sir I acknowledg your late kindnes & hartely wishe good meanes of requightal wherof if fayling, yet to be thankfull I will not fayle.

This inclosed was pursued & (to use your owne woorde) governed by your direction for he first subscribed «this» & then (after some other speeches) I shewed him the other. Only I tould him you pleased to allow my reasons, & had at your meeting forgotten Mr Richers, he curtuosly yealded, & gave me much cause to honor him.

If you vowtsafe to joyne I pray advise me in the sending it to him, least knowing his income in the per [*on average*], he postdateth good meaning. I heer not of the knight in ower late conference, nor can learne that Mr Thomas Windham is at Felbrig, or Mr Layer at Booton. Sir Ri[*chard*] Gressom is at Thorpe in the Northe Hundred & in either hundred be jentelmen of good estate & ther resident. Whom

---

[569] See below, pp.210–11.

with my sealfe I refer to you[r] wisdome & ernestly desier to be accounted yours in all good offices. Norwood Barningham this 18 of August 1605.[570]

Signed: Austin Palgrave. *Holograph*.

Addressed: To the right worshipfull Sir Nathaniel Bacon knight deliver thes at Stifkey.

Endorsed in Martin Man's hand: Sir Awsten Pagrave.

½ p. BL Add. 41140 ff.56–7.

Roger L'Estrange to Sir Nathaniel Bacon

1605, August 20. *One of two letters referring to a muster in the Hundreds of Gallow and Brothercross. "There were many difficulties over arms, and many defaults by contempt and otherwise."*[571] *From Hempton, 20 August 1605.*

1 p. Barnard, 51 (c.1912), item 92.

Memorandum concerning an accusation of paternity

[**1605, post September 7**].[572] Memorandum that the vii daye of September 1605 Elizabethe Fenn of Wiveton travailing with childe did send for Mistres Ann Brigges Mistres Sara Jenkenson Mistres Elizabeth Kynge Mistres Elizabeth Gould Mergaret Grogon Mergaret Warnes Alice Thurlowe wydowe Marye Braddock Jone Catton Honour Willson & Hellen Reve her mother who were all there present at the birth of her childe. Mistres Brigges with others chardged her that she had bene a lewd wench & nought[573] with diverse men and that she had slaundered Mr Pointer. And being much urdged in her travaile by them all to speak the truth whose the child should be, she sayd that never no man had to doe with her but Mr Poynter and that the child is his. And moreover in her travaile they asked her wher he <had> got it. She answered he had to doe with her in Blackney church. Then they sayd howe could that be, the clarck kepeing the key therof. She answered that he had then the key & opened the dore therwith, also «she said» he had to doe with her in Wiveton parsonage. Then they asked her why she layd it upon the brollmans boye[574] and she desired that God would forgeve her for she had slaundered hym by Mr Poynters meanes who willed never to bring his name in question and gave her mony to that end upon the reckoneing day at Wiveton in the morning and promysed her if she would lay it to any other she should never want so long as she lived and that daye «at the reckoning she being sent for by the parishioniers» she

---

[570] This is a difficult letter to interpret, but given the perceived threat of Catholic unrest it is likely that Bacon was taking steps to ensure that as many gentlemen as possible had a presence in their locality. To this end Pagrave—although apparently not a J.P. until 1613 (Smith, *County and Court*, p.367; but see *BP*, iv, p.88)—seems to be reporting on the situation in the Hundreds of North and South Erpingham rather than the recently appointed John Richers.

[571] The other letter was sent by Roger L'Estrange on 20 September 1605 (below, p.209). The section of the Catalogue entry quoted appears to relate to both letters.

[572] Dating from internal evidence. For the result of previous proceedings, see letter from the Commission for Causes Ecclesiastical of 15 June 1605, above, pp.185–6, and also 30 September 1605, below, pp.211–13.

[573] In the sense of bad, morally wicked.

[574] That is, Sander Dove. "Brollman" does not appear in the *OED*, but as the boy is described on 23 April 1605 as a comber (above, p.176), it may derive from "burl", a knot in wool or cloth.

layd it to the brollmans boye. Also in her travaile she cryed out and sayd woe worth Mr Poynter that ever she knew hym for the child is his and noe mans els. Then she was asked, the child being his, wherfore she went then to Blackney to aske hym forgivenes. She answered & her mother likewise that it was by meanes of the wydowe Thurlowe, whereupon she denyed that she did not aske hym forgivenes but did desire that God would forgive her for slaundering the boye. And Mr Poynter haveing served a warrant upon the wyddowe Thurlowe, she went to hym, who sayd if she could bring the wench to aske hym forgivenes he would clere her, who prevailed with the wench & her mother to goe with her to Blackney to satisfy her mynd but did not ask hym forgivenes as she sayd in her travaile.

Undated. Unsigned.
Endorsed in Martin Man's hand: Elizabeth Fenne her affirmacion upon the delivery of her childe touching Poynter.
1 p. Chicago 4449–C; photocopy in NRO FX 245/12/3.

Henry Howard, Earl of Northampton, Lord Lieutenant of Norfolk, to the deputy lieutenants

1605, September 15. After my <verie> hartie commendacions. Synce your letters of the 12 of August, which came not to my handes before Frydaie last, I receaved a letter from the Maior & Aldermen of Norwich wherby I perceave that defect is observed by them which you mencioned in yours concerning the want of speciall wordes in my commission for that citye & the countie of the citye. Thei seeme to attribute it to some purpose in me to spare them, out of consideracion of the course formerly holden with them, both by the late Queens Majesty & the last Lord Liuetenaunt[575] that exempted them from out of the authority of the deputies of the shire (as thei alleadge) and gave them power for the citye & countie of the citye, by a warrant particuler.[576] The like favour thei desire of me for the cityes countenaunce, promising all dutifull care & <diligence> willingnes to performe the service required, to make view of the armes for the present, & to retourne me a true & perfect certificat accordingly.

This offer, considering how the case standes, I have thought fitt to accept of, that the service maie receave no hinderaunce, whiles I take a course to rectifye myne owne power and authority by amending the comission. In the meane tyme I have promised them to write unto you to forbeare to presse them further with your authority in that behalf, untill I shall signifye my pleasure how farre I shall thinke fitt to favour them in their suite. This I praie you let them knowe I have

[575] Henry Carey, Lord Hunsdon, Lord Lieutenant 1585–96; after a long intermission, Henry Howard, Earl of Northampton, was first appointed Lord Lieutenant on 16 July 1605 (J. C. Sainty, *Lieutenants of Counties, 1585–1642*, 1970, p.28). He replaced the local Commissioners for Musters who were relegated to the rôle of deputy lieutenants, marking part of the reinstatement of the Howards at Court and an attempt at the re-establishment of some of their old influence in East Anglia.

[576] Between 1404 and 1974, Norwich enjoyed the status of a county separate from Norfolk. It was a privilege that was jealously guarded, just as the reacquisition of an equivalent status is still assiduously pursued. Northampton's commission was renewed on 16 November 1605, possibly in order to insert a reference to the city of Norwich (Sainty, *Lieutenants*, p.28).

performed, and that you will accordingly spare them untill I shall give you <further> «other» order.

Your opynions concerning the needles service of a mustermaster hath so confirmed me in my first purpose, that I am resolved so farre as it may rest in me to spare the contrey the charge. And this caution I must adde to your direccions, out of the same care, that if anie generall supply of armes shall be needfull to be made by the countrey, I maie knowe it, and how it maie best be done, with least cost, least otherwise it be made more burdynous to them then needes, to benefitt or advantage anie person particuler that shall undertake to furnishe them. Which concerne me in myne honour to respect next the well serving of his Majestie and you in the trust I have reposed in you in an aunswerable degree for your owne reputacions, which I knowe you are so tender of as I shall not neede to doubt, but will ever rest confidently & assuredly your verie faithfull & assured frynde. From the Cort at Whithall 15 September 1605. [*Signed*:] H. Northampton.

Copy in Martin Man's hand.

Addressed: The dep[*uty*] lieutenauntes of Norfolk: Sir Arthur Hevenyngham, Sir Philip Woodhouse, Sir Bassingbourne Gawdy, Sir Nathaniel Bacon.
Endorsed: The Lord Lieft[*enants*] letters 15 September 1605.
1½ pp. Folger L.d.446.

John Coppledyke to Sir Nathaniel Bacon

1605, September 15. Sir understanding that yow have graunted a warrant for the peace againste me,[577] wherin I holde myself muche grieved that yow will offer me that wronge before yow heare the truthe of the cause, but I imagine the best of yow, and the worste of him. In the meane «time» I was so deeply wronged, as I could not at that time have so digested it, had it not beene that I had my wife behind me. To write the whole circumstance were too tedious, but this bearer (who was then present) can dilate the truthe of the matter to yow at large, and had he not beene before me with yow, I had desired a warrant for his men. Thus being to ride forthe upon some earnest buisines (otherwise I would have come to yow my self, and at any time herafter when you please, I will be ready, without a warrant) I humbly take my leave. Your worshippes to commaunde.
Stody this xv of September 1605.[578]

Signed: John Copuldyke.[579]
Addressed: To the right worshipfull Sir Nathaniell Bacon knight at Stuky.
Endorsed: Mr Copuldyck.
½ p. *slightly clipped on r.h.s.* NRO MC 1872/5, 866X1. Calendared, *Supplementary Stiffkey Papers*, p.23.

---

577 The warrant against Coppledyke was granted on 13 September 1605 to Edward Scamler gent (Bacon memoranda book 1602–7, NRO BL/BC/5/22, p.71). This was probably Edward Scambler of Burston, second son of Edmund, the late Bishop of Norwich (Rye, *Norfolk families*, p.777).
578 Written below in the same hand as the signature.
579 Probably the son of Humfrey Coppledyke of Hethersett and grandson of the John Copeldike buried at Kirby Cane in 1593 (Blomefield, viii, pp.31, 36; Rye, *Visitation of Norfolk*, p.84).

Examination in a case of attempted rape

1605, September 16. The examinacion of Alice Large taken the 16 of September 1605 before Sir Nathaniell Bacon knight.

Shee saith that yesternight shee being at Clay late was brought back towardes her fathers house dwelling at Lerringsett [*Letheringsett*] by one Richard Alburgh a lyme burner of Lerringsett who offered to carrie her behinde him upon his horse. And shee saith that by the waie he lighted of the horse and drew her of with him and did by violence offer to defile her which shee withstoode. And in Hurle Lane[580] he threw her into the busshes and so contynued his violence towardes her <unles> that one John Goodson hearde her crye out.

Shee also saith that the meanes wherby shee escaped from him was bicause the said Alburgh stayed to looke after his horse and his cloake which he had lost in strugling with her.

Shee saith that he did not defile her though he sought with violence to have don it.

Signed [*by mark*]: Alice Large. *In Martin Man's hand.*
Endorsed: Examinacion of Alice Large.
½ p. NRO MC 1872/19, 866X2. Calendared, *Supplementary Stiffkey Papers*, p.20.

Roger L'Estrange to Sir Nathaniel Bacon

1605, September 20. *Letter concerning a muster in the Hundreds of Gallow and Brothercross. From Hunstanton, 20 September 1605.*[581]

1½ pp. Barnard, 51 (c.1912), item 93.

Agreement concerning a rate for horse and foot armour

1605, September 23. An agrement made «att the Kinges Head in Norwich» by the deputie lieutenantes the xxiii of September 1605 touchinge a rate for horse & foote «armour» what proporcion every man shalbe laid within the county, and this to be due at the uttermoste value.[582]

Imprimis, that eche man whose estate in landes is at £200 *per annum* or £2,000 in goodes be layd a launce, besides his foote armour, which shalbe a corslett & a muskett, to be mustered therwith [*two words deleted*] before the captain whear he is resiante.

Item that every <and> man <that may> whose estate in landes is 100 markes *per annum,* or 1,000 markes in goodes shalbe laid a light horse, and one foote armour, at the discretion of the captain.

Item that every man whose estate is in landes £40 *per annum* or in goodes £500 shalbe laid to a petronell, and one foote armour at the discrecion of the captain.

Item that every man whose estate in landes £15 *per annum* or £200 in goodes shalbe laid to a muskett «or» a corslett [*two words deleted*] at the discretion of the captain.

---

580 Probably what is now 'Hurdle Lane', in Glandford, between Cley and Letheringsett.
581 See also letter from L'Estrange to Bacon of 20 August 1605, above, p.206.
582 For further discussion of this subject, see Memoranda of 3 December 1605, below, pp.220–1.

Item that every man whose estate in landes £10 *per annum* or be worthe in goodes 200 markes shalbe laid a caliver at the discretion of the captain.

Memorandum that whatsoever anie man is alredy charged & have yelded therunto be not altered, but if anie man hereafter finde himselfe greved, that then the rules above said «be considered upon» <by> the direccions of the deputie lieutenantes.

Memorandum also that the towne armours shall stande as before hath ben agreed.

Unsigned.

Endorsed in Martin Man's hand: Orders *per* d[*eputy*] lieut[*enants*] 23 September 1605.

1 p. NRO MC 1872/80/1, 866X3. Calendared, *Supplementary Stiffkey Papers,* p.25.

Findings of an inquisition of the goods of certain recusants

1605, September 25. An indenture of the goodes of John Dike of Kellinge[583] William Reve of Wickmere and Thomas Seppins of West Rudham founde by the oath of Christofer Parr Robert Miller Edmond Sheringham John Worttes William Rice Thomas Gilbert Roger Warner gent Nicholas Skey John Cooper William Baynyarde William Newarke John Thurlowe John Gaseley Mathew Bensley Thomas Gilberte Edmonde Dike James Beckham Robert Buck Phillip Browne John Framingham Leonard Constable Richard Doe Richard Thurroll and Edmond West gent jurors, as appeareth by inquisicion taken at Walsingham the five and twenteth daie of September in the yeare of the reigne of our sovereigne lorde James by the grace of God Kinge of Englande Fraunce and Irelande defendor of the faith etc the thirde, and of Scotland the nyne and thirtieth, before Sir Nathanael Bacon knight, John Pagrave and Rice Gwynne esquires, by vertue of his Majesties writt of commission to them the said Sir Nathanael Bacon John Pagrave and Rice Gwynne amongst others directed to inquire of the goodes landes and tenementes of divers recusantes mentioned in a certain scedule to the said commission annexed.[584]

John Dike possessed of one shodd carte [*with iron-tyred wheels*]. One milch cowe, two worke horses. Thre combes of rye. Thre combes of barley. One table. Fouretene peces of pewter. Seaven peces of brasse. Thre speetes, one firepan and tonges, one bedsteede, and a flockbed. One coverlet. Thre chestes and two paire of sheetes. *Et valent in toto,* £8.

William Reve possessed of tenn combes of wheate. Tenn combes of rye. Twenty combes of barley and five combes of bucke [*buckwheat*]. One olde geldinge. Two mares. Five milch neate, and two year[ling] calves. *Et valent in toto,* £21.

Thomas Seppins possessed of twenty combes of wheate. Twenty combes of rye.

---

[583] John Dike, yeoman, of Kelling was convicted of popish recusancy at the Quarter Sessions at Norwich in October 1610 (R.H. Box 71).

[584] For Bacon's letter of 31 July 1605 concerning this commission, see above, pp.201–2, and the arrangements to meet at Walsingham, made on the 10 August 1605, above, p.205.

Forty combes of barley. Thre worke horses. Five milch neate, and divers implementes of houshold. *Et valent in toto,* £36.

Unsigned. 2 indented copies with three seals on each.
2 pp. RH Box 71. Printed, *Stiffkey Papers,* pp.183–4.

Rental. Manor of Methwold

[*1605, post September 29*]. *Summary.* "Rental of Methwold for the year ending
Michaelmas 1605".[585]

From entry in *Supplementary Stiffkey Papers,* p.38.

Sir Nathaniel Bacon to the Commissioners for Causes Ecclesiastical

1605, September 30. Yt maie please your Grace and the rest of his Majesties
Commissioners for Causes Ecclesiasticall to be advertized that I have receaved your
letter «of the 15 of June last» touching Mr James Poynter parson of Blakeny &
Wyveton in the countie of Norfolk.[586] And though the same letter of yours be
directed by name to severall others besides my self yet in asmuch as I dwell neerest
unto Mr Poynter and therby am the more privie to his course of life I have thought
my self more tyed then perhappes the rest doe, to whome also your letter is written,
to make knowen <what the course of Mr Poynters life hath ben> «how he hath
lived», which perhappes is not so well understode by the rest as by my self. Mr
Poynter <manie «sondry»> yeares sinc <placed> «was called» to be parson of
Blakeney & Glamford two distinct charges and yet united by some auncient
unyon and sone after was, though not openly, yet secretly, suspected to be the
father of a childe begotten of a base poore woman, which was not publickly called
in question, and so passed away. After this he fell into the liking of one Alice
Whitby, notwithstanding that he had a wife of his owne, and shee being «by him»
gotten with childe as most men, who were acquaynted with the cause, did thinke.
And shee being examined before my self for the father of her childe did accuse one
[*blank*] Penthery a man whome no man knew.[587] And shee being bounde by
recognizance to appeare at a Sessions for the aunswering of the bastardy was caryed
being great with childe by Mr Poynter from Blakny here in Norfolk to Bury in
Suffolk and from thence to London or nere therunto where the woman was delivered of her childe. After this the said Whitby had severall children, and all
supposed to be by Mr Poynter by reason of his contynuance of conversing with
her. And «he» was called in question for the same, both before the Chancelour of
Norwich, & before B[*ishop*] Redmayn by authority of his high comission, and yet
passed through all, so as his charges thereby have growen such, as for dett he hath
lien no litle tyme together in <our comon gaole> «the prison» of this county.
During his troubles touching this Alice Whitby, his wife reputed an honest woman
did departe from him, and so hath lived a great while at Cambridge. Also whiles

---

[585] Methwold was part of the Duchy of Lancaster lands in Norfolk, of which Bacon was steward.
[586] See above, pp.185–6.
[587] And not traceable in earlier volumes of these papers.

this his suspected conversacion with Alice Whitby did last, he was accused of a rape with a younge mayde to be comytted in the high way, and for this he was indicted & publickly arraigned, and though he was acquited of the rape, bicause the yonge woman had taken a groate of him, yet the comitting of the fact was upon the evidence stronge against him, and so also was the rape, though not so pregnaunt in evidence, as the other fact. And this I do the more boldly write, bicause I was present at the evidence giving before my Lord Chiefe Justice of England.

It is reported that the said Alice Whitby is some yeare or more past maryed. And Mr Poynter not calling home his wife who liveth at Cambridge some 50 myles from him is now accused by one Elizabeth Fenne of Wyveton wher Mr Poynter is also parson, being a charge by him obteyned to his other lyvinges, all three of them being neere together, to be the reputed father «of a childe» wherof shee hath lately ben delivered. <And> This Fenne is the daughter of a poore woman in Wyveton who liveth of the almes of the towne, and upon her examinacion before me before her delivery shee did accuse Mr Poynter, and so contynued it at the tyme of her delivery as shall appeare unto your Grace & the rest by examinacions, the coppies wherof I sende up by this bearer, yf it shall stande with the pleasure of your Grace & the rest <overreadinge> «to» reade them over.[588] I compleyned to my Lord Bushop of this diocesse of this his last cariage and <did hope that he would have proceeded against him and yet Mr Poynter hath used some meanes to stay him> «his Lordship was mynded to have examined the cause». Two of his charges Blakny & Wyveton be greate, and the third called Glamford is also a distinct <parrish> charge. And he causeth thes three parrishes to be served by 2 curates, who preache not, and the one of them is scarse able to reade. And seing Mr Poynter hath dwelt so longe in this kynde of synne of his, and no warning will reforme him, your Grace & the rest in my meane judgment shall performe a pleasing service to God in removing him from hence for this his scandalous life, that some better man may be placed in his roometh. It is like that Mr Poynter will except against me, and yet I knowe not whie he should, unles yt be bicause I call him in question for this his evil corse of living, and am more bolde to speake when I know, then other men. For as he dealeth with Mr Bradock, who is an honest man, so he doth with poore persons as the widdow Ringold & citeth them up that <by> «the» very extremity of charge may feare [*frighten*] them from speaking anie thing touching this his manner of life.[589] The suggestion made unto your Grace & the rest of pracktise by Bradock & the rest is verie untrue for anie thing that I can discover and therefore your Grace shall do very well to dismisse them & «to» leave <him> «Mr Poynter» to the Bishop of the dyoces & to the justices for the bastardy, where the causes with <lesse> more ease of charge may be examined, and I will forbeare acording to your Graces letter to proceede against him, untill it shall appeare, what corse yt shall please you to take with him. Thus referring the cons[*ideration*] herof to your better wisdomes I besech God to direct you to do that which shall be most to his glory.

[588] Above, *post* 7 September 1605, pp.206–7.
[589] See 5 July 1604 and 15 June 1605, above, pp.111–12, 185, where Poynter has cited Bradock before the High Commission, and immediately below.

From St[*iffkey*] this last of September 1605. Your Graces and of the rest at commandment.

Unsigned. Draft in Martin Man's hand.
4 pp. Chicago 4449–B

Sir Nathaniel Bacon to Robert Rich, Baron Rich

[*1605, post September 30*].[590] It maie please your honour to understande that one James Poynter parson of Blakeney Wiveton and Glamford thre severell chardges, and chaplin to the Erle of Northumberlande, beinge a man notoriously defamed for his vitious life continually led since he came into the chardge of the ministery and now lately accused by a pore womans daughter of Wiveton to have gotten her with childe hath cited the bearer herof John Braddock and «allso» divers <others> «pore persons» of Wiveton into the High Commission courte that by extremitie of chardge he might feare them to speake againste him. The course of his life ledd, your honour maie understand by the coppie of my letter written unto the B[*ishop*] of Canterberrie and to the reste of the commissioners which this bearer can shew you, and himselfe sufficiently informe your honour of. My humble sewte unto your honour is that you will be pleased to informe the Erle of Northumberland[591] of the lewde conversacion of this his chaplin, that his honour maie no longer countenance so bad a member, and to geve this bearer your furtherance for his dismission out of the courte. Thus committinge your Lordshipe to the keping of Allmighty God I take my leave. Your honours at commaundment.[592]

Undated. Unsigned. Copy in William Sanders' hand.
Endorsed: Copy letter to the Lord Rich.[593]
½ p. NRO MC 571/14, 778X4. Printed, *Stiffkey Papers*, pp.19–20.

Certificate in the case William Croppe and his wife against Thomas Hastings and others

1605, October 7. *Calendar*: By commission from the court of Chancery Bacon has heard the allegations of William Croppe and his wife, plaintiffs, against Thomas

[590] Dating: dated from the reference to Bacon's letter of 30 September 1605 to the Commissioners of Causes Ecclesiastical, immediately above.
[591] Henry Percy, ninth earl of Northumberland (1564–1632). Although himself a conformist the attachment of his predecessors to Catholicism had blighted their lives. In the early months of James' reign he had advocated toleration for Catholics. Through his patronage of Thomas Harriot, Percy was associated with atheism and forbidden knowledge. Possibly Rich's connection with Percy had been through the second earl of Essex. The situation confronting Bacon was a difficult one: following James' accession Northumberland had received royal favour and had for a time occupied a position of influence at Court. Presumably, this had also bolstered the confidence of his dependant, Poynter. However, by this point Northumberland was again in disgrace and was soon to be suspected of involvement in the gunpowder treason (*ODNB*).
[592] Despite Bacon's efforts, Poynter apparently remained at Blakeney and Wiveton until his death in 1621 (Venn, *Al. Cant.*, iii, p.390).
[593] Bacon's appeal to Rich was an astute move in his campaign against Poynter. Rich was the hot-headed lay leader of the godly in Essex and his followers had in their time been prosecuted by the High Commission. Furthermore, he had a very personal reason for antagonism towards the ecclesiastical hierarchy. At this very moment he was engaged in divorce proceedings against his wife, the adulterous Penelope, before Richard Bancroft, the Archbishop of Canterbury (*ODNB*).

Hastinges and others, defendants, counsel on both sides being present. But he was unable to persuade the parties to end their differences, and therefore certifies his opinion of the case as follows.

The wife of the plaintiff William Croppe had an estate of free lands and leases in Hindringham from her former husband, Martyn Hastinges, but released her right in it before a judge of Assize. In return she was to receive either a rent charge of £40 a year, or an estate in the free lands for life and for 60 years in the leases if she lived so long and such a conveyance was made soon afterwards.

By his will[594] Martyn devised the lands and leases to her for 50 years if she lived so long provided that she entered a bond of £1,000 to observe the conditions of the will. The executors accepted her bond and this entitled her, in equity though not in law, to claim the income from the lands and leases.

If Martyn's intention was that his wife should have the land and leases, as proved by some of the witnesses, then he did not mean her to be limited to the annuity of £40. All agree that she was not to have both the annuity and the lands.

Nevertheless Bacon's opinion "under your Lordships reformacion" is that the plaintiff should not be relieved. First, his wife clearly should not have both lands and annuity and both the plaintiff and his wife, by their actions, had chosen the annuity. During her widowhood the wife entered a bond of £100 and accepted £80 in money or money's worth together with the wardship of her child; her husband the plaintiff having taken advice did not deal with the lands but chose the annuity, as proved by two witnesses.

Secondly, the plaintiff did not press his claim for 27 years, therein tacitly accepting the annuity, and it is now too late, especially as the defendant has settled the property and has had the expense of defending his title to the lease "which was litigeous". Moreover his second wife, by whom he has several children, "was married unto him in regard of this his estate" and has a jointure in part of the lands. So it would be inconvenient to alter the position now.

Bacon sought to persuade the plaintiff to content himself with the annuity and £80 of arrears due at Michaelmas last, and that his wife assure to the defendant any interest she has in the leases, but William Croppe hopes for more from the Lord Chancellor.

The defendant would not give security to the plaintiff for the annuity or arrears because of the charges incurred by the suit. Bacon intended to order that the wife's bonds of £1,000 and £100 should be cancelled if she barred her claim to the lands and leases.

"Stifkey 7 *Octobris* 1605".

Copy in Martin Man's hand.
Addressed: To the right honorable the Lord Ellesmere Lord Chauncelor of England.
Endorsed in a different hand: Certificat touching the cause betwen Mr Croppe & Hastinges in Chauncery.
2 pp. NRO RAY 267.

---

[594] The will of Martin Hastinges of Hindringham was proved in 1574 (TNA PRO prob/11/56 Martyn f.44).

John Richers to Sir Nathaniel Bacon

1605, October 8. Good sir, I was promised to have Sir Bassingbourne Gawdye his accompt theise last sessions of the mony receaved and disbursed for the Kinges Benche, Marshallse etc. but I neyther have it, nor yet soe much as eny note for what tyme the country hath payed, that thereby I might knowe what to demaund. Onely he hath delivered me £60 which me thinckes showld not be all that is due by him, for the yearely receipt comes to £124 7s. 1d. for which he is accomptable 6 or 7 yeares (as I heare) therefore I suppose there must needes be a greater remayne. I doe also fynd that slacknes in the cheife constables, that without the assistance of the justices in their severall lymittes, or sending about my servant into the severall Hundreds to distreigne (which wilbe to chargeable and troblesome) I shall not bring this buisines into that even coorse that I would. Therefore before I use the extremitye, I praye you to be pleased to send for the cheife constables of the Hundreds of Northerpingham, Northgrenehoe, and Holt (except for Mr Frauncis Symones, whoe hath payed) and appoynt them to bring presently unto me all such mony, as they have receaved for the use aforesaid, due at Michaelmas last, which they ought then to have payed (and hereafter must paye quarterly according to the lawe) and also that they certefie unto me the names of all defaulters, and likewise the severall parishes within their severall Hundreds, together with the some taxed on each parish, for this service. Wherein it wilbe good to geve them in charge to make their taxacions severall, and not to put the assessement for the Kinges Bench, the lame souldiers, the prisoners, the composition for his Majesties diett, the poore, and all other parish charges whatsoever, together, as they doe in that Hundred where I dwell. Which must be done (albeit the common people conceipt [*conceive*] it not) because as the occasions for which those taxacions are made are divers, and severall, soe are the meanes to come by them from those that refuse payment, also divers <and severall> cannot by one measure to all be compelled.[595] I am requested by this bearer, to let you understand, that both in respect of the smallnes of his living (his charges increasing) and also for some other privat respectes, he is desirous to change his place for a better, & hearing that there is a benefice lately fallen into your handes, is desirous of your favour therein, hoping your good opinion of him is noe lesse nowe then heretofore. The matter is your owne, therefore were I better acquainted with you then I am, I would not importune you for eny man, onely I have undertaken to lett you understand that he lives paynefully in his place & calling here, and that he seemes to me (being better knowne to your selfe) by this little acquaintance I have with him, to be a man of honest lyfe and conversacion, but to intermedle eny further in this your privat businesse I intend not. Therefore with remembrance of my diuty I take my leave. Swenington Hall this viii of October 1605.

Signed: Yours assuredly John Rychers.

Addressed: To the right worshipfull Sir Nathaniell Bacon, knight, at his howse, at Styfkeye.

---

[595] Effectively, these were the various heads under which local taxation was raised and which, because of the means by which they were levied, in time became know as 'rates'.

Endorsed in Martin Man's hand: [*1*]Mr Richers. [*2*] Letter to Mr [*word illegible*]
N. Erp[*ingham*], N. Grenho, Holt.
1½ pp. Folger L.d.497.

Reckoning between Robert Stileman and Richard Spratt

1605, October 15. A reckoninge made the xv of October 1605 betwene Robert
Styleman thelder[596] and Richard Spratt gent for money receyved and paid by the
said Robert Stileman towardes the dischardge of the said Richard Sprattes debtes
beinge £320.[597]

Robert Stilemans disbursmentes.

Imprimis to Mr Farrington	£113 10s.	
Item to Mr Hawse	£39 10s.	
Item to Tomson	£6	
Item to Mr Paston	£23	
/[?]nb: 15d./[598]		
Item to Sir William Read for rent of 2 yeares		13s. 4d.
Item to [?]Pit & one other in Swanton for corne inning [*harvesting*]		16s.
Item to Jhon Sprat for Mr Dawes	£4	
Item for toune charges		6s. 8d.
Item for the tilth & sed of the Red Close nowe sowen with rie	£30	
/*Soma*	£206 14s. 9d./	
/Item to Rogers for looking to the kill [*kiln*]		30s./
/*Soma totalis*	£208 4s. 9d./	

His receiptes

Imprimis for corne 142 comb of rye at 6s. 8d. the comb	£47 6s. 8d.	
/Allowed by his own reckoning/		
Item for the feed of the stuble		30s.
Item for two yeares feede of pasture		£4 16s. 8d.

/The one close was accepted for 1 yeare for 46s. 8d. & for the last yeare so mutch
as the same maie nowe be leat for which is to be feed by Stilmans till our Lady
& to all[*ow*] 50s. & 10s. for the other close – £4 16s 8d./[599]
/Mr Pecock of his offer & that to be all[*owed*]/

Item for Yorkes meddowe		£3 all[*owed*]
Item for the wood in Collins olland		£23

---

[596] Robert Stileman the elder of Field Dalling (d.1610). Stileman had acted as witness together with
Martin Man to one of Bacon's earlier arbitration agreements in 1593 and served as chief constable of North
Greenhoe in 1602 (*BP*, iii, p.244; *BP*, iv, p.269). In 1610 he appointed Nathaniel Bacon as supervisor to
his will, in which he left property in Field Dalling, Hindringham, Salthouse, Wiveton, Kelling and
Sharrington (NRO, NCC Harman f.54).

[597] This account is difficult to interpret in places because of poorly written marginalia. It should be
considered together with the Memoranda of 7 November 1605, below, p.218.

[598] This seems to be a deduction.

[599] This appears to be 10s. short.

/All[owed]: viz. in some allowance to Fleming 10s. or [?]therabout/
Item for the wood in Millfeild   £5 11s.10d.
/The wood [?]mairs[600] saye   £10 10s.
   for the other close   £3 16s.8d./
Item for the wodde in the square close   £6
   /Ther is no fell therof and so the valew uncler to me/
Item for 7 trees   46s. 8d. all[owed]
Item for tymber of Wortley & Gilbert   £3 5s. 4d.
   /20s. received of Gilbert & the rest unp[aid]/
   /Wortly asketh all[owance] for 24 daies worke & so stoppeth all which is of
   him demaundeth/
Item of Flemming «resp[ite] £5» for wood and barke   £19 13s. 4d.
   /Saving £10 in Fl[emings] handes because he hath not all his bark/
Item for two thowsand and halfe of tyle «which he had himself»   25s. all[owed]
Item of Mr Hunt for two thowsand tyle   20s.
   /This some due to Webster/
   /Yf Mr Hunt saie that he hath allowed Stilman then he is to aunswere the 20s./
Item for a killware of brick and tyle   £10
   /Confessed 6000 brick, 3000 tile/
Item for the profittes of the brickkill this yeare   £20
   /4 brent & 1 not brent. Rogers to witnes for the rest/
   /It is agreed that Blog do set downe upon his honest word, what the profites of a
   kill, & therafter Stilman is to allowe/
Item for Rogers for rind [?bark]   £3 10s.
   /& 1 to burne/
                 Summa totalis   £169 10s. 4d.
/ <£135 3s. 6d.> £132 10s. 2d./[601]

So ther remaine in his handes £13 10s. 4d. besides his gaine.

In a close of rye «now sowne» conteyninge 40 acres with £20 allowed him for seede and tylth and £22 for the ferme of that close and other groundes, the increase of the rye estemated at 200 combes and valewed at 6s. 8d. a combe £80 out of which the £42 for seede tylth and ferme being deducted there remaine unto him in cleare gaine £38

Item received by him more for wood and other thinges £23
So ther rest in his handes £74 10s. 4d.

In William Sanders' hand, with marginal annotations in Nathaniel Bacon's hand.
Endorsed in Martin Man's hand: The reckoning betwen Mr Spratt & R. Stileman.
1 p. Folger L.d.740.

---

[600] Perhaps timber growing at the edges (mires=boundaries) of the wood.
[601] This is the accepted total of Spratt's demands (see Memoranda of 7 November 1605, below, p.218).

Christopher Reve to Martin Man

[*Post 1605, November 5*].[602] Mr Martyne ther is due to your mauster £3 remeyning of the twenty powndes, and he demaundeth of me, for half a yeares rent of the stywardshippe £7 15s. Of this Mr Bedyngfild did enforce me to pay to him the one half and had moch adoe to escape for the other half so that I [?]falle dowble charged for the half of £7 15s. I did travayle <with> uppe to London when he went to the first session of Parliament and did contynue ther a fortnytt at myne owne chardge which cost me aboute £3 10s. and I leyd out in the sute for him agaynst the two Yarmouth men for the mast & rope 28s. 9d. of which ther is but one fee the rest disbursed. And you spake to me for a wrytt for one of your maisters men which I broke uppe and after sent downe an *alias ca.*[603] which cometh to 8s. 4d. I hope your maister will allowe me towardes my chardges for yt was in Lent out of the term tyme and his promyse was to allowe all, but I requyre but 40s. And I send by this bearer £7. If theis thinges will not content him lett me be advertised therof by you and I will content him. So with my harty comendacons I rest. Your very lovyng freind.

Undated.

Signed: Chr[*ist*]ofer Reve. *Holograph.*

Addressed: To my very lovyng freind Mr Martyne Man at Mr Peckevers[604] in Norwich.

½ p. NRO BCH 27/9/74 I (35).

Memoranda concerning the reckoning between Robert Stileman and Richard Spratt

1605, November 7. Remembrances falling out upon the conclusion of the reckoninges betwen Mr Richard Spratt & Robert Stileman. 7 November 1605.[605]

Inprimis the demaundes on R. Stilemans behalf as appeareth by a particuler note fall out to be £208 4s. 9d.

Item the demaundes on Mr Sprattes behalf fall out to be £132 10s. 2d.. So there resteth due to R. Stileman £75 14s. 7d.

For this arrerages Mr Thomas Fairfaxe is to be procured to become bounde and to paie use for the same money from the date hereof untill it be paid.

Memorandum that the wood in the Square closse is to be dealt withall by Mr Spratt upon this assuraunce made.

Also R. Stileman is to feede until <Christmas> «or Lady next» the Busshie closse the [?]Raunde closse & Yorkes meadowe.

---

[602] Dating: there is no evidence that Bacon used the services of Christopher Reve before the death of his former attorney, Stephen Drury, in 1599, so it is probable that Reve's reference to Parliament concerns that of 1604–10. This is confirmed by the fact that there had been only one session in the last Elizabethan Parliament of 1601. His reference to the "first session" suggests that he is writing after the commencement of the second session of the first Jacobean parliament which began on 5 November 1605. Reve was Duchy of Lancaster bailiff in the hundreds of Gallow and Brothercross (*BP*, iv, p.229) and steward of Methwold, a Duchy manor, while Bacon was high steward of all Duchy lands in Norfolk.

[603] *Alias ca*[*pias*]. A further writ to seize a defendant when a previous writ has had no effect.

[604] Edmund Peckover, husband of Cecily Man. See 12 June 1604, above, p.110n.

[605] See also Reckoning of 15 October 1605, above, pp.216–17.

Item there is allowed to Mr Spratt by R. Stileman but 20*s*. for Wortly & Gilbertes reckoning.

Also £5 is due from Flemyng & to be allowed to Mr Spratt upon Fleming his enjoying his wholle bargayne for the barke.

Also if Mr Hunt saie that he hath allowed R. Stileman for 2000 brick, there is to be allowed more to Mr Spratt 20*s*.

Item Rogers is promised his dwelling, paying his farme to Mr Spratt untill Michaelmas next.

Also a kyll of brick now unburnt is to go to R. Stilemans use allowing to Mr Spratt £4.

Also wheras R. Stileman & Webster have given their wordes to enter into bondes of £20 a pece to morowe at Holt for abiding Mr William Huntes order, who ending the same and that above being performed, then «generall» acquittances to be sealed as well on Mr Sprattes & Websters parte to «R.» Stileman, as on R. Stilemans parte to them.

Memorandum the arable closse sowen with rye upon the performaunce of that above on Mr Sprattes parte is to go to Mr Sprattes use.

Memorandum if Mr Fairfaxe do not become bounde and Mr Spratt can procure payment of the money betwen this & Christmas, then that to be in lieu of Mr Farfaxes bond.

Item the close lett to R. Stileman by Mr Paston called the Bushie close must be sett over to Mr Spratt and he to give sufficient security to discharge him against Mr Paston.

Memorandum that 10*s*. or 15*s*. must be allowed by Mr Spratt to the buyers of the wood for their satisfaccion about the standes felling.

Memorandum if anie question fall out concerning the articles afore set downe, the parties do agree to have it decided by Sir Nathaniel Bacon.[606]

Memorandum Mr Spratt is to allowe £4 to Mr Gwyn, which is behinde & was promised by R. Stileman & L. Webster to be paid to Mr Gwyn.

In Martin Man's hand. Signed: Na[*thaniel*] Bacon.
1½ pp. Folger L.d.741.

Petition. Townsmen of Wells and Burnham to Robert Cecil, Earl of Salisbury

[*1605 <-Θ-> 1611*], November 8.[607] Our dueties in humble wise remembred. Wee dwellinge neare unto the townes of Welles and Burnham in the countye of Norfolk are bould to be sewtors unto your Lordship for <the furtheraunce> «your favour in allowance» of <this> «a» peticion which the marchantes and owners of manie ships, belonginge to the same townes, beinge members of the porte of Kinges Lynne, doe make. That <a porte wherin both customer and other officers might be> «with your honours choice of a customer and other officers, a porte might be [?]metely [*word deleted*]» erected, at the said towne of Welles, for both

---

[606] An instance of informal mediation by Nathaniel Bacon between two of his clients.

[607] Dating: the limits are set by Cecil's promotion to the earldom of Salisbury, 4 May 1605, and his death on 24 May 1612 (Fryde *et al.*, *British Chronology*, p.481).

the said townes, being within thre miles the one of the other, wherby they should not be compelled (as now they are) to travell for the cocket of every ship neare twenty miles, which is both chardgable and very troblesome to seafaringe men.[608] Besides if this be effected, it will be a meanes herafter, to further the Kinges profitt, because an immediate officer will better looke therunto, then a substitute or deputie, and will recompence the Kinges chardge, by the better collecting of custome and such other duties. The profitt of the Kinge «for his custome» being now more, then hath bene, <for his custome> will aske a [*require*] more care, in the lookinge therunto, and withal a more chardg in attendance. <We offer thes reasons to your Lordships wise consideracion> Though this sewte be a diminution to the porte of Lynne, to have thes two townes taken from it, and made a distinct member by it selfe, yet, it beinge a beneficiall thinge for the Kinge, and greatly for the ease of the subject, wee hope that thes co[*n*]sideracions will weigh more with your Lordships wisdome, then the private respect of that porte alone. Thus comittinge your Lordship to the proteccion of Almightie God we take our leave. Your Lordships at comaundement.

Undated. Unsigned. Draft in William Sanders' hand.
Endorsed: Copy letter to my Lord of Salesbury 8 November for a customes house at Welles.
1½ pp. NRO MC 1872/31, 866X3. Calendared, *Supplementary Stiffkey Papers,* p.18.

Memoranda for discussion of militia administration with the Earl of Northampton

1605, December 3. Remembraunces for conference with the Lord Northampton.[609]

To praie his direccion touching the raising of a nomber of horses within Norfolk that the same maie be don with most indifferency & least offence. Herin it must be shewed unto his Lordship that his advise is prayed what allowance he doth give to have the statute for armes [*4 and 5 Ph. and Mar., c.2, 1558*] duely observed inasmuch as the statute doth appointe a man of 100 markes a yeare to finde a l[*ight*] horse & a man of £1,000 to fynde [*blank*] horses wherin it is to be regarded when the statute was made. Then 100 markes by yeare did amounte to more lande then perhappes 300 markes a yeare now doeth, & so of other valewes. And the statute is construed as the utter valewes of landes be by improvement.

---

[608] For the purposes of both maritime and customs jurisdiction the coast of Norfolk was divided into two stretches, one under the headport of Lynn, the other of Yarmouth. As is evident here, this could create practical problems for the subsidiary 'creeks' such as Wells and Burnham.

[609] The justices were clearly unhappy with the rates agreed on 23 September 1605 (above, pp.209–10). The statute of arms of 1558 had been interpreted to mean that individuals were to contribute towards the expenses of the militia only in their place of residence, regardless of where the lands from which they drew their income lay, with the actual amount paid being based on an individual's assessment for the subsidy. This system tended to penalise areas with large numbers of absentee landlords. The repeal of the provision in the General Act for renewing or repealing legislation (1 James I c.25) left the system open to reform on the equitable model of poor relief rates. Nathaniel Bacon, in the name of the commissioners for musters, had argued for this principle in 1598, but for the next quarter century a workable basis of assessment remained elusive and disputed (see Smith, 'Militia Rates', pp.93–110).

It is also to be considered if a man of £1,000 be laid [*blank*] horses then whither a man of £2,000 or £3,000 shalbe laid 2 or 3 so many, & accordingly of other valewes.

Also it is to be argued upon in like sort for the laying of foote armour. And bicause many of the armes prescribed by the statute are out of use, what is to be don in the lieu of those armes.

Besides it is to be considered what rule shall be taken to lay upon a Hundred. [*Blank*] armes or [*blank*] horses. Whither the rule of the subsidy or what other rule. For men are laid to armes by their valewes so as the same must be guided either by the subsidy or by a particuler ex[*aminati*]on of every mans estate, which seemeth to be the best corse. Wherin the d[*eputy*] lieftenantes must be informed of the estates of men by others of whome thei make choice for their faithfull informacion.

Also some rule must be set downe how to proceede against them who being charged with horse or foote do comytt contemptes in not providing.

Direccion also would be how to proceede with them who are appointed to places of charge, as capteynships, & do make refusall.

Also to be directed whither anie beacon watche shalbe kept to the charge of the contrey.

To consider if it be meete to speake of the coate & conduct mony wherof my Lord Chief Justice [*Sir John Popham*] at an Assises made inquiry and no more was don therin after.

To consider of them which dwell in cittyes & townes and have valew of landes in the contrey, whither it be not meete to have them laid to horses if their valewes be accordingly.

Whither a lawyer or an att[*orney*] who make gayne by their pracktise be not in some sort to be laid to armes in regard of their pracktise.

Whither it be meete to have the clergy laid to armes & mustered by the l[*ieu*]tenantes or by the Bishop. And if thei be mustered by themselves their charge is the greater by defrayeing the officers charges, & by their comyng from all partes of the shire to one place.

To consider in regard of the late treason[610] what the fittest corse is to take for the safe forthcoming of the store of powder which is allotted to be in a readynes in every Hundred.

Unsigned. In Martin Man's hand.

Endorsed: Matters to be [?]remembered upon conference with the E[*arl*] of Northampton.

1½ pp. NRO MC 1872/80/2, 866X3. Calendared, *Supplementary Stiffkey Papers*, p.25.

Chancery order in a suit between Edmund and Anthony Penning

1605/6, February 11. *Calendar*: Hearing in a suit between Edmund Pennynge gent and Anne his wife, plaintiffs, and Anthony Pennynge esq, defendant,[611] with

---

[610] The plot to blow up Parliament on 5 November 1605, familiarly known as the Gunpowder Plot.

[611] See letters to Bacon and others of 20 October 1604 and ?March 1605/6, above, p.134, and below, pp.225–6.

counsel for both parties present, concerning a legacy of £4,000 given to Edmund by the will of Arthur Pennynge, his father.[612] This legacy the defendant sought to satisfy by conveying lands and paying Edmund £560, but the plaintiffs are not satisfied and have applied to the court. The plaintiffs previously petitioned Parliament by Bill,[613] where the committees to whom the matter was referred felt that it was necessary to establish whether the terms of the conveyance were suitable and whether the lands and money were sufficient recompense for the legacy. By mutual agreement the matter was referred to Sir Charles Cornwallis and Sir Nathaniel Bacon, named by the plaintiffs, and Sir John Higham and Robert Kempe esquire, named by the defendant, and Sir Robert Jermyn[614] was chosen by the committees to be umpire if necessary. If the arbitrators found the lands and payment of £560 not to be sufficient, the defendant was to alter the conveyance or to make up the value according to their recommendation. The court considers their order, in which the committees "cleered the saide defendant of any imputacion laide to his chardge", to be just to both parties. Because Sir Charles Cornwallis is now on his Majesty's service in Spain, the court refers the case, with consent of both counsel, to Sir Robert Jermyn, Sir John Higham and Sir Nathaniel Bacon, to consider in town. If Jermyn is not in town, the other two may end the dispute if they can before going down, but otherwise all three are to deal with it in the country. What they decide should be done is to be put into the hands of friends to preserve the interests of the plaintiff, his wife and children.

Signed: *Per* Henry [*name obliterated*], *deputatum Regis*.
Endorsed: Penninge and Penninge xi Feb. 1605. Hill[*ary*].
3½ pp. Folger L.d.464.

Breviate for a Bill in Parliament concerning relief for the ministers of Norwich

[*1605/6, post February 13*].[615] Reasons to inforce «the Bill» for the ministers of Norwich rather than any other «Bill» whatsoever.

---

[612] Arthur Pennynge of Kettleburgh, Suffolk, whose will was proved on 5 February 1593/4 (TNA PRO prob/11/83 Dixy ff.166–7).

[613] The Bill "for the frustrating of a release unduly procured by Edmond Penning" was introduced on 6 June 1604 and had a second reading on 8 June. Nathaniel Bacon was not appointed to the committee. (*CJ*, i, p.234).

[614] Sir Robert Jermyn of Rushbrooke, a 'godly' Suffolk magistrate and friend of Sir John Higham (*ODNB*).

[615] Dating: the history of the Bill is somewhat puzzling. A general measure "For the better relief of preachers and ministers within cities and towns corporate" had been introduced in the 1604 session, but did not progress further than its first reading on 21 June (*CJ*, i, p.244). Probably it is the text of this Bill that was entered in Anthony Harison's *Registrum Vagum* (i, pp.137–9). Two days later a Bill to relieve ministers specifically in Norwich and Gloucester was presented. This was read a second time on 29 June, but no committee was appointed and it was "ordered to sleep till the next session" (*CJ*, i, pp.245, 249). In the autumn of 1605 the corporation of Norwich was holding discussions on the issue with the clergy of the city, and resolved on 4 November to "send some convenyent man or moe to London to solycyte & follow the busynes which concerne the Byll exhibited to the parliament howse by the mynisters" (NRO NCR Case 16c (5) Norwich Assembly minute book 1585–1613, ff.322–3). A Bill limited in title to the ministers and preachers of Norwich had its first reading on 30 January 1605/6, and on 13 February was referred to a large committee including the burgesses of Norwich, Yarmouth and Exeter, and the three addressees of this breviate. Mr Nicholas Overbury was member for Gloucester, which suggests that the previous session's alliance between

1. The Court of Aldermen (after long deliberacion and consultacion had with the ministers) held it the best course of all. «2s. in the pownd.»

2. The authorizing the maiour, & som justices of the citie, to rate at their discretions, is to continew the ministers still in uncertainties causing them to dispend (as now) more by £20 *per annum*, then they can receave of their parishioners.

3. Men worth a thowsand «pownd» who gaine very much yearely ar not ashamed to pay their minister 2s. or 2s. 6d. a quarter at the moast, for all their tythes, except their offerings.

4. Landlordes of good hability will pay but 4d. a quarter, & bid the ministers com by more as they can <when in truth they eate up the ministers bread>.

5. Many ministers in Norwich ar so poore, as they are not only constrayned to borrow bookes when they studdy,[616] & cloakes for their journeyes, but also to abstaine from warme meat 10 dayes togither.

6. Divers parishes ar so deepe in arerages to the Crowne, as three yeares profittes ar not sufficient to discharg them.

7. Chauncells[617] & parsonages ar so fallen into dilapidacions, as will forc the ministers to forsake their places, except this acte relieve them.

8. Whatsoever can be objected against the Bill as inconvenient, we <promise to make a sufficient aunswere unto it> «desire our aunswer may be hard» speedely.

[*Added subsequently:*] 9. They expect that in tymes of infection we should attend upon them, & yet stand to their curtesye.

We have lived in hope these 20 yeeres to have our estates bettered by a Parliament & done our endeavours, but as yet nothing is effected.

Undated. Unsigned.

Addressed: For Sir John Higham, Sir Nathaniel Bacon, & Mr Overbury our worshipfull committees.

Endorsed in Martin Man's hand: Concerning Norwich ministers.

1 p. NRO SOTH 28/12/67.

Warrant for grant of rectorial revenues to Ludovick Stuart, Duke of Lennox

1605/6, February 20. *Calendar.* Warrant from James I to Sir John Fortescue, chancellor of the Duchy of Lancaster. In consideration of the service done by his cousin and counsellor Ludowicke, Duke of Lennox, and of his surrender of lands in Scotland at the King's request, James is granting to Ludowicke such rectories or

---

the cities was not dead. No report from the committee is recorded and the Norwich Bill went no further (*CJ*, i, pp.261, 267). However, the Privy Council wrote to the mayor and corporation of Norwich on 15 February 1606/7 ordering that a tax be levied on the inhabitants of the city to provide a decent maintenance for the established ministry (*CSPD 1603–10*, p.348).

[616] In part this problem was solved by the establishment in 1608 by the City of what was to become known as the Old City Library. The Library was intended to meet the needs of the local clergy and it was housed over the porch of 'New Hall', the old Blackfriars, and adjacent to the civic preaching yard. Its establishment may have been prompted by the problems outlined here. (See Clive Wilkins-Jones, ed., *The Minutes, Donation Book and Catalogue of Norwich City Library founded in 1608*, NRS lxxii, Norwich, 2008).

[617] The chancel was the responsibility of the minister whereas the nave was the responsibility of the congregation.

parsonages impropriate, tithes and glebe lands within the survey of the Exchequer and Duchy of Lancaster as amount to the yearly value of £1,100, net of reprises, to hold for ever in fee farm as of the manor of East Greenwich in free socage, paying such rents and reservations as are now paid. A book or books containing the grant is to be drafted, subscribed by the chancellor and sent to the King for signature and seals. Given under the privy seal at the palace of Westminster 20 February 3 James.[618]

/"The like warrante was directed to the Lord Treasorer"./

Copy. Unsigned.

Addressed: To our trustie and welbeloved counsellour Sir John Fortescue knight chancellour of our duchie of Lancaster.

Endorsed in Martin Man's hand: Warrant for the D[*uke*] of Leneax.

1 p. Folger L.d.915.

Breviate for a Bill in Parliament concerning regulation of building timber

[*1605/6, March*].[619] Abuses used concerning the heawing, sawing, and measuring of timber, boords, laths, quarters, joystes, puntions [*puncheons*], rafters, and stable-plankes, and such other like stuffe belonging to buildings.

Imprimis timber, boordes and such like stuffe as is above rehearsed is bought and soulde within this realme of England not heawed, sawed, sized or measured to any lawfull size or true measure, by reason evill minded persons by subtill practises, knowing there is no law to the contrary, to binde them to keepe any size or true measure, doo therefore sell it to his Majestie and his loyall subjects, what measure or size they please. Whereby his Majesty and his loving subjects are greatly deceived and abused, not onely in paying for the stuffe, but also for land and water carriages with the wharfage therof, a great deale more then they receive any ware [*merchandise*] for. For by custome timber should be well heawed, and keepe true measure, *viz.* 50 foote of assize or more to a loade and as it is measured and soulde there wanteth by true measure 8, 10 or 12 feete of assize more or lesse in the most loads.

Item, all boords and planckes, that are sawed, are measured so insufficiently, that in every thousand of boords and planckes by true measure there wanteth one hundreth or more. Besides, quarter boords & seeling boords are sawed so thinne, that they performe not a quarter of the service, which otherwise they might, and in right ought.

Item all laths are so insufficient in breadth and thicknesse, that tilers and

---

[618] On 10 February 1605/6 Bacon had been placed on the Commons committee to consider granting subsidies. The next day the same committee was also empowered to examine the grievances of the realm, apart from purveyance (Bowyer, *Parliamentary Diary*, p.33; *CJ*, i, p.266). This gift to Lennox probably came within the committee's purview in relation to the question of naturalization of Scots, but the Duke was also being attacked over his patent as King's Alnager of new draperies—a matter of considerable significance in Norfolk (see early April 1606, below, p.226).

[619] Dating: a Bill "for the true measuring, marking, and assising of timber, and other stuff incident and belonging to building" had its first reading on 10 March 1605/6. At the second reading on 13 May it was refused committal or ingrossment (*CJ*, i, pp.351, 373).

laborers are in great danger to stand upon them, on the roofes of houses. Besides in number there wanteth in a bundle which should conteine 5 skore laths of 5 foote long to the hundreth, and 6 skore and 5 laths of 4 foote long to the hundreth, 12, 16 or 20 lathes more or lesse in the most bundles.

Item there are a number of unskilfull, covetous, and greedy persons, who for the most part of them doth not know the true measure and assize of the same stuffe aforesaid, nor dooth know how to transport or alter the property therof either by workmanship or otherwise, but only by making a kind of merchandize of the same, being of late time used by them. Which persons for their owne greedy and covetous gaine, doe not onely buy all such kind of stuffe as is above rehearsed that is brought to be sould for the provision of the city of London, and for all other places neere unto the sayd city, to builders or workmen, but dayly doe ride and goe into the counties, and like forestallers, regraters or ingrossers doo buy all that is to bee had, so farre as their purses or credits will stretch, neither regarding the true measure or assize. The which evill merchaunts or evill members have greatly enhaunsed the prices of all the aforesayd stuffe, to the great charge and hinderance of all builders, and to the utter undooing of all poore workmen and labourers incident and belonging to buildings, with their wives and children, unlesse reformation be had in this present Parliament.

Undated. Unsigned.
Printed in italic.
Endorsed in Martin Man's hand: Abuses in timber sawers etc.
1 p. NRO BL/BC/6/14.

Sir Nathaniel Bacon and other arbitrator or arbitrators to surveyors chosen in the case of Penning v. Penning

[*1605/6, ? March*].[620] After our hartie commendacions. Upon a suite comensed in the cort of Chauncery by Edmund Pennyng gent & his wife «plaintiffs» against Anthony Pennyng esqr «defendant» concerning a legacy of £4000 given unto the said Edmunde by Arthur Pennyng his father. «And upon» satisfaccion <of the said legacy being offered and accepted of> «<being> offerd by the <re> defendant» for the same legacy «by conveyaunce of landes» <and the plaintiffs willing «content» to accept therof so as the value of the landes may be aunswerable therunto and> it hath pleased the right honourable the Lord Chauncellour by order «in the said cort» to referre unto us the examinacion of the value of the landes so offered <to be so> to be conveyed <by the defendant. And to deale further betwen the parties for ending of the controversy.> Wee have thought good «<for our helpe therin>» to make choice of you <(for our helpe therin)> «*steb*» praying you to take a perfect view and survay of the landes which shall be set out <by the plaintiffs>. And to set downe <& certefye us> particulerly <of> the true state of them as namely their

---

[620] Dating: in their letter of 12 April 1606 (below, p.227) the surveyors appointed as a result of this letter report that they met to begin their work on 7 April. By that date they had already enlisted the help of a third surveyor who is mentioned only as a possibility here. For the order in Chancery of 11 February 1605/6 authorising Nathaniel Bacon, Sir Robert Jermyn and Sir John Higham as arbitrators, see above, pp.221–2.

«nomber of acres ««with»» their» natre & tenure, and your estimate of their values «and to sende us a certificat therof <before the [*blank*] next> ««so soone as conveniently you can»» ». <And for your assistaunce herin wee have also required [*blank*] to joyne with you in the survey.> /«Yt may be wee will intreate a third man to joyne with you for your assistaunce in the survey.»/ <All your charge about this busynes «as well for your payment as [?]agenst»> «Your charge & travell taken herin» shall be <borne> «satisfied» by the parties «to your contentment». And so <not doubting for> «assuring ourselves of» your faithfull<nes> & upright<nes in the> carriag «in the busynes» wee hartely bidde you farewell.

Undated. Unsigned.
Draft in Martin Man's hand.
Endorsed: Draught of a letter to the survayors *in causa* Penning.
Note in a different hand on dorse: Artycles offered to the commyttees about the framing of a Byll «to be» intituled an Acte to establysh trew religion or any other tytell that shall beste like the Howse which may by the tytell shew [?]that.
1 p. Folger L.d.70.

Breviate for Parliament concerning the patent for sealing new draperies

[*1606, ?early April*].[621] The pattent of the crowne seale is a generall hurte to the common wealth, for it imposeth a subsidie of all our labors, of every cloth a half peny, & of every grosse of lace an half penny.

A deputie of this pattent deposed, that he raised £400 a yeare by thes subsidies and that the poorer sort of men of that trade did weepe bitterly at the payment thereof.

That the offyce is needlesse, for the statute of 7 Edw.4 hath appoynted wardens to be chosen & sworne to searche, & seale such as be sufficient, & punishe such as be defective by the oath of 12 men of the said crafte, before the mayour or steward.

But it is usuall for the alnager to sett the crowne seale to such clothes as the owners dare not bringe before the wardens, by reason of their insufficiency.

And further it is usuall with the alnager, to compounde with divers men what thei shall paie quarterly, never seing what wares thei make, but onely give them every weeke a tickett to passe their wares by, taking besides the said composicion for every such tickett 2*d.*

Statutes concerning the worsted weavers 7 Edw.4, 33 Hen.8 & 1 Edw.6.

---

[621] Dating: a patent as King's Alnager, for searching and sealing new draperies, had been granted to the Duke of Lennox in September 1605 (*CSPD, 1603–1610*, p.233). A new Commons committee "to consider and dispute of the grievances", of which Bacon was a member, was appointed on 8 April 1606, and the patent was raised as a specific issue when the committee reported the following day. It was agreed that counsel for the Duke should be heard, and the legal arguments both for and against the patent were presented on 16 April. The grievance was adopted, and was among those presented to the King on 14 May (Bowyer, *Parliamentary Diary*, pp.112, 129, 165–6; *CJ*, i, pp.295, 299). Despite the King's assurances that abuses would be remedied, the Commons' petition of grievances of July 1610 complained that the situation was unchanged (Foster, *Proceedings*, ii, pp.268–9). See also Brentnall, 'Regional Influences', pp.198–201. For Bacon's earlier involvement in Parliament with a similar issue relating to the regionally important textile industry see *BP*, iv, pp.39–40.

Undated. Unsigned. In Martin Man's hand.
Endorsed: A note touching the worsted weavers.
1 p. NRO SOTH 28/12/67.

John Osborne, Clement Paman, and John Darby to Sir John Higham and Sir Nathaniel Bacon

1606, April 12. May it please yow to understand that wheras yow have desyred us to take the viewe of the landes and tenementes that Mr Anthonie Pennynge hath layd out and assured to his brother Edmond and his wyfe, as parte of the porcion of £4,000 gyven to him by his father Mr Anthony [*sic*] Pennynge deceased,[622] as also to consider of the severall tenures valewes and natures of the sayd landes and tenementes, and to certyfye yow therof before Easter next yf we could, we in satis-faccion of your requestes only (which otherwayes without other aucthoritye for dyvers respectes we had cause enoughe to have refused) did assone as our leysours would permytte meete at Bawdessey [*Suffolk*] *viz.* the vii daye of this present moneth of Aprill being Mondaye, and hoping there that both parties would have mette (as to some of us by some of the plaintiffes frendes yt was promised) both to have measured the sayd landes and tenementes and to have objected all their doubtes therby to have given some light to our proceedinges for both their satisfac-cions. The plaintifes fayled eyther to come or send and the defendant whoe mette there, cowld not delyver to us any certein measure of the landes, notwithstandinge we spent three wholle dayes there «and twoe at Parham [*Suffolk*]» in perusing, viewing and enquyringe by all such convenient meanes as we could to satisfye your requestes. Soe as thoughe our opynyons of the severall natures and valewes of the sayd landes are satisfied therin yet not beinge trewly informed of the quantitye of the severall kindes therof done by a trewe measure we cannot sette downe any thinge therin to any good purpose for an ende. And therfore we «will &» have laboured with the parties to performe this by some indifferent course, the which when as we shall see effected we shalbe willinge to our best skylles to sette downe our opynions therin in all thinges. And we doe thinke yt very convenient yow did both wryte to the plaintiffes and defendant to performe this measure spedilye and to let one of us named John Derby understand of the tyme when they purpose to make this measure, whoe is willinge to be present at the doing therof for the better effectinge of this busines, but not willing to doe yt him self for some respectes which he hopethe will not be thought but reasonable. And even soe desyringe your speedye answer heerto we commend yow both to the grace of thalmightie. From Ipswiche this xii of Aprill 1606. Your duetyfull frendes.

Signed: John Osborne, Clement Paman, John Darby.[623]

[622] In fact, Arthur Penning. See Chancery order of 11 February 1605/6 and letter from Bacon and the other arbitrators of March, 1605/6, above, pp.221–2, 225–6.

[623] These men appear to be Suffolk gentry with surveying experience rather than professional surveyors. John Osborne is probably the John Osborne of Wattisfield, gent, named in the Suffolk visitation of 1612 (Metcalfe, *Visitations of Suffolk,* p.154). Clement Paman of Chevington acted as Sir Robert Drury's trustee in 1613 (Bald, *Donne,* pp.89, 143–4). He only features as a possible witness in the will of Clement Paman of Ubbeston, Suffolk, clerk (d.1599) but may have been related (NRO NCC 1599 Pecke f.196). John Darby

Addressed: To the right worshipfull Sir John Heigham and Sir Nathaniell Bacon knightes.
Endorsed: Letter from Mr Osborne Mr Paman and Mr Derby.
1 p. Folger L.d.450.

Sir Nathaniel Bacon to Anthony Penning and Edmund Penning

[*1606, post April 12*].[624] Whereas by an order of the ii of Februarie last it pleased the right honourable the Lord Chancellor to appointe Sir John Higham and me to consider of an order formerly made betwyxt you by certeine committies of the lower house of Parliament concerning a legacie of £4,000 demaunded by the plaintiff and to eand the matter if we could. In our regard of that order and for the better satisfaction of our judgmentes therein we directed our letters to Mr Osborne, Mr Paman and Mr Darbye requiring their paines to viewe and surveie <the> such lands as the defendant Mr Anthony Penning shold set forth in recompence of the said legacie, and to make their reporte unto us. I perceive by their letters sithence directed unto us that accordingly they have taken paines therein and have well considered of the value, and nature of the land, but by cause they know not what quantitie of acres the same conteines they have forborne to yeld their opinions of the value, <and> desiringe us to write unto you the plaintiff and defendant that you cause the land to be measured. And by cause Sir John Higham is not in towne, and I could wishe we might travaile in yt before our coming downe and eand the cause if it be possible, I have thought it good to requier you boeth to cause it to be measured forthwith and to geve knoledge unto Mr John Darbye of your tyme when to thend he might be present for soe it is desired by them, and uppon your performance hereof I doubte not but that theye will make «their» spedie reporte unto us.

Undated. Unsigned.
Endorsed in Martin Man's hand: Sir Nathaniel Bacons letter to Mr Anthony & Edmund Pennyng.
1 p. Folger L.d.68.

Giles Bridges to Sir Nathaniel Bacon

1606, April 28. Good Sir Nathaniell Bacon. Forasmuch as I am nowe restrayned from coming to London, by reason of some sicknes which ys happened unto me, I shall desire yow (yf my presence be required or my consent demaunded by the Parlyament howse, for the passing of myne honorable brothers act)[625] that yow

---

belonged to a family connected with Tuddenham and Bramford (Metcalfe, *Visitations of Suffolk*, pp.148–9). None of the three are recorded in Eden, *Surveyors*.

[624] Dating: dated with reference to the letter from Osborne, Paman and Darby of 12 April 1606, immediately above. For a subsequent meeting of the arbitrators, see Jermyn and Higham to Bacon, 11 June 1606, below, p.236.

[625] The brother was Grey Bridges, fifth Baron Chandos. His uncle, the third Baron, had reserved certain lands to provide for his youngest daughter, Katherine, but the Lords authorised the substitution of a payment of £7,000 in trust to Katherine's mother. The Bill to settle the estate was brought to the Commons on 27 March 1606, and the House was requested to add a proviso that the dowager Lady Chandos give

will, not only make knowene unto the«m» <Lords and the rest> the cause of myne absence att this tyme, but will allso signifie unto them my full and free consent thereunto, which I pray yow for me (as from myne owne mowth), to deliver unto the whole howse yf cause require, that myne absence may be no staye or hinderaunce to my brothers proceedinges, which I desire yow by your best meanes, to further and effect, to his good liking. And I will ever rest thanckfull to yow for hitt. And so with my kyndest comendacions doe comitt yow to God. From Sudeley [*Castle, Glos*] this xxviii of Aprill 1606. Your assured loving frend and cosen.

Signed: Giles Briges.

Addressed: To my verie «loving cosen» & good frend Sir Nathaniell Bacon knighte.

Endorsed in Martin Man's hand: Cozen Bridges.

1p. NRO BL/BC/6/15.

Sir John Popham, Lord Chief Justice, to Sir Nathaniel Bacon and John Palgrave

1606, May 17. With my verye hartie comendacions. Complaynt beinge made unto me by one Thomas Fayrfexe «gent»[626] this bearer of dyvers assaultes & outrages made upon hym by Sir Henry Sidney knighte and his servantes & followers tendinge greatly to the breache of his Majesties peace, whereof (as I am also informed) complaynt hath of late ben made to the justices of peace in the last sessions before whome the said Sir Henrye hathe refused to appeare to aunswere the same, I have therefore thought good to sende unto you this inclosed peticion conteyninge the said complayntes, prayeng & requiringe you to call the said Sir Henry Sidney & his said servantes before you & to examyn the truethe of the saide complayntes by such proffes & witnesses as to you shalbe thought expedient. And yf upon examinacion thereof you shall «find just» proffe of the said complayntes then I thincke it fitt that you bynde over the said Sir Henrye Sidney and such of «his» said servantes soe offending to appeare at the next Assises to be holden within the countye of Norfolk to aunswere the same and in the meane tyme that you take such speciall order that his Majesties peace be dulye observed amongst them. And evenso not doubtinge your sufficient & diligent care herein as to your places apperteyneth I bid yow hartelye farewell. From my chamber at Serjeantes Inne in Fleete Strete London this xvii of May 1606. Your verye lovinge frinde.

At the foot in Popham's hand: I am informed that he used speches <that he used speches> contempnyng to come before som of the justices. Yf that apeare to be trew and well proved I hold yt then fytt he be bownd to his gud behavyor for the indyngst [*most indigent*] justice of the peace must in hys place be obeyd by as gud a man as Sir Henry Sydney for he may not contempne the auctoryte.[627]

---

sufficient security for her part in the transaction, over which she had made difficulties. The second reading had taken place on 7 April. Bacon was not nominated to the committee, but had a family obligation in the matter, in that the mother of Grey and Giles Bridges was Mary Hopton, the aunt of his second wife, Dorothy (*GEC sub* Chandos). The Bill was passed on 7 May, and sent back to the Lords on 10 May (Bowyer, *Parliamentary Diary*, pp.94–5; *CJ*, i, pp.290–1, 292, 294, 306–7).

626 For Fairfax see 17 February 1604/5, above, p.153n.

627 See also Sidney to Bacon, 24 May 1606, below, pp.230–2.

Signed: Jo[*hn*] Popham.

Addressed: To the worshipfull my verye lovinge friendes Sir Nathaniell Bacon knight and John Palgrave esquier two of his Majesties justices of peace in the countie of Norfolk & to either of them geve thes.

Endorsed: Lord Chief Justice touchinge Sir Henry Sidney and Mr Fairfaxe.

1 p. BL Stowe 150 ff.208–9.

Jonas Pitts to Sir Nathaniel Bacon

1606, May 20. Sir. Yt have pleased my Lord Ambassador[628] for some reasons which maye concerne him selfe, not onely by his letters to nominate mee to be the man whome he intende to truste with the collectyon of the taske within his devisyon, but to <requyer> «beseeche» my Lord of Northampton to speake unto you for the same, & to Mr Rogers to putt his Lordship in mynde, yf happely there shoulde be any diffycultye by reason of his owne absence for the obteynynge of the same. I have not prosecuted this course for that Sir William Cornwalys[629] (uppon his motyon) fownde your owne inclynacyon sortynge [*agreeable*] to doe that or any other kyndnes to his father, & so he have advertysed him by his late letters. I wyll attende your worshipp as presently as my busynes wyll from hence geve me leave, and acquaynte you with everye circomstaunce pertynente to my Lord his desyer in this behalfe, untyll when with my humble duty remembred I take my leave this xx of *Maii anno* 1606. Your worshippes ever att comandement.[630]

Signed: Jonas Pytts. *Holograph*.

Addressed: To the righte worshipfull Sir Nathanyell Bacon knyght att Stewky Hall.

Endorsed: Letter of Jonas Pittes *pro collect*[*ione*] *subsid*[*ii*].

½ p. Folger L.d.490.

Sir Henry Sidney to Sir Nathaniel Bacon

1606, May 24. Sir I can not but <yt> take yt very kyndly and that this motion procedes of your love to me to make a peace betwyxt Thomas Fayerfax and me but such ar his late wronges unto me that I can not yet disgest them, for he hath as I understand informed my Lord Chefe Justice with many lies & untruthes in his peticion, wherin ther is nothyng true in <every> «the most» part only I confess that I did rather gave [*sic*] hym a frendly correction then a violent beatyng and had that care of hym that I would not suffer a man to stryke hym «but my self» and wheras he hath informed my Lord that I refused to com befor the justices and gave contemptyble wordes of them in som sort they ar both false as the justices them selves and the messengers that went betwyxt us can best wytnes, for uppon ther first sendynge for me the bayly mett me in <the> my hall and towld me that the justices had sent hym for me tellyng me the cause. And in good manner my aunsuer was that I desired to be excused unto them for my head did ake excedyngly and that I

---

[628] Sir Charles Cornwallis, appointed resident ambassador to Spain in 1604 (*ODNB*).

[629] Sir William Cornwallis the older (see 16 June 1606, below, p.237n.).

[630] A letter from an over-anxious client seeking a minor county office. For a further letter with the same intent, see Pitts to Bacon, 16 June 1606, below, pp.237–8.

was goyng to take <my> «som» rest and desired hym further to delyver <hym> unto them <further> my protestation that I had no purpose or meanyng to use any more violenc to Fayerfax and that I would command my men that not any one should lyft up an hand agaynst them. And afterwardes sent my cosyn Drury[631] unto them, sync I understod that Fayerfax had sworne and that they could not deny hym the peac, to desier «unto» them that they would be pleased that my apparanc should not be before Mychelmas next because I was commanded by my Lord Generall of Flusshyng[632] to repayer to Flushyng, which they did well accept of and I have bene always readie to be bownd and do protest before God I have used no meanes or have [?]placed any impediment agaynst the servyng of the warrant and <have> «do» verryly beleve that Fayerfax have stayed the procedyng of yt being not contented as appeareth by his petition with the procedyng of the jus-tices. And for the other part that I should use contempty[ble] <of> wordes of the justices I assure you of my creadit yt is altogeather most false as <all> many gentle-men can well wytnes with me which wear at that tyme with me but such a bowld proud impudent fellow being like his companniones Thomas Balles and Thomas <Ball> Cloudsly[633] wyll most shamefully devyse and affirme any <thyng> untruth to serve ther owne turnes not sparyng any man with ther slanderows raylyyng tonges.

I could have bene verry well content that you should have hard the differences betwyxt us had not this last wrong bene more then intollerable for he hath spred abrod that my Lord Chefe Justice hath directed his letters unto you and Mr Pagrave to bynd me to my good behavowr[634] which he hath mysreported as Mr Fotherbie telleth me. I have always accompted the good behaviour next the halter therfor I should thynck my self not worthy of lyfe if I had so farr overshot my self as myght fully deserve to be bownd to my good behavowr but the lying informa-tions of this lewd fellow shall not mak me thynck the worse of my self and I hope through his owne lyes <and mysreport> and mysreportyng my Lordes letter to my great disgrac to procure hym to be bownd to his good behaviour besydes many other reason that ar now to long to wryght.

I am sorry your clark hath made hym a gentleman both in your warrant and also in your letter to me. I asure you of my creadit his grandfather kept an alehowse in Berry [?Bury St Edmunds], his father was the netherde in <Myldenhall> «Brandon [Suffolk]», an whole year and afterwardes so pore a vickar that he was dryven to

[631] The family connection probably derived from the marriage of John Drury of Godwick to Eleanor, daughter of Thomas Sidney (Rye, Visitation of Norfolk, p.115).

[632] Sir Robert Sidney (1563–1626), the younger brother of Sir Philip Sidney and, as a result of the latter's death at Zutphen, the unexpected heir to the family estates. He became Baron Sidney of Penshurst 13 May 1603 and Lord Chamberlain of Queen Anne's Household, being created Lord Lisle 4 May 1605 and earl of Leicester in 1618. In 1589 he had been appointed Governor of Flushing (Vlissingen). It served as one of the cautionary towns that the United Provinces had granted Elizabeth as security for a loan that she had made to this nascent state. He served in this office until 1616. However, after his Court appointments under James he spent more time in England (ODNB).

[633] Thomas Cloudsley of Cley and Thomas Fairfax of Walsingham were brothers-in-law via Cloudsley's marriage to Joan Fairfax (Rye, Visitation of Norfolk, p.118). On 1 July 1605 Thomas Balles had been ap-pointed muster-master for the county (above, p.196).

[634] See Sir John Popham to Bacon and Palgrave, 17 May 1606, above, p.229.

mak a dublet for this yong gentleman of the coverynges of 2 bybles and now no man howldeth hym to have any worth or honestie in hym.

I would most wyllyngly com unto you uppon Monday next to satisfie my Lordes [*word deleted*] «pleasure» in his letter but that the shypp is sayled this mornyng but now I must mak hast away, I lynger only because the wynd is contrary. I hope he wylbe out of fear when I am on the other syde of <seal> «the» sea and at my returne I wyll fre hym from that feare by your censuer and Mr Pagraves according to my Lord his letter. For the meane tym I desier much to be contynued in your good opinion and love and wyll ever rest your asured frend. Walsingham this xxiiii May 1606.

Signed: Henry Sydney. *Holograph.*
Letter headed in a late 17th century hand: Mr [*sic*] Henry Sydney's assault upon Mr Fairfax.
Endorsed in Martin Man's hand: Sir Henry Sydney.
4 pp. BL Stowe 150, ff.210–11. Printed in part, *HTM*, i, pp.125–6.

Examination in a case of paternity

1606, June 3. The examination of Dorothie Rose of Holte taken before Sir Nathanael Bacon knight the thirde of June 1606.

She confesseth that she is with childe, and begotten with childe by John Bright a taylore, and that about thre weekes after Christmas she fell with childe, and denyeth that anie other man hath defiled her besides the said Bright.

She sayth that the said Bright went from Holte sone after Christmas to his father in Hilderstone,[635] and since came often tymes to her masters house to worke with him, and now lately within this fortnight the said Bright is gone to London.

Signed: Na[*thaniel*] Bacon, [*by mark*] Dorothie Rose.
In William Sanders' hand.
Endorsed: [*1*] Examination of Dorothy Rose; [*2 in Martin Man's hand*] touching John Bright.
½ p. NRO BL/BC/6/16.

Verdict concerning Methwold manor and warren

1606, June 5. *Calendar*: "The verdicte att Methwold *5 Junii 1606*". Answers are returned to articles concerning the manor and warren of Methwold.[636] Article numbers are given in brackets.

(1) The jurors find Sir Nathanyell Bacon to be fermor of the royalty of the King's manor of Methwold and Sir Edmund Mandford (*sic*) fermor of the King's demesne lands apart from the coney warren.

(2) "The names and surnames" of all the freeholders and copyholders. 82 names are listed, headed by the Earl of Arundel, Sir Edmund Mundford, the master and

---

635 Hindolveston, south of Melton Constable, and on the road between Holt and Guist.
636 The manor was part of the Duchy of Lancaster and as such under the supervision of Bacon as High Steward of the Duchy in Norfolk.

fellows of Christ's College, Cambridge, and Richard and William Badgecrofte gents. The last eleven given are stallholders.

(2, *sic*) The boundary of the manor "beginneth at a ditche att Southrey townesyde westward and soe goeth eastward to a place called Broadgappe, which in estimacion wee take to be five myles. From Broadgappe to a place called Gallowhawe to the Severall Fenn westward, by estimacion two myles, and the Severall Fenn westward extend other two myles, from the North Ryver soe to Southrey Burrs southward by estimacion one myle and a half. And then the Common Fenn extendeth from the Severall southward half a myle".

(3) The fermor to the King's warren is Thomas Wright gent at a reported rent of £30 a year; he lets it to others for £100 and certain conies. It is so full of conies that six towns and the King's tenants suffer a yearly loss of 120 combs of corn. The fishing severally is called the King's land; the tenants have always had the other fishing about the common and usually the fowling, as the profit is small. No abuses are known of. They further find that at least 400 acres which used to be arable are now made warren. As evidence of this they have a precedent which mentions a headland at Sandgall where some furlongs run east-west and others north-south, and the boundary between the warren and the arable as leading east to a place near Ashebrackes and through a valley to Black Lands, then north to Stonye Valley and further north to Mundforde Waye. There is a piece of the lord's demesne of some six score acres, part of which has been ploughed by William Younges one of the jury. Most of the rest is demesne but they also have abuttal evidence from tenants' deeds. According to ancient doles, the warren begins near Feltwell Headlonge "that is the west parte of our boundarie" and leads east to Grayestone, leavinge Feltwell ground to the south, and so east to Broadgappe. From Broadgappe northward a ditch leads to Mundford Waye. Then west a little, then south to Stonye Valley, leaving the landes which were formerly arable to the west, and so to Blacke landes. Then west to Folden Waye and south to a place near Feltwell Headlong again. They estimate the warren at 600 acres, besides the 400 acre encroachment. At least 300 acres of this encroachment are from the demesne and formerly ploughed "as appeareth by that ground".

(4–6) They know nothing concerning concealment or exchanges and of no escheated lands. As regards buildings or inclosures, there are ten separate buildings on the common, which are "poore shuddes for beggars".

(7, 8) Rents and suit are rendered at the court according to the custom of the manor. Thomas Ollett, William Rumbold, Thomas Baker, Thomas Parsley and Thomas Rustey usually throw in sheep at the King's sheep wash. The custom for surrenders is to surrender to one copyholder in the presence of two others. Copyhold tenements are subject to waste, but woods and timber on them can be used at pleasure. Fines used to be certain, but somehow this was broken and they are now arbitrable. They know of no felons' goods.

(9) There is a drain called Bordede Bridge which should be kept by Hilgay men but is neglected, as is a common drain between Methwold and Northwold which should be kept by the tenants of Northwold from the Barres to the main river.

(10) "Concerninge fold courses wee cannot saye anye thinge as for abuses wee have none".

(11) "As for the common wee have att a place called Fenns End and att the Whynns and soe it goes on westward over the Litle Whomes and soe goeth on still westward to a place called the Kinges Severall. From thence it goeth on south ward still to a place called Feltwell Load. This place of common is called the Nether Fenn, and then another place called Sowe More which lead westward to Southray. And if it weare drawne into a square wee thinke it would be a myle everye waye."

(12) Two shops made into a dwelling house cause an annoyance to the market place.

(13) They refer themselves to the rental which they believe accurate.

Jurors: John Aynger, Robert Tuddyn, Thomas Younge, John Bull, Richard Younges, John Younge, Richard Terington, Robert Wake, Robert Martyn, William Younge, Edward Huyn, Mathew Mynn, Thomas Watson, Richard Younge, William Russell.

At the foot: "By verdicte at Helgaye it was found 7 of the late Queene that the free-hold of the common of Helgaye was in the Queene. The coppies are *curia cum leta domine regine.* There stood a pound called the Kinges pound and the tenantes had common feed in all the common fenns there as appeares by divers deposicions taken there by me."

Signed: *ex*[*aminatus*] Chr[*istopher*] Grimeston.[637]

Endorsed in Martin Man's hand: [1] Notes concerning Methwold & Helgaye; [2] The verdict of the tenantes uppon Mr Grimstons survey.[638]

5 pp. NRO NNAS S2/16/24.

Accusations concerning maladministration of the poor rate at Blakeney

1606, June 5. *Memorandum 5 Junii 1606.* Yt was shewed by Thomas Barker,[639] that Robert Makyns[640] had omytted out of his last accompt yealded since Easter

---

[637] Most likely Christopher Grimston (1564–1608), son of Thomas Grimston of Grimston, Yorks, who was appointed surveyor of the southern lands of the Duchy of Lancaster for life on 24 July 1604 (Somerville, *Lancaster Office Holders*, p.77). However, allusions to the searching out of concealed lands in a later letter in this sequence (31 July 1606, below, p.249) might indicate that the signatory was a member of the East Anglian family of this name. With his father, Edward I, Christopher Grimston, the second son, was a patentee for concealed lands (MacCulloch, *Suffolk*, p.268). From a Suffolk family, it is likely that he had settled in Norfolk following his marriage to Elizabeth, the daughter of Martin Barney of Gunton (MacCulloch, *Suffolk*, p.160; *Visit. Of Norf. 1563*, i, pp.175–6). The Grimstons shared the religious convictions of the Bacons and had close connections with them. Christopher's older brother, Edward II, had been a client of Sir Nicholas Bacon. An attorney in Star Chamber, he was the contemporary of Nathaniel and Edward Bacon and kept the latter informed of affairs at Court during the 1570s (*BP*, i, *passim*).

[638] See below, 6 July 1606, p.246.

[639] Thomas Barker of Blakeney and Morston was a ship-owner who did considerable business with Nathaniel Bacon. In 1597 he was described as collector of relief for the poor of Blakeney, Wiveton and Cley (Stiffkey Database; *BP*, ii, p.146; *BP*, iv, p.190). There is a possibility that he was a retainer of Bacon's protagonist, James Poynter, rector of Blakeney, whose misdeeds are recorded above, pp.211–12.

[640] Robert Makins of Blakeney, tailor, (d. 1637) undertook considerable work for Bacon, on one occasion lodging at Stiffkey Hall for six weeks. He was aged 68 in 1631 (Stiffkey Database *sub* Makins, erroneously recorded as of Walsingham; *BP*, iii, p.15; TNA PRO DL 4/80/1; NRO ANW 1637 f.225).

last 2s. 1d. of the monethly rate taxed upon the towne by the rest of the overseers of Blakeny.

Also that he had suffered an abatement of Francis Sturges monethly charge towardes the poore without the allowaunce of the rest of the overseers, and forborne to collect accordingly. Also that Mr Campe being taxed 23d. monethly, he had taken but 20d. a moneth, & not sought to get the rest.

Also, that many of the poore people complayne, that thei were not satisfied their allowaunce for 3 monethes.

Also, that in the yeare before there rested an arrerage of 20s. & more in Edward Daynes handes one of the overseers with Robert Makyns, which is not sought to be levied.

Ordered. That Makyns cause Daynes to repayer to Sir Nathaniel Bacon forthwith for the aunswering of the said arrerag.

And Makyns enjoyned to appeare at the next sessions for Holt Hundred to aunswer the complaynt above.

Unsigned. In Martin Mans hand.
Endorsed: Matters against Robert Makyns.
½ p. Folger L.d.742.

The inhabitants of Wissett to Sir Nathaniel and Lady Dorothy Bacon

1606, June 10. After remembrance of our humble dueties.[641] We acknowledge great thankfullnes right worshipfull for that worthie respect and care which you have ever shewed towardes us and nowe espetiallie that your worship is pleased to appoint unto us soe worthie and learned a man for our minister and teacher, wishinge our poore towne were fitt to afford him such intertainement as would aunswer his desertes. But entringe into a consideracion of our unfittnes for him in regard of the poverty of our towne and our want of howseromth [*house-room i.e.lodging*] for his intertainement, and fyndinge not onely our towne, but alsoe the cuntry nere about greatly affectioned to a brother of our late minister Mr Swallow,[642] a man approved unto us to be noe lesse qualified with good giftes, & furnished with the like facullties, then his said brother was, whoe in regard he is a single man, and is suer to retaine the same schollers which his brother had (for that he alsoe teacheth singinge and musike) shall by that meanes purchase a greater benefitt for his yearely intertainement then a stranger shall, and by helpe thereof with your worships accustomed allowance, may attaine to some resonable yearly liveinge for a single man without our further chardge. We be all therefore humble sutores unto your good worship and our worshipfull lady that ye wilbe pleased to vouchsafe to graunt unto us this our likinge and choise of Mr Swallow, wherein

---

[641] From Wissett, Suffolk. Bacon is here presenting as the lay impropriator on behalf of his step-son, William Smith. Lady Dorothy may be included because of her life interest in the Suffolk properties (see 21 May 1605, above, p.182n.).

[642] The "late minister" referred to here is probably George Swallow, the curate in 1604 (NRO DN/REG 31 p.975). His brother might be Edward Swallow, ordained in 1600 and later curate of Ixworth and rector of Elmswell, or just possibly Abraham, ordained deacon in 1604, curate at Westhall and rector of Ilketshall St John from 1609 (Venn, *Al. Cant.*, iv, p.189).

your worships may afford not onelie comfort and ease unto our poore towne but alsoe much contentment to our selves and our neighbours cuntry gentlemen nere about. And soe craveinge pardon for our bouldnes, desiringe your worships favourable acceptance and aunswer hereunto, we humbly take our leaves. From Wyssett this 10 of June 1606. Your worships to comaund in all duety.

Signed (not autograph): Fraunces Claxton, Ciprian Sallowes, Nicholas Harvy senior, Valentyne Coppyn, Henry Balles, William Dawson, Nicholas Harvy junior, Thomas Dawson, Roberte Wright, Roger Michells, William Sampson, Alberte Kennett, George Mowser, William Mowser, James Burrow, John Larrance, Thomas Michells.

Addressed: To the right worshipfull our very good lord and lady Sir Nathaniel Bacon knight and Lady Dorothy his wife at Styfkey.

Endorsed in Martin Man's hand: Wissett inhabitantes.

1 p. NRO RAY 268. Printed, *Stiffkey Papers*, pp.191–2. Calendared, *HMC Townshend*, p.17.

Sir Robert Jermyn and Sir John Higham to Sir Nathaniel Bacon

1606, June 11. Sir Nathaniell Bacon, though we colde never have with lesse contentment ymploied our travaile then nowe, being oppressed with multitude of business and the same of no small weighte, yeat for satisfyinge of our duties to the Lord Chauncelour and the cuttinge of an unkinde sute betwene two brethren, and that in a cawse nerelie concerninge either of them, we have appointed to mete with you at Norwich uppon Tewsdaie at nighte nexte [*17 June*] and so to spend that eveninge and the two nexte daies doinge our best endeavours to determine the cawse yf yt maie be, or otherwise to praie from the Lord Chauncelour a longer respite, orels to certefie our opinions in whose defalte the end cold not be effected. And so with our verie hartie commendacions to your selfe and your ladie, we committ you to God whoe keape us ever his. From Burie this 11 of June 1606. Your verie lovinge freindes.[643]

[*Postscript*]: We thinke yt were more convenient for your sealfe and for us to have appointed Sopham [*Swaffham*] for the place of meetinge beinge both nearer to you and us which yf you agree to and can so appointe the parties we praie you maie stand.

At the foot in Martin Man's hand: Memorandum 14 June aunswer retorned for meeting at the George in Tombland in Norwich at the daie above mencioned.

Signed: Rob[er]te Jermyn, Jo[hn] Heigham.

Addressed: To the righte worshipfull our verie lovinge freind Sir Nathaniell Bacon knighte give this. Enquyer to Stukey & the next way thether.

Endorsed in Martin Man's hand: Sir Robert Jermyn & Sir Jo[hn] Heigham.

1 p. Folger L.d.377.

---

[643] For the previous and subsequent documents in this arbitration, see Bacon to Penning, *Post* 12 April 1606, above, p.227 and 17 June 1606, below, p.239.

Memorandum concerning parish funds at Langham

1606, June 13. Directions for the gathering up of certayn dettes due to the towne of Langham. 13 June 1606.

1. Allan Lampkyn to become bounde with a suertie <to the churchwardens> «forthwith to» Robert Tolye and John Parsons for 40s. to be paid at midsummer 1607 & 3s. for use.

2. Mary Man to pay unto Robert Toly & John Parson before midsomer next 13s. 4d. rem[aining] of the stock of the poore in Richard Mans handes. The same oweth for breaking up the church 6s. 8d.,[644] to be paid to the churchwardens.

3. Rest in John Grickes junior his handes for corne solde 52s. Item for a cowe given by John Grix thelder 45s. Item for rent of the cowe for 4 yeares 16s. Total £5 13s. /A warrant for John Grixe./

4. Richard Lodes oweth upon a reckoning when he was constable 6s. 6d. He promiseth to pay it presently to the persons above appointed.

5. Widdow Massingham, now wife of Bar. Barnard, oweth 10s. due from her husband Massingham.

6. Mistres Barnard oweth 40s. received by her husband of John Pynchin which shee promiseth to pay before midsomer.

Memorandum. Given by William Gassingtons will to the poore of Langham £7 to be paid 20s. a yeare by the discretion of the executors.[645] The comissary to be moved for resolucion herin.

Unsigned. In Martin Man's hand.

Endorsed: Direccions concerning somes of mony in the handes of sondry inhabitantes of Langham.

1 p. NRO RAY 269.

Jonas Pitts to Sir Nathaniel Bacon

1606, June 16. Sir, presentlye uppon my retourne from your worshipp I dyd meete with the convenyencye of suche a messanger to London, as I thought fytt not to omytt. By him my letters were att London one Satturdaye laste. I did dyrecte them to Sir William Cornwalys the older (whoe nowe doe stande in good termes with his brother)[646] & to Sir John Hobart.[647] I signefyed your wyllyngnes to the full accordyng to the truthe of <of> the speeche you had with me, which letter or the effecte therof, I verely thynke wyll very shortely be made knowne to my Lord Chauncellor [*Thomas Egerton*], and therefore although you nowe be pleased to take this course in your certyfycat yett yf by some showe in your letters you shall lett my Lord [*Northampton*] understande your wyllyngnes to Sir Charles

---

[644] For a burial inside the church.

[645] This was not the only bequest in Gassington's will that seems to have led to problems. See *BP*, iv, pp.1–2.

[646] William Cornwallis (1551–1611) was uncle to the essayist of the same name (1579–1614), with whom he is sometimes confused (*ODNB*). Presumably this is an allusion to his younger brother, Sir Charles Cornwallis. (The relevant entries in *ODNB* would benefit from some further clarification.)

[647] Sir John Hobart (1593–1647), second son and ultimately heir to Sir Henry Hobart of Blickling.

his nominacyon, for the one, so yt maye be without your owne prejudyce, yt wyll make a consente with that that he shall be acquaynted with before. For Mr Payne[648] or any other so to be nominated & certefyed, althoughe your worshipp shall therein bewraye your wyllyngnes to Sir Charles his desyre so furre fourthe, yett I am (as I was of mynde «when I was» with your selfe) not intendynge to come to the place as a suter for my selfe, either from your worshipp or any other, & so referrynge the consideracyon hereof to your worshippes experyenc & wysdome, with my humble duty rememberd I take my leave this present xvi of June 1606. Your worshipps in all dutye.

Signed: Jonas Pytts.[649] *Holograph.*
Addressed: To the righte worshipfull Sir Nathanaell Bacon knighte att Styfkey Hall.
Endorsed in Martin Man's hand: Mr Pyttes.
1 p. Folger L.d.491.

Sir Anthony Browne to Sir Nathaniel Bacon

1606, June 16. Good sir, as I appoynted with your man att Norwich for meetynge youe of Frydaye next att Fakenham for appoyntynge the [*word deleted*] sessers and such lyke for the subsedye, so ment I by God his favor to have done had not an unexpected occation of great wayte enforced my present and hastye repayre unto London, which (God willynge) I intend to morrowe mornynge, which by no meanes I can delaye. I praye therfore for this tyme hold me excused, and let me be so bold of youe that by your care one other <maye> commissioner for the subsedye maye be assured to meete youe, for dispatche wherof I have the lesse doubte respectynge I heare that daye the sessions shalbe there. Neverthelesse for that I was willynge for your more ease to promysse by your man my meetynge «that day», and that divers for the sessions ar not commissioners for the subsedy nether somme appoynted I take it can deale in the subsedye, I thought good to lett youe in tyme knowe my so important busynes, wherby yf neede be my faylinge may not hynder the servyce. And whom youe shall appoynt for sessors I shall wyllynglye alowe, intretyng 2 or 3 words from youe of your daye for the gyvynge in the bookes by this bearer. And so with remembrance of my kyndest rememberrance to God I leave youe. Elsynge this xvi of June 1606. Yours ever assured.

Signed: Antho[ny] Browne.
Addressed: To the ryght woorshipfull my verye assured frynd Sir Nathaniell Bacon knyght hast thes. Styffkeye.
Endorsed in Martin Man's hand: Sir Anthony Brown.
1 p. BL Add. 41140 ff.58–9.

---

[648] Probably John Payne esquire of Tunstead. In 1583, Bacon had appointed one of this name, as a young man, to an understewardship of the Duchy of Lancaster estates in Norfolk, Suffolk and Cambridgeshire. He appears still to have been in office in 1608 (*BP*, ii, pp.257, 334n.299; Somerville, *Lancaster Office Holders*, p.198). See also p.66n.

[649] Sir Charles Cornwallis, acting as an MP and Commisioner for the Subsidy, had nominated him as collector of the subsidy in his division (see 20 May 1606, above, p.230).

Examination in a case of paternity

1606, June 17. The examinacion of Katheryne <Beeston> Todde, taken the 17 of June 1606 before Sir Nathanaell Bacon knight.

She saith, that a moneth before Christmas last, shee was retayned before the chief constables of the Hundred of Northgrenhoe to serve Richard Riplingham sheppard at Warham for a yeare. And during her being in service with her master shee was by him gotten with childe.

She saith also that shee did accuse one John Yonger to be the father of her childe but shee confesseth that shee did so accuse him by the persuasion of her master, and denyeth that ever the said Yonger did defile her.

Shee saith that her master laie three or fower tymes with her, and that shee contynued not above six weekes with her master, and departed bicause shee was not able to do her work as shee was at her first comyng.

Shee saith that shee hath not ben in service with anie other since her departure from Riplingham.[650]

Signed: Na[*thaniel*] Bacon. *In Martin Man's hand.*
Endorsed: Examination of Katherine Todde *pro* bast[*ardy*].
½ p. NRO NRS 24659, 125X3.

Notes concerning a settlement of the case of Penning v. Penning

[*1606, June 17*].[651] Remembr[*ances*].

A letter to my Lord Chancellor for certefying whatt our proceding hath bene, & the cause of no full conclusion.

A protection for joynter both present & herafter, yf his wife die.

A setting downe the entaile with a remainder in Mr Anthonie Pennyng.

A direction for the evidens or copies.

To agree of a time for the survey, by Mr Frogmorton & Mr Agas[652] with Mr Derby.

For the present maintenaunce & for the satisfying the arrer.

To agree upon lawers to drawe the conveiaunce.

Undated. Unsigned. In Nathaniel Bacon's hand.
Endorsed in Martin Man's hand: Rem[*embrances*] *inter* Pennyng & Pennyng upon the hearing.
½ p. Folger L.d.652.

Sir Robert Jermyn, Sir John Higham, and Sir Nathaniel Bacon to Thomas Egerton, Baron Ellesmere, Lord Chancellor

1606, June 18. Our duties verie humbly remembred unto your Lordship. Whereas

---

[650] Riplingham was bound over on 25 September 1606 to appear at the next sessions for North Greenhoe (Bacon memoranda book 1602–7, NRO BL/BC/5/22, p.87).

[651] Dating: 17 June was set as the date of the hearing in the letter from Jermyn and Higham to Bacon of 11 June 1606 (above, p.236), and the arbitrators wrote to the Lord Chancellor on 18 June, immediately below.

[652] Ralph Agas, land surveyor (see 10 March 1603/4, above, p.80n.).

there was referred unto us by your Lordships order of the xi of February last past, a controversie depending in the court of Chauncery betwen Edmond Pennyng gent & Anne his wife complainantes & Anthony Pennyng esquire defendant concerning a legacy of £4,000 bequeathed unto the said Edmond, by Arthur Pennyng his father, that wee should deale in the hearing thereof, & set downe some ende therin. It maie please your Lordship to be advertized, that wee have mett about the cause, & hearde the allegacions on both sides (having the parties before us) and have drawen the cause to a conclusion with their consentes, saving for the conveyaunces & assuraunces making by the defendant of certayn landes unto the plaintiffs in parte of recompenc for the said legacy, which is referred to be don by learned councell, named by us indifferently with the parties allowaunce. So wee humbly take our leave. From Norwich this 18 of June 1606. Your Lordships at commandement. [*Signed:*] Robert Jermyn, Jo[*hn*] Heigham, Nathaniel Bacon.

Copy in Martin Man's hand.
Endorsed: Copie of a letter to the Lord Chancelour. 18 June 1606.
½ p. Folger L.d.108.

Articles of agreement between Edmund and Anthony Penning

1606, June 18. *Calendar:* Terms of an agreement in the dispute between Edmond Penninge gent and his wife Ann, complainants, and Anthony Penninge esquire, the older brother of Edmond, defendant, made at Norwich on 18 June by Sir Roberte Jermey, Sir John Higham, and Sir Nathaniel Bacon. The agreement was made under an order of Chancery dated 11 February last and was assented to by both parties.

1. Anthony Penninge is to convey all his freehold lands in Bawdsey and Alderton, Suffolk,[653] to Sir Nicholas Bacon, Sir Harry Glemham, Sir Edmond Bacon, Sir John Craftes, knights, and Edward Bacon and Thomas Wingfeld, esquires, in trust to the use of Edmond and Ann during their lives, free of all incumbrances created by Anthony or by Thomas Denney.

2. The feoffees shall have power to assure such land as they see fit to any second wife Edmond may have, provided its value does not exceed £100 a year, the rest remaining to Edmond's heirs in tail with reversion to Anthony Penninge and his heirs. And after the deaths of Edmond and any second wife, the feoffees are to stand seized of all the lands to the use of his heirs in tail, with reversion to Anthony in fee simple.

3. As various of the lands are held by lease of the King's manor of Bawdsey Butley,[654] it is agreed that Anthony is to purchase the reversion of the leaseholds as soon as he may before expiry of the term, and to convey them to the feoffees at his own cost. Meanwhile he is to convey to them his tenement in Parham and Framlingham, Suffolk,[655] now or late in the occupation of John Thrower; this conveyance to be void once the lease lands have been assured to the feoffees.

---

[653] Two adjacent parishes in the Hundred of Wilford, just north of the mouth of the River Deben.
[654] On the coast adjacent to the mouth of the River Deben.
[655] Inland, about 15 miles north of Bawdsey and Alderton.

4. Since for speed the arbitrators have taken the lands at Anthony's valuation, it is agreed that Anthony shall warrant them as worth £180 a year when let and for the next 50 years, net of all outrents and annuities, with proviso against negligence by Edmond or his lessees.

5. As the mansion (dwelling) house in Bawdsey is reported to be unfit for use, Anthony is to "roughe cast,[656] glase, plancher[657] and furnishe with dores and staiers the said insett house[658] and all the roomes thereunto belonginge" at his own expense so that it is habitable by All Saints next.

6. The copyhold lands are to be surrendered to the uses aforesaid and the fine to be paid equally by the parties.

7. If Edmond shall die in Ann's lifetime she is to allow £40 a year towards the bringing up of his children.

8. This conveyance shall be made with the advice of Sir Harry Hobart, Mr Sergeant Hawton and Richard Godferie esquire.[659]

9. Anthony has already paid Edmond £460 as part of £4,000 due; it is agreed that he shall pay a further £300 and also £360 for arrears of rent.

/Added in the margin opposite this entry: "Yt is ordered <by> uppon motion made by Sir Nathaniel Bacon (as Sir John Higham informed the plaintiffs) sithence this order set down, that of the said £660, £200 shalbe alowed for the plaintiffs' debts & £200 for stocking of their ground & £260 to be kept by the defendant at 8 in the hundred untill a purchase can be found". The whole entry is crossed through, and Martin Man has written above: "This is put out by Sir Robert Jermyn & Sir John Heigham since the first meeting"./

10. Of these sums £100 is to be paid within 10 days, £200 on 16 October next, £160 within 20 days after Christmas, and £200 within 20 days of Our Lady following, to be paid at the sign of the Greyhound in Ipswich.

11. Bonds are to be entered to Edmond Penninge for payment of the above.

12. Any ambiguities or omissions are to be left to the interpretation of the arbitrators.

On the dorse in Martin Man's hand: "Added upon a meeting of Sir Robert Jermyn & Sir John Heigham since the former articles were agreed upon.

Memorandum it is agreed that of the said some of £660, £200 shall go to the payment of Mr Edmond Pennyng his dett, £200 to the stocking of his grounde, if he stock the same, and the residue, as it shall grow due, to remayne in the handes of Mr Anthony Pennyng allowing after the rate of £8 for the £100 untill lande may be purchased therwith to thuse of the said Edmond & his heires.

Subscribed: this is a true coppie of the order aforenamed. In witnes wherof wee have herunto set our handes. Robert Jermyn, John Heigham, Nathaniel Bacon."

---

[656] In the period considered to be essential for excluding water penetration (*BP*, iv, p.152).

[657] "Plancher": boarded flooring, but also sometimes an inner timbered roof (see *BP*, iv, p.151n.).

[658] Inset house: a house built in the curtilage of an existing dwelling.

[659] Sir Henry Hobart of Blickling, at this point Attorney of the Court of Wards, and just about to be appointed Attorney General on 4 July 1606; Robert Houghton of Gunthorpe, serjeant-at-law; Richard Godfrey of Hindringham, counsellor-at-law.

Unsigned. Copy.
Endorsed: Articles *inter* Pennyng & Penning.
3½ pp. Folger L.d.464 (3).

Robert Michell to Sir Nathaniel Bacon

1606, June 18. Right worshipfull, my moste humble duty remembred. I received your worships letter wherin I received commandemente to inquire whether the maste at Eastone [*Bavents, Suffolk*] was founde flottinge or not and whether theye that did sease it did sease it flottinge or not, for the which cause I did ride unto the finders them selves, bycause I would certifie your worship with the truthe of this cause, and they did tell me that they did finde it firste ner unto Walderswick haven, and did follow it as it was flottinge upon the sea, untill they came at Eastone, and all that way never could come ner to towtche it, and presenteley after it came on to Easton side, ther came a mightie sea and did drive it upe so fare, that at the fall of the seae they mought go round abought it, and did lye all one the dry londe, untill the seae came againe and then it did lye jottinge [*bumping*].[660] The finders did presentley send worde to Henry Bennefice of Easton, and he did come presentley downe and did sease it to the lordes use of the mannor of Easton,[661] the which was the firste seasur that was made of the said maste. It was found by sixe men of <Sowlde> «Southowld» and they have sowlde ther partes being the halfe as they doe challenge it <to one> to one Mr Hoddes of the same towne for 2*s*. 6*d*. a pece, the which doth come to 15*s*. wherof he paid unto them 18*d*. a pece, and they shall have the reste when he have his halfe of the maste. This Mr Hoddes dothe make a great spetche of his halfe and that whoo soever dothe injoy hir that he shall have but the one halfe which halfe he him selfe will by and so drives of other men that would very willingly have dealt for hir. She dothe lye in great dispayer [*disrepair*] by reason of the sune in chickine of hir.[662] Thus leavinge thes thinges unto your worships consideration I humbly take my leave. From Wissite [*Suffolk*] this 18 of June 1606. Your worshipes pore sarvaunte to commaund.

Signed: Rob[*er*]te Mighells.
Addressed: To the right worshipfull my very good master Sir Nathanniell Bakone at Stifkey.
Endorsed in Martin Man's hand: R. Myhelles.
1 p. Folger L.d.426.

Anne Penning to Sir Nathaniel Bacon

[*1606, post June 18*].[663] Sir, wheras by your order my husbandes brother shold

---

[660] The significance of determining these precise circumstances arose from the fact that goods cast on the shore as wreck belonged either to the Crown or to the lord of the manor, whereas when they were still at sea they came under the jurisdiction of the Admiralty.

[661] Easton Bavents, just north of Southwold, was one of the manors in which Bacon had an interest through his ward and stepson William Smith (see 21 May 1605, above, p.182n.). The mast appears to have floated north from Walberswick up the coast past Southwold to Easton Bavents.

[662] "In chickine": from "chick", to sprout or to crack; i.e. the timber is splitting.

[663] Dating: dated with reference to Articles of agreement of 18 June 1606, above, pp.240–1.

have put us in band [*bond*] for payment of the monie at the dayes therin mencioned, hee sinc refuseth and will pay the monie but to Sir John Higham and Sir
Robert Jermine and tels us that excepte they thinke yt fitt hee will not pay yt to us.
Accordinge to the order wee have prepared a stock which wee must pay for, and
land to be purchased with the £260 accordinge to the direction sett downe by yow.
So wee know not what to doe. He delaies our assuranc untill the ould feffees have
released so that if they will not release as they are att his disposing then wee shall
have noe assuranc. Wherfore I humbly besech yow to sett your hand to the order,
to the end wee «may» procuer my Lord Chanclers order to compell them to release.
Our casse is very dangerous, and therfore good sir I beseech yow consider of us, for
if hee die before eyther hee hath made the assuranc or payd the monie wee are
remedilesse. Hee hath sinc perswaded Sir John Higham to allowe of a lease which
hee tels him hee had formerly made to one parson Williams, wheras before hee had
(in the presens of the said Williams) confidently affirmed that the land was cleare
of all incombrances and that possession of all shold bee delivered us at Mihelmas.
And besides this now comes an other and saith hee hath a foremer lease for 7 yeares
so that if these may bee admitted wee shall have noe possession. I beseech yow for
Godes cause suffer us not to bee «thus» oppressed nor compelled to goe anie more
to law for wee are not able to give an £100 at a day of hearinge as yow heard him
say hee did. If yow cannot compell him to performe this order I besech yow leave
us att libertie to appeale to my Lord who honorably promised that if yow ended it
not, hee wold bee pleased to heare our cause & end yt him selfe. I hope yow will bee
pleased to remember that yt was agreed that hee shold give us some allowanc for the
remainder, which though yt bee omitted in the order, in equitie yow will help us.
And so dependinge uppon your justice I humbly take leave. Your most distressed.

[*Postscript*]: Good sir lett mee have your letter to the other knightes of that yow
thinke fitt, that the order may certainely bee agreed uppon, for Mr Pennynge saies
that ther is nothing agreed by yt as yt is nowe, as this messenger cann informe yow
truly of.

Undated. Signed: Ann Pennynge.
Addressed: To the right worshipfull Sir Nathaniell Bacon knight.
Endorsed in Martin Man's hand: Mistres Pennynges.
1 p. Folger L.d.464 (1).

Referral of petition. The heirs of John Moretoft to Sir Edward Coke, Chief Justice

[*1606, June 30 <-Θ-> August 11*].[664] *Calendar*: Petition to Sir Edward Coke as
Chief Justice of the Common Pleas. William and Thomas Mortofte and their five
sisters (Fraunces wife of Robert Appleton, Dyonis wife of John Tylour, Mahelle
wife of Stephen Morse, Mary Denis, widow, and Ursely wife of William Tverd),
being orphans, complain that their brother John Mortofte, deceased, about three

---

[664] Dating: the limits are set by Coke's appointment as Chief Justice of the Common Pleas (30 June
1606) and the Memoranda and Agreement relating to the case dated 11 August 1606, below,
pp.245–50).

years ago deposited £40 with Thomas Thetford esquire of Hevingham to the use
of his two brothers and five sisters whenever they should lawfully demand it, to be
divided equally among them together with the profits for any unclaimed period.
But Thetford unjustly detains all their shares contrary to the trust reposed in him.
They intreat his Lordship's direction for some course to come by their money,
being very poor and unable to sue for their rights. *Unsigned.*

At the foot: "This is referred to Sir Nathaniel Bacon, he to end or certifie". *Signed:*
Edw[*ard*] Coke.

Undated.

Endorsed: The humble peticion of William Mortofte & others.
1 p. Folger L.d.755.

Referral of petition. Robert Anderson to Sir Edward Coke, Chief Justice

[*1606, June 30 <-Θ-> 1613, October 25*].[665] To the right honorable Sir Edward
Cooke knight lord cheiffe justice of the Common Pleas.

Right honorable, maie it please your good honor. I your dailie orator, a poore
distressed man, humblie complaines me to your good honor of one Christopher
Davye who under the title of authoritie doe grynd the faces of your poore country
men, whose cry ascendes to god, and will returne to your honorable censure err
long. Ah my good Lord amongst which number of poore men I am one as a marke
sett upp to shoote att and maie saie with Job my conscience cleare me butt my
enimie is cruell. Therfore his menacing did nott dismaye me, knowing that the
sword of authoritie hurtes nott the well doer. God knowes I owe him nothing, butt
would have bribes which I would never give him, and therfore hee sues me as hee
saith upon dyvers mercimentes [*amercements*], mercilesse pointes maie I saie, if
God and your good honor prevent him nott. First he stole out a *nihil dicit* against
me well knowne to Mr Gybsonne[666] my attorney who waite on your honor. Next
he gott a jurie last assize of his owne appoyntment, wherby he did evict me before
I cam to Norwich or had any notice of it, God to wittnes. Lastlie he hath gott judgment and execution upon judgment of eight or nine poundes for none payment of
a bride noble[667] demanded. So that now poore Naboath must sell his vynyard to
give Gehezi[668] a bribe. Now as the harmlesse bird right honorable finding no rest
for the soole of hir foote flew to Noah Arke for succor, so I advised by a multitude
of poore men humblie seeke to your honor for favour. Assuring my selfe that God

---

[665] Dating: the limits are set by Coke's tenure of the office of Chief Justice of the Common Pleas.

[666] Probably John Gibson, mentioned in the letter from Matthew Plumb to Martin Man of 15 April
1607, below, p.274. His name also appears as witness in a number of documents during Bassingbourne
Gawdy's first shrievalty in 1594 and he may well be related to Henry Gibson who was Gawdy's under-sheriff
(*HMC Gawdy, passim*). Probably he was an attorney working in the Exchequer.

[667] "Bride noble": presumably for a "broad noble", on analogy with the slightly later "broad-piece" for
a 20-shilling piece (*OED*). As such it probably refers to the gold ryal or rose-noble issued late in Elizabeth's
reign (worth 15s.). This was a larger coin than the angel—another type of noble worth 10s. (C. H. V. Suther-
land, *English Coinage 600–1900*, 1973, plate 73, p.154).

[668] Naboth, a poor man, refused to sell his vineyard to King Ahab and was murdered for it (1 Kings 21).
Gehazi, the servant of Elisha, claimed not a bribe but an unmerited reward from Naaman the Leper (11
Kings 5).

hath seated your honor as one of his steward upon earth, to do justice amongst men, to the punishment of wickednes and vice and advancment of Godes glorie. In hope herof having God and a good cause on my side I humblie preferr my petition to your honorable consideration. Now the lord of lyffe the rewarder of all good workes prosper you in this liffe and possesse you with the joyes of heaven. Amen. Your humble orator for ever. *Signed:* Robert Andersonne.[669] *Holograph.*

At the foot in Coke's hand: I desier Sir Nathaniel Bacon to enforme himselfe of the true state of this case and to ende it or certifie. *Signed:* Edw[*ard*] Coke.

Further note at the foot in James Wilshere's hand: Sir I was reteyned in this cause & I spake to Mr Gibson to appere for Anderson by reason it was in the Kinges Benche & the cause was brought downe & tryed at the Assizes without eny knowledg gyven to eyther of us. *Signed: Per me Jacobum Wilshere.*

Undated.

Endorsed: Robert Anderson.

1 p. BL Add. 63109 f.19. Printed, *Stiffkey Papers*, pp.43–4.

Referral of petition. Robert Colles to Sir Edward Coke, Lord Chief Justice

[*1606, June 30 <-Θ-> 1616, November 15*].[670] *"Petition from Robert Colles against John Man and William Gardener, who had taken alleged wrongful possession of his house." With endorsement in the hand of, and signed by, Sir Edward Coke, referring the matter to Nathaniel Bacon.*

Tregaskis, 720 (n.d.), item 149.

Sir Nathaniel Bacon to Robert Radcliffe, Earl of Sussex

1606, July [*5 <-Θ-> 31*].[671] My verie good Lord, I humbly thank you for your kinde remembraunce of me as appeareth by your letter of the v of this present which I have lately receaved. And I wishe that I dwelt neerer to your Lordship then I doe that I might oftener shew my love to you in doing you the service which lieth in me to performe.

The gentlewoman Mistres Amy Gurney whome her brother bringeth now over to attende upon my Ladie[672] had before this tyme made her repayer but there was «by a gent» offer made <by a gentleman> of mariage to her, the successe wherof is uncertayne.[673] And this was the cause of her staye. I hope that shee will be to my

---

[669] Anderson appears not to be a graduate, but he is certainly colourfully articulate.

[670] Dating: dated by reference to the period during which Coke was successively Lord Chief Justice of the Common Pleas and then of the King's Bench, although it is not clear from the catalogue entry that Coke was referred to as Chief Justice in the document.

[671] Dating: dated from internal evidence.

[672] Robert Radcliffe, fifth earl of Sussex, was married to Bridget (d.1623), the eldest daughter of Sir Charles Morison of Cassiobury, Hertfordshire. By 1602 his wife was living separately, though there may have been a brief rapprochement between 1602 and 1610. Although Robert Radcliffe was based in Essex, he held an estate at Attleborough, which he left in his will to his illegitimate daughter, Jane. (*ODNB*).

[673] Possibly she did indeed escape genteel service by marriage. The gentlewoman under discussion may have been the Amy Gurney, sister of Anthony, of the family of that name in West Barsham and Cawston, who married George Sybsay of Boston, Lincs. (Rye, *Visitation of Norfolk*, p.275).

Ladys liking for her condicions are verie good and shee hath ben acquaynted with service and so «much» I thinke my wife hath heretofore signiffed <so much> unto my Lady.

Thus comytting your Lordship to the favour of Almightie God, I take my leave. From Stifky this [*blank*] of July 1606. Your Lordships at comandment.

Unsigned. Draft in Martin Man's hand.
Endorsed: Copy letter to the Earl Sussex.
1 p. Folger L.d.109.

Christopher Grimston to Sir Nathaniel Bacon

1606, July 6. Right worshipfull, my hartiest commendacions in all kindnes premised, with as many thankes for my kind entertaynement as good will can measure from the best meaninge mind.

I will send you the copy of the verditt at Methold soe sown as I can and will attend your worship in it.[674] I found the fines ther to be arbitrable and that Mr Wright had encroched 300 acres from the demayne which I have layd agayne to the mannor and left to Mr Wright «what he» can challenge by lease or charter. Yf he stir in it, the event will sho he hath leardnedly disceived himself in taken his lease. When I came att Helgay thay toke great exceptions to me that I would come wher his Majestie had nothinge but whitrentes [*quitrents*], which Mr Willoughby[675] whom thay termed sole lord of the mannor did truly pay, but err I came away I found his Majesties court lete and baron and that he is lord of the frehold ther. I found wher the Kinges pound is to stand and that thay ar his wastes. Thay ar mutch desierus to enclose and it is mutch to your good but I will take noe cuorse till I speake with you for my better direction. Your tenantes att Methold would now have you feed the cattell you sent, yet soe as it may not be a president agaynst them hearafter yf you doe part from the lease. I refer you to the letter thay writ to you by this bearer. Of all these more when I attend you for your direction. Thus I humbly take my leave. vi *Julii.* Yours att command.

Signed: Chr[*istopher*] Grimeston. *Holograph.*
Addressed: To the right worshipfull my very worthy frend Sir Nathaniel Bacon.
Endorsed in Martin Man's hand: Mr Grymston. 6 July 1606. Concerning Helgay & Methwold wastes.
1 p. NRO NNAS S2/16/25.

Manor of Methwold. Bailiff's account

1606, July 15. *Summary.* The account of Roger Barham, bailiff of the manor of Methwold, for two and a half years ending at Our Lady 1606.

The receipts amounted to £46 19s. 5¼d. This included rents, outrents and rent-

---

[674] See 5 June and 22 July 1606, above, pp.232–4, and below, pp.247–8. This inquiry was the result of the wider strategy initiated by Lord Treasurer Buckhurst for increasing revenues through a more effective exploitation of Crown lands.

[675] John Willoughby of Risley, Derbyshire, and Wiggenhall, part of whose manor in Hilgay belonged to the Duchy of Lancaster lordship of Methwold. See short biography in *BP*, iv, p.212n.

corn paid for various lengths of time, 38s. 1d. from Hilgay for 2 years, and 55s. 8d. from fines and profits of court. Rent still owed is noted in the margin. 3 lambs and 2 calves listed as strays were charged on Francis Reymond[676] and not in this account. Disbursements came to £43 14s. 6d., leaving £3 4s. 11¼d. on 15 July 1606, which was paid to Martin Man.

In Martin Man's hand.

Endorsed: Roger Barhams accompt for Methwold *pro annis 1604 & 1605 & de anno ad festum annunciationis 1606.*

6 pp. NRO MC 1872/16, 866X2. Listed, *Supplementary Stiffkey Papers,* p.38.

Christopher Grimston to Sir Nathaniel Bacon

1606, July 22. Right worshipfull, I send you enclosed the verdett from Methwoold together with a breif for Helgay, in both which I pray your mature deliberation and soe refer my self to your direction in them.[677]

Concerninge Watson I pray your best conceit, that in regard I seeke to redress and not revenge wronges you would the rather right me from those base terms of cowardly boy and rascall where with he hath soyled me, and that it would please you to make his acknowledgement of his wronge to me as notorius as the injury. You see how I forbear with temper, thow I cannot bear his distemper. I know you shall have fayre speaches from him, but they will be as fruitles as his promises wear to Mr Rugge who both speake, writ, and sent his son to signefie his opinion, all which was answered by him with contempt, which Mr Rugge would have redressed but that he was unwillinge to deale within the limitt.[678]

I pray you to consider the great want I have of those howses sett forth to be in common, besids the bruehowse dayrye howse and other romes that stand upon the grundes allotted to me and ar to goe with the soyle beinge not otherwise ordred. I pray you let the continewall necessity of them, quickne your relief of me in my right that I may have it without these extream provocations wherby they seeke noethinge but breach of peace and quarrelles. The kitchin and court yard is sett down in comon and I delivered Watson a note under the surveiors hand that the grundes wheron the other houses stand ar allotted to me as parcell of the wood and new grunds. I pray you to cause him to deliver your worship the keies of them, for in this vacation I am destitute of other relief, and I cannot live without water and other necessaries not to be had but in those romes. Thus referringe these contentes to your consideration I take my leave. Yours att command.

[*Postscript*]: I received a letter even now wherin I am advertised that the Spanish embass[a]dor is confined to his own howse.[679] The rest as you formerly hard. I

---

[676] Francis Raymond of Feltwell, incoming bailiff of the Duchy manor of Methwold.

[677] See 5 June and 6 July 1606, above, pp.232–4, 246, and 31 July 1606, below, p.249.

[678] William Rugg, J.P., lived at Felmingham in Tunstead Hundred, in north-east Norfolk, a long way from the south and west Norfolk "limits" that included Methwold and Hilgay (see Map 1).

[679] There is no evidence that the Spanish ambassador, Pedro de Zuñiga, was "confined" but his Irish secretary, John Ball, had been arrested and interrogated on 10 July concerning plans to betray one of the Dutch fortresses still receiving assistance from English auxiliaries. Tomasio de Franceschi, a captain in Spanish service, had been sent from Flanders to liaise with Ball, and was arrested at the same time. It was also alleged

pray your worship to send me down the writinges for Mistres Berny brings an *nisi prius* agaynst me and I must use them.

/22 *Julii*./

Signed: Chr[*istopher*] Grimeston. *Holograph*.

Addressed: To my very honourable frend Sir Nathaniel Bacon at Stukye.

Endorsed in Martin Man's hand: Mr Grymston. 22 July 1606.

1 p. Folger L.d.324.

Sir Anthony Browne to Sir Nathaniel Bacon

1606, July 22. Good sir this daye Nycholas Suffield Mr Bramptones[680] man of Brampton was brought unto me, whoe accordynge to our warrant hath entered bond with suertyes to appere at thes Syses [*Assizes*]. Also this daye John Allyn of Buxton came unto me alone with infformations (hereinclosed sent youe) ageynst his accusers Lionell Toplyff I take it Custe and the other. Which albeit it goethe neere the manner of recrymination, yet differynge by reason Allyn tellynge them (he sayth) of thes inclosed (which they intended to conceale) made them so to complayne of Allyn for the mattre of disordre at the watche. And beynge also (he sayth) sent unto me with the same from Sir Myles Corbet, I receyvd them and do thynck them well worthy the tryinge oute agaynst Toplypp [*sic*] and his felowe complaynants of Buxton, and them worthy to answer at thes Syses such apparant necglect (yf so it prove) otherwyse we ar worthy to fall the heviar of Allyn yf fayned. And to that end Allyn comynge alone and remarkeynge his name, thoughe not when his apparance ether at the Syse or sessions, I thought good to trye this Allyn and so have I onlye bound «hym» to thes Syses to maynteyne thes enclosed to be tried. Wherby we shalbe suer to have hym, and then may we laye hold further of Allyn as cause shall fall oute. Yf your leysure wold permytt I wyshe youe wold send for this Toplyffe and the other complaynants of Buxton that either together before youe, or at the Syses the truth herof may appere. Were not my present rydynge into Suffolk and so to Bury I wold make somwhat of it. I had yestreday a newe attempt for the apparant bastardy I told youe of in the coche to Holt wards. And so with my best remembrance I betake you to the Allmyghty. Elsynge this 22 of Julye 1606. Yours ever assured.

Signed: Antho[*ny*] Browne.

Addressed: To the ryght woorshipfull Sir Nathannell Bacon knyght Styffky.

Endorsed in Martin Man's hand: Sir A. Brown.

1 p. BL Add. 41140 ff.60–61.

that they conspired to assassinate the King at Royston. Franceschi confessed to a design against Sluys, but denied that there was any plot against James (*CSPD, 1603–10*, pp.324–5). Ball seems to have remained a prisoner well into 1607, despite promises to return him to the embassy (*HMC Salisbury*, xviii, pp.261, 355; xix, p.163). However, by December that year he was in Brussels, and being solicited to return clandestinely to England (*CSPD, 1603–10*, p.389).

680 Probably Edward Brampton of Brampton (d.1622), esquire (Blomefield, vi, p.435).

Christopher Grimston to Sir Nathaniel Bacon

1606, July 31. Sir I thinke my self muche beholden to you for your paynes with Watson, and wishe it might have better prevailed with him.[681] I knowe your wisdome did sowne discover the weakenesse of his delatorie aunsweare aunswearlesse, as also his untruthe in enforminge you his councell should advise him to stand against the occupyinge in common, for it is not our fashions to devise anie thinge contrarie to «soe» peremptorie a resolucion of soe honourable a courte. Concerninge the landes at Methould it is probable they will fall to Sir Edmund Mumford [*Moundeford*] as parcell of the Kinges demeanes, but for the landes at Helgaye and the encrochementes enclosed by Mr Skipwith I doe assure my self they must eyther come to you by vertue of your lease, or to me by reason of his Majesties grante of concealmentes emprovementes & encrochementes or to both of us.[682] I make no question but att my next goinge I shall have a verdicte for the Kinges Majestie which I will presently returne into the Dutchie and soe drawe an informacion as cause shall requyre. It is not within my comprehension what eyther Mr Willabee or Mr Skipwith should have to saye for a juste defence for soe unjust encrochinge. Mr Skipwith did acknowledge his error and offered composicion and still solliciteth for it but I will doe nothinge without your privitie & advyse. I thinke it very fitt if it maye stand soe with your pleasure that I might have your assistance & presence there, that you might see both the qualitie and quantitie of those groundes, which I knowe will farre exceed your expectacion of them. You shall see soe muche as lyeth in me, I will deserve your best opynion in my proceedinge. I praye you to sende my writinges by this bearer for I shall use them att the Assisses. Thus with my hartiest comendacions in all kindnesse remembred I take my leave this laste of July 1606. Yours very assured.

Signed: Chr[*istopher*] Grimeston.
Addressed: To my very honourable frend Sir Nathanyell Bacon att Stifkye.
Endorsed in Martin Man's hand: Mr Grymeston *ultimo* July 1606. Concerning Helgay & Methwold commons concealed by Mr Skipwith & *al.*
1 p. Folger L.d.325.

Memoranda concerning the dispute between Thomas Thetford and the heirs of John Moretoft

1606, August 11. Remembraunces upon hearing of the cause between Moretoftes kyndred & Mr Thomas Thetford. 11 August 1606.[683]

The peticioners charged Mr Thetford to detayne from them about £40, which remayned in his handes of certayn money comytted to him in trust by John Moretofte deceased. Saving that thei confessed certayn somes paid to ech of them, for the use of their partes etc.

Mr Thetfordes defence was thus, namely, that about 17 yeares synce the said

---

[681] See 22 July 1606, above, p.247.
[682] See note to 5 June 1606, above, p.234.
[683] See Referral of petition, 30 June<-Θ->11 August 1606, above, pp.243–4.

Moretofte upon sale of his lande appoynted <assured> «bonde» to be <made> «taken» for £60 of the money (received for his lande) <& taken> in Mr Thetfordes name <by> «of» one Wilson, who borrowed the money & paid the use therof to the said Moretofte. And that Moretofte before his death tooke into his handes £20 of the said £60, and at his death there remayned £40 in Wilsons handes still. And that Mr Thetford hath put Wilson, & one Deane (who is suertie for Wilson) in suite and recovered upon the bond. And when he hath the money upon execution, he will satisfie their partes, & not before.

Unsigned. In Martin Man's hand.
Endorsed: Remembrances concerning Mr Thetford & Moretoftes.
½ p. Folger L.d.744.

Agreement between Thomas Thetford and the heirs of John Moretoft

1606, August 11. A remembraunce of the agreement set downe the 11 of August 1606 by the mediation of Sir Nathaniell Bacon knight between Thomas Thetford esquire of thone parte and Steven Mosse, William Tuert, John Tyler, Mary Dennys widow, Frances the wife «of» Robert Appleton, William Moretofte & Thomas Moretoftes wife.[684]

That where there remayneth in the handes of William Wilson and John Deane & William Jervys about £40 of the mony of one John Moretofte deceased and bonde for the same is taken by Mr Thetford in his owne name, and the said John Moretofte gave the said mony at his death to the parties above named, being his brothers & sisters.

The said Mr Thetford agreeth to disburse presently 20*s.* a pece to 4 of them, *viz.* Mosse, Tuert, Tyler, & Dennys, which is accordingly paid them. And <the rest> agreeth to satisfie equally to every of them (deducting reaonable charges, & allowances already given) their portions out of the said remaynder upon Thursday the [*blank*] of this instant moneth at Stifky in the house of the said Sir Nathaniell.

Memorandum a letter to Deane Wilson & Jervys to be then at Stifky, either to deliver the mony out of their handes, or new security.

Signed: Na[*thaniel*] Bacon. *In Martin Man's hand.*
Endorsed in Martin Man's hand: Agreement betwen Mr Thetford & Moretoft etc.
½ p. Folger L.d.743.

Sir William Cornwallis to Sir Nathaniel Bacon

1606, August 12. Sir, the jentlewoman whose praiers you have bound unto you for your paynes taken in hers and her housbonds busines, the wife of the younger brother of the Pennings,[685] perceyving the perswatitions [*sic*] of the ellder brother likely to wourke more to ther prejudice then what was agreed on and sett down under your hands, with some other the commissioners, writes a lamentable letter to me, desiring [?]myne to you, that you will not suffer any part of the order

---

[684] See also the Settlement of 21 August 1606, below, p.253.
[685] See Anne Penning's letter of *Post* 18 June 1606, above, pp.242–3.

allredy sett down and signed by your own hand to be alltered, or diminished in
«the» good to her and her housbond, wherin«to», as I am easily perswaded, you
will assent. So these do most ernestly intreat you, not to be intreated otherwise
which I do assure you sir I will attempt, as a just and jentle point of frendshipe
from you to me, who you shall never find strang in any occasion of yours wherin I
may shew requitall. The jentlewoman I know hath served my daughter 10 yeers in
good and honest fashion, and in my opinion, deserves as good a man as this
Penning, though he had his fathers £4,000 given him by will, fully perfourmed in
redy money. Sir I dare presume my Lord Chancelor before whom this cause hath
been shall thinke well of your indifferent ending of it, for the good of the younger
brother and his wife who can make no such frinds haply as the ellder hath, and can
make. And so with my verye kind commendations unto you I committ you sir to
God and this to the Chancery of your own conscience, and curtesy for my sake.
From Brome this xii of August 1606. Your well assured to my powr.

Signed: Willia[*m*] Cor[*n*]waleys.
Addressed: To the right wourshipfull my assured good frind Sir Nathaniell Bacon
knight.
Endorsed in Martin Man's hand: Sir W. Cornwallys.
1 p. Folger L.d.243.

Sir Nathaniel Bacon to Sir Edward Coke, Chief Justice of Common Pleas

1606, August 13. It maie please your Lordship to understande, that according to
your direction, I <called> «caused one» Clement Lambart[686] to come unto me togither with the bearer John Utting,[687] a peticioner to your Lordship for relief in
regard of mony due to him from one John Lambart father of the said Clement, and
the said Clement alledgeth that he hath fully administred, & refuseth to satisfie
this dett. Which in conscience (in my judgment) he ought to <do> «pay», both in
respect of the poverty of the man, who lent the mony to old Lambart, and also, of
the porcion of lande which was left to the young man by his father being of the
value of £40 by yeare «being copiehold. I would have had him repayer unto your
Lordship with the bearer but he refused to do it without warrant». I have thought
it fitt to certefy thus much unto your Lordship referring the poore man to your
further consideracions, and so I take my leave. From Stifk[*ey*] this 13 of August
1606. Your Lordships <at commandment> verie assured.

Unsigned. Draft in Martin Man's hand.
Endorsed: Copy of a letter to my Lord Coke concerning Utting. 14 August [*sic*].
½ p. Folger L.d.111.

---

686 Possibly Clement Lambert (d.1622), yeoman, of Binham. By his will he left property in Binham, Hindringham, Briston, Melton Constable, Field Dalling, Gunthorpe and Bale (NRO NCC 1622 Bradstritt
f.64).
687 John Utting: perhaps one of at least two men of this name from Warham. A John Utting served as
overseer for the poor there in 1600/1 (*BP*, iv, p.191).

Jo. Pepys to Sir Nathaniel Bacon

1606, August 13. Sir this bearer Well and his adversarye Roper hath bene before my Lord[688] who hath heard the cause betwixt them and hath ordered it thus *viz.* that Roper should come before you and bring suerties with him «to be bounde» for his good behaviour «and for his appearance at the next Assisses» and that the speciall *supplicavit*[689] which the Bayliffes of Yarmouth have against Well should be stayed and that yf Roper doe require the peace against Well that upon his oath it be graunted him. And thus <being> my humble dutye remembred to your self and your good lady I take my leave. In haste from Godwick this 13 of August 1606. At your woorshipps service.

Signed: [?]Jo. Pepys.[690]
Addressed: To the right woorshipfull his very good frend Sir Nathanyell Bacon knight at Stiffkey.
Endorsed in Martin Man's hand: Mr Pepys concerning Roper & Well.
½ p. BL Add. 41140 ff.62–3.

Samuel Stallon to Sir Nathaniel Bacon

1606, August 20. Right wourshipful, my very humble dutie remembred. I can not as yett understand any other circumstances of this suspected murder, then formerly I have acquaynted your wourship withall, saving that the common speache in Sharington ys that George Mason was not at home that night (*sed qua fide nescio*).[691] Sir I have delivered your wourships letter to Robert Morris who ys to testifie of Masons talking with the widowe both the tyme, place, and how long.

George Allen: for saying (as he went to the buriall) that he gave him his last drinke *viz.* Cobbell.[692]

Risborowgh: whether he have harde of the clamour raysed of him, that he shold kill Cobbel and uppon what occassions such speaches shold arise. This partie ys one that layde him into the grave, when as he bledd freshlye.[693]

As I do heare of any other liklyhoods I will certifie your wourship and so in all humble dutie I commend you to thalmightie. Brinton this 20 of August 1606. Your wourships in all duty.

Signed: Sam[uel] Stallon.[694]

[688] Presumably Sir Edward Coke, who acted as judge of assize on the Norfolk circuit from summer 1606 to summer 1612 (Cockburn, *Assizes*, pp.268–9).
[689] "*Supplicavit*": "he has entreated". A writ directed to the sheriff or the J.P.s by a party fearing violence and requesting a recognizance against a breach of the peace.
[690] "Jo. Pepys": probably John Pepys (1576–1652) of Creake and London, but possibly for his father Jerome (Fermor) Pepys (*Visit. of Norf. 1563*, i, p.381), active in Brothercross Hundred (*BP*, iv, p.259).
[691] "*Sed qua fide nescio*": "with what justification I know not".
[692] Possibly Peter Cobble, listed as a ratepayer at Sharrington in 1604/5 (NRO MC 1872/21, 866X2).
[693] An expression of the popular belief that the body of a murdered man could identify his murderer.
[694] Samuel Stallon (d.1613), rector of Sharrington. Stallon was rector of North Barsham from 1589, and Barton also has him as rector of Sharrington from this date (Venn, *Al Cant.*, iv, p.144; Barton, *Anthony Harison*, i, p.195). In fact he was not instituted to the benefice until 18 January 1601/2 (NRO DN/REG 14, f.297). Stallon had a long-standing connection with Bacon. A puritan minister, he preached at the weekly "exercises" held at Wiveton in the 1580s, in relation to which he is later described as of Walsingham

Addressed: To the right wourshipful Sir Nathaniell Bacon knight at his howse in Stiffkye.

Endorsed in Martin Man's hand: Mr Stallon. 20 August.

½ p. Folger L.d.560.

Settlement between Thomas Thetford and the heirs of John Moretoft

1606, August 21. 21 August 1606. Memorandum that Mr Thetford hath agreed to satisfy the parties undernamed before the next term.[695]

[*Written above:*] The partie [*share*] for ech of them «being *viz.*»	£7 2s. 11d.
The dividend. First due at Candlemas 1604	£44
at Candlemas 1605	£4
Since Candlemas for half a year	40s.
Summa	£50
Paid to William Moretofte at severall tymes	£4 5s. 6d.
[?]Paymentes upon a reckoning	[*blank*]
So rest to him	57s. 5d.
/Memorandum the partie absent./	
To Thomas Moretofte. [?]Paymentes upon a reckoning	48s. 5d.
So rest	£4 14s. 6d.
Agreed to be paid to his wife upon her repayer	
/Memorandum the partie absent./	
To Steven Mosse	£3 <7s.> 3s. 2d.
Rest	£3 <15s. 11d.> 19s. 9d.
Before Michaelmas terme upon his repayer	
To William Tuerd. Present.	47s.
Rest	£4 15s. 11d.
To Mary Dennys	45s. 4d.
Rest	£4 17s. 7d.
Before the terme	
To John Tyler	37s.
Rest	£5 5s. 11d.
Before the terme	
To Frances Appleton	27s.
Rest	£5 15s. 11d.

Promiseth to send of to Bylney to her husband before the terme

At the foot: Memorandum ech of them to seale acquittaunces upon the receipt of their mony.

(*BP*, ii, p.316; *BP*, iv, pp.16–17). Although Stallon is naturally involved here as the rector of Sharrington, it would not in any case be surprising to find him acting as the eyes and ears of Bacon as a leader of the north Norfolk theocracy.

[695] See also Memoranda and Agreement, 11 August 1606, above, pp.249–50.

Signed: Per me Tho[mam] Thetford.
In Martin Man's hand.
Endorsed: The agreement betwen Mr Thetford & the Moretoftes. 21 August 1606.
1 p. Folger L.d.746.

Agreement between Robert King and Robert Mundy

1606, August 25. Memorandum 25 August 1606. Yt was agreed before Sir
Nathaniell Bacon knight as followeth betwen Robert Kynge & Robert Mundye of
Thursforth [*Thursford*], *viz.*

That in consideracion of a liberty claymed by Mundye to drawe water at a well
within Kinges yarde, the said Kynge shall paie 10*s.* unto Monday towardes the
making of a well in his owne grounde, and Mondy to forbeare to drawe water at
Kinges well hereafter.

And the 10*s.* is agreed to be left in Robert Walkers hande, and 5*s.* therof to be
paid to Mundy so sone as he doth begyn the well, & the rest after it is finished.

And ech partie releaseth the peace taken against one another & against the rest
conteyned in the warrantes made & granted by Sir Nathaniel Bacon & Mr Gwynne.

Signed: Na[*thaniel*] Bacon.
In Martin Man's hand.
Endorsed: An agreement betwen Mondye & Kinge.
½ p. Folger L.d.747.

Agreement between William Wild and Nicholas Ringall

1606, August 25. Memorandum 25 August 1606. It was agreed betwen William
Wylde & Nicholas Ringold [?]junior, that upon the payment of 40*s.* to Wilde by
Ringold, and upon the delivery to Wilde of a bond remayning in Wolseys handes
wherin Wilde standes bounde with N. Ringoldes sonne, both parties shall seale to
ech other generall releases.

Signed: Na[*thaniel*] Bacon. *In Martin Man's hand.*
Endorsed: An agreement betwen Wilde & Ringold.
½ p. Folger L.d.745.

Complaint against the bailiff of North Greenhoe

1606, September 8. Memorandum 8 September 1606. Andrew Pyle was arrested
by <the bailiff of Northgrenho> one [*blank*] as deputie for John Clerk at the suite
of John Whoode. And upon his arrest he was caryed to the said Clarkes house who
is <also> bailiff of the Hundred and there kept as prisoner for about an houre,
untill he gott suerties for his apperaunce. And John Clerk tooke of him for fees for
the house (as he said) 10*s.* & 12*d.* for garnishe, 2*s.* 4*d.* for the arrest & bond, 3*d.*
for a coppie out of the warrant, & 2*d.* besides.

Unsigned. In Martin Man's hand.
Endorsed: A complaint against John Clerk by Andrew Pyle.
½ p. NRO BL/BC/6/17.

Anthony Penning to Sir Nathaniel Bacon

1606, September 8. Right wourshipfull, maye itt please you to understand, thatt some three weekes synce I received from my brother a drawght of a conveyaunce, upon the order made betwene us by Sir Robertt Jermyn Sir John Hygham and your selfe, and fynding therin diveres just causes of exception, I did assone as I could possible gett another drawghte made, and have entreated this bearer (whome I have acquainted, with the causes of exception in the first drawght) to attend you bothe with thatt my brother sentt unto me and also, with the drawght made by my owne councell, humbly prayinge you to peruse them bothe. And whattsoever itt shall please Sir Robertt Jermyn Sir John Hygham and your selfe to thinke fitt for me to doe, I will willinglye performe. And soe beinge very sorye thatt I must still be soe trowbellsome unto you, I humbly take my leave. Kettelburghe [*Suffolk*] this 8 of September 1606. Your wourships alweyes att commaunde.[696]

Signed: Anthony Pennynge.
Addressed: To the right wourshypfull Sir Nathaniell Bacon knight.
Endorsed in Martin Man's hand: Mr Anthony Pennyng September 1606.
½ p. Folger L.d.465.

Sir John Higham to Sir Nathaniel Bacon

1606, September 9. Sir I have perused two draughtes of conveyance for the [land] to be assured by Mr Anthony Pennyng to his brother Mr Edmund Pennyng & his wiffe, with certeyne exceptions to the draught sent by Mr Edmund Pennyng,[697] which exceptions I have perused & advisedly consydered of, and I think them fytt to be regarded, for I hold yt not reasonable that the wooman yf she survyve hir husband should hold the land without impechment of wast. For the 2 I thynk yt ys contrary to my Lord Chancellors order & our meanyng, that Edmund Pennyng shold have interest in the land for terme of his lyffe, for then he maye through hys want of experyence, be brought to passe awaye that interest & so lyve full meanely all his lyffe after & therfore fytter to have the profytes duryng his lyffe, without interest in the land. I thynk the rest of the exceptions very worthe consyderation, & espetially the last exception. For Mr Wyll[i]mas [*sic*] leas I well remember yt was agreed upon, & yf I be not very forgettful, you toke a note therof in your paper. For the «draught of» conveyance made by Mr Anthonye Pennyng I hold yt agreable with our order, only therin ys wantyng that yf the wife overlyve hir husband, she should geve a yearly anuyty to hyr children. And in that draught I praye yow consyder of the covenant for the assuerance to be made at ther equall charges for I think, although I do not perfectly remember yt, that the charges of assuerance should be borne by Mr Anthony Pennyng. And this ys all that at this tyme I remember and therfore do end with my most kynd commendacion to yow & your good ladye. From Barrow [*Suffolk*] this 9 of September 1606. Your very assured frend.

---

[696] See the Articles of Agreement, 18 June 1606, above, pp.240–1, and Higham to Bacon, immediately below.
[697] See Anthony Penning's letter, immediately above, and correspondence between Higham, Jermyn and Bacon, 30 October and 1 November 1606, below, pp.261–3.

At the foot in Martin Man's hand: Memorandum I have written to Sir John Heigham 11 September 1606 that wee may meete after Michaelmas, & that the remembrance concerning Mr Wyll[*ia*]ms lease is like to be in Mr Throgmortons handes.

Signed: J. Heigham.

Addressed: To the right worshipfull my verye lovyng frend Sir Nathanyell Bacon knight.

Endorsed in Martin Man's hand: Sir John Heigham 9 September.

1 p. Folger L.d.343.

Certificate of church attendance

1606, September 14. May it please your good worshupe to understand that at the request of the berer herof Mr Strange Godfray I am to certyfye unto your worshupe that he doth come to the church as ordinarily as «what» other the parishoners of Gunthorpe do and moreover my father in law Mr Armitsted[698] servinge the cure for me in my absence can testifie the same. In witnes hereof I William Warren the curate ther[699] for the confirmation of the truth hereof have subscribed my name with my owne hand the xiiii of September in *anno domini* 1606. Your worshipes in all dewty to commaund.[700]

Signed (in William Warren's hand): William Warren and James Armitsed the parson of Bale «who» did see hym at church this present Sabboth. *In William Warren's hand.*

Addressed: To the right worshupfull Sir Nathaniell Bacon.

Endorsed in Martin Man's hand: Certificate for Straunge Godfry & Anne Godfry.

1 p. NRO BL/BC/6/18.

Petition. The townsmen of Southwold, with Cyprian Sallows and William Girling, to Sir Nathaniel Bacon

[*1606, c. October*].[701] *Calendar.* According to the petition, there is a bill preferred in the Court of Star Chamber against Richard Gooche for maintaining a cause in Chancery against the bailiffs and sundry inhabitants of Southwold and against Cyprian Sallouse and William Gyrling, in the name of Margaret Raphe, widow of Thomas Raphe. The Star Chamber has referred the bill to Sir Francis Bacon[702] for report at the beginning of this next term. In supporting the widow Raphe, mostly

---

[698] James Armistead, rector of Bale from 1576, non-graduate (Barton, *Anthony Harison*, ii, p.208; *BP*, iii, p.237).

[699] In June 1606 William Warren is described as the curate of North Barsham, having been ordained in 1604 aged about 24 (Barton, *Anthony Harison*, i, p.187). In that capacity he served under Samuel Stallon the rector there, one of Bacon's clerical acolytes (see note to 20 August 1606, above, p.252).

[700] Presumably a certificate of attendance in connection with recusancy.

[701] Dating: dated with reference to the letter of 21 October 1606 from Sallows and Girling to Martin Man, below, p.259.

[702] Francis Bacon, Nathaniel's half-brother, had recently been thwarted once more in his careerist aspirations to significant office. Nonetheless, he was busily engaged in work for the government on matters large and small, as here. Referral to him of this matter by Star Chamber may have occurred because he already had a reversionary interest in the clerkship of that Court (*ODNB*).

at his own expense, Gooch has greatly hindered the township by commencing various frivolous suits in Star Chamber and Chancery, calling 20 persons to answer. The township is lately much impoverished "fyrst by fyer dystroyinge a third parte of the towne, s[e]condly by the late <pestilent> pestylent sycknes, thirdly by the greate losses susteyned by the Dunkerkers[703] and hostyle enemyes of Spaine, and forthly by hard vyages in fysher fare and badd markettes, whereon the state of the said towne wholly dependeth".[704] Sir Francis Bacon has formerly been counsel to Gooche concerning the bill in Chancery, and Gooche does or has served Sir Nicholas Bacon, both matters likely to influence Sir Francis in his favour. The petitioners request Sir Nathaniel Bacon to write to Sir Francis, urging him either to undertake his examination as judge rather than advocate or to refuse it so that it may be referred to some other person.

Undated. Unsigned.
Addressed: To the right wourshipfull Sir Nathanyell Bacon knight.
Endorsed in Martin Man's hand: Sould [*Southwold*] peticion concerning R. Goche. 1 p. Folger L.d.756.

Sir Edward Coke, Chief Justice of Common Pleas, to Sir Nathaniel Bacon[705]

[*1606, October <-Θ-> 1606/7, January 26*].[706] After my verie hartie commendations. «I have received» your letters of the eight of this instant moneth together with copies of divers examinations concerning the poisoning and death of Thomas Cooke of Claye in Norfolk. Which examinations I have perused and uppon consideration thereof I do much commend your judgment in 2 respectes, first that you have not bailed her, 2, that the matter is to be heard at the Assises. For «of» al murdres poysoning is the most detestable, and of all poisoning, that of the woman of her husbond is the most damnable, and therfore by lawe it is petit treason. I will not enter into any judgment of the fact, for it is nowe no tyme for it, since I find there is vehement suspicion, and consequentlie she ought to be imprisoned. And when she is once in prison, it may be that more will be discovered, and parties will speak more confidentlie then when the partie accused is at large. And I doubt not but God (who is the author of truth) assisting your painfull and discreet laboure herein the truth will appeare, and having theise groundes of further examination I knowe you will not pretermitt no good meanes eyther of [?]determination (which is most necessarie seing there is so much contrarietie) or of examination of any other not yet known or examined if any further shall come to your knowledg. It

---

[703] Dunkirkers: privateers operating out of the port of Dunkirk, then part of the Spanish Netherlands.

[704] Nathaniel Bacon also had some interest in this area and its economic plight as a result of his wife and stepson's ownership of nearby manors, especially that of Easton Bavents just up the coast from Southwold (see 21 May 1605, above, p.182n.).

[705] The letter is described as addressed to Sir Nathaniel Bacon when offered for sale on the internet by Alan Boyer, New York, on abebooks.com. on 5 March 2000.

[706] Dating: 10 witnesses from Cley and Weybourne, including Katherine Bradfelde, together with Samuel Stallon, rector of Sharrington, were bound over between 21 October and 10 November 1606 to appear at the next Assizes in connection with the indictment of Joan Cooke the widow (Bacon memoranda book 1602–7, NRO BL/BC/5/22, pp.89–91). In a letter to Coke, Bacon listed the case as due to be heard at the Lent Assizes (26 January 1606/7, below, pp.269–70).

were in myne opinion necessarie to get that blacke stone that was <sus> supposed to be brought out of Iceland and to sift out that matter of the ratsbane, and it were necessarie to reexamine Bradfeldes wife concerninge the ratsbane and if she persist in her former examination it were good to confront the widowe & her in that [?]event onlie and then to reexamine the widowe where and when she bought it where she layed it upp etc. I much marvaile what moved the widowe to shewe the deade body of her husbond (and to handle it so boldly) to her neighbours. The matter of unkindnes betwen her & her husbond would be thoroughly examined. Wherof and of all due circumstances I have no doubt seing the matter is under your examination wherein you shall doe service in fynding out the trothe pleasing to the Almightie unto whose blessed [?]protection I [?]directe you and will ever remayne. Your true & loving frind.

At the foot and barely legible. Item to reexamine whether her husbond [?]charged [?]another with ther [?]promise etc.

Item whether he chewed any tabacco that morninge & whether he had any in the house.[707]

Item who were those that sawe the body to [?]know it after he was dead.

Undated. Signed: Edw[*ard*] Coke.
1 p. Maggs, 497, plate VIII.

Information concerning the death of an apprentice

1606, October 10. The informacion of Agnes Howsigo widdowe of Welles[708] taken before Sir Nathanael Bacon knight the 10 of October 1606.

Shee saith, that her sonne Peter Howsigo now deade was about the age of 20 yeares, and was put fourth apprentice to one George Phillips of [*Dunton cum*] Doughton about 5 yeares since to serve in the science of a tanner. And the said Phillips was severall tymes threatned to be complayned of for his no better usadge of his said apprentice and yet no redresse was had.

Shee saith, that upon Tuesday last the said Peter came from his master and, as he said before his death, for weaknes & want of attendanc & succor in his sicknes. And the same night was not able to reach from Doughton to Welles being but about 8 myles and so laie in the fieldes all night and the next morning came to this examinates house in Welles about 8 of the clock and cryed out at his comyng for drynk and the same afternoone about 2 of the clock dyed.

Shee saith that his apparrell was of leather rent & torne «&», as he said, he had no other. And was so exceeding full of lice as thei who sawe his garmentes had not seen the like. And when his shirte was plucked of he said that he had no cleane shirte of a moneth before.

Shee saith, that he could reade upon the bible, and yet tolde this examinat that he had not ben at church since Easter, & for want of clothes.

---

[707] Interesting evidence of the rapid familiarisation with this newly imported and loathsome substance. Evidently it aroused suspicion.

[708] Various members of the Howsego family were resident in both Wells and Salthouse (*BP*, ii-iv, *passim*).

Memorandum the said Phillips had £4 10*s*. with the said apprentice.

At the foot: Agnes Howsigo is enjoyned to appeare at the next sessions at Fakenham to informe etc.[709]

Signed: Na[*thaniel*] Bacon, [*by mark:*] Agnes Howsigo.
In Martin Man's hand.
Endorsed: Informacion of Agnes Howsigo touching Phillips.
1 p. Folger L.d.748.

Evidence concerning a theft of fruit

1606, October 10 – 12. 10 October 1606. John Hallymont saith, that John Crosby his fellow servant & he doe lodge [in] an outhouse of thes Mr Franyngham,[710] and the said Crosby doth use many nightes to come late to bedd, sometyme at 11, & sometyme at 12 & after.[711] And he hath not sen anie peres or apples brought by him, at anie tyme into the said chamber. But confesseth that now & then he hath given him 2 or 3 peres out of his hose, which were mellow. And the peres were rounde like the bargemot Dutch peres.

He saith that one morning he sawe a sack laid on a bedd in their chamber, with something in «it» to the quantity of 3 peckes. And that night Crosby came to bedd after he was fallen asleepe. And whither there were pears or apples in the sack he knoweth not but thinketh there was one of them.

12 October. He further saith that the first tyme that he sawe anie peres was in a morning. And Crosby had laid in the chamber about 30 greate peares.

He saith that the sack of 3 peckes before spoken of by him were litle rounde peares.

He saith that at another tyme there were brought into the chamber another <chamber> sack with pares or apples in the night by the said Crosby.

Unsigned. In Martin Man's hand.
Endorsed: Concerning Crosby.
½ p. Folger L.d.749.

Cyprian Sallows and William Girling to Martin Man

1606, October 21. We have caused our neybour this bringer to come over for aunswer of the petytion lately made unto Sir Nathanyell by the townsemen of South[*w*]old and ourselves[712] prayinge yow to furder our purpose, what lyeth in yow. So with our very hartie comendacions we take our leave. Brampfeild [*Suffolk*] xxi *Octobris* 1606. Your loveinge frindes to theire poweres.

---

[709] George Phillips was bound over the same day in £20 to appear at the next sessions for Gallow Hundred (Bacon memoranda book 1602–7, NRO BL/BC/5/22, pp.89–91).

[710] Framingham was a common surname in north Norfolk (see *passim* and *BP*, iv, *passim*) and it is not clear which Framingham was of sufficient status to be given the status "Mr".

[711] "Nightwalking", as it was euphemistically called, was a recognised feature which worried early-modern society (see, for instance, Paul Griffiths, 'Meanings of Nightwalking in Early Modern England', *The Seventeenth Century* 13, 1998, pp.212–38 and Antoinette Wattebot, 'The experience of time in early modern England, with special reference to Eastern England', UEA PhD, 2000).

[712] See Petition of c.October 1606, above, pp.256–7.

At the foot: The partyculers of our greifs.

Injuries done by Gooch to the towneshippe of Southold

    1. He hathe «wrongfully» entred theire towne landes of £50 rente and held that same this 2 yeres against theire willes and paieth no rente.

    2. He felleth theire tymber.

    3. He felleth «& selleth» of theire wood.

    4. He harryeth the groundes with the ploughe.

    5. He pretendeth a concealement against the same landes.

/All the said injuries are wrought «contynued» by reason of an injunction obteyned grounded uppon a reporte made by a doctor beinge one of the Masters of the Chauncery./

Injuries done by him to Sallouse and Gyrlinge

    1. He suborneth one for whose debte they stand condempned in £140 and he haveinge spente her estate in shiftes against them they are left without remedy.

    2. He hath drawne them and tenne of theire servantes and workemen into the corte of Starr Chamber uppon very fryvelouse matters which suite still dependeth at great charge to the poore servantes and workemen.

Signed: Cuprian Sallose, W[*illia*]m Gyrlinge.

Addressed: To our verie lovinge frind Mr Martyn Man.

Endorsed in Martin Man's hand: Ciprian Sallowes letter with a particler of Goches wronges.

1 p. Folger L.d.935.

Sir Nathaniel Bacon to Sir Francis Bacon

1606, October 25. Good brother, I understande, that there is a reference made unto you out of the cort of the Starchamber, of a byll there exhibited by the township of South[*w*]old in Suffolk against R. Goche my brother Bacons servant & your clyent.[713] And thei of the towne being not <verie> riche, by reason of the great pestilence, which hath ben lately amongst them, & by other occasions of pyracy & fire, are loathe to holde on a chargable contencion, and therefore have intreated me to be a meanes unto you in their behalf, that some good corse might be taken, whereby there might be no contynuance of the suites betwen them. The consideracion hereof causeth me hereby to be a suitor unto you, that you will take knowlege of the grievaunces of both sides, and as a judge, advise & move such a proceeding, as a peace may be concluded betwen them. And in so doing, as well Goche as the townsmen of Soulde shall have greate cause to holde themselves beholding unto you, and will be readie to do you anie kyndnes or service for your travell so bestowed, and I also take it kyndly at your handes. When I was at the last parliament I did heare some of them & R. Goche also speake touching the differences betwen them, and I then thought Goche in fault and did tell him that I would complayne to his master for the «unquiet» cariage of himself. So I commende you to the grace & favour of God. From Stifky 25 October 1606.

---

[713] Sir Nicholas Bacon. See c.October and 21 October 1606, immediately above and pp.256–7.

Unsigned. Copy in Martin Man's hand.
Endorsed: Copy of a letter to Sir Francis Bacon on the behalf of Sould [*Southwold*]. October 1606.
1 p. Folger L.d.112.

Affirmation concerning an accidental injury

1606, October 27. The affirmations of William Scabburne upon some conference had betweene him and those men whose names are under written.

Inprimis that ther was never any quarrell grudge or mallice betwixt them but that they were perfect frends.

2ly that <as> the sayd William comming from Burnham Markett accompanied with George [?]Bond the 12 day of this moneth ther met with him in the field Thomas Stephenson Andrew Purvys William Cooper and the sayd Stephenson being next <him> «the sayd Scabburne» and Purvys next him and Cooper one the outside in some throwst of one or all of them the <was> sayd William Scabburne was cast into Gallow way and soe by that meanes had his thigh broken upon which hurt the sayd William affirmeth that he hath much paine but is somewhat recovered and findeth not himselfe to be mortally hurt.

Lastly [*two words deleted*] the sayd William Scabburne averreth that upon this condition he may be mainteyned and succoured during the time of his inhabilitie to worke for his living he forgiveth them all this injurie, and further if it soe please God that he dye <before> «of» this sicknes he freely and heartily forgiveth them all.

Signed: Edward Ceney *clericus*, Edw. Thurlow cheif constable, Samuell Boston graduate, Robert Bastard [*and*] Edward May[714] constables [*of Burnham*] Norton, Edward Pearson, Paul Mawbie, Richard Lane.
Endorsed: The speches of Scabborne touching those that hurte him.
1 p. NRO MF 4/1.

Affirmation of allowance to be paid to a disabled man

1606, October 27. Memorandum that Richard Lane of Burnham Westgate this present day being the 27 day of October 1606 doth affirme a promise during the time of <his> «the» unfittnes and disability <to worke> of the sayd William Scabburne to worke for his living as in times before his hurt to allow the sayd Scabburne 2s. 6d. every weeke and that the [*sic*] Scabburne is contented therewith.

Signed: [*by mark:*] Richard Lane, Edoward Ceny, Edwarde Thurlowe, Samuele Boston.
½ p. NRO MF 4/1.

Sir John Higham and Sir Robert Jermyn to Sir Nathaniel Bacon

1606, October 30. After our harty commendacions.[715] Thes are to advertize yow that Mistres Pennyng, the wiffe of Edmunde Pennyng gent, hath byn with us at

---

[714] "Edward May": the reading is doubtful. It is possible that it should be "Man".
[715] For the previous and subsequent letters in this case, see 9 September and 1 November 1606, above, p.255, and immediately below.

Bury, & have shewed hyr great mislyke of our order <th> because we would have the land to remayne in the feoffees of trust to dispose of the profytes therof duryng the lyffe of Edmunde Pennyng the husbond only. Hyr importunytye was so great as we sent for Mr Anthony Pennyng to come to us to Bury [*St Edmunds*], wher we labored hym to yeld so to assuer the landes as that his brother might have the very land yt self duryng his lyffe, which we the rayther endevered to perswade Mr Anthony Pennyng to yeld unto because a cownseller at law (whom the gentel-wooman entertayned) dyd affyrme that yt might be saffely done with a proviso that yf by leas or otherwise Edmunde hyr husbond should charge the land so as a certeyne yearly rent (of leesse valew then the land) should not be reserved that then the landes should returne to the feoffees they to dispose of the profytes of the land to the use of Edmunde the husbond duryng his lyffe. Herupon Mr Anthony Pennyng desyered to be advised by his cownsell, who fully resolved us, that yf the land were assuered for lyffe <as> of the husbond as yt should be to the wiffe, with remaynder to the issue etc. that then the husbond & wiffe might by recovery cut of the intayle, & so in short tyme, the husbondes estate would quyckly be over-throwen. The gentelwoman mislyked of this, & urged us to a certifycate, and we perceyvyng hyr disposytion & that nothyng wyll content hyr but the sale of the land, we have in a letter set downe the wholl truth & asserteyned my Lord Chancellor therof, whereto yf yow lyke we pray yow to subscribe, to prevent the malytios purpose of the wooman. And so we betak yow to God this 30 of October 1606. Your very lovyng fryndes.

Signed: Jo[*hn*] Heigham, Rob[*er*]te Jermyn. *In John Higham's hand.*
Addressed: To the right worshipfull our lovyng frynd Sir Nathanyell Bacon knight.
Endorsed in Martin Man's hand: Sir R. Jermyn & Sir Jo. Heigham concerning Pennynge.
1 p. Folger L.d.378.

Sir Nathaniel Bacon to Sir John Higham and Sir Robert Jermyn

1606, November 1. Sirs, I have perused the certificate sent unto me under your handes, touching the cause betwene Mr Antonie Penninge and Mr Edmond Penninge his brother and have considered allso of your letter written unto me, and yet I muste intreate you to excuse me, though I forbeare now to joyne in the cer-tificate. You have had your judgmentes satisfied by hearinge the parties on both sides to speake before you, and it maie be, I shall be of your judgment, when I heare the like. But I am doubtfull at this present, how to judge of this pointe *viz.* how farre forth Edmonde Penninge shalbe barred duringe his life. I allowe well, that he be barred to doe no acte to overthrowe the inheritance, and this semed upon our firste meetinge to be agreed upon betwene us, and the other pointe was lefte doubtfull. Therfore I thinke it beste, that a cause of this importance be at London determined upon wher the best councell in lawe maie be had, and where you Sir John Heigham and I are like shortely to meete, and then upon more advice, we maie certifie Sir Roberte Jermi[*n*]e what ther falleth out best to be allowed upon and in the meane tyme the causes maie rest as they be. Thus I hartely comende you both to the grace and favour of God. From Stifkey this firste of <October> November 1606. Your very lovinge frinde.[716]

Signed: Na[*thaniel*] Bacon. *Copy in William Sanders' hand.*
Endorsed: Copy of a letter to Sir John Heigham an[*d*] Sir Robert Jermyn.
1 p. Folger L.d.110.

Certificate. Sir Nathaniel Bacon to Sir Edward Coke, Chief Justice of Common Pleas

1606, November 5. My duty remembred unto your Lordship. Whereas it pleased you at the late Assis in Norfolk to referre unto me «(with the consent of the parties <then [*word illegible*] > ««then being [*?*]present »»)» <certayn> the causes in «suite &» varyaunce <& suite> depending betwen Robert Bullen Robert Laseby & one Thomas Shaxton,[717] wherupon the tryall of severall «writtes of» *nisi prius* «then» brought downe by Laseby & Shaxton against Bullen were by your Lorships order staide after a verdict was passed for Bullen against Laseby « <at the said Assis>» <Now yt may please you to be advertised> «These are <now> to signifye unto your Lordship» that the said Bullen notwithstanding <his consent given to abide my order «arbitrement»> refuseth to enter into bonde to performe <the same> «my arbitrement as touching the matter passed by verdict <for him> as befor then befor you» <as> «which» your Lordship also <ordered>«referred to be ordred & Bullen assented therto» so as <the> «my» proceding <to arbitrement> «betwen them» is thereby stayd. Thus <much referring> «leaving» the cause to your Lordships further consideracion, I take my leave. From Stifky this <16> 5 of November 1606. [718]

Your Lordships at comandement.

Unsigned. Draft in Martin Man's hand.
Endorsed: Certificate *inter* Bullen & Lasby to my Lord Coke.
½ p. Folger L.d.113.

Counterpart of lease. Sir Nathaniel Bacon to John Dickerson, blacksmith

1606, November 14. *Calendar*: indenture dated 14 November 4 James. Sir Nathaniel Bacon of Stiffkey, knight, lets to John Dickerson of Stiffkey, blacksmith, a built tenement in Stiffkey with a smith's shop or forge, a little walled yard, and a piece of ground 42 ft. broad lying to the north. The premises lie next to Cattes Lane on the west and Sir Nathaniel's land called Guildhall Yarde on the east, and abut on the king's highway to the south and land of Mary Baker, widow, to the north. The lease is for 16 years from Michaelmas last, at 30*s.* a year payable at Lady Day and Michaelmas. Certain tools (or their value) are to be delivered up with the buildings in good repair at the end of the lease.

---

[716] This is a response to the letter from Higham and Jermyn of 30 October 1606, immediately above.
[717] All three parties were of Bale.
[718] For further proceedings in this arbitration, see Certificate of 2 November 1607, below, p.300.

At the foot: "A particuler note of the implementes and tooles above mencioned with the value of them.

A payer of bellowes at	5*s*.
A bickiron at	3*s*.
Two payer of tonges	18*d*.
Two vices	7*s*.
One poynting stake	12*d*.
A broken stithe[719]	4*s*.
A grindston cranke[720]	20*d*."

Witnesses to sealing and delivery: Martyn Man, John Walker.[721]
Signed by mark and sealed. Probably in Martin Man's hand.
Endorsed in Martin Man's hand: Counterpart of a lease to John Dickerson of a tenement in Stifkey. *Redditus per annum 30s.*
1 p. NRO NNAS S2/16/26.

Reply to the grievances of the House of Commons

[*1606, November 19*].[722] *Summary:* "A memorial of such resolucions as his Majesty hath taken with the advise of his Pryvy Counsell, assisted with the two Cheef Justices the Lord Chief Baron and his Majesties counsell at law, upon examynacion of those greevances which were presented to his Majesty by the lower howse of Parlyament at the last session". Answers are given to sixteen grievances concerning: patents for fines and other payments granted to Lord Danvers and Sir John Gylbert, to Sir Roger Aston, and to Sir Henry Bronker [*Bruncard*], including Greenwax payments[723] from the tenants of the Duchy of Lancaster; licences to sell wine by retail at a higher price; patent allowing use of a mixture of logwood or blockwood for dyeing; raising the rate of the customs; impositions on currants and on tobacco; patent to the Duke of Lennox for searching and sealing the new draperies;[724] charges that sheriffs are put to on rendering their accounts; mustermasters;[725] pre-emption of tin; making of blue starch; purveyance; transportation of iron ordnance and bullets; digging or working of saltpetre.

Undated. Unsigned. Copy.
Endorsed: [*1: in Martin Man's hand*] His Majesties aunswer to the grievaunces. [*2*]

---

[719] "Bickiron", "stake" and "stithe" are all types of anvil. "Stake" is a small portable anvil used for items such as nails (Yaxley, *Glossary*, p.199).

[720] A detachable handle for turning the grindstone.

[721] John Walker of Stiffkey, a household servant to Nathaniel Bacon for 28 years until Bacon's death in 1622 (TNA, PRO C 21/K7/7). He was resident in Bacon's house until he married in 1594 and had become coachman by 1597. In 1614 he was described as "yeoman" when he leased 2 acres in Stiffkey from Nathaniel (Stiffkey Database; NRO BRA 926/63, 372X9). In later years an overseer of the poor and churchwarden, he emerges as a reliable servant who intergrated Bacon's household with the local community (NRO MC 1872/23, 24, 26, 866X2).

[722] Dating: dated from *CJ*, i, pp.316–18.

[723] Profits from judicial proceedings (see Somerville, *Duchy of Lancaster*, p.66).

[724] See Breviate of ?early April, 1606, above, p.226.

[725] A matter of concern within Norfolk. See, for example, Howard to the deputy lieutenants, 15 September 1605, above, p.208.

A 64 pound weight of wool 4*d*. subsidy.
16 pp. NRO RAY (6) 44. Printed, *CJ*, i, pp.316–18.

Manor of Methwold. Bailiff's account

[*Post 1606/7, January 6*].[726] *Summary*: The account of Francis Rayman, bailiff of Methwold, for the half year ending Michaelmas 1606, annotated by Martin Man.

    The account shows assize rents totalling £8 17*s*. 9*d*. These include outrents paid for a whole year. Profits of court received from Christopher Reve,[727] entry fines and strays (a steer and a lamb) total £5 16*s*. 6*d*. Disbursements amounted to £4 13*s*. 5*d*. and two payments of £9 10*s*. and 10*s*. 10*d*. were made to Martin Man as *receptor domini* on 12 October 1606 and 6 January 1606/7. A further account gives rents uncollected, namely 55*s*. 10¼*d*. from Methwold for the half year, 3 combs 3 bushells of corn rent for the year, 13*s*. 9*d*. outrents from Waterwell[728] and 19*s*. ½*d*. from Hilgay for the year.

Endorsed in Martin Man's hand: Compotus Francisci Raymond pro dimidio anno finito ad Michaelem 1606.
6 pp. NRO MC 1872/16, 866X2. Listed, *Supplementary Stiffkey Papers*, p.38.

Christopher Grimston to Sir Nathaniel Bacon

1606/7, January 14. Good sir Mr Willowghby Mr Atho and my self mett att London concerninge Helgay.[729] Mr Atho mutch urged a decre out of the Dutchy which I answered was but *quousque* and that now by the copies his Majesties title did better apear. The conclusion was that Mr Willowghby mutch desiered inclosure, referringe him self and tenantes to Mr Atho who shuld supply his place. I would earnestly pray your presence ther and would apoynt the time att sutch time as might be best to your likinge befor which time I will attend you as I had now don but that I am sent for. Thus with my hartiest commendacions I rest. Yours att command.
    xiiii January.

Signed: Chr[*istopher*] Grimeston. *Holograph*.
Addressed: To the right worshipfull my approved frend Sir Nath[*aniel*] Bacon at Stufky.
Endorsed in Martin Man's hand: Grimston. January 1606.
1 p. Folger L.d.323.

Privy Council to the subsidy commissioners

1606/7, January 17. After our very harty commendacions. We are very sory to have just cause to write unto you in a matter wherein both his Majestie and our selves in steede of thankes for your expected travell doe justly thinke you worthy of

---

[726] Dating: dated from internal evidence.
[727] The steward for the manor.
[728] Upwell, Outwell and Welney, on the eastern edge of the fens near Hilgay.
[729] See 6 July 1606, above, p.246, and 26 September 1607, below, pp.290–1.

blame and reprehention for your careles and remisse proceedinge in the assessment of the first paiment of the first subsidie, to the great diminishinge of that valewe which his Majestie had reason to expect should rather have bene increased in regarde of his extraordinarie urgent occacions to use money both towardes the paiment of the loane and for other great debt of the Crowne wherof we knowe you cannot be ignorant, the valewe of your late certificates appearinge to be much lesse then in former tymes except the remaine of the late subsidie graunted in the <tyme> Quenes tyme deceased and paid in the first yeare of his Majesties reigne, wherin allso what partiall course was held the bookes them selves with the other of the former tymes doe make manifeste by the multitudes of abatementes and those of manie of the principall and wealthyest of the countie, which president you have now followed as it seemeth in your last assessment, a thing so full of private respectes and prejudice to his Majestie as we must tell you that it makes you unexcusable when it shall be brought in question. But for that it maie be you will indevour to transferre the fawlt from your selves to the sessors or presentors whose billes you were to receive, and so to passe the assessment, it is fitte you knowe that this maie no waie excuse you, well knowinge the authoritie geven you by Act of Parliament as well to punish by waie of fine all such particuler assessors as allso to reject such bills, and to inquire of and examin ther better valewes as by the Act is prescribed, which if you had done and made some example by punishment, no doubt the service had better succeded, and yet without anie just greivance of the inferiour sorte.

And wher some of your selves commissioners of the subsidie and other commissioners of the peace being seassed at so extreme lowe rate farre under your knowne valewes cann be but a spetiall cause of your connivencie in others who might take themselves to be the [*word deleted*] harder dealt with if they should be sett above or equall with you, beinge of your owne rancke, wee thinke it nott convenient that anie of your selves or anie in commission of the peace though some of them be [?]towardes the lawe, be from henceforth sett under £20 land at the least. And therfore if wee finde anie assessment under that valewe his Majesties meaninge and resolucion is to forbeare them herafter eyther in that service as justices of the peace or any other of trust and credit, nothinge beinge more offensive and scandalous in all this kinde of service then that men of place and valewe should «be rated so much to spare themselvs with their owne» so little benefite and so apparant great prejudice to and losse to his Majestie. We find likewise your books filled «up» with multitudes sett out at 20s. and which beinge the very lowest rate, wee maie with reason conceive to growe out of parciallytie and favour to the parties so assessed though manie of them are not persons landed but farmors artificers and tradesmen, and consequently to be done with intent to defraude his Majestie being but halfe the valewe of £3 goodes as you knowe which is allso expedient to be reformed.

The like abuse is allso comitted in makinge up your books at your metinge wher it is not meant anie person of what degree or qualitie soever should allwaies chalenge the doinge therof to himselfe for anie respect whatsoever nor that anie alteracion or abatement be made in anie sorte but with the generall consent, and that upon juste cause of all the commissioners presente at the assessement. And that the same books be by tourne made up by the clarkes of such commissioners as shall be present and attende the service.

And wher allso divers persons of good estate and abilitie doe eyther of purpose or by chaunce, as their other occacions doe require remove them selves from the places wher their abilities are beste knowne into other sheires and places wher their estate is not so well understode, and this beinge done before the tyme of the taxacion of the subsidies, and they gettinge certificates from the other places of their knowne abilities doe therby defraude the trewe intent of the Act by gettinge themselves to be sett at very lowe and under valewes, wher by the Act, ech ought to be sett and taxed, wher he and his familie were resident for the moste parte the yeare next before such taxacions, and not elswher not beinge commissioners. Thes are to require you to looke carefully to it, that the taxacion maie be made accordingly, and that you make no certificates for anie that are taxed before you, except for such only as have made their residence with their family in the place wher they are taxed by the moste parte of the yeare next before such taxacion. And for such as have removed from their former habitacions and yet have made their residence with their famyly in the place wher they are taxed by the space of one yeare next before such taxacion, we require you to take a dewe examination of such according to the Acte, wherby they maie in no wise falle from that which they were sett or taxed in their former taxacions of that or other subsidies [*except*] wher you shall finde juste cause of their decaies.

And wher you are to nominate the assessors and to assesse them it shall be very requisite that according as the Acte doth prescribe, you appointe such in every place to be assessors as are moste able and discrete and those to be a competent nomber and that your selves according to the Acte assesse them at reasonable and convenient rates. And for our better satisfaccion of your good service herin wee advise you to put the adicion of Sessor to the name of every assessor whereby we maie be certefied from the Exchequer by the estreates to be sent thither how the assessors them selves of every township or place are sett. Another kinde of practise as straunge as the reste is allso much put in use by the inhabitantes of sondry townes and parishes amongst whome some one or two only are usually presented and assessed in subsidie and all the rest contribute to that chardge, and by this meanes are exempted from this paiment of any subsidie savinge that smale porcion which they so contrybute, whereas in truth manie of those inhabitantes are of sufficient abilitie to be assessed, and paie with the rest that are so assessed, an abuse such and so greate as is fitt to be moste severely reformed and punished. We might remember unto you manie other undue courses held by <you both> you the commissioners as in the like manner in the assessors to the hindrance of this so important service, but wee forbeare the same in hope your future indeavours will geve testimonie of your more care and diligence in a matter of such consequence wherof his Majestie intendeth to take an accompte and so make his judgment of every mans good or yll desert.

And lastly because divers of you the commissioners are of the Parliament house, and therfore your best indeavours is to be imployed before your cominge out of the countrye, it is very needefull that your firste sittinge be before the firste of Februarie and that the commission be therupon proceded in as you maie not faile to send unto us by the v of March next cominge in wrytinge aswell the severall rates at which your selves the commissioners are assessed and allso of all such as are knightes or in commission of the peace for those partes which you are to deale with, that wee maie perceive how farreforth this admonition hath prevailed with you and therby to be able to geve his Majestie the better satisfaccion in his Majesties service. And so we bid you hartely farewell. From the courte at Whitehall the 17 of Januarie 1606.

Postscript. Wee doe well consider that in the laste clause of our letters touchinge the tyme of settinge and sendinge certificates we have foreprised the tyme precisely lymited by the statute which beinge in regarde to the extraordinarie occacion of speede in the service in the cominge of some of you to the Parliament <who> we wish <is> it maie to be observed, if not, yet the spediest tyme to be taken. Your very loving frendes. [*Signed:*] Thomas Elsmere *Canc.*, Gilbert Shrewsburie, Thomas Dorset, H. Northamton, Edw. Worcester, Thomas Suffolk, E. Wotton, Salisbury, John Stanhope, Popham.

Copy.
3½ pp. *stained.* NRO RAY 270. Printed, *Stiffkey Papers*, pp.78–82.

Order by Sir Nathaniel Bacon in a suit between Augustine Bretland and William Muskett

1606/7, January 20. *Calendar:* A suit in the Duchy Chamber between Augustine Bretlande, plaintiff, and William Musket, defendant, has been referred to Nathaniel Bacon with the consent of both parties. Bacon adjudges that at or before Our Lady next, whenever Bretlande gets Musket to surrender his rights in a tenement with "orteyearde" (vegetable/fruit garden) in Fakenham held of the manor of Fakenham, Bretlande shall pay Musket £3 6s. 8d., and the same sum at Christmas next. This will be in full satisfaction of money due under any cause now depending in the Chamber; and at the time of the first payment Bretlande shall give good security for the second. Dated 20 January 1606.

Signed: Na[*thaniel*] Bacon.
Endorsed in Martin Man's hand: Order *inter* Bretland & Muskett.
½ p. BL Add. 63081 ff.92–93.

Examination in a case of paternity

1606/7, January 25. The examinacion of Emme Howse taken the 25 daie of January 1606 before Sir Nathaniell Bacon knight.

Shee saith that shee is with childe by one Thomas Emerson who used her bodie last, a forthnight before Lammasse last, at which tyme shee dwelt with John Dey of Old Walsingham, and Emerson with Thomas Bullock, and that he did not use her since.

Shee saith that shee founde her self to be with childe before Michaelmas last, and shee never made it knowen to anie til about a forthnight since, to her mistres, who suspected her to be with childe, & asked her the question.

Shee saith that since the tyme that Emerson used her, shee neither sawe him nor sent to him, nor he to her till about a sevenight since, at which tyme shee went to him to tell him of it. And he denyed the fact.

Shee saith that her fryndes were unwilling to have Emerson marrye her. And this matter for mariage with him was moved about Whitsontide last and then not liked of by her fryndes.

Signed: Na[*thaniel*] Bacon. *In Martin Man's hand.*
Endorsed: Ex[*aminatio*] *Emme Howse de bastardia per Emerson.*
½ p. NRO NRS 24659, 125X3.

Sir Nathaniel Bacon to Sir Edward Coke, Chief Justice of Common Pleas

1606/7, January 26. It maie please your Lordship to be advertised, that certayn causes be appointed to be dealt in at the Assises next «in» which, bicause thei be of some importaunce, and I make doubt, that your Lordship maie faile of your being in the contrey yf the Parliament be not the soner ended, I desire to receave your Lordships direction, whether you will be pleased to have them proceeded in in your absence, or rather respited untill the somer Assises. For in two of the causes no justice of peace «of the countie» besides my self, hath dealt in the examinacion <of them> and in the third, which is the widdow Cookes, onely Mr Gwynne was a litle acquaynted therwith, and manie poore persons are <to be> «bounde & to be» bound, as witnesses, which if your Lordship shall so allowe maie be newly bounde to the somer Assises «before my comming up to the Parliament» and so spared from travell to thes Lent Assises. The first cause is concerning the rape, «for» which James Poynter clerk was indyted before your Lordship in somer last, and then no witnesses were bounde over, bicause the tyme of his comyng to aunswer the cause, was uncertayn.[730] The second cause is touching the Widdow Cooke, for the poysoning of hir husbond, and about 14 witnesses, wherof many be poore, are bounde to give evidence.[731] The third cause is against one William Wursted of Sidestrond,[732] upon suspicion of murthering his wife, and he is indyted by the crowners inquest, and divers poore <men> «women» bounde to give evidence. Myne owne attendance <upon> «at» the hearing of the causes will be necessary,

[730] Agnes Cooper, widow, and Priscilla Cooper, spinster, of Blakeney, had been bound over on 22 and 23 July 1606 to appear at the next Assizes in order to accuse James Poynter of rape. Priscilla Cooper was bound over again, along with Margaret Cooper, spinster, and John Cooper, mariner, on 5 February 1606/7 (Bacon memoranda book 1602–7, NRO BL/BC/5/22, pp.82, 98). But evidently the case was postponed again to the summer Assizes of 1607, when Priscilla and two other female witnesses were bound over on 8 July and Hill the constable of Blakeney ordered to come to Stiffkey 3 or 4 days before the Assizes "to be directed for the womens conduction etc" (Bacon recognizance book 1607–21, Folger V.a.273, p.7).

[731] See Coke to Bacon, October 1606 <-Ө-> 26 January 1606/7, above, pp.257–8.

[732] Eleven witnesses from Sidestrand, Northrepps and Trimingham had been bound over between 28 and 30 December 1606 to appear at the Assizes to give evidence against William Worsted. The majority of the witnesses were women; James Matchet, rector of Mundesley and Trimingham, was one of three men named. (Bacon memoranda book 1602–7, NRO BL/BC/5/22 pp.93–4).

and my <attendance> «service» at the Parliament may be occasion of my absence, and «even» the last fact of Wurstedes is not so apparant but the judge had neede to have informacion. Therefore, if it may please your Lordship upon consideracion of these reasons, which I have set downe, to signify your pleasure unto me, I shall pursue such direction as you shall give. Otherwise I shall let the causes rest as thei bee, and upon the appearance of the witnesses at the Assises thei maie then be bounde over agayne, as it shall seeme good to him, who shall governe the cort, «& yet I rather wish that the witnesses, in respect of ther povertie & farre travell might be spared, untill ther service shold be used». Thus holding it my dutie to put your Lordship in remembrance of thes <causes> «thinges», I comytt you to the keping of Almightie God. From Stifky this [*blank*]. Your Lordships at commandement.

Unsigned. Draft in Martin Man's hand, with alterations in Nathaniel Bacon's hand. Endorsed: Copie of a letter to the Lord Coke 26 Jan[*uary*] 1606.
1½ pp. Folger L.d.114.

List of commissioners and divisions for the subsidy

1606/7, January 31. *Ultimo die Januarii anno domini 1606.* A devision of the shire agreed upon by the justices comissioners appointed for the taxacion of the second payment of the first subsidy graunted to his Majestie *anno 3 regni sui* into lymites as followeth.[733]

Est Flegge, West Flegge, Happing & Tunstead. Blofeild, <Walsham>, Loddon, Claveringe, Walsham, Taverham[734]

The Lord Byshopp, Sir Henry Gawdy, Sir Wm Paston, <Sir Myles Corbet>, Sir Henry Woodhouse, <Sir Thomas Berney>, Richard Jenkinson esqr, [*in another hand*] Tho Corbett esqr

Dysse, Depwade, Earsham, Henstead
Sir Henry Gawdy, Sir Arthour Hevenyngham, Sir Phillip Woodhouse, Sir Henry Hobart, Sir Thomas Knyvet, Sir Henry Clare, Sir Clippesby Gawdy, Edmond Doyley esqr

Mytford, Fowerhooe, Humbleyard
Sir Arthour Hevenyngham, Sir Phillip Woodhouse, <Sir Henry Clare>, Sir Anthony Browne, Tho. Richardson esqr

South Greenhoe, Wayland, Grymshoe, Shropham, Gilt Crosse
Sir Phillip Woodhouse, Sir Edmond Bell, Sir Edmond Mumford, Sir Clement Spilman, Sir Roberte Mansfeild, Sir Anthony Browne

Frebridg *ex parte* Marshland, Frebridg Lynne, Clackclosse
Sir Robte Mansfeild, Sir Edmond Bell, Sir Edmnd Mumford, Sir Clement Spilman, Sir Hamond le Strange, Thomas Athoe esqr

Landiche, Smethdon, Gallowe, Brothercrosse
Sir Phillip Woodhouse, Sir Anthony Browne, Sir Nathaniell Bacon, Sir

---

[733] For the background to this list, see Privy Council to the subsidy commissioners, 17 January 1606/7, above, pp.265–8.
[734] These two groups of Hundreds are taken together.

Hamond le Strange, Wm Rugge *ar*[*miger*], Jo. Pagrave *ar.*, Lord Coke, Ro. Houghton serjeant at law

South Erpingham, No[*rth*] Erpingham, Eynsforde, Holt, No[*rth*] Greenhoe
    Sir Anthony Browne, Sir Nathaniell Bacon, Wm Rugge *ar.*, John Pagrave *ar.*

On same sheet and with same endorsement and reference as a list of commissioners and assessors dated 4 August 1610.
Endorsed in Martin Man's hand: Devision & assessors.
1 p. NRO RAY 317.

Sir Robert Gardiner, Sir John Higham, and Sir Nathaniel Bacon to Thomas Egerton, Baron Ellesmere, Lord Chancellor

1606/7, March 4. *Calendar:* The signatories received a commission from the Chancery authorising them to sell such lands of Robert Cotterell[735] as would satisfy William Le Grys[736] to the sum of £807 7s. 4d. as formerly decreed by his Lordship and confirmed by Act of Parliament[737] in the last session and by another order of the court. With the consent of both parties they have dealt with one Slegge about the purchase, who offered only £700. Le Grys was willing to accept this, but they supposed the lands to be of better value, and having commiseration for Cotterell's poor estate urged Slegge to give him a further £50, which he agreed to do. But as the words of the order specify that the money is to be disposed by his Lordship, and Slegge offers his bond to this effect, they have no authority to add any conditions when they assure the land to Slegge, "whose estate wee suppose meane", and thus no certain means to relieve either Le Grys, whose poverty is also great, or Cotterell after his land is sold. All parties therefore agreed to await the Lord Chancellor's further order for assurance of the money after conveyance. Dated 4 March 1606. Signed: Robert Gardener,[738] John Heigham, Nathaniel Bacon.

[*Postscript*]: At the examination various poor creditors claimed considerable sums due to them from Le Grys, which he did not deny, and sought help in getting a settlement if Le Grys received the money. The signatories mention the matter although Le Grys said that it was not within their authority to deal with it.

On the dorse: "A note sent with the letter to my Lord Chancellor. Alter, amende, or add or diminishe at your pleasure, and subscribe my name. And by this I assent. Robert Gardener."

---

[735] Robert Cotterell of South Repps, gent (Rye, *Visitation of Norfolk*, p.87).
[736] Probably William le Grys of Brockdish (Rye, *Visitation of Norfolk*, p.188), not to be confused with the le Gros family of Crostwight (*ibid.*, pp.185–6).
[737] "An Acte for the performance and execution of a Decree in the Chauncerie made between William le Gris Plaintiffe and Robert Cottrell Defendant", no.29 in the list of Private Acts for 3 and 4 James I (1605–6). The Act had been passed by the Commons on 21 March 1605/6 and returned from the Lords with amendments on 13 May. Bacon was not involved in the committee stage. (*CJ*, i, pp.269, 275, 288, 308).
[738] Sir Robert Gardiner of Elmswell, Suffolk (d. 1620). Knighted 1591, Chief Justice of the Irish Queen's Bench and, like Sir John Higham, a Suffolk J.P. (Shaw, *Knights*, ii, p.88; MacCulloch, *Suffolk*, pp.379–80, 414).

Copy.

Endorsed: Le Grys v. Cottrill. Report to Lord Chancellor as to proceeding in this matter & negotiations for sale of C[*otterells*] land etc.

Calendared from a transcript by H. W. Saunders, NRO MC 934/1, 800X5.

Petition. Robert Cotterell to Thomas Egerton, Baron Ellesmere, Lord Chancellor

[*1606/7, March 4* <-Θ-> *19*].[739] *Calendar*: Following an Act made in the last Parliament, his Lordship ordered Sir Robert Gardner, Sir Robert Jarmyn, Sir John Higham, Sir Philipe Woodhowse and Sir Nathanell Bacone, or any three or four of them, to sell the lands and tenements of the petitioner, Robert Cottrell, in accordance with a decree of Chancery on behalf of Wylliam Legryce, plaintiff. The Act also required that money raised from his lands or his debts should be disposed of by the Chancery for performance of the decree.

Sir Robert Gardner, Sir John Higham and Sir Nathanell Bacone have now sold the land for £750, "which is a good penyworth in respecte of the hansomnes of the howsses being belte of lyme and stonne and well wooddid for the nesesarye provysion of the said howse". The land could be let for £45 per annum on a lease of 21 years. The purchasers are also to receive the half year's rent due at Our Lady next and have fifteen months to pay.

All Cottrell's debts are kept from him by Legryce, so that he has no means for his maintenance nor "so much as a beed of his owne to lye one". He desires the Lord Chancellor to consider his poverty in disposing of the money to be raised, "he being thre skore and five yere of agge and never brought up to laboure and having syxe children". *Unsigned.*

At the foot in ?Ellesmere's hand: "Yf ther «be» any cause that maye move the commissioners to have better consideracion of hym, he is to informe them of yt, and therupon they are to procede according to justice, and as the commission directeth them." *Signed*: T[*homas*] E[*llesmere*] C[*anc*].

Undated.

Endorsed: The humble petycion of Robert Cottrell.

1 p. NRO MC 571/11, 778X4.

Bargain and sale. Sir Robert Gardiner, Sir John Higham and Sir Nathaniel Bacon to Edward Slegge and Christopher Woodhouse

1606/7, March 19. *Calendar*: Indenture dated 19 March 4 James. Sir Robert Gardener, Sir John Higham, and Sir Nathanyell Bacon, knights, to Edward Slegge of Cambridge and Christopher Woodhowse of Hackney, Middlesex, gent. After a lengthy suit in Chancery between William Le Grys, plaintiff, and Robert Cottrell, defendant, it was decreed on 24 July 1601 by Sir Thomas Egerton, Lord Keeper, that Cottrell should pay Le Grys £807 7s. 4d.; and by a private Act made in the second session of this Parliament it was enacted that if Cottrell did not perform or

---

[739] Dating: dated with reference to the letter of 4 March 1606/7, immediately above, and the bargain and sale dated 19 March 1606/7, immediately below.

give security to perform this decree within three months of the session then his lands should be sold. By order of 30 October last, the three months having elapsed, the court of Chancery appointed Sir Robert Gardener, Sir Robert Jermyn, Sir John Higham, Sir Phillippe Woodhowse, and Sir Nathanyell Bacon (or any three or four of them) to make the sale. The lands could not be sold for the specified value and Gardener, Higham and Bacon now bargain and sell them to Slegge and Woodhowse for £700 to be paid in instalments, namely £300 at St John Baptist next (probably the Nativity, 24 June), £200 at All Saints following (1 November), and £200 on 1 May after that. The whole sum is to be applied according to the decree and Act of Parliament. The lands in question are the copyhold and freehold lands lying in South and North Repps, Thorpe Market, Antingham or elsewhere, of which Cottrell was seised or in which he had a beneficial interest on the first day of the first session of this Parliament.

Signatures and seals have been cut off the bottom of the document.
1 parchment, *hole in centre and torn.* NRO RAY (6) 23.

Agreement concerning the sale of Robert Cotterell's lands

1606/7, March 19. The xix day of Marche 1606. Memorandum that before the ensealing of the indentures for the sale of Robert Cotterelles lande in Norfolk to Christofer Woodhouse and Edward Slegge gent according to the Act of Parliament & by force of an order in the Chauncery yt was by William le Grys gent condiscended unto in manner following. First the lande was solde both free & coppie for £750 paiable at severall dayes as by the said indentures appeareth. Next yt was also agreed by the said Grys that £50 of the said somme should be payd by the said purchasors at two severall dayes to the said Cotterell for the relieving of his decayed estate. Thirdly the sale of the lande is made to the said purchasors with the consent of the said Grys and to be subject to the incombrances of Mr Chamberleyn & Capteyn Parker «if he cannot otherwise avoide the same by law or equity». Fourthly yt is agreed unto by the said Grys that a statut of a thowsand powndes knowledged by the said Cotterell & remaynyng in the handes of the Lord Coke shall be cancelled.

At the foot: Memorandum there was delivered into Sir John Heighams handes 3 bondes made by Mr Slegge & Mr Woodhouse to Mr Gris for £700.

Also delivered to Sir Nathaniel Bacon the counterpane of the indenture for sale of the landes abovesaid, and the peticions of Mr Cotterell & Mr Gris.

Signed: Will[*ia*]m Le Gris. *Witnesses to signing:* Jo[*hn*] Heigham, Robert Wingfeilde, Na[*thaniel*] Bacon. *In Martin Man's hand.*
Endorsed: Mr Grys his agreement.
1 p. NRO MC 571/12, 778X4.

Documents concerning the Assizes

1607, March 25 <-Θ-> 1607/8, March 24.[740] *Letter from Sir Edward Coke, " 1607, to Sir Nathaniel Bacon concerning the Norfolk Assizes and other papers s[igned] by Sir Nathaniel, etc., relating thereto".*

9 docs. Sotheby, (18–19 December 1911), lot 108.

Subsidy assessment for Gallow Hundred

1607, March 25 <-Θ-> 1607/8, March 24. *Summary:* Assessment for Gallow Hundred, 1607, rating lands at £188, goods at £81.[741]

Taken from Stiffkey Papers, p.85, note 1.

Matthew Plumb to Martin Man

1607, April 15. Mr Man. Wheras one Randell a verye pore man and one Parke his suertye, were arrested in Trinitye vacacion last at the suite of Sir Nathaniel Bacon uppon a bande of apparance when Sir Nathaniel was sheryff of Norfolk. In regarde of the povertye of the man, and that ther was noe amerciament estreated,[742] I intreated Sir Nathaniel when he was at Fakenham sessions at Michaelmas, that he wolde be pleased to staye the suite untyll his worship might be fullye satisfied whether ther wer any amerciament or not which Sir Nathaniell Bacon was contented with, and soe willed me to speake with Mr John Gibson[743] that followed the suite (from him) that all procedynges sholde ceace untyll he & I sholde mete together before Sir Nathaniel. Yet albeit I informed Mr Gibson soe mutche, Mr Gibson wolde not surceace, but in Michaelmas terme did procede & declare against bothe, and saide that he had bene with Sir Nathaniel and that he had gyven him warrant & wylled him to procede, which I informed Sir Nathaniel of in the ende of that terme, and Sir Nathaniel then saide that Mr Gibson had not bene with him, and that he had gyven noe sutche warrant to him to procede, and then alsoe willed that we sholde mete before him, which I toulde Mr Gibson of the last terme. Yett he then wolde not be perswaded to staye untyll Sir Nathaniel his comynge upp to London, but with many wordes protested that Sir Nathaniel had gyven order to procede and that he wolde procede, which he did with all the advantages that he could take, and althoughe it be the use in the Kinges Benche that if the defendant aunswere and pleade any tyme durynge the terme tyme, it is accepted & no advantage taken yett he because he had non aunswer in the begyninge of the terme, entred a judgement uppon a *nichil dicit.* And yett I had gyven a warrant to the <attorney> clarke for to pleade (*comparuit ad diem prout patet per recordum*)[744] a seavenight at

---

[740] Dating: dated from internal evidence. This may be Sir Edward Coke's reply to Bacon's letter of 26 January 1606/7 (above, pp.269–70).

[741] Dating: dated from internal evidence. Any one of three instalments of the subsidies granted in November 1605 may have been involved here. The second part of the first subsidy was due to be assessed by 20 March 1606/7, and certified by 20 April following. The first part of the second subsidy was to be assessed by 20 September 1607 and the second part of the second subsidy by 20 March 1607/8 (3 James I, c.26).

[742] That is, returned to the Exchequer to be prosecuted.

[743] See note to Referral of petition, 30 June 1606<-θ ->25 October 1613, above, p.244.

[744] "He appeared on the day as is shown by the record".

the least before thende of the terme, which aunswere was often offered Mr Gibson but he refused the same against all the course of the court, but toke all the advantage he coulde gett, which I partlye informed Sir Nathaniel of the last daye of the last terme but not then knowinge he had entred a judgement. And then againe Sir Nathaniel willed me to tell Mr Gibson he wolde speake with him and that we sholde bothe goe downe together to him to his lodginge, which I did, but Mr Gibson did often apponyte [*sic*] but never kept promyse, or if he did he never tould me of his goeinge. But nowe this Lent he have caused the pore mans suertye to be arrested uppon an execucion and <have> «there is» taken of him £6 10*s*. by Mr Gibsons appoyntment. Nowe in regard that there was no amerciament and that Sir Nathaniel was never indampnified and that the pore man that must pay all is not worth the third parte of this money that is taken, and that he vave [*have*] alsoe bene putt to greate chardges for he was once suede before & his suerty & then it was pleaded unto & then Mr Gibson surceased & went not forward, in Mr Sprattes lyfe tyme, I pray lett me request you to be a meanes to Sir Nathaniel, that he wolde yett be pleased to examyne the cause and to take it into his handes and not to gyve any warrant to the sheryff to delyver the money unto Mr Gibson untyll the cause be examyned and then I am suer Sir Nathaniel will take that course that the pore man shall not sustayne that greate wronge that otherwyse he is lyke to doe. And thus beinge overboulde to troble you & in hast I ende with my dutye remembred to Sir Nathaniel & most hartye comendacions unto your selfe I comytt you to the Almightie. From Norwich this 15 of Aprill 1607. Your frynde to use.

Signed: Mathewe Plombe.[745]
Addressed: To his verye good frynde Mr Martyne Mann at Stukey.
Endorsed in Martin Man's hand: Mr Mathew Plombe.
2 pp. Folger L.d. 473.

Memoranda concerning land at Worstead

[*Post 1607, April 23*].[746] *Calendar*: Information taken from title to four acres in Worstead, noting the following transactions:

   Grant by Robert Toppes to W. Groundsborough and others of one piece of arable land containing four acres in Dilham called Whetely Pittes with a pit at the east end. 5 Henry VIII.

   Will of Jo. Grene dated 10 April 1546.

 Confirmation by Geoffrey Yemes to Anne Grene widow of a built messuage with lands in Dilham for life. 38 Henry VIII.

 Grant by Edward Yemes to W. Pory gent of four acres of "ferrgrund" (furze ground) called Wheatly Pittes in Worstead, to take effect if Yemes does not acquit Pory against Thomas Husbond upon a bond of £40 for the payment of £22 entered into by Pory with Yemes as surety. Witnesses: Clement Pollard, Thomas Husbond junior. 28 February 1606/7.

---

[745] Matthew Plumb served as undersheriff of Norwich in 1604 (Hawes, *City Officers*, p.122).
[746] Dating: dated from internal evidence.

Grant by Edward Yemes to William Pory of Dilham gent of four acres called Wheatly Pittes with a pit in Worstead. Witnesses: Thomas Husbond junior, Andrew Glaunford, Clement Pollard. 23 April 1607.

Part in Latin. Undated. Unsigned. In Martin Man's hand.
Endorsed: A note of the writinges concerning 4 acres in Worsted belong[*ing*] to Mr Pory.
½ p. NRO RAY 271.

Account for the relief of the poor in Morston

1607, April 25. *Summary:* Account of Thomas Kinges gent and John Powdiche, chosen as overseers by the justices of the peace, and of Robert Powdyche and John Powdiche the younger, churchwardens, made to Sir James Calthorpe, J.P. Rate collected for 13 months: 47s. 9d. 14 ratepayers named. Principal contributor: Thomas Kinges gent. Expenditure: 46s. 8d. 6 poor named. In hand: 13d. "due by Peter Shorten". Town stock in the hands of Robert Powdyche: 20s.[747]

Signed: Per me Thomam Kinges, John Powdich the younger, [*by mark:*] the other John Powdich.
Endorsed: Morston account for the poore 1607.
1 p. NRO BCH 27/9/74 I (96)

Thomas Hewar and Thomas Hunston to Sir Nathaniel Bacon

1607, May 1. May yt please yow wheras we understand that ther hath ben motions maid, in the Parlayment howse for the reliefe of Somersetshire, Monmothshire of Wales, and some other partes of the West contrye, that hath sustayned losse by the late overflowing of waters, the like inundacion having happened to this poore contrye of Marshland[748] which is daylye distressed both with the raging of the sea, and fresh waters, that the inhabitantes live in great perill of ther estats, therfore our desire is that yow, being selected to have care of the good estate of the whole contrye, would be pleased to make the like mocion for us in the Parlayment howse, to which intent we have sent unto yow a trew certificate of the losses that the contrye hath sustayned both by the sea and fresh waters which is like daylye to increase, not doubting but in your especiall care of the good of this contrye, yow would doe your best indevors eyther for some contribucion to be yealded to this contrye of Marshland, owt of some other parts of the realme, who are not subject to the like daungers, or at lestwise to be eased of those usuall charges which is dayly payed out of this place, hoping that we, being in as great and daungerous estate as the other places, may by your good means have the like helpe, to be imployed for the generall good of this contrye. So not doubting of your frendly care and indevors herin, for which not only our selves shalbe much behoulden unto yow, but also the whole inhabitants much obliged for your care

---

[747] For the conventions used here, see Poor accounts of *Post* 24 April 1603, above, p.28.
[748] "Marshland": as the places named in the Petition immediately below make clear, the reference here is restricted to the Hundred of Freebridge Marshland in Norfolk and does not extend to the entire topograhical area of Marshland that straddled the boundaries with adjacent counties.

and paynes therin, refering the matter to your wise and carefull ind[*e*]vors we rest. Your lovinge frendes. Emneth this first of Maye 1607.

Signed: Your lovinge frendes Thomas Hewar,[749] Tho[*mas*] Hanston.[750]
Addressed: To the right wourshippfull our verye loving frend Sir Nathaniell Bacon knight.
1 p. NRO BL/BC/6/19.

Petition. Inhabitants of Marshland to the Knights of the Shire for Norfolk

1607, May 1. To the right wourshippfull the knightes of the shire of the cowntye of Norfolk.[751]

The inhabitantes of the poore disstressed contry of Marshland who have latly sustayned very great losses by the overflowing of the sea and freshwaters, have humbly intreated us to move yow, that in commissiracion of the poore and distressed estate of this contrye of Marshland, yow would be pleased to stand so much all our good frendes as to signify unto the honorable and high court of Parlayment the great losse & daunger which we have sustayned and are likely dayly to increce, except yt will please that honorable plase to compationate our estate and to graunt unto us some releife in this our needfull case, the which we desier yow would be pleased to indevour and solesett [*solicit*] in our behalfes. Which losses as by the particulers of everye townshipp delivered to us appeareth doth amount in the whole to the some £10,000, and more, only in the townes of Emneth, Walsoken, Westwalton, Wallpoole, Terrington, Tyllnye and Eslington. The other townes having also receyvid verye much losse the particuler wherof we doe not certaynly knowe. Emneth this first of Maye 1607.

Signed: Thomas Hewar, Tho[*mas*] Hanston, Robert Balam,[752] Andrew Ogard,[753] Francis Snell,[754] Alexan[*der*] Cockson.
Endorsed in Martin Man's hand: Peticion for relieving Marshland in regard of inundacion.
1 p. NRO BL/BC/6/20.

Examinations concerning suspected criminals at Walsingham and Hempton fairs

1607, May 26. The examinacion of Henry Hopkyns of Burnham Westgate in the said county taken before Rice Gwynne esqr the xxvi of May in the fyfth yere of the raigne of our soveraigne lord King James.

---

[749] Sir Thomas Hewar (d.1630) of Emneth, J.P. (1589 to after 1616) and knighted 1605, was much involved with the sea defences of Marshland (see *BP*, iv, *passim*; *Stiffkey Papers*, p.33; Smith, *County and Court*, p.353).

[750] Undoubtedly Thomas Hunston of Walsoken (d.1646), the son of William Hunston esq, J.P. 1569–79, who had died in 1582. Although Thomas did not succeed his father as a J.P. he was involved in the the management of the repair of the sea banks of Marshland. (Clarke and Campling, *Visitation*, i, p.105; Smith, *County and Court*, p.353; *BP*, iv, pp.235, 239).

[751] Nathaniel Bacon and Sir Charles Cornwallis.

[752] Robert Balam (aged 12 in 1592), son of Charles Balam esq. of Walsoken (Blomefield, ix, p.131).

[753] Possibly Andrew Hogard of the family of that name of Emneth (Smith, *County and Court*, p.383).

[754] Francis Snell (d.1619), rector of Walsoken from 1588 (Venn, *Al. Cant.*, iv, p.117).

Who sayeth that yesterdaye at Walsingham fayre[755] hee mett with one Nichols whome he knewe somtymes at Hertford gaole for a robbery who would not at the first knowe this examinate and therupon hee tooke acquayntance of the said Nichols and drewe him to the house of one Thomas Applegate where hee tooke a pipe of tobacco with him and renewed his said former acquayntance and thence they went to one Tompsons and other houses where they dranck together and the said Nichols at the first sayed hee was a schoolemaster within fyve myles of Norwich, but this examinate knowinge what hee was, gave no creditt therunto but urged him to discover himselfe and in the end hee putting his trust in this examinate confessed that there was some thirty of his company, wherof some were cuttpurses, but hee himselfe and some other of the company are for the highwaye. And of that company this examinate sawe at Walsingham some 15 wherfore the said Nichols sayed hee was sory they were so many as hee sayed they were so as they could doe no good but were as they sayed <smoakd> smoaked. <And after that this examinate acquaynted> And after that the said Nichols acquaynted this examinate with his wyfe who is the daughter of one Hogg a musicion of Ware [*Herts*] and the said Nichols promised this examinate that hee and his wife would goe with him to Burnham the last nighte, yet did not, but one Nicholson a younge fellowe whome they call cosen went with him thither who confessed himselfe to be one of the cuttpurses but sayed hee had no share of their purses at Walsingham and therfore desired this examinate to lend him <21*d*.> 12*d*. untill the next daie and hee confessed that dyverse purses were taken by his company wherof one with 10*s*. odd money another with 5*s*. 2*d*. or theraboutes and another with a 9*d*. and a 6*d*. and for their order that the purses are conveyed from one to another and never remayned with him that cutteth it and that they share honestly at their meeteinge. And that hee tould this examinate that there was a riche person [*or* "parson"] about Norwich whome hee desired to robbe of his estate and yf that might be effected hee would leave purse cuttinge.

The examinacion of Edward Nicholson sonne to Michaell Nicholson clerk parson of Sizeland some fyve miles from Norwich taken the daye aforesaid.

Who sayeth that hee never knewe <Nicholson> «Stephen» Nichols untyll yesterdaye about three or fower of the clock but that hee is of kynne unto him and confesseth that «he borrowed of» the said Hopkyns 12*d*. and promised him payement at the «Hempton» fayre[756] «this daye» oute of money his father <promised him> appoynted him to receave of one Parfield of Wynersham [*Wimbotsham*] towardes Downham at «the said» Hempton fayre and that hee entended to ley at Mr <Michelles> «Medcalfes» within twoo miles of this towne but hee knoweth not the towne where hee dwelleth and never sawe him, only his father willed him to repaire unto him being of his acquayntance, and that upon Sonday he laye at Ba[*w*]deswell with his cosen Nichols and his wyfe and that there was but one more there who is nowe here apprehended upon suspicion <of> but knoweth him not. And sayeth

---

[755] There were two fairs held in Walsingham. Originally one of them had been granted to the prior of Walsingham, to be held—appropriately—on the Nativity of the Virgin Mary, 8 September. Evidently it is the other fair referred to here (Blomefield, ix, pp.269–70).

[756] Hempton near Fakenham. In origin the fair had been granted to the priory there. It was held on the Tuesday in Whitsun week, and was still a "considerable" fair in the early 18th century (Blomefield, vii, p.100).

that hee never confessed to Hopkyns that so many purses were cutt or that he promised him the 12*d.* when hee had his share of them only hee confessed there was one
purse drawen which had a 9*d.* and a 6*d.* and nowe sayeth that purse was
delyvered <to> againe to the owner yet the said Hopkyns being face to face <this
examinate confessed> «justyfied» every point and that hee never spake to him of any
money he was to receyve of any man at the fayre but that hee promised payement
«oute» of his share which he was to have and that hee never spake of Mr
<Michelles> «Medcalfes» that hee heard.

Stephen Nichols of Ely in the county of Cambridge the daye aforesaid «examined»
sayeth, that upon Monday was seavennighte hee came from Ely to Thetford where
hee remayned two dayes at Mistres Snellinges and from thence went to Wyndham
where hee laye one night being Wednesdaye at the Gryffin and thence went to
Newton Bridge[757] where hee remayned untill <Thursdaye> Satterday in hope of
preferment to be a teacher to wryte by one Petingalls meanes of the same towne
who not standing to his promis in preferring of him he went to Norwich on
Satterdaye where hee remayned all Sondaye and upon Monday he came from
Norwich to Walsingham being yesterdaye and the fayre daye which hee knewe not
untill hee came neere to the place by the intercourse of people and from thence
went to <Creak> South Creake and there laye at Mr Michelles house all nighte and
had in company with him his wyfe his brother and another here present whome he
knoweth not whoe overtooke him his wyfe and brother neere Norwich in the waye
to Walsingham, but the mans name he knoweth not nor what hee is and that from
Creake they came to Hempton fayre this daie understandinge therof at Creake and
the rather for that hee was to receave money of one Wright of Lynne who «as» hee
was enformed would be at the fayre. And for the last examinate Nicholson hee
sayeth hee never sawe him untyll this daye that hee sawe him in Hopkyns company
and that hee knoweth no kyndred between him and the said Nicholson for they be
not one name and his first acquayntance with Hopkyns was at Hertford gaole
where the said Hopkyns was a prisoner «but this examinate never prisoner there»
and that hee mett him at Walsingham fayre yesterday when the said Hopkyns
tooke acquayntance of him when they dranck beere and tobacco at sundry houses
and sayeth hee affirmed no such thinge to the said Hopkyns as he chargeth him
withall in his examinacions touchinge his consortes.

Edward Ward examined sayeth hee mett Nicholson yesterday morninge he
knowth not where, nor where hee laye upon Sondaye at nighte last nor upon
Satterdaye but upon Frydaye hee laye at Dickleburrough and hee never sawe
Nicholson before yesterdaye morninge, and that they laye together the last nighte
but knoweth not where.

Signed after each deposition: Rice Gwynne.
Endorsed in Martin Man's hand: Ex[*aminations*] Henry Hopkins, Edward
Nicholson, Steven Nicholls, Edward Warde *coram Ricardo Gwyn armigero*.
3 pp. Brewer.

[757] Newton Flotman or Trowse Newton; probably the latter, on the outskirts of Norwich.

Depositions concerning suspected criminals at Walsingham and Hempton fairs

1607, May 27. *Calendar*: Examinations taken before Sir Nathaniel Bacon on 27 May 1607 of Edward Nicholson of Sisland, of Stephen Nicholles of Iver, Buckinghamshire, of William Mosse of Olney ("Onley"), Northants, of William Craforde, of Edward Warde of Needham Market and of Frances Nicholles, wife of Stephen.[758]

Edward Nicholson says that his age is a little over twenty, and he was apprenticed to one Dowglasse of Bungay as a linen weaver. After serving seven years he finished his apprenticeship at Easter last and has since lived with his father at Sisland. He came here from Norwich to receive 40*s*. from one Parfitt of "Waymerstone" (Wimbotsham) who had promised his father to meet him at Hempton fair, but he did not find him there.

Stephen Nicholles says that his age is about twenty-six. He was brought up to draw and as a scrivener and was sometime a scholar in Oxford. For the half year past he has lived in Ely. Before that he kept shop for a year as a drawer in Golding Lane in London. He married the daughter of Hogge of Ware two years ago last midsummer. Asked why he brought his wife with him, he said that she came with him to see him settled as a school teacher in this country. About Newton Bridge he has acquaintance, but not about Hempton. At Walsingham fair he met Henry Hopkins who acquainted him with several of the country and "tould him of a great lyvinge was fallne unto him". He says he was never a prisoner in Hertford gaol and only came there to see Hopkins; but reconsidering says that he was indicted, came in upon bail and was acquitted there about two years since on a charge of highway robbery. He says that he was not acquainted with anyone at Hempton fair yesterday except Nicholson, Hopkins and one Warde from Suffolk.

William Mosse says that his age is about twenty, and that he was brought up as a linen draper under his father in Northamptonshire, with whom he came to London. He was sent to Hempton fair to seek one Atkins, a servant of his father's who had stolen some goods, but as he is a stranger here he cannot produce a witness. He was at Walsingham fair first and then Hempton.

William Craforde says he is half-brother to Stephen Nicholles, came from the Low Countries about six weeks ago, and came into Norfolk from Ely to accompany his brother. They left Ely "Mondaie was seaven night", reached Walsingham fair last Monday about 2 o'clock and went on to Hempton fair next day. When he left Ely he "had 20*s*. on his brother wherwith he mainteyned his chardge".

Edward Warde says he came from Suffolk to reclaim a debt from one Thornton of North Walsham. He is a clothier by trade, and has been out of his apprenticeship at Ipswich for four years. He has no acquaintance at Walsingham

---

[758] Each examination is recorded on a separate sheet, and their order is therefore conjectural. Nicholson's was clearly taken first, as his deposition carries the date. The names of the other witnesses are listed on the dorse of his evidence, in the order followed here. That Frances Nicholls was the last witness is borne out by the fact that Man's endorsement is on her statement. The examinees were remanded to the gaol and Henry Hopkins of Burnham Westgate was bound over in £10 to inform against them at the next Assizes (27 May 1607, Bacon memoranda book 1602–7, NRO BL/BC/5/22, p.102).

or Hempton, though he was at both fairs. He met Nicholles last Monday near Walsingham, and had only seen him before at Ipswich three years ago, and did not know him in any gaol or at London.

Frances Nicholles says that she is the daughter of Hogge, minstrel at Ware, and that she has been married three years on the Monday after midsummer. Her husband lay in Hertford gaol only two or three nights before his acquittal, and was removed there from Newgate. Otherwise neither of them was ever in gaol. She knew Warde only because he fell into their company between Norwich and Bawdeswell. In London, after living in Goulding Lane for a year, she and her husband had lived in Shoe Lane for half a year before moving to Ely about six months ago.

Signed after each deposition: Na[*thaniel*] Bacon. *In William Sanders' hand.*
Endorsed in Martin Man's hand: Examinacions of Nicolson & others suspected to be cutpurses.
6 pp. Folger X.d.346. Examination of Stephen Nicholles reproduced and transcribed, *Elizabethan Handwriting, 1500–1650*, ed. G. Dawson and L. Kennedy-Skipton (New York, 1966), pp.88–9.

Bargain and sale. Martin Man to William Feake

1607, June 1. *Calendar:* Martin Man of Stiffkey, yeoman, bargains and sells to William Feake of Holt Market, linenweaver, two pieces of land lying together in Stiffkey and amounting to 3½ roods, formerly of Barnabas Banyerd deceased. The land lies between the free close of Robert Skynner late of Barnabas north, unfree land late of Barnabas south, Le Greeneway west, and the common way from Stiffkey to Morston east. Man had acquired the property from the four daughters and co-heirs of Barnabas, namely Alice wife of Robert Skynner, Joan wife of William Kinge, Grace wife of William Feake and Mary wife of John Pells, by deed dated 8 March 1606/7 and fine levied the quindene of Easter 1607. Dated 1 June 1607.

Latin. Signed and sealed: Martinus Man. Seal missing.
Endorsed with memorandum of livery of seisin on the same day.
Witnesses to livery: Thom[*a*]s Kinges, John Framyngham, Edmund Munford, Rob[*er*]t Framyngham.
1 parchment. NRO RAY 272.

Recognizance book

1607, June 1 – 1621, April 13. *Summary:* Entries consisting mainly of recognizances to keep orderly alehouses, to keep the peace and to appear at sessions[759] held for the Hundreds of North Greenhoe, Brothercross, Gallow, Holt, North and South Erpingham, Smithdon and Taverham, and those held at Fakenham, Walsingham and Norwich Castle, at the general sessions and at the Assizes. Also

---

[759] A reference to the petty sessions, by now—as this document makes clear—held within each double limit.

including committals to gaol and occasional related matters such as a shipwrecked
mariner at Burnham and wife beating in 1608 (p.52), problems with the poor rate
at Cley in 1616 (p.116), an accusation of witchcraft against Beatrice the wife of Jo.
Rumbold of Holt in 1619 (p.153), and bastardy cases and apprenticeships.

In Martin Man's and William Sanders' hands.
190 pp. Folger Ms V.a.273.

John Rooke to Sir Nathaniel Bacon

[*1607*], **June 13.**[760] Right worshipffull as my humble dutye bindethe me every
daye to praye for your prosprous estat withe my good ladye whoe I praye to God
to contynewe you bothe together withe longe lyffe and happye dayes to your harts
dessire and comfort of all them that wishe you well. Good Ser Nathaniell Bacon as
I have ever fownd your worshipe lovinge and kinde to me so I beseche you for
Godes sake to stand my worshipffull good master to conffere withe Mr Trenche[761]
concerninge me at this tyme. Ser maye yt pleasse to understand the casse rightly.
You knowe that on Worstead was attached for killinge his wiffe. Mr Trenche
sending for me to Norwiche wher he laye to charge me to make hast home agayne
to ceisse the goodes that wer Worsteades and did undertak to save me harmles.
Good ser amongst other goodes ther was growinge upon the grownd five acers of
whett and rye whiche my Lord Cook his man did by advice challenge to be my
Lordes and did com to me to tell me that yt did belonge to his master therffor
willed me not to medle withe yt. I sent to Mr Trenche to acquaynt him with
[th]esse speches and Grime my Lordes man did cary my letter and ment upon
[pu]rposse to conffer withe him at my request about yt but Mr Trenche forbode
[Gri]me not to medle withe the corne for yt did belonge to him and that he would
[d]effend me agaynst all men that wold mak any challenge to yt and so sent me a
nother letter by my Lordes man withe speciall words to get yt felled and caried to
some howsse fittinge to kepe yt only to his usse and he wowld deffend «me»
agaynst all men. I did acordinge to his dereccions and the corne was by Mr Trenche
his assignment th[r]esshed and by his men and hired a cart and caried to Aylsham
and I <not> medled not withall since yt was caried and layed in the barne. Well
presently after my Lord sent proces agaynst me Mr Trenche cawssed Mr Blowfeild
to put in bayll and afterward cawssed him to conffes yt and then cam downe a writ
of inquiry of damages to the sheriffe. Mr Trenche was then at Walsham him selff
to followe the casse and nowe he have suffered me to be arested upon execucion
and redye to be caryed to Ip[s]wiche Jayll but have gotten frindes to staye «me»
untyll I have answer from him howe he will deall withe me and therffor I most
humbly besseche your worshipe to conffere withe Mr Trenche howe he will deall
withe me for my discharge whiche must be presently. Yt ys a great [?]discreted [*dis-
credit*] to me bessides my losse of tyme in my procedinges therffor I besseche your

---

[760] Dating: Nathaniel Bacon mentions the indictment against William Worstead of Sidestrand for the
murder of his wife in a letter to Chief Justice Coke of 26 January 1606/7 (above, pp.269–70) and the
accused was probably convicted at the following Lent assizes.
[761] "Mr Trench": possibly John Trench of Barney. From his actions, he would appear to be either the chief
constable of the Hundred or to be operating on behalf of the coroner's office.

worsshipe for Godes sake to move him very erneslye to send me mony for to discharg yt or els to mak an end withe Mr Bullen her in the cowntrye and so get a discharg to the shriffe for me and let me not leye in the jayll to be utterly undone and this hopinge of your worships favour and love toward «me» I hope to r[e]ceive present answer to my joye and comfort by your worshipe good meanes.

And I besseche your worshipe to stand my good master for the grantinge of a newe licence for my howsse [*alehouse*] to my wyffe nowe at this sessions. I was in Norffolk at this Whitsontid and conffered with Mr Kempe[762] who willed me to com to Norwiche to have my lycenc renewed and cary my suerties whiche I did and moved the matter to Mr Knevet[763] who answered me that it must be granted by thosse justices of the same limit that did grant yt the last yeare and that your worshipe was on withe Ser Henry Sydnye at Facknem [*Fakenham*] and I acquaynted Mr Knevet that I was to be in Suffolk at oure sessions that very day and he promysed me that yff my wyff cam ther showld be some cowrsse taken that Mr Kempe showld take the bond as sone as the tearme was ended when I cam into Norffolke and I beseche «you» let me have your worshipe furtherance in my behalf in regard it have bene contynewed withe my howss and becawsse I have layed out a great deall of mony in a brewhowsse with other furnitur belonginge to the furnishinge of my howsses hoping your worshipe will have dewe consideracion of me.

I beseche your worshipe give me leave once agayne to move you to make a mocion for me to Bowlton of Wells for the inne the widowe dwelt in and if your worshipe will stand my good master herin I knowe I shal have yt. I wowld willingly by yt yff he wowld sell yt yff not I will give him a good rent for yt and pay him his mony every halffe year beffor hand and yff he will have suerties I can put him in bond in five hundred powndes and this dessiringe your worshipe furtherance hearin I in this and many others kindnes heartoffore have fownd do still dayly praye for your worshipe longe and prosperous dayes. From Melton in Suffolke this xiii of June. Your poor orator for ever to comand.

Signed: John Rooke.[764] *Holograph.*

Addressed: To the right worshipfull Ser Nathaniell Bacon.

Endorsed in Martin Man's hand: John Rooke.

1 p. *page torn in upper l.h.s.* NRO RAY 477.

John Kemp to Sir Nathaniel Bacon

1607, July 6. Sir, wheras uppon the sute of this pore man Thomas Curtis of Fi[e]ld Dawling he bringing a certificate from all the chiefe of thinhabitantes of the same town in that behalf I have thought good to geve my allowance unto him to be a cannaker in the said towne of Fyld Dawling and have drawen him his licence and put to my hand and seale. My desire is that it would «please» you to

---

[762] "Mr Kempe": John Kemp of Antingham esq (d. 1610), J.P. 1601–10 (Smith, *County and Court*, p.253, incorrectly described as of Gissing in the Index; *BP*, iv, p.230).

[763] Edmund Knyvett, clerk of the peace in Norfolk 1584–1616 (L. E. Stephens, *The Clerks of the Counties 1360–1960*, Warwick, 1961, p.137).

[764] John Rooke, constable of South Repps (see Bastardy memorandum of 19 October 1607, below, p.295).

joyne with me hearin and to tak suertyes of him for kepeing and observing his orders and thus not doubting of your allowance hereof with my harty com[*mendations*] I tak my leave from Holt this vi of July 1607. Your loveing frinde.

Signed: J. Kemp.[765]

Addressed: To the right worshipfull my very good frend Sir Nathanael Bacon knight.

Endorsed: Mr Kempe for Curtes at Dawlinge.

½ p. Folger L.d.381.

John Richers to Sir Nathaniel Bacon

1607, July 6. Sir, your being at London the last sessions, and myne this terme, is the cause I have not heatherto lett you understand, that you were (at those sessions) chosen treasurer for the Kinges Bench, Marshallsee & pore of the cownty, for those Hundredes that were in my receipte. The monyes have bene so slacklie paide by the cheife constables, that I have bene constrayned to complaine of them to the benche at the sessions divers tymes, yet no redresse.[766] And theise last sessions there was an order made and signified unto them that every of them should come unto me this last weeke, and perfect their accomptes, but fowre onely came. Could I have compelled them according to the lawe, I would not have taken this course, but aswell this, as other thinges, have bene to slieghtlie passed over. The taxacion made by the justices cannot be founde, by anie meanes that I cann use, therefore a distresse cannot be justified. No doubte there was one made at the beginning, but yt was not putt into a booke and kepte with the recordes of the peace, there to be alwaies extant, but delivered aboute in papers, and soe came to private handes & is now lost. I have heretofore moved the justices both at the Assizes and sessions, that they would informe themselves of the severall parishes within there severall lymittes and according to their values to make an equall taxacion of them against the last sessions, then to have bene ratified, and soe entered into a booke. Every one sayeth yt were well done, but none did yt. Then I requested againe yt might be done against the next yere, which was consented unto, but unlesse you doe now follow yt in tyme, yt wilbe to doe when the sessions come, and then yt wilbe to late, to doe yt rightlie there.

I have sent you fiftye poundes by my mann, and also such a note as was delivered me at randon [*sic*], of the chardge of every Hundred within your receipte, which doeth not consent with the cheife constables paymentes, nor they with themselves, for somtymes they pay more and sometymes lesse. And also I sende you such \<sp\> steadye paymentes as you are chardged with all, and the tymes when. And at the Assizes I shall deliver you my accompte, if you be there. In the meane tyme I thought good to lett you understande that because my yere entered

---

[765] There were some who considered that John Kemp was too generous in his licensing of establishments for the supply of alchohol. Apart from the practicality of requiring two signatures to the licence it may be that it was Bacon's involvement in the settlement of these past complaints that prompted Kemp's choice of Bacon as the other signatory (see *BP*, iv, pp.230–1).

[766] Richers is complaining about the inadequacies in the collection of what, effectively, were the county funds based on a rating (see 8 October 1605, above, p.215).

from the Annunciacion of Our Lady 1605 I have not therefore receyved, or paid, anie monies but such as was then due, unlesse yt be of two constables (as I now remember) of whom my mann did receive, at the Assizes in Lent in my absence, for halfe a yere ending at midsomer 1607 whereof there is onely one quarter due to me.[767] Eaven so I leave you to the mercyes of the Allmightie & take my leave. Swenyngton, this vi of Julye 1607. Your assured loving freinde.

Signed: John Richers.

Addressed: To the right worshipfull Sir Nathaniell Bacon, knight, at Styfkye.

Endorsed in Martin Man's hand: Mr Richers.

1 p. BL Add. 41140 ff.64–5.

Memorandum concerning the maintenance of a bastard child

1607, July 19. 19 July 1607. Memorandum. Valentyne Barnard of Ketleston delivered this much to my master in the presence of John Walker and mee, *viz.* that a bastard childe was put to him to keepe by Pynchins[768] servant «& yealded by him the rather» at the motion & request of his wyves kinsman one Tailor of Hunworth and for that the young woman is of kynne to his wife. And upon his receiving of the childe shee told him there should be 10*d.* a week paid by Stewky towne.

And he after coming to Stewky for his mony demaunded it of Edmund Monforth who went to Sir James Calthorp and tooke his hand to an order for Greves payment of mony weekly, and undertooke to pay Barnard the mony due to him at a day after, at Wals[*ingham*], and performed it accordingly.

Wherupon my master referred him to Edmund Monforth to receive the mony of him according to his promise.

Unsigned. In Martin Man's hand.

Endorsed: A remembrance of Valentine Barnardes speeche.

½ p. NRO MS 20527, 132X6.

Thomas Sackville, Earl of Dorset, Lord Treasurer, to Sir Nathaniel Bacon

1607, August 1. *Calendar*: The King has authorised Bacon and others to survey various royal manors and lands in Norfolk. Now the Lord Treasurer gives notice that he has appointed Mr John Hercye[769] and the other commissioners to meet Bacon at Burnham Overy on 1 September. From the Court. Dated 1 August 1607.

At the foot: "Alsoe to be at Snettesham the 2 and 3 and at Terrington the 4 and 5 dayes of September."[770]

---

[767] Assuming the Annunciation of Our Lady 1605 mentioned by Richers is 25 March 1606 (the day following 24 March 1605/6), his accounting year included the first 'quarter' of 1607 (to 25 March).

[768] The Stiffkey connection, evident herein, identifies this as John Pinchin. John served as overseer of the poor there in 1601/2 and as churchwarden in 1607/8. This memorandum may relate to his responsibilities as a parish officer (*BP*, iv, p.238; Pitman, 'Stiffkey', p.145). On the other hand, he was later involved himself in bastardy allegations concerning his servant Anne Robinson (NRO MC 1083/9, 803X1).

[769] Probably John Hersye of Middlesex, surveyor, active 1596–8 (Eden, *Surveyors*, ii, no.311).

[770] This postscript, and the location "Burnham Overy" in the body of the letter, are entered in a different hand.

Signed: T. Dorset.
Addressed: To my verie lovinge freind Sir Nathanyell Bacon knight.
Endorsed in Martin Man's hand: L[ord] Tres[urer].
½ p. Folger X.d.502 (21).

Francis Raymond to Sir Nathaniel Bacon

1607, August 22. Right wourshipfull so yt is that I cannot make payment of your wourships half yeres rent till I have geven assuerance of my howse, whereuppon I shall receyve seven score poundes at which tyme your wourshippe shall eyther have £20 or £20 bestowed in cattell at your wourships plesure for the performinge whereof we stey but for a court onlie. Therefore these are to desyre your wourshippe that your half yeres court maie be on Mondaie come fortnett[771] whiche is but three wekes afore St Mychell & we have often tymes had the court as longe before. I would crave of your wourshippe yt maie be so bycause I desyre aswell your wourshippe had your money as also I would be at Sturbiche [*Stourbridge*] fayer[772] to see howe the pryses of cattell rule there. Thus humblie cravinge your wourships assystance herein, with your wourships direccion eyther to Mr Reve or Mr Goodwyn[773] to that effecte, to whom I will presentlye repaier accordinge to your wourships dyreccions or yf yt please your wourshippe you maie send my boye to eyther of them. With my humble dutie I comytt your wourshipp to the tuicion of the Almightie. Methwold this 22 of August 1607. Your wourships humble & obedient servant.

Signed: Fra[ncis] Reymonde.[774]
Addressed: To the right wourshipfull & his verie good master Sir Nathaniell Bacon «knight» at Stifkey.
Endorsed in Martin Man's hand: Francis Raymond.[775]
1 p. NRO RAY 273.

List of assessors for the subsidy in north-west Norfolk

1607, August 28. *Calendar*: Assessors for the first payment of the second subsidy granted by Parliament in 1605 appointed by Sir Nathaniel Bacon and Sir Anthony Browne, commissioners for the same, on 28 August 1607.

Launditch: Roger Bozome esquire; Nicholas Mynne, Peter Barker, Henry Farrer, gents; Thomas Goche and William Alee, chief constables. Delivered by ("*per*") Sir A(nthony) B(rowne). Thomas Utber gent added.

---

[771] That is, 7 September.

[772] The international fair held just outside Cambridge, 24 August to 29 September each year.

[773] Christopher Reve was steward of Methwold, see 11 January 1603/4, above, p.66. It is not clear which Mr Goodwin was under-steward. John, the surveyor, acted as such in 1601 (*BP*, iv, pp.211–2). His brother Christopher, however, was written to as steward on 21 September 1607, although he seems to be reporting back to John five days later (below, pp.290–1). They may have split the office between them.

[774] Bacon's bailiff of the Duchy manor of Methwold.

[775] Above the address in the same hand is the date 22 October 1605; presumably the paper had originally been intended for some other purpose.

Smithdon: Richard Stubbe esquire; Robert Drury, Roger Warner, gents; John Reade and Thomas Cremer, chief constables. Delivered by Manser (?absent). Ha[mon] Strange added.

Gallow: Thomas Townshend, Phillip Russell, Thomas Gurnay, Thomas Lynford, gents; Mathew Bensley and Richard Kinge, chief constables. Delivered by Mr ("*Magistro*") Perefoy.

Brothercross: Clement Hoe, Richard Norton senior, gents; Edward Thurlow and Thomas Lane, chief constables. Delivered by Mr Norton.

North Erpingham: William Wynter esquire; William Plumsted, John Holl, Robert Doughty, gents; Francis Symondes (unwell) and Thomas Cooke, chief constables. Delivered by Mr Parre.

South Erpingham: Thomas Thetford esquire; Robert Kempe, Henry Norgate (unwell), Anthony Page, gents; Erasmus Buck and Clement Rolffe,[776] chief constables. Delivered by Mr Godfrey.

Holt: Christofer Hunt, Thomas Sherwood, Christofer Houghton, Thomas Kinges, gents; John Jenkinson and William Kinge, chief constables. Delivered by Mr Parre. Thomas Asteley esquire added.

Eynesford: William Rokewood, Raphe Symondes (absent), esquires; Jo. Founteyn (unwell), Edward Bulwer (added), Arthur Founteyn, William Croppe, gents,[777] Thomas Outlawe and Thomas Thompson, chief constables. Delivered by Sir A(nthony) B(rowne).

North Greenhoe: Thomas Hastinges, Christofer Bedingfeld, Nicholas Browne, gents; John Grene and Robert Purlond, chief constables. Delivered by Mr Browne.
Marginalia in Latin.
Signed: Na[*thaniel*] Bacon, Antho[*ny*] Browne. *In Martin Man's hand.*
Endorsed in Martin Man's hand: [1] Assessors *pro prima solucione 2 subsidii*; [2] The bookes to be delivered in 18 September at the Faulcon *hora* 8.
1 p. BL Add. 38508 ff.20–21.

Petition. The inhabitants of Bodham to Sir Nathaniel Bacon and other J.P.s in Norfolk

1607, September 10. To the right worshipfull Sir Nathanyell Bacon knight and other the Kynges Majesties justyces of the peace within the countye of Norfolk. To whome it maye apperteyne.

Maye it please your good worships to be advertised. That forasmuche as it is requysyte that one alehous or victellynge house should be admytted within this throughfare towne of Bodham bothe for readye provisyon of beare and breade for suche as doe want it within the same towne, & also for relief & ease of suche as be travellers to & from dyvers & sundry places & townes therabout. And for that our neighbour Rychard Jervys of Bodham aforeseyd, beynge an auncyent man & of

---

[776] Written in this order, but Buck marked "b" and Rolffe "a".
[777] Rokewood, Symondes, Jo. Founteyn and Croppe are numbered 1–4.

good government mete to be imployed in suche a trade & exercise, ys desyrous to undertake the same, he havinge seated him self in his owne purchased house which heretofore hathe ben used for trade of victellynge, & very aptlye scituated for the same, hathe desyred of us his neighbours our furtheraunce therin unto your good wourships, that it might please you by your lycence to admytte him therunto, which maye not onely be a relief to the mayntenaunce of his aged yeres & charge of wyef and chyldren but also be an occasyon to restreyne others that heretofore have unlawfullye resisted auctoritye in lyke case. And he in no wise willinge to offer suche offence, but to use it by orderlye meanes, and for performance of this his sute, we joyne with him in intreatye unto your good wourships. And so humblye take our leaves. From Bodham this x of September 1607. Your wourships humbly at commaund.

Signed: Henry Armiger, Thomas Armiger, John Jervis, James Smyth; [*all by mark:*] Robert Hemblinge, James Tynker, Rychard Balle, Anthonye Tynker, Thomas Shepard the elder, William Shepard the elder, Anthony Bacon, Wylliam Andrewes.
Endorsed in Martin Man's hand: Bodham cert[*ificate*] for Richard Jervys.
1 p. NRO RAY (4) 38. Printed, *Stiffkey Papers*, pp.53–4.

Subsidy assessment for the Hundred of North Greenhoe

1607, September 14. *Summary*: Assessment for the first payment of the second subsidy of three granted in 1605, made 14 September 1607. By Thomas Hastinges, Christofer Bedingfeild, and Nicholas Browne, gents, and John Greene and Robert Purland, chief constables, for the Hundred of North Greenhoe. 164 names. Lands assessed at £317, paying £42 5s. 4d. Goods assessed at £169 10s., paying £14 2s. 6d. Aliens: two Danes and two Scotsmen (Wells) and one Dutchman (Little Walsingham).

Signed: Thomas Hastinges, [*Christopher*] Bedingfeild, Nycholas Brown, *per me Johannem Greene* & Rob[*er*]t Purland.
Endorsed in Martin Man's hand: Northgrenho. *Prima pars 2. subs*[*idii*] *anno 3 Jac.*
5 pp. NRO RAY 275.

Subsidy assessment for the Hundred of Holt

1607, September 18. *Summary*: Assessment for the first payment of the second subsidy of three granted in 1605, made 18 September 1607. By Thomas Asteley esquire, Christofer Hunte, Thomas Sherwoode, Christofer Holton, and Thomas Kinges, gents, and William Kinge and John Jenkenson, chief constables, for the Hundred of Holt. 200 names. No totals given.

Signed: Chr[*istopher*] Hunte, Thomas Sherwoode, Christofer Houghton, Thomas Kinges, William Kinge.
On cover: Holt Hundred 1 payment 2 subs[*idy*].
7½ pp. BL Add. 38508 ff.22–6.

Subsidy assessment for the Hundred of Gallow

1607, September 18. *Summary:* Assessment for the first payment of the second subsidy of three granted in 1605, made 18 September 1607. By Phillip Russell, Thomas Towneshend, Thomas Gurney, and Thomas Lynford, gents, and Mathew Benslye and Richard King, chief constables, for the Hundred of Gallow and delivered to Sir Nathaniell Bacon, Sir Hamon Le Strange, and Sir Anthony Browne. 112 names. Lands assessed at £188, paying £25 1*s.* 4*d.* Goods assessed at £81, paying £6 15*s.*

Signed: Thomas Touneshend, Phyll[*ip*] Russell, Tho[*mas*] Gurnay, Thomas Lynford, Math[*ew*] Benslye, Richard Kinge.
On cover in Martin Man's hand: Hundred de Gallow. *Prima pars secundi subsidii. Anno 3 Regis.*
6 pp. RH Box 71. Listed, *Stiffkey Papers,* p.85, n.1.

Sir Edmund Moundford to the steward of the Duchy manor of Methwold

1607, September 21. Sir so it is that as I had just occacion «of grefe» so I complayned to the honourable Sir John Fertescue Chanceler of the Duchie of offences comitted by the inhabitants of Methwold for breakeinge & spoylinge the Kinges soyle & destroyinge of his shepes course ther by digginge flagges[778] & turffes ther, from whome I receyved dyrection that I should geve notice of the said matter unto the stewerd of the courte & to requier him in his Majesties behalfe to geve the said offences in charge unto the homage & all other annoyances committed by any of the said inhabitants ther, & that you geve knowlege unto the said homage that yf they refuse to present such offences or shall conseale them wilfully it shall brede a forfiture of theyer coppihold estates. Wherfore I have adressed theyes fewe lynes to advertize you of Sir John Fostecues pleasure herein, and for your better procedeinge therein I have thought it good to specefye the places wher the offences be committed & the maner therof.

Imprimis the digginge of flagges in the comon betwen Harvest Home & Morwold comon on the north and also betwen the said feld called Harvest Home & the feldes of Metwold.

Item the spoile of the firres [*furze*] ther which should be the safegard of the shepe fedeinge uppon the Kinges shepes course ther, against both which offences ther be lawes made in that courte longe sinse.

Item the breakeing of the soyle & <make> «makeing of» turfe-pitts wher none have ben made he[*re*]tofore to the hinderance of his Majesties ryght of drifte & hinderance of «the» shepes fede ther, parte therof being firme grounde & good pasture.

Item theier [*sic*] kepeinge of an herd of [*s*]wyne & the same unringed both to the great spoile of the comon & the fede of the shepe in the feldes.

Item that such as have no shepes course or shepe walkes doe kepe shepe uppon the comons & feldes to the spoile of the shepe of such «as» have shepe courses & also of other cattell fedeinge uppon the said comons.

---

[778] "Flagges": light surface peat.

I pray you to certefy me of your procedeinges therein & what the jury presenteth that according to the dyrection geven to me I may advertize Sir John Fortescue therof.

I hadd ben at the courte my selfe yf my travell to the sessions & other «my» necessary busines hadd not hindred <this> me, & so I committ you to God. Feltwell the xxi of September 1607. Your loveinge frend.

Signed: Ed[*mund*] Moundeford.

Addressed: To <the> his loveinge frend the stewerd of the courte of his Majesties manner of Methwold.

Endorsed: Sir Ed[*mund*] Mondefords letter to the steward of Methold courte dated xxi September.

Enclosed with letter of 26 September 1607 from Christopher Goodwin, immediately below.

1 p. NRO NNAS S2/17/18. Calendared, *HMC Townshend*, pp.17–18.

Christopher Goodwin to John Goodwin

1607, September 26. Brother John.[779] You maie lett Sir Nathaniel Bacon understand that the sale of his man [*Francis*] Reymonds house did not procede at Methwold because one Mr Crosse of Brandonfery who should purchase the same, doth doubt the title, and therefore desireth that a seizure for wast be made thereof, & then he will have it graunted unto him out of the lordes handes.[780] He tasted[781] me for the fyne & I told him £10 should be the very least & unto which I thinck I could easelie have drawn him if wee had proceded. That cort is adjourned tyll Thursday the viii of Octobre next. The admittances there were only of a ruinous tenemente or stalls in the market place the fine whereof (with much holdinge) I brought to 13*s.* 4*d.*, & the other fine of 3½ acres, 3*s.* 6*d.* During my being there I perused the fewe cort rolles, and I found both <ref> reliefes, herriottes, bondmen of the names of Mountford & others with other thinges whereof Anger the prolocutor of that manor denyed all manner of notice. Sir Ed[*mund*] Mountford sent me a letter which I send herewith, but the tenantes esteme him not as they say, but understand (as I heard) he giveth countenance to the tenantes ageinst Sir Nathaniel for the comon.

At Hellgay there was nothinge done, for Mr Hawes and Sir John Willoughbies steward came to me but excused all matters by Mr Henry Will[*oughby*] being highe shreffe «in Darbyshire».[782] Surelie I am much deceyved if there be not greate wronge offered to the mannour of the Duchy there. As for the leete Mr Hawes will (as he saith) presently cary over a decree which he hath of Michaelmas terme *anno x Regine Elizabethe* which doth mencion only an article of a leete for thassize of bread and beere there to belong to the Duchy. There hath bene a pounde for Lanc[*aster*] within memorie. They saie they are not to be amercied, and for their

---

[779] For John and Christopher Goodwin see note to 22 August 1607, above, p.286.

[780] Effectively what is being proposed is a collusive action: that is, where an action is brought against another by his own agreement. Here, the procedure would have assured the purchaser of his title. Instances such as this should give pause to the too ready reading of court proceedings at face value.

[781] In the sense of 'taxed', inquired or asked of me.

[782] See 6 July 1606, above, p.246.

fynes Sir Nathaniel Bacon, as Reymond saith, will have them arbitrable as Methwold is, since Hellgay is parcell of Methwold, & I could finde but 2 copy-holders enfeoffed, which both impugne ther tenementes in that [?]matter. Sir John Willoughby hath of late used to purchase all the bandes[783] he could of the Duchy mannour, & questionlesse he hath much conceled land thereof. I heare that Mr Skipwith of Fordham hath an extent of the whole towne.[784]

For Well I gott (with faier wordes) an auncient rentall made *secundo Elizabethe* & renued & abbutted what I could in so smale tyme. & there I delivered the bayliffe an extract of defalters, & reliefs, & so was much trobled a whole afternone thereabout. I wrote a copy of all that I did & gave it Reymond. And I desier God to blesse us & all ours. Downham much payned in my legge this 26 of September[785] 1607. Your loving brother.

[*Postscript*]: There are 6 to be admitted besides Mr Willoughby at Hellgaye. I made proclamacion ageinst them all.

Signed: Christo[*pher*] Goodwyn.
Addressed: To his lovinge brother John Goodwyn at Helloughton.
Endorsed: Christofer Goodwins letter to his brother John Goodwin. *In Martin Man's hand*: Methwold.
Enclosure: Letter of 21 September 1607 from Sir Edmund Moundford, immediately above.
1 p. Folger X.d.502 (25).

Manor of Methwold. Bailiff's account

1607, September 29. *Summary*: Account of Frauncis Reymond to Michaelmas 1607. Total receipts, consisting of Methwold assize rents for one year, cornrents, Hilgay and Well rents for two years and the sale of a steer, amounted to £23 17*s.* 11*d.* No details are given of the rents. Disbursements came to £3 12*s.* 4*d.*, excluding 2*s.* 6*d.* for conies, teal and mallard bought and sent. The accountant has paid in £20 and so owes 5*s.* 7*d.* He has yet to account for the profits of court and a stray mare.

Draft.
Endorsed: [*1*] Francis Raymondes notes; [*2 in Martin Man's hand*] Notes of Raymondes reckoning at Michaelmas 1607.
1 p. NRO MC 1872/16, 866X2. Listed, *Supplementary Stiffkey Papers*, p.39.

Memorandum concerning the pier at Cromer

[*? 1607, c. October*].[786] What benifitt in tymes past was by havynge a peare at Cromer.[787]

---

[783] "Bandes": that is, bonds.   [784] In the sense of 'township' of Hilgay.   [785] Written "7er".
[786] Dating: this date is suggested by the letter of 22 October 1607, to Chief Justice Coke from Sir Nathaniel Bacon, Sir James Calthorp, and John Kempe (below, pp.296–8). This mentions a survey made by them at Cromer following a petition by its inhabitants, and gives the views of the surveyors on the need for a new pier or piers there.
[787] Past attempts to improve the sea defences at Cromer and Sheringham had confronted those involved with more than a practical problem. They also gave rise to corruption and had been a major issue in the politics of Norfolk in the 1580s (Smith, *County and Court*, pp.235, 247–53).

Fyrst it dyd save the towne from wastynge by the seae whiche nowe for wante therof is a great hynderaunce to [*the*] Kynges Majestye his subjects and tenants there beinge lord therof.

That the pore mariners belonginge to the towne beinge at seae in small botes. And others comynge from all partes bothe wythin the realme and from beyounde the seaes fyshynge for hearynge [*herring*] being the chefe place in the begenyng of fyshynge have in sudyn distress put in there to the saftye of ther leyves & goods. And synce the decaye therof manye hundreds have perished besyds the lose of ther goods. And not only fyshers but all other pasengers comynge therby as of nesesite thay must.

That in tyme of ware manye pasengers which have bene loden wyth all kynde of comoditis and beinge pursued wythe ther enemye have bene there rescued to the saftye of ther goods.

That the countrye nere adjoynynge had then all ther provicion brought to that place. And ther comoditis convayed from thence wythe <small> fare smaler chergis then nowe thaye have beinge noe other haven or port wythin tene myles therof.

That Kinge Edward the forth in the sevill warres betwixt hyme and Henrie the sixt, beinge forced to flee, dyd take a small shippe at Lyne. And beinge at seae and the Easterlyngs[788] at ware wythe this realme a shipe of that countrye havyng the shipe in chase wherin the Kynge was by puttynge in to that place was [*sic*] defended from <thos> «his» enemis, as the cronnicles report. And afterwerds he became a good benefactor to the towne. And there caused hym selfe to be sett upp in monument whiche doe yett remayne.

Unsigned. Undated.
Endorsed in Martin Man's hand: Reasons for maynt[*aining*] a peere at Cromer.
1 p. NRO RAY 513. Printed, *Stiffkey Papers*, p.124.

Mathew Clark to Sir Nathaniel Bacon

1607, October 10. Right wourshipfull. Theare is one John Athill who hathe sould unto this bearer John Warde thre acres and a half of coppyhowld land lying in Emneth which he hathe in the right of his wyffe, and therfore cannot make any assurance therof unlesse his wyffe be examyned before <the> a st[*e*]ward by patent, or else in open court. I would therfore intreat your wourship, to take her examinacion, and to accept of his surrender and his wyves, to the use of John Warde and his heyours yf they shall comme to make offer of the same.[789] And to delyver the sayd surrender soe taken under thear handes unto John Warde who will bringe the same unto me, and att the next court howlden for that manour I will perfect the recorde. So with humble remembrance of my dutie I rest. Lynne 10 October 1607. Your wourships to be commaunded.

Signed: Mat[*hew*] Clarck.

---

[788] "Easterlyngs": natives of the Baltic coast and more specifically inhabitants of the Hansa towns.
[789] Copyhold (native) land was conveyed through the manor court, by means of surrender to the use of the purchaser. Married women had to be examined separately to ensure their agreement to the transaction.

Addressed: To the right wourshipfull Sir Nathaniell Bacon knight at Styffkey.
Endorsed: Mr Ma[*thew*] Clerk.
½ p. NRO BL/BC/6/21.

Memorandum of surrender out of court

[*1607, October*] **14**.[790] *Calendar.* The land held by John Athill and Alice his wife of the manor of Emneth *Regis* is described as three and a half acres of native land in Emneth in the field called Knopmore next to land belonging to Emneth church north, with land of Sir Henry Gaudy east and Knopemore Lane west, and paying the King 7 *d.* a year. This is followed by a memorandum that on Wednesday 14 Alice was examined in the absence of her husband by Sir Nathaniel Bacon, chief steward of all the King's manors and possessions in Marshland. Afterwards John and Alice unconditionally surrendered their land into the hands of the King through Sir Nathaniel to the use of John Warde and his heirs and assigns. Signed: Nathaniel Bacon.

Latin. Undated. Copy in Martin Man's hand.
Endorsed: John Athill & his wifes surrender of lande in Emneth.
½ p. NRO BL/BC/6/22.

Bastardy Sessions memoranda

1607, October 19. Proceedinges at Holt before Sir Nathaniel Bacon & Sir James Calthorp knightes & John Kempe esquire in causes of bastardy.

1. Margaret Clipwell of Brinton delivered of a daughter «named» Dorothy, wherof one Thomas Browne of Hindringham charged to be father.
The said Browne is departed & cannot be come by.
Order. The cause respited till the man may be gott. And Mr Plaiforth is directed to repayer to Sir Nathaniel for a warrant for his apprehension. /Respited./

2. Cicely Holmes daughter of Thomas Holmes of Burningham delivered of a daughter named Elizabeth wherof Robert Loades «servant with D[r] Hunt the» reputed father. /Ordered./
Evidence. <Eliz.> «Cicely» Holmes *jurata.* Was servant with Loades of Burrogh when his sonne abused her, & first bewrayed[791] it to Robert Loades half a yeare before her delivery. Was delivered a forthnight afore Lammas last. Upon examination before Mr Pagrave shee accused him, & to be gotten a forthnight afore Hallowmas & so contynueth to accuse. Was sent away out of her «masters» service without cause about Christmas.
Pro def. Robert Cheseny sonne in lawe to Jo. Loades. Touching the cause of departure of Elizabeth Holmes. Stoutnes etc. That shee was not thought with childe then.
Thomas Holmes *juratus.* Shee bewrayed herself to him at Our Lady being sent home by Curson of Melton. And then shee [?]declared R. Loades to be father.

---

[790] Dating: dated by reference to the letter from Mathew Clark of 10 October 1607, immediately above.
[791] In the sense of to reveal, expose, discover unintentionally, and usually what it is intended to be concealed (*OED*).

Jo. Millers wife, Morrys wife *juratae*. Were at the labour. Goodwife Purvys gracewife[792] examined her «& helde her hardly to it». Shee named onely R. Loades. The childe full borne.

Memorandum. R. Loades dwelt in the house togither with him. The tyme agreeth.

Pro def. Reporte of evill shamles speches whirby the woman is touched in creditt.

Order. Robert Loades reputed the father. The childe to remain with the mother. Loades to contribute weekely 8*d.* till the age of <8> «10» yeares from the birth. To enter bond with suertyes to the church wardens of Bur[*gh*] in 20 markes. The punishment. Loades to be imprisoned 14 daies & the woman stockd at Holt Markett 3 hours.

/Shee submitteth. Loades comited to the constable of Briston to go to the gaole *quousque* etc. <Shee> at Bur[*gh*] from [?]Tues. [?]All during preyer next Sonday./

3. Elizabeth Fuller of Sharingham delivered of a daughter, Alice, wherof Nicholas Wilson of Beckham charged.

Order. Wilson to finde suerties to be forthcoming. The matter respited. /Respited./

4. Cicely Hooke of Southreppes delivered of a daughter named Margaret. Mr James Hartstong[793] defalted nothwithstanding the appointment made by his owne consent. /Ordered./

Evidenc. Cicely Hooke *jurata*. <That> «According to» her examination & confession in January last before Mr Kempe shee saith that Mr James Hartstong usd her about Shrovesonday <till Tueday> «& Shrove Tuesday till Michaelmas» was twelvemonth, & was delivered about Christ[*mas*] in his house. Served him 12 monethes 5 weekes. Departed on New Yeares day. Shee tolde him of it. He promised mariage. Gave her 2*s.* a shirt & sheete upon his going to London. /Promysed allowance of furres[794] meslyn & mony yearly if shee would conceale him, but shee never would consent to leave his house./

Ann Hooke widdow *jurata*. The mother of Cicely. Mr Hartstonges speech to her *viz.* /Offered to give Jo. Bacon his servant £20 to mary her, as Bacon tolde one Bateman of S. Reppes./

The women at the birth *ex relacione Magistro Kempe*. Declared upon former [?]hearing «upon their oath», the wench charged her master to be father etc.

Peter Lawson *juratus*. That 4 women swore that Cicely named her master. Rookes wife & Thomas[*in*] Curakeper. Shee charged him lying in her childbedd to be father. That Mr Hartstong said he would kepe it as a bastard. The women after explain their meaning that shee meant her master Harstong. /Mr Harstong hath had divers delivered in his house. Mr Harstonges answers, 1. not her master. 2. for the tyme. Excommunicated by the Bishop./

---

[792] Another term for a midwife. This pre-dates the instances given in *OED*.

[793] James Hartstongue: possibilities are the barrister of this name, James Hartstongue of Southrepps (see Venn, *Al. Cant.*, ii, p.321) or the assessor for the subsidy and chief constable for North Erpingham Hundred in 1602 (*BP*, iv, p.228).

[794] "Furres": furze for firewood.

Uxor Jo. Rooke jurata. Was at the travell. Shee examined the woman *coram reliquis* [*in the presence of the rest*], charging her etc. Her execration upon her self if shee wronged Mr Harstong prey[*ing*] shee might not be delivered etc.

That before, shee heard of Cicely being with childe by Mr Hartstonges folke & that being dealt with privatly shee charged her master onely.

Mr Lawson. That Mr Harstong concealed the matter etc. though it were manifested to him by his brother Raph Harstong *& al.*

Jurati Robert Blofeld, Mr Bateman. Understande of the womans being with childe a forthnight *ante partum* [*before the delivery*]. Thei in their judgment thinke Mr Hartstonge the father rather then anie other.

Ex relacione Magistro Kemp. Shee confessd it to Mr Otes.[795] *Ut ipsi afferunt super sacramentis etc.* [*As they affirm on oath*].
Order. That Mr James Hartstong is father. The child to remain with the mother. He to contribute 12*d.* a week from the birth during 10 yeares & to enter bonde «with surties» in £20 to the churchwardens of S. Reppes. To be imprisoned *sans* baile one moneth. Shee to be set in the stockes the next market dey at Cromer «3 houer» & the next Sonday at S. Reppes *ut ante.* A warrant to bring him before one of the Justices to finde suerties to performe an order for the said bastardy. /V.O./[796]

Memorandum the warrant delivered to Jo. Rooke constable of S. Reppes.

The woman submitteth her selfe.

5. Alice Harwyn at Sheringham delivered of Thomasyne a bastard wherof shee chargeth one Edmund Coxon *de* Estbeckham. /Respited./
Order. That Mr Kemp call him & binde him over.

6. Margaret Hillington of <Towne Barningham> «Kelling» delivered of Alice a bastard wherof shee chargeth to be father Robert Pynchin of Kelling. /Ordered./[797]
Evidenc. Margaret Hillington *jurata.* Delivered a forthnight after midsummer last. Protesteth the childe to be Pinchins. Shee revealed it to a woman of Bar[*n*]ingham. /Was delivered alone. Shee said shee had [*word illegible*] for it with Pinchin./

Pro def. Thomas Gilbert *juratus.* Jo. Ransome master of the parties, tolde him that a cooke & the woman were taken togither in the fact in Ransomes house.
Order. Robert Pinchin the reputed father. The childe to remain with the mother. Pinchin to pay weekly 4*d.* The rest to be borne by the woman & the towne. To be both whipped <presently> in Holt.

Memorandum both were whipped. And a warrant «[?]under the order» delivered to the constable of Kelling with Pinchin to be caryd to the gaole till he finde suertyes according to the order which was sent therwith.

Unsigned. In Martin Man's hand.
Endorsed: Procedinges in bastardy 19 October 1607.
3 pp. NRO NRS 24661, 125X3.

---

[795] Samuel Oates senior, rector of Southrepps from 1588 (Barton, *Anthony Harison*, i, p.197).
[796] "V.O.": meaning unknown, although from their position in the margin the letters are likely to refer to action to be carried out.
[797] Probably not related to Memorandum of 19 July 1607, above, p.285.

Sir Nathaniel Bacon, Sir James Calthorpe, and John Kemp to Sir Edward Coke,
Chief Justice of Common Pleas

[*1607, c. October 22*].[798] *Summary:* Draft letter concerning repairs to sea defences
at Cromer.[799]

Undated. Unsigned. Unaddressed.
Draft alternately in Martin Man's and Sir Nathaniel Bacon's hands, with Man's initial
section heavily corrected in Bacon's hand.
Endorsed in Nathaniel Bacon's hand: A part of Cromer certificat 1607.
2 pp. NRO RAY 278.

Sir Nathaniel Bacon, Sir James Calthorp, and John Kempe to Sir Edward Coke,
Chief Justice of Common Pleas

1607, October 22. Our dueties remembred unto your Lordshipe. It appeareth by
the peticion inclosed,[800] which hath bene exhibited by the inhabitantes of the
towne of Cromer in Norfolk to the Kinges Majestie and by direccion referred to
your Lordships consideracion, that your desire is to be informed by us of the trewe
estate of the cause, and accordingly wee doe now signifie, what wee doe finde
therin.

Wee made our repaire to the towne of Cromer, and by the examinacion of witnesses, and by sight of the cliftes, it is manifest, that the sea hath brought to ruine
manie howses «there», and hath utterly decaied a peere, which was built not longe
since of tymber with great chardge, and that in fewe yeares much more of the
towne together with the church, which is faire and very large with a high steeple,
is like to be overthrowne, if some helpe in tyme be not had. For within this twelve
yeares, the force of the sea hath wonn upon the lande wher manie howses did
stande betwene the decayed peere and the towne neare the bredth of six acres, and
the church is now within twelve score[801] of the cliffe, upon which the sea doth

---

[798] Dating: the date, intended signatories—other than Bacon—and the destination of the letter are inferred from the finalised version of 22 October 1607, immediately below. There are considerable differences
of spelling and phraseology between the two documents, and the draft omits altogether the section "And yet
we cann this farforth certefie your Lordshipe that there is one olde peere standinge" to "and maie justly
move compassion". See also the Memorandum of *c.*October 1607, above, pp.291–2.

[799] See Memorandum of *c.*October 1607, above, pp.291–2.

[800] This might be the petition from the tenants of Cromer recorded as having been made to the King
complaining of abuses. It was referred to the Lord Chief Justice "to consider of the conveniencie of this and
to certifie what is meet for the relief of the petitioners" (Hoyle *et al.*, *Heard Before the King*, p.71, no.984).
However, if this is the case there had been a considerable delay before the issue was considered as the record
of this petition is dated to 1 November 1605. Moreover, at that point in time Coke had not yet become Chief
Justice.

[801] Possibly with the sense of score = 20, in which case the distance referred to would be 240, but initially
the unit of measure itself looks as if it is not specified. "Score" could also have the sense of a number as
counted, thus used after a numeral it could mean precisely so many. However, it is most likely that it is used
here in the sense of twenty paces (*OED*), thus specifying the unit of measure. Also, there is a specifically East
Anglian usage—recorded as being associated with Lowestoft—where it refers to a narrow, steep path or
street leading to the sea and formed into steps (*OED*, 'score' as noun, 1c). It is the case that at Cromer the
modern descents of the cliff near to the church do take the form of steep slopes and also steps. The adoption
of this unit of measure here may have been prompted by the association of both of the latter meanings in
the mind of the writer.

continually more and lesse worke. So as the decaie of this populous towne which is the Kinges inheritance in parte, and the inheritance of manie private persons beside, wherof manie have bene men tradinge to the seas, is so well knowne all the countrye over, as no gainesaying therin can be made. But the matter of difficultie wherin men of more skyll then our selves were fitt to be used, is to set downe, how the towne maie be preserved from the force of the sea, and what the chardge therof will arise unto, and herin, though we have the speciall direccion to meddle, yet beinge so pertinent to the state of the cause, wee thinke it not amisse to certefie our opinions. The helpe must be eyther in making a great peere, which maie be the safety both of the towne and small ships, or in making severall smalle peeres or jetties, which can only succoure the towne. But the chardge of a great peere will be such in regarde of the largenes of the tymber, and the quantyty therof to be used together with the workemanship, and maintenance therof after the finishinge, as we dare not advise that to be attempted, least the chardge exceede the benefitt. Therfore the smalle peeres & jetties, though they be the more, will yet be the lesse chardge, and must, as wee thinke, be the waie for helpe. What the chardge will be to make thes smalle peeres, and to mainetaine them, when they be made, wee leave to the judgement of men experienced in busines of that kinde: And yet we cann this farforth certefie your Lordshipe that ther is one olde peere standinge and lowe built, the length wherof is about one hundred yardes, and two men <off> of the towne affirmed unto us, that they did worke the same, and did estemeite the chardge to be two hundred poundes, and this lowe peere doth now preserve the cliffes, wherupon a little parte of the towne doth stand, so as if two or thre at the moste of the like scantlinge [*dimensions*] were built and maineteyned, the whole towne might be preserved. The peeres must be made of tymber, because the cliftes yeeldeth no stone or rockes wherof to make them, and this timber cutt at scantlinges for that purpose, maie be provided with lesse losse to the kingdom out of Norwaie <then here> and with lesse chardge, then here in Englande.

The towne hath much buildinge in it, and is a market towne, and maie justly move compassion.

Moreover wee holde it meete to make knowen unto your Lordship that most of the townesmen of Cromer be pore, and thei which be of the best ability amongst them, are needy & wanting, whereby wee feare, that thei of the towne, who preferred the peticion do rather seeke their private lucre then the publick good, and wee have cause to suppose this, bicause the towne had a gifte from our late soveraign Queen Elizabeth towardes the building of peers by the transportacion of much corne for which greate somes of mony were due, wherof (as wee be informed) much is unimployed, & converted to private uses. So as wee assure ourselves, that your Lordship knowing thus much from us, will have a care to foresee, that, if the Kinges Majestie give them anie gifte, yt may be so governed, as the former abuse may not agayne be suffered.

Thus being loath to serve anie private turne, and yet willing to give our best furtherance to the upholding of the towne, which is like to perishe without some provision be had, more then the towne can yealde, wee referre the consideracion herof to your Lordships better wisdome, and so take our leaves. From Stifky this 22 of October 1607. Your Lordships at comandment. [*Signed:*] Nathaniel Bacon, James Calthorp, John Kemp.

[*On the dorse:*] Memorandum this letter was sent to Mr Kempe to be conveyed etc. & that some of Cromer, *viz.* Mr Blofeld or Baxter might attende my Lord Cokes aunswer.

Copy in William Sanders' and Martin Man's hands.
Endorsed in Martin Man's hand: Coppie of a letter to the Lord Coke concerning Cromer.
2½ pp. NRO RAY 189. Printed, *Stiffkey Papers,* pp.124–6.

Exemplar of a certificate of militia companies

1607, October 22. Norfolk. The forme of the certificate.[802]
Imprimis Foote
The band of Thomas Cleer esquire within the Hundred of Estfleg strong in 30 pikes, 30 muskets, 20 caliveres. Total 80.
The band of Sir Drew Drewry knight within the Hundred of Westfleg strong in 35 pikes, 35 muskets, 20 caliveres. Total 90.

Sir Thomas Grosse knight captain of the light horses and petronelles raised out of the Hundreds of Estfleg, Westflegg, Happing and Tonsteade, stronge in 25 light hors, 15 petronelles. Total [*blank*].
Sir Clement Heigham knight captain of the launces which are to be raised out of the county of Norfolk, 80 launces. Total 80.

Unsigned. Copy in William Sanders' hand.
Endorsed: The forme of Sir Arthur Heveninghams certificates for the musters 22 October 1607.
Enclosed with Heveningham's letter of 23 October 1607, below p.299.
1 p. Folger X.d.502 (34).

The deputy lieutenants in Norfolk to Henry Howard, Earl of Northampton, Lord Lieutenant[803]

1607, October 22. Our dueties in all humble manner remembred. According to your honours direccion by your letteres the laste of Maie we have caused the captaines both of foote and horse to vewe the severall companies unto them allotted. And we doe finde by the certificates of the captaines of the foote bandes that their severall companies are not so compleate and fully furnished now, as they hope to supply and make readie in all pointes by the next vewe, as in former tymes they have bene chardged.

As for the launces light horses and petroneles, they are greatly decayed and will hardly be raised againe, except some course be taken by lawe, what every person

---

[802] In the original the numbers are given in columns.
[803] As his letter of 23 October 1607 to Sir Nathaniel Bacon (immediately below) makes clear, this communication was drafted by Sir Arthur Heveningham on behalf of his fellow deputies, and though no addressee is specified it is almost certainly directed to the Lord Lieutenant.

shall finde according to their severall valewes. Because ther is no lawe as we conceive to chardge anie man, by reason the statute of Phillip and Mary and other statutes are repealed.[804]

Wee send unto your Lordship a certificate of the forces both of foote and horses, and the names of the captaines and in what Hundredes they raise their severall companies. Wherby it maie appeare unto your honour what nomber of men & horses every captain hath bene chardged with heretofore, that the same number maie continue «fully» compleate under your honours commaunde, as was in the former Lord Lewetenauntes tymes, which God willinge we will use all care and diligence to performe when it shall be your honours pleasure to geve us direccions. If it maie stande with your honours lykinge that a vewe maie be taken twise a yeare, and some strict order geven for them that shall make defaulte, and that the powder and all other necessarie thinges to every severall companie be renewed as was commaunded *anno* 1602 no doubt your honour maie have the whole forces of Norfolk fully compleate in a short tyme. For the citty of Norwich wee cannot make anie certificate because they saie they are priveledged, and the [*word illegible*] geven to us from your Lordship little regarded. Thus cravinge pardon for our bouldnes, wee humbly take our leaves.

Norwich this 22 of October 1607.

Unsigned. Copy in William Sanders' hand.
Endorsed: The mustires.
Enclosed with Sir Arthur Heveningham's letter of 23 October to Sir Nathaniel Bacon, immediately below.
1 p. Folger X.d.502 (33).

Sir Arthur Heveningham to Sir Nathaniel Bacon

1607, October 23. Good knight I have thought it good to send unto yow a drafte both of the certificate and the letter to peruse,[805] and if any thinge shall mislike yow herin, yow may ade or demynishe if it please yow, for Sir Henry Gaudy and Sir Phillipe Woodhowse have had a sight therof. If yow like them I praie put to your hand, and send them to me againe by this bearer, and they will subscribe therunto, wherby we maie send it up to my Lorde so speedelie as maie be. And so with very hartie comaundacions to yow, and to your good ladie, I comitt yow to God. Ketteringham this xxiii of October 1607. Your very lovinge frend.

Signed: Arthur Hevenyngham.
Addressed: To the right worshipfull his very lovinge frend Sir Nathaniell Bacon knight.
Endorsed: Sir Arthur Heveninghams letter.
Enclosures: Draft letter from the deputy lieutenants and muster certificate dated 22 October 1607, immediately above.
½ p. BL Add. 41140 ff.66–7.

[804] See note to Memoranda, 3 December 1605, above, p.220.
[805] Immediately above.

Certificate. Sir Nathaniel Bacon to Sir Edward Coke, Chief Justice of Common Pleas

1607, November 2. My dutie remembred unto your Lordship & the rest.[806] It may please you to be advertised that by force of an order set downe in the cort of Common Pleas betwen Robert Bullen & Robert Laseby of Batheley in the county of Norfolk I have had the said parties sondry tymes before me and have hearde their contencions at large debated betwen themselves togither with their proofes by witnesses & otherwise and had also the helpe of two other men of good under-standing for the more through examining of the differences betwen them. And both in their opynions & myne owne yt was holden fitt that ech of the said parties should set downe with their losses & charges and when I had made manifest by my speche unto them both that this should be my order betwen them then Bullen refused and withdrew himself in a froward & obstinate sort. And Laseby did condiscende to that which I moved and yet yf I should have given anie considera-cion from the one party to the other I thinke it were rather due from Bullen to Laseby then otherwise. The causes betwen them were many. And all of small moment and yet their charges on both sides in suite of lawe were growen greate. I founde that the «greatest» grownde of their contencions grew by Bullens keping «in Bale alone by him self» 120 or 140 shepe and herin I moved Bullen to a most reasonable corse «(as I thought)» for ende. But his wilfullnes was such, as he would not be conformable in anie sort, which will breed him greate trouble from others of his neighbors, aswell as Laseby. Moreover at one tyme this sommer past when they came before me about their causes I pressed them to be bounde «to abide my order» for so seemed to be the direction of the cort and Bullen directly <refused> «denied» and yet gave his promise to abide it, which now he hath refused. Thus being sorie that my labour hath brought fourth so litle fruite, I <leave to> «yet hope that» the wisdome & better consideracion of your Lordship & the rest <how to> «will» bridle this Bullen, who spareth not to hazard his owne undoing for the tryall to have his will. <From. And so> «I» tak my leave. From St[*iffkey*] 2 November 1607. Your Lordships at commandment.

Unsigned. Draft in Martin Man's hand, with emendations in Bacon's hand.
Endorsed: Certificate to the Lord Coke *inter* Bullen & Laseby.
1½ pp. Yale (Beinecke) MS195.

John Palgrave to Sir Nathaniel Bacon

1607, November 6. Sir. For as mutch as by his Majesties orders the justices of everye divission are to assemble themselves together, betwene everye quarter ses-sions of the peace nere about the myd tyme betwene eatche suche sessions for the exicucion of his Majesties orders conceived (well knowen unto yow) which now approtchethe, I doe thinke good hereby to put yow in mynd that some daye may be appoynted for that purpose at the usuall place at Holte being the sessions howse theare, the xxi daye of this instant monthe of November by eight of the clocke of

---

[806] See also Bacon's previous certificate in relation to this case, 5 November 1606, above, p.263.

the fore noone of the same daye if yow shall so thinke good, but if yow doe not like of that daye then I praye yow appoynt some other daye for that purpose and therof advertise me, to the end I may discharge my dutie in that behalfe, for God willing I meane then to mete with yow «then» theare. And as touchinge the warrants to be directed to the chieff constables of the Hundreds of Northgrenho, Holte, and <Southerpingham> «Northerpingham» and to the petty constables chirchwardens & overseers of the poore of everye «of the townes» of the said Hundreds, yf I shall understand from yow to which of them yow have directed your warrants «unto» I will find the meanes that other warrants shalbe directed to the rest.

Northwood Barningham the sixte daye of November 1607. Yours well assured.

Signed: J. Pagrave.
Addressed in a ?different hand: To the right worshipfull Sir Nathanyell Bacon knight at Styfkey.
½ p. NRO BCH 27/9/74. I (95).

Information by Thomas Locksmith against Nicholas Towling and John Crisp

1607, November 7. *Information of Thomas Locksmith taken 7 November 1607, giving evidence of gambling by Nicholas Towling and John Crisp at the former's house at Langham.*

1 p. Dobell, 46 (1925), item 72.

Examination in a case of paternity

1607, November 18. The examination of Amie Ducker taken before Sir Nathanael Bacon knight the xviii of November 1607.

She saith that she is with childe, by one Edmonde Ixworth servant to Edmonde Danham, who went awaie from Walsingham in harvest last, and saith that he hath had the companie of her a twelve moneth and more.

She saith that she looketh to be delyvered of her childe within this fortenight.

Signed: Na[*thaniel*] Bacon, [*by mark*] Amie Ducker. *In William Sanders' hand.*
Endorsed: Examination of Amie Duckre 18 Novembr 1607.
½ p. NRO NRS 24659, 125X3.

Chancery order for the administration of a charitable bequest

1607, November 25. *Calendar*: Order made 25 November 5 James in the case between Christopher Bedingfeld and others, plaintiffs, and Richard Farrington and John Smith, defendants, Mr Godfrey being counsel for the plaintiffs. The defendants are the executors of Gregory Smith, merchant tailor of London,[807] who devised £120 to purchase land of the clear yearly value of £5 4s. for the maintenance of the poor of Wighton and Hindringham. The named trustees, Robert Tudnam and Henry Rose, have died and the defendants wish to bestow the

---

[807] The will of Gregory Smythe, Merchant Tailor of London, born at Wighton, was proved in 1597 (TNA PRO prob/11/90 Cobham f.89).

£120 so as to be discharged by order of the court. It is ordered that the money be paid to Sir Nathaniel Bacon, Sir Henry Sidney, Sir Anthony Browne and Sir James Calthorp on Ascension Day next (5 May 1608) at Bacon's house and be laid out to provide weekly relief according to the will. Signed: Richard Edwards, deputy registrar.

Copy in Martin Man's hand.
Endorsed: Order in the Chancery for £120 by Mr Smithes will given to Hindringham & Wighton.
½ p. NRO MC 1872/5, 866X1. Calendared, *Supplementary Stiffkey Papers*, p.21.

Edward Coke and William Daniell, Justices of Assize, to the J.P.s in North Norfolk

1607, November 25. After our verie hartie comendacions. Forasmuch as wee are credibly informed of diverse robberyes burglaryes & other notorious fellonyes lately don within the countie of Norfolk and the confynes thereof, the cause whereof wee ascribe aswell to your negligence and want of providence whome his Majestie in that case hath specially trusted, as also to the remisse pursuite of the offendours, wherin also you are justly to be blamed. Least therefore others through presumption of their impunity be incouraged to the like, and you maie through your connyvence & negligence incurre danger to your selves, these shalbe to praie & require you, as you tender his Majesties service and will aunswer the contrary at your perilles, that you take a present & speedie course of redresse herin, as well by effectuall prosequution of such as rest already suspect, as by diligent & carefull examinacions & sifting of all others, within your severall lymittes, which by reason of their idle course of life may give cause of suspicion. And so resting in hope of your due performance hereof, wee comytt you to the blessed protection of the Almightie. 25 November 1607. Your loving frendes. [*Signed:*] Edward Coke, W. Danyell.

Copy in Martin Man's hand.
Addressed: From the Justices of Assize. To the very worshipfull the justices of peace for the lymittes & Hundredes of South Erpingham N. Erpingham Northgrenhoe Einsforth Holt Landishe Smethdon Gallow & Brothercrosse from one to another with all speede.
Endorsed: Concerning the apprehending of disordered persons.
1 p. NRO BL/BC/6/23.

Francis Raymond to Sir Nathaniel Bacon

1607, December 4. Right wourshipfull. So yt is that wheare I should have ben at your wourshipps aweytt [*?audit*] the nynth of November, so yt is that I was then at London, & have ben almost ever sythens, and bycause the courtes at Methwold & Helgaie are not yeat fynished & there is a great fyne due to your wourshippe for the howse I sould I doe stey my accompt till after the court whiche is on Weddnesdaie nexte.[808] Therefor these are to desyre your wourshippe to send

---

[808] 9 December.

dyreccions for the same fyne what course shalbe used in the ratinge thereof, the value of the thinge sould is £12 ayere & the better parte is copiehould, therefore yf yt please your wourshippe to sett downe the rate of the fyne, I shall then be fytt to certyfie the steward your wourshipps pleasure and make paiment thereof with rest of my accompt at your wourshipps appoyntment presentlie after the court be ended. Also Helgaie court is on Thursdaie next, yf yt please your wourshippe to send your dyreccions what shalbe done there, yt shalbe the better performed. And where I should have bought quenches [*quinces*] for my ladie, I could not at Elye fayre[809] gett anye, but suche as were not worth the preservinge neyther can as yeat enquire anye havinge sent by my good fryendes bothe into Suffolk & Cambridgshire. Pleaseth your wourshippe further wheare as Sir Henrie Gawdie is highe sheryf of Norfolk & I dwell almost in the mydest of the Hundred of Wayland & Grimshoe, these are humblye to desyre your wourshipps letter in my behalf to Sir Henrye Gawdye his wourshippe, & to Sir Robert Gawdies wourshippe on my behalf, that I maye have the preferement of the same balywicke for my money & uppon good securytie.[810] Thus hopeinge of your wourshipps favour herein I humblie take my leave. Methwold this 4 of December 1607. Your wourshipps humble servant in all dutie at comaund.

Signed: Fra[*ncis*] Reymonde.

Addressed: To the right wourshipfull & his verie good master Sir Nathaniell Bacon at Styfkey.

Endorsement in Martin Man's hand: [*ms damaged*] December 4.

Dorse used for jottings for an account of meslin, barley and malt headed [*?*] *Brampton.*
1 p. NRO RAY 277.

Elizabeth, Lady Peryam to Sir Nathaniel Bacon

1607, December 6. My good brother[811] I thanke God my trobles with my lordes childre [*sic*] are nowe so nere an end as that I hope in the Lords mercye I shall have yowr bandes discharged this next terme. I am «to» request yow to calle to mynd whatt end yow made with Brandsbye for my part of Pawlinge[812] as alsoo whatt was concluded for my sisters parte with him. I remember yow complayned heretofore of a payne yow had in yowr arme. I besetche yf yow had any meddisyne that dyd yow good lett me understand <yf> yt from yow for I am trobled as I thinke with the lyke payne. My nese Killegre[813] hathe bin of latte very sicke but now God

---

[809] St Awdrey's fair, originally held to celebrate the translation of the abbey's foundress, St. Ethelreda, on 17 October.

[810] The under offices of the sheriffwick were evidently worth obtaining. See entries relating to Miles Baspoole and Richard Spratt in *BP*, iv.

[811] Elizabeth was Nathaniel's thrice-married sister and by this stage was the widow of her third husband, the judge Sir William Peryam, who had died in 1604.

[812] On the arrangements made for the manor of Sea Palling, see *BP*, iv, *passim*.

[813] Possibly one of the daughters of Sir Henry Killigrew by his first marriage, as the children of his second marriage would be too young at this time. Sir Henry had first married Katherine, the sister of Anne, the second wife of Sir Nicholas Bacon, the father of Nathaniel and Elizabeth. This made his daughters Elizabeth Peryam's cousins rather than her nieces. However, the terms 'nephew' and 'niece' were used far more loosely in this period than they are today. In this instance this usage may have been encouraged by a difference in age.

bethanked well recovered, she hathe a boye and a girle most fine children the Lord blesse them. Thus desyringe to be most kindly remembred to my good sister I rest. vi of December. Yowr lovinge sister.

Signed: Elezabeth Periam. *Holograph.*
Addressed: To the ryght worshipfull and my very good brother Sir Nathaniell Bacon at Styfkye.
Endorsed in Martin Man's hand: Lady Peryam. December 1607.
½ p. Folger L.d.468.

Sir Edmund Moundford to Sir Nathaniel Bacon

1607, December 18. My very good unkle[814] this bearer cominge to Styfkye aboute my wyfe her busines, I thought it good to advertize you of some badd dealinge of Frauncis Reymond your baylyfe of Methwold[815] *viz.* that after he had seised to your use a meare with a foale and allso mony which was in his handes, for a nagge which he bought of one whoe was suspected to have stoallne them all, and so much made knowne to him with sufficient reason of the vehement suspicion, he himselfe without bringinge the partie suspected before any justice of peace to be examined (and after he himselfe had gyven warninge to other whoe would have bought the sayd meare and foale, that they should not buy them for that it was suspected that they were stoalne) he hath not only delivered the meare and foale to the fellon, but allso he himselfe hath bought them of him, receyvinge of him an untrue certificate with names sett therto of which he knoweth but one man, but the handes of none subscribed under the certificate. The felonies be proved directly & the fellon by necligence suffered to escape. The name of one of the parties whose beast was stoallne was sett to the certificate to testifie that the sayd beaste was the parties suspected to have stoallne the same. Thus remembringe my selfe in all kyndnes to you & my good aunte your lady with my syster Knyvett I committ you to God.

Feltwell this 18 of December 1607. Your loveing nephewe.

Signed: Ed[*mund*] Moundeford.
Addressed: To the right worshipfull Sir Nathaniell Bacon knight at Styfkye.
Endorsed in Martin Man's hand: Sir Ed. Mondford concerning Raymond.
½ p. BL Add. 41140 ff.68–9.

Petition. Richard Douglas to the J.P.s in Norfolk

[*Post 1607, December 19*].[816] *Calendar*: The bearer, Richard Dudglas of Holt, was bound for the appearance of Thomas Joanes at the sessions held at Fakenham on Friday and Saturday, 18 and 19 December 1607. Joanes made his appearance and

---

[814] Moundford had married Abigail Knyvett, sister of Bacon's son-in-law, Sir Thomas Knyvett (*The Knyvett Letters 1620–44*, ed. B. Schofield, NRS xx, 1949, p.26).

[815] There was considerable scope for conflict between the officers of Nathaniel Bacon, who was fermor of the Duchy manor at Methwold, and Edmund Moundford, who was fermor of the demesne lands. See also 31 July 1606, above, p.249.

[816] Dating: dated from internal evidence.

was discharged in open court, as his neighbours can testify, but the clerk of the sessions mistakenly returned his recognizance as forfeit to the value of a hundred shillings. He is unable to pay, having a wife and "a great charge of children" and no income apart from his labour. He craves that they will be satisfied by 20s. already paid to the Norfolk commissioners for levying his Majesty's debts. The commissioners are willing to accept this if the justices certify their approval.

At the foot in William Sanders' hand: "A letter was written to Mr Neave to accept of the 20s. that was paid".

Undated. Unsigned.
Endorsed: Duglas his peticion.
1 p. NRO Townshend Additional, Box 113.

John Duck to Sir Nathaniel Bacon

1607, December 20. If it please your worshipp there is one Middleton in our towne[817] which at the last courte holden for your worshipp did present in his verdict a boulspritt [*bowsprit*] which came up at the sea side, & upon his othe did saie then that he found it upon the drie ground which was true, & delivered it into my handes to your worshipps use, but he had sett the Admiralls marke upon it & upon Thursdaie was seavenyght at the Admirall cort he did there find it for the Admirall. But it is challenged by a merchant of London, & the Doctor upon Myddletons enformation have promised his warrant to deliver it to the marchaunt, wherbie your worship is like to loose your groundidge by his meanes. Therfore I beseche your worship to direct me some course what I maie doe in it. For I have drawen it up the clife & the same Myddleton have certefied the Doctor that Goodman Smythe would not suffer him to burie a man that came up naked & was eaten with doges, wherbie the doctor said that he had enformed his Majestie withall. Which is false for I was with Goodman Smyth when he entreated him to burie him & commanded him to burie him. Thus remembring my dutie unto your worship I comitt you unto Allmightie God. Hembesbie this xx of December 1607. Your worshipps to commaund.

[*Postscript*]: Martin Man did heare what the same Myddleton did speake at the courte.

Signed: John Ducke.[818]
Addressed: To the right worshipfull Sir Nathaniell Bacon at Stifkie Hall. Deliver this letter at Mr Peckifers a silkman.
Endorsed in Martin Man's hand: John Duck.
½ p. Folger L.d.278.

---

817 Hemsby was a Bacon manor, hence Bacon's right to wreck. (Compare a similar case in Suffolk where he also had an interest, 18 June 1606, above, p.242). This instance is a further example of the ongoing disputes over foreshore rights between Bacon and Dr Burman, judge of the Admiralty Court in Norfolk (see *BP*, iv *sub* 'Burman, John'). Middleton, it would seem, was an informer for the Admiralty Court (for other such see *BP*, iv, p.197n.). Smith may have been the parish constable.

818 John Duck, a man of some education, came of established yeoman stock in Hemsby. For the Lord Admiral's reaction, see Charles Howard to Bacon, 20 February 1607/8, *BP*, vi, forthcoming. Robert Duck had been bailiff of the manor of Hemsby in the 1580s (*BP*, iv, p.27n.).

Sir Nathaniel Bacon and others to Thomas Egerton, Baron Ellesmere, Lord Chancellor

1607, December 29. Our humble duties remembred. Yt may please your Lordship to be advertized that upon differences falling out betwen Sir Chr[*istopher*] Heydon knight & Thomas Thetford esquire in causes of great weight thei referred themselves to our <order> arbitrement and became bound ech to other in the some of £10,000 to abide our order. And therupon wee bestowed our travell therin 3 severall dayes and yet could not bringe their causes to such ende as wee wished partly bicause some witnesses were desired to be examined by oath which wee had no power to do. Therefore wee did move them to yealde their consentes that upon bill «to be» exhibited before your Lordship «this next terme» thei might after joyne in comission for thexaminacion of witnesses which thei have condiscended unto. So as if it may stande with your Lordships pleasure to thinke well of this their proceeding for the more speedy ending of their contencions both the said parties <are by us persuaded to put forward the same> «will acknowledg them selves bounden unto your Lordship for your favour therby shewed unto them.»

Unsigned. Draft in Martin Man's hand, with emendations in Nathaniel Bacon's hand. Endorsed: A draught of a letter to the Lord Chancellor begon at Holt 29 December 1607.
½ p. Yale (Beinecke) MS 195.

Thomas Sackville, Earl of Dorset, Lord Treasurer, to Sir Nathaniel Bacon

1607, December 31. *Calendar:* The Lord Treasurer's former letters[819] ordered that no tenants were to be admitted to copyholds of inheritance in the manor of East Dereham, until they were surveyed, which is now done. The Council has therefore resolved that Bacon, assisted by a neighbouring justice of the peace and by the Surveyor of his Majesty's possessions in Norfolk[820] (or by two justices in the Surveyor's absence), may now admit tenants. As common persons are allowed to take fines of three years' rent from their customary tenants, fines henceforward must be assessed at no less than two years' full profit of the land, and in the case of dwelling houses assessed on the quality of the buildings. The assessors are to return certificates of their decisions from time to time, with details of tenements, ancient rents, late holders and new tenants. If any tenant refuses payment, the bailiff is to seize the land and profits to the King's use. Particulars of those not admitted at the time of the late survey are enclosed. Since negligence and fraud by sundry bailiffs of the King's manors have much impaired Crown revenue, Bacon is to take greater care in preservation of rents, reliefs, services and the quality of heriots, charging homage and jury to this effect. The bailiff is to pay monies arising into the Exchequer at the feast of the Annunciation next. From Dorset House. Dated last of December 1607.

At the foot: Steward.

---

[819] Of 15 February 1603/4, above, p.73.
[820] Presumably John Hersye (see 1 August 1607, above, p.285).

Signed: T. Dorset.
Addressed: To my lovinge freind the steward of the Kings Majesties mannor of East Dereham in the countye of Norfolk or to his deputie.
Endorsed in Martin Man's hand: Lord Treasurer for East Dereham.
1 p. NRO MS 21508/6, 368X5.

COMBINED GLOSSARY AND WORDLIST[1]

a – from

ac – and

agistment – (payment for) putting in livestock to feed

al (*ios*) – others

al (for *au*) – to (the)

anno (domini) – (in) the year (of the lord)

anno regni regis – in the year of the reign of the king

Annunciation – see *Lady Day*

ante – before

armiger – esquire; i.e. a man qualified to bear arms (heraldic)

assize rents – fixed rents similar to a ground rent

averment – a statement to make the position clear

band – frequently used for *bond*

bargain and sale – an agreement to purchase land which could also, if enrolled in
the Courts of Record at Westminster or at Quarter Sessions, operate as a
conveyance

bays – heavy wool fabric of plain weave

bond – a written promise to pay used to secure the payment of a debt or the performance of an action. Generally for twice the amount owed, and including
a condition that the promise becomes void if the debt is paid or the action
performed

buffin – coarse cloth used for gowns

caliver – light musket, or the soldier bearing one

cancellarius – chancellor

Candlemas – the feast of the Purification; 2 February

canniker – a person licensed to sell beer or ale without keeping an alehouse or
providing food. Presumably from 'cannikin', a small can or drinking vessel.
See also p.127n.

cape (seize!) – a writ concerning pleas of land used to summon the defendant.
Both the *cape magnum* (grand *cape*) and *cape parvum* were used particularly
where the defendant has already failed to appear

cepi for *cepi corpus* (I have seized the body) – the return made by the sheriff that
he has taken a named defendant

clericus – clerk

cocket – a written acknowledgement of custom paid, usually under seal

Common Law (Law) – the system of law applied in the common law courts (e.g.
King's Bench and Common Pleas)

(vera) copia – (true) copy

---

[1] Many of the legal definitions are based on Jacob, *New Law-Dictionary*.

compotum – account

conies – rabbits

contra (leges) – against (the law)

coram – in the presence of

country – a term used variously for farming regions, wider rural areas, or in the sense of *county*, but not generally in the sense of *nation* or *state*

customers – customs officers

de – concerning

debet – he/she owes

del – of the

deputatum/us – deputy

dimidius (*di.*) – a half

distringas (you should distrain) – a writ to the sheriff ordering him to distrain to compel (for instance) appearance in court. *Distringas juratores* was a writ to distrain a jury to appear

domine/i – of the lady/lord

durance – a stout durable cloth

durante beneplacito – during pleasure

egrotus – ill, unwell

entail – a method of tranferring land so that it can only pass to the descendants of the original grantee. When an entail is broken it is said to be *barred*

Equity – the system of law applied, for example, in the courts of Chancery and Requests

error, writ of – a writ used to correct errors apparent in the record of a case. This served as a limited form of appeal

etc. – used, often at the end of a sentence, in the place of a standard phrase or of information already given

(*ex*) *parte* – on the part of/behalf of

examinata/ur/us – examined

exigent – see *outlawry*

farmer/fermor – the person taking on any property or office for a fixed term in return for rent

farm/ferm/firm – rent, or the taking of a property or office in return for the payment of rent

festum – feast

fine – (1) An action in the Court of Common Pleas acting as a form of conveyance (final concord). A fine was said to be 'levied'. (2) A downpayment made, for instance, at the beginning of a lease or when taking over a copyhold tenement

formedon in the remainder – a writ to be used by the person entitled to the land (the remainderman) after an entail comes to an end

generosus – gentleman

grogram – a coarse fabric made variously of silk, mohair or wool or a mixture of the three, often stiffened with gum

Hallowmas – All Saints Day; 1 November

heriot – payment of money or chattels made to a feudal lord on the death of a tenant

Hilary term – the law term between Christmas and Easter

Hundred – an administrative division of the county established before the
    Norman Conquest

ignoramus (we do not know) – the return made by any inquest or jury that they
    did not know the answer to the question

imprimis/in primis – in the first place

impropriation – an impropriation occurred when a religious house, in effect, took
    over as the incumbent of a benefice. After the Dissolution the successor in
    title became the lay rector, with the right to receive the rectorial tithes and
    to appoint a vicar or curate to serve the parish

in capite (in chief) – a tenant in chief held directly from the Crown and was
    liable to increased feudal dues

in forma pauperis – as a poor man. On oath that he was worth less than £5, a
    plaintiff could bring a case *in forma pauperis* without paying the usual fees

in toto – in full, altogether

inde – of which

inquisition post mortem (inquisition after the death) – an enquiry after a land-
    holder's death into the property held of the Crown

inter – between

(*inter*) *partes* – between the parties

juratus/a/i – sworn

kersey – coarse narrow cloth woven from long wool

King's Bench, Marshalsea and Maimed Soldiers – taxes levied for the relief of pris-
    oners and for pensions for soldiers and mariners injured in war

Lady Day/Our Lady – the feast of the Annunciation of the Blessed Virgin Mary;
    25 March

Lammas – 1 August

latitat – see *Middlesex*

le – the

leet – minor criminal jurisdiction, often exercised by the manor court

limit and *double limit* – also known as 'divisions'. Administrative areas created
    within the county to facilitate the work of the justices of the peace between
    Quarter Sessions. Although the Act of 1530 setting up such areas was
    repealed in 1545, the system was in place in Norfolk by the end of the six-
    teenth century, each *limit* consisting of a number of *hundreds*. (See map 1
    and Smith, *County and Court*, pp.103–105.) The system was a flexible one,
    and when conditions were appropriate and the presence of a larger group of
    justices would reinforce the system, as with the proclamation of James as
    king in March 1603 (p.26), they worked in *double limit* units

maslin – mixed grain, especially rye mixed with wheat

match – cord or rope prepared for burning

members – in the context of King's Lynn and Great Yarmouth, "members" refers to outports. The customs at King's Lynn covered all the smaller ports along the North Norfolk coast as far as, and including, Wells; Blakeney and the coast to the east fell within the jurisdiction of the customs at Great Yarmouth

meslin – mixed grain

Michaelmas – the feast of St Michael the Archangel; 29 September

Middlesex, Bill of – the Bill of Middlesex was part of a procedure that enabled the Court of King's Bench to extend its jurisdiction. The issue of the Bill on a generally fictitious allegation of trespass *vi et armis* (by force and arms) brought the defendant (on the fictitious supposition that he resided in Middlesex) within the jurisdiction of the court. If the defendant was not in Middlesex, the sheriff returned *non est inventus* (he is not found) and a writ of *latitat* (he lurks) was sent to the sheriff of his county of residence.

mortuus – dead

neat – cattle

new draperies – specialist cloths introduced by the Walloon and Dutch refugees who settled in Norwich in the later sixteenth century

nihil dicit – he says nothing. A failure by the defendant to put in an answer to the plaintiff's plea by the day assigned, leading to judgement against him

nisi prius – a writ initiating the trial of civil cases at the Assizes. It required attendance at one of the courts at Westminster unless beforehand (*nisi prius*) the itinerant justices arrived in the locality specified to try the case.

non est inventus (he is not found) – the return by the sheriff when a writ could not be served on a defendant. See also *Middlesex*

non obstante – not withstanding

nota – note

obulus (*ob.*) – a halfpenny

olland – arable land laid down to grass

outlawry – where the defendant to a personal action could not be found, and he had no personal goods in the county to be distrained by, the sheriff was sent a writ of *exigent* (they shall demand) requiring him to call the defendant to appear on five county court days. The last call was the *quinto exactus* (called for the fifth time). If the defendant did not appear then he was outlawed. A writ of *supersedeas* could be used to set at liberty someone taken on an *exigent*

outrents – rents from outside the main geographical location of the manor

particular licence – licences granted to individuals rather than to the community at large

per – by, through

petronel – large pistol or carbine used especially by horse-soldiers, or the soldier bearing one

post – after

postea – afterwards

primo – the first

pro – for

Purification – see *Candlemas*

quietus (quit) – an acquittance

quindene – 15th day after

quinto exactus – see *outlawry*

quousque – until. Often used with the implication of 'until' some action has been performed or event occurred

rash – a smooth fabric made of silk or worsted

receptor – receiver

recognizance – bond with condition to perform/or not perform an action

recovery (for *common recovery*) – a fictitious court action used in particular to bar (defeat) an entail. A common recovery was said to be 'suffered'

redditus – rent

regine/regis – of the queen/king

(*ex sua*) *relacione* – (by his) report

remainder – a right to property in the future

replevy – to recover distrained goods on payment or on giving security

reversion – a right to property in the future, where the right is held by the original grantor or his heirs

says – fine wool cloth sometimes containing silk

seisin – legal possession

serges – woollen fabric similar to *says* but also a durable fabric worn by the less well off

shack – right of pasturage on arable land after the harvest

si – if

stranger – in Norfolk used specifically for Dutch and Walloon immigrants

summa (totalis) – sum, total

summer corn – grain sown in the spring, as opposed to *winter corn*, sown in the autumn

supersedeas (you should desist) – a writ to stay proceedings. Could be used to free on surety persons taken e.g. in cases of breach of the peace and *Outlawry*

taske – tax; used both generally for the subsidy and, more specifically, for the medieval 10ths and 15ths, often granted at the same time as the subsidy but which did not need individual assessment

temp(*ore*) – in the time

teste/testibus – witness(es)

ultimo – last

unde – of which

usque – until, up to

ut – as

uxor – wife

vale(*n*)*t* – it is/they are worth

videlicet (*viz*) – namely

wethers – adult male sheep, usually castrated

Whitsun – Pentecost; the seventh Sunday after Easter

CURRENCY, WEIGHTS AND MEASURES

Currency

2 farthings (¼d.)	= 1 halfpenny (½d., *di.* or *ob.*)
2 halfpennies	= 1 penny (d.)
12 pennies	= 1 shilling (s.)
20 shillings	= 1 pound (£)
1 mark	= 13*s.* 4*d.*

Measurement (approximate, there were local variations)

(a) *of volume*

2 gallons	= 1 peck
4 pecks	= 1 bushel (approx. 63lbs of grain)
4 bushels	= 1 co(o)mb
2 co(o)mbs	= 1 quarter (qr)
4 quarters	= 1 chalder/chaldron of grain (32 bushels)
4½ quarters	= 1 chalder of coal or lime (36 bushels)
10 quarters	= 1 last of grain or malt
1 cade	= a barrel containing 720 herring
1 firkin	= a small cask, about a quarter of a barrel
1 warp	= a unit usually of 4 fish, but sometimes of 2 or 3

(b) *of weight*

16 ounces (oz.)	= 1 pound (lb., *li.*) = weight
14 pounds	= 1 stone
8 stone	= 1 hundredweight (C, cwt., 112 lbs)
1 tod of wool	= 2 stone (28 lbs)

(c) *of land*

4 roods	= 1 acre

BIOGRAPHICAL NOTE: NATHANIEL BACON[1]

Nathaniel Bacon (?1546–1622) was the second son of the Lord Keeper Sir Nicholas Bacon and his first wife Jane, the daughter of Thomas Ferneley, a Suffolk merchant. Nathaniel had two brothers, Nicholas and Edward, both of whom became county figures in Suffolk, and two half-brothers, Anthony and Francis, the sons of Sir Nicholas and his second wife Anne, the cultured daughter of Sir Anthony Cooke.[2]

Nathaniel was educated at Trinity College, Cambridge, and Gray's Inn. In 1569 he married Anne, the base daughter of Sir Thomas Gresham and Mistress Dutton, the wife of Thomas Dutton, one of Gresham's factors in Antwerp. After renting a modest house at Cockthorpe, Nathaniel began in 1576 to build Stiffkey Hall where the couple took up residence in 1578 despite its unfinished state. They had three daughters, Anne, Elizabeth and Winifred, and two sons, both of whom died in infancy. Elizabeth married Thomas Knyvett in 1592, Anne married John Townshend in 1593/4, and Winifred married Robert Gawdy in 1597. Their mother Anne died in 1595 and two years later Nathaniel married Dorothy, the daughter of Arthur Hopton and widow of William Smith of Burgh Castle, by whom she had had three children (William, Owen and Mary).[3] Sir John Townshend, the husband of Anne, Nathaniel's eldest daughter and heiress, was killed in a duel in 1603.

Through his family Nathaniel had close connections with leading figures at Court, especially through his father Sir Nicholas, Lord Keeper to Elizabeth I, and his father-in-law, Sir Thomas Gresham, who was the Queen's principal financial agent. When his father married Anne Cooke, he became a nephew by marriage of William Cecil Lord Burghley, Sir Thomas Hoby (ambassador to France), Sir Henry Killigrew (ambassador to Scotland), and Lord John Russell, son of the second earl of Bedford. Through this marriage he also became a cousin of Robert Cecil, later earl of Salisbury. His two famous brothers were well-connected at Court: Anthony became secretary to the earl of Essex, while Francis rose to be Lord Chancellor and a philosopher of European renown. His sisters extended this network of Court contacts. The eldest, Elizabeth, was married three times: her first two husbands, Sir Robert D'Oyly (d.1577) and Sir Henry Neville (d.1593), were minor figures at Court, while her third, Sir William Peryam, was chief baron of the Exchequer. Another sister, also named Elizabeth, married first Francis Wyndham (d.1592), who became a judge of Common Pleas, and secondly Sir Robert Mansell, courtier, monopolist and admiral. The third sister, Anne, married a Norfolk gentleman, Henry Woodhouse of Waxham.

Despite these connections, Nathaniel remained essentially a county figure, apparently never seeking any office at Court or in central administration. In 1574 he

---

[1] This biographical note is largely based on *BP*, iv, pp.304–6, which see for references.
[2] For the Bacon family pedigree see *BP*, i, *inter* pp.xvi–xvii.
[3] For the Hopton and Smith family pedigrees see Key, 'Dorothy Bacon', pp.110–11.

was appointed a J.P. in Norfolk, an office he held for almost fifty years and which he discharged assiduously both at sessions and through his out-of-sessions activities. As a carpet-bagger he represented Tavistock in the parliaments of 1571 and 1572, probably as a result of religious affinity and family connections with the earl of Bedford. But once settled at Stiffkey he was returned as knight of the shire for Norfolk in 1584, 1593 and 1604, and as burgess for King's Lynn in 1597. His keenness to use legislation as a means to redress the ills of society no doubt prompted him to stand yet again as knight of the shire in 1620 at the age of 74, but this time unsuccessfully. The concern for a range of local issues evident in his papers is reflected in his membership of parliamentary committees and such evidence as survives of his parliamentary speeches. Twice sheriff of Norfolk and for many years collector of the loan there, he regularly figured as a subsidy commissioner, and as a member of innumerable special commissions was especially valued by the Council for his "uprightness and indifferency". He evinced less enthusiasm for military affairs, apparently never commanding his local militia company, and only being appointed to the muster commission in 1596 and the deputy lieutenancy in 1605, an office he proceeded to discharge with more concern for legal and constitutional niceties than for the raising of an efficient militia. He was knighted in 1604.

A zealous puritan in religion, Nathaniel is to be classed with those who supported reform from within the Anglican church. He disliked the practices and procedures of church courts; bishops, in his view, were to be pastors of their flocks, primarily concerned with preaching and teaching rather than with administration of laws such as those against recusancy or with the policing of morals. "For", as he informed the House of Commons in 1593, "bishoppes and their officers being men utterly unacquainted with theis proceedings, or being no parte of their studie or exercise, it were not fitt to use them in this cause, but to leave it to the justices of the peace and others of the laitie". Hence his own involvement in administration which was designed to secure social and moral reform. But his puritanism was most explicit in the efforts he made to secure the appointment of Godly preachers. After the death of the rector of Stiffkey in 1574, he spent more than a year trying to persuade such well-known puritan figures as Hugh Booth, Walter Travers and Edmund Chapman to accept the benefice. Under his encouragement prophesying flourished at Wiveton, Holt and Fakenham, and under his patronage John More, the famous 'apostle of Norwich', continued to catechise after being suspended by Bishop Freke in 1578.

Nathaniel Bacon emerges from his papers as an earnest, severe and rather self-righteous man: more concerned with business than with pleasure, and above all assiduous in establishing the puritan ethic in north Norfolk. His letters, although frequently lengthy, contain none of the news and gossip which characterise those which he received from his brother Edward, nor the enthusiasm for falconry which is a feature of the rare missives from his elder brother Nicholas; they contain none of the introspective agonising of a Thomas Knyvett nor any abstract discussion of politics or of religion. In his single-minded concern for the business of government and practicalities of life, he showed a greater affinity with his father than did his brothers, but even Sir Nicholas senior displayed a keener interest in the details of family life than his son evinced through his pen. For Nathaniel to write was to do business: hence the superb archive he amassed, an archive which reveals politics and religion in action.

INDEX

Abbreviations

b.	born	da.	daughter	m.	married	s.	son
br.	brother	f.	father	mo.	mother	Sfk	Suffolk
bur.	buried	gr.	grand	n.	niece/nephew	sis.	sister
cr.	created	h.	husband	N.B.	Nathaniel Bacon	w.	wife
d.	died	knt	knight(ed)	Nfk	Norfolk	wid.	widow(er)

The index does not include all variants in the spelling of surnames. Christian names given in the index are not always given in the text.

Green (Grene), John, *chief constable of North Greenhoe Hundred*, subsidy assessor, 287

Green, John, *merchant*, account for sale of malt in Holland, 133

Green (Grene), Roger, land of, in Alethorpe, 69

Green, Thomas, surety for bond, 198

Green, (Grene), Thomas, parish officer for Cley, 161

Green (Grene), Thomas, *of South Creake*, impropriator of tithes, 39

Green (Grene), William, *of Mattishall*, imprest as mariner for Blakeney, 6

Greenhoe Hundred *see* North Greenhoe

Greenwich, document dated at, 193

Greenwich, East, property held of manor, 84

Gregges *see* Grigg(es)

Gresham (Gressom), Sir Richard, *knt 1603, of Thorpe Market*, resident, 205

Greve, ..., to pay for keep of illegitimate child, 285

Greve, Henry, land of, in Alethorpe, 69
   owed money by Edmund Newby, 51
   signs Warham petition, 183

Greve, John, parish officer for Warham, 32

Greve, Ralph, parish officer for Cley, 165

Greve, Thomas, creditor of Rokesby, 47
   parish officer for Cley, 29
   signs Warham petition, 183

Grey, Anne de, *w. of Sir William, da. of James Calthorpe*, 100n.

Grey (Graye), Edmund, parish officer for Blakeney, 165

Grey, Thomas, *Baron*, reprieve of, 60

Grey, Sir William de, *of Merton*, introduces Bill to relieve penalties on recusants, 100

Grice *see* Le Grice

Griffeth, Owen, suspect recusant at Wells, 204

Grigges, (Gregges), Edward, land held of the manor of Walpole, 136, 141, 174–5

Grigges, (Gregges), Thomas, *br. of Edward*, land held of the manor of Walpole, 136, 141, 174–5

Grime, ..., servant to Sir Edward Coke, 282

Grimes (Gryme), George, *gent, of Foulsham*, trustee for disputed bond 121–2

Grimshoe (Grymshaw) Hundred, bailiwick of, sought for purchase, 303
   jury to be summoned from, 201
   subsidy commissioners, 270

Grimston, Christopher, letters from, 246–9, 265
   survey of Methwold signed by, 234

Grimston, Christopher, *s. of Edward, m. Elizabeth Barney*, 234n.

Grimston, Christopher, *surveyor for the Duchy of Lancaster, s. of Thomas of Grimston, Yorks*, 234n.

Grimston, Elizabeth, *w. of Christopher, da. of Martin Barney of Gunton*, 234n.

Grimston family, 234n.

Grimston, extent of Castle Rising warren in, 138, 140, 150
   persons associated with (listed), 137, 140
   Wyvelings in, 140, 150

Grix (Grickes, Gryx), John, *junior, of Langham*, town funds held by, 31, 133, 237

Grix (Greyx), John, *senior, of Langham*, cow given to town by, 133, 237
   parish officer for Langham, 31, 162, 165

Grixe, ..., *chapman, of Aldborough*, offers to buy grain, 123

grocers, 36n., 85, 128n.

Grogon, Margaret, present at Wiveton birth, 206

Grogon, Thomas, signs Wells petition, 79

Grosse, Sir Thomas, captain of light horse and petronels, 298

Groundsborough, W..., land in Dilham conveyed to, 275

Growte, E...., householder, 70

Growte, Mary, warrant against, 70n.

Gryme *see* Grimes

guildhall *see* Stiffkey

Guiltcross (Gilcrosse) Hundred, jury to be summoned from, 201
   subsidy commissioners, 270

Gunder, John, *brewer, of Wells*, accused of fathering child, 70

Gunpowder Plot *see* Catholic plots

guns and gunpowder *see* military affairs, troops and equipment

Gunthorpe, complaint concerning poor accounts, 177
   curate, 256
   overseers, 165
   poor accounts of, 30, 161
   property in, 251n.
   ratepayers in (listed), 178

Gunton, 12n., 156n., 234n.
   church of, damaged, 155
   letter dated at, 155

Gurlington, ..., *fermor of Congham*, 140

Gurney, Amy, to attend on Bridget, Countess of Sussex, 245
   see also Sybsey, Amy

Gurney, Anthony, *of West Barsham and Cawston, br. of Amy Sybsey*, 245n.

Gurney, Thomas, *gent*, subsidy assessor for Gallow Hundred, 287, 289